Springer Proceedings in Business and Economics

Springer Proceedings in Business and Economics brings the most current research presented at conferences and workshops to a global readership. The series features volumes (in electronic and print formats) of selected contributions from conferences in all areas of economics, business, management, and finance. In addition to an overall evaluation by the publisher of the topical interest, scientific quality, and timeliness of each volume, each contribution is refereed to standards comparable to those of leading journals, resulting in authoritative contributions to the respective fields. Springer's production and distribution infrastructure ensures rapid publication and wide circulation of the latest developments in the most compelling and promising areas of research today.

The editorial development of volumes may be managed using Springer's innovative Online Conference Service (OCS), a proven online manuscript management and review system. This system is designed to ensure an efficient timeline for your publication, making Springer Proceedings in Business and Economics the premier series to publish your workshop or conference volume.

More information about this series at http://www.springer.com/series/11960

Alina Mihaela Dima · Fabrizio D'Ascenzo
Editors

Business Revolution in a Digital Era

14th International Conference on Business Excellence, ICBE 2020, Bucharest, Romania

Springer

Editors
Alina Mihaela Dima
Bucharest University of Economic Studies
Bucharest, Romania

Fabrizio D'Ascenzo
Dipartimento di Management
Sapienza University of Rome
Rome, Italy

ISSN 2198-7246 ISSN 2198-7254 (electronic)
Springer Proceedings in Business and Economics
ISBN 978-3-030-59971-3 ISBN 978-3-030-59972-0 (eBook)
https://doi.org/10.1007/978-3-030-59972-0

This Springer imprint is published by the registered company Springer Nature Switzerland AG
The registered company address is: Gewerbestrasse 11, 6330 Cham, Switzerland

Preface

This proceedings constitutes a selection of best papers from the 14th International Conference on Business Excellence, Business Revolution in the Digital Era, ICBE 2020, held in Bucharest, Romania, in June 2020.

The idea of this new proceedings published by Springer is an initiative to respond to the recent education challenges related to digitalization, innovation, creativity, and performance.

During the 18 sections of the conference, more than 200 young and experienced researchers from 17 countries presented their research papers online. This was a great opportunity to very interesting and productive discussions regarding future research subjects for excellence in research and business. This book is based on the selective collection of the most representative research findings and working papers related to education and business environment, digitization and international finance, entrepreneurship and innovation, energy business and accounting, human resources and data science.

The main goals of this book are the following:

- Introduces new and revolutionary concepts, like knowledge entropy; by measuring knowledge entropy researchers can find the ways for developing intellectual capital and creating intelligent organizations and managers can develop new strategies which leads to enhancing innovation.
- Presents the novel soft computing methods in digital coaching environment allowing better intuition-building and learning results for strategic investment decision-makers.
- Introduces new financial instruments like the Price Probability Predictor, which can be used to build reliable trading signals and limit conditions to automate the investment activity.
- Disseminates research results regarding trending topics like electric vehicles, sentiment analysis via Twitter, econometric analysis for tourism industry, or finding the determinants of economic growth for the European Union countries.

The valuable partnership with the Faculty of Economics of Sapienza University of Rome is based on a long-lasting relationship built on trust and commitment toward responsibility, research and performance, excellence, and international prestige. This book is another opportunity to strengthen this higher education cooperation between our institutions, in both teaching and research as well. The research and innovation created through this partnership play a crucial role in individual and societal development. This book of proceedings is a valuable final product of this mutual and productive collaboration.

Nevertheless, many projects are to be developed in the future, and we will continue cooperation in teaching and research based on friendship and mutual respect.

Rome, Italy Fabrizio D'Ascenzo
Bucharest, Romania Alina Mihaela Dima

Contents

Bad Counter Knowledge: Case Studies and Countermeasures

Ettore Bolisani and Juan-Gabriel Cegarra-Navarro

1 Introduction

Today, there is an increasing production and spread of contents that are difficult to verify and tend to mix with imperfect elements of knowledge, or even fakes (Gosa 2011; Thompson 2008)]. This problem is serious in the case of some public services, like healthcare, where these contents can be spread even deliberately and for tendentious purposes (Cegarra-Sanchez et al. 2017). When people, being ill, feeling vulnerable and seeking for some cures, are prone to believe rumors, myths or urban legends (Beveren 2003), some may try to take advantage of this and to influence their decisions. So, scientific institutions and public "authorities" are often confronted by individuals, groups, or companies who contest the "official truth" and propose alternative views even when these are not supported by facts or rational examinations (Lee 2004).

A key problem is that the intellectual capital of a person or organization is the sum of their knowledge (Darroch and McNaughton 2002) and can also develop from counter-knowledge, i.e. a mix of rumors, gossip, unsupportable explanations or justifications, partial truth, or lies (Cegarra-Navarro et al. 2015). Since counter-knowledge becomes an intertwined component of intellectual capital, this leads to new threats to organizations and companies, with negative effects on their reputation and recognized value (Dumay and Guthrie 2017).

In societies, counter-knowledge can trigger a vicious circle of mutual distrust, social turmoil, and potential problems for organizations and institutions in their effort

E. Bolisani
Università Degli Studi Di Padova, Padova, Italy
e-mail: ettore.bolisani@unipd.it

J.-G. Cegarra-Navarro (✉)
Universidad Politecnica de Cartagena, Cartagena, Spain

A. M. Dima and F. DÁscenzo (eds.), *Business Revolution in a Digital Era*,
Springer Proceedings in Business and Economics,
https://doi.org/10.1007/978-3-030-59972-0_1

to maintain objectivity and control for public interest. Social media amplify these negative effects (Sánchez-Casado et al. 2015). But the issue of counter-knowledge is complex because, under another perspective, it can also have positive effects for someone. Drawing upon a reading of (Yerkovich 1977) and (Baumeister et al. 2004) (Cegarra-Navarro et al. 2014) propose that counter-knowledge may be useful for social influence, entertainment, and even business: social media platforms contain a lot of unverified and even false information, which increase the number of their followers and therefore contribute to their particular market.

Recently, this issue has raised the interest of knowledge management (KM) scholars (Cegarra-Navarro et al. 2014). The purpose of this study is to use KM concepts and models to shed light onto mechanism and effects of production and diffusion of counter-knowledge, the role of social media, and the measures that can be taken by organizations to handle this phenomenon. The study draws inspiration from three cases regarding the Italian healthcare sector. These are paradigmatic because they show the problems faced by public organizations due to the diffusion of counter-knowledge. In particular, the weakness of the "official" sources of knowledge (when they must face the upsurge of so many producers of counter-knowledge, whose messages are amplified by media and social media) is examined, and useful lessons for public institutions and policy-makers are drawn.

2 Background

The term "counter-knowledge" was coined by (Thompson 2008) as "mis-information packaged to look like facts". This refers to the existence of sources of unverified information, gossip, partial truths, or deliberate lies, which are transformed and presented in a way so that they can be mistaken for true facts (Cegarra-Navarro et al. 2015; Sánchez-Casado et al. 2015): people may think they have acquired some kind of "true knowledge", can change their mental representation of reality (Lee and Pistole 2014) and their decision processes (Martínez-Ortiz et al. 2017).

In principle, as with any other knowledge elements, the people should critically assess any kind of knowledge they receive or develop. However, while counter-knowledge may often result in frustrations, misunderstandings, or misled decisions, this is not always the case. Not only is counter-knowledge the result of unproven theories or spurious claims, but it may also be the result of popular proverbs, colloquial expressions or sayings (Cegarra-Navarro et al. 2014) which may "contain some truth", although unverified scientifically. In addition, by extrapolating the concept of "emotional knowledge" proposed by (Bratianu and Orzea 2013), we can assert that uncontrolled emotions such as happiness or comfort based on groundless trust of positive evaluation could lead people to share jokes and inappropriate comments with friends and colleagues (Bratianu 2015; Paradiso 1998). Some people may use jokes or gossip because they wish to socialize or protect themselves from receiving rejection or negative evaluation (Taylor and Bright 2011). This implies that counter-knowledge is part of a complex system and cannot only consist of a simple list of inappropriate behaviours, but it also involves responding to other people's emotions (Bratianu and Orzea 2013).

For managers, counter-knowledge is a challenge. To cultivate and develop positive relationships inside or outside their organizations, they need to be aware of the misuse of counter-knowledge. Especially, public institutions such as universities, scientific research organizations, health organizations, courts, etc. base their credibility on the recognition of professional competence and deontological ethics of their members, and this credibility can be undermined by counter-knowledge. This can cause wrong decisions and provoke doubts about efficacy and appropriateness of official messages and instructions of institutions and public authorities (Hargreaves and Hargreaves 2005).

To sum up, the phenomenon of misusing the counter-knowledge is associated with: (a) the production and delivery of elements of mis-information (Baumeister et al. 2004); (b) their possible transformation into wrong elements that are believed to be true and become integral part of a person's view of reality (Thompson 2008; Cegarra-Sanchez et al. 2017; Beveren 2003; Lee 2004; Darroch and McNaughton 2002; Cegarra-Navarro et al. 2015, 2014; Dumay and Guthrie 2017; Sánchez-Casado et al. 2015; Yerkovich 1977; Baumeister et al. 2004; Lee and Pistole 2014; Martínez-Ortiz et al. 2017; Bratianu and Orzea 2013; Bratianu 2015; Paradiso 1998; Taylor and Bright 2011; Hargreaves and Hargreaves 2005, 2017), and (d) the influence that this can have on the decisions that individuals takes and/or on the way they perceive the role of official institutions (Cegarra-Navarro et al. 2015).

The issue of counter-knowledge has gained momentum due to the emergence of social media (Sánchez-Casado et al. 2015), which bring about new processes of knowledge construction and exchange, in an open environment not controlled by official institutions. For example, Wikipedia is not based on the official delivery by an institutional source (like, e.g., a university, a scientific journal, etc.) but, rather, on a communitarian consensus of users. Social media also lead to an increasing diffusion of fake news: fake news include many phenomena—e.g. news satire, news parody, fabrication, manipulation, advertising or propaganda— (Tandoc et al. 2017) and especially refer to deliberately fabricated contents, typically by anonymous sources "that spread falsehoods by manipulating [...] emotions and tapping into deeply held partisan beliefs" (Gelfert 2018).

Some Internet-based companies, for their business purposes, facilitate the spread of fake news, either intentionally or not: their technical and business system require that more and more people are attracted by their websites, and there is no better way to do that than a tendentious piece of news (maybe fake) that stimulates curiosity, rage, and viral reactions (Thompson 2008). In conclusion, the proliferation of fake news by means of social media can contribute to the misuse of counter-knowledge.

It can be concluded that counter-knowledge can cause damage to human relations (Hislop et al. 2014) because it can be a source of errors and negative attitudes. This can also affect the performance of organizations and companies (Coombs et al. 2013; Fiol 2017; Reese 2017). Misusing counter-knowledge can also pose challenges to liberal societies (Greenhill and Oppenheim 2017) because it undermines the authority of those institutions that are generally recognized as providers of "credible" knowledge

(Cegarra-Navarro et al. 2016). For this reason, analyzing and developing countermeasures that can contrast the phenomenon is increasingly important.

3 Research Questions and Method

KM models can be of great use to analyze the processes of counter-knowledge, and to derive useful lessons for contrasting it. When someone consciously uses unverified information to manipulate people's expectations in his (her) own interest, it is possible that this results in bad knowledge (Cegarra-Navarro et al. 2015).

As shown in Fig. 1, counter-knowledge misuse can be treated in relation to three aspects: its ingredients, its misuse/transformation process, and its effects. Its ingredients can be a mix of unsupported/unsupportable explanations and justifications, which have not necessarily harmful effects because many people may use them simply in a "fun" way. As regards its misuse, there are different forms of manipulation (more or less credible, more or less convincing, more or less official, etc.) that can deliver partially true/false knowledge contents in varying proportions (i.e. truth plus intentional lies, unverified plus official information, objective information plus gossips, etc.): this makes it difficult (especially for uneducated or ingenuous people) to distinguish "real or reasonably plausible facts" from fakes. Its effects can be seen in cognitive terms (namely, the new knowledge constructions that individuals build on the basis of the bad counter-knowledge absorbed and/or developed) and in decisional terms (i.e.: the consequent decisions that are taken based on these cognitive constructions). In other words, although counter knowledge is not in itself a guarantee for misleading decisions, one thing, for sure, is that bad counter knowledge adversely influence the decision process. This is what the lower part of Fig. 1 means: ingredients themselves of counter-knowledge are not necessarily negative in terms of their possible effects, but when they result in negative effects, these effects may, in turn, lead to misleading decisions.

This paper addresses these questions:

a. How can the misuse of counter-knowledge impact on the behavior of the public and, in turn, of scientific institutions?

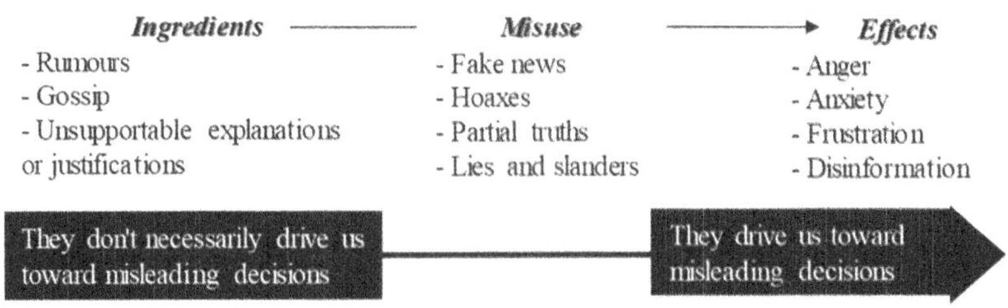

Fig. 1. Flow of misusing counter-knowledge

b. Seen under a KM perspective, what are the main lessons that can be drawn?

We refer to "knowledge" as informative elements based on verified/verifiable facts or that, at least, are available in a form that can be checked transparently. We refer to "(bad) counter-knowledge" as the content of manipulated messages that are unverified/unverifiable, may simply represent allegations and gossip, can be fake, and—intentionally or not—spread over a great audience.

Three cases are examined, which summarize the events concerning three medical treatments in the recent history of Italy and the consequent processes of misusing counter-knowledge. Qualitative research, and particularly an analysis based on documentary research (Ahmed 2010; McCulloch 2004), was used. The purpose was substantially explorative, i.e. to provide preliminary elements for a debate about the emerging issues, and to set the grounds for further research. The available data are in multiple form and from different sources, i.e.: (a) existing case-studies, books, press releases, and newspaper articles, especially to reconstruct the chronology of events and collect other factual data; and (b) newspaper articles, websites, video interviews, especially to analyze opinions and statements expressed by involved players. The following sections report the cases in the form of a chronological narration, with an emphasis on the elements that are crucial from a KM viewpoint.

4 Cases

4.1 The "Di Bella Method"

Di Bella (1912–2003) was a physician who became popular due to insisting rumors that had been spreading over at least one decade that "a doctor had found a cure for cancer". At the end of the 90s, press and televisions started to throw a spotlight on Di Bella and his "Method" (DBM), even at international level (Nadeau 2002). Di Bella's home was assaulted by patients, desperately looking for a cure, and journalists. The virtuous lifestyle of Di Bella contributed to build his credible image (Grazia 2011).

However, many medical researchers repeatedly affirmed there was no clinical evidence of the efficacy of DBM: they claimed that DBM had never been tested in a standard clinical trial, nor his proposer had ever published his works in a medical journal for "public scrutiny". Di Bella and his supporters claimed that the evidence was clear, simply because "the method had cured many people"; they blamed other physicians (including a Nobel Prize and a worldwide-known oncologist) and the pharmaceutical industry to exert their power for personal reasons or just a myopic vision, and that the methods of official science were untrustworthy. Di Bella was not completely isolated in the medical community (there were doctors affirming that some of the points made by Di Bella could have some foundations). What's more, official medical institutions had some failures in terms of reputation (e.g. cases of malpractice, corruption, etc.).

For these reasons, the public authorities felt forced to play defensively, and the media didn't help to make things clearer because, according to some observers (Minerva 1998), the position of the "official science" in public debate was just presented as "one possible opinion" with an equal weight of all the others (including rumors, unverified facts, or emotional opinions). A frank debate was impossible, and the case became a matter of "cheers and beliefs by the different supporters" rather than honest "judgements" based on factual elements.

In 1997, a judge of a small court, decided in favour of some appellants and imposed the free administration of Di Bella's treatment at the expenses of the public national healthcare system. The Government was brought up and, despite the repeated opposition of the official healthcare Commissions, the Health Ministry (Rosi Bindi) declared that the "willing of the people" was to give DBM a chance. An experimentation protocol was implemented, but it brought no evident benefit to patients. While Di Bella claimed that the failure was due to a bad implementation of the trials (www.metododibella.org) – and indeed, it seems that the police forces had found some evidence of misconduct—on the other hand, many doctors underlined that the trial had been implemented under the direct supervision by Di Bella himself, and accused the physician to have never provided complete and objective information.

Time passed, and a new government decided to re-open the case, but after an ultimate round of analysis, DBM was finally rejected (Vickers and Cassileth 2001). Di Bella, until his death in 2002, kept affirming that his cure was effective, and so are doing his heirs, family, and supporters (https://metododibella.org/it). The official science (Vickers 2004) maintained that DBM had been subjected to a good quality clinical trial with no effective results.

4.2 Stamina

"Stamina" refers to a medical treatment proposed by Davide Vannoni. According to some observers (Lepore and L. 2013) he was just a professional in media and communications, with experience in persuasions and marketing in medicine (Vannoni and G. 2002). Vannoni used to tell the people that he himself was cured with a special treatment based on staminal cells in Ukraine, and he just intended to bring this cure to Italy (Mautino 2014). His personal suffering may have contributed to the construction of a credible reputation.

Vannoni founded a "laboratory" in the basement of his marketing company (Mautino 2014) and hired two Ukrainan biologists. He also started a communications campaign in local television channels, which made him gain the favour of public opinion and especially seriously ill people who, so far, had not found effective cures in the official medicine.

While the Public Prosecutors started investigating on his controversial activity (especially about his credentials to administer a treatment), Vannoni was, anyway, able to involve more doctors and even a public center for cancer treatment ("Spedali di Brescia"). There, his cure was administered to a growing number of patients. All this increased the pressure on public authorities and helped Vannoni to obtain an official permission and even public funds.

The cures and the experiments with patients went on, but always on the spotlight of the public authorities and prosecutors. Vannoni was asked to illustrate his therapeutic protocol publicly and to provide evidence of the results really obtained. According to some observers, he just replied with a mix of contrasting communications (Mautino 2014) who could grasp the attention of non-careful readers but attracted the criticism of experts (Pini 2013). In September 2013, a report by a special public Commission declared that Stamina was an ineffective and even a potentially dangerous method (Pini 2013).

Finally, Vannoni was condemned in 2015 for fraud and administration of dangerous drugs. He settled with the court, but despite his promises, he went on administering his treatment in a non-EU country. So, he was arrested in 2017, and died in 2019.

4.3 "No-Vax" Movement

This term identifies those that oppose to the compulsory administration of vaccines to humans. Anti-vaccine movements have a long history that starts just after Edward Jenner, the pioneer of smallpox vaccination, proposed his method. In recent times, there has been an upsurge of this phenomenon, strictly related to the advent of Social Media. There is a proliferation of websites, forums, and blogs related to "No Vax" topics (Weniger and Papania 2012).

Some think that the No Vax position is just a matter of prejudice, false beliefs, or ideological opinions. However, opponents to vaccines claim that their motivations derive from the "official science" itself (Kata 2012; Mazzucco 2016). Indeed, in a paper published in a famous medicine journal (Wakefield, et al. 1998)– which, it must be admitted, underwent the scientific peer-review assessment—the authors claimed that there was evidence of correlation between vaccines and the upsurge of autism and other diseases. The study gained resonance and fueled the protests of No vax communities all around the world, although lately, it was discovered that the study was simply a fake (Deer 2010), and the paper was retreated by the journal editors (but only after 12 year).

The No vax movement has gained strength in Italy, so much to affect political decisions. A growing number of people claimed their right to avoid vaccines for them and their children. Despite bold statements and pro-vax campaigns by doctors and authoritative physicians (see e.g. www.robertoburioni.it), the No vax position gained consensus also thanks to the massive role of social media. Especially in some areas of the country, the total amount of vaccine administration to children dropped under a minimum level, with risk of epidemies.

Concerned with these consequences, in 2017 the Ministry of Health (Beatrice Lorenzin), supported by her official consulting committees, promulgated a bill to impose vaccination to all children attending schools. This raised a turmoil of protests

(Caporale 2018) that were not sedated by the voices of the official science. Indeed, some wonder why there is such a climate of distrust towards the medical community. In the case of Italy, despite some data show that the national health system is, on average, good enough for the people, the few cases of malpractice and corruption may have contributed to a negative image of the medical profession (Caporale 2018).

5 Discussion and KM Implications

The KM implications can be illustrated by considering the three main aspects mentioned in Sect. 3, i.e.: the ingredients of knowledge and counter-knowledge, the processes of misusing, and the effects in cognitive and decision terms.

In terms of ingredients, all the three situations show that highly sophisticated scientific knowledge requires complex structures to be described and understood. Also, no scientific knowledge can be considered ultimate, and the research process itself proceeds by continuous steps of validation. Scientific knowledge is not an act of faith but, rather, a rational and progressive process of assimilation and internalization (using Nonaka's term) that requires a special attitude, a cognitive background, and constant application. Scientific knowledge is always partial and incomplete, and in continuous construction, step by step. This is hard to accept for the "common people", especially when they are in a fragile situation and simply need fast and "easy" answers, which, at the same time, may not be possible.

The official science makes advances only in a frank and lively debate between different positions and schools of thought, which reflects the complexity of scientific knowledge previously recalled. But it can be interpreted by the people as a sign that "there is something rotten" in the medical community, or that the academics simply have "time to waste in sterile debates" sitting in their ivory tower.

Consequently, the efforts by the scientific community (like in the DBM or Stamina cases) to "explain" the rationale behind a scientific trial protocol and its statistic, conflict with much simpler messages such as, for example, "patients have the right to experiment any available treatment they like". Indeed, rational, emotional and spiritual implications of knowledge (Bolisani and Bratianu 2018), are mixed and difficult to separate. Counter-knowledge—in terms of fake elements, gossips, rumors, and beliefs—can easily spread, intentionally or not.

Furthermore, counter-knowledge sometimes derives from the "official science" itself, deliberately or not—as in the No VAX case. But while scientists can have the resources to detect and correct false statements, this is much more difficult for the common people. When they get information from a source that they think is reliable, they may lack the time or capability to check it, to consult other sources, to cross-check data, etc. In short, their final interpretations are based on a narrow frame of reference and may result in an abuse or improper use of the source itself. Later, these inappropriate interpretations spread and become established opinions and beliefs. In short, counter-knowledge is also "knowledge that we assume it is right" when, in fact, it is wrong.

Considering the misuse process, as the cases show, there are many actors (i.e. researchers, doctors, pharmaceutical companies, politicians, and patients) that have different cognitive backgrounds and even conflicting interests. The success of a medical treatment (e.g. a vaccine) requires that a positive knowledge exchange occurs between all the parties. This can be affected by inappropriate attitude and distorted messages, that can be misunderstood by the others. Bad counter-knowledge is the result of misusing unsupportable explanations and justifications (Thompson 2008), so we can find three potential triggers based on the level of subjectivity inherent in misusing this unverified information, and the pervasive influence of peer pressure in the spreading and manipulation of information. While in the first case, the DBM promoters believe in their own opinions regardless their "formal scientific demonstration" (i.e. *unintended misuse of counter-knowledge*), the "Stamina" case involves fraudulent or dilatory intent (i.e. *intended misuse of counter-knowledge*), and in the "No VAX" case, social pressure is the force that accelerates the fears of side effects of vaccination and enhances bad knowledge creation (i.e. *peer pressure to misuse counter-knowledge*).

As regards the effects, the presence of bad counter-knowledge induced the people to build their own "special knowledge" about an issue. In the "No vax" case, they tend to build a sort of "alternative knowledge" about the problem of vaccines, and this cognitive process is not necessarily based on a "scientifically correct" approach but, nonetheless, represents a base for decision-making. In addition, in the absence of a strong supreme authority that is publicly recognized, there is no more "official knowledge", and personal beliefs become more important than "demonstrations". As the cases show, the official scientific authorities are not unaffected by cases of malpractice or corruption, and in the eyes of the public these sources of knowledge are put, in the end of the day, on an equal footing of any other source—including gossips and false messages. The issue of trust emerges clearly: in all the cases examined, a key reason of the proliferation of counter-knowledge is the lack of reciprocal trust between the involved parties.

The implications of the above-mentioned findings are that healthcare managers may need to be aware of the possibility that patients and carers do access manipulated information. This means, for instance, that a doctor must not simply administer a vaccine, but should also "convince" a patient that the treatment is appropriate, inform about risks, etc.; but the doctor must also be able to "listen to" the possible objections and fears. Similarly, drug companies that simply deliver marketing messages can be interpreted as "just minding their own profits". A physician that refuses to support unverified treatments (like it happened for Stamina and DBM), may be perceived as "not empathic" with the people and their sufferance, if she/he is not able to explain the plausible reasons for this refusal. A quotation from Ben-Hur film (1959) suits perfectly in this context: "one idea is only fought with another idea". If Judah Ben-Hur was a businessman, the ideas of unlearning and putting aside outdated knowledge could have well been born in the first century. These results support the extant literature that argues that as a result of replacing or unlearning, organizations can discard or revise obsolete routines and embrace new understandings (Cegarra-Navarro and Sánchez-Polo 2008; Ransbotham and Kane 2011; Starbuck 1996). The problem is that old knowledge can be replaced by bad counter-knowledge, with all the negative effects that this can bring about.

Finally, the upsurge of social media amplifies the negative impacts of counter-knowledge; any news (true or false that it can be) moves fast in the social media networks, while scientific knowledge requires time to be understood, assimilated, and maybe even reasonably criticized. In addition, Internet companies can favour any message that attracts users, regardless its truthfulness.

6 Conclusion

The paper highlights key KM issues related to the emergence of bad counter-knowledge. The origin of counter-knowledge can be not only intentionally fake news (deliberately diffused for some reason or personal interest) but also supposedly verified sources of information, or "honest" beliefs. In other words, an implicit risk in scientific activity is the fact that its results can be misunderstood or used even contrarily to their meanings. This study provides insights into the possible implications for scientific institutions and policy-makers. These lessons are here expressed in the form of "working ideas" rather than ultimate conclusions.

a. Complexity of knowledge. The awareness that medical problems are complex can help scientists and policy-makers to avoid mistakes. The emotional and irrational components that unavoidably affect the cognitive processes should be clear in the mind of doctors when they try to explain the reason of a treatment (or its refusal).
b. Knowledge for decision processes. Professionals should be aware that the decisions of common people (and not only) are based on a mix of knowledge contents, that includes rational and factual elements, but also emotional and irrational aspects, personal beliefs, etc. The presence of counter-knowledge, in any possible form, can affect it. So, it can be hard, for scientific institutions, to develop a climate of mutual respect and calm debate where the people can carefully ponder all factual elements. The continuous rebound of accusations between "parties" —which tends to be exacerbated by social media—should be avoided because it especially harms the credibility of public authorities and tends to poison decision processes. On the other hand, a "bureaucratic" attitude (as is typical of public institutions) is not a shortcut because it may be perceived as "technocratic arrogance".
c. Trust, transparency, and openness to admitting mistakes. When it is not possible to show the "true knowledge" conclusively and incontrovertibly, it may be appropriate to be open to honest reservations and fears. Especially, when a mistake is done (and science is not error-free) it may be better to admit it. Transparency in decision-making should be essential. In addition, for building a trustworthy climate, any potential conflict of interest should be avoided.

d. Communication skills and use of social media. The scientific community is often unprepared for public communications: scientists and physicians may be easily fall in the perverse traps of social media. Education of doctors and scientists should include these competencies, which is an aspect rarely considered.

The results of this research should be interpreted with caution, as it has some limitations. The cases were selected because they highlighted the presence of bad counter-knowledge and its harmful effects, but different findings might have been obtained from a different sample. As regards the method, a documentary research approach implies that several direct sources have not been included, such as fresh direct interviews with key informants, etc. These limitations may, however, be addressed in future studies, and this paper just represents an initial contribution. For example, a line of research can be to examine the different ways of creating counter-knowledge. Another option can be to develop a longitudinal study that examines the changes in the definition of counter-knowledge over time.

Acknowledgements The authors would like to thank the Ministerio de Economía, Industria y Competitividad of the Spanish Government for financing the research project ECO2017-88987-R (MINECO/FEDER;UE), co-financed from the European Union FEDER, and the European Union COST action "INDCOR"—CA18230—"Interactive Narrative Design for Complexity Representations".

References

Ahmed, J.U.: Documentary research method: new dimensions. Indus. J. Manage. Soc. Sci. **4**(1), 1–14 (2010)

Baumeister, R.F., Zhang, L., Vohs, K.D.: Gossip as cultural learning. Rev. Gen. Psychol. **8**(2), 111–121 (2004)

Bolisani, E., Bratianu, C.: Emergent Knowledge Strategies: Strategic Thinking in Knowledge Management. Springer International Publishing, Berlin (2018)

Bratianu, C.: Organizational Knowledge Dynamics: Managing Knowledge Creation, Acquisition, Sharing, and Transformation. IGI Global, Hershey (2015)

Bratianu, C., Orzea, I.: The entropic intellectual capital model. Knowl. Manage. Res. Pract. **11**(2), 133–141 (2013)

Caporale, E.: La battaglia sui vaccini tra pericoli e fake news. La Stampa, 8 Feb 2018 (2018)

Cegarra-Navarro, J.G., Sánchez-Polo, M.T.: Linking the individual forgetting context with customer capital from a seller's perspective. J. Oper. Res. Soc. **59**(12), 1614–1623 (2008)

Cegarra-Navarro, J.G., Eldridge, S., Wensley, A.K.P.: Counter-knowledge and realised absorptive capacity. Euro. Manage. J. **32**(2), 165–176 (2014)

Cegarra-Navarro, J.G., Cepeda Carrión, G., Wensley, A.: Negative aspects of counter-knowledge on absorptive capacity and human capital. J. Intell. Capital **16**(4), 763–778 (2015)

Cegarra-Navarro, J.G., Soto-Acosta, P., Martinez-Caro, E.: Linking counter-knowledge to goal orientation through an unlearning context—a study from a Spanish University. Learn. Ind. Differ. **45**, 260–267 (2016)

Cegarra-Sanchez, J., Cegarra-Navarro, J.G., Wensley, A., Diaz Manzano, J.: Overcoming counter-knowledge through telemedicine communication technologies. J. Health Organ. Manage. **31**(7/8), 730–745 (2017)

Coombs, C.R., Hislop, D., Holland, J., Bosley, S.L.C., Manful, E.: Exploring types of individual unlearning by local health-care managers: an original empirical approach. Health Serv. Deliv. Res. **1**(2) (2013)

Darroch, J., McNaughton, R.: Examining the link between knowledge management practices and types of innovation. J. Intell. Capital **3**(3), 210–222 (2002)

Deer, B.: Truth on the MMR vaccine scandal. The Sunday Times, 24 January (2010)

Dumay, J., Guthrie, J.: Involuntary disclosure of intellectual capital: is it relevant? J. Intell. Capital. **18**(1), 29–44 (2017)

Fiol, M.: Unlearning established organizational routines—part I. Learn. Organ. **24**(1), 13–29 (2017)

Gelfert, A.: Fake news: a definition. . Informal Logic. **38**(1), 84–117 (2018)

Gosa, T.L.: Counterknowledge, racial paranoia, and the cultic milieu: decoding hip hop conspiracy theory. Poetics **39**(3), 187–204 (2011)

Di Grazia, S.: Dossier Di Bella (2011). Retrieved from www.medbunker.it/p/dossier-di-bella.html

Greenhill, K.M., Oppenheim, B.: Rumor has it: the adoption of unverified information in conflict zones. Int. Stud. Quart. **61**(3), 660–676 (2017)

Hargreaves, A.: The emotions of teaching and educational change. In: Hargreaves, A. (ed.) Extending Educational Change, pp. 278–295. Springer, Dordrecht (2005)

Hislop, D., Bosley, S., Coombs, C.R., Holland, J.: The process of individual unlearning: a neglected topic in an under-researched field. Manage. Learn. **45**(5), 540–560 (2014)

Kata, A.: Anti-vaccine activists, Web 2.0, and the postmodern paradigm—An overview of tactics and tropes used online by the anti-vaccination movement. Vaccine **30**(25), 3778–3789 (2012)

Lee, J.J.: Comparing institutional relationships with academic departments: a study of five academic fields. Res. High. Educ. **45**(6), 603–624 (2004)

Lee, J., Pistole, M.C.: International student sociocultural adaptation: gossip and place attachment contributions. J. Mental Health Couns. **36**(4), 345–359 (2014)

Lepore, F., Piana L.: Mr Stamina, solo marketing, L'espresso, 5 July 2013 (2013)

Martínez-Ortiz, P.J., Moffett, S., Cegarra-Navarro, J.G., López Hernández, F.A.: Modelling the relationship between counter-knowledge and open-mindedness for policy development. J. Pub. Aff. **17**(3) (2017)

Mautino, B.: Stamina: una storia sbagliata, Padova: CICAP (2014). Retrieved from www.cicap.org/new/files/Stamina_una_storia_sbagliata.pdf

Mazzucco, M.: Il vaccino può causare autismo. Lo dice il bugiardino. Nexus Edizioni, October 2016 (2016). Retrieved from www.nexusedizioni.it/it/CT/il-vaccino-puo-causare-autismo-lo-dice-il-bugiardino-5313?parentSlug=medicina-e-salute-23&fixed_cms=sezioni

McCulloch, G.: Documentary Research: In Education, History and the Social Sciences. Routledge, Abongdon (2004)

Minerva, D.: La leggenda del santo guaritore. Il caso Di Bella: Una storia italiana. Editori Riuniti, Roma (1998)

Nadeau, B.: Doctor of Hope. Newsweek, 28 April (2002)

Paradiso, S.: Emotional brain: the mysterious underpinnings of emotional life. Am. J. Psychiatry **155**(4), 570–570 (1998)

Pini, V.: Stamina, l'appello degli scienziati: i malati non sono cavie, vanno tutelati. La Repubblica, 21 May 2013 (2013)

Ransbotham, S., Kane, G.C.: Membership turnover and collaboration success in online communities : explaining rises and falls. Manage. Inf. Syst. Q. **35**(3), 613–627 (2011)

Reese, S. (2017). Putting organizational unlearning into practice: a few steps for the practitioner. Learn. Organ. **24**, 167–69

Sánchez-Casado, N., Cegarra-Navarro, J.G., Tomaseti-Solano, E.: Linking social networks to utilitarian benefits through counter-knowledge. Online Inf. Rev. **39**(2), 179–196 (2015)

Starbuck, W.: Unlearning ineffective or obsolete technologies. Int. J. Technol. Manage. **11**, 725–728 (1996)

Tandoc, E.C., Lim, Z.W., Ling, R.: Defining fake news. Digital Journalism, 1–17 (2017)

Taylor, S.N., Bright, D.S.: Open-mindedness and defensiveness in multisource feedback processes: a conceptual framework. J. Appl. Behav. Sci. **47**(4), 432–460 (2011)
Thompson, D.: Counter-Knowledge. Atlantic Books, London (2008)
Thompson, N.: Our Minds Have Been Hijacked by Our Phones. Tristan Harris Wants to Rescue Them. Wired, 26 July (2017)
Van Beveren, J.: Does health care for knowledge management? J. Knowl. Manage. **7**(1), 90–95 (2003)
Vannoni, D., Tardivo, G.: Psicologia della comunicazione e marketing nella prevenzione sanitaria. Communication Report to Regione Piemonte (2002). Retrieved from https://tinyurl.com/qa4gw2z
Vickers, A.: Alternative cancer cures: "unproven" or "disproven"? CA: A Cancer J Clin **54**(2), 110–118 (2004)
Vickers, A.J., Cassileth, B.R.: Unconventional therapies for cancer and cancer-related symptoms. Lancet Oncol. **2**(4), 226–232 (2001)
Wakefield, A.J. et al.: Retracted: Ileal-lymphoid-nodular hyperplasia, non-specific colitis, and pervasive developmental disorder in children. Lancet (1998). Retrieved from https://doi.org/10.1016/S0140-6736(97)11096-0
Weniger, B.G., Papania, M.J.: Alternative vaccine delivery methods. In: Vaccines, 6th edn. Elsevier, Amsterdam (2012)
Yerkovich, S.: Gossiping as a way of speaking. J. Commun. **27**(1), 192–196 (1977)

Sources of Information Used by Teachers and Reseachers from Romanian Universities in the Knowledge Flows of Bioeconomy

Andrei Ștefan Neștian, Silviu Mihail Tiță, and Alexandra Luciana Guță

1 Introduction

This is the second article published for disseminating the results of a research conducted in the field of knowledge flows in bioeconomy. In the first article, published in 2018, about the intensity of involvement of teachers and researchers from Romanian universities in bioeconomy knowledge flows (Neștian et al. 2018), we argued on the fact that the involvement of teachers and researchers in the bioeconomy knowledge flows is different based on the intensity of their involvement in knowledge flows related to bioeconomy development. The specific sets of activities were named: Bio-Academic, Bio-Tech and Science, Bio-Entrepreneurship, Bio-Ambassador and Bio-Expert. These components can be understood as five different behavioral compounds or roles that can be used to understand their involvement in knowledge flows related to bioeconomy.

The instrument for collecting data for the first article contained supplementary scales for measuring other aspects of the knowledge flows, not used in the first article. These supplementary scales are built on the perspective that the knowledge flow can be described as a passage of knowledge from a source to a beneficiary. Hence, defining extremities of the flows are the sources of the knowledge involved, as objects or persons from which the information is originating.

A. Ș. Neștian (✉) · S. M. Tiță · A. L. Guță
Alexandru Ioan Cuza University, Carol I. 11, Iasi, Romania
e-mail: nestian@uaic.ro

S. M. Tiță
e-mail: silviu.tita@uaic.ro

A. L. Guță
e-mail: luciana_guta@yahoo.com

A. M. Dima and F. DÁscenzo (eds.), *Business Revolution in a Digital Era*,
Springer Proceedings in Business and Economics,
https://doi.org/10.1007/978-3-030-59972-0_2

2 Literature Review

2.1 Bioeconomy Knowledge Flows and Universities

The largest context of this research is the Bioeconomy, a concept holding revolutionary economic promises that has brought it in the focus of both scientists and public institutions. In an OECD document we find that "a bioeconomy can be thought of as a world where biotechnology contributes to a significant share of economic output" (OECD 2009).

The Bioeconomy is defined as a particular kind of economy, characterized by some distinctive features. First of all, it relies on renewable natural resources. Kuisma (in Näyhä 2012) states that "bioeconomy can be defined as the exploitation and management of renewable natural resources in a sustainable way."

Another important feature is that bioeconomy is a new kind of economic system. Maciejczak (2017) considers that "bioeconomy is widely understood as an economic system that combines in a synergic way both natural resources and technologies, together with markets, people and policies" (Maciejczak 2017).

A third feature of the Bioeconomy is that it creates a very diverse array of products and services, categorized as products of different economic sectors, some for direct consumption of humans, some for industrial use or for producing indirect benefits to human beneficiaries. Dabbert et al. (2007) state that "bioeconomy refers to the sustainable production and conversion of biomass into a range of food, health, fibre and industrial products and energy".

This double complexity of the Bioeconomy makes it a perfect field of study for analyzing the knowledge flows related to its development. Knowledge from remarkably different sciences needs to get together to facilitate economic activities resulting in an equally diverse array of products and services, also with a remarkable divergent potential uses. This requires the existence of knowledge flows, with a paramount role in the development of science and technology for bioeconomy.

The concept of knowledge flow is coined by Bolisani and Oltramani in 2012. They state that "knowledge flows can be seen as a metaphor that is useful for analysing the knowledge transfer that takes place between two different economic players" (Bolisani and Oltramani 2012). The idea of a knowledge flow as a passage of knowledge from a source to a beneficiary is based on Bratianu's (2011) statement, who mentions that "knowledge flows only due to a pressure difference between the emitter and the receiver". In another publication, Bratianu and Orzea (2013) are developing the previous idea into a practical explanation about the flow of knowledge between two persons: "The knowledge flow should be oriented from an individual with a higher level of knowledge and understanding towards an individual with a lower level of knowledge and understanding" (Bratianu and Orzea 2013). This supports our perspective that the knowledge flow originates in a source and is potentially beneficial for the receiver.

Universities are entities recognized for three core activities: providing educational services through educational programs, providing scientific services through the creation and diffusion of scientific knowledge, and providing other services to students, for facilitating their living and learning style. From this we can see that the involvement of the universities in knowledge flows will be specific to their main activities. In order to understand this specificity we rely on Bolisani and Oltramani's (2012) analysis, which points out that there are three different forms of knowledge flows: "knowledge transferred through consulting services or trainings, knowledge incorporated in services or products that are delivered and knowledge transferred through the exchange of services and products, before, during and after the exchange has taken place". We used this specificity in developing the methodological framework of our study, by separating different types of activities in which the academic staff takes an active role in the Bioeconomy.

2.2 *Knowledge Sources in Bioeconomy*

For the development of the scientific instrument for data collection about the knowledge sources, the literature review process has lead to the discovery of several criteria differentiating the sources used by the teachers and researchers in Bioeconomy. According to Schwartz et al. (2011) the organization of object knowledge can be done using the category-based view. This assumes that object knowledge is organized by taxonomic and thematic categories.

In this process of categorization, we were bound by the need to design a research instrument based on the result of the categorization process. Additionally, our knowledge also includes links between concepts that play complementary roles in the same scenes or events, referred to as thematic categories.

Our process of categorisation was based on the scientific literature and our experience as academic staff, and the purpose of it was to achieve a clear taxonomy, respecting principles of dichotomous differences between categories.

First of all, we find out that the scientific approach that led to the creation of the knowledge available at the source is important. For that, a difference is made between knowledge emerging from scientific activities, being published or disseminated in a scientific manner, practical knowledge and institutional knowledge. This criterion is significant since it assumes different ways of involvement of the academic staff in the related processes. This separation is based on several theoretical opinions.

According to Mauser et al. (2013), in one perspective, knowledge is considered as being composed of different configurations and validated practices that emerge as a result of agents' learning within their natural and/or societal contexts. The origin of knowledge is in the practical activity and people involved in that activity are learning it through repeated application and through interpersonal sharing. From this point, Nonaka's opinion on categories of knowledge is relevant. The practical knowledge can be seen as either tacit or explicit knowledge. Tacit knowledge is highly personal and hard to formalize, making it difficult to communicate or share with others. It is deeply rooted in an individual's actions and experience as well as in the ideals, values or emotions he or she embraces (Nonaka and Konno 1998). "Explicit knowledge is formal and systematic. For this reason, it can be easily communicated and shared, in product specifications or a scientific formula or a computer program" (Nonaka 2007).

In the scientific activity, knowledge is transferred as explicit knowledge using a formal and systematic language and vocabulary, using data and scientific formulas in order to argument and to prove new knowledge. Mauser et al. (2013) state that "knowledge should ultimately be put in a formal framework and thus be universally recognizable and to a large extent exchangeable across contexts." (Mauser et al. 2013). The role of science is precisely to generate such kind of knowledge that has the universality and the expression necessary to make it understandable and reusable by as many recipients as possible.

The combination stage of the SECI model gives us an insight on the fact that some knowledge, shared between an important parts of the members of an organization and able to be found in various explicit copies in documents issued by the company, can be considered institutional knowledge (Nonaka 2007). Examples of institutional knowledge source generally used by scientists are studies and secondary data published by public institutions or professional organizations.

One condition for the knowledge to be externalized and shared is the codification in a shared language. Boisot (1998, p. 233) has developed an abstract model of knowledge dynamics, in which the space for sharing knowledge is characterized by three dimensions: codification, capture and diffusion. He explains that, in a general formulation, codification is a process throughout which we shall create conceptual categories that facilitate the classification of events and phenomena.

Codification is an individual activity that depends on the existence of a common language, already shared by the emitter and the receiver of the information. From a practical point of view, in sharing scientific knowledge and in accessing scientific sources, the concept of codification leads to two issues: the form of the codified knowledge and the limitations of using different mother tongues in sharing the scientific output.

In this perspective, the form of the codified knowledge means the material form on which the knowledge is to be found or to be transferred, and the three possible forms are: written, oral or experiential. The first two forms are typical for explicit knowledge. The written form comprises books, articles, conference proceedings, graphical representations, secondary data etc. The oral form of the knowledge sources comprises all conversations with other scientists and practitioners in scientific conferences, in project teams, in consultancy activities etc. The experiential knowledge comprises all types of tacit knowledge that the scientist manages to acquire through his individual involvement in practical activities related to his scientific field: on-site visits at companies or public institutions, his own consulting activity, interpretations of secondary data, participation in project teams etc.

Hence, we found that the language used to codify the information is a defining characteristic of the source. The limitations of using different mother tongues in sharing the scientific output are related to the codification strategy chosen by the scientist. Publishing the results of research in a language that has a large number of native and taught speakers around the world will make it a potential knowledge source for a greater number of potential users compared with publishing it in a language spoken only by the natives of a certain country, a language that only a few people from other countries are taught to speak. Publishing in English will make the scientific content easier available for a greater number of potential readers than publishing in Romanian.

Language plays a restrictive role in scientific production, insofar as production itself is concerned, as well as in the areas of publication and dissemination. "English is generally considered to be the lingua franca of the scientific community. For example, roughly 80% of all the journals indexed in Scopus (one of the important scientific data based) are published in English" (Meneghini and Packer 2007; Van Weijen 2012).

The publication of scientific articles in the lingua franca generates paradoxical situations. Even publishing in journals with a high impact factor, which are recorded in the main databases and which are published in English (i.e., prestigious international journals), can be counter-productive if they are not read by the researchers to whom the paper is mainly directed or these papers hardly become known in the very country in which the research was performed—where potentially the main readers may be and where the work may be of greatest use (Bordons 2004).

Publishing in a language such as Romanian raises a problem of international relevance for the researcher because his scientific creation is very little accessed by specialists in order to represent something in a field, contradicting the idea that "the creation of knowledge and their dissemination, for the benefit of society, is why researchers benefit from public funds" (Florian and Florian 2006). A search on Google Academic with the key words "Bioeconomie + Romania" for the years 2019 and 2020, revealed 128 results. "Bioeconomie" is the Romanian word for bioeconomy. The search was performed in January 2020. Amongst the results, only 21 were in Romanian and 13 of these 21 were in Amfiteatru Economic Journal, a journal published in two versions, Romanian an English. Hence, we can state that only 8 publications were only in Romanian (6.3%), 13 were available simultaneous in Romanian and English (10.2%) and 107 were only in English (83.6%). The same search on Scopus database retrieved only one article, an article from Amfiteatru Economic Journal, listed because the title was doubled in English and Romanian. In fact, no publication in Romanian language was to be found on Scopus. In Clarivate Web of Science Core Collection, the same query returned zero results.

In order to be comprehensive, the list of sources of information used by the Romanian teachers and researchers was compiled based on a mix of criteria related to the form of the source (written, oral or experiential), the language of the information (in mother tongue or other languages), the scientific approach (scientific knowledge, practical knowledge, institutional knowledge) and the way the person gets in contact with the source (by reading, by hearing, by relating with other persons). The initial list of sources was pre-tested with professors and researchers in fields like Machinery Building, Economics, Management, who were asked to assess the entire questionnaire and to provide feedback. The participants proposed improvements in order to ensure that the questionnaire was understandable and easy to complete and that the variables are realistically designed, based on their experience. Based on their opinions and on the mix of criteria stated already, a realistic and holistic list of 13 sources emerged, which are included in the Results and discussions section of this paper.

3 Methodology

3.1 Hypotheses

The methodology of the present research was built in order to discover the importance of the sources of information on the bioeconomy that are used by teachers and researcher in Romanian universities. We are formulating the following hypotheses:

H1: There are differences between the level of importance of different sources of information about bioeconomy used by teachers and researchers in Romanian universities.

H2: Sources of information about bioeconomy in mother tongue are more important than sources in other languages.

3.2 The Instrument

The present study is part of a larger research. In this paper, we focus on the sources of information that the respondents use in order to develop their knowledge that is applicable to bioeconomy and on the importance of those sources. The scale for the latent variable "sources of information" ranges from 0 (zero) to 4 (four), with the following meanings: 0 (zero)—"Null importance (You do not use)"; 1 (one)—"Low importance"; 2 (two)— "Medium importance"; 3 (three)— "High importance"; 4 (four)—"Critical importance"; the scale contains thirteen items.

3.3 The Sample

Being part of a larger research, that is focused on knowledge flows in bioeconomy, this research was conducted on teachers and researchers from Romanian universities, taking into consideration only faculties that are related to the field of bioeconomy from 15 Romanian universities. Thus, 15 universities from all the regions in Romania have been identified, which are specialized in:

- Agriculture and veterinary medicine: Banat University of Agricultural Sciences and Veterinary Medicine of Timisoara, University of Agricultural Sciences and Veterinary Medicine Iaşi, University of Agricultural Sciences and Veterinary Medicine Cluj-Napoca, University of Agronomic Sciences and Veterinary

Medicine of Bucharest, from which teachers and researchers from the fields of agriculture, horticulture, agricultural management and veterinary medicine were targeted.

- Economics: Bucharest University of Economic Studies.
- Medicine: Grigore T. Popa University of Medicine and Pharmacy Iaşi, Iuliu Haţieganu University of Medicine and Pharmacy Cluj-Napoca—faculties of medicine, pharmacy and biotechnologies.
- Science: Alexandru Ioan Cuza University of Iaşi, Babeș-Bolyai University, University of Bucharest, West University of Timișoara, from which we have selected faculties from the fields of biology, chemistry, economics, geography and geology, physics.
- Technology: Gheorghe Asachi Technical University of Iași, Politehnica University Timișoara, Technical University of Cluj-Napoca, University Politehnica of Bucharest, from which the faculties of Chemical Engineering, Textiles and Leather, Materials Science and Economic faculties were selected.

A number of 2530 e-mail addresses of faculty members and researchers have been collected from the 15 mentioned universities. Two e-mails were sent to each e-mail address between February and March 2018. After the first e-mail, a number of 2462 valid e-mail addresses were reached and after the second e-mail a number of 2463 e-mails were sent. Due to various reasons, a small number of e-mail addresses were invalid. We received a total number of 354 responses out of which 336 responses could be validated. A number of 18 responses have been eliminated due to the following reasons:

- One respondent did not check on the questionnaire whether he or she was involved in the field of bioeconomy.
- Two persons did not complete any of the items in the questionnaire.
- One person completed only the academic title, without completing any of the items in the questionnaire.
- 14 respondents failed to complete the items although they reported that they were involved in activities related to the field of bioeconomy.

These led to a percentage of valid responses of 13.64%. Out of the 336 valid responses, a number of 171 respondents responded to the questionnaire items—whether to all the items, or to a part of them—these respondents were involved in bioeconomy, more or less, which means a percentage of 6.94% out of the sample. A number of 165 respondents mentioned they were not involved in bioeconomy.

3.4 Methods and Techniques Used in Analyzing the Data

For data processing and analysis, we used Microsoft Excel (version 2007) and Statistical Package for the Social Sciences (SPSS; version 20). We conducted the following types of analyses: reliability analysis, factor analysis (principal components analysis—PCA) and descriptive analysis. Reliability analysis was used for determining the internal consistency of the whole instrument, the scale presented in this paper and the results obtained regarding the construct's components. PCA was used for extracting the components ("factors") for the latent variable. Since we could not identify similar studies and since the scale used for the variable "sources of information" has been proposed by the authors of the research, we applied exploratory factor analysis. There are two types of factor analysis, according to Hair et al. (2006): exploratory and confirmatory. For interpreting the results we used descriptive statistics. The missing values have been treated passively.

4 Results and Discussions

4.1 Consistency Analysis

Table 1 shows the results of reliability analysis for the entire questionnaire (except dichotomous and nominal variables) and for the latent variable "Sources of information". The reliability analysis showed that the entire instrument (which, excepting the nominal and dichotomous variables, is formed of three scales: Sources of information; Types of organizations and people; Involvement in bioeconomy) and also the scale included in this paper showed internal consistency, thus were reliable, as Cronbach Alpha coefficients exceed 0.70 (Hair et al. 2006). This study is part of a broader research and focuses on one latent variable from the whole questionnaire, namely "Sources of information". The latent variable "sources of information" refers to sources that the respondents use to develop the knowledge applicable to the bioeconomy and their importance.

Table 1. Consistency analysis for the whole instrument and the scale "Sources of information"

No.crt	Scale	Cronbach alpha coefficient	Cronbach alpha coefficient—standardized items
1	Whole questionnaire (57 items), except dichotomous and nominal variables	0.971	0.971
2	Sources of information (13 items)	0.926	0.926

4.2 "Sources of Information"—Results from PCA

The components resulted from factor analysis (PCA) of the latent variable "Sources of information" are presented in Table 2.

Varimax rotation with Kaiser normalization was used. The items are shown in Table 2 in descending order of their loading to the appropriate component. It needs to be mentioned that items 7, 8 and 10 were also loaded to another component (loadings between 0.508 and 0.564), but, due to the relevance of these items for the research as well as the fact that the four components of the chosen solution explained a sufficiently large percentage of the total variance (79.756%), it was decided to keep these three items. Only loadings higher than 0.565 are displayed in Table 2. Normally, it is enough to display the loadings that are of at least 0.50, due to the fact that, according to one of the acceptations in the literature, only loadings that are over 0.50 have practical relevance (Hair et al. 2006).

Table 2. Components resulted for "Sources of information"

Rotated Component Matrix

	Component			
	1	2	3	4
SInfo10—Firms—source of applicative knowledge for teaching use	0.773			
SInfo11—Firms—source of applicative knowledge for scientific research activities	0.750			
SInfo13—Studies and secondary data published by public institutions or professional organizations	0.742			
SInfo12—Exchange of ideas with members of project teams in the field	0.726			
SInfo9—Own consulting activity	0.692			
SInfo2—Scientific articles in English		0.856		
SInfo5—Books in English		0.827		
SInfo8—Conferences and professional meetings		0.655		
SInfo7—Academic conferences		0.653		
SInfo3—Scientific articles in other languages of international circulation (without English)			0.918	
SInfo6—Books in other foreign languages (without English)			0.893	
SInfo1—Scientific articles in Romanian (mother tongue)				0.801
SInfo4—Books in Romanian (mother tongue)				0.734

Extraction Method: Principal Component Analysis
Rotation Method: Varimax with Kaiser Normalization
[a]Rotation converged in 7 iterations

The value of Kaiser-Meyer-Ohlin (KMO) test is 0.830, thus the solution obtained by applying factor analysis is very good (Pintilescu 2007).

Sig value of Chi-square (Bartlett's Test of Sphericity) is 0.00, which guarantees (with a likelihood of 95%) that there are statistically significant correlations between the variables (Pintilescu 2007).

The Cronbach Alpha coefficient for the five items in component 1 is 0.883 (0.885 for the standardized items), for the four items in component 2: 0.906 (0.908 for the standardized items), for the two items in component 3 the value of the coefficient is 0.908 (0.910 for the standardized items) and for the two items in component 4 the value of the coefficient is 0.865 (0.868 for the standardized items).

Considering the items that were grouped in each of the four components, the components were named in the following way: component 1—Sources from the business environment; component 2—Scientific sources predominantly in English; component 3—Scientific sources in other languages (without English and mother tongue); component 4—Scientific sources in mother tongue (Romanian).

Regarding the scientific sources predominantly in English (component 2), we need to mention that most conferences take place in English, which may be an explanation of why the two items referring to academic conferences (item 7) and to conferences and professional meetings (item 8) may load on this component. It is also an additional argument for the fact that we kept these two items in the analysis.

4.3 *"Sources of Information"—Descriptive Statistics*

Regarding the sources of information that the respondents use to develop their knowledge that is applicable in the field of bioeconomy, we measured the importance that the respondents gave to these sources, at perception level. The items in the scale were synthesized into four components. As a result of the respondents' perception regarding the importance of each source, the four components are hierarchized as follows: scientific sources predominantly in English (mean value 2.69, which means that, in average, this category of sources of information has a medium to high importance, but closer to a high importance), scientific sources in mother tongue—Romanian (mean value 2.00, which signifies that, based on the obtained answers, this category of sources has, on average, a medium importance), sources from the business environment (mean value 1.75, from which it follows that, on average, the importance of this category of sources is low to medium, but closer to medium), scientific sources in other languages, without English and mother tongue (mean value 1.35, which means that, on average, the importance of this source is rather low). The results are presented in Table 3.

H1 hypothesis testing. Considering the four components obtained by applying PCA and the results obtained at the level of the descriptive analysis, we can conclude that hypothesis 1 has been partially validated. There are differences between the level of importance of different sources of information about bioeconomy used by teachers and researchers in Romanian universities; however there are two components that,

Table 3. "Sources of information"—descriptive analysis for the components

Descriptive Statistics			
	N	Mean	Standard deviation
S_Info_C1	162	1.75	1.13
S_Info_C2	168	2.69	1.15
S_Info_C3	146	1.35	1.27
S_Info_C4	158	2.00	1.24
Valid N (listwise)	142		

based on the mean values obtained, have a medium importance (component 4—scientific sources in mother tongue—Romanian) or, by approximation, a medium importance (component 1—sources from the business environment).

H2 hypothesis testing. Hypothesis 2 states that the sources of information about bioeconomy in mother tongue are more important than sources in other languages. The results show that scientific sources predominantly in English obtain the highest mean value (2.69), while scientific sources in mother tongue (Romanian) is second, after the importance given by the respondents. Concluding, hypothesis 2 has not been validated.

5 Conclusions

A number of four components resulted, regarding the sources of information that the respondents use to develop their knowledge that is applicable in the field of bioeconomy, by applying Principal Components Analysis. The components regarding the sources of information have been named in the following way: Sources from the business environment; Scientific sources predominantly in English; Scientific sources in other languages (without English and mother tongue); Scientific sources in mother tongue (Romanian). These four components that resulted comprise two main types of sources of information: sources from the business environment (reflected within the first component) and scientific sources. The second type of source—scientific sources—contains three components that differentiate themselves based on the language in which the sources can be found: sources that are predominantly in English; sources in other languages, without English and mother tongue; sources in mother tongue (Romanian).

The results showed that scientific sources that are predominantly in English are the most important for the respondents (a medium to high importance, but closer to a high importance), followed by those that are in mother tongue—Romanian (medium importance), by sources from the business environment (very close to a medium importance) and by scientific sources in other languages, without English and mother tongue (which have a rather low importance).

One possible explanation for the results obtained, which places scientific sources that are predominantly in English on the first place, with a medium to high importance but closer to a high importance, is the fact that most research is available in English. Also, there seems to be a tendency of focusing on scientific sources (and not on those from the business environment), since on the second place are the scientific sources in mother tongue (Romanian), with a medium importance.

Our research focuses on the sources of information of bioeconomy that teachers and researchers in Romanian universities use to develop their knowledge that is applicable in the bioeconomy and on the importance of those sources. The sources that have been considered in this study refer both to sources from the business environment and to scientific sources, that the respondents use, more or less.

However, for developing the field of bioeconomy, both the academic and the business environments should be involved, and also a transfer of knowledge from the business environment to research should be taken into consideration.

References

Boisot, M.H.: Knowledge Assets: Securing Competitive Advantage in the Information Economy. Oxford University Press Inc., Oxford, New York (1998)

Bolisani, E., Oltramani, A.: Knowledge as a measurable object in business contexts: a stock and flow approach. Knowl. Manage. Res. Pract. **10**(3), 275–286 (2012)

Bordons, M.: Towards International Recognition of Spanish Scientific Publications. (Editorial). Revista Española de Cardiología **57**(9), 799–802 (2004)

Bratianu, C.: Knowledge and Intellectual Capital. Business Excellence, Bucharest (2011)

Bratianu, C., Orzea, I.: The entropic intellectual capital model. Knowl. Manage. Res. Pract. **11**(2), 133–141 (2013)

Dabbert, S., Lewandowski, I., Weiss, J., Pyka, A.: Knowledge-Driven Developments in the Bioeconomy Technological and Economic Perspectives. (e-book)Springer International Publishing AG. Homepage https://www.springer.com/de/book/9783319583730 Cham (2017)

Florian, R., Florian, N.: Majoritatea revistelor ştiinţifice româneşti nu servesc ştiinţa. Ad Astra **5**(2), 1–26 (2006)

Hair, J.F., Black, W.C., Babin, B.J., Anderson, R.E., Tatham, R.L.: Multivariate Data Analysis, 6th Edition: Pearson Prentice Hall, New Jersey (2006)

Maciejczak, M.: Bioeconomy as a complex adaptive system of sustainable development. J. Int. Bus. Res. Mark. **2**(2), 7–10 (2017)

Mauser, W., Klepper, G., Rice, M., Schmalzbauer, B.S., Hackmann, H., Leemans, R., Moore, H.: Transdisciplinary global change research: the co-creation of knowledge for sustainability. Curr. Opin. Environ. Sustain. **5**(3–4), 420–431 (2013)

Meneghini, R., Packer, Al.: Is there science beyond English? EMBO Rep. **8**(2), 112–6 (2007)

Näyhä, A.: Towards bioeconomy: a three-phase Delphi study on forest biorefinery diffusion in Scandinavia and North America. Jyväskylä Studies in Business and Economics. Homepage https://jyx.jyu.fi/dspace/handle/123456789/40500. Last Accessed 18 Mar 2020

Neștian, A.Ș., Tiță, S., Guță, A.L.: Intensity of involvement of teachers and researchers from Romanian universities in bioeconomy knowledge flows. Amfiteatru Econ. J. **20**(49), 567–582 (2018)

Nonaka, I., Konno, N.: The concept of "Ba": building a foundation for knowledge creation. California Manage. Rev. **40**(3), 40–54 (1998)

Nonaka, I.: The knowledge-creating company. Harvard Bus. Rev. **85**(7/8), 162–171 (2007)

Organisation for Economic Co-operation and Development.: The bioeconomy to 2030: designing a policy agenda. Paris: OECD. Homepage from https://www.oecd.org/futures/long-termtechnologicalsocietalchallenges/42837897.pdf 28 Jan 2018
Pintilescu, C: Analiză statistică multivariată. Iaşi: Alexandru Ioan Cuza" University Publisher, Iasi (2007)
Schwartz, M.F., Kimberg, D.Y., Walker, G.M., Brecher, A., Faseyitan, O.K., Dell, G.S., Mirman, D., Cosleett, H.B.: Neuroanatomical dissociation for taxonomic and thematic knowledge in the human brain. Proc. Natl. Acad. Sci. **108**(20), 8520–8524 (2011)
Van Weijen, D.: The language of (future) scientific communication, research trends. Homepage. https://www.researchtrends.com/issue-31-november-2012/the-language-of-future-scientific-communication/ last accessed 2020/03/18

Regional Convergence in the European Union: A Success Story or an Unaccomplished Goal?

Dumitru Miron and Ana-Maria Holobiuc

1 Introduction

European Union remained a very challenging global actor in the contemporary economic and political scene that gathered together more and more European states in the last decades. With the enlargement of the European Union, convergence started to be a very complex, but sensitive topic, given the asymmetries between the founding countries and the newcomers from Central and Eastern Europe. More and more, both theoreticians and practitioners shifted their perspectives from the national to the regional level. One of the biggest challenge for European Union's member countries is to reach an appropriate level of economic, social and territorial cohesion between and within them, while enhancing the external competiveness of their economies. The main purpose of the paper is to offer a multi-level and multi-parameter picture on the regional convergence within the European Union, by focusing on the NUTS 2 regions and to assess the possibility to create business clusters in Romania. In this respect, we have analyzed the main patterns of convergence or divergence using β- and σ-convergence tests and focusing on four clusters of regions: from the Old Member States, New Member States, Euro New Member States and Non-Euro New Member States. Another objective of our study was to assess the business activity in Romania's NUTS 2 regions, trying to identify industrial clusters by taking into consideration the share of persons employed in each sector.

D. Miron · A.-M. Holobiuc (✉)
The Bucharest University of Economic Studies, Bucharest, Romania
e-mail: anamaria_holobiuc@yahoo.com

A. M. Dima and F. DÁscenzo (eds.), *Business Revolution in a Digital Era*,
Springer Proceedings in Business and Economics,
https://doi.org/10.1007/978-3-030-59972-0_3

2 Literature Review

2.1 *Some Perspectives on the Regional Dimension of the European Union*

The concept of convergence has become increasingly captivating both in the academic institutions and the governmental chancelleries with the establishment and deepening of the European Union. The enlargement of the European Union with the ex-communist Central and Eastern states has created both challenges and opportunities for each European Union member country and for the group as a whole. One of the main challenge derives from the different levels of economic development between the founding countries and the Southern and Central and Eastern European countries, that can pose into question one of the main pillar of the European integration process: the cohesion between and within the Member States. It became more and more complex to maximize synergy between two congruent processes, the deepening of integration and the enlargement with the most of the European countries. Without doing this, it could become unimaginable to strengthen the economic and political role of the European Union on the international stage.

The process of convergence has been analyzed mainly from two perspectives: nominal and real. Nominal convergence is referring to a specific set of economic parameters, initially defined in the Maastricht Treaty (1992) as prerequisites for the Euro adoption, namely price stability, exchange rate sustainability, long-term interest rate stability and high level of health in public finances. Additionally, real convergence doesn't take into consideration a strict determined set of parameters, but usually is referring to the welfare of the nations and citizens, compensation of employees, productivity, investments, competitiveness, standard of living and quality of life. Although in the second half of the last century, academics and policy makers have analyzed convergence mainly at national level, since the moment of entering the New Millennium, experts started to be more interested in the regional axis of convergence. Taking into consideration the complexity of the topic, convergence has been studied from different perspectives. For example, some analysts examined the catching up process in the regions at NUTS 2 level (Tondl and Vukšić 2003; Artelaris et al. 2010) or at NUTS 3 level (Goecke and Hüther 2016). Moreover, convergence has been examined taking into consideration the income by Tondl and Vuksic (2003), Marelli (2007), Petrakos and Artelaris (2009), Artelaris et al. (2010), Goecke and Hüther (2016), Alcidi et al. (2018), while other researchers tried to identify the business specialization and industrial clusters at regional level (Geppert and Stephan 2005; Ezcurra et al. 2006).

Tondl and Vukšić (2003) analyzed the process of economic growth and catching up in Central and Eastern Europe at the end of the last century, taking into consideration a number of 36 NUTS 2 regions from Czech Republic, Slovakia, Slovenia, Poland and Hungary. The main purpose of the analysts was to study if the accumulation of capital, the transfer of technology and the improvement of the quality of education programs contributed to the acceleration of the economic growth in the selected regions. The results of the study showed that foreign direct investment had a major role between 1995 and 2000, accelerating the catching up in the regions. From another perspective, Artelaris et al. (2010) empirically demonstrated that the regional inequalities significantly increased after the collapse of the communist regime in Central and Eastern Europe, reaching the level recorded by the NUTS 2 regions from the Old Member States. By applying non-linear econometric tools, analysts have identified convergence clubs in almost all the New Member States.

Goecke and Hüther (2016) studied regional convergence between NUTS 3 regions using the σ and β-convergence tests. In this respect, they identified significant asymmetries between regions in countries such as Germany and Italy, offering relevant evidences supporting the β-convergence hypothesis, namely that the poorer regions of the European Union grew faster than the more developed ones. Regarding σ-convergence, the analysis conducted by Goecke and Hüther showed that between 2000 and 2009, the coefficient of variation between the NUTS 3 regions had a predominantly downward trend, subsequently increasing. According to these findings, the economic performances of the regions are influenced mainly by factors, such as: proximity to national borders, subsidies, sectorial structure of the economy and quality of infrastructure.

Moreover, Ezcurra et al. (2006) examined the industrial specialization in the European Union's regions, combining non-parametric methods with techniques used in space econometrics. Taking into consideration the period 1977–1999, analysts have shown that usually neighboring regions have similar productive specializations. Moreover, the analysts identified a number of highly specialized regions, which tended to be located in the southern periphery, while regions with similar patterns with the Community's average were located in the central area of the European Union. At the same time, the analysts identified a decrease of the productive specialization within the Community, which was determined by the change of the specialization model of the regions, from a high to medium specialization.

Geppert and Stephan (2005) studied regional disparities at Community's level, building an econometric model in order to identify convergence and agglomeration in the Old Member States (15). In this respect, analysts illustrated that disparities between regions decreased between 1980 and 2000. However, Geppert and Stephan identified absolute convergence at national level, but not between regions. In the view of the authors, the national infrastructure, the institutional environment, as well as the economic and political framework significantly influence the growth path of the states and the related regions. However, divergences between regions still persist, as metropolitan areas maintain or improve their position relative to other regions of the countries. Consequently, agglomeration forces attract productive activities in metropolitan areas.

Similarly, Tondl and Vukšić (2003) identified strong agglomerations in the capitals of five Central and Eastern European countries, where human, R&D and financial resources are efficiently used. Consequently, analysts concluded that the capital regions are the main winners of the catching up in the New Member States. Similar conclusions were reached by Alcidi et al., who illustrated that the capital regions in Central and Eastern Europe registered significant increases of the GDP per capita since 2000. However, with the accelerated convergence process of the capitals in the Central and Eastern European, the other regions at national level are laying behind, the discrepancies between them becoming prominent.

From another perspective, Blahó (2005) tested convergence hypothesis, concluding that the European Union should find an equilibrium between two seemingly contradictory objectives: economic growth and prosperity at national level and regional cohesion. Reaching a balance between economic growth and prosperity on one hand and catalyzing convergence between the European regions on the other hand will remain a challenge for the European decision-makers in the upcoming years and a subject of discussion in the academic institutions.

2.2 *Industrial Clusters and Their Role in Economic Growth and Development*

In the last few years, researchers interested in the topic of economic growth and development have emphasized the defining role of industrial clusters in creating jobs and catalyzing regional competitiveness. Porter (2008) and Ketels (2013) have studied the relationship between regional clusters and economic growth. Clusters are a network of economic links that create competitive advantages for companies in a region. These advantages also determine other industries to relocate or develop their activity in the region. From the perspective of Slaper et al. (2018), the establishment of industrial clusters represent the foundation for the economic development, considering the positive influences on the entrepreneurial and investment environment of the country of region. Consequently, according to Slaper et al., industrial clusters positively influence the increase of productivity and create favorable framework for the development of new business opportunities.

Sölvell et al. (2008) examined the industrial specialization in the New Member states, trying to identify the existence of industrial clusters. The analysts have concluded that the geographical concentration of industrial activities is randomly distributed. In spite of the incipient phase of the concentration in the New Member States, Sölvell et al. have identified a stronger tendency comparing to the Old countries.

The appropriate equilibrium between competition and cooperation within clusters is a fundamental driver of economic policies. According to Newlands (2003), if policy makers seek to enhance cooperation between companies, the economic policies will favour the localization of key sector enterprises to certain locations. In contrast, promoting competition on the market can be achieved by adopting policies that create a level playing field for all companies. Newlands (2003) considers that over time, the policies adopted by the main poles of power, including European Union, have combined the two seemingly contradictory directions.

According to McDonald and Vertova (2001), with the deepening and expansion of the European Union, companies that are included in an industrial group will be able to tap the advantages offered by the single market and by the policies which aim to catalyze the regional cohesion. Moreover, the economic actors that are able to respond to the redefinition of the competitive pressures as a result of market integration by concentrating the economic activities can benefit from first-mover advantage.

3 Methodology

The main purpose of this paper is to study regional convergence at Community's level. In this respect, we have used the β- and σ-convergence concepts, (Barro and Sala-i-Martin 1992) trying to test the neoclassical growth model assumptions, which were initially stated by Solow (1956). The β-convergence test assesses the relationship between the initial level of income of a country or region and the subsequent growth rates. The σ-convergence is used to asses if the divergences between countries and regions diminish over time. According to Beylunioğlu et al. (2018), the β-convergence model is based on the hypothesis of decreasing returns to capital. Consequently, low-income countries have a higher return on capital, which promotes faster accumulation and economic growth.

In order to assess if the poorer regions from the European Union recorded higher growth rates, we have included in our study regions from 24 Member States, with the exception of France, Lithuania, Netherlands, Poland as relevant data was not available for the entire period. The β- and σ-convergence tests were applied based on the values of the GDP per capita by NUTS 2 regions (as percentage of the EU average), as provided by Eurostat, and the data series aimed the 2000–2017 period. In order to assess if disparities diminished during the 18-years period (σ-convergence), we have grouped the NUTS 2 regions in four clusters: NUTS 2 regions from the Old Member States (Belgium, Denmark, Germany, Ireland, Greece, Spain, Italy, Luxembourg, Austria, Portugal, Finland, Sweden, United Kingdom), NUTS 2 regions from New Member States (Bulgaria, Estonia, Croatia, Cyprus, Latvia, Hungary, Malta, Romania, Slovenia, Slovakia), NUTS 2 regions from Euro New Member States (Estonia, Cyprus, Latvia, Malta, Slovenia, Slovakia) and NUTS 2 regions from Non-Euro New Member States (Bulgaria, Croatia, Hungary, Romania).

Another purpose of our study was to identify potential industrial clusters in Romania. In this respect, we have taken into consideration the share of persons employed in each business activity for the eight NUTS 2 regions in 2017. We have considered that a proportion equal or above 10% of employees in one business sector, calculated as a percentage of the total number of persons employed in the region, is representative for identifying business clusters. The share of persons employed in each sector is detailed for all the eight NUTS 2 regions: Nord-Vest, Centru, Nord-Est, Sud-Est, Sud-Muntenia, Bucuresti-Ilfov, Sud-Vest, Oltenia and Vest. The computation is based on the data provided by Eurostat.

4 Results and Discussions

4.1 *Regional Convergence*

Figure 1 illustrates the β-convergence calculated based on GDP per capita for the European Union's NUTS 2 regions. The negative slope of the trend line illustrates a negative relationship between the initial level of income and the average growth rates between 2000 and 2017. According to our calculations, the highest GDP growth rates were recorded in the Romanian NUTS 2 regions, respectively Nord-Vest and Bucuresti-Ilfov (8%), Vest (7.9%), Sud-Muntenia (7.8%) and Sud-Vest Oltenia (7.5%). Other Central and Eastern European regions that recorded significant annual GDP per capita growth rates were: Yugozapaden (7.3%), Sostines regionas (6.3%), Eesti (6%), Bratislavský kraj (5.9%) and Vidurio ir vakaru Lietuvos regionas (5.7%). In contrast, the regions from the developed Western countries had modest performances during the analyzed period, mainly below 1%. Moreover, some of the NUTS 2 regions recorded negative economic growth rates, exceeding −2% per year: Dorset and Somerset (−2%), Lincolnshire (−2.1%), Outer London—East and North East and Outer London—South (−2.4%). Consequently, there still persist significant discrepancies between the NUTS 2 regions. Our analysis suggests that while the Central and Eastern European regions are making important progresses in terms of increasing their income per capita, the developed regions from Western Europe cannot keep pace with them.

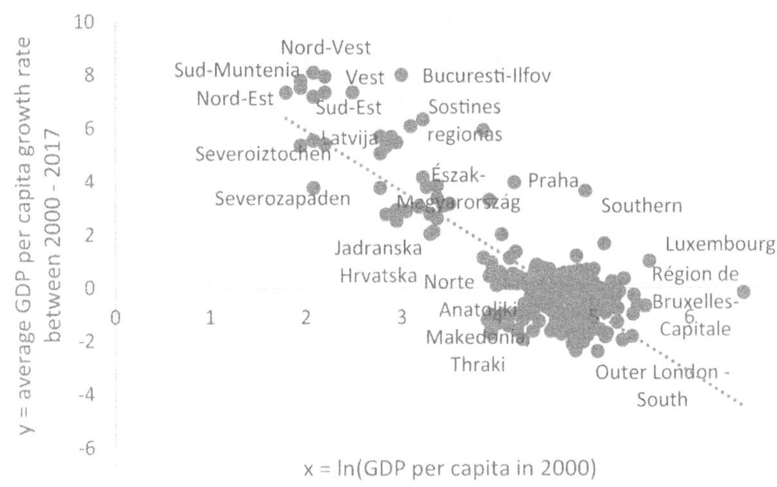

Fig. 1 β-convergence in the regions at NUTS 2 level (GDP per capita as % of EU average). *Source* Authors' computation based on data provided by Eurostat

Fig. 2 σ-convergence in the regions at NUTS 2 level (GDP per capita as % of EU average). *Source* Authors' computation based on data provided by Eurostat

Figure 2 illustrates the σ-convergence calculated for four groups of regions: from Old Member States, New Member States, Euro New Member States and Non-Euro New Member States. We have divided the regions from New Member States in two subgroups in order to study if the adoption of the single currency had a defining role in increasing the economic performances of the NUTS 2 regions. Our calculations suggest that within NUTS 2 regions from the Old Member States, the divergences slightly increased between 2000 and 2017. In contrast, in the regions from the New Member States, income gaps decreased with 24%. Within the regions from the New Member States, there still persist some differences. In this respect, the NUTS 2 regions from the Euro New Member States recorded a significant process of convergence, as divergences decreased with 36% between 2000 and 2017. In contrast, the coefficient of variation of the NUTS 2 regions from the Non-Euro New Member States decreased with only 17%. Overall, we found evidences in favor of the σ-convergence hypothesis for the NUTS 2 regions from the New Member States, as the income gaps between these regions diminished between 2000 and 2017.

4.2 *An Analysis of the Business Activity in the Romania's NUTS 2 Regions*

Another purpose of our study was to assess the business structure of the Romania's NUTS 2 regions, trying to identify the existence of appropriate conditions to create industrial clusters. In this respect, we have examined the structure of business activity in Romania in 2017, based on the data provided by Eurostat for the eight NUTS 2 regions: Nord-Vest, Centru, Nord-Est, Sud-Est, Sud-Muntenia, Bucuresti-Ilfov, Sud-Vest Oltenia and Vest. In order to study the existence of industrial regional clusters, we have calculated the share of persons employed in each business activity. We have considered that a proportion of employees in a business activity above 10% of the total number of persons employed in the region suggests the existence of an industrial cluster. In order to capture the representative activities for each region, the figures below illustrate the share of activities above 5%.

Figure 3 depicts the share of each business activity in Romania's Nord-Vest region. According to our calculations, in the Nord-Vest region, the main business activity was manufacturing, with almost 36% of persons employed from the region in this sector. Besides manufacturing, we have identified industrial clusters in wholesale and retail trade (21% persons employed), transportation and storage (10% persons employed) and construction (10% persons employed).

Figure 4 illustrates the industrial structure in another NUTS 2 region: Centru. Similar to the Nord-Vest region, we have identified an industrial cluster in manufacturing, with more than 40% of persons from the region working in this field of activity in 2017. Moreover, the Central region from Romania had another industrial cluster in wholesale and retail trade; repair of motor vehicles and motorcycles, with a percentage of 20% persons employed in this sector in 2017.

Figure 5 illustrates the industrial structure in Nord-Est NUTS 2 Region, where the main business activity was also manufacturing, with more than 31% of total employees from the region working in this sector of activity. Moreover, we identified an industrial cluster in wholesale and retail trade (27% of employees) and construction (11% of employees).

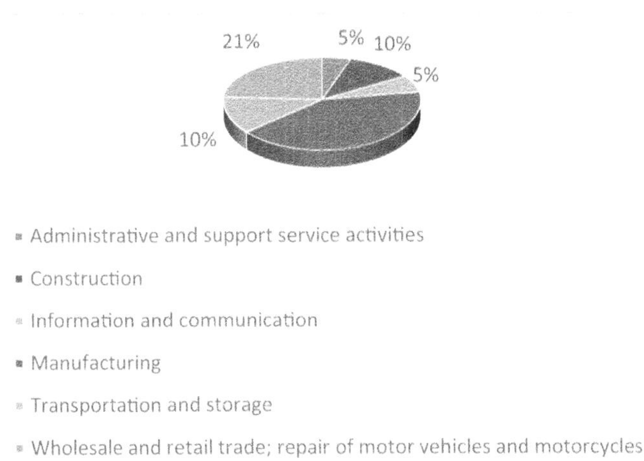

Fig. 3 Industrial structure in Nord-Vest NUTS 2 region in 2017 (% of persons employed). *Source* Authors' calculations based on data provided by Eurostat

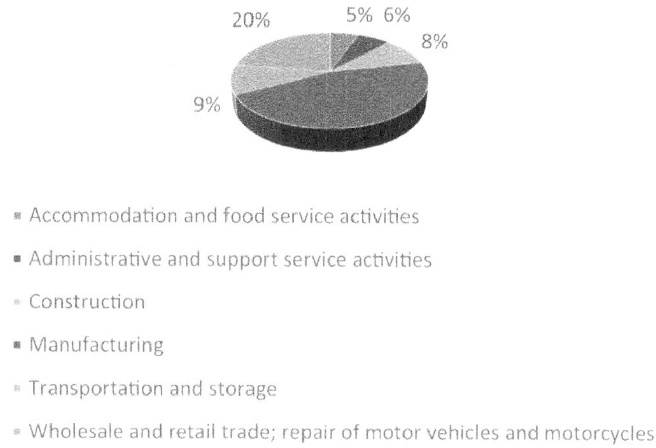

Fig. 4 Industrial structure in Centru NUTS 2 region in 2017 (% of persons employed). *Source* Authors' calculations based on data provided by Eurostat

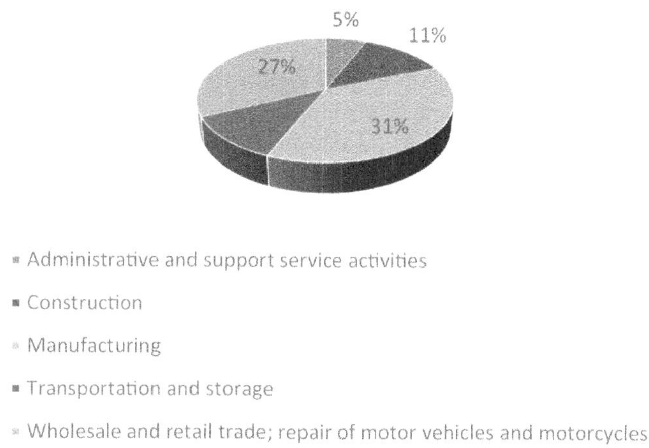

Fig. 5 Industrial structure in Nord-Est NUTS 2 region in 2017 (% of persons employed). *Source* Authors' calculations based on data provided by Eurostat

Another NUTS 2 region is Sud-Est, where the main economic activities were manufacturing and wholesale and retail trade, with shares representing 29 and 26% of the total number of employees from the region. Moreover, a percentage of 11% of the total persons employed from the region were involved in transportation and storage activities in 2017 (Fig. 6).

In Sud-Muntenia region, 39% of the persons employed were working in manufacturing in 2017, which suggest the existence of an industrial cluster in this field

Fig. 6 Industrial structure in Sud-Est NUTS 2 region in 2017 (% of persons employed). *Source* Authors' calculations based on data provided by Eurostat

of activity. Also, a large percentage of employees (22%) were working in wholesale and retail trade in 2017, while almost 10% in transportation and storage (Fig. 7).

Bucuresti-Ilfov is the most developed region from Romania, where the main economic activity is wholesale and retail trade; repair of motor vehicles and motorcycles (26% of persons employed). Moreover, Bucuresti-Ilfov was the only region from the country where more than 10% of the employees were working in administrative and support service activities (15%). Manufacturing has a less importance

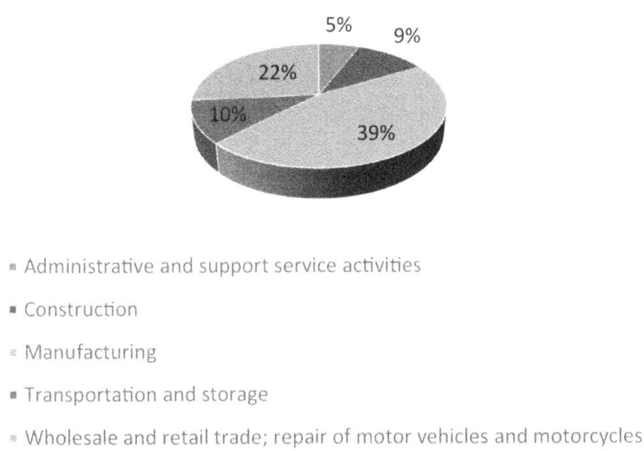

Fig. 7 Industrial structure in Sud-Muntenia NUTS 2 region in 2017 (% of persons employed. *Source* Authors' calculations based on data provided by Eurostat

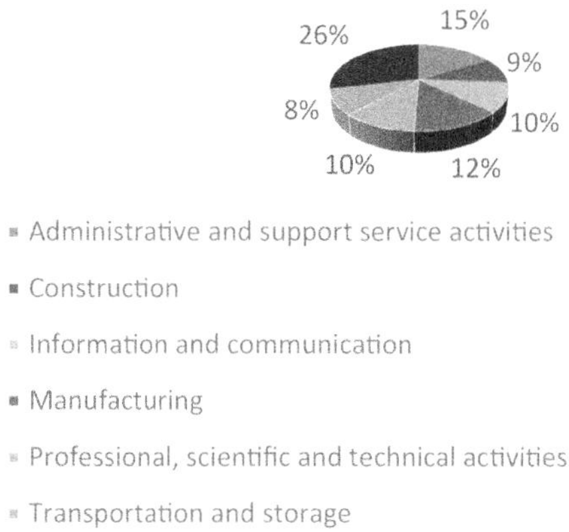

Fig. 8 Industrial structure in Bucuresti-Ilfov NUTS 2 region in 2017 (% of persons employed). *Source* Authors' calculations based on data provided by Eurostat

comparing to the other Romania's regions as a share of only 12% of persons out of the total number of employees from Bucuresti-Ilfov were working in this field. Moreover, a percentage of 10% of employees were involved in professional, scientific and technical activities (Fig. 8).

In Sud-Vest Oltenia region, the largest proportion of persons employed were involved in manufacturing (30%), wholesale and retail trade (25%) and transportation and storage (10%). The rest of business activities recorded in 2017 a share of persons employed of less than 10% out of the total number of employees in the region (Fig. 9).

Last but not the least, in Vest region, the share of persons employed in manufacturing was 42% in 2017, which suggests the existence of an industrial cluster in this activity. The second business activity, taking into consideration the share of employees was wholesale and retail trade, with 18%, being followed by transportation and storage (10%) (Fig. 10).

In conclusion, in this section of the paper we have studied the industrial structure of Romania, trying to identify industrial clusters at the level of the NUTS 2 regions. Our study suggests that the main economic activity in seven out of eight regions (excepting Bucuresti-Ilfov) was manufacturing, being followed by wholesale and retail trade.

5 Conclusion

The main purpose of this paper was to examine real convergence in the European Union, taking into consideration its regional dimension. In this respect, we have studied the β- and σ-convergence assumptions, illustrating that the poorer regions

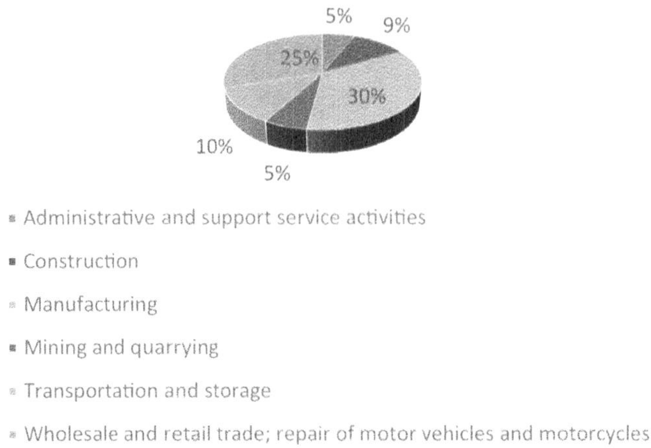

Fig. 9 Industrial structure in Sud-Vest NUTS 2 region in 2017 (% of persons employed). *Source* Authors' calculations based on data provided by Eurostat

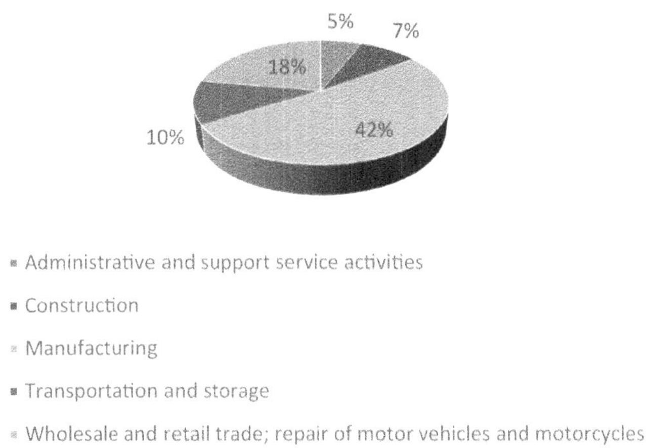

Fig. 10 Industrial structure in Vest NUTS 2 region in 2017 (% of persons employed). *Source* Authors' calculations based on data provided by Eurostat

from Central and Eastern Europe recorded higher GDP per capita growth rates than developed ones between 2000 and 2017. Moreover, we have found evidence in favour of the σ-convergence hypothesis, as the divergences within the regions from the New Member States decreased during the analyzed period, which suggests a catching up process also between Euro and the Non-Euro regions. This section of the study could be expanded by including other variables that might have influence on income convergence. In the second part of the paper, we have assessed the industrial structure of Romania, illustrating that the main business activities in 2017 were manufacturing and wholesale and retail trade. However, in the most developed region from Romania, Bucuresti-Ilfov, a large proportion of employees were working in administrative and support service activities given the concentration of the public institutions in this region. Our study suggests that manufacturing will remain the main business activity in Romania in the upcoming years and the capital region, the main pole of attraction. However, our findings should be interpreted with cautious as they reflect a preliminary analysis regarding the industrial specialization in Romania. Taking into consideration these conclusions, the paper could be expanded by studying the business activity in all the NUTS 2 regions from Central and Eastern Europe in order to find similarities, differences and futures directions of development of the industrial clusters. Our results are in line with the previous findings in this field of study, which confirm a higher catching up speed of the poorer Central and Eastern European economies and the tendency to establish high-value business activities in the capital regions. Taking into consideration the results of our research, we might conclude that although the European Union has reached important performances in the last years, real convergence has not been achieved so far at regional level.

References

Alcidi, C., Ferrer, J.N., Musmeci, R., Di Salvo, M., Pilati, M.: Income Convergence in the EU: Within-Country Regional Patterns. Centre for European Policy Studies, Policy Contribution, Brussels (2018)

Artelaris, P., Kallioras, D., Petrakos, G.: Regional inequalities and convergence clubs in the European Union new member-states. Eastern J. Euro. Stud. **1**(1), 113–133 (2010)

Barro, R.J., Sala-i-Martin, X.: Convergence. J. Polit. Econ. **100**(2), 223–251 (1992)

Beylunioğlu, F., Yazgan, M., Stengos, T.: Detecting convergence clubs. Macroeconomic Dynamics, 1–41 (2018)

Blahó, A.: Some aspects of european economic area and competitiveness. Soc. Econ. **27**(1), 63–90 (2005)

European Commission: Eurostat. Database. https://ec.europa.eu/eurostat/web/regions/data/database

Ezcurra, R., Rapún, M. Regional disparities and national development revisited: the case of Western Europe. Euro. Urban Reg. Stud. **13**, 355–369 (2006)

Geppert, K., Happich, M., Stephan, A.: Regional Disparities in the European Union: Convergence and Agglomeration, DIW Discussion Papers 525. Deutsches Institut für Wirtschaftsforschung (DIW), Berlin (2005)

Goecke, H., Hüther, M.: Regional convergence in Europe. Interecon. Rev. Euro. Econ. Policy **51**(3), 165–171 (2016)

Ketels, C.: Recent research on competitiveness and clusters: what are the implications for regional policy? Cambridge J. Reg. Econ. Soc. **6**(2), 269–284 (2013)

Marelli, E.: Specialisation and convergence in European Regions. Euro. J. Comp. Econ. **4**(2), 149–178 (2007)

Mcdonald, F., Vertova, G.: Geographical concentration and competitiveness in the European Union. Euro. Bus. Rev. **13**(3), 157–165 (2001)

Newlands, D.: Competition and cooperation in industrial clusters: the implications for public policy. Euro. Plann. Stud. **11**(5), 521–532 (2003)

Petrakos, G.: Artelaris, P: European regional convergence revisited: a weighted least squares approach. Growth Change **40**(2), 314–331 (2009)

Porter, M.E.: The five competitive forces that shape strategy. Harvard Bus. Rev. **86**(1), 78–93 (2008). (Special Issue on HBS Centennial)

Slaper, T.F., Harmon, K.M., Rubin, B.M.: Industry clusters and regional economic performance: a study across U.S. Metropolitan statistical areas. Econ. Dev. Q. **32**(1), 44–59 (2018)

Solow, R.: A contribution to the theory of economic growth. Q. J. Econ. **70**(1), 65–94 (1956)

Sölvell, O., Ketels, C.H.M., Lindqvist, G.: Industrial specialization and regional clusters in the ten new EU member states. Competitiveness Rev. **18**(1/2), 104–130 (2008)

Tondl, G., Vukšić, G.: What makes regions in Eastern Europe catching up? The role of foreign investment, human resources and geography, ZEI Working Papers B 12–2003. ZEI—Bonn: University of Bonn—Center for European Integration Studies (2003)

Systemic Risk Dynamics in the EU—A Conditional Capital Shortfall Approach

Cristina Georgiana Zeldea

1 Introduction

In the last decade, the extreme events generated by the global financial crisis and the sovereign debt crisis have had a negative impact on financial stability. These periods of systemic turmoil incurred high economic and social costs, thus representing turning points for research in the field.

Against the background of the obvious and repeated underestimation of systemic risk, the authors' interest was directed to identifying the causes and risk-enhancing vectors, as well as to risk monitoring and mitigation tools. The banking sector, recognized as a primary source of systemic risk, has become a central theme of quantitative studies on financial stability. As detailed in the upcoming section, a consistent body of literature relies on Conditional Capital Shortfall methods to assess systemic risk in various contexts.

This paper addresses systemic risk empirically, focusing on the banking and real estate sectors in the European Union. We use a Conditional Capital Shortfall method, namely SRISK (Brownlees and Engle 2016) to obtain daily systemic risk estimates. The European Union provides a suitable ground for this analysis, considering the impact the global financial crisis and its particularized form, the sovereign debt crisis, have had on its financial markets. For a long time, academia and decision-makers have focused on the banking system particularly, as the main source of financial instability. We start, as well, in the study we undertake, from the premise that banks represent, traditionally and in accordance with the results of the reference works in the field, primary sources of systemic risk. To compare and contrast, we employ the same methodology for the real estate sector. The importance of the real estate sector

C. G. Zeldea (✉)
Bucharest University of Economic Studies, 010374 Bucharest, Romania
e-mail: zeldeacristina@gmail.com

Institute for World Economy, Romanian Academy, 050711 Bucharest, Romania

A. M. Dima and F. DÁscenzo (eds.), *Business Revolution in a Digital Era*,
Springer Proceedings in Business and Economics,
https://doi.org/10.1007/978-3-030-59972-0_4

as a risk driver during the global crisis cannot be neglected. However, the literature employing Conditional Capital Shortfall methods for this sector is rather scarce.

The results we obtain represent, first and foremost, a tool for analysing the dynamics of systemic risk in the targeted financial markets. As it was expected, the results confirm the high systemic importance of the banking sector. Systemic risk in the real estate sector runs lower. We find that the crisis period corresponds to an increase in risk in both sectors. We notice certain common patterns for the two sectors which suggest potential co-movement episodes.

The remainder of this paper is organized as it follows: Sect. 2 provides a brief overview of the literature on the topics of financial stability and Conditional Capital Shortfall methods for systemic risk measurement, Sect. 3 presents the data and methodology used, Sect. 4 discusses the results. We draw conclusions in the latter section.

2 Literature Review

2.1 Financial Stability

There is no unanimity in the literature in what concerns the significance of financial stability. Most often, financial stability is described in contrast to its very absence and defined in relation to systemic risk and financial instability. In either case, financial stability is usually explained by the absence of systemic episodes during which the financial system fails to function in normal parameters (2004). Allen and Wood (2006) analyze financial stability from a distinct perspective, drawing an analogy between it and the physical properties of a system. Thus, the laws of physics, which state that a system is stable if it returns to its equilibrium state, reacting in order to mitigate the perturbations to which it is exposed, can be successfully used in defining financial stability. More specifically, a financial system is stable if it does not amplify the shocks, but absorbs and tempers them. The European Central Bank (2011) defines financial stability as "the state in which the financial system, including intermediaries, markets and market infrastructures, is able to withstand financial shocks and imbalances". In other words, a stable financial system reduces the likelihood of interruptions in financial intermediation activities that are likely to affect capital flows for investment.

Most of the central banks record as intrinsic features of a stable financial system the following: offering the possibility to make payments for the sale and purchase of goods and services, allowing risk management and risk hedging; providing income-saving opportunities; allowing access to finance for both households and businesses in order to invest and grow.

From another perspective, a financial system is stable, in its natural and desirable state, when it contributes to achieving the following objectives: allocating resources as efficiently as possible, managing financial risks, keeping the unemployment rate as close as possible to its natural rate and maintaining price stability (World Bank 2020). In a previous study, Mishkin (1991) also devoted the state of financial stability to the efficient allocation of financing resources.

We particularly recognize the latter objective as the stability target assumed by a great number of central banks at the global level. This objective has actually driven a consistent body of studies. Broadly put, the core of the debate is that by focusing exclusively on price stability, the effects of monetary policy measures on financial stability are overlooked (Issing 2003; Woodford 2012), while, conversely, other authors advance the view that price stability is intrinsic to financial stability and a sufficient condition for it (Wood 1998). Moreover, financial stability should be an indirect goal in itself for central banks. Stein (2012) and Smets (2014) argue in this respect, recognizing the role that monetary policy plays in maintaining financial stability. Adrian and Shin (2008) also suggest that there is a close link between financial stabilization policies and monetary policy, especially because of the influence they exert on the indebtedness of financial institutions.

In virtue of their implicit or explicit function of maintaining financial stability, most central banks publish semi-annual or annual financial stability reports. In general, these reports represent the main official communication channels of the central banks regarding the risks to financial stability. Correa et al. (1203) use the text of these reports for 35 countries to build a Financial Stability Sentiment Index (FSS), which they evaluate in correlation with economic cycle indicators. They highlight that most of the words with positive or negative connotations refer to the banking system, and the main finding is that the calculated sentiment index deteriorates before the onset of a banking crisis. In a relatively similar manner, Born et al. (2011) study the market reaction to the release of the financial stability reports of 37 central banks over a 14-year period. Their results demonstrate that the publication of stability reports has a persistent effect on stock returns, providing evidence that they do disclose relevant information to financial markets.

2.2 *Systemic Risk Modelling*

Conditional Capital Shortfall approaches play a significant part in the wider body of literature dealing with systemic risk measurement. In the aftermath of the 2008 financial crisis, a special attention has been given to the seminal works of Brownlees and Engle (2012) and Acharya et al. (2010). SRISK of the first, and Marginal Expected Shortfall of the latter, have soon become reference methods for authors addressing systemic risk.

Brownlees and Engle (2016) measure systemic risk as the potential loss of an institution, conditional on a significant market decline. They calculate SRISK for 94 US financial institutions classified in banks, insurance companies, brokers, dealers and others. We mention that they do not analye the real estate sector per se, but they include it in the others category, together with non-depositary institutions. Same authors reiterate later on the methodology on a sample of US financial institution with a market capitalization greater than 5 billion dollars (Brownlees and Engle 2012). Engle et al. (2014) apply the SRISK methodology to a wide range of large European financial institutions and argue that, in some cases, the bailout costs become so high for the authorities that some banks may be "too big to be saved".

Allen et al. (2012) use Expected Shortfall in parametric and non-parametric forms in order to estimate systemic risk. They find that CATFIN—as the method is named—able to signal crises six months in advance. Coleman et al. (2018) apply a modified version of SRISK, for the banking and insurance sectors in Canada. The modification consists, on one hand, in the exclusion of the actuarial debt from the total debt of the insurance companies, and on the other hand, in the change of the prudential capital threshold according to the national requirements. Their results show that SRISK tends to overestimate systemic risk in the insurance sector.

Chang et al. (2018) apply SRISK to analyze the systemic importance of the insurance sector in Taiwan and conclude that the degree of indebtedness of the insurers and their size are key determinants of the systemic risk that this industry generates. Cipra and Heyndrich (2017) estimate the systemic risk in the Czech financial market, using the Marginal Expected Shortfall methodology. Battaglia and Gallo (2013) assess the effects that securitization has on systemic risk in Italy. They calculate both Expected Shortfall and Marginal Expected Shortfall, for Italian banks during the 2000–2009 and show that, despite the recognized valences of risk dispersion, securitization actually generates higher potential losses for the primary institution. Ben Ameur et al. (2017) study the simultaneity of Marginal Expected Shortfall in the United States and the European Union based on high frequency data.

Pederzoli and Torricelli (2017) test the predictive power of the Marginal Expected Shortfall, analyzing it in comparison to the results of the stress tests performed by the European Banking Authority in 2014 and find that using a financial market index as benchmark, rather than a global one, improves the obtained results. Bănulescu and Dumitrescu (2015) present a modified version of Marginal Expected Shortfall, which they call CES—Component Expected Shortfall. They provide evidence that CES identifies correctly the systemically important institutions during the global financial crisis of 2007–2009.

Grundke and Tuchscherer (2018) investigate the performance of benchmark systemic risk measurement instruments, including MES and SRISK, in respect of their predictive power of a systemic event that results that would lead to the bankruptcy of a bank. Their results show that SRISK has the greatest economic significance.

A strand of recent literature ran the methodology on several sectors, and tried to identify and explain connections between them. Studies as such focused, for the most part, on the banking-insurance pair (Gehrig and Iannino 2018). Lin et al. (2016) estimate CoVaR, ΔCoVaR, SRISK and Marginal Expected Shortfall for the banking system, the insurance sector and other financial companies in Taiwan and then rank the institutions of systemic importance according to the results by the four methods. Other studies assessed the nexus between systemic risk and sovereign bond yields (Pagano and Sedunov 2016), or between systemic risk and a sample of real variables (Stolbov and Shchepeleva 2017).

We emphasize that although the literature dealing with systemic risk is extremely wide—and we by no mean intended to make a comprehensive survey here—the literature relating real economy sectors in a Conditional Capital Shortfall framework is rather narrow.

3 Methodology

The analysed period is from January 2004 to March 2019. The selection of banks and companies in the real estate sector from Stoxx Europe 600 was made by the author according to the ICB classification of FTSE Russell. The sample includes 27 banks and 16 real estate companies. The daily frequency data is sourced from Bloomberg and consists in daily closing prices based on which log differences were computed, market capitalization and total debt.

The methodology proposed by Brownlees and Engle (2016) first requires to define the Capital Shortfall-CS. CS is the difference between the value of the prudential capital reserve required and the market capitalization of the institution:

$$CS_{it} = kA_{it} - W_{it} = k(D_{it} + W_{it}) - W_{it} \tag{1}$$

where W_{it} is the market capitalization, D_{it} is the value of the debt, and K is the required percentage of prudential capital reserve.

SRISK depends on the size of the institution (market capitalization), the degree of indebteness and the loss caused by a systemic event. It is necessary to define the systemic event as the market decline below a threshold C, within a time interval h:

$$SRISK = E_t(CS_{it+h}|R_{mt+1:t+h} < C = kE_t(D_{it+h}|R_{mt+1:t+h}) \tag{2}$$

where $R_{mt+1:t+h}$ is the average return from $t + 1$ to $t + h$ and $R_{mt+1:t+h} < C$ is the systemic event.

It follows that:

$$\begin{aligned} SRISK &= kD_{it} - 1(1-k)W_{it}(1 - LRMES_{it}) \\ &= W_{it}[kL_{it} + (1-k)LRMES_{it} - 1] \end{aligned} \tag{3}$$

where L is the leverage $\left(\frac{D+W}{W}\right)$, and LRMES is the stock return conditional on the systemic event.

LRMES is estimated using the DCC-GARCH approach of Engle (2009).

4 Results and Discussions

The analyzed period is heterogeneous, covering both periods of financial stability and recession. The graphical representations of the systemic risk estimates reveal, as it was expected, specific patterns of dynamics during periods of crisis. However, there are differences between the two sectors that will be detailed. Figures 1 and 2 show systemic risk estimates in the banking and real estate sectors of the European Union.

The dynamics of systemic risk displays some common patterns, but with a number of specific elements to each sector. The global financial crisis, with its particular form in the European Union—the sovereign debt crisis of the Eurozone-, seems to cause a synchronized increase of risk in both sectors. In fact, since the onset of the global financial crisis and until now, Greece has been a pole of instability for the European financial market, raising concerns for creditors and investors alike. Therefore, events related to the economic and financial evolution of Greece delimit episodes of financial instability on European markets, marking episodes of increased risk with the preparation of austerity programs (e.g. launch of the bail-out programme). Returning to financing on the capital markets through treasury bonds was a sine qua non condition for recovery, after Greek bonds had previously been downgraded to junk-bond status. Following the dynamics of risk during the debt crisis, we observe that it certainly represented a period characterized by high financial instability for European markets. The risk level reaches around 2011–2012 values similar to those of 2008, suggesting the severity of the problems faced by the Eurozone.

Specifically to the EU, we observe a persistence of risk in the banking system even after the end of the crisis. It is known that the revival of economic activity took place at a slower pace in the EU and this can be attributed to the underdevelopment of some European capital markets. In EU, companies rely heavily on bank financing. As such, the economic recovery in the community area lagged behind on the background of recurring liquidity issues in the European banking systems. In contrast, while companies in United States recovered more quickly, benefiting from easy financing on the capital markets, economic activity in the European Union suffered due to the limited number of loans granted by banks in the aftermath of the crisis. In fact, the low degree of integration and the deficient functioning of financial markets is a recognized issue of the European Union, which is why the projects of the Banking Union and the Capital Markets Union were launched relatively recently, in 2014 and 2015, in addition to the Economic and Monetary Union that was launched in 1999. We observe that SRISK in the banking system remains high even after the sovereign debt crisis ends, in line with the liquidity problems of the banking systems that persist in certain European markets (e.g. Greece). However, systemic risk is not marked by sharp volatilities.

The systemic risk shows a downward trend from 2012 to 2016, amid the positive signals from the market regarding the end of the crisis. In general, the period between July 2012 and the end of 2013 signals the decrease or even the end of the tensions induced by the sovereign debt crisis. Greece's return to financing on financial markets, in october 2014—event J, would actually mark the end of a long period of economic turbulence in Europe.

The descending risk slope is due to the end of the recession (successive quarterly GDP growth), to the recovery measures announced and to some events that led to an increase in investor confidence (July 2012—the President of the European Central Bank announces that all measures will be taken to maintain the euro; December 2013—Ireland leaves the bailout program, giving a first signal of the end of the sovereign debt crisis). Subsequent exits of Spain and Portugal from the bailout programs of their banking systems, give an important positive signal about the onset of the post-crisis financial recovery, after an extremely turbulent period for the capital markets.

The well-known Brexit referendum determines another pattern of dynamics specific to the EU (event m, June 23rd, 2016).

We find interesting the dynamics of risk in the real estate sector (Fig. 2), which shows two major episodes of instability: the first delimited by the global financial crisis, and the second that begins with the spread of financial tensions to Spain and

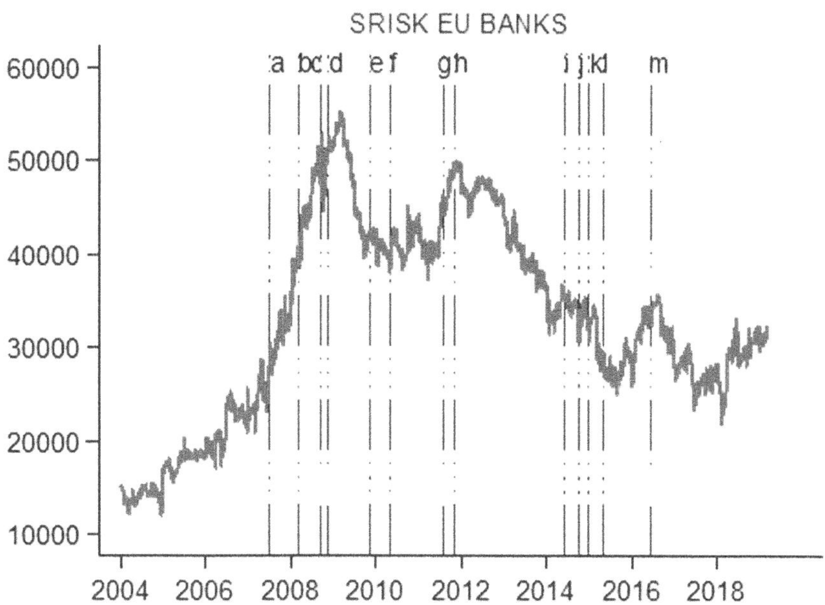

Fig. 1. Systemic risk dynamics in the banking sector of the EU. **a** BNP Paribas suspended three of its investment funds. **b** Bear Stearns is bought out by JP Morgan. **c** Lehman Brothers files for bankruptcy protection. **d** U.S. financial authorities agree to rescue Citigroup. **e** Greece's 12.7% budget deficit announcement. **f** The bail-out programme for Greece is launched. **g** Financial tensions spread to Italy and Spain. **h** Greece's 50% of debt is cut. **i** BCE introduces negative interest rate. **j** Greece returns to financing on capital markets. **k** Greek government collapse. **l** Deposit outflows accelerate in Greece. **m** Brexit referendum

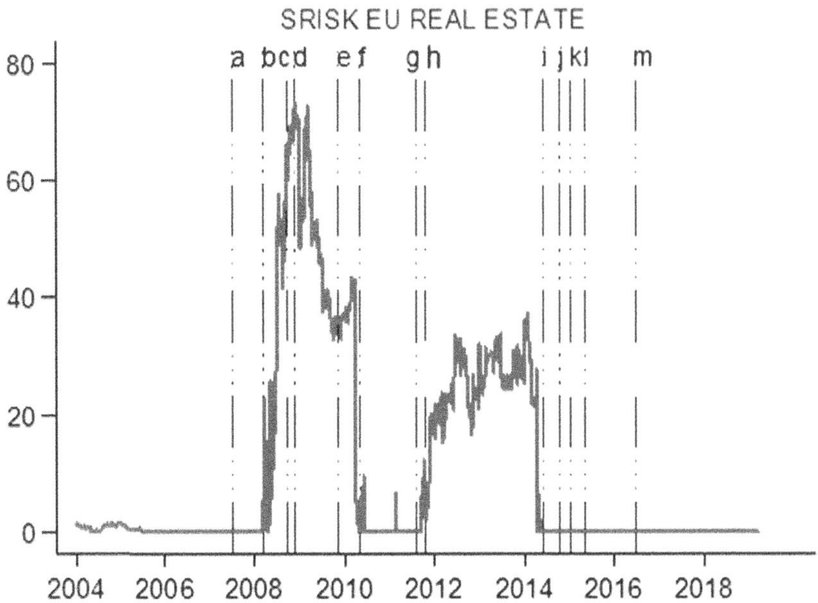

Fig. 2. Systemic risk dynamics in the real estate sector of the EU. (a) BNP Paribas suspended three of its investment funds. (b) Bear Stearns is bought out by JP Morgan. (c) Lehman Brothers files for bankruptcy protection. (d) U.S. financial authorities agree to rescue Citigroup. (e) Greece's 12.7% budget deficit announcement. (f) The bail-out programme for Greece is launched. (g) Financial tensions spread to Italy and Spain. (h) Greece's 50% of debt is cut. (i) BCE introduces negative interest rate. (j) Greece returns to financing on capital markets. (k) Greek government collapse (l) Deposit outflows accelerate in Greece. (m) Brexit referendum.

Italy during the second half of 2011. Around the same time, the European Central Bank began to buy Italian and Spanish bonds, in an attempt to temper financial market tensions.

We note that the real estate sector does have systemic importance, but it is much lower than that of the banking sector. We observe extended periods of time when the systemic risk in the real estate sector is 0. Considering that SRISK measures the capital needed during a crisis period, so that the prudential capital fraction is kept at the established level, these periods imply the existence of a capital surplus.

5 Conclusion

Systemic risk has been a constant for financial markets in contemporary history. However, over the last few decades, it has generally been overlooked during accumulation periods, gaining attention late and usually when actually materializing in systemic crises. The global financial crisis of 2007–2009 has generated a particular wave of interest in developing, consolidating and analyzing risk-mitigation methods. Benoit et al. (2017) tried to develop a definition with universal applicability of systemic risk: the risk that several market participants will be affected simultaneously by financial losses, which later extend into the system. This general and minimal definition captures to a very large extent the fundamentals of systemic risk, as they have been depicted in the literature of the field in the recent years.

This paper addressed systemic risk dynamics in the European Union, during the 2004–2019 interval, with a focus on the banking and real estate sectors. We examined the above-mentioned dynamics via daily estimates derived from a Conditional Capital Shortfall approach.

On one hand, the dynamics showed that the instability episodes were generally synchronized in the analyzed samples, so the crisis period corresponds to a sharp increase in systemic risk. Although these common patterns do not empirically demonstrate a nexus, they do suggest the existence of co-movement, causality and/or contagion episodes of the banking-real estate pair in turbulent times. These simultaneous reactions give a hint of the connections between the two sectors, which can be explained, to an extent, by the common exposures of banks to the housing sector.

On the other hand, we have found that there are certain heterogeneities regarding systemic risk in the banking and real estate sectors. Moreover, the banking sector displays risk patterns and ranges that support the assumption of it being a primary source of systemic instability. This is in line with the findings of many studies that identified banks as main systemic risk drivers in the real economy (Engle et al. 2014; Billio et al. 2012; López-Espinosa et al. 2012). Engle et al. (2014) go as far as concluding that in certain cases, systemically important banks' bail-out costs become so high that it becomes rather impossible to save them.

These findings can lay the foundation for further research on network connectedness and risk dependencies between financial markets. The broadest body of literature focused on financials as main risk drivers in the economy. Identifying risk connections between real economy sectors, other than financials, may also provide valuable insights for academia and policy makers, into finding main risk senders and receivers.

References

Acharya, V., Pedersen, L., Philippon, T., Richardson, M.: Measuring systemic risk Federal Reserve Bank of Cleveland Working Paper (2010)

Adrian, T., Shin, H.S.: Financial intermediaries, financial stability, and monetary policy. Staff Report No. 346, Federal Reserve Bank of New York (2008)

Allen, W.A., Wood, G.: Defining and achieving financial stability. J. Financ. Stab. **2**(2), 152–172 (2006)

Allen, L., Bali, T.G., Tang, Y.: Does systemic risk in the financial sector predict future economic downturns? Rev. Financ. Stud. **25**(10), 3000–3036 (2012)

Bănulescu, G.D., Dumitrescu, E.I.: Which are the SIFIs? A component expected shortfall approach to systemic risk. J. Bank. Financ. **50**, 575–588 (2015)

Battaglia, F., Gallo, A.: Securitization and systemic risk: an empirical investigation on Italian banks over the financial crisis. Int. Rev. Financ. Anal. **30**, 274–286 (2013)
Ben Ameur, H., Jawadi, F., Louhichi, W., Idi Cheffou, A.: Modeling international stock price comovements with high-frequency data. Macroecon. Dyn. 1–29 (2017)
Benoit, S., Colliard, J.E., Hurlin, C., Pérignon, C.: Where the risks lie: a survey on systemic risk. Rev. Financ. **21**(1), 109–152 (2017)
Billio, M., Getmansky, M., Lo, A.W., Pelizzon, L.: Econometric measures of connectedness and systemic risk in the finance and insurance sectors. J. Financ. Econ. **104**(3), 535–559 (2012)
Born, B., Ehrmann, M., Fratzscher, M.: How should central banks deal with a financial stability objective? The evolving role of communication as a policy instrument. In: *Handbook of Central Banking, Financial Regulation and Supervision after the Financial Crisis*, vol. 245, (Issue 68) (2011)
Brownlees, C.T., Engle, R.: Volatility, correlation and tails for systemic risk measurement. Retrieved from SSRN, 1611229 (2012)
Brownlees, C., Engle, R.F.: SRISK: a conditional capital shortfall measure of systemic risk. Rev. Financ. Stud. **30**(1), 48–79 (2016)
Chang, C.W., Li, X., Lin, E.M.H., Yu, M.T.: Systemic risk, interconnectedness, and non-core activities in Taiwan insurance industry. Int. Rev. Econ. Financ. **55**, 273–284 (2018)
Cipra, T., Heyndrich, R.: Systemic risk in financial risk regulation. Czech J. Econ. Financ. **67**(1), 15–38 (2017)
Coleman, T.F., LaPlante, A., Rubtsov, A.: Analysis of the SRISK measure and its application to the Canadian banking and insurance industries. Ann. Financ. **14**(4), 547–570 (2018)
Correa, R., Garud, K., Londono, J. M., Mislang, N.: Sentiment in Central banks' financial stability reports. International Finance Discussion Papers 1203, Board of Governors of the Federal Reserve System (2017)
Engle, R.: Anticipating Correlations: A New Paradigm for Risk Management. Princeton University Press (2009)
Engle, R., Jondeau, E., Rockinger, M.: Systemic risk in Europe. Rev. Finan. **19**(1), 145–190 (2014)
European Central Bank: Financial Stability Review, December (2011)
Gehrig, T., Iannino, M.C.: Capital regulation and systemic risk in the insurance sector. J. Financ. Econ. Policy **10**(2), 237–263 (2018)
Grundke, P., Tuchscherer, M.: Global systemic risk measures and their forecasting power for systemic events. Euro. J. Financ. 1–29 (2018)
Issing, O.: Monetary and financial stability: is there a trade-off? Bank of International Settlements Working Paper (2003)
Lin, E.M.H., Sun, E.W., Yu, M.T.: Systemic risk, financial markets, and performance of financial institutions. Ann. Oper. Res. **262**(2), 579–603 (2016)
López-Espinosa, G., Moreno, A., Rubia, A., Valderrama, L.: Short-term wholesale funding and systemic risk: a global CoVaR approach. J. Bank. Financ. **36**(12), 3150–3162 (2012)
Mishkin, F.: Anatomy of financial crisis. NBER Working Paper no. 3934 (1991)
Pagano, M.S., Sedunov, J.: A comprehensive approach to measuring the relation between systemic risk exposure and sovereign debt. J. Financ. Stab. **23**, 62–78 (2016)
Pederzoli, C., Torricelli, C.: Systemic risk measures and macroprudential stress tests: an assessment over the 2014 EBA exercise. Ann. Financ. **13**(3), 237–251 (2017)
Schinasi, M.G.J.: Defining financial stability. International Monetary Fund Working Paper No. 4–187 (2004)
Smets, F.: Financial stability and monetary policy: how closely interlinked? Int. J. Central Banking **10**(2), 263–300 (2014)
Stein, J.C.: Monetary policy as financial stability regulation. Q. J. Econ. **127**(1), 57–95 (2012)
Stolbov, M., Shchepeleva, M.: Systemic risk in Europe: Deciphering leading measures, common patterns and real effects. Ann. Financ. **14**(1), 49–91 (2017)
Wood, G. E.: Money, prices and the real economy. Edward Elgar Publishing (1998)
Woodford, M.: Inflation targeting and financial stability. NBER Working Paper, No. 17967 (2012)

World Bank. Key terms explained—financial stability. https://www.worldbank.org/en/publication/gfdr/gfdr-2016/background/financial-stability. Last Accessed 20 Jan 2020

Nonrenewable Energy Prices and Stock Prices of EU Financial Companies: A Short Versus Long-Term Analysis

Alexandra Horobet, Georgiana Vrinceanu, Consuela Popescu, and Lucian Belascu

1 Introduction

The global economy is faced for a number of years with the serious and action-provoking reality of climate change, fueled to a large extent by the economic model that supported worldwide development, based on the extensive and intensive use of nonrenewable energy sources, such as coal, oil and gas. Although the use of renewable energy sources has intensified recently (World Energy Council 2019), enterprises and households alike are still heavy consumers of nonrenewable energy, which generates an economy-wide impact of changes in the prices of these energy sources. This puts pressure on public and private decision-makers alike to address the environmental issues that could challenge the global quest for economic opportunities (OECD 2011).

Fig. 1 depicts the evolution of the prices for oil, coal and gas between 2009 and 2019, where it can be easily observed the rather high volatility of both oil and gas prices, compared to coal prices. Thus, oil prices plunged after 2014 and reached a minimum level in February 2016 (30$ per barrel for Brent crude oil price), but the volatility diminished after 2016, with a price rising to 86.29$ per barrel in January 2018, only to subsequently drop to 52.16$ per barrel in December 2018. The volatility of gas prices is even more striking, with a spike in mid-2014 (6$ per million BTU) but followed by a drop to less than 2$ per million BTU towards the end of 2015. After 2015, gas prices resumed their volatility, but at lower levels, to stay within the band of 2$ to 4$ per million BTU. For what concerns coal prices, their volatility

A. Horobet (✉) · G. Vrinceanu · C. Popescu
Bucharest University of Economic Studies, Piata Romana 6, 010374 Bucharest, Romania
e-mail: alexandra.horobet@rei.ase.ro

L. Belascu
Lucian Blaga" University of Sibiu, Victoriei Street 10, 550024 Sibiu, Romania

A. M. Dima and F. DÁscenzo (eds.), *Business Revolution in a Digital Era*,
Springer Proceedings in Business and Economics,
https://doi.org/10.1007/978-3-030-59972-0_5

Fig. 1. Nonrenewable energy prices. *Source* Federal Reserve of St. Louis

was much lower compared to oil and gas in the last decade, fueled mainly by the increasing renewable energy generation capacity (IRENA 2019).

The European Union is in a concerning situation regarding its energy mix, consisting of both production and imports, since 74% of energy in 2017 was represented by nonrenewable sources (petroleum products, including crude oil—36%; natural gas—23%; solid fossil fuels—15%). The remaining 26% of the energy mix was split between renewable energy (14%) and nuclear energy (12%). At the same time, EU countries differ significantly in terms of the share of various energy sources in the total energy; i.e. Cyprus, Malta and Luxembourg have high shares of petroleum products use (between 64% and 93%), while Italy, the Netherlands and United Kingdom see a share of approximately one third for natural gas. On the other hand, France and Sweden are leaders in the use of nuclear energy, with shares higher than 30%. To this picture we add that the EU dependency ratio—which measures the share of net imports (imports–exports) in gross inland energy consumption—was 55% in 2017 (rising since 2000, when it was 47%), but with high disparities across countries—the ratio is above 59% for Cyprus, Luxembourg and Malta, but below 15% in Estonia and Denmark (Eurostat 2019). In this framework, nonrenewable energy sources volatility has the potential of generating changes in prices and inflation, on currencies' values and on the performance of the financial and non-financial components of the economy. The report of the European Commission concluded that EU is exposed to external market forces that leave businesses and households at risk of nonrenewable energy sources prices volatility, which in turn is reflected in worsening trade balance terms and a lower overall economic performance (European Commission 2019).

Our paper addresses the economic impact of nonrenewable energy prices and their attribute as shock transmitters, as evidenced by the influence they have over the short- and long-run stock returns of financial companies and institutions. The analysis we propose is built on the hypothesis that financial companies stock prices and returns' exposure to energy sources changes in prices is an indication of systemic risk at country, region and global level. Moreover, financial institutions may be seen as potential transmitters of shocks in nonrenewable energy prices towards the real economy, given their lending, borrowing and investing relationships with non-financial companies and households.

We contribute to the academic debate on the links between nonrenewable energy prices and firms' market value, as we reinforce the previous conclusions on the exposure of financial companies to commodities' prices. The paper is structured as follows. The next section presents and discusses the main findings of the empirical literature on the relationship between energy prices and stock prices. Further, the Methodology section describes the data used in our research and details the research methodology, followed by the presentation of the most important and relevant results. The Conclusions part at the end of the paper discusses the implications of our findings, as well as the limitations of our research and a few directions for future research.

2 Literature Review

The academic literature has paid particularly close attention in the last years to the examination of the impact of energy prices and volatility on stock prices. Moreover, the effect of oil prices on stock prices has been researched intensively compared to the effect of other nonrenewable energy sources prices, such as coal price.

Overall, the existing evidence proves that oil price movements lead to fluctuations in stock prices even if the findings are rather mixed. No significant relationship between oil price changes and stock market returns was found by authors like Cong et al. (2008), Jammazi and Aloui (2010) or Mohanty et al. (2010). On the other hand, authors like Sadorsky (1999), Ciner (2001), Tuna et al. (2017), Cevik et al. (2018), Drachal (2018), Dominioni et al. (2019) or Horobet et al. (2019) provided completely different findings.

Thus, back in 1999, Sadorsky (1999) applies a vector autoregression model to show that oil prices and their volatility influence real stock returns and conclude that the dynamics of oil price has changed after 1986 and to evidence the asymmetric effect that shocks in oil price volatility have on the economy. The dynamic linkages between oil prices and stock prices were also examined by Ciner (2001), with results showing that oil prices impact stock returns, in the economic output logic, and identifying a stronger relationship in the 1990s. More recently, Tuna et al. (2017) use the

Pedroni panel cointegration model and the Dumitrescu-Hurlin causality test (2012) to find a long-term relationship between oil prices and stock prices and a bilateral causality between the two in the case of developing countries; at the same time, the causality relationship in developed countries is unilateral, from oil prices to stock prices. An interesting result is identified by Wang et al. (2013), which conclude that the stock markets' response to various oil price shocks depends on oil's importance for a specific economy and that oil-exporting countries experience higher degrees of co-movement between oil prices and stock prices, while lower levels of co-movements exist in oil-importing countries.

Cevik et al. (2018) employ time-varying causality tests in mean and variance on two samples of emerging and developed countries, to find that the relationship between oil price changes and stock market returns depends on the phases of the economic cycles, as the causal relationships between oil prices and stock returns are time-specific and depend on the level of stock market volatility. In the same vein, Drachal (2018) examines the causal dynamics between spot oil price, exchange rates, and stock prices in Central and Eastern Europe (CEE) countries using several causality tests. His findings revealed that oil price impacts both stock prices and exchange rates for these CEE countries. One year later, Dominioni et al. (2019) analyzed the link between oil and renewable energy stock prices over a period of ten years (2006–2016), using the Lotka-Volterra integrable non-autonomous model. The authors found that this link is described by major structural breaks that happened in 2008 and around 2013, with causes that are not fully understood yet. As a result, the authors advise that researching the interaction between oil and renewable energy sources prices or stocks should capture the changes in this interaction through appropriate methods.

For what concerns the financial sector, which is a non-oil-related sector, the results provided in the academic literature seem to be indecisive until now. Overall, the authors' findings demonstrate that there are positive effects of the oil price changes on oil-related and oil-substitute sectors, negative effects on oil-using sectors and insignificant effects on non-oil-related sectors. Narayan and Sharma (2011) examined the link between oil prices and stock returns of US companies listed on the NYSE employing a GARCH model. Their findings showed that oil price fluctuations have sector-related asymmetric effects on stock returns. In his research, Gogineni (2010) confirmed and explained these findings by the supply chain dependency to oil markets which is essential in indicating the impact of oil price changes in any sector of economy. Horobet et al. (2019a) have shown that the EU financial sector is substantially exposed to oil price movements over the long-run and this type of exposure should be understood in the context of financial companies' exposure to real economy risk factors, which reveals the major role of the financial sector in the EU economy in transmitting systemic shocks. Moreover, Horobet et al. (2019b) analyze the exposure to oil price risk of listed CEE financial companies with the help of panel methodology. Their findings show that oil price movements impact the stock prices of CEE financial companies, but the relationship between stock price return and oil price risk presents some particularities and it is mostly detectable on the long run analysis. Arouri (2011) investigated the relationship between oil price movements and European stock returns using the Dow Jones Stoxx 600 index and twelve industrial sector indices from European countries. His findings show that Financial, Oil and Gas, Industrials, Basic Materials, and Personal and Household Goods sectors display positive responses to oil price changes. Furthermore, in a subsequent paper of Degiannakis et al. (2013) it is shown that Financial and Consumer Goods sectors present a negative response to oil price movements.

Despite the importance of coal as a source of nonrenewable energy, there seems to be a weaker interest of researchers towards analyzing the connection between coal prices and stock market returns until now. To the best of our knowledge, there are only a few studies that address this subject. Thus, Ratti and Hasan (2011) studied the effect of oil and coal price shocks on coal sector stock returns and the effect of oil prices on the stock prices of oil and gas companies using the panel data methodology. Their findings show that both increases in coal and oil prices lead to increases in the stock prices of oil and gas companies but nuanced based on the country and time period investigated. A few years later, the same authors have expanded the research and investigated the risk factors of Australian coal companies' stock returns—Hasan and Ratti (2014). They examined the impact of coal and oil prices on stock returns of listed Australian coal companies using a GLS panel data model and monthly data between 1999 and 2010 and their results showed that coal and oil prices present positive effects on coal companies' stock returns.

As far as we are aware, our work pioneers the research that attempts to explain the short and long term relationship between financial companies' stock returns, nonrenewable energy prices and several macroeconomic variables using an ARDL model. Horobet et al. (2019a) were the first authors who employed this model when investigating the relationship between stock returns of financial companies, oil price and several macroeconomic variables using the same methodology.

3 Methodology

Our research investigates 76 EU headquartered financial companies stock prices' exposure to nonrenewable energy sources prices volatility, i.e. oil and coal. The selected financial companies, with an overall market capitalization of 1,594.1 billion US dollars at the end of 2018, are included in the Forbes' 17th Annual Global 2000 Ranking of The World's Largest Public Companies. They originate from six financial services industries and 16 EU countries, as shown in Table 1.

We investigate the exposure of these financial companies' stock returns to changes in oil and coal prices in a macroeconomic framework that includes other variables besides nonrenewable energy prices, in order to get more insight into the interactions between the internal and external market forces that configure this exposure. The set of variables includes the following: (i) Brent crude oil price; (ii) Coal price; (iii) local stock market indices (ATX for Austria, BEL20 for Belgium, OMX Copenhagen all shares for Denmark, OMX Helsinki for Finland, CAC Large 60 for France, DAX for Germany, ATG for Greece, BUX for Hungary, ISEQ Overall for Ireland, FTSE

Italia All Share for Italy, AEX All Share for Netherlands, WIG for Poland, PSI 20 for Portugal, IBEX 35 for Spain, OMX Stockholm for Sweden and FTSE-All Share for the United Kingdom); (iv) the EUR/USD exchange rate, with EUR as the base currency; (v) long-term interest rates, with a 10-year maturity; and (vi) a measure of global financial market volatility incorporated by VIX, which represents the US market expectation of 30-day forward looking volatility, frequently used for this purpose.

Table 1 Financial companies' distribution across financial services industries and countries of headquarters

Industry	Name of the financial company
Consumer financial services 2 companies	Fastighets Balder (SW), Melrose Industries (UK)
Diversified Insurance 16 companies	Vienna Insurance Group (AU), Uniqa (AU), Aegeas (BE), Sampo (FI), AXA Group (FR), CNP Assurances (FR), Scor (FR), Allianz (GE), Munich Re (GE), Nuernberger Beteiligungs (GE), Generali Group (IT), Unipol Gruppo (IT), Cattolica Assicurazioni (IT), Aegon (NL), Mapfre (SP), Willis Towers Watson (UK)
Investment Services 12 companies	Sofina (BE), Wendel (FR), Deutsche Boerse (GE), Wuestenrot & Wuerttembergische (GE), Exor (NL), Investor AB (SW), Industrivarden (SW), London Stock Exchange (UK), Investec (UK), 3i Group (UK), St. James's Place (UK), TP ICAP (UK)
Major banks 18 companies	Erste Group Bank (AU), Dexia (BE), Danske Bank (DK), BNP Paribas (FR), Societe Generale (FR), Natixis (FR), Deutsche Bank (GE), ING Group (NL), Santander (SP), Nordea Bank (SW), SEB AB (SW), Svenska Handelsbanken (SW), Swedbank (SW), HSBC Holdings (UK), Lloyds Banking Group (UK), Royal Bank of Scotland (UK), Barclays, Standard Chartered (UK)
Regional Banks 27 companies	Raiffeisen Bank International (AU), KBC Group (BE), Jyske Bank (DK), Credit Agricole (FR), Commerzbank (GE), National Bank of Greece (GR), Piraeus Bank (GR), Alpha Bank (GR),Eurobank Ergasias (GR), OTP Bank (HU), AIB Group (IR), Bank of Ireland (IR), Intesa Sanpaolo (IT), Unicredit (IT), Mediobanca (IT), UBI Banca (IT), Banco BPM (IT), BPER Banca (IT), Credito Emiliano (IT), Banca Popolare di Sondrio (IT), PKO Bank Polski (PL), Bank Pekao (PL), Banco Comercial Portugues (PT), BBVA-Banco Bilbao Vizcaya (SP), CaixaBank (SP), Banco de Sabadell (SP), Bankinter (SP)
Thrifts and Mortgage Finance 1 company	Aareal Bank (GE)

Note AU Austria, *BE* Belgium, *DK* Denmark, *FI* Finland, *FR* France, *GE* Germany, *GR* Greece, *HU* Hungary, *IR* Ireland, *IT* Italy, *NL* Netherlands, *PL* Poland, *PT* Portugal, *SP* Spain, *SW* Sweden, *UK* United Kingdom
Source Forbes' 17th Annual Global 2000 Ranking of The World's Largest Public Companies

Data was collected with monthly frequency from Forbes, Bloomberg, Eurostat, Comtrade.un.org website and OECD and was included in logarithmic form with the goal of managing the different measurement units of the variables. The period under analysis is January 2010 to December 2018, thus avoiding the turbulent years of the Global financial crisis.

It is difficult to hypothesize a positive or a negative relationship between oil and coal prices, on one hand, and financial companies' stock returns, on the other hand, as increases in the former might generate increases in the stock prices of companies operating in the oil and coal industry, but it would also fuel increases in the costs of companies located downstream from both industries. Overall, a clear-cut relationship is not easy to detect, as it depends on the country's economic structure and its production versus imports ratio, as well as on how market investors view the relationship between the non-financial businesses cash flows and financial companies' stock prices. Local stock market indices are included in our investigation to reflect general economic prospects and a positive link between changes in indices and financial companies' stock returns is expected, given the strong exposure of the financial sector to market risk.

Since most of the EU economies are net oil importers, a depreciation of the EUR against the USD indicates a significant concern for them, which reflects in a negative expected sign of the exposure. Moreover, an increase in imports of oil would generate a higher market risk and a lower stock return. On the other hand, an increase in oil price would cause a decrease in oil imports. Still, taking into account that oil represents an essential and not simply replaceable resource, it is possible that no effect is noticed in the short-term. VIX would ordinarily impact in a negative manner stock returns given that empirical evidences show that higher market volatility is commonly associated with lower returns.

We use the panel data as the base econometric model as it is able to control for heterogeneity of cross-section units—financial companies in our research—over time and to result in more unbiased estimations. For our purpose, an ARDL (Autoregressive Distributed Lag) technique is used, which represents a standard least square estimation that consists of lags of both the dependent and independent variables. Moreover, the ARDL framework explores cointegrating relationships between variables and allows for a long-run versus short-run perspective on the link between variables.

The general equation of the ARDL (p, q, q … q) model is the following:

$$Y_{it} = \sum_{j=1}^{p}(\alpha_{ij}Y_{i,t-j}) + \sum_{j=0}^{q}(\delta'_{ij}X_{i,t-j}) + \mu_i + \varepsilon_{it} \tag{1}$$

Where Y represents the stocks' price and the dependent variable, while X is a vector matrix which includes the set of explanatory variables: Brent crude oil price, coal price, local stock market indices, EUR/USD exchange rate, long-term interest rates and VIX. $\alpha_{i,j}$ and δ'_{ij} represent the coefficients associated with a linear trend, lags of Y, and lags of the q regressors X for $j = 0, \ldots q$, μ_i denotes the short-run coefficient and ε_{it} represents the error term (the white noise residuals).

Equation (1) permits for the parameters to vary between units which can be estimated by employing the Mean Group estimator per financial company and then the average for the whole group of companies. The Pooled Mean Group (PMG) permits for the short-run parameters to vary across financial companies but keeps the long-run parameters homogeneity. Our model can be reparametrized (in order to demonstrate the short-run dynamics and also the long-run relationship of the underlying variables) as follows:

$$\Delta Y_{it} = \varphi_i(Y_{i,t-1} - \beta_i' X_{i,t} + \sum_{j=1}^{p-1} (\alpha_{ij}^{*} \Delta Y_{i,t-j}) + \sum_{j=0}^{q-1} (\delta_{ij}^{*\prime} \Delta X_{i,t-j}) + \mu_i + \varepsilon_{it} \quad (2)$$

Where Δ denotes the first difference operator, β_i represents a vector of interest used in order to measure the long-run impact of the regressors on the stocks returns, φ_i represents the error corrector mechanism impact on the dependent variable, ε_{it} is the error term (the white nose residuals) and the rest of the parameters are short-run coefficients (μ_i, δ_{ij}'). We obtain the order of lags on the first-differenced variables from the ARDL model by means of the AIC (Akaike Information Criterion).

Considering that the regression equation offers only the short-run relationship between the variables and we are also concerned about the long-run relationship between the variables, the concept of cointegration and reparametrization of the ARDL model into an ECM (Error Correction Model) becomes indispensable. The ECM can be obtained from an ARDL model through a simple linear transformation that is able to incorporate the short-run adjustments with long-run equilibrium without sacrificing the long-run information. Consequently, the advantage of the ECM is that Eq. (2) ensures both short-term and long-term information regarding the relationship between the dependent variable and the set of independent variables.

4 Results and Discussions

For the purpose of establishing whether the variables can be good predictors, tests for unit root were performed in Eviews. Therefore, Levin, Lin, Chu test (LLC), Breitung t-stat, Im, Pesaran and Shin W-Stat (IPS), ADF—Fisher Chi-square and PP—Fisher Chi-square tests were selected to be used. The benefit of using these tests is that, in their case, the null hypothesis supposes common/individual unit root process.

The results in Table 2 demonstrate that the series of VIX are stationary in level, while the series of the other variables of our model (oil price, coal price, company' stock returns, EUR/USD exchange rate, local stock market indices and long-term interest rate) are stationary at the first difference. Taking into account that not all of the series are integrated at the same order, the use of an ARDL model is optimal.

We have estimated the long-run and short-run coefficients using AIC as lag length criterion in Tables 3, 4 and 5. We discuss the results based on the lag length evidenced by the panel ARDL model. It is important to mention that the long-run coefficients are constrained to be the same across the financial companies, while the short-run coefficients are allowed to vary between cross-sections. The estimations are performed by changing the independent variables as a test for results' robustness. For this purpose, we have implemented ten panel models. Therefore, we vary regressors in order to examine the presence of both oil price and coal price exposure when the panel regression specification is changed.

Table 3 displays the results of the long-run panel ARDL estimations. We notice that five out of ten panel models present a significant relationship between oil price changes and companies' stock returns in the long-run, while in all models the coefficients for coal price changes are statistical significant. Also, we remark statistically significant coefficients for all the other independent variables employed, with signs that are consistent across the models. As a result, the foreign exchange rate, the long term interest rate and the local stock market index return present positive correlations with the stock prices, while VIX represents the only variable showing consistent negative correlation with the latter.

Source Authors' results

At the same time, we do not find consistent and statistically significant coefficients in the short-run equations for these variables (in Table 4). An explanation for this can be that it takes time for investors to adjust their risk premiums to the changes in the risk environment as shown by the changes in the before analyzed variables. Moreover,

Table 2 Unit Root Test of the variables

Variables	Order of integration	LLC	Breitung	IPS	ADF	PP
Stock returns	1	67.964 (0.000)	28.608 (0.000)	−65.278 (0.000)	3019.6 (0.000)	4511.3 (0.000)
Oil price	1	−57.337 (0.000)	−6.597 (0.000)	−51.805 (0.000)	2272.75 (0.000)	3493.71 (0.000)
Coal price	1	−58.388 (0.000)	−23.907 (0.000)	−51.673 (0.000)	2265.15 (0.000)	2689.04 (0.000)
Local indices	1	−72.942 (0.000)	−23.0325 (0.000)	−62.553 (0.000)	2893.06 (0.000)	4327.37 (0.000)
EUR/USD	1	−61.924 (0.000)	−50.218 (0.000)	−58.963 (0.000)	2686.40 (0.000)	4874.68 (0.000)
LT Interest Rate	1	−34.211 (0.000)	−29.264 (0.000)	−31.473 (0.000)	838.89 (0.000)	1038.18 (0.000)
VIX	0	−27.210 (0.000)	−3.611 (0.000)	−18.856 (0.000)	618.617 (0.000)	1081.68 (0.000)

Note The null hypothesis is that the series is a unit-root process; p-values are reported in parentheses

if we explore the relationships between oil price movements, coal price movements and companies' stock returns in the long term, we find that oil price returns are always negatively influencing the companies' stock returns, while coal price changes are positively influencing the stock returns—all these signs are consistent across the models. Furthermore, no significant relationship has been found between these variables in the short term (see Table 4), except for one panel model, where the second lag of the coal price changes is negatively influencing the stock returns of the EU companies.

Regarding the particular short-term exposure of EU financial companies' stock returns to oil and coal price movements, the distribution of cross-section coefficients across companies does not divulge any certain pattern based on signs, origin of the headquarters or financial services industry (see Table 4).

Concerning the panel regressions' standard errors (SE), smaller values are superior for the reason that they suggest that the observations are closer to the fitted line. On the other hand, in the case of log likelihood (LL), the higher the value, the better is the model. Considering these, we choose the panel model 1 (where SE value is 49.640) as the best model from our panel ARDL estimations. The panel model 1 is the one that includes all the variables (see Table 4).

Table 5 illustrates the numbers and signs for the short-run statistically significant cross-section coefficients only for oil and coal price changes. In the case of oil price returns, the number of cross-sections in whose case the short-run coefficients are positive is higher than the number of cross-sections with negative coefficients. On the other hand, in the case of coal price movements, we notice an inverse situation. This might be explained by the specific exposure of these financial companies to oil and coal price changes, based on their specific assets and liabilities portfolio, as well as country and/or countries or operations.

Overall, both oil and coal price fluctuations seem to be important determinants of stock price returns of EU financial companies, which confirms similar results in the existing literature for oil price have been found in previous works by Horobet et al. (2019a, b).

5 Conclusion

The main purpose of our paper was to examine the relationship between financial companies' stock prices and nonrenewable energy sources prices as Brent crude oil price and coal price using a sample of major financial companies headquartered in EU countries. We have addressed the economic impact of nonrenewable energy prices and their role as shock transmitters, as evidenced by the influence they have over the short- and long-run on financial companies and institutions' stock returns. We have built our research on the hypothesis that financial companies' stock prices and returns' exposure to energy sources price volatility represent an indication of systemic risk at the country, region and at global level. Furthermore, financial institutions may be seen as potential transmitters of shocks in nonrenewable energy prices towards

Table 3 Results of long-run panel ARDL estimations

Variable	1 ARDL (4, 3, 3, 3, 3, 3, 3)	2 ARDL (2, 2, 2, 2, 2, 2)	3 ARDL(4, 3, 3, 3, 3, 3)	4 ARDL(4, 3, 3, 3, 3, 3)	5 ARDL(1, 1, 1, 1, 1, 1)	6 ARDL(1, 1, 1, 1, 1)	7 ARDL(1, 1, 1, 1, 1)	8 ARDL(4, 2, 2, 2, 2)	9 ARDL(1, 2, 2, 2, 2)	10 ARDL(3, 3, 3, 3, 3)
Oil	**−0.034**	**−0.025**	**−0.037**	−0.005	−0.014	0.012	**−0.007**	−0.004	−0.012	**−0.008**
Coal	**0.032**	**0.046**	**0.033**	**0.016**	**0.027**	**0.016**	**0.009**	**0.014**	**0.031**	**0.017**
EUR/USD	1.284	**4.663**	–	−0.283	1.168	**6.426**	**0.986**	0.647	–	–
Interest rate	0.378	**0.737**	0.377	–	0.122	0.385	–	–	**0.603**	–
Index	**0.002**	**0.003**	**0.003**	**0.000**	–	–	–	**0.000**	**0.003**	**0.000**
VIX	**−0.032**	–	**−0.029**	**−0.010**	**−0.054**	–	**−0.014**	–	–	**−0.008**

Notes Bolded coefficients are statistically significant at least at 5% level and "–"indicates that the variable was not included in the model

Table 4 Results of short-run panel ARDL estimations

Variable	1 ARDL (4, 3, 3, 3, 3, 3, 3)	2 ARDL(2, 2, 2, 2, 2, 2)	3 ARDL(4, 3, 3, 3, 3, 3)	4 ARDL(4, 3, 3, 3, 3, 3)	5 ARDL(1, 1, 1, 1, 1, 1)	6 ARDL(1, 1, 1, 1, 1)	7 ARDL(1, 1, 1, 1, 1)	8 ARDL(4, 2, 2, 2, 2)	9 ARDL(1, 2, 2, 2, 2)	10 ARDL(3, 3, 3, 3, 3)
CQ1	**– 0.797**	**–0.826**	**–0.820**	**–0.721**	**–0.967**	**–0.977**	**–0.966**	**–0.743**	**–0.902**	**– 0.733**
CO (1 lag)	**– 0.140**	**–0.080**	**–0.125**	**–0.186**	–	–	–	**–0.124**	–	**– 0.183**
CO (2 lags)	**– 0.089**	–	**–0.083**	**–0.130**	–	–	–	– 0.027	–	**– 0.138**
CO (3 lags)	– 0.005	–	0.008	– 0.008	–	–	–	– 0.001	–	–
Oil (0 lags)	0.111	0.070	0.103	– 0.587	0.749	0.802	1.637	– 0.641	0.045	– 0.276
Oil (1 lag)	0.251	0.108	0.243	0.006	–	–	–	0.338	0.095	– 0.145
Oil (2 lags)	– 0.158	–	– 0.083	– 0.760	–	–	–	–	–	– 0.728
Coal (0 lag)	– 0.454	– 0.908	– 0.637	**–0.558**	– 0.986	– 0.865	– 1.455	– 0.102	– 0.711	– 1.503
Coal (1 lag)	– 0.487	– 0.575	– 0.852	– 1.672	–	–	–	– 1.466	– 1.024	– 1.478
Coal (2 lags)	0.233	–	0.465	0.631	–	–	–	–	–	1.135
EUR/USD (0 lags)	61.625	5.372	–	47.453	– 36.876	26.335	107.456	192.904	–	–
EUR/USD (1 lag)	90.004	92.104	–	– 145.660	–	–	–	**124.987**	–	–
EUR/USD (2 lags)	– 42.273	–	–	– 296.439	–	–	–	–	–	–
Interest rate (0 lags)	– 8.355	– 8.830	– 8.912	–	– 8.646	– 8.680	–	–	– 7.082	–
Interest rate (1 lag)	**1.025**	1.353	– 1.959	–	–	–	–	–	1.871	–

(continued)

Table 4 (continued)

Variable	1 ARDL (4, 3, 3, 3, 3, 3, 3)	2 ARDL(2, 2, 2, 2, 2, 2)	3 ARDL(4, 3, 3, 3, 3, 3)	4 ARDL(4, 3, 3, 3, 3, 3)	5 ARDL(1, 1, 1, 1, 1, 1)	6 ARDL(1, 1, 1, 1, 1)	7 ARDL(1, 1, 1, 1, 1)	8 ARDL(4, 2, 2, 2, 2)	9 ARDL(1, 2, 2, 2, 2)	10 ARDL(3, 3, 3, 3, 3)
Interest rate (2 lags)	1.245	–	– 1.911	–	–	–	–	–	–	–
Index (2 lags)	0.094	0.093	0.092	0.268	–	–	–	0.190	0.079	0.286
Index (1 lag)	0.069	0.066	0.067	0.253	–	–	–	0.131	0.048	0.244
Index (2 lags)	0.025	–	0.018	0.165	–	–	–	–	–	0.119
VIX (0 lags)	0.514	–	0.230	– 0.479	– 1.648	–	– 4.988	–	–	– 1.925
VIX (1 lag)	– 0.915	–	– 1.300	– 2.570	–	–	–	–	–	– 2.959
VIX (2 lags)	– 0.746	–	– 0.398	– 1.577	–	–	–	–	–	– 1.064
SE	49.640	57.863	51.093	252.297	76.956	79.157	330.182	272.316	62.443	290.423
LL	– 5982.37	– 6454.13	– 6090.81	– 15556.90	– 7052.99	– 7273.61	– 18626.90	– 16171.27	– 6543.373	– 16084.92

Notes Bolded coefficients are statistically significant at least at 5% level and "-" indicates that the variable was not included in the model. Source: Authors' own research results
Source Authors' results

Table 5 Short-run statistically significant cross-section coefficients—number and signs

Model	Variables											
	Oil (0 lags)		Oil (1 lag)		Oil (2 lags)		Coal (0 lags)		Coal (1 lag)		Coal (2 lags)	
	+	−	+	−	+	−	+	−	+	−	+	−
1	19	9	21	7	9	19	2	26	11	17	16	12
2	17	11	6	22	na		5	23	8	20	na	
3	8	20	7	21	14	14	0	28	2	26	19	9
4	43	33	50	16	34	42	16	62	48	28	43	33
5	27	1	na		na		1	27	na		na	
6	28	0	na		na		4	24	na		na	
7	72	4	na		na		10	66	na		na	
8	41	35	50	26	na		17	59	29	47	na	
9	15	13	23	5	na		1	27	4	24	na	
10	46	30	54	22	34	42	9	67	13	63	47	19

Note "na" —not available; " + " indicates positive coefficients and "−" indicates negative coefficients
Source Authors' own research results

the real economy, given their lending, borrowing and investing relationships with non-financial companies and households.

We integrate the analysis on energy prices volatility and stock prices of financial companies in a wider macroeconomic framework, by including a number of macroeconomic variables in our tests (Brent crude oil price, coal price, local stock market indices, the EUR/USD exchange rate, long-term interest rates and VIX), so that we provide a more comprehensive view on this subject. In order to gain insight into the short- versus the long-run relationship between nonrenewable energy prices and financial companies' stock prices we implement a Dynamic Panel estimation in an ARDL framework, which is suited for this purpose. Our findings reveal that the EU financial sector is pervasively exposed to the nonrenewable energy sources price fluctuations over the long-run and we interpret this as a component of financial companies' exposure to real economy risk factors. In addition, the short-term exposure is specific to financial companies and highlights a different behavior of market investors compared to the long-run valuation of financial companies' stock prices. These results point towards the fundamental role of the financial sector in the EU economy in transmitting systemic shocks, which raises serious challenges for the EU financial authorities.

We contribute to the academic debate on the relationship between nonrenewable energy prices and corporations' market value, as we reinforce the previous conclusions on the exposure of financial companies to commodities' prices and determine the role of financial sector as transmitter of shocks to the real economy.

Concerning the main limitations of our study, they reside firstly in the sample used, since we have applied our analysis to big EU companies, but the effects of oil price changes may be more vigorous on medium and smaller size companies. Secondly, they reside in the time frame employed (applying the same methodology out of sample might offer more insight into our results) and, inherently, in the econometric model employed. Nevertheless, given the complexity of the panel ARDL methodology used, our results are robust and point towards the need to thoroughly investigate the unexpected links between the real and financial economy. Future research directions include extending the investigation to companies from other countries outside the EU and from other industries, such as transportation, chemical and pharmaceutical products, etc. and using more sophisticated econometric methodologies. For example, quantile regressions and random forests may be used to enhance our findings.

References

Arouri, M.E.H.: Does crude oil move stock markets in Europe? A sector investigation. Econ. Modell. **28**(4), 1716–1725 (2011)

Cevik, E.I., Atukeren, E., Korkmaz, T.: Oil prices and global stock markets: a time-varying causality-in-mean and causality-in-variance analysis. Energies **11**(10), 2848 (2018)

Ciner, C.: Energy shocks and financial markets: nonlinear linkages. Stud. Nonlinear Dyn. Econ. **5**(3), 1079–1079 (2001)

Cong, R.G., Wei, Y.M., Jiao, L.J., Fan, Y.: Relationships between oil price shocks and stock market: an empirical analysis from China. Energy Policy **36**(9), 3544–3553 (2008)

Degiannakis, S., Filis, G., Floros, C.: Oil and stock returns: evidence from European industrial sector indices in a time-varying environment. J. Int. Fin. Mark. Inst. Money **26**(C), 175–191 (2013)

Dominioni, G., Romano, A., Sotis, C.: A quantitative study of the interactions between oil price and renewable energy sources stock prices. Energies **12**, 1693 (2019)

Drachal, K.: Exchange rate and oil price interactions in selected CEE countries. Economies **6**, 31 (2018)

Dumitrescu, E.I., Hurlin, C.: Testing for Granger non-causality in heterogeneous panels. Econ. Model. **29**(4), 1450–1460 (2012)

European Commission.: Energy prices and costs in Europe. Brussels: European Commission. Available online: https://ec.europa.eu/energy/sites/ener/files/epc_report_final_1.pdf. (2019). Accessed on 29 Jan 2020

Eurostat.: Shedding light on energy in the EU 2019—A guided tour of energy statistics. Available online: https://ec.europa.eu/eurostat/cache/infographs/energy/index.html. (2019). Accessed on 29 Jan 2020

Forbes.: The world's largest public companies—2019 ranking. Available online: https://www.forbes.com/global2000/list/#tab:overall. (2019). Accessed on 30 Oct 2019

Gogineni, S.: Oil and the stock market: an industry level analysis. Fin. Rev. **45**(4), 995–1010 (2010)

Hasan, M.Z., Ratti, R.A.: Australian coal company risk factors: coal and oil prices. Int. J. Bus. Fin. Res. **8**(1), 57–67 (2014)

Horobet, A., Vrinceanu, G., Popescu, C., Belascu, L.: Oil price and stock prices of EU financial companies: evidence from panel data modeling. Energies **12**, 4072 (2019)

Horobet, A., Vrinceanu, G., Belascu, L.: Oil price exposure of CEE financial companies. Rev. Socio-Econ. Perspect. **4**(2), 1–15 (2019)

IRENA: Renewable Power Generation Costs in 2018. International Renewable Energy Agency, Abu Dhabi (2019)

Jammazi, R., Aloui, C.: Wavelet decomposition and regime shifts: assessing the effects of crude oil shocks on stock market returns. Energy Policy **38**(3), 1415–1435 (2010)

Mohanty, S., Nandha, M., Bota, G.: Oil shocks and stock returns: the case of the Central and Eastern European (CEE) oil and gas sectors. Emerg. Mark. Rev. **11**(4), 358–372 (2010)

Narayan, P.K., Sharma, S.S.: New evidence on oil price and firm returns. J. Bank. Finance **35**(12), 3253–3262 (2011)

OECD.: OECD Green Growth Studies—Energy. OECD Publishing. Available online: https://www.oecd.org/greengrowth/greening-energy/49157219.pdf. (2011). Accessed on 29 Jan 2020

Ratti, R.A., Hasan, M.Z.: Oil and coal price shocks and coal industry returns: international evidence. In: 24th Australasian Finance and Banking Conference, Sydney, Australia (2011). https://papers.ssrn.com/sol3/papers.cfm?abstract_id=1914347

Sadorsky, P.: Oil price shocks and stock market activity. Energy Econ. **21**, 449–469 (1999)

Tuna, G., Göleç, N., Tuna, V.E.: The relationship between oil and stock prices: the case of developing and developed countries. Theor. Appl. Econo. **24**(4), 97–108 (2017)

Wang, Y., Wu, C., Yang, L.: Oil price shocks and stock market activities: evidence from oil-importing and oil-exporting countries. J. Comp. Econ. **41**(4), 1220–1239 (2013)

World Energy Council.: World Energy Scenarios 2019. Available online: https://www.worldenergy.org/assets/downloads/Scenarios_Report_FINAL_for_website.pdf. (2019). Accessed on 29 Jan 2020

Designing Better Policies for a Cleaner Air: The Case of Electric Vehicles in Europe

Camelia Ghiurcă

1 Introduction

In Europe, last June was the warmest June in history, average temperatures being more than 2 °C above normal. Even though the phenomenon cannot be directly related to climate change, it is believed that such events will happen more frequently due to increasing greenhouse gas (GHG) concentrations in the air. (Copernicus Climate 2019) Although efforts are being made by both European and national authorities, reducing the GHG quantity remains a great challenge.

The European Environment Agency claims that transport sector is responsible for about ¼ of Europe's greenhouse gases (GHG) emissions of which 82% has its source in road transport. (European Environment Agency 2016) In order to reduce this quantity, European Commission has created a Strategy for low-emission mobility in which one of the main elements is the adoption on large scale of low and zero-emission cars, electric or otherwise. (European Commission 2016) Furthermore, the European Commission decided that the transport sector must reduce by 60% its GHG emissions levels by 2050 compared to 1990. (European Commission 2011) Other measures include, targets for fuel quality (European Commission 2008), GHG targets for new passenger cars (European Commission 2009) and GHG targets for new light commercial vans (European Commission 2011) that were introduced in order to reduce the impact of transport sector on climate. Until now, only the target for vans seems to be a realistic one to be reached in 2020.

C. Ghiurcă (✉)
University Alexandru Ioan Cuza, Iaşi, Romania
e-mail: camelia.ghiurca@yahoo.com

A. M. Dima and F. DÁscenzo (eds.), *Business Revolution in a Digital Era*,
Springer Proceedings in Business and Economics,
https://doi.org/10.1007/978-3-030-59972-0_6

2 Literature Review

In order to reach proposed targets, Europeans need to change their behavior. On one hand, they have to change their daily behavior by adopting new mobility solutions such as car-sharing or use more frequently public transport. On the other hand, a change in their buying behavior is needed, so that people buy more personal cars with zero or low emissions—electric or otherwise. Unfortunately, the term "electric" raises confusion among consumers, and combined with the lack of information about the impact of electric cars on the environment, half of them declared that they don't even take into account to buy an electric vehicle in their next purchase. (Gómez Vilchez et al. 2017) The same study identifies as the most important factor when purchasing an electric vehicle, the price, followed by distance with one recharge, recharge at home without private charging, recharging time, fuel costs, maintenance costs, insurance costs and maximum speed.

Regarding consumers' decision on buying a new car, a recent study (ICCTE 2018) that included five European countries indicated that these are suboptimal. The authors compared the monetary effects that national public policies have on the price of four variants of VW Golf cars—VW Golf on petrol, VW Golf on diesel, VW e-Golf 10 (Battery electric vehicle—BEV) and VW Golf GTE (Plug-in hybrid electric vehicle- PHEV on petrol). All four have an emission level between 114g/km CO_2 for the diesel variant, followed by 112 g/km CO_2 the petrol version, 36 g/km CO_2 the PHEV and 0 g/km CO_2 the BEV. The analysis showed that over a 4-year period, taking into account all national fiscal measures, in all five European countries the best cost-effective option is the electric option BEV, VW e-Golf. In conclusion, the suboptimal decision people make when buying a car does not only affect their health, but also their personal finances.

Usually, information regarding emissions of a car are provided to Europeans with the help of an environmental component that is part of many national motor tax policies. In Europe this component can take the form of: (a) emissions standards—cars are classified from EURO 1 to EURO 6, where EURO 1 includes the most polluting cars (BE0); (b) a bonus/malus scheme where the polluter must pay and the non-polluter is rewarded (BE1); and (c) a tax based on the quantity of emissions where polluter must pay while non-polluter is exempted and electric vehicles are used as reference point (BE2). There are countries that do not use any form of this environmental component, basing their motor tax policies only on physical attributes of car like engine power or other self-made values that make no references to emissions (T). (ACEA 2016,2017,2018).

Apparently, providing information about emissions raises awareness about the carbon footprint of a car. It can be observed that between 2016–2018 countries as Poland (0.2%), Italy (0.3%) and Denmark (1.22%) that did not include any environmental component in their motor tax policies have the lowest market share of electric vehicles compared with countries with similar purchasing power and charging infrastructure such as Hungary (0.97%), Spain (0.6%) and Finland (2.84%) respectively.

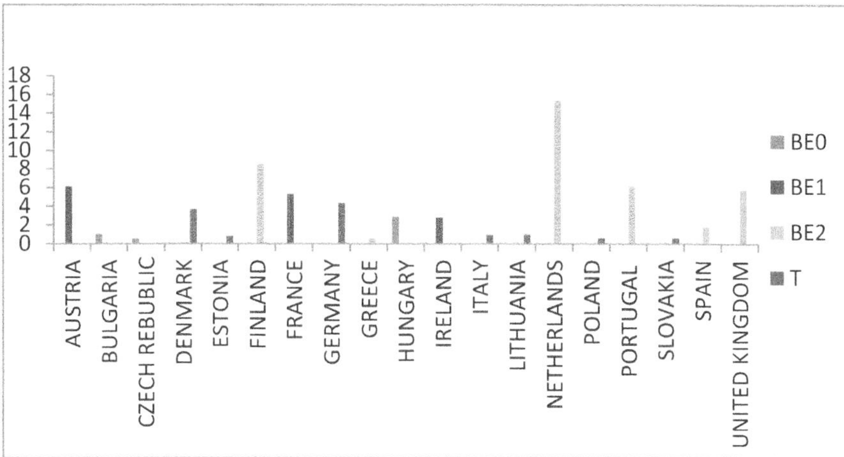

Fig. 1 Adoption rate (3 year) by country and policy. *Source* Author's own contribution

Furthermore, using a certain design of the environmental component seems to influence people's behavior when purchasing a car, having a positive impact on the adoption rate of electric vehicles. Normally, early adopters of innovative products such as electric vehicles are people with a high purchasing power, and in this particular case, living in countries with a developed charging infrastructure. However, data show that along with countries that satisfy these conditions, there is an anomaly: Portugal (2.05%). A country with an inferior purchasing power and charging infrastructure that has a greater adoption rate of electric vehicle than Germany (1.43%), France (1.76%) and Denmark (1.22%). Figure 1 summarizes the way each one of the 19 European countries considered frames its motor taxation policy between 2016 and 2018 and their correspondent rate of adoption.

At first sight, it could be believed that the difference among countries could be explained through two factors influencing purchasing behavior, selling price and culture.

Five years apart, two studies (Thiel et al. 2012; Gómez Vilchez et al. 2017) identified price as being the most important factor in buying an electric vehicle, followed by infrastructure and product related factors. As any other innovation, electric vehicles have a high selling price, which prevents people from buying it. In order to overcome this barrier many countries such as France or Germany adopted the standard economics approach of creating demand by diminishing the price and offer subventions that range from 3.000 euros for a PHEV and 4.000 euros for a BEV in Germany to a maximum of 5.000 euros for any electric vehicle in France[1]. The most common way to make electric vehicles more price convenient is by offering different monetary incentives at the time of acquisition. This kind of measure had a positive impact on the sales of electric vehicles, but these countries rate of adoption remains

[1] Data on subvention www.acea.be. Last Accessed October 2019.

lower compared with similar countries that use electric vehicles as a reference point, as in the case of the third form the environmental component can take. The gap between the two groups becomes even greater when the latter also offers monetary subventions or when people show an active involvement in fighting climate change as in case of Finland.

Another factor that could have a significant impact on the rate of adoption of electric vehicles is culture. When classifying observed countries in cultural clusters we notice that in four out of five groups the country with the highest rate of adoption during 2016–2018 is the one that uses electric vehicles as a reference point[2]. In the Anglo-Saxon cluster (Ireland—0.92% and United Kingdom—1.92%) United Kingdom has the largest adoption rate, followed by Netherlands in the Germanic cluster (Germany—1.43%, Austria—2.03% and Netherlands—5.10%), Portugal in Latin cluster (Italy—0.3%, Spain—0.6%, Portugal—2.05%, France—1.76%) and Finland in Nordic cluster (Finland—2.84% and Denmark—1.22%). A different situation is in the Eastern European cluster (Hungary—0.97%, Poland—0.2%, Greece—0.19%, Slovakia—0.19%, Czech Republic—0.19%, Bulgaria—0.34%, Estonia—0.26% and Lithuania—0.95%) where even though Greece is the only country using electric vehicles as a reference point, Hungary has the biggest rate of adoption. It is also true that the low rate of Greece can be the result of the poor charging infrastructure, this being the country with the lowest number of charging stations among the observed countries, with only 46 stations in 2018[3].

Under this circumstances, it seems that neither the acquisition price nor the culture are the reasons why anomalies such as Portugal appear. Rather, it is believed that the high rate of adoption registered by Portugal can be explained by the way authorities design their motor tax policy, especially by the form the environmental component takes. When the latter takes the form of a tax based on the quantity of emissions and electric vehicles are treated as a reference point being assigned a zero or a minimum value of the tax, the rate of adoption increases.

This abnormal phenomenon could be the result of the way people perceive electric vehicles. The importance of perception in the adoption rate of an innovation is not new. Rogers (1983) underlines its role stating that changing people's behavior starts by changing their perception. Perception is important not only in the way change agents—in our case policymakers—are positioning an innovation as electric vehicles with respect to other options available in the considered set, but also in the way people make decisions. In the case of electric vehicles, positioning them as a reference point and assigning the best value as it does it the case of the third design of the environmental component, improves their perceived attributes. First, it gains a relative advantage because is perceived better than conventional car. Secondly, by being included in the car category facilitates comparison between old and new technology. Third, the idea behind electric vehicles has a higher compatibility with older ideas about cars and as a result it is easier to be accepted.

---

[2] Adoption rate is the market share of electric vehicles. Data retrieved from https://www.acea.be/statistics/tag/category/registrations-and-press-release-calendar. Last Accessed Octomber 2019.

[3] Data from https://www.eafo.eu/countries. Last Accessed November 2019.

Perception is also the starting point in behavioral decision theory. According to behavioral economics a person's decisions are based on mental representations of reality as he or she subjectively perceives it. (Kahneman 2012) Behavioral economics also states that people's preferences are constructed (Lichtenstein and Slovic 2006) and their decisions can be influenced by the way a decision problem is framed. (Tversky and Kahneman 1981) When facing a decision people evaluate the outcomes as gains or losses considering their own subjective reference point. (Kahneman and Tversky 1979) The latter is influenced by a person's experience and can change in the light of new information. In addition to this, people's decisions can be affected by anchors (Ariely et al. 2003) or default options (Johnson and Goldstein 2003) provided by different choice architects. (Thaler and Sunstein 2008).

In the following section we present the methods we used to investigate if a certain form of the environmental component has an influence on the rate of adoption of electric vehicles.

3 Methodology

In order to verify if the way national authorities design their motor tax policies has an impact on the adoption rate of electric vehicles, we investigated 19 European countries which did not change the way they design their tax policies between 2016 and 2018. (Appendix 1).

We started by defining four categories of policy designs used in Europe: (a) T-for policies that make no reference to emissions; (b) BE0—for policies based on emissions standards; (c) BE1—for policies that are using a bonus/malus scheme and (d) BE2—for policies based on the quantity of emissions in which electric vehicles are treated as a reference point. The statistical analysis was perform using STATA.

In our analysis we first compared the adoption rate between countries that are using at least one form of the environmental component (BE0, BE1 or BE2) and those that are not using it at all. (T) By comparing the means of the two groups we found out that the difference between them is about 1.9816% in favor of the first group. Levene test has a Sig. = 0.013 (<0.05) and the value of T statistic for Equal variance not assumed from the Independent-Sample T- Test table is −2,871 with Sig. = 0.012 < 0.05, value showing us that the means of the two groups considered are significantly different. Figure 2 illustrates the differences between the means of the two groups.

Secondly, we analyzed our data using a multiple regression analysis where we considered the adoption rate for electric vehicles as a dependent variable. The model also includes three dummy independent variables representing years—$\alpha 0$, d2016, d2017—with 2018 as a base and one dummy indicator variable for the use of BE2 policy (1 = yes; 0 = no). The model is completed with other four independent variables describing the purchasing power (GDP), the available national charging infrastructure (Stations), active involvement of people in fighting climate change (ActiveInvolvement) and one variable for Electricity price (ElectricityPrice). Also,

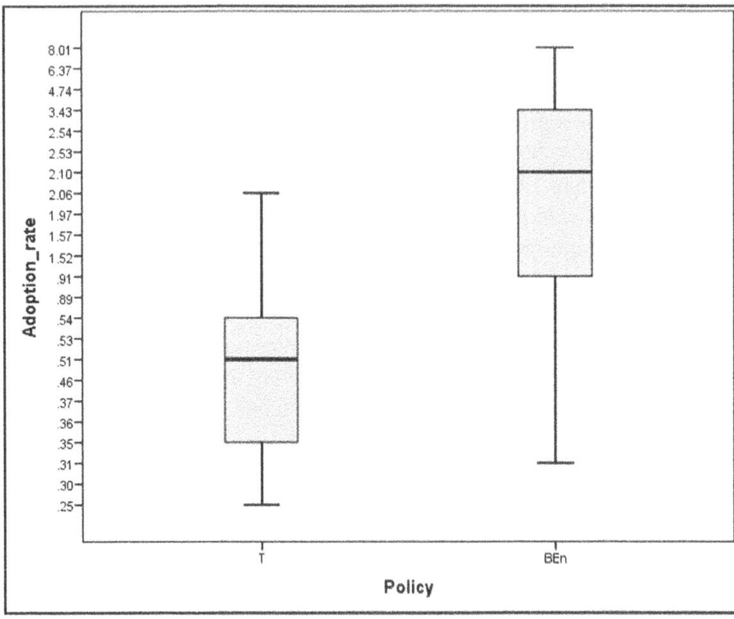

Fig. 2 Boxplot graph that illustrates the differences between the means of the two groups. *Source*Author's own research results

Subventions (Subventions) is considered an independent variable. As most countries offer different sums for BEV and PHEV, we treated it as a dummy variable. (1 = yes; 0 = no). All other factors are considered equal, ceteris paribus. Our model is similar with that developed by Johnson and Goldstein (2003) to demonstrate the power of defaults options in organ donation and takes the following form:

$$\begin{aligned}\text{Adoption rate}_{it} = {} & \alpha_0 + \beta_1 X_{BE2} + \beta_2 X_{GDP} + \beta_3 X_{Stations} \\ & + \beta_4 X_{Subventions} + \beta_5 X_{ActiveInvolvement} + \beta_6 X_{ElectricityPrice} \\ & + d_{2016} X_{2016} + d_{2017} X_{2017} + \varepsilon\end{aligned}$$

Table 1 describes the resulting multiple regression model. The econometric modelling was based on panel data with $N = 19$; $T = 3$ and a total number of observations considered of $N = 57$. From the statistical analysis was obtained an R2 that equals 0.727, and an F-statistic $F(8,48) = 16.01$ with a probability $p = 0.000 < 0.5$. Table 2 describes the correspondent ANOVA of the resulting regression model.

The resulting multiple regression model confirms that the way the taxation policy is designed influences the level of market share of electric vehicles, suggesting that the buying behavior of people can be influenced by policymakers if they design their policy using electric vehicles as a reference point, as it is in BE2 policy design. When using BE2 design, the adoption rate of electric vehicles can increase in average with

Table 1 Multiple regression model

Source	SS	df	MS			
				Number of obs	=	57
				F(8, 48)	=	16.01
Model	78.7414887	8	9.84268608	Prob > F	=	0.0000
Residual	29.5034874	48	.614655988	R-squared	=	0.7274
				Adj R-squared	=	0.6820
Total	108.244976	56	1.932946	Root MSE	=	.784

Adoption_rate	Coef.	Std. Err.	t	P>|t|	[95% Conf.	Interval]
Policy						
BE2	.8519833	.2395687	3.56	0.001	.3702983	1.333668
GDP	.0000506	.0000109	4.62	0.000	.0000286	.0000726
STATIONS	.0000617	.0000117	5.29	0.000	.0000383	.0000852
Subventions	-.6178303	.26502	-2.33	0.024	-1.150689	-.0849718
ActiveInvolvement	.0259255	.0119679	2.17	0.035	.0018625	.0499885
ElectricityPrice	-9.356763	2.696286	-3.47	0.001	-14.77801	-3.935516
d1	-.4343747	.2977524	-1.46	0.151	-1.033046	.1642965
d2	-.422402	.2814958	-1.50	0.140	-.9883873	.1435833
_cons	-.038972	.6244134	-0.06	0.950	-1.294439	1.216495

0.85% ($P = 0.001 < 0.05$) compared with other design options, with some significant differences across years.

4 Results and Conclusions

Handling climate change will require public policies that can change people's behavior. Creating awareness about the consequences of it and also designing effective public policies that improves people perception about goods that are less harming for the environment can make the difference in handling current climate challenge. For this reason, policymakers need to include in their policy design insights from behavioral sciences about how people perceive innovation and make decisions.

The present study illustrates how the way national policymakers choose to design a national motor tax policy influences the purchasing behavior of people when they decide to buy a new passenger car. Our analysis included 19 European countries that did not change the way they frame their motor tax policy between 2016 and 2018. Our results show that positioning electric vehicles as a reference point helps consumers to avoid suboptimal decisions that not only affects their health, but also their personal finances.

Apart from the standard solution of diminishing the price in order to increase demand, innovative products such as electric vehicles can be pushed on the market by improving people's perceptions about them, positioning them as the best option

Table 2 Analysis of variance

Number of obs = 57		R-squared = 0.7274			
Root MSE = .784		Adj R-squared = 0.6820			
Source	Partial SS	df	MS	F	Prob>F
Model	78.741489	8	9.8426861	16.01	0.0000
Policy	7.7738176	1	7.7738176	12.65	0.0009
GDP	13.121938	1	13.121938	21.35	0.0000
STATIONS	17.217899	1	17.217899	28.01	0.0000
Subventions	3.340513	1	3.340513	5.43	0.0240
ActiveInv~t	2.8843867	1	2.8843867	4.69	0.0353
Electrici~e	7.4020395	1	7.4020395	12.04	0.0011
d1	1.3081297	1	1.3081297	2.13	0.1511
d2	1.3840127	1	1.3840127	2.25	0.1400
Residual	29.503487	48	.61465599		
Total	108.24498	56	1.932946		

available. This second solution is more efficient, as the case of Portugal demonstrates it and also involves less costs for authorities.

In the future, if they want to reach their climate change targets, authorities must react to the changes happening in the automotive sector. The right positioning for electric vehicles could mean attracting a market segment that until now preferred diesel cars, technology that at the moment is under great pressure due to the scandals it involved. Also, the way people perceive electric vehicles can be an advantage when they are compared with cars based on petrol technologies. For these reasons, the way authorities will design their policies will have a major impact on the speed with which people will adopt electric vehicles in the near future.

Among the limitations of current research, we can include the small sample included in the analysis. Another limitation we can mention is the fact that in the present study only cars from M1 category are included. Future research can address these limitations and furthermore can also include measurements regarding the quality of air in order to see if there is a correlation between adoption of less polluting cars and the values of GHG. Also, an analysis at a national level will also be a good extension of current analysis. In this case, Belgium seem to be the best candidate because each of its three regions has a different design for their motor tax.

Appendix 1 Panel Data Used for Statistical Analysis

Date	Country	Adoption rate EVs (%)1	Policy[2]	GDP per capita (PPS—€)[3]	Stations[4]	Subventions[5]	Active Involvement[6] (%)	Electricity Price[7] (€ per kWh)
2016	AUSTRIA	1.54	BE1	40800	3467	Yes	60	0.201
2017	AUSTRIA	2.02	BE1	42100	3664	Yes	66	0.1978
2018	AUSTRIA	2.54	BE1	43700	3885	Yes	72	0.2012
2016	BULGARIA	0.05	BE0	6800	21	No	27	0.0938
2017	BULGARIA	0.34	BE0	7300	82	No	33	0.0983
2018	BULGARIA	0.64	BE0	7800	91	No	44	0.1005
2016	CZECH REPUBLIC	0.08	BE0	16700	408	No	41	0.1421
2017	CZECH REPUBLIC	0.11	BE0	18100	559	No	42	0.1488
2018	CZECH REPUBLIC	0.38	BE0	19600	572	No	48	0.1586
2016	DENMARK	0.93	T	49200	2455	No	55	0.3084
2017	DENMARK	0.61	T	50800	2469	No	64	0.301
2018	DENMARK	2.14	T	51500	2541	No	77	0.3123
2016	ESTONIA	0.16	T	16500	383	No	33	0.1238
2017	ESTONIA	0.17	T	18000	383	No	42	0.1319
2018	ESTONIA	0.46	T	19500	388	No	52	0.1418
2016	FINLAND	1.2	BE2	39300	885	Yes	68	0.1545
2017	FINLAND	2.58	BE2	40700	885	Yes	67	0.1599

(continued)

(continued)

Date	Country	Adoption rate EVs (%)1	Policy[2]	GDP per capita (PPS—€)[3]	Stations[4]	Subventions[5]	Active Involvement[6] (%)	Electricity Price[7] (€ per kWh)
2018	FINLAND	4.74	BE2	42100	898	Yes	83	0.1698
2016	FRANCE	1.45	BE1	33400	20106	Yes	59	0.1711
2017	FRANCE	1.75	BE1	24200	21672	Yes	59	0.1756
2018	FRANCE	2.1	BE1	35000	24339	Yes	65	0.1799
2016	GERMANY	0.75	T	38400	24289	Yes	75	0.2977
2017	GERMANY	1.59	T	39600	24422	Yes	75	0.3048
2018	GERMANY	1.97	T	40800	26196	Yes	74	0.3
2016	GREECE	0.04	BE2	16400	32	No	41	0.1723
2017	GREECE	0.23	BE2	16800	37	No	50	0.162
2018	GREECE	0.3	BE2	17200	46	No	55	0.1646
2016	HUNGARY	0.36	BE0	11600	197	No	53	0.1125
2017	HUNGARY	1.03	BE0	12700	257	No	49	0.1134
2018	HUNGARY	1.52	BE0	13500	572	No	67	0.1118
2016	IRELAND	0.47	BE1	57200	969	Yes	53	0.2338
2017	IRELAND	0.72	BE1	61900	999	Yes	51	0.2355
2018	IRELAND	1.57	BE1	66700	1011	Yes	65	0.2539
2016	ITALY	0.15	T	27900	2664	Yes	38	0.2261
2017	ITALY	0.24	T	28500	2809	Yes	36	0.208
2018	ITALY	0.51	T	29100	3413	Yes	54	0.2161
2016	LITHUANIA	0.31	T	13500	23	No	40	0.1171
2017	LITHUANIA	0.2	T	14900	81	No	50	0.1107

(continued)

(continued)

Date	Country	Adoption rate EVs (%)1	Policy[2]	GDP per capita (PPS—€)[3]	Stations[4]	Subventions[5]	Active Involvement[6] (%)	Electricity Price[7] (€ per kWh)
2018	LITHUANIA	0.44	T	16100	125	No	55	0.1097
2016	NETHERLANDS	5.96	BE2	41600	32629	No	47	0.1592
2017	NETHERLANDS	2.66	BE2	43100	33387	No	59	0.1556
2018	NETHERLANDS	6.69	BE2	44900	36789	No	64	0.1707
2016	POLAND	0.13	T	11100	319	No	37	0.1352
2017	POLAND	0.22	T	12200	507	No	37	0.1451
2018	POLAND	0.25	T	12900	714	No	47	0.1396
2016	PORTUGAL	0.88	BE2	18100	1476	No	58	0.2298
2017	PORTUGAL	1.84	BE2	18900	1506	No	62	0.223
2018	PORTUGAL	3.44	BE2	19600	1524	No	75	0.2293
2016	SLOVAKIA	0.07	T	15000	310	No	48	0.1537
2017	SLOVAKIA	0.22	T	15600	416	No	49	0.1442
2018	SLOVAKIA	0.3	T	16600	459	No	71	0.1462
2016	SPAIN	0.32	BE2	24100	4860	Yes	67	0.2284
2017	SPAIN	0.61	BE2	25100	4938	Yes	63	0.2177
2018	SPAIN	0.89	BE2	25900	5058	Yes	80	0.2477
2016	UNITED KINGDOM	1.37	BE2	36600	13534	Yes	46	0.1831
2017	UNITED KINGDOM	1.86	BE2	35400	15555	Yes	45	0.1856
2018	UNITED KINGDOM	2.53	BE2	36000	17763	Yes	56	0.2024

(continued)

(continued)

Date	Country	Adoption rate EVs (%)1	Policy[2]	GDP per capita (PPS—€)[3]	Stations[4]	Subventions[5]	Active Involvement[6] (%)	Electricity Price[7] (€ per kWh)

[1] https://www.acea.be/statistics/tag/category/registrations-and-press-release-calendar
[2,5] https://www.acea.be/industry-topics/tag/category/tax-guide
[3,7] Eurostat
[4] eafo.com
[6] Eurobarometer on Climate Change (Data from Eurobarometer 2015 used for 2016; data from Eurobarometer 2017 used for 2017 and data from Eurobarometer 2019 used for 2018)

References

ACEA—European Automobile Manufacturers Association: Tax Guide 2016 (2016)
ACEA—European Automobile Manufacturers Association: Tax Guide 2017 (2017)
ACEA—European Automobile Manufacturers Association: Tax Guide 2018 (2018)
ACEA—European Automobile Manufacturers Association: Tax Guide 2019 (2019)
Ariely, D., Loewenstein, G., Prelec, D.: Coherent arbitrariness: stable demand curves without stable preferences. Quart. J. Econ. **118**, 73–105 (2003)
European Commission: Directive 98/70/EC Relating to the Quality of Petrol and Diesel Fuels and Amending Council Directive 93/12/EEC. European Commission (2008)
European Commission: Regulation (EC) No 443/2009 Setting Emission Performance Standards for New Passenger Cars as Part of the Community's Integrated Approach to Reduce CO_2 Emissions from Light-Duty Vehicles. European Commission (2009)
European Commission: Regulation (EU) No 510/2011 Setting Emission Performance Standards for New Light Commercial Vehicles as Part of the Union's Integrated Approach to Reduce CO_2 Emissions from Light-Duty Vehicles. European Commission (2011)
European Commission: Strategy for low-emission mobility. European Commission (2016)
European Environment Agency: Electric Vehicles in Europe. European Environment Agency (2016)
Gómez-Vilchez, J., Harrison, G., Kelleher, L., Smyth, A., Thiel, C.: Quantifying the factors influencing people's car type choices in Europe (2017)
ICCT—International Council on Clean Transportation Europe: Using vehicle taxation policy to lower transport emissions: an overview for passengers cars in Europe. ICC TE—International Council on Clean Transportation Europe (2018)
Johnson, E.J., Goldstein, D.: Do Defaults save lives? Science **302**, 1338–1339 (2003)
Kahneman, D.: Thinking Fast and Slow. Penguin Books, London (2012)
Kahneman, D., Tversky, A.: Prospect theory: an analysis of decision under risk. Econometrica. **47**, 263 (1979)
Lichtenstein, S., Slovic, P. (eds.): The Construction of Preference. Cambridge University Press, Cambridge, Massachusetts (2006)
Rogers, E.M.: Diffusion of Innovations. The Free Press, New York (1983)
Thaler, R.H., Sunstein, C.R.: Nudge: Improving Decisions About Health, Wealth, and Happiness. Yale University Press (2008)
Thiel, C., Alemanno, A., Scarcella, G., Zubaryeva, A., Pasaoglu, G.: Attitude of European car drivers towards electric vehicles: a survey (2012)
Tversky, A., Kahneman, D.: The framing of decisions and the psychology of choice. Science **211**, 453–458 (1981)

Outsourcing in International Business: Theoretical and Practical Insights

Alina Mihaela Dima, Adrian Tudor Tudorache, and Monica Teodora Tudorache

1 Introduction

Globalization strongly contributes to the increase in the linkages between the world's economies. In the context of an increased importance of the knowledge economy (Hadad 2017), the need for both efficiency and excellence determines many companies to make use of specialized external providers, therefore getting involved in outsourcing activities. The importance of outsourcing has grown in the last decades, especially in the context of offshoring that took prevalence in the recent years. Outsourcing is inevitably linked with the globalization of businesses and is a phenomenon expected to further grow and develop in the future.

Outsourcing is a complex business to business relationship in which a company contracts another company for services that can include only one activity, a group of activities or a whole end-to-end business process. Outsourcing is seen to be a long term and result oriented relationship, in which the customer company (client/outsourcer) intends to divest its capacity to do the work itself and instead buys the service from the market place and the service provider (outsourcing provider/vendor/supplier/insourcer) that assumes the responsibility to offer the results for which it was contracted by employing people, processes and technologies (OPBOK 2010, p. 4; Nicolescu and Iamandi 2018). The external service company is usually a specialized provider for the service being contracted. When the outsourced activity/process takes place in a foreign country, the activity is called offshoring. While at present globalization connects the world's economies, there will be less and less companies able to cope with the growing environmental challenges by

A. M. Dima · A. T. Tudorache (✉)
Bucharest University of Economic Studies, Romania, Piața Romană 6-8, Bucharest, Romania
e-mail: tudortudorache@yahoo.com

M. T. Tudorache
Otto Friedrich University of Bamberg, Kapuzinerstraße 16, 96047 Bamberg, Germany

A. M. Dima and F. DÁscenzo (eds.), *Business Revolution in a Digital Era*,
Springer Proceedings in Business and Economics,
https://doi.org/10.1007/978-3-030-59972-0_7

conducting their activities solely on their own and by relying only on internal resources. Consequently, companies will turn to business partners, in many cases via outsourcing.

This chapter has the purpose to study the outsourcing activity conducted in Romania.

2 Outsourcing Literature Review

2.1 The Typologies of Outsourcing

Outsourcing activities are of different kinds and they can be classified according to different criteria. This section presents the different types of outsourcing as acknowledged by the literature. According to the *type of activity* that it is outsourced, there are (OPBOK 2010; Friend et al. 2002; Lacity et al. 2009; Dhillon et al. 2017):

(a) Information Technology Outsourcing (ITO) that refers to transferring IT operations (such as server management, data center operations, desktop services, application development) that previously were conducted in house to external service providers.
(b) Business Process Outsourcing (BPO) that refers to the transfer of business processes (both in terms of management and execution) or entire business functions (such as finance, accounting, procurement, human resources) to external service providers.
(c) Knowledge Process Outsourcing (KPO) that refers to the transfer of performing highly knowledge related activities to external service providers. These can include highly specialized knowledge producing operations such as the analysis of capital markets or legal advice (OPBOK 2010).

According to the *place* where the outsourced activity takes place, there are also a large variety of outsourcing options (Oshri et al. 2009; OPBOK 2010):

(a) Onshore outsourcing that takes place when the service provider is situated in the same country with the client company. It is a home country outsourcing, as the services are contracted from an external provider that resides in the home country.
(b) Offshore outsourcing (as a generic term) that takes place when the service provider is situated in another country than the client company, often in low-wages countries. Further on, there are different types of offshoring outsourcing:
    - Nearshore outsourcing that takes place when a service provider in a nearby country is contracted for the services.
    - Offshore outsourcing (as a specific term) (also seen as farshoring) that takes place when the service provider contracted is situated in a geographically distant country.

(c) Onsite outsourcing refers to the situation when an IT operation stays where it is and the outsourcing provider takes over the facilities of the client and operates them on site, from distance.

According to the *number of companies* to which the job is outsourced (Dibbern et al. 2004; Oshri et al. 2009):

(a) Single sourcing depicts the situation when the client company outsources activities only to one external provider. In this case the ITO and BPO processes might be integrated and governed in a centralized manner by just one vendor.
(b) Multisourcing depicts the situation in which the client company outsources different tasks/jobs to more external service providers. In this case, the client company might use more specialized and usually smaller vendors.

Other important terms that have been developed in relationship with outsourcing are the following:

(a) Backsourcing, when the client company transfers assets, skills and activities needed to perform an operation, that were previously outsourced, back in house. It takes place a change in ownership back to the client company, regardless of the location of the services operations (Nujen et al. 2015).
(b) Global outsourcing depicts the expansion of a service provider at international level, a multinational company that offers outsourcing and offshoring services from a different number of countries to different client companies also with operations in a variety of countries (Oshri et al. 2009). Well known US based global outsourcing companies are Accenture, IBM and Hewlett-Packard, while Indian based global outsourcing companies are Wipro, Infosys and TCS.
(c) Captive offshoring refers to the situation when a company opens a branch of its own in a foreign market to make use of the best economic conditions there (Oshri et al. 2009). There is an offshoring activity that it is organized in house by opening in a foreign market a center owned by the organization, through which the organization locates some of its activities in another country, usually for lower costs.

The present chapter focuses on offshoring for both Information Technology Outsourcing and Business Processes Outsourcing having Romania, as an outsourcing destination market.

2.2 *Choosing a Location for Offshoring*

For a company willing to choose an outsourcing location there are two elements that are considered (Oshri 2009, p. 33): the attractiveness of the sourcing location (the country and the city) and the attractiveness of the supplier (the company). As far as countries as locations are concerned the evaluation frameworks consider factors such as costs, business environment, availability of workforce and specific skills (Carmel

2003) or similarly costs, skills, risk profiles, market potential, business and living environment, quality of infrastructure (Farrell 2006).

These factors are shortly presented as they were considered by Oshri (2009). *Costs* will include labour costs, infrastructure costs and corporate taxes. The *availability of skills* will consider the size of labour pool that possesses the required skills (technical skills, soft skills, etc.), in terms of number of yearly university graduates with the needed skills. The *environment* will consider: (a) the business environment in terms of compatibility of business culture and ethical behaviour; (b) the governmental support in terms of legislation, level of corruption, bureaucracy, foreign investment support; (c) living environment in terms of quality of life, crime per capita and (d) accessibility in terms of travel possibilities, flight frequency and time difference. The *quality of infrastructure* will consider aspects such as transportation, reliability of power supply, availability and quality of real estate and telecommunication and IT. *Market potential* is evaluated based on local market potential in terms of GDP and GDP growth rate, as well as in terms of access to close geographical markets. The *risk profile* will include the study of: (a) security issue (fraud, crime, terrorism); (b) disruptive events such as political unrest, natural disasters, labour strikes; (c) intellectual property risk depending on how strong the intellectual property protection is; (d) macroeconomic risks such as inflation and currency fluctuation; (e) regulatory risks such as stability of legal framework (Oshri 2009, pp. 33–44).

Romania as an outsourcing destination is presented later in the chapter by considering some of the above criteria.

3 Methodology

The present study analyzes the outsourcing activity that takes place in Romania, as a country of destination. The main research method is documentation, based on the search of internet based information. The unit of analysis refers to the outsourcing service provider located in Romania, both as a branch of a global outsourcing company and as a local Romanian national company that offers outsourcing services, considering both ITO and BPO.

The first part of the research envisages the study of the first 30 outsourcing global companies (according to revenues) operating in EMEA (Europe, Middle East and Africa) region. They were selected based on the ISG Index 2019 and include two categories: The Big 15 (with annual company revenues of over 10 bill. $) and the The Building 15 (with annual company revenues between 3 and 10 bill. $). An analysis of the web site content for these companies is conducted with the purpose to identify, their presence on the Romanian market, the type of services offered from Romania, the extent of development in Romania (in terms of number of employees and/or number of cities where they opened offices). Appendix presents the list of the global outsourcing companies included in the study.

The second part of the research is based on the study of a sample of the service business providers operating in the Romanian market. The research is based on the analysis of the offers of a sample of Romanian located service companies, offers included in an international business directory. The sample of service providers have been selected from the US internet business service directory Clutch[1] that includes service providers from all over the world. Clutch is a US based business directory that assists organizations from all over the world in buying business services located in different countries. Service providers get listed in the directory based on their own subscription. The registration in an international service business directory was considered a good indicator for the willingness of Romania located companies to offer outsourcing services to other companies at world level. The analysis of the web site content of the Clutch business directory is conducted in order to identify the type of services that are outsourced by the companies operating in Romania and listed in the directory. All companies registered for Romania are considered, totaling to 1181 companies.

4 Outsourcing Companies in Romania

4.1 Romania as an Outsourcing Destination

Since the beginning of 2000, Romania started to develop as an outsourcing service market that grew continuously up to present and will continue to grow. In 2007 in the industry were working 15.000 employees, while in 2018 there were approximately 125.000 employees working in the outsourcing industry in Romania (ABSL 2018). Also in 2017 the industry's turnover in Romania was nearly 4 billion Euro (ABSL 2018), illustrating that Romania is a good outsourcing destination for both ITO and BPO services.

The main advantages that Romania presents as an outsourcing destination include (Telus 2015; ABSL 2018; InvestRomania 2018; Evozon 2018): a good price-ratio quality (the average wage is 600–700 Euros); multilingual skills (English for all graduates and also French, German, Spanish, Italian); good aptitudes of employees and soft skills; a qualified and experienced IT workforce; a large number of university graduates (more than 300.000 graduates per year out of which 8.500 are IT specialists) that assures the continuity of talent pool; political and economic stability (economic growth has been registered in the last years—7% in 2017); geographical proximity to Western Europe and time zone convergence with clients; cultural similarities with western cultures easing the communication with client companies; is a EU member state, fact that allows to simplify legal and financial aspects of the activity. Other advantages related to ITO refer to the high speed internet (especially in the capital); the tax exemption of IT specialists' salaries encouraging working in the field; the IT sector has an annual growth of 15–20% since 2000, there are over 20.000 companies operating in the IT industry in Romania (Andras 2018) and IT based social networks

[1] https://clutch.co/.

are highly developed (Vătămănescu et al. 2018), while the need for IT skills also increases (Foerster-Pastor and Golowko 2018). Half of the outsourcing activities are run in Bucharest, but also in other cities, mainly university centers (Cluj-Napoca, Timișoara, Iași).

Romania is even called "the outsourcing valley", due to its rapid development in BPO, ITO, software development, research activities, knowledge process outsourcing and shared services centers (Telus 2015). Romania continues to be seen as having a huge outsourcing potential due to its lower wages, good education and skilled labour force. On Kearney Global 2017 Services Location Index[2] Romania ranked the 18th worldwide and the 5th location in Europe and in 2016 according to BPO Index of Cushman and Wakefield,[3] Romania was on the first place for countries that became mature outsourcing markets.

In this context an analysis of the companies involved in outsourcing activities in Romania becomes of interest.

4.2 Global Outsourcing Providers in Romania

The largest 30 global outsourcing companies with operations in the EMEA region (according to revenues and classified by ISG Index 2019) were studied for: the presence on the Romanian market, the number of employees hired in the Romanian market, the number of Romanian cities in which they operate and the type of services they offer (ITO and/or BPO).

The analysis of the first 30 global outsourcing companies from EMEA revealed that the majority of those, respectively 23 (representing 77%) have operations in Romania. Among those two (United Internet—Germany and TechMahindra—India) have only one employee in Romania, indicating that at the moment they are only prospecting the market.

Table 1 presents the structure of the outsourcing companies in terms of country of origin.

It can be observed that the majority of the large global outsourcing companies present in the Romanian market are from US (39%), followed by the European ones (34%) with the French ones leading (17%). Indian global outsourcing companies are also well represented in Romania with 17% in total.

Table 2 illustrates the structure of the 30 companies according to the number of employees at world level.

The largest group of companies (37%) have between 100.000 and 300.000 employees at world level and all of them are present in Romania. There are 5 companies with over 300.000 employees at world level and only 3 of them (60%) have operations in Romania, representing 13% among the global outsourcing companies

[2]https://www.multivu.com/players/English/8179851-at-kearney-2017-global-services-location-index/.

[3]https://ozb.ro/2018/05/16/the-next-step-for-romanian-tech/.

Table 1 Country of origin of the first 30 global outsourcing companies

Country of origin	Number	Number in Romania	Present in Romania (%)	Percentage in Romania (%)
USA	10	9	90	39
France	5	4	80	17
Germany	5	3	60	13
India	5	4	80	17
Israel	3	1	33	4
Other countries Europe	1	1	100	4
Other countries world	1	1	100	4
Total	30	23	77	100[a]

[a]*Note* Figures do not add up to 100%, due to approximation to integers
Source Authors' own research

Table 2 Number of employees worldwide of the first 30 global outsourcing companies

Number of employees at world level	Number	Number in Romania	Present in Romania (%)	Percentage in Romania (%)
Under 50.000	10	5	50	22
50.001–100.000	4	4	100	17
100.001–300.000	11	11	100	48
Over 300.000	5	3	60	13
Total	30	23	77	100

Source Authors' own research

studied operating in Romania. It can be noticed that most of the global outsourcing companies operating in Romania are companies with large operations at world level: 78% have over 50.000 employees world-wide.

Table 3 illustrates the number of countries in which the studied companies operate. Five of them are literally global companies operating in more than 100 countries of the total of 195 existing countries in the world.[4]

Out of those, four are also present in Romania (IBM, Cognizant, Accenture and CBRE) representing 18% of the global outsourcing companies operating in Romania.

The majority (67%) of the studied outsourcing companies operate worldwide in between 26 and 100 countries. Out of those 85% operate also in Romania, representing 73% of the total number of companies operating in Romania.

In our analysis we also looked at the specific activity conducted by these companies in Romania. Table 4 presents the number of employees working in Romania at

[4]https://www.worldometers.info/geography/how-many-countries-are-there-in-the-world/.

Table 3 Number of countries of operation of the first 30 global outsourcing companies

Number of countries of operations	Number	Number in Romania	Present in Romania (%)	Percentage in Romania (%)
Under 25 countries	5	2	40	9
26–50 countries	9	8	89	34
51–100 countries	11	9	82	39
101–150 countries	2	2	100	9
Over 150 countries	3	2	67	9
Total	30	23	77	100

Source Authors' own research

Table 4 Number of employees in Romania for global outsourcing companies

Number of employees in Romania	Number	Percentage in Romania (%)
Under 5	4	18
5–250	5	23
251–500	1	4
501–1000	2	9
1001–2000	7	32
Over 2000	3	14
N/A	1	4
Total	23	100

Source Authors' own research

company level and Fig. 1 depicts the structure of companies according to the number of employees in Romania.

It can be noticed that 47% of the global outsourcing companies operating in Romania are very large companies that hire in Romania, over 1000 employees and other 41% companies operate as Small and Medium Sized (SMEs) companies with less than 250 employees in Romania. The companies that have large number of employees at world level (over 100.000) are the ones that have 1000 or more employees in Romania, too.

Table 5 and Fig. 2 consider the number of cities from Romania in which the global outsourcing companies operate.

The majority of the global outsourcing companies studied (52%) operate only in one city and this is Bucharest, the capital. The number of companies operating in 3 and more cities is 7 (representing 31% of the global companies operating in Romania) and generally the cities of operations, besides Bucharest, would be Cluj,

Fig. 1 Number of employees in Romania for global outsourcing companies. *Source* Authors' own research

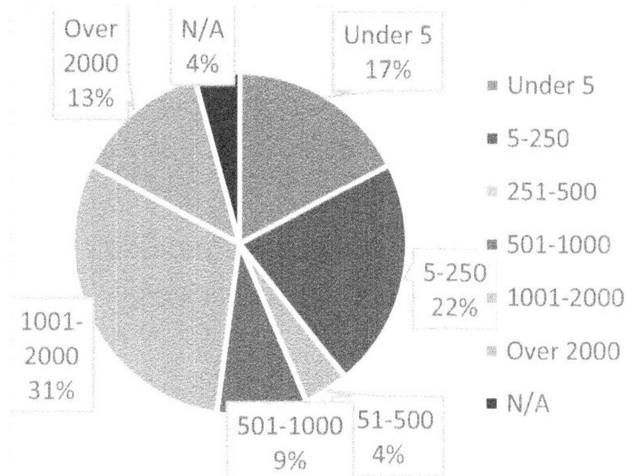

Table 5 Number of cities of operation in Romania for global outsourcing companies

Number of cities in Romania	Number	Percentage (%)
1 city	12	52
2 cities	4	17
3 cities	2	9
4 cities	2	9
5 cities	3	13
	23	100

Source Authors' own research

Fig. 2 Number of cities in Romania for global outsourcing companies. *Source* Authors' own research

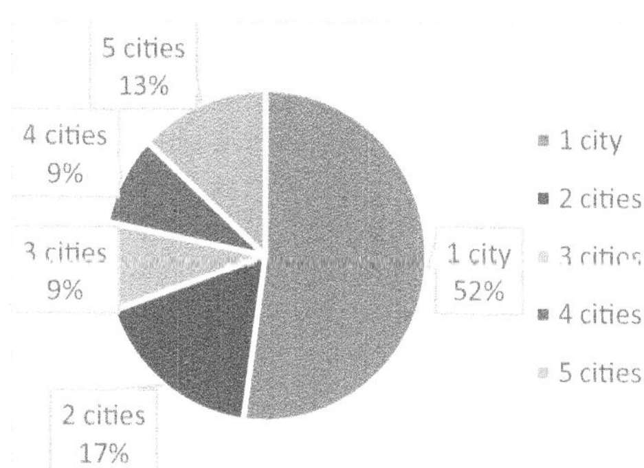

Timişoara, Iaşi, Braşov, Sibiu and Constanţa. There is also an Indian company (HCL Technologies) that did not open an operation in Bucharest, only in Iaşi and Braşov, but the company has a very low number of employees in Romania (5), suggesting that it is still prospecting the market.

The majority (78%) of the global outsourcing companies operating in Romania, offer both ITO and BPO services. There are 2 companies that focus only on ITO and 3 companies that focus only on BPO (usually involving call centers).

It can be concluded that the majority of the major global outsourcing companies are present in Romania and they have extended operations here in terms of number of employees, number of cities in operation and types of operations.

4.3 Service Outsourcing Providers in Romania—The Clutch Internet Business Directory

The second part of our analysis is based on a sample of business service providers located in Romania that registered in the international services business directory Clutch for which it is conducted the analysis of the services offered by them at international level. The self registration in the international business directory is an indication of the willingness of these companies to offer their services at international and global level.

The information included about the companies registered in the directory allows us to make an analysis of their offer in terms of type of services offered, location within Romania and the size of the company according to the number of employees. Table 6 presents the synthetic information about the companies found in the Clutch service business directory.

At the same time, there are a number of aspects related to the information available in the web based business directory that are to be mentioned: (a) the information included in the directory is not always complete at company level; (b) the companies included in the directory are both local Romanian business service companies and branches of multinational business service companies; (c) many companies offer multiple services and are listed under different categories of business services. The consequences of these peculiarities of the data collected are that the figures on services categories are not always adding up to the totals and the available data allows us to make a rather qualitative analysis of the offerings of the sample of business service companies operating in Romania.

As observed in Table 6, the companies that registered in the business directory are dominated by the ones that offer ITO services, 1160 entries in total under information technology related services, whereas the BPO related services have less entries (only 246 for the specific business service considered).

The analysis of the ITO services offered by the sample of companies located in Romania illustrates that:

- companies from Romania offer services under all IT service categories included in the directory: (a) Search Engine Optimization; (b) Mobile app development; (c) Web and Software development; (e) Web design and (f) IT Services and Solutions.
- most of the information technology companies offer more than one type of business service, the majority having on offer a combination of at least 4–5 IT related services.
- the main towns in which the providers are situated are Bucharest, Cluj, Timișoara and Iași, with Bucharest holding most of the providers.

- the majority of the companies registered in the directory are Small and Medium Sized Enterprises (SMEs) with up to 250 employees. More than half of the registered companies have up to 50 employees, being small companies, but with good innovative capacities as also acknowledged by the literature (Nicolescu and Nicolescu 2012; Vătămănescu et al. 2017). The Romanian services companies have generally between 2 and 50 employees. Many companies with more than 50 employees are branches of multinational companies. Larger companies with more than 250 employees are very few and in general they are also branches of multinational companies operating in Romania.

The analysis of the BPO services offered by the sample of companies located in Romania illustrates that:

- the number of BPO providers registered to the business directory is very limited, varying between 24 (voice/call center services) and 92 (consultancy services) for the whole country.
- providers in Bucharest and Cluj seem to be the ones most willing to register in the directory.
- most of the companies offering consulting, accounting and human resources services are smaller in size (between 2 and 50 employees), while many companies offering call center services are larger in size (over 50 employees).

On overall, it can be observed that more than 80% of the companies registered in the directory are small companies with up to 50 employees, these being mainly Romanian business service providers.

5 Conclusions

The analysis of the outsourcing activity in Romania based on three sources of data (data from different reports, data from web sites of global outsourcing companies operating in Romania and data from an international business directory) lead to the following conclusions:

(a) Romania is seen as a good outsourcing market based on a number of advantages (lower costs, availability of technical, language and soft skills, continuity of pool of talents, cultural and geographical proximity of Western European markets, a developed IT industry, advantage of being a EU country). Romania was even called the "outsourcing valley".

(b) the fact that Romania is a good outsourcing destination is proved by the fact that the majority of the largest global outsourcing companies are present in Romania: 77% of the first 30 large global outsourcing companies in terms of revenues.
Most of them are from US, followed by the European ones, but also by some of the major Indian outsourcing providers.

(c) the global outsourcing companies present in the Romanian market have an extended development in Romania both in terms of number of employees (46% of them have over 1000 employees in Romania) and in terms of number of Romanian cities in which they operate (31% operate in more than 3 cities).
(d) Bucharest is the preferred city by most global outsourcing companies, as only one global outsourcing global company does not have operations in Bucharest.
(e) the majority of the global outsourcing companies (78%) offer a diversified range of services from Romania including both ITO and BPO, while only few are specialized in either ITO (9%) or BPO (13%) (mainly call centers).
(f) the case study based on the international service business directory analysis revealed that the majority companies that self registered in the service business offering their services at international level are SMEs and are local Romanian companies, as companies that are willing to offer their services internationally.
(g) ITO providers are more proactive in searching for clients at international level, by registering themselves in an international business service directory than the BPO providers.

As a general conclusion, it can be mentioned that outsourcing activities in Romania are conducted by both global outsourcing companies, but also by small Romanian SMEs (especially in the IT field). It is expected that the outsourcing sector will continue to grow in Romania and will become an even more important sector for the Romanian economy. This takes place in the context in which outsourcing business strategies represent a strategic option for an increasing number of companies that want to take advantage of facilities and opportunities offered through outsourcing.

However, in the light of the recent medical outbreak at global level, one aspect one should reflect to is: How the new medical conditions would affect the outsourcing as a business strategy and the outsourcing industry at world level? In a broader context, it might be the case that outsourcing in the conditions of increasing teleworking activities to increase, but this can be the case only in places were the IT infrastructure is very well developed.

The present study has a number of limitations, among which an applicative part that looks at only one national market. Also, the research methodology is mainly based on the analysis of existing secondary data and limits the results of the research according to the availability of data. Based on the existing limitations of the study, further research can be developed by collecting empirical data from more national markets that represent good destination countries for outsourcing. Also, in the context of the present pandemic, research on how telework and other changes in working conditions and business conditions can affect outsourcing (both as a business strategy and as a whole industry) can be of interest.

Table 6 Services of outsourcing companies located in Romania—location and company size (Clutch directory)

Service category	Services in the category	Number of providers in Romania	Towns in Romania					Size of company (employees)			
			Bucharest	Cluj	Iași	Timișoara	Others	2–9	10–49	50–249	Over 250
ITO	Search engine optimization	220	118	173	4	14	20	121	74	19	1+
	mobile app development	211	84	51	18	15	37+	76	96	25	8+
	web and software development	325	132	84	18	12	51+	140	140	35	3+
	Web design	297	119	89	12	13	46+	151	112	24	3+
	IT services and solutions	107	26	17	8	6	17+	26	46	15	15+
BPO	Business services	31	21	6	2	1	1+	4	4	7	13+
	voice/call center services	24	16	4	1	0	1+	3	1	5	12+
	consulting	92	27	53	11	0	1+	31	43	14	2+
	Accounting	48	11	34	0	2	0	10	29	7	0+
	human resources	51	21	27	2	0	1+	22	19	9	1
Total number of service providers in Romania (Clutch directory)		1181	N/A	N/A	N/A	N/A	N/A	480	467	167	33+

Source Authors' own research based on data collected from https://clutch.co/

Appendix

The first 30 global outsourcing companies in EMEA region (according to revenues, based on ISG Index 2019).

Category at world level	Name of the company	Web link
THE BIG 15 (revenues over 10 bill.$)	Accenture	https://www.accenture.com/ro-en/careers/accenture-romania-offices
	Atos	https://atos.net/en/about-us/company-profile
	BT Global Services	https://www.globalservices.bt.com/en
	Capgemini	https://www.capgemini.com
	CBRE	https://www.cbre.com/
	Cognizant	https://www.cognizant.com/
	DXC Technology	https://www.dxc.technology/
	IBM	https://www.ibm.com/ro-en
	Infosys	https://www.infosys.com/
	ISS A/S	https://www.issworld.com/
	TCS	https://www.tcs.com/
	T-Systems	https://www.t-systems.com/de/en
	Amazon Web Services (AAS)	https://aws.amazon.com/
	Google (AAS)	https://about.google/
	Microsoft (AAS)	https://www.microsoft.com/ro-ro
The building 15 (revenues 3–10 bill.$)	Amdocs	https://www.amdocs.com/
	Arvato (new company Majorel)	https://www.bertelsmann.com/divisions/arvato/ https://www.majorel.com/
	Bechtle	https://www.bechtle.com/
	CGI	https://www.cgi.com/
	HCL Technologies	https://www.hcltech.com/
	Indra Sistemas	https://www.indracompany.com/
	Kuehne and Nagel	https://home.kuehne-nagel.com/
	Orange B. Services	https://www.orange-business.com/
	SopraSteria	https://www.soprasteria.com/
	TechMahindra	https://www.techmahindra.com/
	Teleperformance	https://www.teleperformance.com/
	Wipro	https://www.wipro.com/

(continued)

(continued)

Category at world level	Name of the company	Web link
	Adobe Systems (AAS)	https://www.adobe.com/
	Equinix (AAS)	https://www.equinix.com/
	United Internet (AAS)	https://www.united-internet.de/

Source: Authors' own research.

References

ABSL: Business Service Sector in Romania 2018, https://www.absl.ro/wpfd_file/absl-romania-industry-report-2018/. Accessed on 01 Oct 2020 (2018)

Atkearny homepage, www.atkearny.com. Accessed on 15 Dec 2019

Andras, S.: A Guide on IT Outsourcing to Romania, https://www.evozon.com/wp-content/uploads/2019/01/A-guide-on-IT-outsourcing-to-Romania.pdf. Accessed on 01 Sept 2020 (2018)

Carmel, E.: The new software exporting nations: success factors. Electron. J. Inf. Syst. Devel. Countries **13**(4), 1–12 (2003)

Clutch homepage, https://clutch.co/. Accessed on 15 Dec 2019

Dibbern, J., Goles, T., Hirschheim, R., Jayatilaka, B.: Information systems outsourcing: a survey and analysis of the literature. DATA BASE Adv Inf Syst **35**(4), 6–102 (2004)

Dhillon, G., Syeed, R., de Sa-, F.: Information security concerns in IT outsourcing: identifying (in)congruence between clients and vendors. Inf Manage **54**(4), 452–464 (2017)

Evozon: A Guide on IT Outsourcing to Romania. https://www.evozon.com/wp-content/uploads/2019/01/A-guide-on-IT-outsourcing-to-Romania.pdf. Accessed on 01 Oct 2020 (2018)

Farrell, D.: Smarter offshorig. Harvard Business Rev. **84**(6), 85–92 (2006)

Friend, M., Lucacs, M., Snowdon, J.: European business process outsourcing forecast and analysis 2001–2006. IDC, Framingham, USA (2002)

Foerster-Pastor, U.S., Golowko, N.: The need for digital and soft skills in the Romanian business service industry. Manage. Market. Challenges Knowl. Soc. **12**(3), 416–430 (2018)

Hadad, S.: Strategies for developing knowledge economy in Romania. Manage. Market. Challenges Knowl. Soc. **13**(1), 831–847 (2017)

InvestRomania: Romania's Business Service Sector IT&C, SDC&BPO. https://investromania.gov.ro/web/wp-content/uploads/2018/10/InvestRomania-ITC_BPO-SSC_EN_.pdf. Accessed on 01 Sept 2020 (2018)

Lacity, M.C., Khan, S.A., Willcocks, L.P.: A review of the IT outsourcing literature: insights for practice. J. Strat. IS **18**(3), 130–146 (2009)

Nicolescu, L., Iamandi, I.E.: Outsourcing and business networks in top southeastern European Banks: the quest for competitive advantage. In: Vătămănescu, E.M., Pînzaru, F.M. (eds.). Knowledge Management in the Sharing Economy, pp. 209–234. Springer International Publishing (2018)

Nicolescu, L., Nicolescu, C.: Innovation in SMEs-findings from Romania. Econ. Sociol. **5**(2a), 71–85 (2012)

Nujen, B., Halse, L., Soli-Saether, H.: Backsourcing and knowledge re-integration: a case study. In: IFIP, Sophia Antipolis, France, June 29–July 3 2015, pp. 191–198 (2015)

Oshri, I., Kotlarsky, J., Willcocks, L.P.: The Handbook of Global Outsourcing and Offshoring. Palgrave MacMillan Publishing, Hampshire, UK (2009)

OPBOK: Outsourcing Professional Body of Knowledge. Van Haren Publishing, The Netherlands (2010)

OZB homepage, https://ozb.ro/2018/05/16/the-next-step-for-romanian-tech/. Accessed on 1 Dec 2019
Telus: Romania: the new outsourcing valley of Europe. https://www.absl.rodownloadreportsromania-the-new-outsourcing-valleyofEurope. Accessed on 01 Sept 2020 (2015)
Vătămănescu, E.-M., Andrei, A.G., Nicolescu, L., Pînzaru, F., Zbuchea, A.: The influence of competitiveness on SMEs internationalization effectiveness. Online versus Offline Business Networking. Inf. Syst. Manage. **34**(3), 205–219 (2017)
Vătămănescu, E.M., Andrei, A.G., Pînzaru, F.: Investigating the online social network development through the five Cs model of similarity: the facebook case. Inf. Technol. People **31**(1), 84–110 (2018)
Worldmeters homepage, https://www.worldometers.info/geography/how-many-countries-are-there-in-the-world/. Accessed on 15 Dec 2019

Sustainable Management of IT Enterprises

Florina Pînzaru, Wioletta Wereda, Ion Moldoveanu, and Victor-Emanuel Ciuciuc

1 Understanding Business Sustainability in the Digital Era

The need to boost up economic development in a sustainable way is a challenge for the 21st century's companies. We are in a connected reality, in which environmental, social, and economic concerns are in the limelight for all activity sectors—and even more for those pushing further the social and business transformation at all levels, such as the IT sector. It could seem common sense to bring together digital opportunities and sustainable practices at the forefront of any strategic business thinking, but there are concerns that an opposite reality could emerge. For instance, unguided AI development could accelerate the environment's degradation, even if the technology itself already presents the transformative capacity to positively address the planet's environmental challenges (PwC 2018). Similarly, if not properly designed and executed, the perceived positive digital contributions to the development of the circular economy (Berg and Wilts 2018) could lead to negative effects on society.

Although digital technologies and sustainability have the potential to reinforce each other, they do not easily match, mainly because they are used to answer to different functions: driving efficiency and ensuring social, economic, and environmental resilience.

F. Pînzaru (✉)
Faculty of Management, National University of Political Studies and Public Administration (SNSPA), 012104 Bucharest, Romania
e-mail: florina.pinzaru@facultateademanagement.ro

W. Wereda
Institute of Organizational Management, Military University of Technology (MUT), 00-908 Warsaw, Poland

I. Moldoveanu · V.-E. Ciuciuc
The Doctoral School of the National University of Political Studies and Public Administration (SNSPA), 012104 Bucharest, Romania

A. M. Dima and F. DÁscenzo (eds.), *Business Revolution in a Digital Era*,
Springer Proceedings in Business and Economics,
https://doi.org/10.1007/978-3-030-59972-0_8

1.1 A Brief Literature Review on the Concept of Sustainability in Business

Sustainability and sustainable development (used as synonyms in this paper) are concepts extensively discussed. The World Commission on the Environment in 1987 (Brundtland et al. 1987) defined sustainable development as the development that meets the needs of the present without compromising the ability of future generations to meet their own needs. Sustainability has multiple dimensions to be considered, such as social, environmental, economic, technical and human (Becker 2015) and requires multi-level action and long-term thinking, therefore being a prerequisite of strategic management approaches. If all dimensions of the sustainability are equally and simultaneously implemented, a strong sustainability (Figge et al. 2001) is developed.

The concept of sustainability faced many debates over time, meaning different things for public institutions, corporations, and scholars. When considering the understanding of sustainability at the level of the enterprise, most definitions build on the stakeholder theory (Freeman 1984), implying simultaneous obligations of the company towards both the inside and outside, including the wider community and, by consequent, a vision on the long term.

Business models for sustainability The current understanding of sustainability is multi-dimensional, as internal and external factors push companies to embrace it actively despite tensions, dilemmas and trade-offs (Wannags and Gold 2020)—inherent to a full transformation of a business logic into a model that creates value to various stakeholders, and the natural environment. The concept of the business model for sustainability itself is relatively recent, and the literature on the topic varies from an idealistic approach (Stubbs and Cocklin 2008), to highlighting its potential for various industries (Wüstenhagen and Boehnke 2008) or the methodologies to develop it (Bocken et al. 2013; Sommer 2012). Adopting sustainability as a dominant paradigm of the business logic depends of external factors and managers' mental models (Abdelkafi and Täuscher 2016), while its development is influenced by different organizational characteristics.

The dimensions of sustainability in business The parallel implementation of the sustainability's dimensions (economic, social, human, environmental and technological) can be complementary or rival (Müller and Pfleger 2014), depending on a variety of factors (i.e. regulations, public opinion's pressure, perceived value by customers, education of stakeholders, personal beliefs of managers and entrepreneurs, corporate values etc.), but with a strong influence of the economic and financial ones.

The economic and the environmental dimensions of sustainability are largely discussed in the literature: for instance, the involvement in socially responsible activities does not maximize the present value of a firm's future cash flow, but it does maximize its market value (Mackey et al. 2007). Managers' approach of sustainable development considers how to mitigate risks that affect cost of equity (Ng and Zabihollah 2015), while consumers tend to declare that they prefer firms which invest in sustainable actions, but in a nuanced manner—consumers respond more negatively to the company's poor commitment to caring for the environmental sustainability than to economic sustainability (Choi and Ng 2011).

As for the social and human dimensions of sustainability, the most frequent associated concepts are education, training, income, social contacts, communication, participation, and social security (Spangenberg 2004; Metzner 2000)—generally linked to employment. The social and human sustainability is directly influenced by the economic one, as social sustainability requires a necessary minimum of economic growth (the concept of the inequality of sustainability) and managerial commitment.

The environmental dimension of sustainability is widely discussed in literature, covering various aspects, such as the consciousness for sustainable consumption related to environmental protection (Balderjahn et al. 2013) or the sectorial approaches—logistics and industry (Pyecik et al. 2015; Centobelli et al. 2017). The orientation towards environmental sustainability is strongly determined by economic factors in some countries (Omri et al. 2019) and secondary determined by values, education and policies.

The technological dimension of sustainability is discussed in literature both from the perspective of the potential of some technologies to sustain the sustainable development (Molla et al. 2009; Meyers 2012), and from the one of the associated risks. For instance, inducing large-scale technological transitions involves fundamental changes in production, organization and the way in which people live their lives (Kemp 1994), posing numerous issues to sustainable development models as understood until the technological disruption.

1.2 The IT Challenges of Sustainability at Present

In a world in full digital transformation, sustainability is even more related to technology and more concretely to IT. Mobile technology is considered to have the greatest impact on sustainability in all industries, while other disruptive technologies specific to the current digital transformation (i.e. nanotechnology, simulations and drones) have various degrees of potential impact on the sustainability of diverse industries (Bai et al. 2020). Smart technologies are directly connected with the economic dimension of sustainability, but not with the environmental and social ones (Saunila et al. 2019).

Concepts of sustainability associated to IT Currently, two different terms are used to cover the multiplicity of edges associated with computing and sustainability: Green IT (Green Information Technologies) and Green IS (Green Information Systems). The concept of green IT is understood as initiatives that focus on the remodeling of information technologies in environmentally friendly ways and promotes the design, manufacturing and management of equipment and services, which consume a minimum of energy throughout their entire life cycle (Tuskeentushi et al. 2013). The concept of green IS can be defined as the processes of the organization for the improvement of environmental behavior (Watson et al. 2010), contrasting with the concept of green IT, as it is not limited to energy efficiency and the use of IT equipment, focusing on the design and implementation of information systems that contribute to the implementation of sustainable business processes. Ahmad et al. (2014) define "sustainable software engineering" as the development of software products for long life systems that can meet the needs of the present and future generations with the integration of the three pillars of sustainability (environmental, economic and social) to comply with basic requirements.

2 Sustainable Management in the Romanian IT Industry: An Empirical Exploratory Research

The Romanian IT industry is one of the most visible sectors of the national economy, globally open and constantly expanding, with a rate of more than 300% increase in terms of output between 2009 and 2018 (Eurostat 2019), but behaves as the majority of the national economy, and is often a sub-assembly producer, creating low added value, while remaining heavily foreign-dependent (Păun and Pînzaru 2019). As a source of innovations both at technological and business levels, the IT actors can be considered catalyzers of new management approaches that could influence the generic business environment by the force of the example, such as adopting sustainable management strategies, with respect both to financial objectives and societal-environmental issues. Starting from the aforementioned framework, we explore furthermore the factors that influence executives of the Romanian IT sector in adopting sustainable management strategies, as well as the challenges they confront in this endeavor.

2.1 Research Context

Romania's IT industry started under the communist regime following a policy of isolationism imposed by the local Coordinating Committee for Multilateral Export Controls (Cocom), blocking the export of many IT technologies to communist regimes (Grundey and Heeks 1998), encouraging the development of local capabilities and production, such as the mini and microcomputers that were mostly copies of western technologies and pirated software. After the fall of the communism, the market was opened for foreign investments, including IT investments, even if initially education in the IT was scarce and limited to some higher education institutions. For instance, in 1996 there were 333 software companies and only 478 registered IT workers at national level (National Institute of Statistics 2019).

In 2001, the Romanian government decided to introduce a new legislation allowing software developers that have graduated a technical university, working for a software company and exporting software, to be tax-exempt. Because of the positive implications such as the increase of the number of high skills employees to the IT industry (Manelici and Pantea 2019), the tax break was extended in 2018 to all IT professions involved in the process of delivering software solutions like testing and functional analyses. The significant impact of this legislation is also mentioned in a report by the National Bank of Romania, confirming the growth in the number of employees being one of the highest in the region, making the IT industry the most profitable sector of the economy (Veaceslav et al. 2017). The IT industry represents 5.5% of the GDP (Eurostat 2019), generates 20% of all national exports, and is expected to employ 111.000 people by the end of 2020 (ANIS 2019)—all, impressive figures for an industry located in a country which is next to the last country in the EU on the Digital Economy and Society Index (European Commission 2019a).

The Romanian IT industry is oriented mostly towards outsourcing, despite of the emergence of some local actors creating innovations at global scale in the Robot Process Automation and software and hardware security sectors. Nevertheless, the Romanian IT industry is challenged by its open competition with India, while being confronted to a real workforce deficit and a fierce competition for talents that leads to limitations in the available skillset and to a salary growth spiral with direct implications on productivity. The Romanian IT industry's competitive advantage comes from being geographically and culturally close to western European countries, but it could be considered to be at a cross-road in order to restructure its business models towards a sustainable development.

2.2 Research Methodology

In order to explore the main factors influencing the adoption of sustainable management strategies in nowadays' context of the Romanian IT market, we conducted 10 semi-structured filed interviews with middle and top management executives (CEOs, General Managers, Managing Directors, Business Development Managers or Technology VPs) from all across the Romanian IT market and an executive representing the most important professional association of the sector.

Semi-structured interviews The choice of conducting semi-structured interviews was made in order to explore diverse dimensions of sustainability in various organizational context, as identified in the literature review process, allowing us to ask follow-up questions whenever we deemed necessary (Frejes and Thornberg 2015). This technique is called "probing" (Saunders et al. 2009; Frejes and Thornberg 2015), and its application and implementation in research is of great use especially when the researcher wants to further explore the topic discussed. The chosen qualitative approach made possible to delve into the factors that determine the adoption of any type of sustainable (economic, environmental, social, technological) dimension in the daily activities of the investigated IT enterprises.

Respondents Our sample covers all types of IT companies in Romania, such as resource vendors, service companies, internal development centres, and product companies (see Table 1). With intrinsically heterogeneous experiences, our interviewees' profile added pluriperspectivism to this study.

It is important to mention that the age of the respondents is between 34 and 65 year old, with an average of 45, and that nine of the ten respondents included in the interview are men, a possible characteristic of the industry itself—in order to comply to the bias-related enactment, we have not selected specific persons, but companies and positions. Further research can confirm if the high percentage of male managers is representative of the lack of diversity in the IT company, in particular in executive positions.

Topics. The main aspects we explored in the interviews were the managers' understanding of sustainability in order to have an insight on their direct experience with the topic (theoretical or practice based) and the actual factors influencing the respondents in adopting sustainable management approaches beyond the economic aspect

Table 1 Respondents' profile

Name	Sex	Age	Company	Size of the company (no. of employees)	Company type	Position held within the company
MP	M	65	DB Technology	900	Corporation	CEO
MM	M	40	Esensys Software	70	Startup	CEO
VD	F	35	Simple Capital	2	Technology Investor	Managing Director
CI	M	34	Structural Management Solutions	20	SME	Director
VF	M	41	Luxoft	1500	Corporation	Manager of Software Development Center
MC	M	49	ANIS	10	Industry association	Public Affairs Manager
IM	M	43	DB Technology	900	Corporation	VP Technology
SL	M	51	Brush Serviuces	40	SME	General Manager
AF	M	47	Alten	320	SME	Business Development Manager
RP	M	47	Qualysoft	35	SME	General Manager

Table 2 Dimensions of sustainability in respondents' answers

Dimension	Item	Quotations
Economic	Tax (taxation, fiscal exemption)	26
	Investments	8
	Economic crisis	4
	Costs	4
Social and human	Education (school, university, teaching)	40
	Employees (human resources, workforce, specialists, skills)	51
	Values	4
Environmental	CSR (responsibility)	18
Technological	Software	8
	Internet speed	2

(the only one studied until now, to our knowledge, for the Romanian IT in terms of sustainability), structured on four dimensions of sustainability: economic; social and human; environmental; technological.

Analysis The collected data were analysed using the Atlas.ti7 software, in order to identify the key topics and the most frequently used words (see Table 2). Annotations were used in order to tag the responses on the selected dimensions.

For the interviewed managers, the most important dimensions of the sustainable management of the IT enterprises are the social one (expressed mainly by the concern regarding the need for a more extensive IT education, due to the specialized workforce deficit) and the fiscal exemptions (as a result of the costs pressure under the effect of global competition). Details are presented furthermore.

2.3 *Findings*

The economic dimension of the sustainability. The definition of sustainability in the perception of managers includes protecting the environment (VF, MC, CI), avoiding unwanted externalities (IM, RP). Economic sustainability is only mentioned by one manager (CI). However, nine out of ten answers, except for (IM) do cover economic sustainability in their definitions. On the contrary, profit and business development objectives are seen by as hindering the efforts to address other types of sustainability goals (RP), such as the social and environmental ones.

There are three answers related to long-term strategies (BP, IM), in a general way, as part of a strategic management view. However, the topic of long-term team company strategy extends throughout any dimension of sustainability.

Considering the high demand for IT services and the scarcity of available workforce, managers are not concerned so much about economics, but more about their ability to respond to the demand. The one divergent opinion comes from CI, which considers shareholders' profit as the main determinant of sustainability. CI's role is to manage investments and HiTech. For her, the economic factors are more important. The other managers (RP, VD, IM) are targeting long-term growth but only as a mean to deliver on a vision.

Even if the economic dimension is not part of most managers' perceptions of what sustainability is, the topic regarding fiscal legislation was covered in all answers (13 quotations). It is linked to the topics in the literature review (Manelici and Pantea 2019), covering the impact of the tax deduction on the IT sector. This is seen as a factor for Romania's development (VF, MP, CI, SL, MM, VD), and a factor of business sustainable growth (VV, AF, VF).

The word "tax" was the most frequently used in explaining the Romanian IT economic sustainability, showing up 26 times, with references to the tax exemption legislation included in all ten answers. In the context of the tax exemption legislation, the high salary level in the IT industry was mentioned by two respondents (AF and VF).

Considering that the tax break applies since the year 2000 and remains such a critical factor in managers' perception of their organization's economic sustainability, the open question remains if Romania's IT sector itself is economically sustainable and if it is competitive even in its absence.

The social and human dimensions of sustainability

The social and the human dimensions of sustainability are the most important ones according to the interviewed managers, both as a conceptual part (more or less related to CSR) and as factor influencing managerial strategies (with reference to the specialized workforce deficit, the global competition and, therefore, the need to invest more in educating future employees in the IT sector).

The impact on society of the activities of their companies was largely mentioned by three respondents (MC, SL and MM). MC considers that Romanian companies are not concerned with social issues "I doubt that the Romanian companies (no matter what sector, IT included) are genuinely concerned with social or environmental factors beyond the "going-through-the-motions, feel-good CSR programs", sharing the point of SL who stated, at his turn: "I do not think that IT companies in Romania are concerned with the social and/or environmental factors."

At the opposite end, MM highlighted that the company that he represents is "actively and continuously involved in social activities".

All identified companies (large and small) engaged in CSR programs see the subsequent activities as a means to involve the employees, while also having a human dimension: according to AF, CSR activities are often organized and implemented by the employees themselves, the concrete examples being, for instance, the blood donations at Essensys and Luxoft.

A particularly important topic for the social and human dimensions of sustainability proved to be education, spontaneously discussed by all ten respondents (40 quotations). The reason why the management focuses on education in IT is explained by VD: "Scarcity of resources will push companies to invest more in education, even if the primary motivation is economic". Engineers are the most important asset for the long-term success of the software companies, directly dependent on the number of graduates and their skills. That drives the demand for more software developers: "We need a significant increase the number of positions in universities for students in IT-oriented specializations" (VF).

Seven respondents out of ten reported that their companies are involved in programs of formal or informal teaching, with examples such as the Financial Computing Master by Deutsche Bank and the online platform for baccalaureate preparation by Brush Services.

The environmental dimension of sustainability Environmental concerns were found to be part of all managers' perceptions of sustainability, but understood mainly as an element of the corporate social responsibility (CSR) programs of the enterprises.

The actual preoccupation and organized investment in environmental CSR activities remain mostly an attribute of larger companies, having financial resources allocated to such activities. This fact is recognized by corporate managers—"smaller IT companies do not have such focus" (VF)—, as well as by SMEs—"If Romanian authorities would provide the legal environment for offering benefits" (SL).

The factors influencing the adoption of environmental sustainability in the IT enterprises represented in our study can be summarized as follows:

a. Compliance to regulations, but very rarely—mentioned as a factor only by AF. The software industry (the majority of the Romanian IT industry is a software one, and not a hardware one) is not known as a big polluter and does not have any special environmental regulations;
b. Alignment with employees' values and motivations through a variety of CSR programs designed and implemented not only for the environmental involvement, but also (or mainly) in order to attract employees that want to work for environmentally and socially sustainable companies: "In order to attract people and retain employees that are concerned about environmental and social issues" (VF).

Concrete examples of environmental responsible activities were given, such as planting trees at Luxoft and recycling in Essensys, mentioning the stimulation of volunteering of the employees through such activities.

The technological dimension of sustainability
While all the respondents are managers in technology organizations, none of the answers mentioned technology in itself as a sustainability factor. All the organizations included in the research, representing the cross-section profile of the Romania IT industry, are software houses. The sustainability of software technology is different from what other brick and mortar organizations will consider the sustainability of their hardware tool. Technology is also mentioned in three of the responses, but in a social rather than technological context: "Romanians are a people opened to new technology" (VD).

For software houses, the concept of technology is the software itself. The software applications were not considered in the context of sustainability. One mention of software came from SL, saying that cracked software helped technology adoption in the early 90s, when students had no money to purchase licenses. However, this is an economic argument rather than a technological one. SL pointed out that "because we live in a world in which technology becomes more and more important, a part of our lives, the demand will continue to grow". This confirms the IT managers' perception of technology as an economic factor, even when MP mentions the Internet speed in Romania (ranked 4th worldwide) as an opportunity for externalization of IT development services in the country.

2.4 *Discussions*

The respondents interviewed in this study, large organizations' directors, SME's managers and entrepreneurs, as well as Romanian National Employers Association of Software and Services (ANIS) executives and board members, are primarily interested in the economic and social determinants of sustainability that are influenced by legislation and governmental politics, such as taxation, education and the potential of growing an internal IT labour market.

When addressing the economic dimension of sustainable management approaches, a key element in maintaining a competitive advantage is mentioned to be the tax exemption facility applicable to IT workers, heavily dependent on politics, as it is re-evaluated periodically by each new government. The main concern of the interviewees is about the impact on the organizations and across the industry if the fiscal facility is removed, a political decision that, combined with the labour force deficit and the international competition, could affect negatively the economic sustainability of the Romanian IT industry.

Only 35% of the industry is based on local capital. Most of the IT companies in Romania are working in the services industry, building bespoke software solutions for the parent organization or foreign clients. Respondents tend to agree with the fact that having a larger number of local start-ups building and selling products will make the industry less vulnerable to international competition and economic cycles. Product-based companies will also enable future growth of the companies without having a strict linear dependency on the number of new graduates.

Our findings do not show a coordinated interest in social and environmental factors like climate and social issues. Social and environmental sustainability initiatives are mostly present in large organizations, with more available resources (both financial and human), and are driven by the social pressure of motivating the employees by creating a sense of community. The interviewed companies do also have initiatives enabling their employees to volunteer for sustainability initiatives.

The ability to find enough skilled resources is a critical success factor for IT companies. For this reason, skills availability is seen by all respondents as the most critical factor that can enable sustainable future growth. That is also the reason why all interviewed organizations are engaged in educational programs.

None of the interviewed managers have reported any concern related to green computing aspects related to energy consumption and carbon footprint. That was to be anticipated because most of the industry is in software development services.

3 Concluding Remarks and Future Research

Sustainability is a very concrete concept for the interviewed managers, concerned concretely by the elements that could alter their companies' medium- and long-term advantages, such as the legislation and the labour force deficit. Of all discussed sustainability dimensions, the interviewed Romanian IT executives are mainly preoccupied with the human aspect. That was expected considering that in IT, despite the rise of automated coding facilities, the intellectual capital remains the most important success determinant. The social dimension is also considered when addressing the public education system outcomes and threats, leading back to the human factor.

From an economic perspective, the software development sector is the rising star industry of Romania, with a continually increasing number of employees, growing revenue and export. However, the growth depends on governmental fiscal facilities and on foreign investment, with limited available local capital. The limited adoption of the digital infrastructure by the public authorities and the overall local economy, as highlighted by the DESI ranking, is also a constraint for the local IT sector, forced to reorient towards international markets, with some implications on the sustainability orientation.

Social and environmental programs of companies are mentioned by the interviewed managers mostly as a way for companies to demonstrate values and principles appreciated by a young and educated workforce. While we interviewed software technology managers, none of them brought up technological sustainability as an important topic, which was understood as intrinsic.

For a more comprehensive understanding of the managers' perception on the subject of Romania's IT industry sustainability, we consider that future studies should include a more significant number of responses. While this paper addressed the perception of upper management, we think that future researches should include younger line managers, in order to assess future possible orientations. The millennial managers are the future leaders of their organizations and have a vested interest in their companies' long-term sustainability and such an approach will create a clearer picture of how the sector perceives the subject. Considering other limits of this study, any future research should also measure the number of women in IT managerial positions and whether the small number of women in the senior jobs positions of IT organizations has an impact on the companies' sustainable management models.

References

Abdelkafi, N., Täuscher, K.: Business models for sustainability from a system dynamics perspective. Org. Environ. **29**(1), 74–96 (2016)

Ahmad, R., Barahom, F., Hussain, A.: A systematic review on sustainability studies in software engineering. Knowl. Manage. Int. Conf. KMICe (2014)

ANIS: Study of Romania IT Industry. DCI Quantitative Research. Association of Software and Services Industry (2019)

Bai, C., Dallasega, P., Orzes, G., Sarkis, J.: Industry 4.0 technologies assessment: a sustainability perspective. Int. J. Prod. Econ. 107776 (2020)

Balderjahn, I., Buerke, A., Kirchgeorg, M.P., Seegebarth, B., Wiedmann, K.P.: Consciousness for sustainable consumption: scale development and new insights in the economic dimension of consumers' sustainability. AMS Rev. **3**(4), 181–192 (2013)

Becker, C.E.: The Karlskrona manifesto for sustainability design. Version 4.0 (2015). https://arxiv.org/abs/1410.6968v4. Accessed on 11 Feb 2020

Bocken, N.M.P., Short, S.W., Rana, P., Evans, S.: A value mapping tool for sustainable business modelling. Corp. Govern. **13**, 482–497 (2013)

Brundtland, G.H., et al.: Report on the world commission on environment and development: our common future. In: United Nations Conference on Environment and Development (1987). https://undocs.org/en/A/42/427. Accessed on 07 Feb 2020

Centobelli, P., Cerchione, R., Esposito, E.: Environmental sustainability in the service industry of transportation and logistics service providers: systematic literature review and research directions. Transp. Res. Part D Transp. Environ. **53**, 454–470 (2017)

Choi, S., Ng, A.: Environmental and economic dimensions of sustainability and price effects on consumer responses. J. Bus. Ethics **104**(2), 269–282 (2011)

Eurostat, NACE A*64. https://ec.europa.eu/eurostat/web/education-and-training/data/database. Accessed on 11 Feb 2020

Freeman, R.E.: Strategic management: a stakeholder approach. Cambridge University Press (2010)

Grundey, M., Heeks, R.: Romania's hardware and software industry: building IT policy and capabilities in a transitional economy. In: Development Informatics (1998)

Kemp, R.: Technology and the transition to environmental sustainability: the problem of technological regime shifts. Futures **26**(10), 1023–1046 (1994)

Manelici, I., Pantea, S.: Industrial Policy at Work: Evidence from Romania's Income Tax Break for Workers in IT (2019). https://www.researchgate.net/publication/332784478. Accessed on 11 Feb 2020

Metzner, A.: Caring capacity and carrying capacity—a social science perspective. In: INES 2000 Conference Challenges for Science and Engineering in the 21st Century (2000)

Meyers, R.A. (ed.): Encyclopedia of Sustainability Science and Technology. Springer (2012)

Molla, A., Cooper, V.A., Pittayachawan, S.: IT and eco-sustainability: developing and validating a green IT readiness model. In: ICIS 2009 Proceedings, vol. 141 (2009)

National Institute of Statistics. Dissemination Standards Bulletin Board (2019). https://www.insse.ro/cms/ro/content/sdds-plus-0. Accessed on 27 Dec 2019

Omri, A., Euchi, J., Hasaballah, A.H., Al-Tit, A.: Determinants of environmental sustainability: evidence from Saudi Arabia. Sci. Total Environ. **657**, 1592–1601 (2019)

Păun, C., Pînzaru, F.: Get It Right This Time? Leaving the Periphery of the European Economic Development. Springer (2019)

Piecyk, M., Browne, M., Whiteing, A., McKinnon, A. (eds.): Green logistics: improving the environmental sustainability of logistics. Kogan Page Publishers (2015)

PwC, Fourth Industrial Revolution for the Earth Harnessing Artificial Intelligence for the Earth, https://www.pwc.com/gx/en/sustainability/assets/ai-for-the-earth-jan-2018.pdf?utm_campaign=sbpwc&utm_medium=site&utm_source=articletext. Accessed on 27 June 2020

Saunila, M., Nasiri, M., Ukko, J., Rantala, T.: Smart technologies and corporate sustainability: the mediation effect of corporate sustainability strategy. Comput. Ind. **108**, 178–185 (2019)

Sommer, A.: Managing green business model transformations. Springer, Berlin (2012)
Spangenberg, J.H.: Reconciling sustainability and growth: criteria, indicators, policies. Sustain. Devel. **12**(2), 74–86 (2004)
Stubbs, W., Cocklin, C.: Conceptualizing a sustainability business model. Org. Environ. **21**, 103–127 (2008)
Tuskeentushi, B., Sedera, D., Recker, J.: Green IT segment analysis an academic literature review. In: Twentieth Americas Conference on Information Systems, pp. 1–15. Association for Information Systems (2013)
Veaceslav, G., Tănase, A., Leonte, A.: Study of IT&C sector evolution in Romania. SSRN 3308591 (2017)
Wannags, L., Gold, S.: Assessing tensions in corporate sustainability transition: from a review of the literature towards an actor-oriented management approach. J. Clean. Prod. 121662 (2020)
Watson, R., Boudreau, M., Chen, A.: Information systems and environmentally sustainable development: energy informatics and new directions for the IS community. MIS Quart **34**(1), 23–38 (2010)
Wüstenhagen, R., Boehnke, J.: Business models for sustainable energy. In: Tukker, A., Charter, M., Vezzoli, C., Stø, E., Andersen, M.M. (eds.), Perspectives on Radical Changes to Sustainable Consumption and Production, pp. 85–94 (2008)

Identifying Circular Business Models Through Traditional and Snowball Sampling

Daniela Staicu

1 Introduction

The transition towards a circular economy offers an opportunity to reduce Europe's environmental footprint through measures of diminishing raw material consumption and reducing waste generation (Council of the European Union 2018; Ellen MacArthur Foundation 2019; European Commission 2019; Whicher et al. 2017).

The progressive introduction of the circular economy in policies in the past ten years determined the European Union, and the Member States to create policies with a strong focus on increasing recycling rates, reducing landfilling and creating new markets dedicated to secondary raw materials. Moreover, a great importance has been given to retaining the value of resources for as long as possible and rethinking the value chain of production—consumption—end of life cycle (Farrant and Olsen 2010; Resta et al. 2016; Seuring and Müller 2008). However, these policies cannot succeed if the business models are not aligning their value chains to the circularity principles. In this perspective, the circular business models are gaining traction (European Commission 2019a, b, c).

Textiles waste is relatively small in terms of weight as compared to other waste streams, but it has a large impact on human health and environment (James and Lings 2018; Koszewska 2018; Sandin and Peters 2018; Stengg 2019), and the limits of the present take-make-waste business model are extremely visible when examining this industry (Jordão et al. 2018; Ewijk and Stegemann 2016). The literature about the circular economy in the textile and clothing sector is flourishing, and more and more business models for particular industries are investigated although there is no standardized circular economy roadmap (Thorisdottir and Johannsdottir 2019).

D. Staicu (✉)
The Doctoral School for Business Administration, The Bucharest University of Economic Studies, 010374 Bucharest, Romania
e-mail: daniela.staicu@fabiz.ase.ro

A. M. Dima and F. DÁscenzo (eds.), *Business Revolution in a Digital Era*,
Springer Proceedings in Business and Economics,
https://doi.org/10.1007/978-3-030-59972-0_9

Although in 2018 Romania adopted a National Waste Management Plan, it does not make any mentions about the textile and clothing sector waste. Being ignored, no actions are forecasted to prevent or deal with this type of waste though thousands of pages of literature predict large quantities of textile waste to be discarded in the following years (Mediului 2019; The Institute for Research in Circular Economy and Environment 2019).

The shift from a linear to a circular model in the textile and clothing sector is associated with the need to implement innovative business models, but the adoption of circular business strategies in the industry has been scarce (Fraccascia et al. 2019; Hall et al. 2010; Thorisdottir and Johannsdottir 2019).

1.1 Statement of the Problem

The transition to a circular economy is associated with circular business models concerned with the sustainability of the value chain, but the adoption of circular business strategies to stimulate the development of such models has been limited (Europe 2019; Ellen MacArthur Foundation 2019; Pardo and Schweitzer 2018). Despite the lack of circular strategies, existing business models are steadily shaping the textile and clothing sector, aligning it to the circular economy principles of reduce-reuse-recycle. These innovators are contributing to the transition to the circular economy through incremental and transformational innovation. Studies about incremental business models (Ballie and Woods 2018; James and Lings 2018; Hall et al. 2010; Jordão et al. 2018; Sousa et al. 2018; Stål and Corvellec 2017) are already being discussed in the public space and studied by academia. However, transformational innovation has not gained the same momentum, although these are offering real business models of applied circularity. In Romania, a roadmap to circular economy has not yet been formulated despite a variety of best practices from other Member States, but a tentative proposal for a Circular Economic Strategy is under development (The Institute for Research in Circular Economy and Environment 2019).

Despite a growing body of research in the area of circular economy in the textile and clothing sector, the researcher identified significant gaps in the literature related to operative sustainable business models. At this time, the literature related to Romanian circular business models is scarce and such best practices in terms of circularity are absent. Moreover, the identity of such innovators is officially not known because it has never been identified. These models certainly exist since they appear spread in various reports of organizations, which are supporting social entrepreneurship (Ashoka 2019; Damaschin-Țecu and Etchart 2019). Therefore, without a database of such stakeholders, it is impossible to move forward with analyzing the circular economy development in Romania and to further develop policies to support the advancement of such innovators.

Empirical research is needed to be performed to identify the population of sustainability-oriented innovators in the textile and clothing sector for displaying the best practices and spark new research questions about circular business models.

1.2 Purpose and Significance of the Study

The purpose of this research study was to identify the population of circular businesses in the textile and clothing sector in Romania. To achieve the scope of the research, the research had three objectives: to analyze through literature review the key concepts related to the circular economy in the field of textile and clothing; to classify the typologies of innovators in the context of the circular economy; to identify the transformative innovators in the transition to the circular economy in textile and clothing sector in Romania.

Mainly, this study has a significant outcome for the circular economy process in Romania: it created the first database of sustainability-oriented innovators in the textile and clothing sector in Romania. With this research paper, Romania contributes to the field of knowledge about circular business models, circular economy and the textile and clothing sector by showcasing how to identify invisible circular business models and their identity.

2 Literature Review

2.1 Data Sources

The researcher defined a list of keywords Table 1 after prior consultation of literature (Ellen MacArthur Foundation 2019; European Commission 2019a, b, Environment and Agency 2017; Gardas et al. 2018; Thorisdottir and Johannsdottir 2019).

The search was performed in the Web of Science databases including ScienceDirect, SAGE Journals, Wiley Online Library, Springer Link Library, and Science Citation Index Expanded and Social Sciences Citation Index were included. An open Web and targeted search was operated in order to capture recent reports or studies, policies, strategies and roadmaps not published in academic journals. The research returned 211 sources Table 2.

Table 1 The list of keywords employed for extensive literature search

Number	Keyword
1	Circular economy in textile and clothing
2	Business models in the circular economy
3	Sustainability in textile and clothing
4	Sustainability in fashion
5	Innovation in the textile and clothing
6	Textile and clothing sector Romania
7	Social entrepreneur textile and clothing

Source Author's own research

Table 2 Characteristics of the literature collected for the literature review

Classification of sources by topic	Number of sources	Timeframe
Circular economy	100	2002–2019
Textile and clothing	32	2001–2019
Sustainable development; sustainability-oriented innovators; sustainability innovation	47	1987–2019
Social entrepreneurship in the textile and clothing	32	2001–2019

Source Author's own research

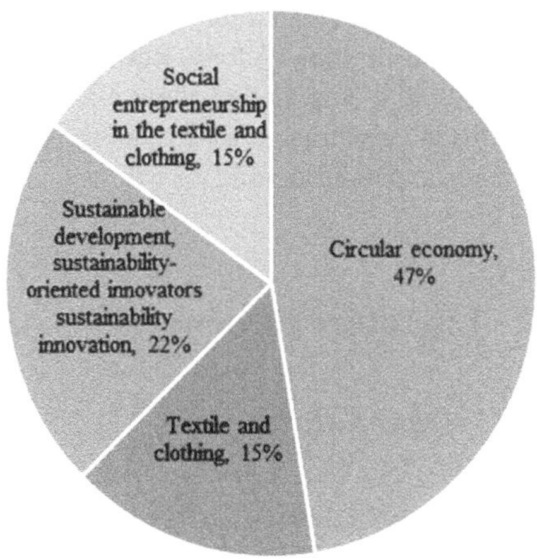

Fig. 1 The classification of literature by topic. *Source* Author's own research

Given the fast-moving transformation of the circular economy, the exhaustive coverage was narrowed to literature published between 2001 and 2019, with three exceptions of papers and reports published in 1987, 1997 and 1999. The results returned 211 sources Fig. 1 of literature in English and Romanian language Table 2.

2.2 *Global Overview of the Circular Economy in the Textile and Clothing Sector*

Moving away from the "take-make-use-dispose" model towards the circular one involves the revival of the end-of-life concept, restoration of resources, the use of renewable energy, the removal of chemicals from various processes along the value chain, and the disposal of waste through efficient design of materials, products, value chains and business models (Ballie and Woods 2018; Bukhari et al. 2018; Franco 2017; Fontell and Heikkilä 2019; Sousa et al. 2018; Apparel and Textile Confederation 2019; Thorisdottir and Johannsdottir 2019). Article 4 of the Waste

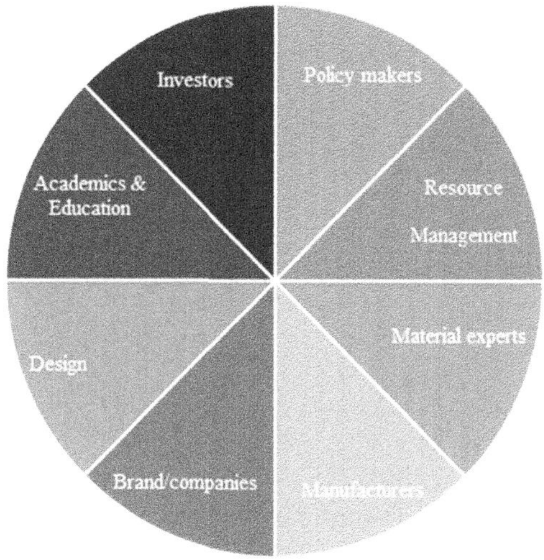

Fig. 2 The circular economy stakeholders. *Source* Author's own research

Framework Directive 2008/98/EC established the waste hierarchy of "prevention—reuse and preparation for reuse—recycle—recovery—disposal" as the underlying principle of waste policies in the EU (Council of the European Union 2019; European Commission 2019a, c; Farrant and Olsen 2010; Fontell and Heikkilä 2019).

Going deeper in understanding the circular economy, the stakeholders in the CE Fig. 2 can be grouped into five to nine categories (Great and Recovery 2019; Whicher et al. 2017).

2.3 Sustainable Development and Agents of Change

Examples of sustainable business models in the T&C sector exist and they help understanding how to shift the textile industry towards circularity (Gardetti and Muthu 2015). However, the understanding of the models available for the T&C sector is scarce with only a few best practices, which can be classified in three categories: "circular" which is a model of creating value from waste, "servitization" which encourages functionality over ownership or "sufficiency" which encourages effective consumption of resources (Smits 2019). According to Hockerts and Wüstenhagen (2010) two types of game-changers (Hall et al. 2010; Schaltegger and Wagner 2011) have been operating on the market: the "emerging Davids" and the "greening Goliaths". While emerging Davids are often new ventures operating in niche markets, with sustainability in their core mission and business model, the greening Goliaths are large companies achieving sustainability through incremental changes.

The researcher revised 35 sources related to sustainable development, sustainability-oriented innovators and business models and sustainability extracted from the 211 sources identified at an earlier stage. Afterwards, the researcher

Table 3 Word frequency analysis using Nvivo

Word	Count	Weighted percentage (%)
Sustainability	151	2.66
Environmental	41	1.28
Innovation	117	1.27
Change	291	1.25
Activities	371	1.24
Models	76	0.97
Study	121	0.71
Practices	89	0.58
Social	44	0.57

Source Author's own research

performed a word frequency analysis using Nvivo qualitative software on the abstracts of these works. The results in Table 3 validated the relevance of these sources at this stage of the research (5).

This analysis was followed by a literature review of these 35 sources and results emerged about the typology of innovators Table 4.

Research on these two types of companies Table 4 has been analyzing both models separately and two distinct concepts arise from this: the new entrants (Fowler 2007; Plieth et al. 2012), or the incumbents (Goldbach et al. 2003). The new entrants also named in the literature "pioneer companies" were perceived as operating in a niche, often not being able to demonstrate relevant impact on sustainability issues. Moving towards the incumbents or "the conventional companies" taking action towards sustainability means launching a product line of eco-or organic fabrics, doing small-impact change to accommodate sustainability. These two forms of sustainable entrepreneurship and their contribution to the transition to the circular economy are also known as "emerging" and "multiplying Davids" or "greening Goliaths" (Hockerts and Wüstenhagen 2010). The literature about functional business models in these two categories of players and their impact on sustainability are scarce and limited

Table 4 Categories of sustainability-oriented innovators

Types of sustainability-oriented innovators	Characteristics
New entrants: sustainable entrepreneurs	Niche players, transformational innovators, pioneer companies, "emerging" and "multiplying Davids" social entrepreneurs, core mission: environmental and social impact
Incumbents: intrapreneurs	mass-market players, incremental innovators, the conventional companies, sustainability manager "greening Goliaths"

Author's own research based on (Ashoka 2019; Goldbach et al. 2003; Hockerts and Wüstenhagen 2010; Plieth et al. 2012)

to incremental environmental innovation with focus on the ecological dimension of sustainability not on the overall business model (Ashoka 2019).

Efforts towards multiplying the examples of business models in the T&C in the transition to the CE done by the C&A Foundation and Ashoka are highlighting innovative insights coming out of a powerful network of social entrepreneurs (Fowler 2007) which corroborates with the literature which points out that the social entrepreneur is seen as a pioneer of the future of the T&C sector. All evidence points out that the game-changers in the T&C sector are the social entrepreneurs.

3 Methodology

To achieve the purpose of this study, the researcher employed the Participatory Action Research, an approach to research in communities that required participation and action, seeking to understand the world by trying to change it, collaboratively and following reflection (Camic and Joas 2003; Chambers 2008). The researcher aligned the research process to the PAR guidelines by involving and consulting throughout the investigation all the nine categories of stakeholders in the circular economy (Thomas 2018) as a measure of ensuring validity of both the input and the results and as a means of creating awareness on the subject of circular economy. Moreover, the researcher itself is an active participant in the field under investigation through its role of social entrepreneur in the textile and clothing sector based in Bucharest, Romania.

In reviewing the literature, and adapting the stakeholders' diagram related to the textile and clothing sector (Thomas 2018) the researcher identified a network of 59 nominal stakeholders from Romania exhibited in Fig. 3.

Before immersing itself in the research process, based on prior literature review, the researcher defined the game-changers targeted by this research Table 4 referred throughout the research also as "sustainability-oriented innovator", "social entrepreneur", "agent of change".

Between September 2018 and March 2019, traditional and virtual sampling research methods were used to identify the sustainability-oriented innovators in the textile and clothing sector. Seen as hard-to-reach populations because of the scarcity of research about this category (Gardetti and Muthu 2015; Stubbs and Cocklin 2008), the researcher employed research methods specific to identify hard-to-reach populations Fig. 4: traditional sampling methods and online virtual sampling (Baltar and Brunet 2012; Boyd and Ellison 2008; Fricker and Schonlau 2002; Time Magazine 2019). The question of sampling hard-to-reach populations partly overlaps with that of rare populations for whom there is generally no sampling frame. This paper will only exhibit the traditional snowball sampling approach. A second paper exhibits the results of the virtual snowball sampling method.

The traditional sampling methods encompass two approaches: first, targeted sampling includes an initial ethnographic assessment in order to identify the networks that might exist in a given population and subgroups are treated as a cluster sample;

Fig. 3 The nine categories of stakeholders in the circular economy adapted to the textile and clothing sector in Romania. *Source* Author's own research

second, snowball sampling: one subject gives the researcher the name of another subject, who in turn provides the name of a third, and so on (Atkinson and Flint 2001), a methodology considered useful in exploratory, qualitative and descriptive research, especially in those studies that respondents are few in number or a high degree of trust is required to initiate the contact (Baltar and Brunet 2012).

3.1 *Traditional Sampling*

The methodology employed for traditional sampling as it is described in Fig. 5 engaged the researcher in a process of first identifying in the literature the categories of stakeholders qualified to recommend sustainability-oriented innovators.

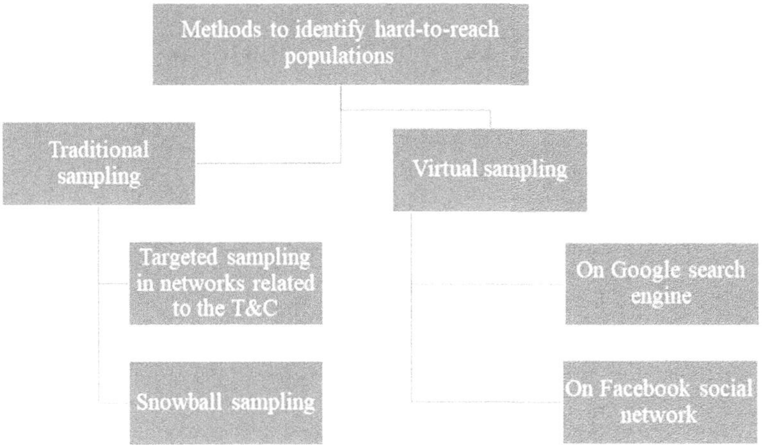

Fig. 4 "Hard-to-reach populations" methodology adapted to this research study. *Source* Author's own research

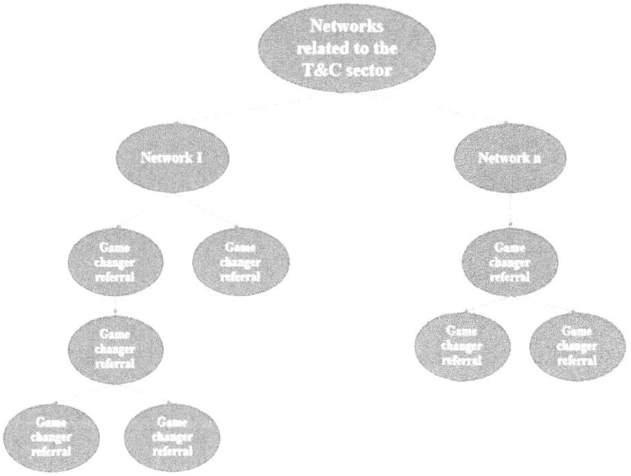

Fig. 5 Traditional sampling methods adapted to game changers in the T&C sector. *Source* Author's own research

The researcher employed simultaneously two traditional sampling methods: targeted and snowball sampling Fig. 5. The research ended when no other subjects were recommended. The networks and individuals considered as potential sources of recommendations in the process of targeted sampling, were identified by populating with data the main categories of the Circular Network Diagram Fig. 2. Based on these categories, the researcher identified specific networks active in Romania within these categories Fig. 6.

Next, to each stakeholder in each network identified, the researcher sent an email explaining the purpose of the research and inviting each stakeholder to recommend

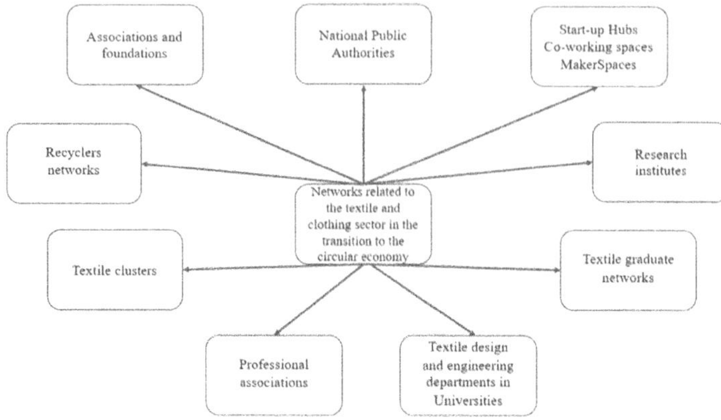

Fig. 6 Sub-categories of networks related to the textile and clothing sector in the transition to the circular economy. *Source* Author's own research

sustainability-oriented innovators. In a first round of results, a list of perceived SOI emerged and later these SOI were submitted through the same process of being asked to recommend other SOI. The process ended when no other recommendations were formulated.

4 Results and Discussions

4.1 Traditional Snowball Sampling

Based on the stakeholders' categories in Fig. 3, eleven sub-categories of networks were identified in relation to the game-changers investigated. Next, for each sub-category, the researcher described the relationship with the textile and clothing in the transition to the circular economy Table 5 to clarify why these networks are relevant to the research topic.

Based on Table 6, in each sub-category, the researcher identified 59 nominal stakeholders in relationship to the game-changers investigated Fig. 7.

For each category of stakeholders, the researcher identified nominal stakeholders for future inquiry about social entrepreneurs in the textile and clothing sector Table 5. The stakeholders in Table 7 were asked to offer recommendations for SOI via e-mail and the recommendations were directly collected by the researcher by e-mail or by filling in a Google form explaining the purpose of the research, giving the definition of a SOI and asking for SOI recommendations. The process ended when no more recommendations were made. A total of 21 SOI were identified and included in a database with perceived SOI resulted (Table 6).

Table 5 Networks related to the textile and clothing sector in the transition to the circular economy

Categories of influencers when designing for circularity	Networks who can recommend game-changers in the textile and clothing	Description of the relationship with the textile and clothing sector or with the circular economy
Policy-makers	The Ministry of the Environment	Author and responsible for the implementation of the national waste management plan
	The Ministry for Business, Commerce and Entrepreneurship	Responsible of programs related to stimulating entrepreneurship development
	The Ministry of labor and social justice	Responsible of the integration of persons with disabilities in the work field and creators of the concept of "Social insertion enterprise" and "Social enterprise"
Resource management	Recyclers networks Reuse networks	Companies or individuals (legally known as PFA) concerned with recycling
Material experts	Universities	Programs textile engineering, composition
Manufacturers	Clusters of manufacturers	Regional textile clusters
	Professional associations	Professional textile manufacturers associations
Brand/companies	Clothing retailers	Retailers in clothing: online and on-site stores
	Startup hubs Co-working spaces	Spaces which host start-ups and/or create programs for start-up development
Design	MakerSpaces	A space for people with shared interests, can gather to work on projects while sharing ideas, equipment, and knowledge
Academics and Education	Universities	Universities with programs in textile design and engineering
	Graduate networks	Graduate networks in textile design and engineering
	Research institutes (public or private)	Textile and circular economy research institutes
Investors	Associations and foundations	NGO's which invest in social entrepreneurship, communities' development, start-ups focusing on sustainability, legislation

Source Author's own research

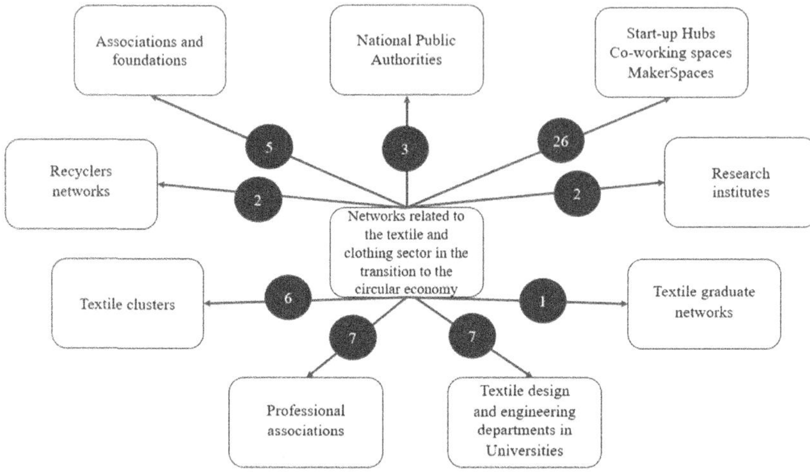

Fig. 7 Number of nominal stakeholders in each sub-category of networks. *Source* Author's own research

Table 6 Perceived sustainability-oriented innovators identified through traditional sampling method

No.	Sustainability oriented innovators identified through the research
1	Made in Roșia Montană (Roșia Montană)
2	Asociația Mai Bine—REDU (Iași)
3	Fundația Speranța (Iași)
4	Utildeco.ro (Iași)
5	Bine Boutique, Crucea Roșie Română, sector 6 (București)
6	H&M Romania (national)
7	Let's do it Romania (București)
8	Yard Sale—Gabi Urda (București)
9	Atelier Merci (București)
10	AnARTivism (Ploiești)
11	Spitalul de blugi (București)
12	Atelierul de pânză—asociația Viitor Plus (București)
13	Mesteshukar ButiQ (București)
14	Pineberry (București)
15	Iuliana Pâslaru Design (Cluj-Napoca)
16	Ana Alexe Design (București)
17	Textilia (Sic, Cluj)
18	Artă și tradiții bisocene (Bisoca. Buzău)
19	Katty Fashion (Oradea)
20	Designer Rhea Costa (București)
21	Pasmatex (Timisoara)

Table 7 Nominal stakeholders in the sub-categories of networks of influencers when designing for circularity

Sub-categories of networks	Nominal stakeholders
National Public Authorities	The Ministry of the Environment The Ministry for Business, Commerce and Entrepreneurship The Ministry of Labor and Social Justice
Associations and foundations	Askoka Romania NESsT Romania Community Foundations World Vision Romania Coaliția pentru Economie Circulară
Start-up hubs Co-working spaces MakerSpaces	Bucharest: Centrul pentru Dezvoltare Durabila Polizu, Impact Hub, 360HUB, Flash Hub, NOD makerspace, The Office HUB, Pura Vida Hub, HUB CAFE Floreasca, Coworking Bucuresti, The Atelier.ro - Cowork Café
	Cluj-Napoca: Impact Hub, ClujHUB, Cluj Cowork, Cluj Makers, Repair Café
	Timișoara: StartUP HUB Timișoara, Cowork Timisoara,
	Sibiu: Tool House—MakerSpace
	Brașov: Hub 1317, OneZero HUB, Alchemy Hub
	Constanța: B.HOUSE
	Oradea: Coworking Oradea, Oradea Tech HUB
	Sfântu Gheorghe: InnoHUB
	Iași: The Grape
Recyclers networks	The Upcyclers' Map
	The Recycling Map
Textile clusters	Romanian Textile Concept
	Clusterul textil Asociatia ASTRICO Nord-Est
	Asociatia Națională a industriei Textilelor din România
	Asociația Clusterelor din România
	Tradiții-Manufactură-Viitor
	Transylvania Textile and Fashion Cluster
Professional associations	Federatia Patronală a Textilelor, confecțiilor și pielăriei
	Asociația Confecționerilor din România
	Asociația producătorilor de confecții textile din România

(continued)

Table 7 (continued)

Sub-categories of networks	Nominal stakeholders
	Asociația de Design pentru Textile—Confecti—Pielărie
	Organizația Patronală a Industriei de Textile—Tricotaje
	Organizația Patronală a Industriei de Textile—Lână
	Asociația Producătorilor de Piele și Blană din România
	Organizația Patronală a Pielăriei și Încălțămintei
Textile design and engineering departments in Universities	Universitatea Tehnica Gheorghe Asachi, Iași
	Universitatea de Arta si Design Cluj-Napoca
	Universitatea Națională de Arte, București
	Universitatea din Oradea
	Universitatea de Vest, Timișoara
	Universitatea Aurel Vlaicu, Oradea
	Universitatea Lucian Blaga, Sibiu
Textile graduate networks	Asociația Absolvenților Facultății de Textile-Pielărie din Iași
Research institutes	Institutul pentru cercetări în economie circulară și mediu "Ernest Lupan"
	Institutul Național de Cercetare Dezvoltare pentru Textile și Pielărie

Source Author's own processing

5 Conclusions

This investigation advanced the knowledge related to circular business models in the textile and clothing sector in Romania. It is imperative to mention that the population investigated was characterized by such terms as „hard-to-reach" or "hard-to-capture" (Baltar and Brunet 2012) because of the scarcity of studies about this category (Gardetti and Muthu 2015; Stubbs and Cocklin 2008), generally characterized by some difficulties: low numbers, members of the population hard to identify, obstacles in identifying commonalities among the members, information about the members rarely recorded and available for consultation, and behavior not entirely known which leads to a poor choice of places or spaces in which to approach them (Marpsat and Razafindratsima 2010).

Since no empirical data about this population was available, the study proceeded in identifying nominally the members of the population and the dimension of the group. To identify the population of sustainability-oriented innovators, traditional sampling methods were employed. A preliminary result of using these research methods specific to hard-to-reach populations was a database of 21 perceived sustainability-oriented innovators.

The main limitations of the study were given by the fact that the population investigated is a hard-to-reach, hard-to-capture population, characterized among others with low numbers.

This is the first exercise of obtaining empirical data about the Romanian sustainability-oriented innovators in the textile and clothing sector and provides valuable information about the distribution and dimension of this category of circular economy stakeholders. Its most important significance may be the discovery of a fundamental agent of change in the circular economy: the circular business models already active in Romania in shaping the textile and clothing sector. The study did uncover the identity of the members of the population of sustainability-oriented innovators.

References

Askoka, C.A.: Foundation: fabric of change. Social entrepreneurs' transforming the apparel industry. https://bit.ly/focreportpdf. Accessed on 05 Nov 2019

Atkinson, R., Flint, J: Accessing Hidden and Hard-to-Reach Populations. Research Strategies. Social Research Update, pp. 33 (2001)

Ballie, J., Woods, M.: Circular sign by De A model for engaging fashion/textile SMEs with strategies for designed reuse. In: Crocker, R. Christopher Saint, G. (eds.) (2018)

Baltar, F., Brunet, I.: Social research 2.0: virtual snowball sampling method using Facebook. Internet Res. **22**(1), 57–74 (2012)

Boyd, D.M., Ellison, N.B.: Social-networking sites: definition, history, and scholarship. J. Comput. Mediat. Commun. **13**, 210–230 (2008)

Bukhari, M.A., Carrasco-Gallego, R., Ponce-Cueto, E.: Developing a national programme for textiles and clothing recovery. Waste Manage. Res. **36**(4), 321–331 (2018)

Camic, C., Joas, H.: The Dialogical Turn: New Roles for Sociology in the Post Disciplinary Age. Rowman & Littlefield, Maryland (2003)

Chambers, R.: PRA, PLA and pluralism: practice and theory. In: The Sage Handbook of Action Research: Participative Inquiry and Practice, pp. 297–318 (2008)

Council of the European Union: Waste management and recycling: council adopts new rules. https://www.consilium.europa.eu/en/press/press-releases/2018/05/22/waste-management-and-recycling-council-adopts-new-rules/. Accessed on 05 May 2019

CSR Europe, Universita Malta: Enablers and Barriers to a Circular Economy, www.csreurope.org. Accessed on 05 May 2019

Damaschin-Ţecu, R. Etchart, N.: Building the Social Investment Industry in Central and Eastern Europe, https://nesst.squarespace.com/s/2016-RO-Bldg-Social-Investment-Industry-ENG-FINAL-web.pdf. Accessed on 07 May 2019

Ellen MacArthur Foundation: A new textiles economy: redesigning fashion's future. https://www.ellenmacarthurfoundation.org/publications. Accessed on 08 May 2019

European Commission: Circular economy: new rules will make EU the global front-runner in waste management and recycling. https://europa.eu/rapid/press-release_IP-18-3846_en.htm. Accessed on 06 May 2019

European Commission: European Circular Economy Stakeholder Platform, https://circulareconomy.europa.eu/platform/. Accessed on 06 May 2019

European Commission: Communication from the Commission to the European Parliament, The Council, The European Economic and Social Committee and the Committee of the Regions on

Closing the loop, www.eea.europa.eu/policy-documents/com-2015-0614-final. Accessed on 06 Sept 2019
European Environment Agency: Waste prevention in Europe—policies, status and trends in reuse in 2017, www.eea.europa.eu/publications/waste-prevention-in-europe-2017. Accessed on 15 June 2019
Farrant, L., Olsen, S.I., Wangel, A: Environmental benefits from reusing clothes. Int. J. Life Cycle Assess **15**, 726–736 (2010)
Fowler, S.J.: Incorporating sustainable business practices into company strategy. In: Strategic Direction, vol. 23 (2007)
Fraccascia, L., Giannoccaro, I., Agarwal, A., Hansen, E.: Business models for the circular economy: opportunities and challenges. Business Strat. Environ. **1**, 430–432 (2019)
Franco, M.: Circular economy at the micro level: a dynamic view of incumbents' struggles and challenges in the textile industry. J. Clean. Prod. 168 (2017)
Fricker, R.D., Schonlau, M.: Advantages and disadvantages of internet research surveys: evidence from the literature. Field Methods **14**(4), 347 (2002)
Fontell, P., Heikkilä P.: Model of circular business ecosystem for textiles, https://cris.vtt.fi/en/publications/model-of-circular-business-ecosystem-for-textiles. Accessed on 08 July 2019
Gardas, B., Raut, R., Narkhede, B.: Modelling the challenges to sustainability in the textile and apparel (T&A) sector. Sustain. Prod. Consump. **7**(15) (2018)
Gardetti, M.A., Muthu, S.S: Sustainable apparel? Is the innovation in the business model?—the case of the IOU project. Textile Cloth. Sustain. J. **1** (2015). https://doi.org/10.1186/s40689-015-0003-0
Goldbach, M., Seuring, S., Back, S.: Coordinating sustainable cotton chains for the mass market: the case of the German mail-order business OTTO. Green. Manage. Int. **43**, 65–78 (2003)
James, K., Lings J.: Life cycle management and circular economy challenges for the textile sector: session wrap up. In: Benetto, E., Gericke, K., Guiton, M. (eds.), Designing Sustainable Technologies, Products and Policies. Springer (2018)
Hall, J., Daneke, A.G., Lenox, M.: Sustainable development and entrepreneurship: Past contributions and future directions. J. Bus. Ventur. **25**, 439–448 (2010)
Hockerts, K., Wüstenhagen, R.: Greening Goliaths versus emerging Davids—theorizing about the role of incumbents and new entrants in sustainable entrepreneurship. J. Bus. Ventur. **25**(5), 481–492 (2010). https://doi.org/10.1016/j.jbusvent.2009.07.005
Jordão, C., Broega, A., Puppim, R., Marques, A.D.: Sustainable entrepreneurship in the reuse of textile waste: H Sarah Trading case study in Portugal. In: IOP Conference Series: Materials Science and Engineering, vol. 459(1) (2018)
Koszewska, M.: Circular economy—challenges for the textile and clothing industry. Autex Res. J. **18**(4), 337–347(2018)
Marpsat, M., Razafindratsima, N.: Survey methods for hard-to-reach populations introduction to the special issue. Methodol. Innov. **5**(2), 3–16 (2010).https://doi.org/10.4256/mio.2010.0014
Ministerul Mediului: Hotărâre privind aprobarea planului național de gestionare a deșeurilor. In: Monitorul Oficial al României, part 1, 186 (11bis). https://www.mmediu.ro/categorie/planul-national-de-gestionare-a-deseurilor-pngd/239. Accessed on 28 Apr 2019
Pardo, R., Schweitzer, J.P.: A long-term strategy for a Europe circular economy—setting the course for success. Policy Paper produced for the Think2030 project, Brussels, Belgium (2018)
Plieth, H., Bullinger, A.C. Hansen, E.G.: Sustainable entrepreneurship in the apparel industry: the case of manomama. Greenleaf Publishing (2012)
Resta, B., Gaiardelli, P., Pinto, R., Dotti, S.: Enhancing environmental management in the textile sector: an organisational-life cycle assessment approach. J. Clean. Prod. **135**, 620–632 (2016)
Sandin, G., Peters, G.M.: Environmental impact of textile reuse and recycling—a review. J. Clean. Prod. **184**, 353–365 (2018)
Schaltegger, S., Wagner, M.: Sustainable entrepreneurship and sustainability innovation: categories and interactions. Business Strat. Environ. **20**, 222–237 (2011)

Seuring, S., Müller, M.: From a literature review to a conceptual framework for sustainable supply chain management. J. Clean. Prod. **16**, 1699–1710 (2008)

Smits, H.: Service-based business models and circular strategies for textiles. www.resyntex.eu/images/downloads/ValrieJBoiten_Textile_collection_strategies.pdf. Accessed on 08 July 2019

Sousa, T., Zomer, A., Magalhães, L., Zancul, E., Cauchick-Miguel, P.A.: Exploring the challenges for circular business implementation in manufacturing companies: an empirical investigation of a pay-per-use service provider. Resour. Conserv. Recycl. **135**, 3–13 (2018)

Stubbs, W., Cocklin, C.: Conceptualizing a sustainability business model. Org. Environ. **21**, 103–127 (2008)

Stål, H., Corvellec, H.: A decoupling perspective on circular business model implementation: illustrations from Swedish apparel. J. Clean. Prod. 171 (2017)

Stengg, W.: The textile and clothing industry in the EU—a survey. https://www.ec.europa.eu/. Accessed on 04 Aug 2019

The Institute for Research in Circular Economy and Environment: Presentation of the activity. https://www.ircem.ro/about-us/history/. Accessed on 23 July 2019

The European Apparel and Textile Confederation: Euratex Annual Report. https://www.euratex.eu/library/reports/annual-reports/. Accessed on 15 July 2019

The Great Recovery: Designing for a Circular Economy: Lessons from the Great Recovery. https://www.thersa.org/globalassets/pdfs/reports/the-great-recoverye-designing-for-a-circular-economy.pdf. Accessed on 09 Aug 2019

Thomas, S.: The great recovery. RSA J. **158**(5550), 42–44 (2018)

Thorisdottir, T.S., Johannsdottir, L.: Sustainability within fashion business models: a systematic literature review. Sustainability **11**(8) (2019)

Time Magazine: Google Tricks That Will Change the Way You Search. https://time.com/4116259/google-search-2/. Accessed on 15 Aug 2019

Van Ewijk, S., Stegemann, J.A.: Limitations of the waste hierarchy for achieving absolute reductions in material throughput. J. Clean. Prod. **132**, 122–128 (2016)

Whicher, A., Harris, C., Beverley, K., Swiatek, P.: Design for circular economy: developing an action plan for Scotland. J. Clean. Prod. 1–12 (2017)

Structural Funds for the Business Environment: The Illusion of Reducing Disparities

Andrei-Alexandru Moroşan and Pavel Stanciu

1 Introduction

The process of accession of a country to the European Union is an overly complex one, involving changes in all areas of activity. However, one of the most difficult issues to be addressed is the reduction of economic disparities between the new member and the older core of the community. One of the solutions identified by the European Commission, since 1973, was the allocation of financial resources to stimulate economic growth and reduce inter-regional disparities. Since its establishment, the Regional Development Policy and implicitly the Structural and Cohesion Funds have recorded varied results, there have been countries and regions that have aligned relatively quickly with the community average, but there have been cases when in spite of important amounts absorbed and a very generous periods of time countries and regions have failed to align with the EU average. Moreover, the EU enlargements of 2004, 2007 and 2013 represented a new challenge for the Regional Development Policy because within these waves of accession countries with a remarkably high disparity of GDP per capita, were accepted in the EU. While in other waves of expansion 1973, 1981, 1986 the differences in GDP per capita were 20–30% of the community average, in 2004, 2007 and 2013 the difference in GDP per capita of the new members was around 70–80% of the community average. In these conditions, more and more authors raise some question regarding the functionality of this instrument to reduce economic disparities and to what extent the Policy for granting these Structural Funds responds to the real needs of the EU members who joined between 2004 and 2013.

A.-A. Moroşan (✉) · P. Stanciu
"Stefan Cel Mare" University, Suceava, Romania
e-mail: alexandrumorosan@gmail.com

A. M. Dima and F. DÁscenzo (eds.), *Business Revolution in a Digital Era*,
Springer Proceedings in Business and Economics,
https://doi.org/10.1007/978-3-030-59972-0_10

2 Literature Review

The theoretical framework underlying the Structural and Cohesion Funds is the neoclassical growth model, based on the accumulation of capital by stimulating the growth rate of investments, but there are certain aspects that need to be considered, for example, projects must fall within certain areas of development, action or priorities, if there are projects that promote cultural or environmental issues, the funds allocated in this direction have a minimum impact on the accumulation of capital, even more, for the implementation of these projects other factors are involved, such as human resources, which are attracted to this sector to the detriment of other directly productive sectors. Another aspect to be considered is the fact that for the absorption of the structural funds it is necessary to provide private co-financing, which implies the allocation of financial resources both from the state budget and from various private sources, thus diminishing the available funds possible to be allocated for productive investments. Thus, it is exceedingly difficult to appreciate the net effect that the Structural Funds have on the rate of economic growth (Ederveen et al. 2002).

In the paper "Micro-efficiency of the EU Cohesion Policy", Peter Wostner concludes that the number of macroeconomic studies regarding the impact of structural and cohesion funds is increasing and the vast majority of them identify an impact conditioned by management practices and the institutional absorption system in the Member State. Peter Wostner later focuses on analyzing the institutional system and the factors that may affect it. The author concludes that major changes are needed within the institutional system, leading to the decentralization of institutions in the absorption system of European funds. In this way, he argues, the operational programs could respond much better to the needs existing in that region and implicitly the impact created by the implementation of these operational programs would be much greater. Another advantage of this decentralization, the author argues, would be the simplification of the institutional system, both vertically and horizontally (Wostner 2008).

In the paper "Socio-Economic Diversity of European Regions: Finding The Impact for Regional Performance", Aistė Palevičienė and Daiva Dumčiuvienė, argue that the impact of the Structural Funds should not be reconciled only in terms of GDP growth, the authors identify a wide range of indicators in various fields (social, educational, labor market practices, demographic aspects) that record favorable developments as a result of the absorption of structural and cohesion funds (Palevičienė and Dumčiuvienė 2015).

The paper "The Evaluation of European Union Structural Support", published in 2014 by Daiva Dumčiuvienė and Indrė Adomynienė, identifies several aspects that diminish the effect of the absorption of structural funds, among them being the lengthy and complex administrative procedures, the project objectives tend to copy the priorities of the operational programs, disregarding the real needs of the community, thus minimizing the long-term effect (Dumčiuvienė and Adomynienė 2014).

Martin Reiner admits in the paper "The Impact of the EU's Structural and Cohesion Funds on Real Convergence in the EU" that the literature does not reach a uniform conclusion, regarding the impact generated by the absorption of EU funds, but in his opinion, the Structural Funds have a positive impact on long-term economic growth. The positive impact of EU funds is also conditioned by a stable macroeconomic environment, microeconomic institutions and structures that support economic growth. Among them, the most important factors being low level of inflation, responsible budgetary policies, taxation system oriented towards supporting companies, efficient transport and communications infrastructure and well-prepared human capital. In addition, Martin Reiner explains, it contributes to the development of domestic economic agents and to the attraction of foreign direct investments, all of which translate into long-term economic growth (Reiner 2003).

Another interesting aspect pointed out by Martin Reiner in the above mentioned research is that at the level of the Regional Development Policy, elements of spatial concentration should be included, the simplification of the procedures should be continued and a more serious coordination with the national and regional policies should be pursued, all these things would, in the author's opinion, lead to a greater impact of EU funds (Reiner 2003).

Similar to Martin Reiner's view, authors Frank Barry, John Bradley, Aoife Hannan, conclude that structural funds have a long-term impact, but this impact is not generated by financial aid to the business environment but by investments in infrastructure and human capital development, these having a direct effect on increasing productivity and profitability at the level of the business environment (Barry et al. 2001).

Ederveen, Groot and Nahuis show in their study, published in 2002, that the Structural Funds cannot fully explain the differences between the growth rates of the beneficiary countries, but they admit that the institutional system represents an essential premise for the efficiency of the structural instruments. The authors point out that there are many aspects that need to be taken into account when analyzing the structural funds and its efficiency, the vast majority of projects must be co-financed, projects must fall within certain guidelines or priorities, thus it is almost impossible to carry out representative analyzes in this area (Ederveen et al. 2002).

In the paper "Impact of Structural Funds on Regional Growth: How to reconsider a 7-year-old black-box" published by Dall'erba, Guillain and Gallo in 2009, the authors outlined some representative aspects for understanding the absorption process:

- Many of the studies done do not make a distinction between the amounts allocated on different priorities, practically the analysis is made on the total amount allocated, but this is not correct the different priorities\areas of intervention contributing differently to the stimulation of the economic growth;
- Many studies do not consider the constraint effect generated by the need for co-financing, the poorer regions have difficulties in allocating the resources needed for co-financing while the richer regions can absorb a larger volume of structural funds.

- The time required to reach the maximum effect, especially in the case of public investments, a lengthy time period is required for the effects of the investment to reach their maximum potential.
- Many analyzes do not consider the spatial effect which, at least theoretically, should have a significant contribution (Dall'erba et al. 2009).

John Bachtler and Sandra Taylor are two other authors who admit that the Structural Funds have a beneficial effect on the economic growth of the beneficiary regions, but they think it is very difficult to quantify this influence. In an article published in 2003, they acknowledge that structural funds act as a catalyst for economic development but emphasize that there are many problematic issues related to bureaucracy, laborious and costly documentation and restricted eligible areas (Bachtler and Taylor 2003).

In the view of the same authors, the most eloquent indication of the efficiency of the structural funds is the diminution of the disparities between the GDP/capita of the beneficiary countries and the EU average, which is observable in most of the beneficiary countries (Bachtler and Taylor 2003).

A very interesting way to define the contribution of the Structural Funds to the stimulation of the economic growth of the beneficiary regions belongs to the authors Wostner and Šlander, in the paper "The effectiveness of EU cohesion policy revisited: are EU funds really additional?" they admit that by means of the econometric methods and techniques it is almost impossible to obtain a conclusive result and consequently the contribution of the EU reimbursable funds must be analyzed through the contribution they make to the growth of investments in the beneficiary regions and through non-financial transfers (know-how, sustainable development, equal opportunities) (Wostner and Šlander 2009).

3 Methodology

Given the fact that many of the authors concerned with the field of structural and cohesion funds consider that the structural funds have a conditional effect (conditioned by the capacity of efficient functioning of the institutions with attributions in this field and by the level of pre-existing development), but they fail to reach a definitive conclusion proves that further research of the matter is needed. The influence exerted by the capacity of the managing authorities to function efficiently is an obvious factor, which in our point of view does not require further demonstration, but the assertion that the economically developed regions/counties will attract more funds than the least developed ones it is somewhat problematic, because, one of the objectives of the EU Regional Development Policy is to reduce the economic disparities between the EU regions, thus, through selection criteria, projects from less economically developed areas are encouraged.

To test this assertion, we will analyze the distribution of the structural funds addressed to the business environment from Romania's North-East Region, considering whether there is a representative difference between the most economically developed and the least developed counties. We choose Romania's North-East Region because, according to EUROSTAT, it is the poorest region of the country, recording the lowest GDP per capita. To perform this test, we have taken data provided by the managing authority, the number of projects and the value of the contracted and implemented projects within the Multiannual Budget Exercise 2007–2013 (Regional Operational Program and Operational Program Increasing Economic Competitiveness; we identified 607 EU funded projects), these data will be tested with data taken from the EUROSTAT application. For the six counties of the North-East Region (Bacău, Botoşani, Iaşi, Neamţ, Suceava and Vaslui), data on GDP/GDP per capita and number of enterprises was collected. Two main objectives are to identify:

1. To what extent the number of companies and their size influence the volume of structural funds attracted;
2. To what extent does the general level of economic development (measured by GDP, GDP/capita) influence the volume of funds absorbed by a sub-region (county).

For the hypothesis testing, we have used the Pearson and Spearman correlation coefficients, both applicable to the scalar variables, the two coefficients take values in the range $(-1; 1)$, as the value tends to -1 the test indicates the existence of a strong inverse correlation, when the value tends to 1, the test indicates the existence of a strong direct correlation, and when the coefficient value tends to 0 then the test indicates the absence of a correlation relation between the analyzed variables. The two coefficients were chosen because they provide a complete picture of the possible links between variables, the Pearson coefficient performs testing on the values of the variables, and the Spearman coefficient analyzes the rank of the variant within the string (Biji et al. 2010).

4 Results and Discussions

By graphically representing the counties of the northeastern region of Romania by the number of active enterprises and the number of projects contracted during the multiannual exercise 2007–2013, we find the existence of a distribution that suggests a directly proportional relationship Fig. 1. In most of the analyzed years, Iaşi county presents a notable deviation from the average, in the sense that in this county there are a much larger number of active enterprises, compared to the average of the Region, at the opposite pole are the counties Botoşani and Vaslui, with a number of active enterprises much smaller than the region average. This distribution only confirms our hypothesis, namely that the structural funds do not contribute to reducing disparities between regions, the richer areas being more advantaged than the poorer ones. A similar distribution is also observed in the case of the correlation between the number

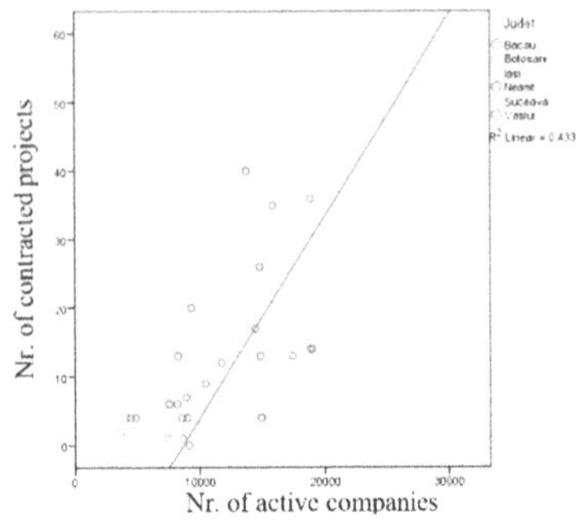

Fig. 1 Correlogram active companies/contracted projects. *Source* Data processed by the author (EUROSTAT; Romanian Ministry of European Funds)

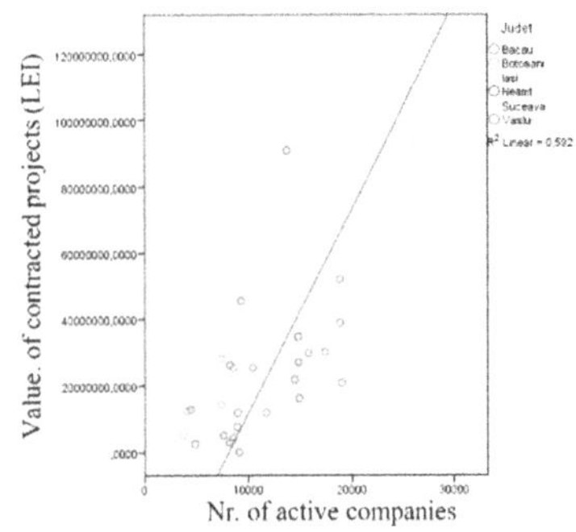

Fig. 2 Correlogram active companies/value of contracted projects. *Source* Data processed by the author (EUROSTAT; Romanian Ministry of European Funds)

of active enterprises and the value of the attracted projects Fig. 2, which suggests that the projects had on average similar values, with no discrepancy between the counties being identified.

Another aspect that we wanted to test is the influence of the concentration of medium and large enterprises in certain counties. According to the statistical data available on EUROSTAT, active companies are classified into: Active enterprises, Active enterprises with at least one employee and active enterprises with more than 9 employees. Given the categories of data available, we will perform a correlation test for each of the three categories, to see if the values of the correlation coefficients differ significantly.

Performing the same test and considering only the companies that register a minimum of 1 employee Figs. 3 and 4, we find a slightly greater dispersion compared to the trend line, which would indicate that the companies without employees contribute to the absorption of the structural funds. Analyzing the value of the coefficients of determination obtained in the two situations (0.433, 0.592 in the case of the first test and 0.422, 0.511 in the case of the test with companies with a minimum of 1 employee), we find that we obtain slightly lower values, which would indicate a weaker correlation between the variables.

Given the assumption that larger companies should attract larger investment projects, we re-performed the analysis considering only enterprises with at least 9 employees. Similar to the previous situation, we find that a correlation relation is

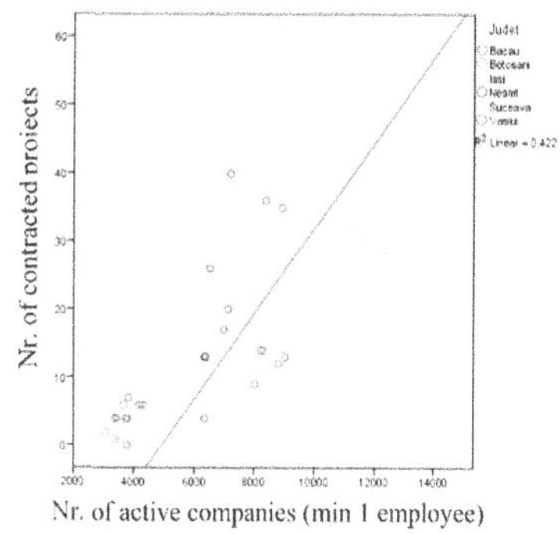

Fig. 3 Correlogram active companies (min 1 employee)/contracted projects. *Source* Data processed by the author (EUROSTAT; Romanian Ministry of European Funds)

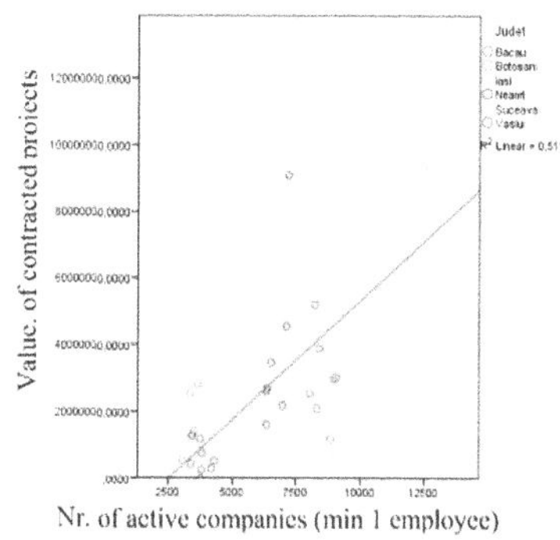

Fig. 4 Correlogram active companies (min 1 employee)/value of contracted projects. *Source* Data processed by the author (EUROSTAT; Romanian Ministry of European Funds)

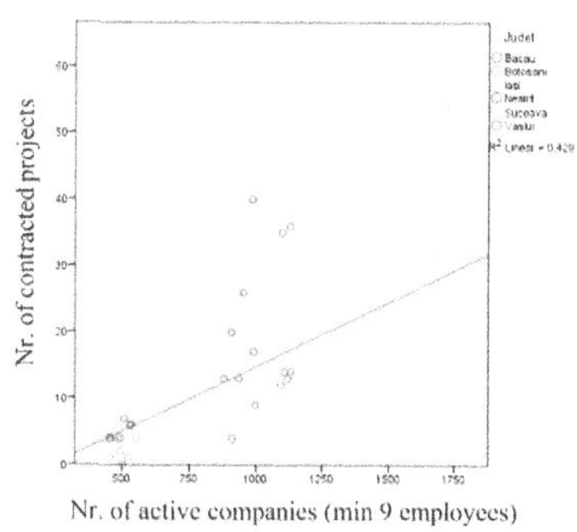

Fig. 5 Correlogram active companies (min 9 employees)/contracted projects. *Source* Data processed by the author (EUROSTAT; Romanian Ministry of European Funds)

formed, but its intensity is lower Figs. 5 and 6. We can conclude that the influence shown by the larger companies is not quite as great as we initially assumed.

However, to test the representativeness of the possible links identified from the graphical analysis, we used the Pearson correlation coefficients Table 1 and Spearman Table 2.

The correlations identified in the graph analysis are statistically representative (the value of the Sig indicator is lower than 0.05 in all cases), and the value of the correlation coefficients indicates the existence of medium to high intensity links. In

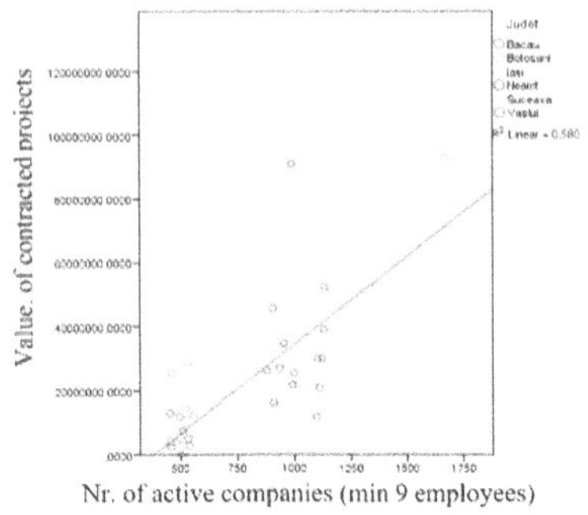

Fig. 6 Correlogram active companies (min 9 employees)/value of contracted projects. *Source* Data processed by the author (EUROSTAT; Romanian Ministry of European Funds)

Table 1 Correlation test—Pearson coefficient

		Nr. of active companies	Nr. of active companies (min 1 employee)	Nr. of active companies (min 9 employees)
Nr. contracted projects	Pearson correlation	0.658	0.649	0.655
	Sig. (2-tailed)	0.000	0.000	0.000
	N	42	42	42
Value of contracted projects (LEI)	Pearson correlation	0.770	0.715	0.762
	Sig. (2-tailed)	0.000	0.000	0.000
	N	42	42	42

Source Data processed by the author (EUROSTAT; Romanian Ministry of European Funds)

the case of the Pearson coefficient the highest value is obtained for the variables "Number of active enterprises"—"Value of contracted projects".

The correlation tests confirm the hypothesis that the more economically developed regions attract more structural funds than the least developed ones (in the case of this first test, we considered the degree of development to be directly proportional to the number of active enterprises in the region).

Regarding the assumption that the presence of larger enterprises in the region implies attracting projects with higher values, the results are mixed, from the perspective of the Spearman coefficient Table 2 this assumption would be confirmed, the highest value of the correlation indicator being recorded for companies with at least 9 employees, while for Pearson Table 1 the value obtained is not the highest in the series, so we can conclude that the presence of larger companies contributes to attracting more structural funds but this influence is clearly conditioned by other factors.

Another indicator that is associated with the economic development is the Gross Domestic Product, so in the first a graph we represented the counties of the North-East Region of Romania according to the annual GDP registered and the number of

Table 2 Correlation test—Spearman coefficient

			Nr. of active companies	Nr. of active companies (min 1 employee)	Nr. of active companies (min 9 employees)
Spearman's rho	Nr. contracted projects	Correlation coefficient	0.713	0.717	0.714
		Sig. (2-tailed)	0.000	0.000	0.000
		N	42	42	42
	Value of contracted projects (LEI)	Correlation coefficient	0.721	0.690	0.755
		Sig. (2-tailed)	0.000	0.000	0.000
		N	42	42	42

Source Data processed by the author (EUROSTAT; Romanian Ministry of European Funds)

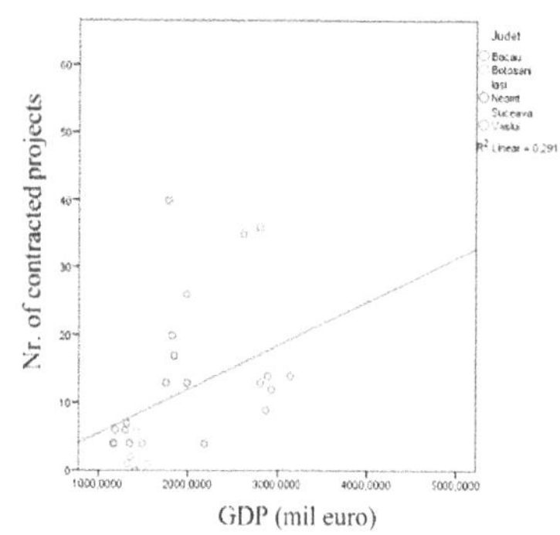

Fig. 7 Correlogram of GDP/contracted projects. *Source* Data processed by the author (EUROSTAT; Romanian Ministry of European Funds)

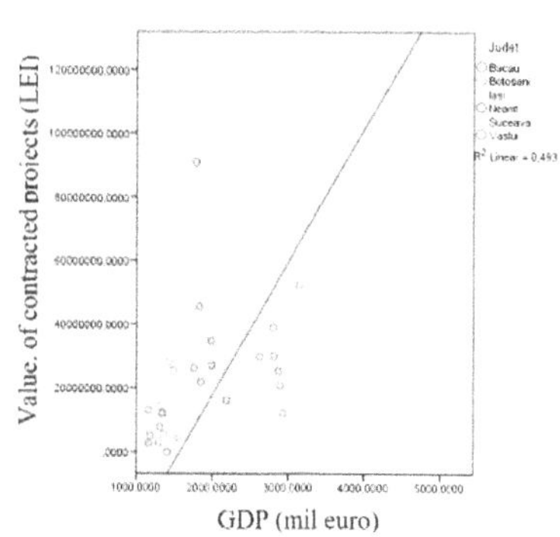

Fig. 8 Correlogram of GDP/value of contracted projects. *Source* Data processed by the author (EUROSTAT; Romanian Ministry of European Funds)

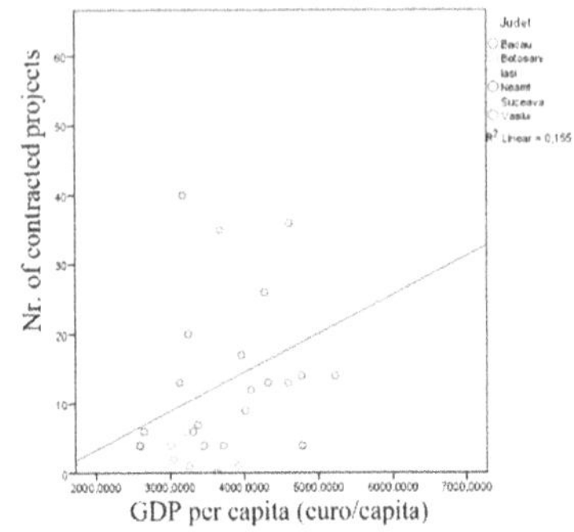

Fig. 9 Correlogram GDP per capita/contracted projects. *Source* Data processed by the author (EUROSTAT; Romanian Ministry of European Funds)

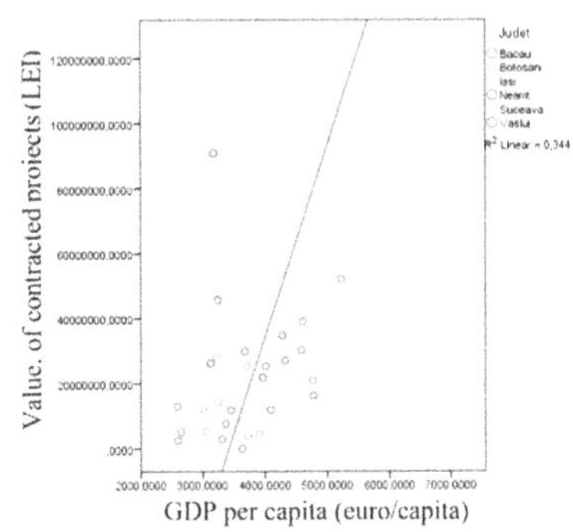

Fig. 10 Correlogram GDP per capita/value of contracted projects. *Source* Data processed by the author (EUROSTAT; Romanian Ministry of European Funds)

contracted projects, respectively the value of the contracted projects. The arrangement in Fig. 7 does not suggest the existence of a correlation between the analyzed variables. The graphical representation related to the value of the contracted projects and the annual GDP Fig. 8 suggests the existence of a directly proportional relationship between the two variables. Counties with a higher GDP (Iasi, Bacău) tend to attract more funds.

In order to have an exhaustive approach, we also performed a test with GDP/capita, in the case of this indicator the results are much weaker Figs. 9 and 10. And the values of the determination ratios (R^2—which indicates the extent to which the variation of one variable can explain the variation of the other variable) in the case of GDP/capita are much lower than in the case of the first test (0.155 for the number of projects contracted and 0.344 for the value of the contracted projects compared to 0.291 for the number of contracted projects, 0.493 for the value of the contracted projects).

In order to quantify the intensity of the correlation between GDP and the volume of funds attracted by the six counties of the North East Region of Romania, we used the correlation coefficients Pearson Table 3 and Spearman Table 4. The correlations identified in the graphical analysis are all statistically representative (Sig. Value is less than 0.05), but they differ in intensity.

The highest values of the correlation coefficients are recorded in the case of the variables value attracted projects—GDP, Pearson Coefficient 0.702 and Spearman

Table 3 Correlation test—Pearson coefficient

		Nr. contracted projects	Value of contracted projects (LEI)
GDP (mil euro)	Pearson correlation	0.540	0.702
	Sig. (2-tailed)	0.000	0.000
	Value of contracted projects (LEI)	42	42
GDP per capita (euro/capita)	Pearson correlation	0.393	0.587
	Sig. (2-tailed)	0.010	0.000
	N	42	42

Source Data processed by the author (EUROSTAT; Romanian Ministry of European Funds)

Table 4 Correlation test—Spearman coefficient

			Nr. Contracted projects	Value of contracted projects (LEI)
Spearman's rho	GDP (mil euro)	Correlation coefficient	0.628	0.696
		Sig. (2-tailed)	0.000	0.000
		N	42	42
	GDP per capita (euro/capita)	Correlation coefficient	0.451	0.568
		Sig. (2-tailed)	0.003	0.000
		N	42	42

Source Data processed by the author (EUROSTAT; Romanian Ministry of European Funds)

0.696, which confirms the hypothesis that the more developed regions, with a higher GDP, attract more structural funds.

5 Conclusion

The analysis carried out at the level of the North-East Region of Romania shows that the structural funds allocated to Romania through the Regional Development Policy of the European Union partially fulfill their assumed objectives. In the analysis we observed that the more developed counties within the Region attract larger amounts of these funds, implicitly the region develops but at its level the inter-county disparities are maintained. Thus, we find that despite the use of selection criteria that, at least theoretically, should have benefited and promoted projects in less developed areas, this is not the case, the more developed areas are attracting a larger volume of funds.

If the process observed in the North-East Region is generalized to other regions or countries, then it is clearly necessary to rethink the way of granting these non-reimbursable financial aids implicitly to the criteria used in the selection process.

Acknowledgement This work is supported by project POCU 125040, entitled "Development of the tertiary university education to support the economic growth—PROGRESSIO", co-financed by the European Social Fund under the Human Capital Operational Program 2014–2020.

References

Bachtler, J., Taylor, S.: The added value of the structural funds: a regional perspective. IQ-Net Report on the Reform of Structural Funds, Glasgow (2003)
Barry, F., Bradley, J., Hannan, A.: The single market, the structural funds and Ireland's recent economic growth. J. Common Market Stud. **39**(3), 537–552 (2001)
Biji, E.M., Lilea, E., Roşca, E., Vătui, M.: Statistics for Economists, Ed. Economică Bucureşti (2010)
Dall'erba, S., Guillain, R., Gallo, J.L.: Impact of structural funds on regional growth: how to reconsider a 7-year-old black-box. Région et Développement nr **30**, 77–99 (2009)
Dumčiuvienė, D., Adomynienė, I.: The evaluation of European Union structural support. Proc. Social Behav. Sci. **156**, 382–387 (2014)
Ederveen, S., Groot, L.H., Nahuis, R.: Fertile Soil for Structural Funds? Tinbergen Institute Discussion Paper TI 2002-096/3 (2002)
EUROSTAT. https://www.ec.europa.eu/eurostat
Palevičienė, A., Dumčiuvienė, D.: Socio-economic diversity of european regions: finding the impact for regional performance. Proc. Econ. Finan. **23**, 1096–1101 (2015)
Reiner, M.: The impact of the EU's structural and cohesion funds on real convergence in the EU. In: NBP Conference Potential Output and Barriers to Growth Zalesie Górne (2003)
Romanian Ministry of European Funds, www.fonduri-ue.ro
Wostner, P.: Micro-efficiency of the EU cohesion policy. European Policies Research Center, Glasgow (2008)
Wostner, P., Šlander, S.: The effectiveness of EU cohesion policy revisited: are EU funds really additional? Eur. Pol. Res. Centre Res. Paper Number 69 (2009)

The Vulnerabilities of the Risk Assessment Model Elaborated by the Basel Committee for Banking Supervision

Paul Baranga and Iulian Zalinca

1 Introduction

Since 1988, when the first Basel Capital Agreement was drafted, and until now, the capital adequacy model has been permanently completed and improved according to the evolution of banking activity, of the factors that generated the 2008 Financial Crisis, as well as and according to the objectives of the European Commission in relation to the banking sector in the European Union.

In this respect, the model "Risk-weighted activity" was initially applied only to credit risk, was subsequently supplemented with market and operational risks and improved with new indicators and additional requirements, including those regarding the quality and structure of own funds. Thus, this model has been continuously improved to surprise to better understand the source of risk factors and their potential impact on capital and cash flows.

With the Third Basel Capital Agreement, the capital adequacy model was supplemented with additional requirements and indicators in order to be used by central banks both in the supervision carried out at the level of each credit institution (micro prudential level) and in the supervision realized at the level of the banking system (macro prudential level).

Although in the last 30 years this model of capital adequacy has been continuously improved and perfected, it still presents a series of vulnerabilities that can affect the relevance of the minimum capital requirements.

P. Baranga (✉) · I. Zalinca
Academy of Economic Studies, 010374 Bucharest, Romania
e-mail: barangalp@yahoo.com

A. M. Dima and F. DÁscenzo (eds.), *Business Revolution in a Digital Era*,
Springer Proceedings in Business and Economics,
https://doi.org/10.1007/978-3-030-59972-0_11

2 The Determination of the Total Risk Exposure Amount

Financial risks have correlated dynamics almost complete in crisis situations, but normally the correlation level is somewhere between certain moderate limits/levels. Due to this, there should have been a risks correlation matrix in the calculation for determining the own funds requirement for all risks, where for every type/category of risks a certain factor of correlation with the other types/categories of risk is provided. This way, the determination of the own funds requirement for all risks would have equally taken into account the correlations existing between the various types/categories of risks.

In the latest form of the formula for determining the capital adequacy ratio is a linear function where the factor 12.5 is used so that the ratio between own funds and own funds requirement may be 8% when they are equal. The capital adequacy ratio is the ratio between the resources of the financial entity and the sum of risk exposures.

The total risk exposure amount is determined according to the following formula:

$$\begin{aligned} TREA = \big(&ER_{Position\,risk} + ER_{large\,exposures} + ER_{Currency\,risk} + ER_{Settlement\,risk} \\ &+ER_{Commodity\,risk} + ER_{Credit\,value\,adjustment\,risk} + ER_{Operational\,risk}\big)*12.5 \\ &+ ER_{Credit\,risk} + ER_{Counterpartyy\,credit\,risk} \end{aligned} \quad (1)$$

where:

TREA = total risk exposure amount.

ER_Position risk = own funds requirement for the position risk.

ER_large exposures = own funds requirement for large exposures exceeding the regulatory limits.

ER_Currency risk = own funds requirement for the currency risk.

ER_Settlement risk = own funds requirement for the settlement risk.

ER_Commodity risk = own funds requirement for the commodity risk.

ER_Credit value adjustment risk = own funds requirement for the credit valuation adjustment risk of OTC derivative financial instruments.

ER_Operational risk = own funds requirement for the operational risk.

ER_Credit risk = own funds requirement corresponding to the amount of credit risk- and dilution risk-weighted exposures.

ER_Counterparty credit risk = amount of risk-weighted exposures for the counterparty's credit risk.

If we assume that any credit operation also requires the debtor to deposit a collateral at least equal to the value of the future exposure, it follows that the default loss will tend to zero. Thus, the value of the expected loss if debtor ends in default will be zero, and the own funds requirement for such exposure will be zero. Any problem having to do with the dynamics of the collateral will be taken into account in the credit value adjustment risk.

If the level of the own funds owned by the credit institution is equal to the level of own funds requirement, the result of the formula will be 8%, as a result of dividing 100 by 12.5. Besides this minimum level of 8%, the prudential legislation on capital adequacy also imposes certain capital conservation buffers, the effects of an anticyclic period, or if the entity is of systemic importance. Added up to the maximum level, the three capital buffers will give an 8% additional level to the original level of the capital adequacy ratio. Thus, in the case of a credit institution of systemic importance, the minimum capital adequacy ratio will be 16%, which means that the relevant entity will own an own funds level at least twice as the own funds requirement.

The level of the leverage effect is determined by dividing the value of the tier 1 own funds of the credit institution by the average value of the global consolidated assets corresponding to the reporting period. The level of the leverage effect must not exceed 3%. In other words, by using the formula for determining the capital adequacy ratio we can indirectly obtain, in certain situations, a maximum leverage effect of 8 times instead of 30 times, which is the limit generally obtained by a credit institution by applying the leverage effect formula.

The lawmaker's efforts to discourage the credit institutions from developing business models based on/oriented predominantly on speculative/treasury activities in favor of credit business lines are limited/reduced by the possibility of reducing the total amount of exposure by moving positions between the two portfolios depending on the entity's interests. Because of this, the elements that can compose each portfolio need to be redefined in order to eliminate any possible confusion in interpreting the relevant legislation.

3 Literature Review

Although, during the 3 decennials that followed the Basel I Accord, various articles have been written about the capital standards, the specialized literature does not include any articles criticizing the relevance of the current minimum capital requirement, their limits, or covering the legal aspects of the non-correlation of relevant significant risks.

Also, there are materials elaborated by the Bank for International Settlements (BIS) and by the European Commission about the reasons, arguments and reasoning that led to the elaboration of the new Basel II global standards or to the current form of the fourth European legislative package on the capital adequacy requirement.

At the EU level, the Directive on capital requirements (2013/36/EU; CRD IV) and the Regulation on capital requirements (575/2013; CRR) have been issued, transposing the new Basel III global standards on bank capital. However, the level 2 measures referring to the own funds requirement of credit institutions have not been thought out yet.

Recently, the legal framework regarding the prudential requirements of the investment firms has been extended by issuing Directive 2019/2034 /EU and the Regulation No. 2019/2033.

On the issue of BASEL III / BASEL IV, several international financial institutions had elaborated materials on this topic of which we mention the following:

- Basel Committee on Banking Supervision. Minimum capital requirements for market risk *Bank for International Settlements January* 2019
- Caio Ferreira, Nigel Jenkinson, and Christopher Wilson. From Basel I to Basel III: Sequencing Implementation in Developing Economies. IMF Working Papers. June 2019
- Sebastian Schneider, Gerhard Schröck, Stefan Koch, Roland Schneider. Basel "IV": What's next for banks? Implications of intermediate results of new regulatory rules for European banks. McKinsey & Company. Global Risk Practice. April 2017.

4 Methodology

4.1 Limitations of the Capital Adequacy Model at the Credit Institutions Level

We are going to present the econometric demonstrations for some of the identified situations, and to propose the solutions for the remedial of such deficiencies.

4.2 Building the Database

In building the database (Barangă and Panait 2018), the specificity and features of the financial entities were taken into account since the value of the financial and prudential indicators vary greatly from one category of financial entities to another. To that effect, three databases were built, which included 150 findings in each database, among which the values of several economic and financial and prudential indicators of the credit institution in Romania, the investment firms in Romania, with fully authorized scope of business, and the investment firms who are only intermediaries.

If the value of an indicator relevant to a reporting date was unknown, it was determined statistically through a linear regression built based on the existing data so that later, when adding the indirectly determined value, the correlations existing between the original data set are not affected.

Based on this historical data, a scoring formula was determined—based on which a reference value can be determined (scoring) for each financial entity assessed within the analyzed category of entities. The best formula evaluated by the Kaiser-Meyer-Olkin Measure of Sampling Adequacy (KMO) evaluation can be used to build a rating system.

To determine the scoring formula, a set of economic and financial and prudential indicators were selected over a time span of at least 5 years. In choosing the time span, the aim was both to ensure the optimal time frame and to make sure that the analyzed prudential indicators are determined through the same procedures established based on the capital adequacy rules—all the indicators are assessed using the same methodology set forth by the capital adequacy legislation. These indicators are reported and included in the database on a biannual basis. Here are some of these indicators: capital adequacy ratio (CAR), liquidity coverage ratio (LCR), largest exposure registered (LER), leverage effect level (Lev), total asset value (TAV), Tier 1 own funds (T1OF), Tier 2 own funds (T2OF), total own funds (TOF), total income (TI), profit or loss (P&L).

Considering that the economic and financial statements are drafted on a biannual basis and the reports on capital adequacy are prepared on a quarterly basis, the data was selected for every six months (biannual) so as to be able to use both the economic and financial data, and the prudential data (the indicators established in the legislation on capital adequacy).

4.3 *Applied Methodology*

Based on the collected data (Barangă and Panait 2018), we made the Principal Component Analysis (PCA) method. Thus, the main elements of the formula are identified and, for each main element, the adjustment (weighting) factors.

One aim of the analysis of the main components is to determine a formula including only one indicator or two at the most, which reflect most of the information, whereas for the analysis of the probability of default of a financial institution applying the capital adequacy rules, this indicator should be the CAR (because it is the most important prudential indicator used in the prudential assessment on capital adequacy).

Also, in the scoring formula, the aim is to include, beside the CAR indicators, T1OF indicator because the level of this indicator shows the size of the financial resources available to such financial institution to cover, over a time span of only a few business days, any debt that could result from the settlement of the transactions made.

To determine the relevance of the data sample, the KMO test is used. For a minimum relevance, the value of this test should be at least 0.60 points. In the analysis of the main component, the following criteria were taken into account:

- Any formula identified to contain at least CAR and the T1OF, where the capital adequacy ratio is the main component—which is mostly reflected by information relevant to the analysed data;
- The identified formula should have reasoning from the prudential and economic points of view (depending on the type of data included in that formula);
- The level of the relevance test of the data sample used (KMO) should be as high as possible;
- The level of information included in the main factor (indicator) (CAR) and of the T1OF should be as high as possible.

Based on the criteria mentioned above, a series of simulations are made by eliminating one indicator at a time or/and later by adding another indicator, thus obtaining a set of PCA analyses on various combinations of the data categories, to determine the most relevant combination of indicators so that the minimum value of each combination exceeds 0.60 points. The highest value of the model ensuring the best relevance in terms of the information it is based on, will be chosen.

4.4 Results Obtained

Following the successive PCA analyses, statistically speaking, the best formula that was obtained is:

1. For credit institutions $= (0.884)*CAR + (0.986)*T1OF + (0.989)*TOF + (0.821)*P\&L + (0.839)*TAV + (0.923)*LER$ (2)

   because: it gives the best result in the KMO, i.e. the value of 0.843;

2. For investment firms with fully authorized scope of business $= (-0.464)*CAR + (0.878)*T1OF + (0.782)*P\&L + (0.937)*TI + (0.904)*TAV$ (3)

   because: it gives the best result in the KMO, i.e. the value of 0.785;

3. For investment firms with partly authorized scope of business (who are only intermediaries) = no statistically relevant formula could be identified. All the attempts ended in formulas where the value of the KMO test was below 0.60.\

Regarding the Credit Institutions. The statistical information regarding the formula identified for investment firms with fully authorized scope of business is shown in Tables 1 and 2.

According to the simulations, if we add or remove/replace the TOF, TAV or LER indicator with other indicators, the resulting equation will have a KMO test level slightly above the relevance threshold (0.60–0.65).

Table 1 KMO and Bartlett's test

Kaiser-Meyer-Olkin measure of sampling adequacy		0.843
Bartlett's test of sphericity	Approx. Chi-Square	869.517
	Df	15
	Sig	0.000

Source The authors' own analyses

Table 2 Extraction method: principal component analysis

	Initial eigenvalues		
	Total	% of variance	Cumulative %
CAR	4.960	82.671	82.671
T1OF	0.484	8.060	90.731
TOF	0.319	5.322	96.053
P&L	0.188	3.141	99.194
TAV	0.047	0.779	99.973
LER	0.002	0.027	100.000

Source The authors' own analyses

The following conclusions can be drawn from the structure of the formula:

- The business model of a credit institution depends on the amounts attracted (through deposits) for financing the main business lines. Because of that, in the formula we will find the following indicators grouped together: the TOF indicator (which includes T1OF and T2OF,), LER and TAV indicator;
- If we add or remove/replace the TOF, TAV or LER indicator with other indicators, the equation no longer has statistic relevance because it no longer has one of the characteristics of a credit institution's business plan, i.e. use the attracted resources in its current activity in a major proportion.

Regarding the Investment Firms with Fully Authorized Scope of Business. The statistical information regarding the formula identified for investment firms with fully authorized scope of business is shown in Tables 3 and 4.

Table 3 KMO and Bartlett's Test

KMO		0.785
Bartlett's test of sphericity	Approx. Chi-Square	463.897
	Df	10
	Sig	0.000

Source The authors' own analyses

Table 4 Extraction method: principal component analysis

	Initial eigenvalues		
	Total	% of Variance	Cumulative %
CAR	3.293	65.868	65.868
T1OF	.849	16.988	82.856
P&L	.528	10.558	93.414
TI	.185	3.692	97.106
TAV	.145	2.894	100.000

Source The authors' own analyses

From the construction of the identified formula it follows that the establishment of the Income and Expenditure Budget of an investment firm depends on the income gained from the trading activity on account/on the clients' account (TI) and from the individual portfolio management (TAV).

If we bring the TOF or LER indicator into the equation, we get an equation with a KMO level slightly below the relevance threshold (0.60) because the business model of investment firms does not include lending activities carried out predominantly from attracted resources. The lending activity is carried out by the investment firms only in view of increasing the exposure experienced by the client in various financial transactions (only for margin transactions where the company lends financial instruments or money to its clients in order to increase the exposure they experience in those financial transactions).

Regarding the Investment Firms with Partly Authorized Scope of Business. We believe that the impossibility of identifying a statistically relevant formula for investment firms with partly authorized scope of business is due to the structure of the business lines these entities may have in comparison with the structure of the business lines existing at the level of credit institutions. After a simple analysis of the two business line structures one can notice that they are significantly different from each other, both in terms of the number of business lines and in terms of the weights relevant to the income those business lines are able to bring to the total income.

4.5 Solution for the Remedial These Deficiencies

We propose the following solutions:

1. **Grouping of positions in the tradeable portfolio or in the bankable portfolio.** One of the weak points of the capital adequacy model is the possibility to reduce the total amount of exposures by moving positions from the tradeable portfolio into the bankable one. Because of this, the elements/positions that can compose each of the two portfolios without leaving room for any legislative interpretation need to be redefined.

Article 4, paragraph 1 of Regulation UE no. 575/2013 on prudential requirements for credit institutions and investment firms and amending Regulation (EU) No. 648/2012 stipulates the following under points 85 and 86:

- "positions held with trading intent means any of the following:

  (a) *proprietary positions and positions arising from client servicing and market making;*
  (b) *positions intended to be resold short term;*
  (c) *positions intended to benefit from actual or expected short-term price differences between buying and selling prices or from other price or interest rate variations;*

- trading book means all positions in financial instruments and commodities held by an institution either with trading intent, or in order to hedge positions held with trading intent;"

Positions that are not included in the tradeable portfolio are included in the bankable portfolio.

To avoid regulatory arbitrage in view of reducing the total amount of exposure, the splitting of positions between the two portfolios should not depend on the intention/purpose of holding and, implicitly, on how long such position is held as long as the exposures on financial instruments are assessed and reported, on a quarterly basis.

The splitting of elements/positions between the two portfolios should depend on whether they are tradeable or non-tradeable. In this respect, the tradeable portfolio should include all positions exposed to the market risks, i.e. all the financial instruments or commodities traded in various trading venues or that are easily tradeable. The rest of the exposures, the receivables deriving from credit operations, as well as any share, bond or fund unit in collective investment undertakings (CIUs) that is not listed in any trading venue or is not easily tradeable, should be included in the bankable portfolio.

Having regard to the above, we believe that the tradeable portfolio must include the following types of positions on financial assets/commodities:

- Financial instruments listed in one of the trading venues regulated by the applicable legislation regarding financial instrument markets;
- Easily tradeable financial assets/commodities.

The category of easily tradeable financial assets/commodities includes the following:

- Financial assets/commodities not listed in a trading venue, but for which there are firm quotations from independent operators/liquidity providers;
- Financial assets/commodities not listed in a trading venue, involving a significant level of bilateral transactions and which could implicitly lead to the formation of an indicative market price.

2. **Formula for determining the capital adequacy ratio**. Since this is a linear function, the various correlations that could appear between the various categories/types of risks are not taken into account. Because of this, the 8% level of the capital adequacy ratio is often not a critical level for the financial entity if the level of liquidity indicators is a good one. The explanation would be that, if the correlations between risks were taken into account, a financial entity with a capital adequacy ratio of 8% has in fact a higher level of prudential sdolvency.

Thus, there should have been a risks correlation matrix in the methodology for determining the own funds requirement for a certain category of risks, where for every risk in that category of risks a certain factor of correlation with the other risks in that particular category should be provided. This way, the determination of the own funds requirement for a certain category of risks would have equally taken into account the correlations existing between the various risks and, implicitly, a lower own funds requirement for such category of risks would have resulted (e.g.: the market risks category).

Also, such a correlation matrix can be used in order to consider the correlation factors between the various risk categories. (e.g.: The Solvency Directive).

3. **Assessment of operational risks**. The own funds requirement for operational risks can be determined by applying the basic indicator to the 3-years mean of the gross revenue indicator. The level of the basic indicator is 15% and has no mathematical relevance. It was decided subjectively after negotiations between BIS and the banking industry. If, for the credit institutions, the value of this basic indicator is 15%, for insurance companies it is 30%.

If we consider the size of the basic indicator applied to the two types of financial entities, it would follow that insurance companies have a much higher level of operational risks than credit institutions. If analysing the importance and role of entities in the real economy, the systemic risk of each category of entities, the relevance of the leverage effect/of the actuarial calculation for determining the premium, we acknowledge that capital requirements for operational risks should be at least equal.

4. **Assessment of the position risk**. The 8% requirement for the general position risk and the 8% requirement for the specific position risk are applied regardless of the volatility level or liquidity level of the equity. In the formula for determining the capital adequacy ratio, the own funds requirement for the position risk is subsequently multiplied by 12.5, resulting in a 200% exposure.

$$The\ exposure = 2{*}8\%{*}12,5 \tag{4}$$

This level of the exposure that relates to the own funds generates the idea that the issuers of the shares would become bankrupt between two reporting dates, i.e. in three months.

The credit risk for shares is determined by weighting the exposure on long-term shares by 100%. Considering that the 100% factor means that we start from an expected loss of 100%, it follows that both the loss in case of default and the probability of default are 100%. Meaning that these exposures are not guaranteed and the issuer is very likely to become bankrupt within a year. Seeing that the own funds requirement is calculated on a quarterly basis, it follows that it is unlikely that an issuer becomes bankrupt within three months, even if the shares it has issued are intended to be held on a long-term (included in the bankable portfolio).

Between the two types of risks that assess the same kind of exposure there should be a high correlation level. The reporting of the own fund requirement is due quarterly, even if the exposure is for different periods of time.

The price of shares is influenced by two categories of factors: the issuer's 'price sensitive' information and the factors pertaining to the microstructure of the market. Any category of factors affecting the price of shares and implicitly the amount of exposure on shares, exposure that will be affected regardless of whether it is intended to be held on the short-term, for speculative purposes, or on the long-term, when their assessment is conducted quarterly. Due to the quarterly reporting, the own funds requirement of the two risks will be strongly correlated.

The quarterly assessment/reporting periodicity abolishes the importance of splitting the portfolio of listed shares into tradeable portfolio and bankable portfolio. Thus, by quarterly assessment, the dynamics of exposures on listed shares, issued by the same issuer and included in both portfolios, is similar. It follows that the dynamics of the own funds requirement for the position risk and for the credit risk on listed shares issued by the same issuer is strongly correlated.

The listed debt securities are taken into account in the assessment of the position risk or of the credit risk, depending on the intention of holding them and, implicitly, on the type of portfolio they are included in. As far as the dynamics of the market price is concerned, the same observations as those made about equity are applicable in general. Considering the influence of the quarterly assessment/reporting, it follows that the own funds requirement for the debt securities listed and issued by the same issuer for the position risk and for the credit risk is similar.

The fund units in collective investment undertakings (CIUs) is taken into account for the position risk and the credit risk, depending on their holding intention and, implicitly, on which portfolio they will be included in. With the position risk, this type of exposure is weighted by 32%, regardless of whether they are listed or not; if they are issued by mutual funds or alternative investment funds, regardless of the type of fund determined by the portfolio structure. In other words, this weight is imposed arbitrarily, without taking into account the type and characteristics of the investment fund that issued them.

Moreover, if we apply a multiplication factor of 12.5 to the 32% weight, a 400% exposure will result, which will be taken into account in the calculation of the capital adequacy ratio. A 400% exposure means that four times more than the amount of the original exposure could be lost, which, in reality, is impossible. Such an exposure, four times than the original one, would make sense with highly risky derivative financial instruments. But not all the fund units issued by CIUs are not exposures on derivative financial instruments.

We believe that the weighting factor of exposures on fund units in CIUs should be significantly reduced and, at the same time, should be differentiated into several categories of fund units in CIUs, depending on the criteria differentiating between the investment funds that issued them. The fund units in CIUs have various risk levels, depending on the time and characteristics of the investment fund that issued them.

5 Conclusion

In the following, as a result of what we have shown above, we will present a series of proposals to improve the methodology for determining the capital adequacy ratio, as well as a series of useful aspects in view of a better applicability of this risk management model even to the investment firms with fully authorized scope of business.

We believe that there should be a simplification of the limitation mechanisms of the speculative/treasury activities existing in the capital adequacy model, which are intended to orient the credit institutions towards lending activities. To improve the capital adequacy model, we propose a series of modifications, namely:

1. **Redefining the elements/positions that could be included in the structure of the tradeable portfolio or of the bankable portfolio**. Thus, to avoid regulatory arbitrage in view of reducing the total amount of exposures, the splitting of the positions held by a credit institution between the two portfolios should not depend on the intention/purpose of holding and, implicitly, on how long such position is held, but on the position/exposure type, as well as on whether they are tradeable or non-tradeable.

In this respect, the tradeable portfolio should include all positions exposed to the market risks, i.e. all the positions on financial instruments or commodities traded in various trading venues or that are easily tradeable. The rest of the positions/exposures that have not been included in the tradeable portfolio will be included in the bankable portfolio.

As a result of this change, the credit institutions will no longer be allowed to perform regulatory arbitrage with a view to obtaining a lower risk exposure amount and, implicitly, a better value of the capital adequacy ratio.

2. **Establishing new weighting factors for the fund units in CIUs included in the tradeable portfolio**. Furthermore, still as an effect of redefining the elements/positions forming the structure of the two portfolios (tradeable and bankable), new weighting factors for the fund units in CIUs could be established depending on the risk level of the investment fund that issued such fund units.

3. **Using the risks correlation matrix**. In determining the own funds requirement, we believe that it is necessary to use some correlation matrixes between the various risk types/categories in order to also take into account these factors occurring between the various types/categories of risks.

4. **Reanalysing the level of the basic indicator used in determining the own funds for the operational risk**. The Fintech has a significant impact on the level of operational risks caused by the IT systems and, implicitly, determines its increase.

By redefining the structure of the two portfolios and through the other measures presented above, the capital adequacy model will be more adapted to the characteristics of the business model of investment firms with fully authorized scope of business. Also, we believe that the current formula for capital adequacy ratio is not applicable to a very large extent to this category of financial entities because of the limitation of the speculative/treasury activities existing at the model level.

Also, so that the 'modified' model for determining the capital adequacy ratio be even more applicable to the business models of this category of financial entities, the additional own funds requirement need to cease being applied based on the level of the requirement applicable for exposures exceeding the 25% limit of exposures on trading book. Considering the structure of the income these financial entities can gain, the potential additional high own funds requirement for these exposures exceeding would only lead to serious constraints in terms of the size of positions held on their own account, seeing that these investment firms will not be able to rely, in an overwhelming proportion, on the income from interests gained as a result of granting lows to clients in margin transactions.

The main conclusion based on the econometric analysis, namely that the methodology of capital adequacy for investment firms must be differentiated from that applicable to credit institutions, is also supported by the recent direction of action of the European Commission to segregate the two methodologies by types of entities. The two legislative acts (*Directive EU 2019/2034* and *Regulation EU 2019/2033)* regarding the capital adequacy, elaborated separately for the investment firms, will enter into force in 2021.

References

Barangă, L.P., Panait, I.: Estimating the credit risk score for nonbank stock exchange intermediaries in the eventuality of changeover to euro currency. Fin. Stud. **22**(4), 25–40 (2018)

Basel Committee on Banking Supervision. Minimum capital requirements for market risk Bank for International Settlements January 2019

Ferreira, C., Jenkinson, N.; Wilson, C.: From Basel I to Basel III: Sequencing Implementation in Developing Economies. International Monetary Fund Working Papers. June 2019

Schneider, S., Schröck, G., Koch, S., Schneider, R.: Basel "IV": What's next for banks? Implications of intermediate results of new regulatory rules for European banks. McKinsey & Company. Global Risk Practice. April 2017

The European Parliament and the Council. Directive 2013/36/EU on access to the activity of credit institutions and the prudential supervision of credit institutions and investment firms, amending Directive 2002/87/EC and repealing Directives 2006/48/EC and 2006/49/EC

The European Parliament and the Council. Directive 2019/2034 /EU on the prudential supervision of investment firms and amending Directives 2002/87/EC, 2009/65/EC, 2011/61/EU, 2013/36/EU, 2014/59/EU and 2014/65/EU

The European Parliament and the Council. Regulation No. 575/2013 on the prudential requirements for credit institutions and investment firms and amending Regulation (EU) No 648/2012

The European Parliament and the Council. Regulation No. 2019/2033 on the prudential requirements of investment firms and amending Regulations (EU) No 1093/2010, (EU) No 575/2013, (EU) No 600/2014 and (EU) No 806/2014

Mission Statements in Top Higher Education Institutions—What Do They Have in Common?

Luminița Nicolescu and Gandolfo Dominici

1 Introduction

Universities started to play a crucial role in the social and economic life, as in the knowledge economy they contribute highly with the scientific, technological and economic knowledge they produce to the development of businesses and of the society as a whole. It is acknowledged that "higher education is facing un-precedent challenges in defining its role in society and in the economy" (OECD 2012) as universities have to perform for both internal stakeholders (Genc 2012; Nicolescu 2011), as well as for external stakeholders, by participating to the improvement of different categories of services at society level (Lopez and Martin 2018; Androniceanu et al. 2020).

In such a context, universities started to use business like practices, so that to be able to adjust their management to the new challenges posed by the environment. This involves the internalization of strategic planning principles and activities at university level, that also involves the design of missions and their written form, mission statements.

The paper aims to provide a thematic oriented understanding of the missions of top universities in the world according to the content of their mission statements.

L. Nicolescu (✉)
Bucharest University of Economic Studies, Piața Romană 6-8, Bucharest, Romania
e-mail: luminicolescu@yahoo.com

G. Dominici
Polytechnic School, University of Palermo, Piazza Marina, 61, 90133 Palermo, Italy

A. M. Dima and F. DÁscenzo (eds.), *Business Revolution in a Digital Era*,
Springer Proceedings in Business and Economics,
https://doi.org/10.1007/978-3-030-59972-0_12

2 Mission Statements in the Literature

Mission statements have been defined in different ways in the literature. Ellis and Miller (2014) consider that the mission statement in an institution represents the purpose of being and even the identity of the institution. At the same time, Lopez and Martin (2018) see mission statements as providing purpose and strategic direction for a company, as well as providing public image. Some authors make the distinction between mission and vision, indicating that the mission statements is about "here and now", while the vision is about the unknown future (Abelman 2014; Ozdem 2011). Both are relevant to present the key areas and directions of development of organizations.

Missions are usually associated with businesses and the private sector. The literature recognizes that mission statements are a core element in the strategic management (Lopez and Martin 2018) as they represent one of the most common management tools (Ellis and Miller 2014). Mission statements represent the foundation for developing institutional strategies (Gordan and Pop 2013), the starting point for every major strategic initiative (Bart et al. 2001; Lopez and Martin 2018) and have the function to guide the entire process of strategic planning (Ozdem 2011). At the same time mission statements are seen as the backbone tool in strategic planning (Cortes-Sanchez 2018) and as laying the foundation for future actions and philosophies that underline those actions (Velasquez et al. 2006).

Generally speaking, mission statements are seen to fulfil few main purposes: (a) inspiring and motivating employees to obtain high levels of performances; (b) guiding the resource allocation in the organization in a unitary manner; (c) creating a balance between the interests of different stakeholders in the organization; (d) providing a sense of direction and a system of values to follow (Campbell 1992; Ellis and Miller 2014). Others see mission statements' role to as being to reveal the identity of the institution (Kosmutzky 2012) and to communicate its unique features and how it differentiates itself from others (Morphew and Hartley 2006).

In higher education missions started to be formulated at the level of 1980s (Wang et al. 2007) and they have developed ever since, so that at present most higher education institutions have formulated mission statements (Hladchenko 2013; Frondizi et al. 2019) as mission statements have been adopted as a strategic planning instrument for universities worldwide (Cortes-Sanchez 2018: 597). The two main reasons favoring this development are: (a) first, the general economic and societal conditions in the last decades (privatization, diminishing public financing, commercialization, marketization, globalization, internationalization) (OECD 2012) that triggered the need for universities to become more entrepreneurial (Clark 2004), more business oriented and to use business specific instruments and methods such as strategic planning, strategic management, total quality management (Ozdem 2011; Cortes-Sanchez 2018; Dedousis 2018) and (b) in many countries and regions in the world, higher education quality assurance became a common practice. In this context most of the national and international accreditation institutions include among their quality standards the requirement for the universities to use strategic planning and to develop institutional missions and strategies. This is the case in most countries and regions as exemplified by authors in Italy (Frondizi et al. 2019), Turkey (Ozdem 2011; Genc 2012), United Arab Emirates (Dedousis 2018), Romania (Nicolescu 2010, 2014), in Ghana (Ganu 2013), in other European countries (Lopez and Martin 2018; Hladchenko 2013), in US (Wang et al. 2007) and in BRIC countries (David 2018).

Mission statements in educational institutions are seen by some researchers as being broad (Dickeson 2010), while others notice a shift of mission statements to more utilitarian focuses (Ellis and Miller 2014). There are authors that consider that mission statements in case of higher education institutions lose their usefulness (Gordan and Pop 2013) as many universities build similar mission statements that fail to identify the particular strengths of an institution and differentiate it from others (Kosmutzky 2012). The fact that mission statements in higher education rather convey an overall image of sameness instead of distinctiveness is also acknowledged by Cortes-Sanchez (2018). However, other researchers found that mission statements allow universities to differentiate and position themselves differently for specific niches they serve (Kosmutzky and Krucken 2015) and that there are significant differences in the rhetoric of mission statements according to institutional culture, but also the environment in which they operate (Abelman 2014). For example, Dedousis (2018) illustrates how differentiation purposes are followed by business schools in UAE.

In this context, the present research looks at the top universities at world level and the way how they identify and differentiates themselves.

3 Methodology

The purpose of the present research is twofold: (a) to identify the main topics included in the recent mission statements of the best universities at world level and (b) to analyze the similarities and the differences between the main directions included in mission statements by the best universities in the world. The hypothesis is that there are more similarities than differences in the mission statements of the top universities in the world. The study looks at the mission statements and universities' strategies for the top 150 higher education institutions at world level, according to rankings.

There were used three prestigious international rankings for the selection of the top 150 higher education institutions at world level, respectively Top Shanghai (2018), QS World University Rankings (2018) and Times Higher Education World University Rankings (2019). These rankings use different methodologies, but studies (Shehatta and Mahmood 2016) found that there is a moderate up to a high correlation between them, resulting that they have more or less consistent results.

The selection method used was based on the following principles: (a) the lowest common denominator in the sense that were selected those universities that were present at the same time in all three university rankings considered and (b) most of the universities considered are part of the rankings in the socio-economic field: economics, management, business administration. Based on these criteria a list of the

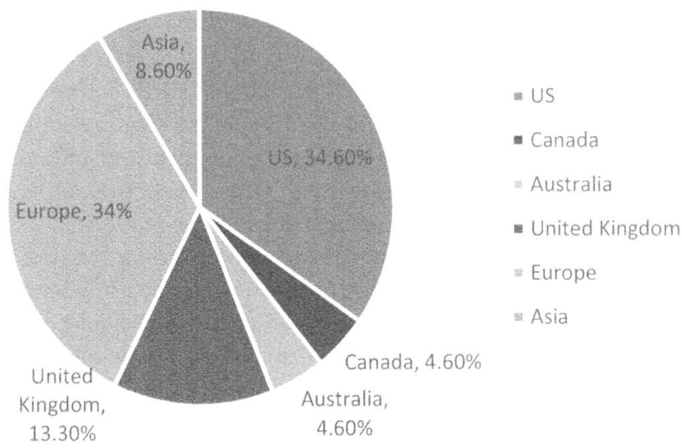

Fig. 1 Top 150 universities' origin

first 150 ranked universities was made and data was collected from these institutions. Appendix 1 includes the list with the top 150 universities included in the study.

Data collection was based exclusively on the information published by universities on their web sites. The web site search envisaged to find information and documents referring to the institution's strategy (strategies, visions, missions, values, strategic objectives, strategic plans, management plans, periodical university management reports). Out of those, for the present paper the analysis was conducted on mission statements and visions published by universities on their web sites. Figure 1 presents the structure of the top 150 universities at world level according to country/region of origin.

The country with the largest number of universities in top 150 is United States (34%) followed by United Kingdom that accounts for 13.3% of the top 150 universities. However as regions, Europe (Europe including UK) holds the largest number of the top 150 universities, respectively 71 universities representing 47.3%, while North America (US and Canada) is the following region with 59 universities representing 39.2% of the total 150 top universities. In Europe, the countries that have universities included in the top 150 universities as part of this study are: United Kingdom (20), Germany (13), Holland (7), Switzerland (6), France (6), Spain (5), Italy (5), Sweden (4), Denmark (3), Norway (1), Austria (1).

Table 1 illustrates the structure of the top 150 universities on countries/regions of origin.

Only 70% of the universities made public on their web sites full strategies, strategic plans and strategic directions. However, in spite of the differences in the level of public availability of full strategic documents, all universities had their missions (or/and visions) public on their web sites.

Table 1 Top 150 higher education institutions

Countries	Universities	
	Number	Percentage (%)
US	52	34.6
Canada	7	4.6
Australia	7	4.6
United Kingdom	20	13.3
Europe (without UK)	51	34
Asia	13	8.6
Total	150	100

Source Authors' own research

Using this methodology, the present paper conducts a qualitative content analysis of the mission statements of the 150 universities with the purposes to identify the main topics and directions stated in their mission statements by the best universities in the world and to compare those.

4 Results and Discussion

4.1 Mission Statements of the Top 150 Universities—Main Ideas

An analysis structured on regions of provenience of the universities, illustrates that in US, universities even though do not make public their strategies, they all offer information on their visions and/or their missions and some of them include also information related to guiding values.

A synthesis of the information included in missions and visions of the most US universities from the top 150 (as presented on their web sites) includes the following aspects: offering excellent education, research and services; attracting excellent teachers, personnel and students; sharing knowledge through education for a diverse community; applying knowledge for the benefit of the nation and of the whole world; educating leader citizens for the society; creating knowledge and educating students in science, technology and other fields that will serve better the nation and the whole world in the 21 century; creating a distinct learning environment so that to create knowledge and disseminate results; creating innovative platforms for learning, teaching and research and inventing new ways of thinking and creating new knowledge to be disseminated globally via an extensive relational platform, so that the humanity's challenges to be addressed; becoming a world top center of education, science and research; improving the today's world and the world of the next generations through research, science, education and practice.

Table 2 Key topics in mission statements

Key topics	Frequency of appearance	Percentage (%)
Excellence	102	68
Leader/top	81	54
Education/learning/teaching/ students	150	100
Research	131	87.3
Innovation/technology	75	50
Knowledge	109	72.6
Services	78	52
Sharing/disseminating	76	50.6
Local community	21	14
Nation/society	103	68.6
International/Global/World	118	78.6
Transformation/discovery/exploration	46	30.6
Values development (trust, responsibility, creativity, sustainability)	44	29.3
Work force formation/employability	57	38

Source Authors' own research

Table 2 presents the statistics of the recurring terms and topics in the mission statements of the top world universities in the period of study. Figure 2 presents the most recurring terms and topics in ascending order according to the frequency of appearance. There are common features of the missions statements of US universities and they refer to excellence, innovation, knowledge, global and world community.

Many of the mission statements were very explanatory in presenting the universities' roles and goals. For instance, Harvard University has as mission: educating citizens and leader citizens for society by engaging in education in exact sciences and in liberal arts that will have a profound transformation power. At the same time, the vision of this university is to set standards for the residential education in sciences and liberal arts for the 21st century. Harvard University is willing to create and support the conditions that will allow students to embark on an educational journey that will transform individuals from the intellectual, social and personal perspectives.

At the same time, Stanford University includes three missions on its web site, corresponding to the three envisages goals and planned commitments: (a) the research mission: to expand the knowledge frontiers; (b) the education mission: to train students to think broadly, profoundly and critically so that to contribute to the world's development and (c) the services mission: to spread the strength of the Stanford university towards the society at the regional, country and world level.

In Canada, for instance Queen's University defines its mission through two central activities: learning and discovery. The university wants the two activities to mutually complete each other, it is a university that defines itself as being centered both on

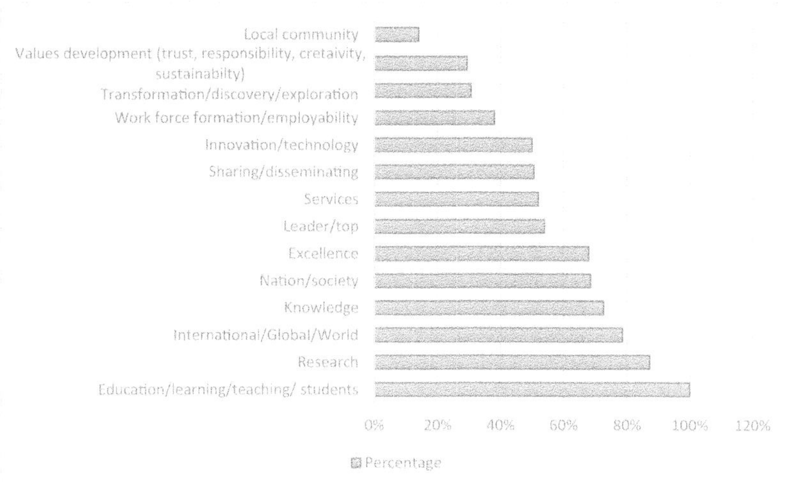

Fig. 2 Key topics in mission statements (ascending order)

student and on research. It wants to offer students an exceptional learning experience both from educational and from extra-curricular point of view.

In Europe, a large part of the universities from top 150 are from UK. Therefore, university missions for UK universities, but also missions from other European universities are exemplified. The Oxford University from United Kingdom has the mission to promote learning through teaching and research and through dissemination by all means. The vision of the university is to unify its staff, students, alumni, colleges, faculties, departments and divisions to provide research and education at top world level. Another university in UK, the Queen Mary University of London defines as its mission promoting social justice and overcoming the borders of previous thinking. The fulfilment of this mission depends on the freedom of academic staff and students to develop and share knowledge in the context of promoting an open, transparent, educated and tolerant society.

Common institutional values presented by UK universities are excellence, academic freedom, integrity, communication, inclusion, innovation, global perspective, responsibility, sustainability, diversity, trust, respect.

Universities in other European countries, also presented publicly their missions and the following examples illustrate some of the main goals of European universities with a focus on those operating in the economic field. Barcelona Graduate School of Economics has as declared mission: the training of future generations of economists and scientists by offering programs at top world level, where the teachers are leaders in their fields. Similarly, Copenhagen Business School (BCS), sees as its mission the responsibility to bring knowledge and new ways of thinking in companies and organizations, for the new generations of business leaders and for the society in its integrity. The vision of CBS is to become a business leading university at world level.

Stockholm School of Economics (SSE) has a more nationally centered mission: through teaching and research the SSE wishes to consolidate Sweden's competitiveness. The vision of SSE is to position itself as one top European business school and to be recognized world-wide as a standard for the collaboration with the industry and for top thinking in certain fields of knowledge. On the other hand, the Norwegian School of Economics has a more internationally oriented mission, as its mission is to be a leader in the development and dissemination of knowledge and expertise at international level. The school wishes to become a vector for the business and society development and to educate people in the spirit of value creation and durable development.

Among the Asian universities, the Tokyo University declared as its vision: the synergy between excellence and diversity with the university acting as a global base for collaboration and knowledge. The University of Hong Kong declared as its mission to create opportunities for the best academic talents to excel and develop human knowledge for the benefit of the society.

The following section envisages to identify similarities and differences between the mission statements of the top higher education institutions in the world.

4.2 Commonalities and Differences in the Mission Statements of the Top 150 Universities

The content analysis of the mission statements, visions and values in all 150 top universities depicts broad similarities among those.

As the qualitative content analysis was structured on the following directions: institutional positioning, activities conducted and services offered, specific aspects and more in depth emphasis related to each activity and geographical scope, the main similarities and differences identified are presented in the following section.

Similarities between the mission statements of the top 150 universities in the world include:

(a) In terms of university positioning, the most common denominator for the mission statements of all top 150 universities from all over the world remains excellence (68%), followed by leadership (54%), illustrating therefore a similarity between institutions.

(b) Regarding the types of services/activities included, all studied higher education institutions included in their mission statements education related topics and the purpose of offering teaching and learning to students. The second university mission (Scott 2006), respectively research was also specifically (by word identification) mentioned by the majority of the universities (87.3%), while some universities referred to innovation and technology (50%) that are also rather research related orientations (Ellis and Miller 2014). The third mission (Scott 2006), the services were specifically included in their mission statements by only 52% of the universities. However, this is a rather narrow and word-related interpretation, as the third mission, seen as the way in which know-how is produced and spread at the level of society (Frondizi et al. 2019), could be interpreted as being present in all those missions that made reference to community and society (78% in total). Frondizi et al. (2019) point that universities need to contribute to the local socio-economic development along teaching and research and this is seen as the third mission of the university that also ensures the shift towards the entrepreneurial university. Similarly, David (2018) sees the third mission of the university to contribute to educational and social progress in a broader sense than the new knowledge production.

It can be stated as a common element that most of the universities included all three missions of a higher education institutions (education, research and services) as presented by the literature (Frondizi et al. 2019; Scott 2006; Hladchenko 2013) and some included what is seen as being the fourth role of universities (Ozdem 2011), namely to develop a qualified work force.

(c) Another rather common element refers to inclusion of the word knowledge in the mission statements (72.6%), this being related with all three universities' activities: knowledge in education (creating and disseminating it to students), knowledge in research (creating it and disseminating it to the research community), knowledge in services (disseminating it to society). This is in line with the role of knowledge broker (Vătămănescu et al. 2018) and knowledge spreader that the academic environment is perceived to have in the knowledge economy (Frunzaru et al. 2018; Burlacu 2011) in which knowledge intensive activities and services are promoters of modernization at regional and societal level (Bușu and Bușu 2017).

(d) It can be observed as another commonality that all universities addressed in their mission statements multiple stakeholders (even though some different from one university to another): students, staff, researchers, communities, as also illustrated by Lopez and Martin (2018).

Differences in the content of the mission statements of the top 150 universities in the world include:

(a) In terms of in-depths and /or specific themes included in the mission statements, there are some differences, as some universities focused on sharing and dissemination (50.6%), others emphasized cutting edge discovery, transformation and exploration (30.6%), while others point out the contribution of the university to the development of a system of values (29.3%). Also, another area specifically included by some of these universities (38%) refers to their role in the developing of the work force and ensuring the employability of their graduates, as one main concern of higher education institutions in general (Nicolescu and Nicolescu 2019; Butum and Nicolescu 2019).

(b) Another difference consists of the geographical broadness specifically included in the mission statements: a part of the top universities (68.6%) defined their scope at national community/society level, while most of the top universities considered that their mission is to educate, research and service for the benefit of the whole world, as the international, global and world level terms and themes have been encountered at 78.6% of the top universities. There was even a limited number of universities (14%) that localized their mission at the level of local community. However, many of the studied universities located their missions at all three geographical levels (50%). Internationalization in higher education is one important development direction for the whole sector (Dima and Vasilache 2016; Butum 2017) and this is reflected in the missions of the best at world level.

Mission statements of top world universities were characterized by both similarities and differences, with the element of commonality illustrating rather a convergence tendency as also reported by other studies (Behm and Berthold 2011) with many reoccurring themes Wang et al. (2007) and similar popular commitments (Hladchenko 2013). However, in spite of the overall similar themes included in their mission statements, top higher education institutions illustrate distinctiveness and differentiation in the way they combine the main themes and in the way they detail these main themes in their mission statements. Higher education insitutions' mission statements are influenced by the external environemnt in which they operate as also presented by Wang et al. (2007), who consider that societal changes, constituencies and geograhical location have a say in the formulation of mission statements of universities in US.

5 Conclusions

The results of the research illustrate that mission statements are used by top higher education institutions to identify themselves and to create an institutional image in the eyes of general public and stakeholders. A certain tendency of isomorphism was also encountered in the present research, as on overall the content of the mission statements included many similar themes. Almost all of the studied institutions made reference to excellence in their positioning and to the three university missions (education, research and public services). However, in spite of the similar themes, a number of differentiating directions were observed. Differentiation came from the way universities have combined and detailed some of the aspects included in the mission statements, as many mission statements were long and offered explanatory details of the major directions they include. Even though many common themes were prevalent (given the specificity of the activity of a higher education institution in general), the emphases of various universities followed different directions. All started from the triple helix, teaching-research-servicing, but some focused more on teaching, some focused more on research, the community servicing being complementary in most of them. Also differentiation came from the geographical scope of their missions, with some institutions declaring a role at all local, national and international levels, while others see their role only at one or two of those levels (international and national or national and local).

The contributions of the present paper stand in: (a) a literature contribution given by the study approach: its transnational character, as opposed to many other studies on the topic that had a national focus and (b) a practical contribution: being focused on the top universities at world level, the present study provides examples of good practice in the strategic planning and mission statement design. The implications of the study can therefore, be related to individual higher education institutions and how they can organize their strategic process. Similarly, higher education institutions around the world can find inspiration for their educational and scientific activities in what the best universities in the world do, without using mimetic approaches, but adapting to their local conditions.

One limitation of the study is that it focuses on only the first 150 top universities in the world and in this context, future research can extend to an even larger number of universities and compare mission statements of universities that are part of different groups in international rankings. Also future research can also comprise the study of universities' strategies by continuing to a more in-depth level the analysis of the strategic management process and its results in the higher education environment.

Acknowledgement This paper benefited of financial support from the ASE institutional project "The Documentation and the Elaboration of the Strategy of the Bucharest University of Economic Studies for 2020–2030", 2018–2019.

Appendix 1

Top 150 higher education institutions, 2018–2019 (3 simultaneous rankings).

No.	Higher education institution	No.	Higher education institution
1	Harvard University	24	University of Toronto
2	University of Chicago	25	Arizona State University
3	University of California, Berkeley	26	National University of Singapore
4	Massachusetts Institute of Technology (MIT)	27	University of Wisconsin - Madison
5	Columbia University	28	Indiana University Bloomington
6	Princeton University	29	University of Warwick
7	Stanford University	30	George Mason University
8	London School of Economics and Political Science	31	Carnegie Mellon University
9	New York University	32	Bocconi University
10	Yale University	33	Washington University in St. Louis
11	Northwestern University	34	Boston University
12	University of Cambridge	35	University of Bonn
13	University of California, Los Angeles	36	Erasmus University Rotterdam
14	University of Pennsylvania	37	University of British Columbia
15	University of Oxford	38	Tilburg University
16	University of California, San Diego	39	University of Zurich
17	Toulouse School of Economics	40	VU University Amsterdam

(continued)

(continued)

No.	Higher education institution	No.	Higher education institution
18	University of Maryland, College Park	41	The University of Melbourne
19	University of Michigan-Ann Arbor	42	Monash University
20	Duke University	43	Aarhus University
21	University of Minnesota, Twin Cities	44	University of Southern California
22	University College London	45	KU Leuven
23	Cornell University	46	University of California, Davis
47	University of Oslo	75	University of Washington
48	The Australian National University	76	Autonomous University of Barcelona
49	University of Toulouse 1	77	Boston College
50	The University of Texas at Austin	78	California Institute of Technology
51	Barcelona Graduate School of Economics	79	Carlos III University of Madrid
52	Brown University	80	Charles University in Prague
53	Dartmouth College	81	Georgetown University
54	Johns Hopkins University	82	Imperial College London
55	Maastricht University	83	Lund University
56	Pennsylvania State University - University Park	84	Michigan State University
57	Pompeu Fabra University	85	Peking University
58	Stockholm University	86	Purdue University - West Lafayette
59	Swiss Federal Institute of Technology Zurich	87	Tel Aviv University
60	The Hebrew University of Jerusalem	88	Texas A&M University
61	The Ohio State University - Columbus	89	The Hong Kong University of Science
62	The University of Manchester	90	The University of Queensland
63	The University of New South Wales	91	Tsinghua University
64	University of Amsterdam	92	University of Bologna
65	University of California, Santa Barbara	93	University of California, Irvine
66	University of Copenhagen	94	University of Cologne
67	University of Groningen	95	University of Essex
68	University of Illinois at Urbana-Champaign	96	University of Gothenburg
69	University of Mannheim	97	University of Sussex
70	University of Montreal	98	University of Virginia
71	University of Munich	99	University of York

(continued)

(continued)

No.	Higher education institution	No.	Higher education institution
72	University of North Carolina at Chapel Hill	100	Utrecht University
73	University of Nottingham	101	Aix Marseille University
74	University of Sydney	102	Catholic University of Louvain
103	Central University of Finance and Economics	127	The University of Tokyo
104	City University London	128	Tufts University
105	Copenhagen Business School	129	Université Libre de Bruxelles (ULB)
106	European University Institute	130	University of Barcelona
107	Georgia Institute of Technology	131	University of Bristol
108	Georgia State University	132	University of Colorado at Boulder
109	London Business School	133	University of East Anglia
110	McGill University	134	University of Florida
111	Pantheon-Sorbonne University (Paris 1)	135	University of Frankfurt
112	Paris Institute of Political Studies	136	University of Goettingen
113	Renmin University of China	137	University of Lausanne
114	Rutgers, St. Univ. New Jersey - New Brunswick	138	University of Leeds
115	Sapienza University of Rome	139	University of Notre Dame
116	Seoul National University	140	University of Rochester
117	Shanghai University of Finance and Economics	141	University of Southampton
118	Simon Fraser University	142	University of Southern Denmark
119	Singapore Management University	143	University of St.Gallen
120	Stockholm School of Economics	144	University of Technology Sydney
121	The Chinese University of Hong Kong	145	University of Vienna
122	The George Washington University	146	University of Wageningen
123	The University of Edinburgh	147	Uppsala University
124	The University of Glasgow	148	Vanderbilt University
125	The University of Hong Kong	149	Western University
126	The University of Sheffield	150	Xiamen University

References

Abelman, R.: Reviewing and revising the institutional vision of U.S. higher education. Rev. Commun. Res. **2**(1), 31–67 (2014)

Androniceanu, A., Sabie, O.M., Pegulescu, A.: An integrated approach of the human resources motivation and the quality of health services. Theor. Empirical Res. Urban Manage. **15**(1), 42–53 (2020)

Bart, C.K., Bontis, N., Taggar, S.: A model of the impact of mission statements on firm performance. Manag. Decis. **39**, 19–35 (2001)

Behm, B., Berthold, C.: Developing strategies for higher education institution and its faculties/departments. In: Bergan, S., Egron-Polak, E., Kohler, J., Purser, L., Vukasovic, M. (eds.) Leadership and Governance in Higher Education- Handbook for Decision Makers and Administrators, vol. 1 (2011)

Burlacu, S.: Characteristics of Knowledge-Based Economy and New Technologies in Education. Administrație și Management Public **16**, 114-119 (2011)

Bușu, C., Bușu, M.: The role of knowledge intensive business services on Romania's economic revival and modernization at the regional level. Sustainability **9**(4), 526 (2017)

Butum, L.: The importance of international experience for Romanian students in establishing career priorities. Management & Marketing. Challenges Knowl. Soc. **12**(1), 155–170 (2017)

Butum, L., Nicolescu, L.: Learn and work in the 21th century. A review of employability models for HE graduates: different levels of analysis. Manage. Dyn. Knowl. Econ. **7**(1), 71–86 (2019)

Campbell, A.: The Power of Mission: Aligning strategy and culture. Plann. Rev. **20**(5), 10–20 (1992)

Clark, B.R.: Sustaining Change in Universities. Continuities in Case Studies and Concepts. Society for Research into Higher Education. Open University Press, London (2004)

Cortes-Sanchez, J.D.: Mission statements of universities worldwide- Text mining and visualization. Intangible Capital **14**(4), 584–603 (2018)

David, S.A.: The relationship between the third mission and the university ranking: exploring the outreach of the top ranked universities in BRIC countries (2018). Available at https://www.researchgate.net/publication/336412656_The_relationship_between_the_third_mission_and_university_ranking_exploring_the_outreach_of_the_top_ranked_universities_in_BRICS_countries. Last accessed 23 Feb 2020

Dedousis, E.: An analysis of mission statements tertiary institutions: business colleges in UAE. e-J. Bus. Educ. Scholarship Teach. **12**(1), 31–51 (2018)

Dickeson, R.C.: Prioritizing Academic Programs and Services: Reallocating Resources to Achieve Strategic Balance. Jossey-Bass, London (2010)

Dima, M.A.; Vasilache, S.: Trends in the internationalization of European higher education in a convergence perspective. Management & Marketing. Challenges Knowl. Soc. **11**(2), 449–457 (2016)

Ellis, J., Miller, P.: Providing higher education in post-modern times: what do university mission statements tell us about what they believe and do? Res. Comp. Int. Educ. **9**(1), 83–91 (2014)

Frondizi, R., Fantauzzi, C., Colasanti, N., Fiorani, G.: The evaluation of universities' third mission and intellectual capital: theoretical analysis and application to Italy. Sustainability **11**, 3455 (2019)

Frunzaru, V., Vătămănescu, E.M., Gazzola, P., Bolisani, E.: Challenges to higher education in the knowledge economy: Anti-intellectualism, materialism and employability. Knowl. Manage. Res. Pract. **16**(3), 388–401 (2018)

Ganu, J.: Institutional mission statements and attitudinal outcomes of selected faith –based tertiary institutions in Ghana. J. Appl. Bus. Econ. **14**(2), 20–30 (2013)

Genc, K.Y.: The relation between the quality of the mission statements and the performances of the state universities in Turkey. Proc.-Soc. Behav. Sci. **58**, 19–28 (2012)

Gordan, C., Pop, M.: Mission statements in higher education: context analysis and research agenda. Ann. Faculty Econ. Univ. Oradea **1**(2), 653–663 (2013)

Hladchenko, M.: Mission Statement—a component of the strategic management of university. New Educ. Rev. **31**(1), 229–240 (2013). https://www.researchgate.net/publication/298160464_

Mission_statement_-_A_component_of_the_strategic_management_of_university_on_the_example_of_German_universities. Last accessed 15 Feb 2020

Kosmutzky, A.: Between mission and market position: empirical findings on mission statements of German higher education institutions. Tert. Educ. Manag. **18**(1), 55–77 (2012)

Kosmutzky, A., Krucken, G.: Sameness and difference: analyzing institutional and organizational specificities of universities through mission statements. Int. Stud. Manage. Organ. **45**(2), 137–149 (2015)

Lopez, Y.P., Martin, W.: University mission statements and sustainable performance. Bus. Soc. Rev. **123**(2), 341–368 (2018)

Morphew, C.C., Hartley, M.: Mission statements: a thematic analysis of rhetoric across institutional type. J. Higher Educ. **77**(3), 456–471 (2006)

Nicolescu, L.: Governance in higher education: theories and practices applied in metallurgical industry. Metalurgia International **XV**(1), 201–205 (2010)

Nicolescu, L.: Student experience in Romanian higher education—a comparative institutional approach. Transform Bus. Econ. **10**, 2B (23B), 664–684 (2011)

Nicolescu, L.: Convergence and internationalization of higher education in Europe: The Case of Romania. In: Dima, A.M. (Ed.) Handbook of Research and Trends in European Higher Education Convergence, pp. 219–240, IGI Global (2014)

Nicolescu, L., Nicolescu, C.: Using PLS-SEM to build an employability confidence model for higher education recipients in the field of business studies. Kybernetes **48**(9), 1965–1988 (2019)

OECD and European Commission. A Guiding Framework for Entrepreneurial Universities. Paris (2012)

Ozdem, G.: An analysis of the mission and vision statements on the strategic plans of higher education institutions. Educ. Sci.: Theory Pract. **11**(4), 1887–1894 (2011)

Scott, J.: The mission of the university: medieval to postmodern transformation. J. Higher Educ. **77**(1), 1–39 (2006)

Shehatta, I., Mahmood, K.: Correlation among top 100 universities in the major six global rankings: Policy implications. Scientometrics **109**(2), 1231–1254 (2016)

Vătămănescu, E.M., Andrei, A.G., Gazzola, P., Dominici, G.: Online academic networks as knowledge brokers: the mediating role organizational support. Systems **6**(2), 11 (2018)

Velasquez, L., Munguia, N., Platt, A., Taddei, J.: Sustainable university: What can be the matter? J. Clean. Prod. **14**, 810–819 (2006)

Wang, J., Gibson, A.M., Salinas, L., Solis, F., Slate, J.R.: Thematic differences in mission statements between four year public institutions and two year colleges in Texas (2007). https://files.eric.ed.gov/fulltext/EJ987299.pdf. Last accessed 25 Feb 2020

Role of Academic Leadership in Building an Open-Lab Teaching and Learning Strategy

Jose Luis Pau and Magdalena Iordache-Platis

1 Introduction: Understanding the Societal Role of Higher Education Institutions

The role of higher education institutions has always been considered a reference point for different industries, due to all research achievements and applied processes that are developed or generated from the academic activity. University voice has become crucial in relationship to public policies' priorities and the academics' and researchers' messages spread rapidly in society due to modern technologies and media channels. The educational and research university contributions are considered as main missions of higher education institutions, but over the last decades the social university engagement has become more and more the focus of the academic leadership.

In processes of social change and sustainable development, universities are considered key institutions, as Sharma (2015) states; he explains that a new role of universities is building of new institutions of civil society, as well as transforming the society through the impact of education. Tandon (2017) also considers the relationship between universities and civil society of crucial importance, the former being producers of knowledge and the latter practitioners; therefore, new knowledge can be discovered from the collaboration with practical units and universities need to reconsider their social role at both local and global scales.

J. L. Pau (✉)
Universidad Autónoma de Madrid, Ciudad Universitaria de Cantoblanco 28049, Madrid, Spain
e-mail: joseluis.pau@uam.es

M. Iordache-Platis
University of Bucharest, Soseaua Panduri. 90, 050663 Bucharest, Romania
e-mail: magdalena.platis@unibuc.ro

A. M. Dima and F. DÁscenzo (eds.), *Business Revolution in a Digital Era*,
Springer Proceedings in Business and Economics,
https://doi.org/10.1007/978-3-030-59972-0_13

Societal role of higher education institutions is not only recognized but confirmed by several changes in topics and actions at different international institutions:

- in 2019 a new ranking was launched—THE Impact Ranking—to measure the university success in the process of acting towards the Sustainable Development Goals; based on the ranking methodology (2020), three main areas are revealed, such as research, outreach and strewardship. In addition, each university is scored according to each focus reflected in 4 objectives, only one being common—the partnership for the goals;
- at the National Co-ordinating Centre for Public Engagement (centre in the UK) engaged universities are those which integrate public engagement into regular activities, more precisely into four areas: research, knowledge exchange, teaching and social responsibility; therefore, students are getting new engagement skills for the public benefit, in general (https://www.publicengagement.ac.uk/about-engagement/what-does-engaged-university-look);
- in 2019 at the European Quality Assurance Forum the main topic for the conference was "Supporting societal engagement of higher education", where discussions encouraged dialogs between practice-specialists and researchers meant to increase professional development for the participants capable to help students to become active citizens (https://eua.eu/events/33-2019-european-quality-assurance-forum.html);
- European University Association (2020) published in 2020 a sector's perspective on the future of the European universities initiatives and promoted the importance of a continuous dialog with society, of academic and non-academic partnerships in an innovative context.

Societal role and actions of higher education institutions are therefore globally considered of utmost importance for the future development of societies, by preparing students and graduates to become prepared for their future careers and active and productive citizens. Stanton (2007) describes a fully engaged institution in the area of education using seven characteristics: improving communities will generate excellence in research, teaching and service; service and research tasks must be cultivated; partnership with community are encouraged; rewarding system is created for engaged staff to get institutional recognition; opportunities for students to achieve civic competences; co-curricular student engagement; creating infrastructure to support and become a public voice for such changes. In addition, Fitzgerald et al. (2015) synthetize the main university forces to become civic engaged: identify economic development needs, make students to commit to applied learning, develop staff propensity for change, receive stakeholder support for shared societal results.

A new model of university is needed to enhance the university-community engagement towards what Goddard and Kempton (2016) describe as civic university, being different than entrepreneurial or triple helix model; civic university is an institution characterized by a flexible limit between higher education institution and society and in which each of the three classical areas—teaching, research and engagement—supports each other and have a societal impact. The authors describe the civic university through seven dimensions: engagement with local community, holistic approach of the university, sense of place, sense of purpose, willing to invest, transparent to stakeholders and public, innovative methodologies. In addition to these, authors admit the need for an active institutional leadership in order to get a leadership and management of place (managerial, political and community leadership).

The importance of higher education institutions of becoming more civic engaged generated some decisions at European level and a funding initiative under an ERASMUS call was established in 2019. Different alliances decided to become more civic and act properly—54 applications for funding, 114 higher education institutions involved from 24 member states were selected and in the end 17 European universities alliances were formed (according to public results, presented later on). All the alliances look for structural and strategic forms of cooperation on long-term towards a new university-society relationship.

Therefore, the societal role of higher education institutions is more and more increasing at all levels of acceptance. The public recognition of being more engaged is definitely unanimous. As many approaches that require important changes, simple declarative engagement does not generate active change. Academic leadership must be totally committed to accept the change from separate, individual, sporadic changes, to transversal, correlated and integrated changes. In order to become more civic engaged, many universities have decided to implement an open lab model; more other universities have committed to integrate this model into regular academic activity of higher education institutions.

2 Literature Review. Open-Lab—Conceptual and Practical Approaches

2.1 Open-Lab Concept

Open lab is not a new concept. Many universities are quite advanced in the open lab implementation and development processes. Others are working with experimented ones to establish the same or similar approach in the university. Main concepts that need to be clarified in relationship with open lab are: open laboratory, living laboratory, living innovation, innovation networks, working open, hubs of innovation, co-production, home-lab.

Birks et al. (2013) admit the role of universities in the country development and growth demonstrating that university itself can be oriented as an open laboratory, when research clusters simply transfer results into practice, diversify funding resources, promote inter and multi-disciplines and develop partners with the community. The authors' conclusion is that open laboratory is a solution to transfer research into practice by providing answers to society needs and solving interdisciplinary challenges.

Many specialists have tried to explain what makes a laboratory open and connected the regular work to the interest of investing in hubs of innovation and similar spaces, where universities allocate substantial resources. DeRosa and Blickensderfer (2017) consider that open lab is meant to connect university to businesses and donors through partnerships which generate sustainability and long-terms objectives; universities should in fact begin to understand that they work for the public, their own graduates being considered future collaborators. Evans et al. (2015) explain living lab, as well as co-production as university platforms for sustainability science; students are engaged in an active environment of teaching and learning, collaborative efforts across sectors and disciplines are put jointly to serve to society challenges. The authors provide clear arguments that the living lab is a generator of solutions to sustainable challenges where students are prepared for competitive job market. Simpler, according to Pop (2018) a living lab is an innovation platform which involves innovation networks and explain the concept as a label, being characterized by two main features—adaptability and responsiveness; thus, the living lab, although it started as a place where people could observe the humans and technology interactions, currently, it is much more than this. In fact, some forms of actions are considered by Ballon and Schuurman (2015) predecessors of living labs, such as: cooperative design based on the involvement of the user and proved in the Scandinavian tradition in 1970s; social experiments, based on experiments outside labs in 1980s; digital cities initiatives, providing internet access to people in 1990s; home labs or smart-home projects during 1970–1990; therefore, living labs are considered to appear in the first years of 2000s.

A clear and synthetic approach of the open lab is reflected in Table 1 describing main features in connection to the literature review.

Many universities have moved from theoretical understanding to practical actions towards an open lab space of sharing knowledge and achieving sustainability goals. Some have decided to enter into alliances to support other higher education institutions to become more visible in the process of addressing to societal challenges.

2.2 Open-Lab—Examples of Good Practices

Academic leadership is facing a lack of materials in the process of going forward towards open lab strategy and approach. Erasmus initiative mentioned previously invited universities to establish strategic partnerships and the alliances became themselves real teaching and learning platforms for members, as sharing of practices and actions became easy. Other open lab responsibles provided free materials to academic community to inspire them to act according to the living lab design. Verhoef and Bossert (2019) provided guidelines in a practitioner handbook explaining the campus of Delft University of Technology, Hochschule für Technik Stuttgart and the dimensions of sustainability; in addition, the material reveals what living labs are and how they can solve real and complex problems by co-creation and co-production, outcomes being valuable in five areas: research, education, campus operations, local community and industry.

Table 1 Open lab—characteristics explained

Literature review	Open/Living lab characteristics	Descriptions
1. DeRosa and Blickensderfer (2017) – Open Lab	Open environment Open to the public Open access Open 24–7 Open for businesses Open thinking	Students can revise their outcomes Students participate at network communities Open resources and licensing for all participants Flexibility for ideas and working time Collaborations with stakeholders Critical thinking and openness about limits
2. Evans et al. (2015) – Living Lab	Strategy Design Holistic approach University model	Sustainability learning and doing Physical, institutional and virtual design Co-production of knowledge Leadership support in decision-making in all areas
3. Ballon and Schuurman (2015) – Living Lab	Active user involvement Real life setting Multi-stakeholders Multi-method approach Co-creation	Characteristics available for previous forms of collaborations (predecessors) All of these are accepted in a holistic approach All of these are integrated in living labs All these actions are promoted under European Network of Living Labs Knowledge sharing + common methodologies

Source Authors' own research

In CIVIS European alliance, the first CIVIS Open Lab was launched in February 2020 and different stakeholders took part at the initiative—municipalities, students, innovation centres, public and private companies etc. This lab's approach is to promote different pilot projects with multidisciplinary approaches at the Universidad Autónoma de Madrid (UAM).

Here are some other examples of living labs:

- An innovative and collaborative approach at the University of Manchester; they dedicate their actions to sustainability and low carbon promoting research and collaboration, developing teaching, courses and projects;
- An opportunity for staff and students, as well as for external parties at University of Leicester dedicated to life sustainability issues; students are becoming responsible citizens;

- A campus as part of the solution at Harvard University; ideas are incubating and new solutions to real problems are promised jointly with the community through a sustainability concrete plan.

Examples can continue in the same approach. The more information is revealed the more questions arise: Is the academic leadership commitment enough to establish an open lab? What happens if at the sharing ideas among external parties, participants share very different opinions? Can students be really engaged in such initiatives? Where resources might come from to support pilot projects?

2.3 *Open Lab Experience in a Civic European University: Case of Universidad Autónoma De Madrid*

The CIVIS Alliance comprises eight European universities that aim to strengthen their contribution to the development of cities and regions where they are rotted by fully understanding and assuming the challenges of their territories. A local permanent dialog between the Universities and the communities must be established to analyze the needs and find solutions, getting key players involved as well as academics and students. Thus, the main tools that the Alliance deploys for the local engagement of the Universities to have true impact on the territories are the Open Labs (OLs).

The CIVIS OLs aim to share knowledge, engagement and intellectual input with stakeholders across the eight territories that form the Alliance, connecting education, research and innovation to local needs and challenges. The main difference with similar initiatives is the extraordinary magnitude of the network including 400,000 students, 55,000 academics/staff. These outstanding figures make the methodology to establish relationships between Universities and citizenship different to other Open Lab approaches and introduces new possibilities to nurture territorial ecosystems and regional development.

The Alliance planned to start implementing a single Open Lab in one of the Universities as a pilot initiative that served to guide the rest of Universities towards the establishment of their own OLs. The Universidad Autónoma de Madrid (UAM) was selected to lead the way, also acting as the coordinator of the OL network later on. A local university team constituted by academics and Directors of University bodies such as the Innovation Unit, the Transfer Office or the Scientific Outreach Unit was built in Madrid for that purpose to give support to the OL activities.

3 Methodology. Academic Leadership Actions and Perceptions on Open Lab Teaching and Learning Strategy—Two Institutional Cases

This section contains two parts—one is a European approach based on public data in order to reveal the leadership support on different forms of open labs and a second one is dedicated to two institutional cases—a Spanish and a Romanian university: Universidad Autónoma de Madrid and University of Bucharest in relationship with the open lab establishment and development.

3.1 European University Initiative—17 Successful Alliances and Academic Commitments

The main facts of the 17 alliances in Europe approved in 2019 to make a change in teaching and learning revealed the following data, as integrated in Table 2.

This European initiative demonstrated not only a declarative interest in working with partners towards a society-based curricula and projects, but a clear responsible commitment with clear activities and outcomes. In fact, it is a new type of university that is built—an open university for society with all stakeholder contributions. All of the 17 alliances include new responses to civic issues, meaning solutions to social needs. It is important to mention that the 17 projects are all considered transnational alliances, based on the structural entities formed around the project purpose, developing strategic cooperation for a long term. In the end—not only the institution wins, but the community involved in all activities, and most importantly, the local community and therefore, the entire society,

Table 2 European University Initiative—2019

European alliance and main objective	Figures: No of universities/students/staff	Open lab or related actions
Total: 17 alliances	113 3,318,236 483,556	Frequent words: collaborative, challenge, network, community

Source Authors' own research (based on https://ec.europa.eu/education/european-universities-factsheets_en)

3.2 *Open Lab Establishment: Case of Universidad Autónoma de Madrid*

3.2.1 Identification of Stakeholders and Kick-Off Event

The local team established some initial criteria to select stakeholders that participated in the OL. Thus, the stakeholders should have a clear link with the local territory because of its location, business area, or social commitment. Their areas of interest should cover one of the five Challenges targeted by the Alliance: (1) Climate, Environment, and Energy, (2) Health, (3) Society, Culture, and Heritage, (4) Digital and Technological Transformations, and (5) Cities, Territories, and Mobilities. The selection also took into account ongoing and previous collaborations of the University and sought to integrate some of those collaborators in the OL.

The UAM team intentionally looked for the aggregation of a broad diversity of stakeholders to ensure that the projects and plans agglutinate different points of view and allow the development of multifaceted approaches. Additionally, they prioritized representatives of minorities and vulnerable groups to consolidate the civic spirit of the OL. Nevertheless, the OL is not seen as a closed circle of entities and it should allow the continuous update of members at any time.

About 30 different stakeholders were identified at UAM and invited to the OL kick off event in February 2020. The event provided visibility in the territory through local communication and social media, and consisted of a brief introduction to the CIVIS project, followed by the general description of the OL objectives. The final part of the event consisted of an open dialog with the audience to probe their interests in participating. To trigger the discussion, one simple question was raised: What CIVIS challenge do you think that requires more immediate action? The audience introduced their answers using Mentimeter App. The results showed that the most voted choice (14 votes) was Climate, Environment, and Energy, and the least voted one (4 votes) was Health. Although the results might be slightly biased by the characteristics of stakeholders selected, it is reasonable to think that the results could have been very different after COVID-19 pandemic that peaked in Spain during April 2020.

3.2.2 Brainstorming Sessions and Project Preparation

Virtual regular meetings were organized to scrutinize territorial problems and discuss about potential solutions through the CIVIS resources. These include the financial support with 1000–5000 €/project to initiate the first activities.

The first step was the collection of ideas from the stakeholders, and their splitting in working groups. Academics got quickly involved in the working groups, with an active participation in providing their view from the frontiers of knowledge. In a second phase, a Call for Projects was officially launched to the stakeholders to get their full proposals about the local issues identified during the brainstorming sessions. Since the preparation of a formal proposal is time-consuming and availability of stakeholders is often limited, the role of academics at this stage became very important. Leadership was in most cases assumed by them since they saw a potential benefit for enriching their research activities within the challenge-driven approach and the CIVIS platform as a bypass to connect with partners from other universities of the Alliance and conform solid international consortia. To make that connection possible, it is required to share the projects selected through the Call with the rest of OLs in the Alliance creating a real network that explore synergies among the different territories. However, project internationalization pathways should not distract from the main purpose of keeping the communication between the University and the local stakeholders active. Hence, it is recommended to distinguish both activities within the local task force and establish a calendar and roadmap to synchronize both objectives in an effective way.

3.2.3 Service Learning: A Valuable Tool for Project Development

One important asset for the implementation of projects in an academic OL is the possibility to design educational methodologies based on learning-by-doing schemes. Service learning is an excellent approach since it joins the realization of activities with strong social impact by the students with their academic recognition. Inclusion, solidarity, reduction of any gender gap, equal access to fundamental rights, sustainability, health, work or economic recovery can be driving forces of Service Learning programs. In them, the students collect data, analyze them and discuss the results with the local communities in a cooperative environment.

The student works need to be mentored by academics, and the management, well integrated in the University structures. The design of those programs in the OL context helps to break barriers towards the introduction of the methodology in degrees and Faculties. Once more, the identification of a responsible person within the local team is a key point to deal with this matter better.

The OL projects also find a valuable resource that can give rise to mobility actions in the same territory or across different regions in Europe, fostering the European identity and the multilingualism among the students.

3.3 Academic Leadership Perceptions on Open Lab—Case of University of Bucharest

Among the 17 alliances, abovementioned, 3 include universities in Romania - University of Bucharest in CIVIS, Technical University of Civil Engineering of Bucharest in EU-CONEXUS and National University of Political Studies and Public Administration in CIVICA. The 3 rectors commit to act according to the project objectives and to increase the higher education competitiveness by promoting the European values

Table 3 Open lab—reflected in the 3 European alliances (Romanian universities part of)

Crt. No	European Alliances Romanian Universities	Descriptions based on institutional web-pages https://unibuc.ro/despre-ub/civis/?lang=en https://utcb.ro/conexus-european-university-for-smart-urban-coastal-sustainability/ https://snspa.ro/snspa-membra-a-consortiului-civica-universitatea-europeana-de-stiinte-sociale/
1	CIVIS University of Bucharest	Long term engagement Civic identity Challenge-driven university Collaboration at all levels
2	EU_CONEXUS Technical University of Civil Engineering of Bucharest	Cooperation for innovation Exchanges of good practices Strategic partnerships New and flexible curricula based on transdisciplinary approach New and innovative teaching and learning based on TIC and professional expertize
3	CIVICA National University of Political Studies and Public Administration	Inter-university European campus Teaching and learning linked with research and society Interdisciplinary experience in teaching and learning Team-work to answer to European and global issues

and identity. Table 3 reveals the main characteristics of the European initiative of going civic at the three Romanian universities that entered in the first financial line; the objectives of the alliances, although different, they follow the same directions of the European initiatives and therefore, the effort of the universities of opening their campuses to public is common.

Source Authors' own research

A questionnaire-based research was applied to understand the academic leadership perception at one Romanian university regarding the conceptual and practicalities of an open lab initiative. It was provided to responsible people on university-industry links from faculties, so the respondents were from the very beginning aware of the importance of moving forward towards more civic engagement. In addition, the questionnaire was meant to make academic leadership understand if the community is ready for a civic change as open lab. The questionnaire was addressed to different level of academic leadership at the University of Bucharest—as seen in Table 4 and although the questionnaire was e-mailed, the collection of the replies was mainly on paper. The distribution of the respondents is described in Table 4. And their answers according to a 5 level Likert scale in Table 5.

Table 4 Distribution of the respondents.

Academic leadership level	Experience (less than 10 year/ more than 10 year)	Total
Institutional or faculty management	8/18	26
Department level	15/20	35
Administrative level	17/15	32
Total	40/53	93

Source Authors' own research

The responses are revealed in Table 5. Respondents were invited to express the level of agreement on 5 levels of Likert scale to 12 questions. The score for each question is shown in the same table.

The respondents proved a high level of agreement on the idea that open lab establishment and functionality would mean allocation of resources and student engagement for which motivational solutions must be found; at the same time, the academic community declares itself willing to accept the change but considers this acceptance difficult in the case of overloading. The respondents showed a lot of reservation in considering students totally available for new voluntary—based projects. In addition to these answers, the respondents were asked to reply if they would act accordingly to an open lab strategy, if this would be the change for the university and most of them (92%) said probably, yes. In addition, at an open question regarding the most relevant measures they vision to implement an open lab strategy, most relevant answers were the following ones:

Table 5 Academic leadership perceptions on open lab initiative

Crt. No	Question	Lickert score
1	Open lab concept is clear for me	2.02
2	I understand the concept of open lab but it needs a lot of resources	3.72
3	Collaborations with stakeholders are not entirely effective	3.76
4	Stakeholders are part of the decision making in university	1.92
5	Students are very difficult to motivate	3.53
6	Professors might be willing to participate, but they are already overloaded	4.24
7	Administrative staff is very open, as long as changes are the right ones	3.72
8	Rewards might be a solution but not in the current legal context	3.70
9	Students care more for curricular activities and less for extracurricular ones	1.79
10	Elaboration of internal procedures takes time	4.04
11	Openness of the university should start from autonomy	4.70
12	Open lab is a teaching and learning strategy based on societal challenges	3.18

Source Authors' own research

- Legislative support (93%)
- Institutional autonomy for real (78%)
- Resources allocated (96%)
- Innovative strategies (74%)
- Team work (87%)
- Physical and virtual space investment (62%)
- Participants' rewards (55%).

Therefore, respondents proved openness to the establishment for an institutional open lab, but at the same time a high level of understanding by providing needed measures to be taken or decided: resources allocated, innovative issues, motivational condition etc.

4 Results and Discussions

Main findings of the paper show a real interest for open lab concept and practical implication of a specific strategy in higher education institutions. As the literature review consists of several explanations and descriptions of open lab, in practice, academic leadership has considered it as a flexible mechanism of open the university to the public. In fact, it is a new university function building up – of sustainability provider/maker. Higher education institution, through all its capacity and expertise, project and staff begins to act a real support for community in both local and global regions, being effective in projects generating sustainable development of society through collaborative actions.

When the academic leadership is institutionally committed, the decision once taken generates concrete implementation steps and outcomes, as in the Spanish university—internal team, brainstorming session, stakeholder classification, open lab event and social needs project elaboration. If the same framework exists, things evolve slower in other universities, as open lab is considered a completely new concept and practical development, but in the context of sharing and partnering, the process is still in place, as in the Romanian university.

Academic leadership is aware of the concept of open lab, but the concept is still unclear for many responsible people. The respondents showed a lot of distrust in the sense of a large change of ways of doing things currently specific and extremely regulated in universities. An open lab strategy would involve collaboration for a long term, support and interest from stakeholders, reward system for participants, new competences for students, as they will be the final receptors of the change towards good citizenship actions.

An open lab teaching and learning strategy would mean a learning by doing approach of students, more flexibility in the curriculum design and effective practical-based learning. In Fig. 1, an open lab strategy reveals main connections that become

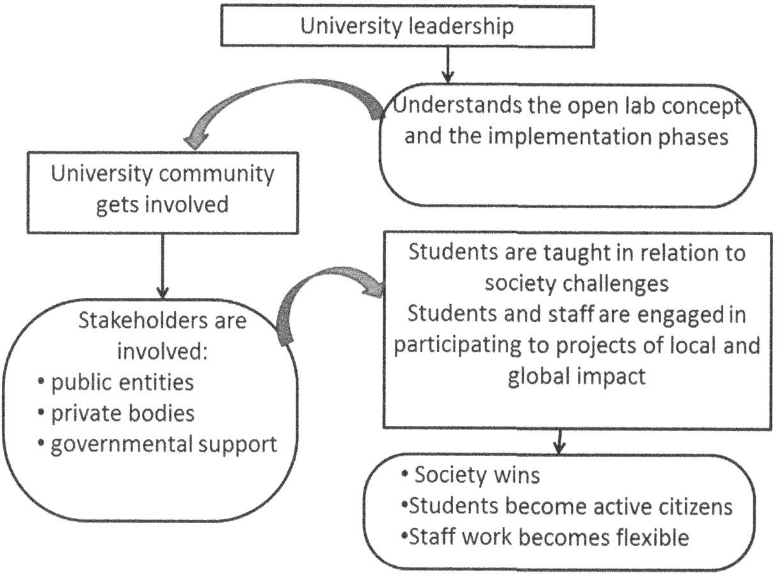

Fig. 1 Open lab strategy model. *Source* Authors' own research

mandatory for successful outcomes. The model starts from the leadership commitment and shows the main steps that should be followed, including the university community involvement and the collaboration to all stakeholders. A general description of the model includes the following phases:

- Leadership commitment
- Stakeholders and university community involvement
- Design of the curricula based on co-creation
- Integration of students in projects
- Students learning by doing
- Society challenges are addressed.

Therefore, the model is based on collaboration among all interested parties—staff, students, stakeholders, society and sustainability. This model can be easily called the 5Ss strategy model and is based on co-production and co-creation for sustainable results in society.

5 Conclusion

The importance of change in educational teaching and learning strategy is all over the world recognized by academic leadership and global institutions. In Europe, the strategic alliances contributed to the creation of several international networks to promote change towards sustainability goals and society development. Complexity of social issues requires flexibility in teaching and learning and more than never, joint actions and collaborative work for local and global achievement.

Society is facing global challenges. Therefore, higher education institutions must change the way they contribute to students' and graduates' competences. In order to become active citizens, students have to learn from concrete action in real projects. An open lab teaching and learning strategy is a solution to future training of graduates.

Academic leadership is committed but particular actions are still needed to create contextual (national and institutional) adequate conditions for such changes. To many still remaining questions, universities and staff, as well as other participants will find answers during working together as effective network and team.

The paper shows an example of an open lab establishment as an example of good or best practice and the power of sharing the experience to another university in the right context which is the ERASMUS framework for the provided example. At the same time, copy and paste experience is not a solution for higher education institution development; therefore, the questionnaire is particularly useful to understand the state of the academic leadership perception of the capacity of an open lab development. In the absence of academic leadership commitment, no decision is efficiently implemented.

The paper has its own limits, as respondents come from only one higher education institution, but it can be considered a pilot study to future analysis on open lab practicalities and impact. Most important aspect is that the new university has started to be built at European and global level.

References

Ballon, P., Schuurman, D.: Living labs: concepts, tools and cases. Info, vol. 17 no. 4., https://www.researchgate.net/publication/277950787_Living_labs_concepts_tools_and_cases. Last accessed 05 Apr 2020

Birks, et al.: The university as an open laboratory. J Res. Admin. **44**(2), 11–37 (2013)

DeRosa, R., Blickensderfer, D.: What makes an open lab 'open'? https://www.insidehighered.com/views/2017/05/02/key-principles-open-labs-essay. Last accessed 20 Mar 2020

EQAF. Supporting societal engagement of higher education. https://eua.eu/events/33-2019-european-quality-assurance-forum.html. last accessed 04 Apr 2020

EUA. The future of the European universities initiative. The sector's perspective. https://eua.eu/downloads/publications/eua%20council%20position%20on%20future%20of%20eui.pdf. Last accessed 25 Mar 2020

European University Initiative. https://ec.europa.eu/education/education-in-the-eu/european-education-area/european-universities-initiative_en. Last accessed 12 Feb 2020

Evans, J. et al. : Living labs and co-production: university campuses as platforms for sustainability science. https://core.ac.uk/download/pdf/82770925.pdf. Last accesses 12 Feb 2020

Fitzgerald, H.E. et al.: The Centrality of Engagement in Higher Education. https://www.aplu.org/library/the-centrality-of-engagement-in-higher-education/File. Last accessed 25 Mar 2020

Goddard, J. and Kempton, L.: The civic university. Universities in the leadership and management of place. https://www.ncl.ac.uk/media/wwwnclacuk/curds/files/university-leadership.pdf. Last accessed 25 Mar 2020

National Co-ordinating Centre for Public Engagement, UK. What does an engaged university look like? https://www.publicengagement.ac.uk/about-engagement/what-does-engaged-university-look. Last accessed 05 Apr 2020
Pop, O. M.: What Is a Living Lab and How Can It Be Used for Open Innovation? https://blog.hypeinnovation.com/living-labs-and-open-innovation. Last accessed 25 Feb 2020
Sharma, R.S.: Role of universities in development of civil society and social transformation. Proceedings of International Academic Conferences. https://ideas.repec.org/p/sek/iacpro/2604181.html. Last accessed 25 Feb 2020
Stanton, T. K. (Ed.).: New times demand new scholarship: Research universities and civic engagement—opportunities and challenges. In: Fitzgerald, H.E. et al Los Angeles, CA: University of California (2015). The Centrality of Engagement in Higher Education, https://www.aplu.org/library/the-centrality-of-engagement-in-higher-education/File. Last accessed 25 Feb 2020
Tandon, R.: University-civil society relations. Public lecture, http://unescochair-cbrsr.org/pdf/presentation/5_Durban_Pub%20Lecture%20May%202017.pdf. Last accessed 25 Apr 2020
THE Impact Rankings 2020: methodology, https://www.timeshighereducation.com/university-impact-rankings-2020-methodology. Last accessed 20 Apr 2020
The Universidad Autónoma de Madrid (UAM), Launch of the first CIVIS Open Lab at Universidad Autónoma de Madrid. https://civis.eu/en/news/launch-of-the-first-civis-open-lab-at-universidad-autonoma-de-madrid. Last accessed 20 Apr 2020
University of Leicester. What is Living Labs, https://www2.le.ac.uk/offices/estates/environment/research/what-is-living-labs. Last accessed 25 Mar 2020
University of Harvard. Our campus is part of the solution. https://green.harvard.edu/series/living-lab. Last accessed 15 Feb 2020
University of Manchester. University Living Lab. https://universitylivinglab.org/. Last accessed 20 Apr 2020
Verhoef, L., Bossert, M.: The university campus as a living lab for sustainability. A practitioner's guide and handbook. https://campusaslivinglab.org/wp-content/uploads/2019/06/new_RZ_Living_Lab_handbook_9.5.19.pdf. Last accessed 28 Mar 2020

Intuitive Fuzzy Real Options in Digital Coaching for Strategic Investment Decisions

Jani Kinnunen and Irina Georgescu

1 Introduction

Digital coaching environment for strategic investments using fuzzy real options models has been recently introduced by Carlsson (2017, 2019). He has further introduced the term into a more general analytics environment as the response to digitalization in Carlsson (2018a, b). The two main motivations have been identified for digital coaching: (i) a complex and changing context, which goes beyond the users' abilities and (ii) the need to support the users to do their task better (Carlsson 2018b).

Carlsson (2017, 2019) discusses how the combination of real options and scenarios has been a success from managerial point of view. The managers have found the fuzzy models more intuitive and resulting in more valuable outcomes, which have been more in line with theory and reality, as well as, the users' experience, when compared to more traditional net-present-value, NPV, methods. The findings have also shown that the earlier types of real options models, such as Black-Scholes formulas (Black and Scholes 1970; Merton 1973) without scenario thinking had been both difficult to grasp and less useful in practice.

Research on decision support systems, DSSs, started in the 1970s and has followed by various technological changes, while the key principles and guidelines have remained for 2010s (Carlsson 2018b): the value of the support systems arises from the help and support they provide for the users rather than their technological level

J. Kinnunen (✉)
Åbo Akademi University, Tuomiokirkontori 3, 20500 Turku, Finland
e-mail: jpkinnunen@gmail.com

I. Georgescu
Bucharest University of Economics, Calea Dorobantilor 15-17, 010552 Bucharest, Romania
e-mail: irina.georgescu@csie.ase.ro

A. M. Dima and F. DÁscenzo (eds.), *Business Revolution in a Digital Era*,
Springer Proceedings in Business and Economics,
https://doi.org/10.1007/978-3-030-59972-0_14

and this is dependent on the understanding what it means to users to do their work better to be able to support it (Keen 1981).

The 1970s and 1980s were seen as a phase where optimization algorithms took over and offered black-box solutions for the users, who were not necessarily able to understand what happened under the hood, while DSSs were to help building the intuition and support their work taking into account their experience (Zeleny 1982). Carlsson (2018b) argues that these lessons should be brought back to the center of the current support systems research as advanced mathematics is often a requirement in today's DSS analytics (cf. Carland et al. 2018; Simon 1980; Sprague 1980). Fern et al. (2014) point out that managers/users of a DSS are often a heterogeneous group with various experiences and technical abilities, while being geographically spread around the globe. To make such groups work effectively, digital coaching can work towards making the groups more homogenous by their analytical skills and experiences (Carlsson 2018b).

The decision support systems of the past will become digital coaching systems. Digital coaching systems will work with data, information and knowledge collected, e.g., from digital services, monitoring tools, data and knowledge bases, and processed for the use in digital coaching to support users (Carlsson 2017). Digital coaching in strategic investments using real options methods is "a way to guide and support users to give them better chances for effective and productive use of real options methods" (Carlsson 2017).

The role of intuition and scenarios in strategic investment analysis, and thus, in supporting digital coaching to achieve more homogenous groups of users within organizations is in the core of this paper. The methodological knowledge and ability to frame strategic investment problems as real options problems, and finally, to value them by utilizing the state-of-art real options methods are the main target.

The rest of the paper is organized as follows. Next, Sect. 2 discusses the development from the Black-Scholes type of models to the recent more intuitive fuzzy real options models and their underlying modelling principles and Sects. 2.1 and 2.2 will take a closer look at the triangular and trapezoidal forms of the center-of-gravity fuzzy pay-off models (GoG-FPOMs) (Borges et al. 2018), respectively. Then, Sect. 3 will discuss through examples how intuition-building can be built into a digital coaching system using single-valued scenarios (Sect. 3.1), interval-valued scenarios (Sect. 3.2) and simulations (Sect. 3.3). Section 4 concludes the paper and discusses the suitability of the presented real options models for digital coaching by reflecting on the requirements set for value-adding digital coaching systems.

2 From Black-Scholes to Intuitive Fuzzy Real Options Models

Carlsson among few others have been pioneers in the field of fuzzy real options modelling and promoting their use in corporations and academy through numerous corporate-academia joint projects and through introducing a number of fuzzy real options models starting from fuzzy version of the famous Black-Scholes models (cf. Carlsson and Fullér 2003; Black and Scholes 1970). The fuzzy real options models discussed by Carlsson (2017, 2019) were still focused on Black-Scholes types of models, where greater uncertainty is, however, allowed by using fuzzy (trapezoidal and triangular) numbers instead of single crisp numbers in the models. The recent developments of fuzzy models are based on fuzzy pay-off model, which are more intuitive and easier to understand, learn and apply. The fuzzy pay-off models are further scenario-based methods, i.e., the scenarios are used as inputs of the real options models. These scenarios are represented by fuzzy pay-off distributions based on triangular or trapezoidal fuzzy numbers and their generalizations to interval-valued fuzzy numbers, IVFNs, which are shown to allow both greater uncertainty and higher impreciseness than the fuzzy forms or Black-Scholes types of models.

The most recent developments in the field of fuzzy real options have been towards so called pay-off methods for real options analysis. The idea of the fuzzy pay-off models for real options has been based on the Datar-Mathews method (DMM) (Datar and Mathews 2007), which suggested that the real options value, ROV, is the weighted probabilistic mean of the positive NPV outcomes, $E(A_+)$, of a pay-off distribution (cf. Collan et al. 2009), i.e.:

$$\text{ROV} = Weight * Expected\ positiveNPV = \frac{\int_0^\infty A(x)dx}{\int_{-\infty}^\infty A(x)dx} * E(A_+). \quad (1)$$

The mean (expected value) of the positive NPV (of type DMM), $E(A_+)$, is replaced by fuzzy expected values of the positive NPV: by the possibilistic mean value, $E_{FPOM}(A_+)$ (Collan et al. 2009), by credibilistic mean value, $E_{Cred\text{-}FPOM}(A_+)$ (Collan et al. 2012) or by the center-of gravity expected value, $E_{CoG\text{-}FPOM}(A_+)$ (Borges et al. 2018) in the case of single-valued scenarios.

Figure 1 presents triangular and trapezoidal fuzzy numbers representing the (NPV) pay-off distributions and shows how they are related to pay-off scenarios. The triangular distribution is a good starting point as the probabilistic triangular distribution can be used as a proxy for a probabilistic normal distribution and it also allows skewness and asymmetry in NPV outcomes, while it is more intuitively obvious (Fairchild et al. 2016). On the left side of Fig. 1, a simple triangular fuzzy number represents cumulative NPV of expected cash flows from a strategic investment. The distribution is based on, firstly, building three scenarios, the pessimistic, the base case, and the optimistic scenario for potential future cashflows discounted to today. The base scenario is represented by the peak, a, of the triangular distribution with the degree of membership 1 (the most possible NPV value to be realized), while the pessimistic case gives the minimum NPV and the optimistic case the potential maximum NPV.

The key real options idea is that the negative NPV (NPV < 0) can be cut off as the investor has the real option, the right to execute the investment, but not obligation. Thus, the expected realized NPV is the expected value of only the positive side of the distribution, i.e. $E(A_+)$, and this must be weighted by the area of the positive NPV

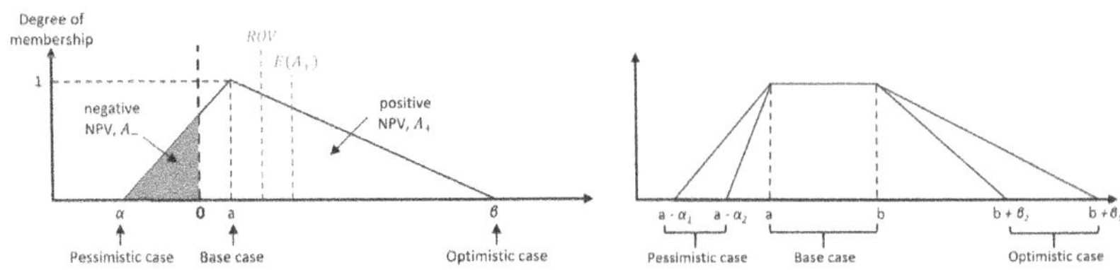

Fig. 1 Fuzzy numbers as pay-off distributions, scenario inputs, and real option valuation

divided by the whole distribution (negative + positive areas). This computation will give the real option value as in Eq. (1).

On the right side of Fig. 1, an interval-valued trapezoidal NPV distribution is shown allowing ranges for the pessimistic, base and optimistic scenarios. This is the most general type of the distributions considered in this paper. It naturally reduces to the interval-valued triangular case, when $a = b$ and further to the simple triangular case if also $\alpha_1 = \alpha_2$ and $\beta_1 = \beta_2$ and all scenarios are represented by single-valued NPVs.

2.1 Fuzzy Real Options with Triangular Numbers

The real option value for the center-of-gravity fuzzy pay-off model, CoG-FPOM, using takes the form (Borges et al. 2018; Kinnunen et al. 2020):

$$ROV_{CoG} = \frac{\int_0^\infty A(x)dx}{\int_{-\infty}^\infty A(x)dx} * E_{GoG}(A_+) = \frac{\int_0^\infty A(x)dx}{\int_{-\infty}^\infty A(x)dx} * \frac{\int_0^\infty xA(x)dx}{\int_0^\infty A(x)dx} \tag{2}$$

The membership function of a triangular fuzzy number $A(a, \alpha, \beta)$ (cf. Left side of Fig. 1) is defined as (Dubois and Prade 1980, 1988):

$$A(x) = \begin{cases} 1 - \frac{a-x}{\propto} & if\ a - \propto \le x \le a \\ 1 - \frac{x-a}{\beta} & if\ a \le x \le a + \beta \\ 0 & otherwise. \end{cases} \tag{3}$$

The expected NPV of the triangular fuzzy number, $E_{FPOM}(A_+)$ is based on Zadeh's possibility theory (Zadeh 1975, 1978) and Carlsson and Fullér's (2001) mean values in the original fuzzy pay-off model FPOM (Collan et al. 2009) for which R codes are presented in (Kinnunen and Georgescu 2019, 2020). In the center-of-gravity case of CoG-FPOM, the expected values, $E_{CoG}(A_+)$ s, and the weight components (cf. The ROV formula (2)), for the 4 cases depending on the location of the zero, become (Borges et al. 2018):

Case 1, $0 \le a - \propto$:

$$E_{CoG}(A_+) = \frac{3a - \alpha + \beta}{3} \text{ and } Weight_1 = 1. \quad (4)$$

Case 2, $a - \propto \leq 0 \leq a$

$$E_{CoG}(A_+) = \frac{\propto (a + \beta)^3 - a^3(\alpha + \beta)}{3\alpha(a + \beta)^2 - 3a^2(\alpha + \beta)} \text{ and } Weight_2 = \frac{2a - \frac{a^2}{\propto} + \beta}{\propto + \beta}. \quad (5)$$

Case 3, $a \leq 0 \leq a + \beta$:

$$E_{CoG}(A_+) = \frac{a + \beta}{3} \text{ and } Weight_3 = \frac{(a + \beta)^2}{\beta(\propto + \beta)}. \quad (6)$$

Case 4, $a + \beta \leq 0$:

$$E_{CoG}(A_+) = 0 \text{ and } Weight_4 = 0. \quad (7)$$

The center-of-gravity expected values for the above 4 triangular cases can be found partly in (Borges et al. 2018) and (Kinnunen et al. 1980) and fully including also R codes in Kinnunen and Georgescu (2020). For the credibilistic case, the formulas are presented in (Collan et al. 2012) and (Georgescu and Kinnunen 2011, 2020).

For the trapezoidal fuzzy number, the expected values have been presented accordingly for 5 cases, where case 3 is an additional case when compared to above. It may be noted that when $a = b$, the trapezoidal distribution degenerates to the triangular distribution and the formulas reduce to formulas (4)–(7). We will not present the non-interval-valued trapezoidal formulas here as they can be found with R codes in (Kinnunen and Georgescu 2020) for different types of models. The next section continues with their interval-valued extensions to the trapezoidal formulations.

2.2 Fuzzy Real Options with Interval-Valued Trapezoidal Numbers

The interval-valued real option values, IV-ROVs, require computing the expected averages and weights of the two fuzzy trapezoidal numbers as seen in Fig. 2 (cf. The right side of Fig. 1): the upper fuzzy number A^U and the lower fuzzy number A^L. The interval-models require still 2 additional cases (cases 2 and 5 in Fig. 2). For the interval-valued triangular fuzzy numbers, Mezei et al. (Mezei et al. 2017) introduced IV-FPOM and Kinnunen and Georgescu (Kinnunen and Georgescu 2020) presented the credibilistic version IV-Cred-POM and Kinnunen et al. (2020) the center-of-gravity version. Kinnunen and Georgescu (Kinnunen and Georgescu 2020) extended the models to trapezoidal forms for all the three considered types: IV-FPOM, IV-CoG-FPOM, and IV-Cred-POM. Here, only the extension of the center-of-gravity pay-off model, IV-CoG is considered.

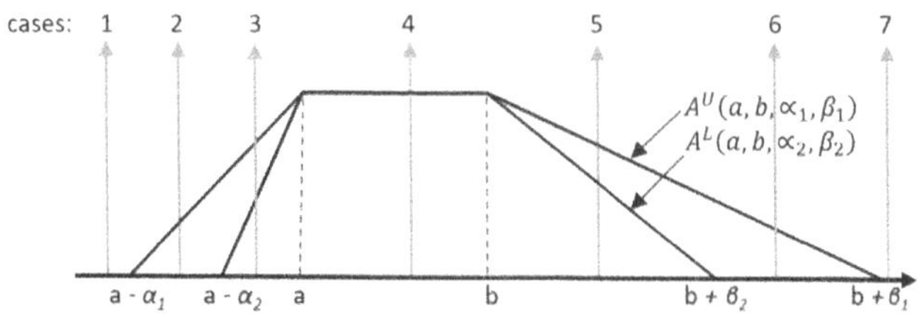

Fig. 2 Cases for interval-valued trapezoidal fuzzy NPV distributions

In the general form, the interval-valued models can be formulated as (Mezei et al. 2017; Kinnunen and Georgescu 2020):

$$IV\!-\!ROV = \frac{\int_0^\infty (A^U(x) + A^L(x))dx}{\int_{-\infty}^\infty (A^U(x) + A^L(x))dx} * E_{IV}(A_+) \tag{8}$$

The interval-valued fuzzy sets introduced by Zadeh (1975) are generalizations of real-valued intervals. By definition, an interval-valued fuzzy set is a function defined on a set X whose values are closed intervals from [0,1]. So, for each $x \in X$ one associates an interval $A(x) = \left[A^L(x), A^U(x)\right]$ included in [0, 1]. $A^L : X \to [0, 1]$ and $A^U : X \to [0, 1]$ will be fuzzy sets, called lower fuzzy set and upper fuzzy set of A and $A^L(x) \le A^U(x)$, for each $x \in X$, as can be seen in Fig. 2.

When A^L and A^U are fuzzy numbers, then A is called interval-valued fuzzy number, IVFN. The center-of-gravity expected value of a fuzzy number introduced in (Borges et al. 2018) is extended naturally to the interval-valued case, IV-CoG (Kinnunen and Georgescu 2020).

The expected value of an IVFN A is defined by $E_{IV}(A) = \frac{1}{2}[\left(E\left(A^U\right) + E\left(A^L\right)\right]$, where $E\left(A^U\right)$ and $\left(A^L\right)$ are the expected values of the fuzzy numbers $A^U(a, b, \alpha_1, \beta_1)$ and $A^L(a, b, \alpha_2, \beta_2)$, respectively. Similarly, the expected value of the positive part of an IVFN A, for IV-CoG is defined as (Kinnunen and Georgescu 2020):

$$E_{IV-CoG}\left(A_+\right) = \frac{1}{2}\left[E_{CoG}\left(A_+^U\right) + E_{CoG}\left(A_+^L\right)\right]. \tag{9}$$

We present the analytical forms of the center-of-gravity expected values of the positive NPV, as well as, the weights for the 6 cases (Kinnunen and Georgescu 2020):

<u>Case 1</u>, $0 < a - \alpha_1$: Both trapezoidal fuzzy numbers, A^U and A^L are fully positive:

$$E_{IV-CoG}\left(A_+\right) = \frac{1}{2}\left[\frac{\beta_1^2 - \alpha_1^2 + 3(a\alpha_1 + b\beta_1) + 3\left(b^2 - a^2\right)}{6(b-a) + 3(\alpha_1 + \beta_1)}\right.$$

$$+\frac{\beta_2^2-\alpha_2^2+3(a\alpha_2+b\beta_2)+3\left(b^2-a^2\right)}{6(b-a)+3(\alpha_2+\beta_2)}\Bigg], \quad (10)$$

$$Weight_1 = 1. \quad (11)$$

<u>Case 2</u>, $a-\alpha_1<0<a-\alpha_2$:

$$E_{IV-CoG}\left(A_+\right) = \frac{1}{2}\left[\frac{-a^3+3b^2\alpha_1+3b\beta_1\alpha_1+\beta_1^2\alpha_1}{-3a^2+6b\alpha_1+3\beta_1\alpha_1}+\frac{\beta_2^2-\alpha_2^2+3(a\alpha_2+b\beta_2)+3\left(b^2-a^2\right)}{6(b-a)+3(\alpha_2+\beta_2)}\right], \quad (12)$$

$$Weight_2 = \frac{\frac{-a^2}{2\alpha_1}+\frac{4b-2a+\alpha_2+\beta_1+\beta_2}{2}}{2b-2a+\frac{\alpha_1+\alpha_2+\beta_1+\beta_2}{2}}. \quad (13)$$

<u>Case 3</u>, $a-\alpha_2<0<a$:

$$E_{IV-CoG}\left(A_+\right) = \frac{1}{2}\left[\frac{-a^3+3b^2\alpha_1+3b\beta_1\alpha_1+\beta_1^2\alpha_1}{-3a^2+6b\alpha_1+3\beta_1\alpha_1}+\frac{-a^3+3b^2\alpha_2+3b\beta_2\alpha_2+\beta_2^2\alpha_2}{-3a^2+6b\alpha_2+3\beta_2\alpha_2}\right], \quad (14)$$

$$Weight_3 = \frac{2b+\frac{\beta_1+\beta_2}{2}-\frac{a^2}{2}\left(\frac{1}{\alpha_1}+\frac{1}{\alpha_2}\right)}{2b-2a+\frac{\alpha_1+\alpha_2+\beta_1+\beta_2}{2}}. \quad (15)$$

<u>Case 4</u>, $a\le 0\le b$:

$$E_{IV-CoG}\left(A_+\right) = \frac{1}{2}\left[\frac{3b^2+3b\beta_1+\beta_1^2}{6b+3\beta_1}+\frac{3b^2+3b\beta_2+\beta_2^2}{6b+3\beta_2}\right], \quad (16)$$

$$Weight_4 = \frac{2b+\frac{\beta_1+\beta_2}{2}}{2b-2a+\frac{\alpha_1+\alpha_2+\beta_1+\beta_2}{2}}. \quad (17)$$

<u>Case 5</u>, $b\le 0\le b+\beta_2$:

$$E_{IV-CoG}\left(A_+\right) = \frac{1}{2}\left[\frac{b+\beta_1}{3}+\frac{b+\beta_2}{3}\right], \quad (18)$$

$$Weights_5 = \frac{\frac{\beta_1+\beta_2}{2}+2b+\frac{b^2}{2}\left(\frac{1}{\beta_1}+\frac{1}{\beta_2}\right)}{2b-2a+\frac{\alpha_1+\alpha_2+\beta_1+\beta_2}{2}}. \quad (19)$$

Case 6, $b + \beta_2 \leq 0 \leq b + \beta_1$:

$$E_{IV-CoG}(A_+) = \frac{1}{2}\left[\frac{b + \beta_1}{3}\right], \tag{20}$$

$$Weight_6 = \frac{\frac{\beta_1}{2} + b + \frac{b^2}{2\beta_1}}{2b - 2a + \frac{\alpha_1 + \alpha_2 + \beta_1 + \beta_2}{2}}. \tag{21}$$

Case 7, $b + \beta_1 < 0$:

$$E_{IV-CoG}(A_+) = 0 \text{ and } Weight_7 = 0. \tag{22}$$

The above situation will be discussed in *Example 2* showing how the model allows using intervals for the scenario inputs in CoG-FPOM following the *Example 1*, which deals with the single-valued scenarios. *Example 3* will further present a situation, where the NPV distribution is a fuzzy set, but not a fuzzy variable. This is done in comparison to the probabilistic model of type Datar-Mathews (Datar and Mathews 2007), for which we also present an R algorithm and we will find out that the ROV from the DM model converges to the recent center-of-gravity fuzzy real option model (Borges et al. 2018).

3 Digital Coaching Through Real Options Examples

The methodological approach of this paper builds on the digital coaching framework for decision analytics introduced by Carlsson (2018a, b) and presented for real options analysis in (Carlsson 2017, 2019). Carlsson (2017, 2019) lays down guidelines for building a digital coaching environment and presents findings from several industry-academia joint projects including why experienced corporate managers and analysts had preferred and adopted fuzzy real options models with scenarios for better and more realistic strategic investment planning than the more traditional net present value, NPV, methods or the earlier stochastic-modelling based real options models.

In this section, we discuss through examples how the latest pay-off based fuzzy real options modelling has improved the practicality, easiness to implement and interpret the results, while accounting for even higher uncertainty and imprecision than the earlier models. The examples focus on certain key properties of the fuzzy pay-off methods using an interactive support tool under construction in R environment. We argue through these examples that fuzzy pay-off models are easy to build into a digital coaching tools and they are more intuitive than the earlier real options models making them particularly suitable for digital coaching. R is a major coding language, along with Python, in today's data analytics, and, for example Excel, supports integrating R code into it just like it supported Visual Basic for Applications in the past.

In this section, we present straightforward applications of the models presented in Sect. 2, i.e. using the recent center-of-gravity fuzzy pay-off model in R environment based on the simplest triangular form in *Example 1*, which is extended to interval-valued scenarios in *Example 2* in a special case, where the base case and the most uncertain upside potential (optimistic case) are dealt with as intervals, while the pessimistic scenario as a single-valued case. *Example 3* presents how simulations of NPV outcomes may be used by utilizing fuzzy sets, as well as, using a simplified probabilistic Datar-Mathews method (Datar and Mathews 2007) developed originally at Boing Corporation for valuing flexible airline development projects. Using the triangular distribution as the basis of simulations improves the industry practice of using uniform distributions by allowing lower possibilities of outcomes in tails than at a peak, while offering an intuitively obvious approach (Fairchild et al. 2016). *Example 3* further demonstrates how the probabilistic model outcome converges to the center-of-gravity real option value.

3.1 Example 1: Single-Valued Scenarios

We consider selected simple properties of a prototype R Shiny interactive application for real option valuation shown in Fig. 3. A user of the support system may select either single-valued or interval-valued scenarios the first one represented by a simple triangular fuzzy number, as selected in Fig. 3, or using intervals for scenario inputs (as done in the subsequent example 2). Building the scenarios can be dependent on the specifics of the application and the preferences of the user. Further, obtaining the cumulative NPV scenarios can be a long and complicated process even with decision support systems and digital coaching environments (cf., Kinnunen and Georgescu 2019; Collan and Kinnunen 2011; Kinnunen 2010; Kinnunen and Collan 2009).

For a general example, a natural starting point is the triangular form of CoG-FPOM (Borges et al. 2018). This requires entering the expected crisp discounted

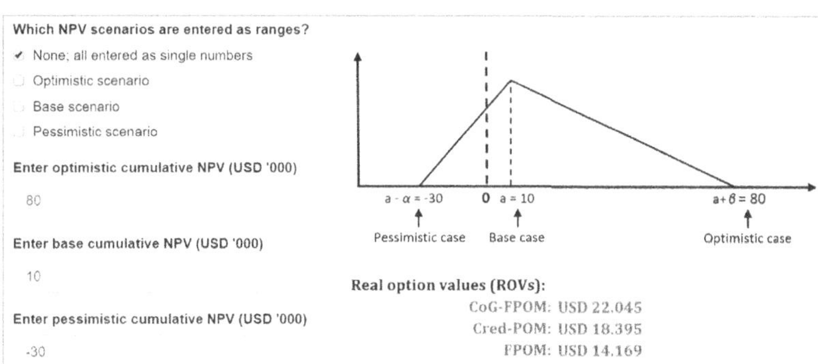

Fig. 3 Single-number scenarios as inputs

payoffs for the three scenarios. Optimistic scenario NPV is USD 80k, the base-case scenario NPV is USD 10k, and the pessimistic scenario NPV is USD -30k. This corresponds to the case 2, $a - \alpha \leq 0 \leq a$, and the ROV of Eq. (5) from the earlier section. The peak a = 10 and the minimum $a - \alpha = -30$, thus, $\alpha = 40$; $a + \beta = 80$, thus, $\beta = 70$. These are all required inputs to Eq. (5) to obtain:

$ROV_{CoG} = \frac{2a - \frac{a^2}{\alpha} + \beta}{\alpha + \beta} * \left[\frac{\alpha(a+\beta)^3 - a^3(\alpha+\beta)}{3\alpha(a+\beta)^2 - 3a^2(\alpha+\beta)} \right] = 79.545\% * 27.714 = 22.045$, i.e., the positive side is 79.545% of the total area of the distribution, giving the weight, and the mean of the positive side, $E_{IV-CoG}(A_+)$, is USD 27.714, and this leads to ROV (GoG-FPOM) of USD 22.045. Figure 3 shows also the credibilistic ROV (Cred-POM) (Collan et al. 2012) and the original possibilistic ROV (FPOM) (Collan et al. 2009) for comparisons.

3.2 Example 2: Interval-Valued Scenarios

In this example, interval-valued scenarios are used for base case and optimistic NPV scenarios; it may be the case that costs are less uncertain and thus the single-valued NPV has been selected for the pessimistic NPV as seen in Fig. 4.

The selection opens up sliders to for the interval-NPV inputs and a number for the single-valued pessimistic scenario. The same NPV inputs are entered for pessimistic scenario, USD -30k, as in *Example 2*; also, the lower limit for base case scenario is the same, USD 10k, but now with the more upside potential the base case NPV ranges from USD 10k to USD 25k, while the optimistic NPV scenario is seen more uncertain with some downside risk compared to previous example: the optimistic scenario ranges from USD 65k to USD 85k.

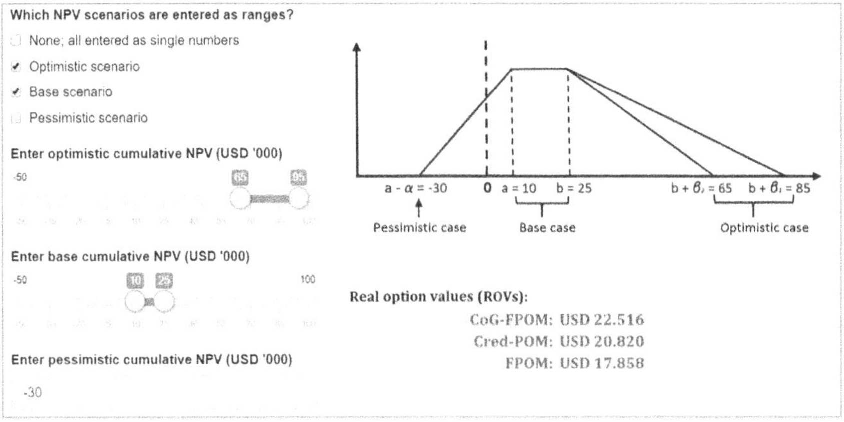

Fig. 4 Interval-valued scenarios as inputs

The selection now corresponds to case 3, $a - \alpha_2 < 0 < a$, represented by Eqs. (14) and (15) for $E_{IV-CoG}(A_+)$ and $Weight_3$, respectively. Now, $\alpha_1 = \alpha_2$, and the interval-ROV becomes:

$$IV-ROV_{CoG} = \frac{2b+\frac{\beta_1+\beta_2}{2}-\frac{a^2}{2}\left(\frac{1}{\alpha_1}+\frac{1}{\alpha_2}\right)}{2b-2a+\frac{\alpha_1+\alpha_2+\beta_1+\beta_2}{2}} * \frac{1}{2}\left[\frac{-a^3+3b^2\alpha_1+3b\beta_1\alpha_1+\beta_1^2\alpha_1}{-3a^2+6b\alpha_1+3\beta_1\alpha_1} + \frac{-a^3+3b^2\alpha_2+3b\beta_2\alpha_2+\beta_2^2\alpha_2}{-3a^2+6b\alpha_2+3\beta_2\alpha_2}\right] = 81.250\% * 27.712 = 22.516.$$

Thus, $IV-ROV_{CoG} = USD22.516$ (with the weight of 81.25% and $E_{IV-CoG}(A_+)$ of USD 27.712), which shows about USD 471, or 2.14% higher ROV than in *Example 1* due to greater upside potential of the base case even the optimistic scenario had more downside than upside compared to *Example 1*'s optimistic NPV.

3.3 *Example 3: Simulating Fuzzy and Probabilistic Real Options Models*

The NPV distribution can be simulated. We introduce the membership function of a fuzzy distribution A based on simulated series of returns as:

$$A(x) = \begin{cases} 0 & x < r_1 \\ \mu_1 & r_1 \le x < r_2 \\ \mu_2 = 1 & r_2 \le x < r_3 \\ \mu_3 & r_3 \le x < r_4 \\ \dots & \\ \mu_n & r_{n-1} \le x \le r_n \\ 0 & r_n < x, \end{cases} \tag{23}$$

which gives the degree of membership for the fuzzy distribution. The simulated return series have been transformed to ranges: the smallest simulated return value r_1 from r_1 gives the minimum NPV for first range from r_1 to r_2 of the obtained distribution, and the range has degree of membership μ_1. The widths of the ranges are equal. We get the width by dividing the range from smallest simulated return r_1 to the largest simulated return r_n by 100, meaning that for 1000 simulations, 10 simulated returns fall between one range on average, for 10000 simulations, 100 returns. The range with the largest number of simulations is the peak range, from r_2 to r_3 in the example (cf. Eq. 23), and the range obtains the membership value 1. The rest of the membership values in our simulation procedure are set relative to the frequency of simulated returns within the range divided by the frequency of the peak range resulting in $\mu \in [0, 1]$ for all μ.

Recalling the ROV formula (2) for the *center-of-gravity* case, we can formulate the components of the center-of-gravity real options formula. The expected NPV of the positive simulated values is:

$$E_{CoG}(A) = \frac{\int_{-\infty}^{\infty} xA(x)dx}{\int_{-\infty}^{\infty} A(x)dx} = \frac{\frac{1}{2}\left[\left(r_2^2 - r_1^2\right)\mu_1 + \cdots + \left(r_n^2 - r_{n-1}^2\right)\mu_{n-1}\right]}{(r_2 - r_1)\mu_1 + \cdots + (r_n - r_{n-1})\mu_{n-1}}, \tag{24}$$

where r_n is the n'th simulated possibilistic return and μ_{n-1} is the degree of membership for the range from the *n-1*'th to the n'th simulated value. The weight component for the simulated return series becomes:

$$Weight = \frac{\int_{0}^{\infty} A(x)dx}{\int_{-\infty}^{\infty} A(x)dx} = \frac{\left[(s_2 - s_1)\varepsilon_1 + \cdots + \left(s_p - s_{p-1}\right)\varepsilon_{p-1}\right]}{\left[(r_2 - r_1)\mu_1 + \cdots + (r_n - r_{n-1})\mu_{n-1}\right]}, \tag{25}$$

where s_p is the p'th simulated non-negative return and $s_p = r_n$, if all the simulated return are non-negative, then s's are replaced by r's in the weight formula; and, similarly, ε_{p-1} is the degree of membership from the *p-1*'th to the p'th non-negative return and $\varepsilon_p = \mu_n$, if all the simulated returns are non-negative.

Thus, the center-of-gravity real option formula for simulated returns becomes:

$$ROV_{CoG} = \frac{\left[(s_2 - s_1)\varepsilon_1 + \cdots + \left(s_p - s_{p-1}\right)\varepsilon_{p-1}\right]}{\left[(r_2 - r_1)\mu_1 + \cdots + (r_n - r_{n-1})\mu_{n-1}\right]} * \frac{\frac{1}{2}\left[\left(r_2^2 - r_1^2\right)\mu_1 + \cdots + \left(r_n^2 - r_{n-1}^2\right)\mu_{n-1}\right]}{(r_2 - r_1)\mu_1 + \cdots + (r_n - r_{n-1})\mu_{n-1}}. \tag{26}$$

For the probabilistic case, withdrawing the simulated return series from the corresponding probabilistic triangular distribution, gives a Datar-Mathews (DM) type of real option value. This ROV_{DM} is obtained using the EnvStats R package with the code shows in Fig. 5. The function *rtri*(n = 1000, min = -30, max = 80, $mode$ = 10) generates 1000 simulated returns from the triangular distribution with minimum NPV = USD -30k, maximum NPV = USD 80k and with the mode (peak) NPV = USD 10k. The function *1- ptri(q = 0, min = -30, max = 80, mode = 10)* gives the weight as *ptri()* is the cumulative distribution function (cdf) of the triangular NPV distribution evaluated at quantile, q = 0, giving the area of negative NPV, which is deducted from the whole area of the NPV distribution, 1. The R algorithm of Fig. 5 returns the weight, 79.55%, the mean, $E(A_+) = 28673$, and the ROV_{DM} of USD 22.808.

Figure 6 shows the positive NPV distributions from above R formula on the right with 1000 simulations (n = 1000 in the *rtri*() function), in the middle with n = 2000 and on the left with n = 10000. It is clearly seen, even the negative NPVs are truncated in the figure, that when the number of simulations increases, the distribution

```
library(EnvStats) # loads the EnvStats library
set.seed(20) # sets the seed for reproducable simulations
Nvect <- rtri(n=1000, min=-30 , max=80, mode=10) # vector of n simulated NPVs
Pvect <- subset(Nvect, Nvect > 0) # vector of the positive simulated NPVs
weight <- (1-ptri(q=0, min=-30 , max=80, mode=10)) # full area (1) minus the negative area
ROV_DM <- weight*mean(Pvect) # computes ROV = weight * mean of the positive area
ROV_DM # returns the ROV with Datar Mathews method: ROV_DM: 22.8087
```

Fig. 5 R algorithm for the probabilistic ROV_{DM} using a simplified Datar-Mathews method.

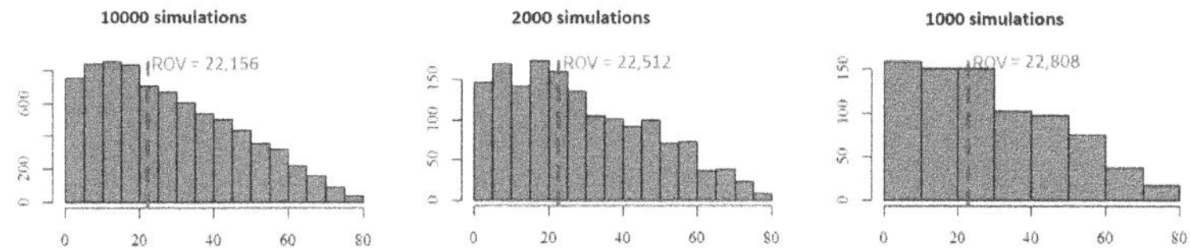

Fig. 6 Simulated payoffs converge to triangular distribution and ROV_{DM} to ROV_{CoG}

converges to triangular shape (with mode = 10, max = 80, and the truncated min = -30). 10000 simulations visually seem to be close to the theoretical triangular distribution, while 2000 simulations still leads to significant deviations from it.

Interestingly, we may note that the probabilistic real option value converges to the center-of-gravity fuzzy real option value for the fuzzy triangular distribution $A(a = 10, a - \alpha = -30, a + \beta = 80)$ (cf. Borges et al. 2018; Kinnunen and Georgescu 2020):

$$ROV_{CoG} = \frac{2a - \frac{a^2}{\propto} + \beta}{\propto + \beta} * \frac{\propto (a + \beta)^3 - a^3(\propto + \beta)}{3 \propto (a + \beta)^2 - 3a^2(\propto + \beta)}$$
$$= 79.55\% * 27714 = 22045,$$

i.e., $ROV_{CoG} = USD\ 22.045$. In Fig. 7, n = 1000 gives $ROV_{DM} = 22808$ (shown on red), 2000 simulations lead to ROV_{DM} = USD 22512, and ten thousand simulations ROV_{DM} = USD 22156, and 1 Mio. Simulations (not shown in the figure) gives $ROV_{DM} = USD\ 22051$. Luukka et al. (2019) have further made transformations between possibilistic means and center-of-gravity means for trapezoidal and triangular fuzzy numbers, which tie up the pay-off models further together.

In Fig. 7, the fuzzy distribution obtained by 1000 simulations replaces the corresponding fuzzy numbers of Figs. 3 and 4 and completes the examples of the real options methods, which may be used as a basis for a digital coaching environment to support strategic investment analysts and decision makers in building intuition

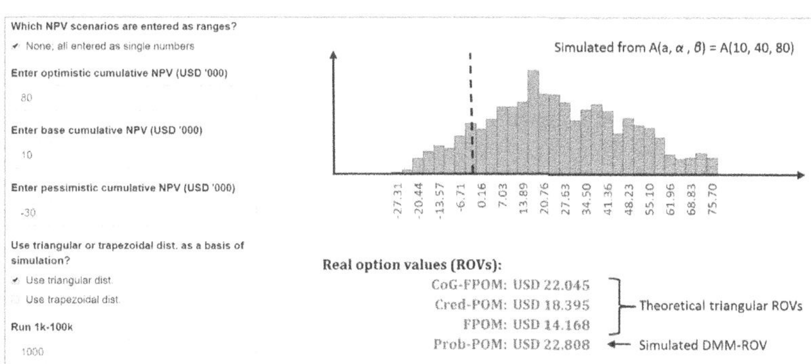

Fig. 7 Simulation-based pay-off distribution

to real options methods and to apply the fuzzy pay-off methods in their application areas.

4 Conclusions

In this paper, the digitalization in financial management practices and valuation methods was considered. The challenges in strategic investment analysis, in the case of flexibility, have been demonstrated to be more suitably handled by real options valuation methods than, for instance, by more traditional net-present-value methods.

The real options methods had been recently developed to be more intuitive but still able to capture the relevant optionalities/flexibilities available for strategic investors, when combined with scenario thinking. The large uncertainty inherent in typical long-run real investments has called for soft computing methods and as a response, particularly, a family of fuzzy pay-off methods, have been developed including the original FPOM (Collan et al. 2009), which, firstly, fuzzified the probabilistic Datar-Mathews Method, DMM (Datar and Mathews 2007), for real options investments, the credibilistic version Cred-FPOM (Collan et al. 2012), and the most recent center-of-gravity model, CoG-FPOM (Borges et al. 2018), which corrected certain inconsistency with the original FPOM found in the context of abandonment options (Borges et al. 2018). Center-of-Gravity and possibilistic means have been shown to be connected, which can further open new modelling developments (Luukka et al. 2019), while we showed numerically (Example 3 in Sect. 3.3) that the real option value from probabilistic DMM converges with the CoG-FPOM.

In the paper, the focus was on the most recent center-of-gravity pay-off method, which was applied through examples to show how a digital coaching environment can be built on fuzzy pay-off models to support and teach by stepwise procedure from intuition-building to actual applications of the practical models. The models were presented in the free open-source R environment allowing, e.g., easy application-specific extensions and integration to common spreadsheet and other analysis software. Extensions and R codes for the presented models are found in (Kinnunen and Georgescu 2020; Kinnunen and Georgescu 2019) and may be requested from the authors.

Carlsson (2019) presented areas of digital coaching, where they had identified the need to produce decision support. Their outlined coaching would start with opening questions about what, why, how and when, and these queries would activate through the user interface. Carlsson (2019) pointed out that coaches will add more value, the better they are calibrated to the cognitive and technical background of the users so that the users get the support they understand and that they can use. They described four main cases, where they had identified need for supports: (i) collecting and guiding estimates of imprecise incoming cash flows and costs; (ii) collecting and guiding market estimates discount rate, value lost over the option, the variance of potential cash flows and downward and upward potential estimates for α's and β's;

(iii) explaining fuzzy ROV, possibilistic mean, variance, and NPV of cumulated cash-flows; and (iv) explaining and guiding ranking of fuzzy ROVs. We argue having presented intuitive real options models for which the required input values are clear although the required data to collect can be very application specific, while we presented the models only in the general context (cf. Cases (i)–(ii)); we find the greatest contributions of this paper with respect to cases (iii) and (iv): The mean values of the pay-off models are all rather intuitive and center-of-gravity ROV was shown to converge with the probabilistic Datar-Mathews type of model with simulated cash flows. This will most likely add to the intuitiveness and easiness to learn and understand the concepts of the mean, variance and cumulated NPVs, as well; Ranking of the investments was seen clear by ranking the obtained ROVs for optional strategic investments, while further allowing several pay-off models (possibilistic, credibilistic and center-of-gravity ROVs and comparable probabilistic ROVs) to help in ranking to identify possible issues needing more attention in the valuation in the case with large differences between the ROVs from different types of pay-off models (cf. Case (iv).)

Further development of the prototype digital coaching tool will be done to account for possible later application-specific needs with the presented real options models.

References

Black, F., Scholes, M.: The pricing of options and corporate liabilities. J. Polit. Econ. **81**(3), 637–654 (1970)

Borges, R.E.P., Dias, M.A.G., Dória Neto, A.D., Meier, A.: Fuzzy pay-off method for real options: The center of gravity approach with application in oilfield abandonment. Fuzzy Sets Syst. **353**, 111–123 (2018)

Carland, C., Goentzel, J., Montibeller, G.: Modeling the values of private sector agents in multi-echelon humanitarian supply chains. EJOR **269**, 532–543 (2018)

Carlsson, C.: Digital coaching for real options support. In: Pelta, D.A., Cruz Corona, C. (eds.) Soft Computing Based Optimization and Decision Models, Studies in Fuzziness and Soft Computing, vol. 360, pp. 153–175. Springer , Heidelberg (2017)

Carlsson, C.: Analytics Mobilized with digital coaching. Intelligent Systems in Accounting, Finance and Management, ISAF1421, 3–17 (2018a)

Carlsson, C.: Decision analytics—key to digitalization. Inf. Sci. **460–461**, 424–438 (2018b)

Carlsson, C.: Digital Coaching to Make Fuzzy Real Options Methods Viable for Investment Decisions. In: IEEE International Conference on Fuzzy Systems (FUZZ-IEEE), pp. 1–6. New Orleans, USA, June 23–26 (2019)

Carlsson, C., Fullér, R.: On possibilistic mean value and variance of fuzzy numbers. Fuzzy Sets Syst. **122**, 315–326 (2001)

Carlsson, C., Fullér, R.: A fuzzy approach to real option valuation. Fuzzy Sets Syst. **139**, 297–312 (2003)

Collan, M., Kinnunen, J.: A procedure for the rapid pre-acquisition screening of target companies using the pay-off method for real option valuation. J. Real Options Strategy **4**(1), 117–141 (2011)

Collan, M., Fullér, R., Mézei, J.: Fuzzy pay-off method for real option valuation. J. Appl. Math. Decis. Syst. **14** (2009)

Collan, M., Fullér, R., Mezei, J.: Credibilistic approach to the fuzzy pay-off method for real option analysis. J. Appl. Oper. Res. **4**(4), 174–182 (2012)

Collan, M., Carlsson, C., Majlender, P.: Fuzzy black and scholes real options pricing. J. Decis. Syst. **12**, 391–416 (2003)
Datar, V., Mathews, S.: A practical method for valuing real options: the boeing approach. J. Appl. Corporate Fin. **19**, 95–104 (2007)
Dubois D., Prade, H.: Fuzzy Sets and Systems: Theory and Applications. Academic Press, New York (1980)
Dubois, D., Prade, H.: Possibility Theory: An Approach to Computerized Processing of Uncertainty. Plenum Press, New York (1988)
Fairchild, K.W., Misra, L., Shi, Y.: Using triangular distribution for business and finance simulations in excel. J. Fin. Educ. Winter **2016**, 313–336 (2016)
Fern, A., Natarajan, S., Judah, K., Tadepalli, P.: A decision-theoretic model of assistance. J. Artif. Intell. Res. **49**, 71–104 (2014)
Georgescu, I., Kinnunen, J.: Credibility measures in portfolio analysis: From possibilistic to probabilistic models. J. Appl. Oper. Res. **3**(2), 91–102 (2011)
Keen, P.G.W.: Information systems and organizational change. Commun. ACM **24**(1), 24–33 (1981)
Kinnunen, J.: Valuing M&A synergies as (Fuzzy) real options. In: Proceedings (CD) of the 14th Annual International Conference on Real Options (ROC-10), pp. 1–23. Rome, Italy, June 16–19 (2010)
Kinnunen, J., Collan, M.: Supporting the screening of corporate acquisition targets. In: Proceedings of the 42nd International Conference on System Sciences (HICSS-09), pp. 1–8. Waikoloa, Hawaii, January 5–8 (2009)
Kinnunen, J., Georgescu, I.: Decision support system for evaluating synergy real options in M&A. In: Proceedings of the International Conference on Management and Information Systems (ICMIS-19), pp. 408–418. Bangkok, Thailand, September 29–30 (2019)
Kinnunen, J., Georgescu, I.: Fuzzy real options analysis based on interval-valued scenarios with a corporate acquisition application. Nordic J. Bus. **69**(1), 44–67 (2020)
Kinnunen, J., Georgescu, I.: Credibilistic real options analysis using interval-valued triangular fuzzy numbers. In: Proceedings of the IRES-WSFASE International Conference, pp. 32–37. Jakarta, Indonesia, February 27–28 (2020)
Kinnunen, J., Georgescu, I., Collan, M.: Center-of-Gravity Real Options Method Based on Interval-Valued Fuzzy Numbers. In: Kahraman, C., Onar, S. Ç., Öztayşi, B., Sari, I. U. Çebi, S., Tolga, A. C. (eds.) Proceedings of the Intelligent and Fuzzy Techniques: Smart and Innovative Solutions Conference (INFUS-20). Izmir, Turkey, July 21-23, 2020 (forthcoming).
Luukka, P., Stoklasa, J., Collan, M.: Transformations between the center of gravity and the possibilistic mean for triangular and trapezoidal fuzzy numbers. Soft. Comput. **23**(10), 3229–3235 (2019)
Merton, R.K.: Theory of rational option pricing. Bell J. Econ. Manage. Sci. **4**, 141–183 (1973)
Mezei J., Collan M., Luukka P.: Real option analysis with interval-valued fuzzy numbers and the fuzzy pay-off method. In: Kacprzyk J., Szmidt E., Zadrożny S., Atanassov K., Krawczak M. (eds) Advances in Fuzzy Logic and Technology 2017. EUSFLAT 2017, IWIFSGN 2017. Advances in Intelligent Systems and Computing, vol. 641, pp. 509–520. Springer, Berlin (2018)
Simon, H.A.: Cognitive science: the newest science of the artificial. Cogn. Sci. **4**, 33–46 (1980)
Sprague, R.H.: Framework for the development of decision support systems. MIS Q. **4**(4), 1–26 (1980)
Zadeh, L.A.: The concept of a linguistic variable and its application to approximate reasoning-I. Inf. Sci. **8**(3), 199–249 (1975)
Zadeh, L.A.: Fuzzy sets as a basis for a theory of possibility. Fuzzy Sets Syst. **1**, 3–28 (1978)
Zeleny, M.: Multiple Criteria Decision Making. McGraw-Hill, New York (1982)

The Influence of Presence of Art in the Life of Individuals and Society

Iuliana Coman and Niculae Mihăiţă

1 Introduction

Noica (1992), presents the Blaga perspective regarding knowledge and culture: "Like some trees of the spirit, raised under unknown threats, to which humans responds by fighting, is the way Blaga sees the creations of knowledge and culture."

Art, in different forms, is one of the daily components of our life, and the convictions regarding the impact of art show a profound influence of art on the lives of individuals worldwide and in Romanian society.

Different convictions regarding the impact of art upon the life of society or upon the life of persons is analyzed in this paper, using the data obtained in the answers of respondents, or analyzing the association between different variables generated by the answer of respondents.

2 Literature Review

The influence of art upon the life of individuals and upon the life of society was the subject of several books or studies published starting with the beginning of last century and up to nowadays.

Gabeaud (1930) consider that the origin of music is lost in the night of time, but, according to the memories of men and the oldest traditions, the art of music manifests itself in two particular forms, each corresponding to a very human state of mind: (1) the art of gesture or dance, which expresses joy; (2) the art of sung speech, from contemplation and prayer.

I. Coman (✉) · N. Mihăiţă
University of Economic Studies, Bucharest, Romania
e-mail: Iuliana.coman.ards@gmail.com

A. M. Dima and F. DÁscenzo (eds.), *Business Revolution in a Digital Era*,
Springer Proceedings in Business and Economics,
https://doi.org/10.1007/978-3-030-59972-0_15

Gombrich (1950) remember that in the past the attitude towards painting and sculpture was often the same. They were considered not so much a work of art as objects created for a specific purpose. Among these primitives, construction and imagery come from the same spirit of utility.

The capacity of art to influence the life of individuals was analyzed in the study moderate by de Sorensen (2011) Dean of the Departments of Art and Humanities at Harvard University, and the study presents the incontestable impact of art on researchers' life, in society and into individuals' life.

Eleonora Pantano published her research "Cultural factors affecting consumer behavior: a new perception model" (2011) reveling the influence of culture on the behavior of consumers of local products in the Calabria area. The results of the study show the major influence which culture has on consumers behavior.

Catherine L. Bachleda and Asmae Bennani describe in the study "Personality and interest in the visual arts", published in 2016, the impact of the psychological components on the visual arts, and the results show that the most powerful influence on the behavior of plastic art consumers are several traits of personality. Rodner et al. (2011) presents how art has already been defined as an economic agent that participates in the evolution of the economic environment.

The Cultural Barometer (2016), presents the tendency manifested at international level to evaluate the impact of art in the social and economic environment. Studies organized in France or Canada, demonstrate that art has a strong influence in society, developing the independence of individuals, expanding the capacity of knowledge, developing the understanding and the ability to act. Also, art participates in building social cohesion and developing society by encouraging civic participation.

Nissley (2010) also shows that art was present in our lives in a multitude of other forms defined in contemporary society, such as decoration—artwork in hallways/corridors and images on office walls (e.g. Art corporate); entertainment—bringing arts/shows into the office space (for example, offering tickets to employees at artistic events); as a tool—when companies use art as a tool for management/leadership development (e.g. equipment, development of communication skills, etc.); and strategic transformation—when the business integrates the arts in areas such as vision and values, creativity and innovation, branding and marketing.

During this period, the influence of art on the feeling of life fulfillment or on convictions regarding art it has aroused some interest, in this paper a more in depth analyze is developed using statistical methods, for assessing the impact of art in nowadays. The aim of this research is to identify the impact that the presence of art has upon the life fulfilment sentiment, upon convictions regarding art influence on individuals or regarding capacity of art to consolidate the society.

3 Methodology

The research was organized using data obtained from an experimental survey, which included 120 respondents from the Southern of Romania.

The sample included persons with higher education for assuring this way a consistent exposure of the respondents to art and assuring this way a more profound analysis of the impact of art in the life of individuals and in the life of society. The influence of education into the behavior of art consumer was also confirmed by the Cultural Barometer 2018 (Croitoru and Becut 2019), where it is confirmed that people with higher education have the greatest participation in cultural consumption.

The 120 answers were obtained by face to face interviews obtained on street, in Bucharest, Alexandria and Brasov, and by answers obtained on-line using a platform promoted in different on-line groups.

This communication is an academic lecture, an example of robustness in the simplest approach starting from the statistical instrumentation of the percentages of contingency tables of the dichotomous variables, found in planes and hyperplanes of interaction or indifference.

For analyzing the association between different variables, the method MONALIS (acronym from the Methodology of Onicescu Analysis in the Language of Informational Statistics) is used according to the description in the Bibliography (Mihăiţă Niculae 1993, 1985, 2001, 2003). MONALIS method had also application in several economics (Dragnea and Mihăiţă 2017) and social domains (Coman 2019).

The method includes the following steps. The contingency tables are used, including the results by intersecting the answers to two questions X with alternatives Xi, where i = 1,....., r placed as rows (r) of the table, and Y with alternatives Yj, with j = 1, ..., c placed in columns (c) of the same table.

The questions considered as segmentation variables (independent, causal, extrinsic, exogenous, stimuli) were placed in the columns of the table.

The tables are cut to 2 × 2 lines and columns. Where: Column 1 presents the alternatives of the influenced phenomenon, or effect, that will be evaluated according to the states of the independent phenomenon, or of the influence (Table 1).

The question analyzed is the next one:

To what extent does the cause (the feeling of Life Fulfilment) influence the effect (the perception of Material Comfort)?

The question can also be asked in the following way: What are the chances that a respondent who has chosen the alternative Partial Agreement regarding Life Satisfaction and Partial Agreement Material Comfort not to change his or her choice regarding the effect variable (Perception regarding Material Comfort).

In Column 1 there are the two alternatives:

- Row 1—event 1 Partial Agreement on Material Comfort and
- Row 1—event 2 Total Agreement regarding Material Comfort perceptions that will be analyzed depending of the influence of the Sentiment of Satisfaction in Life—the second segmentation variable, which was distributed on columns.

Table 1 Life Satisfaction influence upon material comfort

Col. 1	2	3	4	5	6	7	8	9	10	11
Cause (Life Satisfaction)/Effect (Material Comfort)	Partial accord	Complete accord	Total	P1, p2	Partial accord	Complete accord	odds	inter	Ccor	Kcor
Partial Accord	64	20	84	76%	3.2	la o pers	3.4	1792	0.37	0.8
Complete Accord	8	28	36	22%	0.29	pt. 1	0.3	160	0.06	0.51
Total	72	48	120	60%	11.2	OddR	11	11.2	0.44	0.68

In Row 3 is included the total by columns, so the distribution by the second segmentation factor.

Column 2: Frequency in alternatives generated by segmentation by cause phenomenon, (Sentiment of Life Fulfilment); on which is applied the segmentation generated by the effect phenomenon for distribution on rows. In column 2, row 1 there is the maximum number of the four cells.

Column 3: Antithesis of the first alternative. Column 2 and column 3 change alternately, they are conditioned by alternatives.

Column 4: The total on lines, so on the segments generated by the analyzed variable, the variable considered effect.

Column 5: Calculation of Probabilities or Relative Frequencies—Percentages/Chances to which the question refers (Col 2/Col 4).

Column 6: Qualitative Calculation (Col 2/Col 3)—how many times is the frequency of the response higher comparing to the alternative—Col 3. This is the calculation of the Report for the reference segment versus Control (Relative Risk) for being convinced that we have the right answer to the question.

Column 6 Total is the ratio between the subjects interviewed at the event to which the question is addressed and the control group. In our example, it means that 11 times more likely those who chose Partial Accord regarding the Life Fulfilment to choose Partial Accord for Material Comfort over Total Accord regarding Material Comfort.

Column 7: The evidence of the report from 1 to 1, shows that the report in column 6 is possible.

Column 8 (Odds)—Arithmetic calculation of the Magnitude of the analyzed association.

In the first line we have calculated Odds—the chances that a person who has chosen an alternative of the effect variable will move to the other alternative of the effect variable: The maximum between the percentages of column 5 relative to the minimum of the percentages in column 5. In the second line we have (1—max percentages in Col 5) / (1—min percentages in Col 5).

The calculation for which column 5 is constructed is the ratio of Odds calculated on the two lines and thus we obtain the Magnitude of the association.

Column 9: The product of the main diagonal, priority being the first segment from the point of view of the question. The report is calculated to the product of column 2 for relative risk.

Column 10: The Informational Correlation represents for each alternative of the variable Effect: the product of the weights (probabilities) of the alternatives of the causal variable in relation to the total of these in the analyzed universe. For the entire universe: the sum of the above products.

The values of the informational correlation can be found in the range 0–1, where the values close to 1 re-flex the lack of association, and the values close to 0 a very strong association, more precisely it reflects the fact that there is influence between the two variables.

Column 11: Onicescu Informational Correlation Coefficient. In each of the lines we have the Information Energy for the two segments generated by segmentation by the cause factor: The sum of the squares of the weights of the segments generated by the event (the effect factor) within the segments generated by the cause factor.

The coefficient of Onicescu correlation for the entire association is calculated by reporting the Informational Correlation to the radical of the product of the two Informational energies of lines 1 and 2.

The values of the Onicescu Correlation Coefficient can be found in the range 0–1, where the values close to 1 reflect the lack of association, and those close to 0 a very strong association, more precisely reflecting the fact that there is influence between the two variables.

The last row in each table gives us the answer to the question: What is the ratio of the target subjects to the antithesis for which the event will occur?

The conclusion of the table presented above show a strong influence of Life Fulfilment Sentiment upon the Perception of Material Comfort. The Magnitude of association is 11.2. The Odds is 3.4, the Informational Correlation is 0.44, and Onicescu Correlation Coefficient is 0.68, all these indicators reveling a strong association.

When we introduce gender as a control variable, we obtained the same strong association. The Odds for Men is 2.3 and for Women 4.1.

4 Results and Discussions

4.1 Sentiment of Life Fulfilment

The Sentiment of Life Fulfillment was one of the most important variables in the analysis of this paper, in many of the analyzes carried out was considered the association of the various variables with the variable Sentiment of Life Liement to identify their impact on the lives of each of the respondents.

Therefore, in addition to the personal evaluation of the Sentiment of Life Fulfilment, each of the respondents defined the sentiment answering to an open question.

The definition of the feeling of life fulfilment according to the perspective of the respondents is presented below using a table with the most frequently used words in the definition of the sentiment (Table 2).

The most important word used to define the feeling of life fulfillment is "Family". In fact, there are many other studies that identified the Family as the most important value that defines the consumer in Romania (Ex. Consumer Life GfK 2019).

In the next two places are presents the words "Joy" and "Fulfillment".

If the increased frequency of the word "Fulfillment" can be generated by the fact that the question included this word, certainly the word "Joy", placed on the third place is one of the most important words that define the Sentiment of Fulfillment in life from respondents' perspective from the sample of the experimental study.

The next two words in the top are "Health" and "Friends".

Table 2 Top 10 words used for life satisfaction definition

Crt. No	Word	Fervency	Percentages (%)
1	Family	37	31
2	Joy	16	13
3	Fulfilment	16	13
4	Health	15	13
5	Friends	12	10
6	Equilibrium	10	8
7	Material	10	8
8	Living	10	8
9	Travels	9	8
10	Time	9	8

Probably in these moments of Covid-19 pandemic, "Health" would be redefined as one of the most powerful variables in assessing the quality of life and would appear in one of the first 3 positions.

"Friends" are another important variable used to define the sentiment of life fulfilment, followed by "Equilibrium", "Material comfort", "Living" and "Travels".

4.2 *The Presence of Art Influence upon the Feeling of Life Fulfilment*

The results of the experimental study revealed that 39% of respondents expressed their partial accord reading that presence of art influenced their life, and 40% expressed their total accord, that show an influence of presence of art upon the life of respondents.

40% of respondents expressed full agreement on fulfillment in life and 49% expressed partial agreement on fulfillment in life.

The analysis shows that most of the respondents consider that they had a fulfilled life and art was present in their lives.

Going forward was analyzed the influence of the variable generated by the considerations regarding the presence of art upon the variable generated by the considerations regarding the capacity of art to influence the life of respondents.

Analysing the Impact of Sentiment of Fulfilment of Life upon the Perception regarding the Presence of art in the respondent's life a perfect symmetric distribution of data was discovered (Table 3).

The cross table show a perfect symmetry around the first axe. That means in this association both influences are equals. The influence of Presence of Art upon the Sentiment of Life Fulfilment is equal with the influence of Life Fulfilment upon the Perception regarding the Presence of Art. The Informational Correlation 0.45, Onicescu Correlation Coefficient 0.79, and Odds of 1.9 reveal an association.

Table 3 Life satisfaction influence upon perception regarding presence of art

Col.1	2	3	4	5	6	7	8	9	10	11
Presence of art/fulfilled life	Disagreement or Partial accord	Complete accord	Total	P1, p2	Disagreement or partial accord	Complete accord	odds	inter*–	Ccor	Kcor
Disagreement or partial accord	53	19	72	74%	2.79	for one pers	1.9	1537	0.29	0.61
Complete accord	19	29	48	40%	0.66	pt. 1	0.44	361	0.16	0.52
Total	72	48	120	60%	4.26	OddR	4.26	4.26	0.45	0.8

The variable Gender was used as a variable of control, and a similar association was found, with an Odds of 1.7 in the case of Men and 1.9 in the case of Women. The results obtained using the variable of control confirmed that the association exist and is weak.

4.3 The Impact of Presence of Art upon the Convictions Regarding the Influence of Art

In the experimental study conducted 44% of the respondents expressed total agreement on the capacity of art to influence the lives of individuals, and 37% of respondents expressed partial agreement on the capacity of art to influence their lives.

The result of analyses of variable generated by answers to the questions regarding the presence of art and the capacity of art to influence the life of respondents are presented in Table 4.

The results show that the respondents who have expressed Agreement regarding the Presence of Art in their life are 3.6 times more likely not to change their considerations regarding the Impact of Art in their life comparing to those who have expressed their Total Agreement regarding the Presence of Art in their life. Magnitude of association is 22.6, Odds 3.6, Informational Correlation 0.29 and Onicescu Correlation Coefficient 0.403. All coefficient indicates a strong association. The presence of Art in the life of respondents proved that Art has a strong influence on the life of respondents.

But a very interesting fact is that the influence of conviction regarding the Influence of Art upon the life of respondents has an even stronger influence upon the perceptions regarding the Presence of art in the life of respondents. Today art became a part of our daily life, a multitude of songs, images, designs are around us, every of them could be considered a form of art. That is why the perception of presence of art became a very personal and subjective perception.

The impact of conviction regarding the influence of art upon the respondent's life is presented in Table 5.

The conviction regarding the Influence of art upon the life of respondents has a strong influence upon the presence of art in the life of respondents, this could means that these respondents invested time, attention and budget in making art present in their life, but in the same time that means these respondents could have a different perception regarding the presence of life.

When the variable of control is included, gender is used as a variable of control, it was found that influence continues to exist, with a higher Magnitude of association 49 in the case of Men and 71 in the case of Women. Also, Odds calculated for Men and Women indicated a strong influence: Odds of 3.8 in the case of Men and 5.7 in the case of Women.

Table 4 Presence of art influence upon conviction regarding influence on life

Col.1	2	3	4	5	6	7	8	9	10	11
Presence of Art/Influence upon life	Partial accord	Comp. accord	Total	P1, p2	Partial accord	Comp. accord	odds	inter*-	Ccor	Kcor
Partial Accord	59	8	67	88%	7.38	la o pers	3.6	2360	0.14	0.7
Complete Accord	13	40	53	24%	0.33	pt. 1	0.16	104	0.15	0.72
Total	72	48	120	60%	22.69	OddR	22.69	22.69	0.29	0.4

Table 5 Conviction regarding art impact influence upon perception of presence of art

Col.1	2	3	4	5	6	7	8	9	10	11
Influence upon Life/ Presence of art	Partial accord	Comp. accord	Total	P1, p2	Partial accord	Comp. accord	odds	inter*-	Ccor	Kcor
Partial Accord	59	13	72	81.94%	4.54	la o pers	4.9	2360	0.22	0.79
Complete Accord	8	40	48	16.67%	0.2	pt. 1	0.22	104	0.09	0.63
Total	67	53	120	55.83%	22.69	OddR	22.7	22.69	0.31	0.434

Could be mention also that this impact is stronger comparing to the influence of Presence of Art upon the convictions regarding the capacity of art to influence the life of respondents.

4.4 The Impact of Art in the Consolidation of Society

According to Cultural Barometer (Croitoru and Becut 2017) studies organized in France or Canada, revealed that art has a strong influence in society, developing the independence of individuals, expanding the capacity of knowledge, and participates in building social cohesion, encouraging civic participation.

Analyzing the convictions of the population regarding this subject, it was observed that 58% of the respondents from the experimental study carried out expressed total agreement on the ability of art to influence the life of society and 33% expressed partial agreement on the ability of art. to influence the life of the community.

The analysis between the variables generated by the answers regarding the presence of art and those regarding the capacity of art to influence society are presented in Table 6.

The results of the analyses show a weak influence: Odds of 1.9 and Informational Correlation of 0.46.

The presence of art in the life or respondents manifest a weak influence on the convictions regarding the capacity of art to participate to the construction of society.

Including the variable of control, odds registered the value 2.2 in the case of men and 1.6 in the case of women, showing that the convictions of men regarding the capacity of art to build the society is stronger comparing to the same convictions in the case of women.

The analyze of the impact of convictions regarding the capacity of art to participate to the building of society is presented in Table 7.

For this association the magnitude is 5.73, Informational Correlation of 0.46 and Odds of 3.0, reveling that the conviction regarding capacity of art to participate to the building of society manifest a strong influence upon the perception regarding the presence of art in the life of respondents.

This convictions regarding the capacity of art to influence the life of society manifest a stronger influence upon the perceptions regarding the presence of art.

A conclusion of this study is that convictions regarding the capacity of art influence the presences of art, influencing the behavior of respondents, or at least changing the perspective regarding the presence of art in the life of individuals.

5 Conclusions

The research demonstrated once again that art influences the life of respondents, and the role of art goes beyond the aesthetic role, effectively participating in creating the

Table 6 Presence of art influence upon convictions regarding the capacity of art to participate to the construction of society

Col.1	2	3	4	5	6	7	8	9	10	11
Presence of Art/construction of society	Partial accord	Comp. accord	Total	P1, p2	Part. accord	Compl. accord	odds	inter*-	Ccor	Kcor
Partial accord	41	9	50	82%	4.56	for 1 pers	1.9	1599	0.11	0.51
Complete accord	31	39	70	44%	0.79	for. 1	0.32	279	0.35	0.7
Total	72	48	120	60%	5.73	OddR	5.73	5.73	0.46	0.77

Table 7 Conviction regarding capacity of art to participate to the construction of society influence upon perception regarding presence of art

Col.1	2	3	4	5	6	7	8	9	10
Construction of society/Presence of art	Partial accord	Compl. accord	Total	P1, p2	Partial accord	Compl. accord	odds	inter*-	Ccor
Partial accord	41	31	72	57%	1.32	la o pers	3	1599	0.36
Complete accord	9	39	48	19%	0.23	pt. 1	0.53	279	0.1
Total	50	70	120	42%	5.73	OddR	5.73	5.73	0.46

feeling of fulfillment in life or consolidating the communities and developing the society.

Life Fulfilment was defined by the respondents of this experimental survey by words such Family, Joy, Fulfilment, Health or Friends, and 89% of respondents considered that they have a fulfilled life (40% of respondents expressed full agreement on fulfillment in life and 49% expressed partial agreement on fulfillment in life).

On the basis of the analysis performed during this study a perfect symmetry was discovered in the association between the variables Presence of art and Life Fulfilment, that demonstrating that the influence of the Presence of Art upon the sentiment of Life Fulfilment is equal with the influence of Life Fulfilment upon the perception regarding the Presence of Art.

Moreover, the study observed the important role that beliefs play in the life of each of us and of society. Beliefs—manifestations of the depth of the impact of the presence of art—come and participate in their turn in the developing the presence of art, or in the perception regarding the presence of art. The results show that the Presence of Art in the life of respondents has a strong influence upon the convictions regarding the capacity of art to influence the life of respondents. And a very interesting fact is that the influence of conviction regarding the Influence of Art upon the life of respondents has an even stronger influence upon the perceptions regarding the Presence of art in the life of respondents.

Also the presence of art manifest influences upon the convictions regarding the capacity of art to participate to the consolidation of society, and in the same time the influence of the conviction regarding the capacity of art to influence the life of society manifest a stronger influence on the perception regarding the Presence of Art.

The influence manifested by convictions proved to be stronger than the influence manifested by the Presence of Art. In fact, convictions precede actions, and naturally determine actions. At the same time, convictions are determined by the presence of art, and the paper captures this double influence that manifests itself between the Presence of Art and the convictions regarding the influence of art on the life of individuals and of society.

References

Bachleda Catherine, L., Asmae, B.: Personality and Interest in the Visual Arts, Arts and the Market, pp 126–140. Emerald Publishing (2016)

Coman, I.: Life fulfilment influence on art consumption and convictions regarding art. In: Proceedings of the 13th International Management Conference, Bucharest, ASE, Romania (2019)

Consumer Life Report, GfK Romania (2019)

Croitoru, C., Becuț, A.M.: National Institute of Statistics, Barometrul de Consum Cultural 2016 O radiografie a practicilor de consum cultural, Bucharest, Universul academic, (2017)

Croitoru, C., Becuț, A.M.: National Institute of Statistics, Barometrul de Consum Cultural 2018 Dinamica Sectorului Cultural în anul Centenarului marii uniri, Bucharest, Universul academic (2019)

Dragnea, M., Mihăiţă, N..: Customer retention strategies and organizational adaptability, Vision 2020. In: Soliman, K.S. (ed.) Sustainable economic Development, Innovation Management, And Global Growth, Vols. I–IX, pp. 1291–1299 (2017)
Gabeaud, A.: Histoire de la Musique, vol. 1930. Librairie Larousse, Paris (1930)
Gombrich, E.H.: Istoria Artei (The story of art 1950), translation Nicolae Constantinescu. Art Publishing house, Bucharest (2012)
Mihăiţă, N.: Onicescu Information Statistics in a Multiple Marketing Data Processing Methodology, Economic Computation and Economic Cybernetic Studies and Research, review no. 2. (1983)
Mihăiţă, N.V.: Quantitative methods in market research—Information Statistics and Marketing. Editura Economică, Bucharest (2001)
Mihăiţă, N.V., Stanciu Capotă, R.: Relations statistiques fortes, cachées, fausses at illusoires: Applications de la statistique informationelle – edition bilingue. EdituraASE, Bucharest (2003)
Nissley, N.: Arts-based learning at work: economic downturns, innovation upturns, and the eminent practicality of arts in business. J. Bus. Strategy **31**(4) (2010)
Noica, C.: Simple Introduceri la Bunatatea Timpului Nostru, pag 207, Humanitas publishing house (1992)
Onicescu, O., Demetrescu, M.C.: Measuring Structures in Economy. Académie des Sciences Sociales et Politiques de Roumanie. Recherches sur la Philosophie des Sciences. Editions de l' Académie Roumanie (1971)
Pantano, E.: Cultural factors affecting consumer behavior: a new perception model. Euro. J. Bus. pp. 117–136 (2011)
Rodner Victoria, L., Maktoba, O., Elaine, T.: The brand-wagon: emerging art markets and the Venice Biennale, The Business School, Edinburgh Napier University, Edinburgh, UK, published by Emerald, pp. 319–336 (2011)
Sorensen, D.: Dean of the Departments of Art and Humanities at Harvard University, Advancing Fields of Knowledge. Harvard Web Publishing (2013)

The Digital Effectiveness on Economic Inequality: A Computational Approach

Irina Georgescu and Jani Kinnunen

1 Introduction

The digitalization though spreading technology and digital skills are having great well-being effects over the world. If digitalization takes place unevenly, social and economic inequalities can arise from the development.

We study 121 world countries and group them into three clusters seen in Fig. 1: countries in cluster 1 are the most developed in terms of digitalization, competitiveness, GDP and well-being and equality,cluster 3 includes the least developed countries in all these measures (on average), while cluster 2 countries are between the two other groups in all the measures on average.

In the recent Harvard Business Review article (Chakravorti et al. 2017) the index of digital competitiveness for 60 countries as seen in Fig. 2 is measured. They group the countries in 4 classes:

- *Stand-out countries*, like Singapore, New Zealand, UAE, Japan, Hong Kong, UK, Germany are highly digitalized and are leaders in innovation;
- *Stall-out countries*, like Norway, Sweden, Switzerland, Denmark, Finland are also high digitally advanced, but still have to put in their efforts for a sustainable growth;
- *Break-out countries*, led by Russia, China, Kenya, Bolivia, Malaysia are characterized by poor infrastructure, low scores of digital competitiveness, but evolve

I. Georgescu (✉)
Bucharest University of Economics, Calea Dorobantilor 15-17, 010552 Bucharest, Romania
e-mail: irina.georgescu@csie.ase.ro

J. Kinnunen
Åbo Akademi, Turku, Finland
e-mail: jani.kinnunen@abo.fi

A. M. Dima and F. DÁscenzo (eds.), *Business Revolution in a Digital Era*,
Springer Proceedings in Business and Economics,
https://doi.org/10.1007/978-3-030-59972-0_16

Fig. 1 121 World countries grouped to highly developed, developed, and developing. *Source* Authors' own research

rapidly. They have to improve the quality of the institutions who sustain the innovation; and

- *Watch-out countries*, among which Egypt, Pakistan, South Africa, have digital low scores due to low customer demand of internet access mobile phones, precarious institutions and infrastructure.

Some countries are at the border of different zones. Romania and Bulgaria are at the border of break out and watch out countries. According to a recent report of the European Commission from 2019, Romania ranks second to last, only above Bulgaria. The best digitalization indicators are the internet connections and the integration of digital technology by businesses. The cloud services have improved and the use of social media by Romanian enterprises increased.

Countries in Fig. 2 are colored dark blue, light blue or red according to our clusters, CL1, CL2 and CL3, presented in Fig. 1. It can be seen that the highly developed countries (by their well-being, digitalization, competitiveness) belong to stall-out and stand-out categories of Chakravorti et al. (2017). They are the most digitalized and they experienced an average rate of digital evolution, 2008–2015. The developed countries of CL2 have also belonged to these two categories, but generally with lower digitalization than CL1 countries, but countries like Slovenia, Slovakia and Greece had experienced close to zero-growth, while countries like Latvia, Poland, Turkey and Russia experienced a 3–4% rate of digital evolution, 2008–2015, similarly with Islamic countries of United Arab Emirates, Saudi Arabia and Malaysia (which are excluded from out data due to lacking inequality data). The developing countries of our CL3 belong to the watch-out and break-out classes of Chakravorti et al. (2017) and watch-out countries like Egypt, Pakistan, Peru, South Africa and Thailand have all under-average digitalization, as well as, experienced under-average digital evolution, 2008–2015, while borderline countries like Bulgaria, Brazil, Jordan, Vietnam,

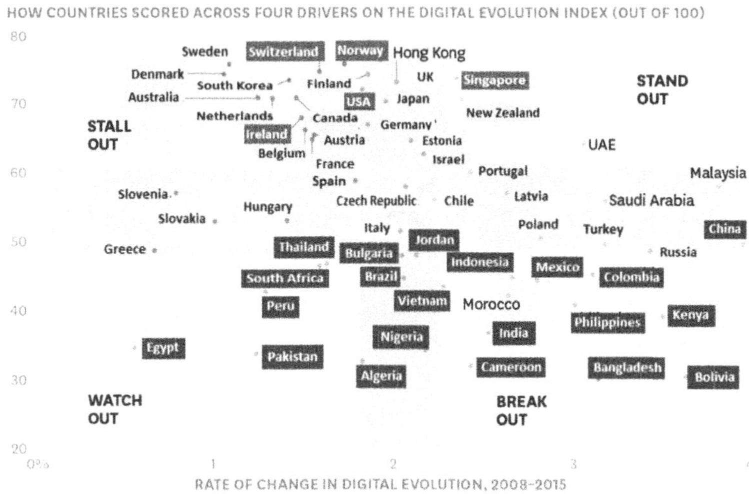

Fig. 2 Four classes of digital evolution. Adapted from Chakravorti et al. (2017)

Algeria and Nigeria have some potential to break-out with their slightly above-average rate of digital evolution. With the very high rate of experienced digital evolution and close to average digitalization, CL3 break-out countries like China, Kenya, Mexico, Philippines, and also the relative fast-growing Mexico, Indonesia and Morocco have the greatest potential to rise towards the league of stand-out countries.

The rest of the paper is structured as follows. In the next section, the relevant literature is reviewed. Then, data and the used clustering and multivariate correlation analysis methods are described. This is followed by the analysis results and their interpretations before the paper is concluded with some suggestions for future research opportunities.

2 Literature Review

In our previous research (Androniceanu et al. 2019,2020; Kinnunen et al. 2019) we proposed a clustering approach to digitalization indicators in order to study the disparities between EU member states. Our findings showed that Romania and Bulgaria positioned in the least digitalized cluster, while in the other clusters, significant differences were discovered in e-government activities, the corporate use of cloud computing and the internet purchase by individuals. Romania and Bulgaria are the weakest performers of EU by almost all considered digitalization indicators.

Digital divide is a very frequent topic (DiMaggio et al. 2004). It refers to the uneven distribution of the ICT access among some groups of populations. These authors distinguish four areas: attitude, access, skills and internet usage. A survey of the Dutch population (Deursen and Dijk 2013) concludes that less educated people and disabled people spend more internet hours than higher educated and employed. Another contribution of their study refers to the internet gap in terms of gender, age, digital skills, income, employment status and residence. Reference (Friemel 2016) shows that in a representative survey for Switzerland, it has been shown that digital divide is an issue among the youngest and the oldest groups: 14–29 year versus 70+ years. The internet usage by old seniors, also called "grey divide" (Morris and Brading 2007) is hindered by the lack of motivation, deficient knowledge or the lack of technical device. Reference (Androniceanu et al. 2020) finds out that consumer attitudes to online purchases in the richest and the most digitalized EU countries, such as Ireland and Luxemburg, are significantly different to the ones in the average EU countries and in the least digitalized EU countries, Romania and Bulgaria.

Reference (Antonio and Tuffley 2014) discusses the gender digital divide in developing countries. Paper (Antonio and Tuffley 2014) is concerned with poor families of workers in which woman does not work and lacks digital skills, e.g. in Southern India or Ghana. In comparison, in West Africa (Burkina Faso, Cameroon, Mali, Senegal, Mauritania) there is no gender digital divide with respect to women with secondary school and above. As seen in Polat (2012), education is a powerful tool to reduce the gender gap in the use of internet.

There is a strong connection between the digital economy and the GDP. The digital economy is closely related to the production and distribution of digital technology. Naumova et al. (2019) note that the contribution of digital economy to GDP for Russia will be from 19 to 34% in future as Russia is only about on the average level of digitalization, it has shown one of the highest development as seen in Fig. 2.

Jovanović et al. (2018) focus on the correlation between the Digital Economy and Society Index (DESI) and other composite indices with sustainability component, for the EU countries. There is a strong positive correlation between these indices, from 0.6 to 0.8, indicating that countries with a high level of digitization contribute more to humanity, therefore, to a higher sustainability.

3 Methodology

The methodology in this research is two-phased: firstly, clustering analysis is applied to the data on the 121 world countries, and secondly, canonical correlation analysis is run on the same data.

3.1 Description of Data

The data consists of four variables, V1-V4 in Table 1, on *digitalization* extracted from the World Bank (WB) and four variables, V5–V8, on *well-being*, i.e., World Economic Forum's competitiveness index (Schwab 2018, 2019), V5, World Bank's monetary well-being measures, GDP per capita (in 2011 US Dollars in purchasing

Table 1 Variables

Variable	Variable label	Source
V1	Digital skills among population	World Bank
V2	Fixed-broadband Internet subscriptions	World Bank
V3	Internet users	World Bank
V4	Mobile-cellular telephone subscriptions	World Bank
V5	Global Competitiveness Index 4.0	WEF
V6	GDP per capita ($ PPP, 2011)	World Bank
V7	Human Development Index, HDI	UNDP
V8	Gini (income inequality)	UNDP

Source Authors' own research.

power parity term), V6, and the United Nations' broad well-being measure, human development index, V7, together with V8, the Gini coefficient measuring the equality of monetary well-being, i.e. the income inequality from the United Nations Development Programme's (UNDP 2018,2019) database for year 2018. The variables of digitalization were determined by the availability of the data on global level.

Below we give the definitions of the eight variables from Table 1:

V1: % of individuals aged 16–74 having basic or above basic overall digital skills and having performed certain activities on the internet.
V2: fixed subscriptions to high-access to the public internet (a TCP/IP connection), at downstream speeds equal to or greater than 256 kbit/s.
V3: % of individuals aged 16–74 who had used the internet within 3 months prior to the survey.
V4: subscriptions to a public mobile telephone provider using cellular technology.
V5: measures national competitiveness defined as the set of institutions, policies and factors that determine the productivity level.
V6: the purchasing power parity value of all final goods produced inside a country in a specified year, divided by the average population measured in the same year.
V7: a composite index of education, life expectancy and per capita income indicators, used to rank world countries in four classes.
V8: a coefficient measuring the income distribution of a country's residents.

3.2 K-Means Clustering

The clustering analysis is conducted using K-means clustering method with SPSS statistical software. The k-means algorithm from (MacQueen 1967) is a very fast algorithm. It computes the Euclidian distances between points and group centers and constructs groups with similar characteristics. The K-means clustering is an iterative process, which starts from some, typically randomized initial center value for each cluster and assigns the closest observations of each centroid (center value) to a cluster,after assignments, new cluster means (centroids) are calculated followed by new assignments. The process is repeated until no new cluster assignments take place.

The number of clusters was selected based on several attempts to determine distinct groups. K-means clustering leads to three clusters, CL1, CL2 and CL3 of sizes 6, 38, and 77 countries, respectively.

3.3 Canonical Correlation Analysis (CCA)

Canonical Correlation Analysis (CCA) is a multivariate statistical technique which investigates associations among two sets of variables. One set is dependent and the other is independent. Linear combinations of variables which maximally correlate are discovered. CCA intends to reduce the data dimensionality by determining a set of canonical variates which are linear combinations of the variables from each set, that explain the variability between and within the two sets. The number of dimensions (canonical functions) equals the number of variables in the smallest set. These functions represent relationships between the dependent and the independent sets.

For CCA, we separate the eight indicators into two classes as seen in Fig. 3:

- Set one (digitalization) contains the indicators V1–V4, and
- Set two (well-being) consists of the indicators V5–V8.

The model consists in predicting 4 dependent variables: Global competitiveness index, GDP per capita, HDI and GINI by four independent variables Digital skills, Fixed broadband subscription, Internet users and Mobile telephone subscriptions.

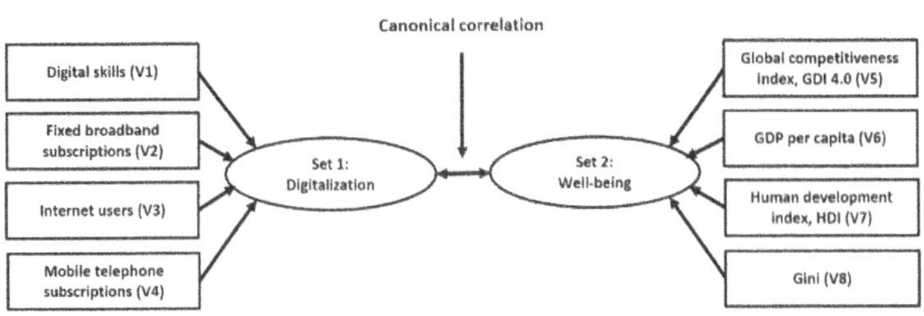

Fig. 3 The CCA model. *Source* Authors' own research

4 Results and Discussions

4.1 K-Means Cluster Analysis

We obtain the following three clusters (CL1, CL2 and CL3) from the applied K-means clustering method (cf. Fig. 1:

- *Cluster 1 (6 highly developed countries)*: Ireland, Luxembourg, Norway, Singapore, Switzerland, and United States;
- *Cluster 2 (38 developed countries)*: Australia, Austria, Belgium, Canada, Chile, Croatia, Cyprus, Czech Republic, Denmark, Estonia, Finland, France, Germany, Greece, Hungary, Iceland, Israel, Italy, Japan, Kazakhstan, Korea Rep., Latvia, Lithuania, Malta, Netherlands, New Zealand, Oman, Panama, Poland, Portugal, Romania, Russian Federation, Slovakia, Slovenia, Spain, Sweden, Turkey, and United Kingdom;
- *Cluster 3 (77 developing countries)*: Albania, Algeria, Angola, Argentina, Armenia, Azerbaijan, Bangladesh, Benin, Bolivia, Bosnia and Herzegovina, Brazil, Bulgaria, Burkina Faso, Burundi, Cambodia, Cameroon, Chad, China, Colombia, Costa Rica, Dominican Republic, Ecuador, Egypt, El Salvador, Ethiopia, Gambia, Georgia, Ghana, Guatemala, Guinea, Haiti, Honduras, India, Indonesia, Iran, Jamaica, Jordan, Kenya, Kyrgyzstan, Lao PDR, Lesotho, Liberia, Malawi, Mali, Mauritania, Mauritius, Mexico, Moldova, Mongolia, Montenegro, Mozambique, Namibia, Nepal, Nicaragua, Nigeria, Pakistan, Paraguay, Peru, Philippines, Rwanda, Senegal, Serbia, Sierra Leone, South Africa, Sri Lanka, Tajikistan, Tanzania, Thailand, Tunisia, Uganda, Ukraine, Uruguay, Venezuela, Vietnam, Yemen, Zambia, and Zimbabwe.

Table 2 presents the data averages for each cluster and as average of all 121 world countries. In addition to the variables V1–V8, we report a *Digi-score* in the second column. This is a simple average of V1–V4 to give us a measure which summarizes the digitalization variables (V1–V4) and shows that the cluster 1, CL1, is the most digitalized (with the Digi-score value of 78.9) followed by CL2 (Digi-score 73.5) and far behind comes CL3 (with the Digi-score of 42.2), while the average Digi-score is 64.9.

Table 2 Cluster means and total averages of the 121 countries

Cluster	DS	V1	V2	V3	V4	V5	V6	V7	V8
CL1	78.9	74.5	70.4	74.9	95.9	80.4	72,388	0.65	0.59
CL2	73.5	62.9	60.5	73.7	97.0	71.9	35,007	0.61	0.56
CL3	42.2	46.8	12.8	28.1	81.0	52.3	8166	0.45	0.35
Avg.	64.9	61.4	47.9	58.9	91.3	68.2	38,521	0.57	0.50

Source Authors' own research

Figure 4 describes the Digi-score for the three clusters and on average (blue bars) together with our dependent variables, V5–V8. It can be seen how the most digitalized cluster, CL1, shows the highest averages to all dependent variables as well: CL1 countries, on average, are the most competitive (by the Global Competitiveness Index, GCI 4.0), are the wealthiest (by GDP per capita) and the most developed (in terms of education, healthcare and wealth measured by the Human Development Index, HDI), but they show also the highest Gini values meaning that their income per capita the most unequally distributed. Similarly, the least digitalized/developed cluster, CL3, shows the lowest performance by all these measures, while CL2 countries' averages are systematically all between the averages of CL1 and CL3 for all measures. It may be further noted that visually one can see that the competitiveness, income inequality and human development decrease in a rather same scale with digitalization from CL1 to CL2 and to CL3, but GDP per capita (PPP, 2011) shows the most radical decrease from CL1's USD 72388 to CL2's USD 35007 to CL3's average of only USD 8166.

Table 3 presents (Pearson) correlations for the same measures presented in Fig. 4, i.e. the Digi-score vs the dependent variables, V5–V8. It is seen that the least developed CL3 countries show the greatest correlations, between 0.813 and 0.869, for the four correlations (and they are statistically significant), the HDI having the highest correlation (0.869) with the Digi-score. CL2 countries show statistically significant correlations between 0.586 (competitiveness, GCI 4.0, vs. Digi-score) and 0.757 (equality, Gini, vs. Digi-score), while clearly lower correlations are seen for CL1. CL1shows even negative correlations between competitiveness and GDP, while correlations are positive between equality and digitalization (0.447) and close

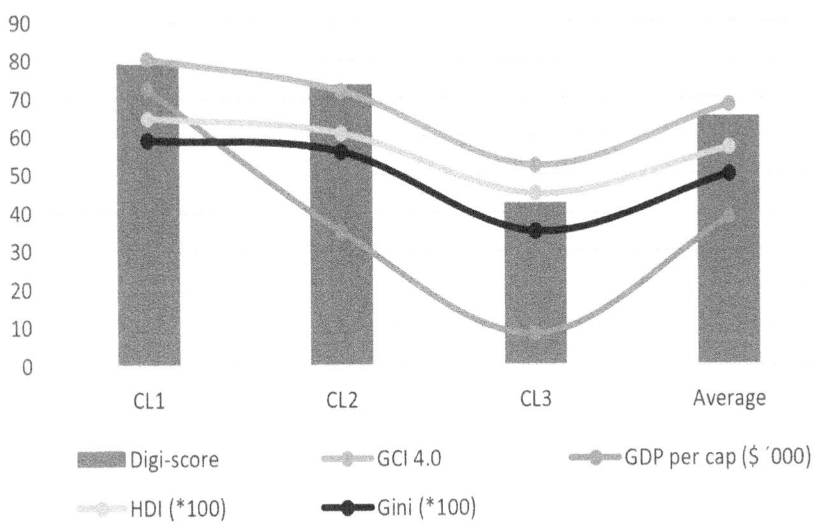

Fig. 4 The digitalization score and the well-being measures. *Source* Authors' own research

Table 3 Correlations between digitalization score and well-being measures

Correlations		Digi-score			
		CL1	CL2	CL3	Average
GCI 4.0, V5	Pearson Cor	−0.206	0.586**	0.813**	0.897**
	Sig.(2-tailed)	0.696	0.000	0.000	0.000
GDP, V6	Pearson Cor	−0.492	0.647**	0.796**	0.814**
	Sig.(2-tailed)	0.322	0.000	0.000	0.000
HDI, V7	Pearson Cor	0.009	0.718**	0.869**	0.919**
	Sig.(2-tailed)	0.987	0.000	0.000	0.000
Gini, V8	Pearson Cor	0.447	0.757**	0.861**	0.927**
	Sig.(2-tailed)	0.374	0.000	0.000	0.000

**$p < 0.01$
Source Authors' own research

to zero (0.009) between HDI and digitalization. It is important to note that correlations in CL1 are *not* statistically significant due to small size of only 6 countries in the cluster.

Next, we proceed with the results of the canonical correlation analysis to dig deeper into the correlations between the set 1 explanatory variables (covariates), V1–V4, and the set 2 dependent variables, V5–V8, as well as, the correlations within the sets.

4.2 Canonical Correlation Analysis (CCA)

The distributions of the set 1 digitalization covariates are seen in Fig. 5 together with correlations within the set 1. It can be seen that digital skills (V1) are the closest to the normal distribution, while the internet users (V3), specifically show two peaks suggesting of world divided into low-use countries and high-use countries. The within correlation ranges from 0.490 (V3 vs. V4) to 0.732 (V1vs. V2).

The distributions of the set 2 well-being variables are seen in Fig. 6 together with correlations within the set 2. The competitiveness (V5) shows the closest to the normal distribution, while HDI (V7) and inequality (V8) show two peaks suggesting the division into low-HDI-high-inequality countries and high-HDI-low-inequality countries. The within correlations are very high ranging from 0.822 (V6 vs. V7) to almost unity of 0.982 between human development and inequality (V7 vs. V8).

The purpose of CCA is to determine the number of canonical variables (dimensions) that are significant in explaining the association between the first set of variables called digitalization and the second set called well-being.

Test of hypothesis 1: There is a statistically significant and positive relationship between the dimensions of digital competitiveness and well-being indicators.

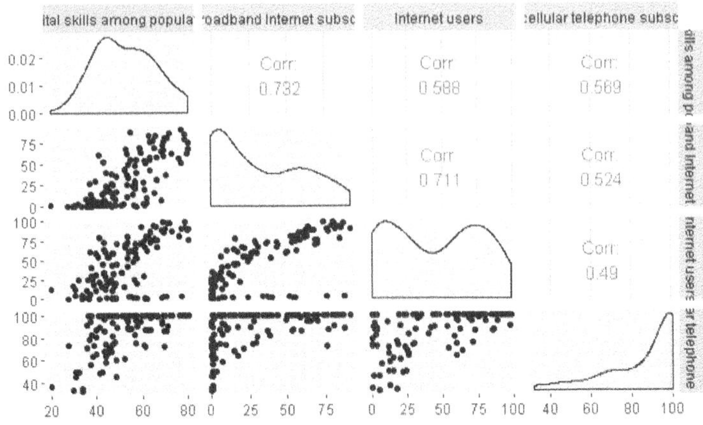

Fig. 5 Set 1: digitalization variables. *Source* Authors' own research

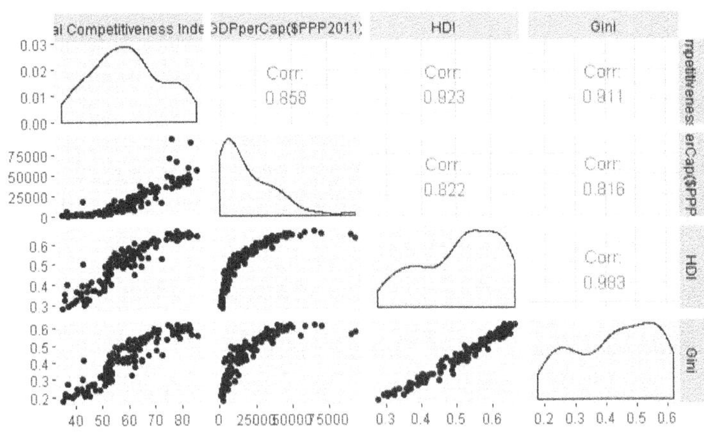

Fig. 6 Set 2: well-being variables. *Source* Authors' own research

Table 4 Multivariate tests of significance (S = 4, M = -1/2, N = 55 1/2)

Test name	Value	Approx. F	Hypoth. DF	Error DF	Sig. of F
Pillais	1.323	14.337	16	464.000	0.000
Hotellings	13.236	92.240	16	446.000	0.000
Wilks	0.047	37.395	16	345.860	0.000
Roys	0.927				

Source Authors' own research

Table 5 Eigenvalues and canonical correlations

Root No.	Eigenvalue	Pct	Cum. Pct	Canon cor.	Sq. cor.
1	12.723	96.125	96.125	0.963	0.927
2	0.367	2.769	98.894	0.518	0.268
3	0.145	1.096	99.991	0.356	0.127
4	0.001	0.009	100.000	0.035	0.001

Source Authors' own research

Table 6 Dimension reduction analysis

Roots	Wilks L	F	Hypoth. DF	Error DF	Sig. of F
1–4	0.047	37.395	16	345.860	0.000
2–4	0.638	6.249	9	277.600	0.000
3–4	0.872	4.068	4	230.000	0.003
4–4	0.999	0.145	1	116.000	0.704

Source Authors' own research

Table 4 shows the fit of the model with Pillai's trace test, Hoteling's trace test, Wilk's lambda and Roy's Greatest Root multivariate criteria. The most frequent test is Wilk's lambda, but one can see that all the first three tests are significant with $p < 0.05$.

All tests test the null hypothesis that the canonical correlations are zero, meaning that there is no linear relationship between the digitalization and well-being indicators. Since $p < 0.05$, all first three tests reject the null hypothesis, so Hypothesis 1 is true.

Table 5 contains the canonical correlations coefficients and the eigenvalues of the canonical roots. The first canonical correlation coefficient is 0.963 with an explained variance of the correlation of 96.125% and an Eigen value of 12.723. The two subsets, the well-being scores and the digitalization measures are positively correlated.

SPSS extracted four canonical roots or dimensions. The first test of significance tests all four canonical roots of significance in Table 6. Since the *p*-value is less than the $\alpha = 0.05$ level of significance, it follows that all the 4 combined dimensions are statistically significant ($p = 0.00$). The second test determines the significance of dimensions 2, 3 and 4 combined. Since $p < 0.05$, it follows that these dimensions are statistically significant.

The third test determines the significance of dimensions 3 and 4 combined. Since $p = 0.003 < 0.05$, it follows that these dimensions are statistically significant.

The fourth test determines the significance of the 4th dimension, which is not statistically significant, since $p = 0.704 > 0.05$.

Next, we obtained for each set of variables the raw canonical coefficients, standardized canonical coefficients, correlations between observed variables, the canonical variant, and the percent of variance explained by the canonical variant.

Table 7 Raw canonical coefficients for COVARIATES

Covariate	1	2	3	4
V1	−0.023	−0.078	-0.053	0.064
V2	−0.021	−0.006	0.020	−0.052
V3	−0.003	0.018	0.024	0.033
V4	−0.008	0.052	−0.043	−0.012

Source Authors' own research

Table 8 Standardized canonical coefficients for COVARIATES

Covariate	1	2	3	4
V1	−0.303	−1.044	−0.707	0.859
V2	−0.598	−0.171	0.572	−1.485
V3	−0.088	0.574	0.780	1.079
V4	−0.142	0.951	−0.778	−0.222

Source Authors' own research

The raw canonical coefficients from Table 7 are similar to the coefficients of linear regression.

According to Table 6, the first three roots are significant. In Table 8, one can see that strongest influence on the first root belongs to variable V2 Fixed-broadband Internet subscriptions with the score −0.598, the second root is strongly influenced by V4 Mobile-cellular telephone subscriptions with the score 0.951, the third root is strongly influenced by V3 Internet users and V2 with scores 0.780, and 0.572, respectively.

For variable V1, Digital skills among population, a one-unit increase in digital skills leads to a 0.023 decrease in the first canonical variate of the covariate set when all the other variables in the model are held constant Table 7. For the same variable, a one standard deviation increase in digital skills leads to a 0.303 standard deviation Table 8 decrease in the score on the first canonical variate for the covariate set when the other variables in the model are held constant.

Canonical loadings measure the correlation between an observed variable in the dependent or independent set and the set's canonical variate as shown in Tables 9

Table 9 Correlations between COVARIATES and canonical variables

Covariate	1	2	3	4
V1	**−0.874**	−0.289	−0.273	0.280
V2	**−0.957**	−0.028	0.200	−0.208
V3	**−0.760**	**0.304**	**0.390**	**0.421**
V4	**−0.672**	**0.546**	**−0.500**	0.016

Source Authors' own research

and 13. The canonical loadings represent the relative contribution of each variable to each canonical function.

The absolute values of loadings greater than 0.3 are shown in bold in Tables 9 and 13. As seen in Table 9, all four variables in the digitization set dominate the first canonical function (Tables 10, 11 and 12).

The canonical variate adequacy coefficients from Tables 10 and 14 measure how well a given set of canonical variate scores describes the variances of the unweighted variables in that set (Chacko 1986). The first canonical function represents 89.883% of the variance in the dependent variables and 67.741% of the variance in the independent set. The second canonical function represents 4.068% of the variance in the dependent variables and 11.869% of the variance in the independent set.

The raw canonical coefficients from Table 11 generate the canonical variates, given by the columns 1, 2, 3, and 4 for each group of indicators. They are interpreted similarly to regression coefficients: for variable V5, Global competitiveness index, a one-unit increase in global competitiveness leads to a 0.038 decrease in the first canonical variate of the covariate set when all the other variables in the model are

Table 10 Variance in COVARIATES explained by canonical variables

CAN. VAR	Pct Var DEP	Cum Pct DEP	Pct Var COV	Cum Pct COV
1	62.805	62.805	67.741	67.741
2	3.184	65.989	11.869	79.611
3	1.635	67.624	12.906	92.517
4	0.009	67.633	7.483	100.000

Source Authors' own research

Table 11 Raw canonical coefficients for DEPENDENT variables

Variable	1	2	3	4
V5	−0.038	−0.108	0.194	−0.027
V6	−0.000	−0.000	0.000	−0.000
V7	4.024	37.656	−3.013	−38.411
V8	−6.376	−14.082	−5.226	38.636

Source Authors' own research

Table 12 Standardized canonical coefficients for DEPENDENT variables

Variable	1	2	3	4
V5	−0.489	−1.380	2.495	−0.340
V6	−0.148	−0.864	−1.634	−0.671
V7	0.436	4.076	0.326	−4.158
V8	−0.833	−1.840	0.683	5.049

Source Authors' own research

Table 13 Correlations between DEPENDENT and canonical variables

Variable	1	2	3	4
V5	**−0.973**	−0.037	−0.169	−0.151
V6	**−0.889**	−0.198	**0.319**	−0.262
V7	**−0.956**	0.283	0.039	−0.060
V8	**−0.971**	0.205	0.063	0.104

Source Authors' own research

Table 14 Variance in DEPENDENT variables explained by canonical variables

CAN. VAR	Pct Var DEP	Cum Pct DEP	Pct var COV	Cum Pct COV
1	89.883	89.883	83.333	83.333
2	4.068	93.950	1.091	84.424
3	3.404	97.354	0.431	84.855
4	2.646	100.000	0.003	84.859

Source Authors' own research

held constant. The standardized canonical coefficients are interpreted similarly to the standardized regression coefficients. For variable V5, Global competitiveness index, a one standard deviation increase in global competitiveness leads to a 0.489 standard deviation Table 12 decrease in the score on the first canonical variate for the covariate set when the other variables in the model are held constant.

Table 15 describes the importance of the effects of the 4 dependent well-being variables (V5, V6, V7, V8). The importance of each independent variable (covariate) can be measured by the Beta value.

Then according to Table 15, the effect of V2, fixed-broadband internet subscriptions, is more important than the effect of V1, digital skills among population, when predicting V5, Global Competitiveness Index 4.0.

When predicting V6, GDP per capita, we find that the fixed-broadband internet subscriptions, V2, has a more important effect than digital skills, V1.

When predicting V7, HDI, we find that V2 has a more important effect than V4 measuring mobile-cellular telephone subscriptions.

When predicting inequality, V8, we find again that V2 has an effect which is more important than V4.

5 Conclusions

This paper studied the effects of digitalization to well-being and inequality of the 121 world countries.

The countries were first clustered into three groups, the most developed/digitalized and richest 6 countries in cluster 1, the well-developed/-digitalized 38 countries in

Table 15 Regression analysis for WITHIN CELLS error term: individual univariate

COV	B	Beta	Std. err.	*t*-value	Sig. t	Lower—95%	CL-Upper
Dependent variable V5							
V1	**0.329**	**0.342**	**0.048**	**6.901**	**0.000**	**0.235**	**0.424**
V2	**0.241**	**0.537**	**0.024**	**9.864**	**0.000**	**0.192**	**0.289**
V3	0,007	0.019	0,018	0,404	0,687	-0,029	0,044
V4	0,116	0,163	0,028	4,079	0,000	0,059	0,172
Dependent Variable V6							
V1	**392,03**	**0,278**	**100.47**	**3.902**	**0,000**	**193.05**	**591,021**
V2	**398.55**	**0.608**	**51.353**	**7.761**	**0.000**	**296.85**	**500.269**
V3	55.22	0.095	38.698	1.427	0.156	−21.43	131.865
V4	−64.29	−0.062	59.640	−1.078	0.283	−182.41	53.839
Dependent variable V7							
V1	0.001	0,115	0.000	2.197	0.030	0.000	0.002
V2	**0.002**	**0.537**	**0.000**	**9.371**	**0.000**	**0.002**	**0.002**
V3	0.001	0,174	0.000	3.568	0,001	0.000	0.001
V4	**0.002**	**0.260**	**0.000**	**6.181**	**0.000**	**0.001**	**0.002**
Dependent variable V8							
V1	0.002	0.160	0.000	3.294	0.001	0.001	0.003
V2	**0.003**	**0.549**	**0.000**	**10.258**	**0.000**	**0.002**	**0.003**
V3	0.001	0.164	0.000	3.619	0.000	0.000	0.001
V4	**0.002**	**0.216**	**0.000**	**5.482**	**0.000**	**0.001**	**0.002**

Bold letters reflect the more important effects of independent variables on dependent ones
Source Authors' own research

cluster 2, and the least developed/digitalized 77 countries with also the greatest inequalities, on average, in cluster 3. All digitalization, as well as, well-being measures showed consistent behavior over the clusters on average.

The greatest correlation within the digitalization variables was between the digital skills and the broadband subscriptions; within the well-being, human development index correlated almost fully (0.983) with inequality (Gini).

Digitalization (score) correlated very strongly with all well-being measures, the most with inequality (0.927).

The digital skills (V1) and broadband subscriptions (V2) were the most important and the only statistically significant predictors of competitiveness (V5) and GDP per capita (V6). Fixed broadband Internet subscriptions (V2) and mobile phone subscriptions (V4) were the most important and significant predictors of human development (V7) and income inequality (V8).

This positive and significance relationship was also confirmed by CCA's tests of significance. 4 dimensions were extracted by SPSS. The first canonical function represents 89.883% of the variance in the dependent set (V5–V8) and 67.741% of the variance in the independent set (V1–V4). It is dominated by all the variables in the two sets, since all loadings have the absolute values greater than 0.3.

The study is limited by the lack of time perspective as it focused on the situation in 2018. The future studies should take the digital evolution over time into account to draw more complete conclusions of the effects of digitalization on well-being and inequality.

References

Androniceanu, A., Georgescu, I., Kinnunen, J.: Digitalization clusters within the European Union. In: Proceedings of the 33rd International Business Information Conference (IBIMA), pp. 1321–1331 (2019)

Androniceanu, A., Kinnunen, J., Georgescu, I., Androniceanu, A.-M.: Multidimensional analysis of consumer behavior on the European digital market. In: Perspectives on Consumer Behaviour: Theoretical Aspects and Practical Applications. Springer, Cham (2020)

Antonio, A., Tuffley, D.: The gender digital divide in developing countries. Future Internet **6**(4), 673–687 (2014)

Chacko, H.E.: An example of the use of canonical correlation analysis. In: The Annual Meeting of the Mid-South Educational Research Association, Memphis, TN, pp. 1–10, 19–21 Nov 1986

Chakravorti, B., Bhalla, A., Chaturvedi, R.S. 60's Countries digital competitiveness, indexed. Harvard Business Review Digital Article (2017).

DiMaggio, P., Hargittai, E., Celeste, C., et al.: From unequal access to differentiated use: a literature review and agenda for research on digital inequality. In: Neckerman, J. (ed.) Social Inequality, pp. 355–400. Russell Sage Foundation, New York (2004)

Friemel, T.N.: The digital divide has grown old: determinants of a digital divide among seniors. New Media & Society **18**(2), 313–331 (2016)

https://ec.europa.eu/digital-single-market/en/news/digital-economy-and-society-index-desi-2019

Jovanović, M., Dlačić, J., Okanović, M.: Digitalization and society's sustainable development-measures and implications. Zb. Rad. Ekon. Rij. **36**(2), 905–928 (2018)

Kinnunen, J., Androniceanu, A., Georgescu, I.: Digitalization of EU countries: a clusterwise analysis. In: Proceedings of the International Management Conference: Management Strategies for High Performance, pp. 1–12 (2019)

MacQueen, J.B.: Some methods for classification and analysis of multivariate observations. In: Proceedings of the 5th Berkeley Symposium on Mathematical Statistics and Probability, pp. 281–297. University of California Press, California (1967)

Morris, A., Brading, H.: E-literacy and the grey digital divide: a review with recommendation. J Inform Literacy **1**(3), 13–28 (2007)

Naumova, O. A., Svetkina, I. A., Korneeva, T. A.: The impact of digitalization on the economic security index of GDP. Digital Age Changes Challenges Future 159–164 (2019)

Polat, R.: Digital exclusion in Turkey: a policy perspective. Gov. Inf Q. 29 (2012).

Schwab, K.: The global competitiveness report 2018. World Economic Forum, Geneva, Switzerland (2018)

Schwab, K.: The global competitiveness report 2019. World Economic Forum, Geneva, Switzerland (2019)

UNDP: Human Development Report 2018. United Nations Development Programme 1, UN Plaza, New York, NY, USA (2018)

UNDP: Human Development Report 2019. United Nations Development Programme 1, UN Plaza, New York, NY, USA (2019)

Van Deursen, A.J., Van Dijk, J.A.: The digital divide shifts to differences in usage. New Media & Society **16**(3), 507–526 (2013)

Ensembles of Convolutional Neural Networks Trained Using Unconventional Data for Stock Predictions

Daia Alexandru, Stancu Stelian, Neamtu (Idorasi) Alina, and Frode Aschim

1 Introduction

The global economy is growing, and current markets are expanding daily. The most significant factor is the expectation of market slants on stock costs, as they decide the net benefit and shortfall to the selected business. As the market advances, unpredictable patterns continue to proliferate, which can lead to increased uncertainty among investors and traders. The capacity to create material that can ease financial exchange forecasts has recently become a significant issue. Errors in financial prediction have led to noteworthy global emergencies, disrupting even the strongest economies. Currently, it is necessary to develop accurate models that can reflect the emerging and unpredictable patterns of financial exchange costs.

In the article "Convolutional Neural Networks And Unconventional Data" (2020), Amunategui reported on the approach of extracting images from quantitative data using convolutional neural networking to facilitate a more accurate understanding of data trends. He revealed that conventional neural networks (CNNs) can better represent varied contexts. Using higher level API for building a convolutional network, he employed three convolutional layers: one that detects edges, one that evaluates the data more deeply, and one that captures higher-level structures. For reducing dimensionality, 2D Maxpooling layer, dropout, and few dense layers were employed. However, in order to report good results, he did not shift the target. This could be interpreted as the need of historical data to predict the next day's closing price.

D. Alexandru (✉) · S. Stelian · N. (Idorasi) Alina
The Bucharest University of Economic Studies, Bucharest, Romania
e-mail: alexandru130586@yandex.com

F. Aschim
Ether Capital Company, London, UK

A. M. Dima and F. DÁscenzo (eds.), *Business Revolution in a Digital Era*,
Springer Proceedings in Business and Economics,
https://doi.org/10.1007/978-3-030-59972-0_17

He instead used data for every period to predict the same day closing price, which does not produce accurate results. Despite these findings, his approach highlights the promising nature of using CNNs and imaging data to establish a more accurate representation of data trends. We chose to apply convolutional neural networking to extracted image data for improved modeling of complex pattern evaluation and determine the utility of CNNs for market predictions.

2 Literature Review

For investors, stock market price prediction is a challenge as markets have random features. Random variations affect markets independently at every point with respect to time. This was found when evaluating variations, and such variations are believed to occur as the result of personal, social, political, business, and economic conditions.

Two methods are primarily used for stock market prices prediction—technical and fundamental analysis (Malkiel 1999). Today, analysts use CNNs, which are considered the most validated and applicable new learning method for technical analysis. This method helps in analyzing visual imagery (Song et al. 2017). Sim et al. (2019) suggested that CNN results for estimating market prediction values were better than those obtained by artificial neural networks (ANN). They designed their study architecture focusing on CNN parameters and technical indicators, which were converted into images. Their findings showed that for stock market price predictions, CNN appears to be more effective. It is more useful for predicting market prices as CNN analyzes time series data as a deep learning method.

Financial data can also comprise image data rather than numeric data, obtained by transforming data in predicting stock market prices. When predicting stock market prices, charts are used for technical analysis, and this method uses chart images of Bollinger bands, oscillators, and stochastic moving averages as technical indicators (Neely et al. 1997). In computer vision segmentation, object detection and fields are used for deep learning in CNN. Recently, significant work has been undertaken regarding stock market price prediction. Chen (2004) revealed that many other data visualization methods such as Germanian Angular Fields and double moving average mapping are used instead of CNN. In this study, it was found that the proposed CNN method was more effective than other visualization methods. Kim and Kim (2019) proposed a model consisting of feature fusion in long short-term memory CNNs (LSTM-CNN). This model included different depictions of the same data, known as stock images and stock chart images, and was used to measure the performance of stock market prices. The results indicate that the error of predicted market prices obtained using this model was lower than that obtained by other methods using images and temporal features.

Gudelek et al. (2017) suggested that using CNNs in predicting stock market process is still new. They evaluate results by calculating and performing paper trading. They compared their methods with traditional trading strategies and concluded that next-day stock market prediction was more than 72% accurate and identified 5:1 realistic values in accounts for transaction values.

In a variety of fields, CNNs are used for the recognition of problems and, in some cases, are more accurate than traditional methods. For financial analysis, CNNs are generally not used to predict stock market prices because they are better suited for use with image data. Hosaka (2019) detailed a method in which set of financial ratios was represented as a grey scale. He utilized the generated image for CNNs for testing and training. Their findings indicate that this method had higher performance in trained networks.

In another study, Duarte-Coronado et al. (2019) demonstrated that deep networks have achieved numerous successes regarding object and image recognition. They utilized CNNs in a deep learning (DL) method successfully for computer vision tasks, object detection, localization, and image classification. Two different models were used, and they successfully illustrated core, petro-graphic, rock, photomicrographic, and mineral hand sample images. Their findings suggest that training algorithms and monitoring the results carefully can address potential unclear and incorrect results. It has been well-established in recent literature that CNN models are novel with a wide range of applications to network applications in data science. While conventional deep learning has been widely applied to stock predictions, previous research has only utilized traditional data (Sezer et al. 2017; Abe and Nakayama 2018; Sarcià et al. 2007; Jiang 2009). Therefore, to evaluate the suitability of evolving CNNs for financial analysis and addressing the gap in the type of data evaluated in previous studies, we developed and applied a CNN trained with unconventional financial data.

3 Subjects and Methods

In the present study, we used daily data of the Apple stock ("AAPL") or the S&P500 index data as listed on the NASDAQ and provided by Yahoo Finance. We used a well-known machine learning method called "bagging" or "bootstrap aggregating" rather than the conventional single neural network approach. Bootstrap aggregating was used as an ensemble method as meta-algorithms were developed to promote machine learning improvement, which further supports good performance and high accuracy in regression or classification. Fig. 1 illustrates the general bootstrap aggregation method.

Model assembling is a groundbreaking method that is useful for expanding exactness on an assortment of ML undertakings. We first investigated a majority vote group ensemble. By doing this, we expected to identify how model assembly lessens the error rate and functions to group low-associated model forecasts effectively. For error correction, it is critical that all signs are effectively handed-off. For example, consider coding required for high-risk applications such as space missions: in the case that we obtain a sign as a double string (e.g., **1**1101100111011110111110111011) and the signal is corrupted (**0**10110011101111011111011011) error identification and correction is significant. A coding arrangement was found in blunder amending

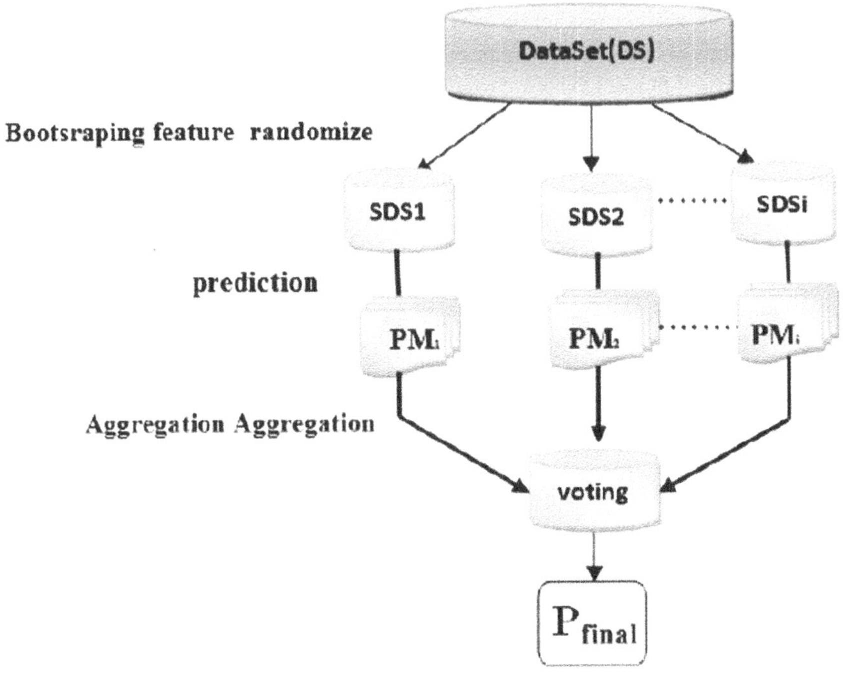

Fig. 1 Bootstrap aggregating method. *Source* Authors' own depiction

codes. Redundant code is the easiest to rectify: the sign should be relayed on numerous occasions in similarly estimated lumps and have a larger part vote.

Averaging and vote majority functions tends to increase performance for a wide scope of issues (both grouping and relapse) and measurements (AUC, squared mistake, or logarithmic misfortune). Averaging expectations frequently minimizes overfitting. It is preferable to have smooth detachment among classes, and the expectations of a solitary model can exhibit jagged edges.

We used neural networks from Keras Library, which is a high-level API over tensor flow that allows the facile prototyping of neural network architectures.

As shown in Fig. 1, the neural network was trained on different portions of randomly selected data to promote diversity in the models by interchanging portions of the dataset for training. After each prediction, the final result was obtained by aggregating results via majority vote.

We used data obtained over a period of 12 year from Yahoo Finance via a corresponding Python API query and shifted the closing price. By shifting the target, our models used data up to and including time **t** to predict the closing price at time **t + 1**.

To create images from prices that we introduced in the ensemble of neural networks, we employed the following procedure:

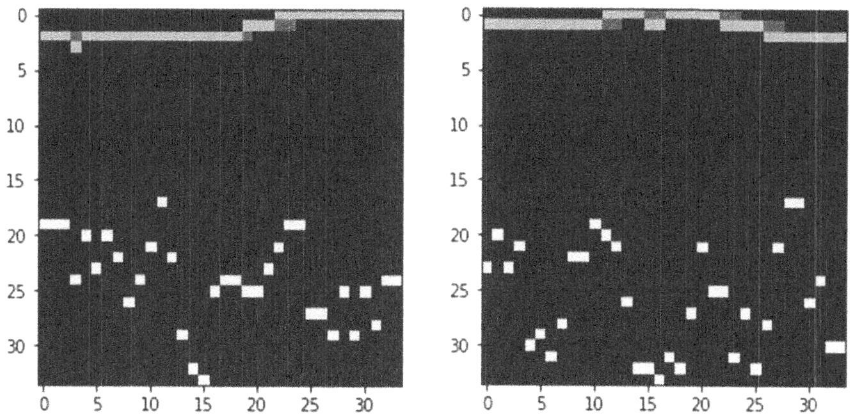

Fig. 2 Graphical illustration of features. *Source* Authors' own work

We created segments of 34 consecutive day periods. We divided that portion into 2 parts. The top part obtained previously was constructed using closing price periods overlaid with rolling averages. The bottom part was obtained in a similar manner, but we choose to use relative strength index. The procedure has been simplified for description.

These images were developed using a new method of feature engineering. Feature engineering is generally unbounded, depending on dataset characteristics. For example, one could obtain new features from current feature spaces by numerous methods such as counting the number of zero and ones. We choose this method because using technical indicators as features does not lead to significant performance or accuracy gains. The features obtained after creating the images were introduced into the ensemble of neural networks, as seen in Fig. 1, and the two neural network architectures we used are illustrated in Fig. 2. These architectures were obtained using the Keras library plot function.

For simplicity of execution and shortened operating time, the image of the neural network that we have presented were obtained using a 34-day period only; it is a medium architecture that contains dropouts to avoid over-fitting. The output reflects that which is expected of dimension 2 meaning a binary one representing the prediction of a particular neural network from the ensemble on a particular day if the price will go up or down compared with previous day as shown in Fig. 2.

The major building blocks of the neural network are the convolutional layers (e.g., spatial convolution over the images), which comprise a convolution portion that is convolved with the layer contribution to create a tensor of yields (Fig. 3).

After initializing the sequential network in Keras, we added the first convolutional layer with a simple line of code: model.add(Conv2D(64, (5, 5), input shape=input shape, activation='relu')).

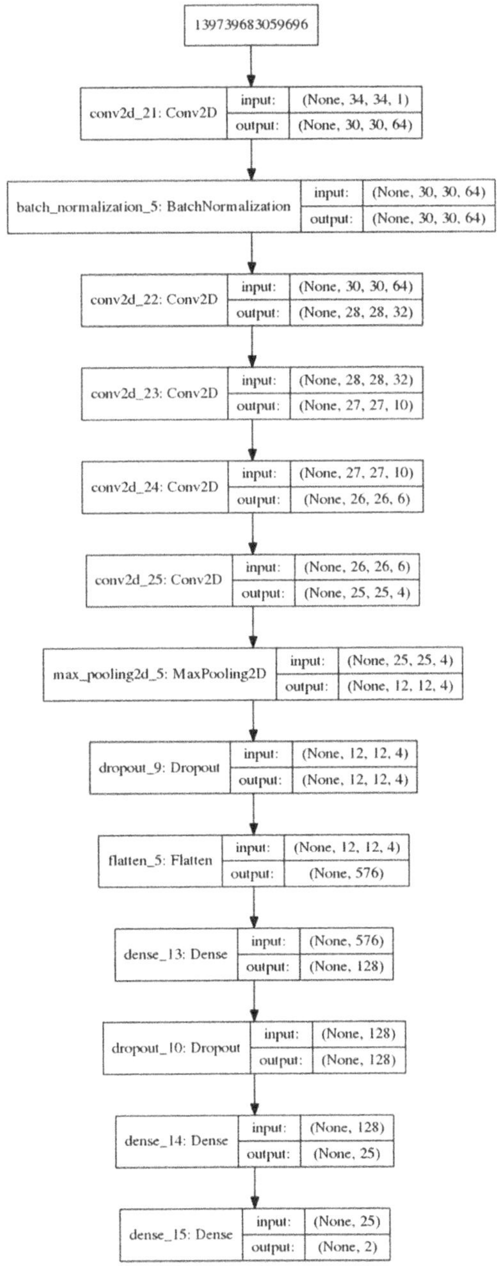

Fig. 3 Neural network design. *Source* Authors' own work

Table 1 Cross-validation results

Cross-validation	Percent (%)
Cross-validation number 1	62
Cross-validation number 2	72
Cross-validation number 3	76
Cross-validation number 4	68
Cross-validation number 5	82
Cross-validation number 6	61
Cross-validation number 7	65
Cross-validation number 8	73
Cross-validation number 9	69
Cross-validation number 10	74

The input shape is designated using the function parameterhas the forma (time_range, time_range, 1) where time_range is a defined period for the image segments. In our study, this value was 34 to reflect the 34-day period.

The activation function selected was **ReLU** (rectified linear unit) (Duarte-Coronado et al. 2019), a widely used activation function known to yield good results. Mathematically, it is defined as y = max (0, x). **ReLU** is the most commonly used activation function in neural networks, specifically in CNNs.

After batch normalization, we added another portion of pooling layers as shown by the following lines of code, which serve as an example illustrating the simple procedure of Keras neural network creation:

```
model.add(Conv2D(32, (3, 3), activation='relu')).
model.add(Conv2D(10, (2, 2), activation='relu')).
model.add(Conv2D(6, (2, 2), activation='relu')).
model.add(Conv2D(4, (2, 2), activation='relu')).
```

After conducting multiple experiments training the bagger for 20, 50, 100, and 500 iterations, we concluded that n_iterations = 100 yielded the most accurate results. We analyzed cross-validation results for the bagger with n iterations=100 (100 models trained with different portions of the data set). Moreover, we conducted 10 experiments in which we randomly used a validation data set containing 10% of the dataset, ensuring that the selected data was different each time. Table 1 shows the results of the cross-validation tests.

4 Discussion

Our findings indicate that it is possible to develop custom pooling layers in a neural network to achieve greater diversity in the model. We present the possibility of reducing overfitting by creating a unique pooling layer based on the Octav Onicescu kinetic energy approach. Contemporary research using neural networks to predict financial trends relies on traditional data, which cannot adequately represent the complexity of continuously changing markets. We developed this model using unconventional data (e.g., open, high, close, low, and adjusted close) and transformed it for image analysis. Feeding convolutional neural nets with image data, we obtained another layer of numeric data, which has the advantage of capturing both visual and quantitative features. Thus, we used convolutional networks to capture varied financial data patterns. Our results indicate the applicability of CNNs on unconventional financial data and highlight future directions for improved modeling that can better address complex datasets.

Existing neural nets are developed using (i) an average pooling layer, a trivial moving grid of dimension n $\times$ n (the value for n is set to three or four on the image) that captures the average values of the pixels, or (ii) a max pooling layer, a trivial moving grid that only captures the highest values of pixels. Both methods are good but trivial, thus exhibiting some limitations. In our future work, we aim to develop a pooling layer based on Octav Onicescu information, or kinetic, energy. This type of pooling layer will create a grid of some dimension n x n and compute the kinetic energy of the pixels in the image. By creating a new type of pooling layer, we can use it in conjunction with a variety of other neural nets to capture different information from the patterns in the image. Thus, we can capture information on averages, maximums, and minimums from the pixels.

Kinetic energy (information energy) for arbitrary vectors (highlights) is similar to motor vitality from material science in probability. Informational energy is a concept inspired by the kinetic expression of classical mechanics. From the informational theory perspective, informational energy formulas measure uncertainty or randomness in a probability system. This approach was introduced and studied for the first time by Onicescu in the mid-1960s. Informational energy and entropy are both measures of randomness, but they describe distinct features. This aspect deals with the informational energy in the framework of the statistical models.

We applied the notion of motor energies to DL by utilizing the new connection coefficient as an execution metric rather than cross entropy. Dynamic energy in neural systems have a wide assortment of utilization cases. For instance, this execution can function in a convolutional neural system for PC vision or a neural system for making inferences from enormous amounts of information.

Changing the connection framework that uses Pearson's R relationship or covariance analyses, with connection lattice dependent on the Onicescu correlation coefficients, we found that it carried more space into the separation between the bunches of the types of the Plant species dataset beneath. It is apparent that using the Onicescu coefficient, or the informational energy, is very useful when describing random vectors, and we must recognize its strengths when dealing with sets of random vectors in machine learning.

It is believed that entropy can be used for estimating bits of data to decide vulnerability. This form of entropy should be considered as 1/2 mv^2 of an irregular vector. It can be used to promote the straightforward depiction whole of squared probabilities.

For a minor model, if X is an irregular vector with comparing probabilities p1, ..., pN the dynamic vitality is equivalent to sum(Pi2). Notice that, if X = 1, 1, 1, 1, 1, 1, ..., 1, 1, 1, 1 KineticEnergy(X) = Sum(prob(1)2) = 1, which means that there is no decent variety and everything is impeccable sure the dynamic vitality is at greatest worth 1. We therefore conclude that this cannot necessarily be acceptable. This model exhibits extreme motor vitality, similar to one in which nuclear cores are extremely close thus leading to significant vitality, which is called atomic combination. If X = $1, 2, 3, 4, 5, \cdots + \inf$KineticEnergy(X) 0, implying that at greatest assorted variety and most noteworthy vulnerability the motor vitality is at low an incentive close to zero. Note that we came about because of past 1, the classifications from the arbitrary vector could be deciphered as nuclear cores came about because of development of the past ones with high vitality bringing about enormous number of particles with low vitality at last, and we could think about that as atomic splitting. This implies active vitality is limited somewhere in the range of (0 and 1). We aim to use a new correlation coefficient as performance metric instead of cross entropy, such as in the case of neural networks or genetic algorithms as fitness functions.

5 Conclusion

In the past several years, international academic and scientific communities have made significant progress in the research and application of neural networks owing to contemporary improvements in computing power and the emergence of innovative computational operations. With these advancements, neural networks can be trained for increasingly long and complex periods and datasets in real time. New layer mechanisms must solve two problems faced by machine learning practitioners:

1. Layers must be developed and applied to yield the highest possible accuracy and performance in terms of area under the curve and F1 score as the weighted average of precision and recall. In some cases, although researchers may have obtained good accuracy, upon inspecting the prediction results, data particularities may result in the model prejudicing only the majority class in situations with unbalanced cardinality of target classes. A suitably flexible and accurate layer mechanism must be utilized to mitigate these types of observational errors.
2. Some models are overly complex, which may lead to overfitting. This limitation was exhibited by the model developed in the present study and significantly lessened the utility of our results. New layer mechanisms must be developed in a manner that disallows for overfitting while ensuring suitable complexity for the applied dataset.

Working with "unconventional" stock data allowed us to identify critical directions for layer development in future research; we aim to create a new type of layer using Octav Onicescu's kinetic energy formulation with the expectation that the developed layer will exhibit suitable complexity in terms of information extraction to yield highly accurate results with minimal overfitting. Through this research, we hope to create an improved deep learning neural network model that can address common issues faced by machine learning practitioners, while enabling the use of ensemble deep learning methods constructed in varying ways to address a multiplicity of issues that emerge in data science and machine learning applications.

References

Abe, M., Nakayama, H.: Deep learning for forecasting stock returns in the cross-section. In: Phung, D., Tseng, V., Webb, G., Ho, B., Ganji, M., Rashidi, L. (eds.) Advances in Knowledge Discovery and Data Mining (PAKDD 2018). Lecture Notes in Computer Science, 10937. Springer, Cham (2018)

Aple Corp. (AAPL): Profile, business summary. Yahoo! Finance. Retrieved from https://finance.yahoo.com/q/pr?s=AAPL (2019)

Chen, C.: Searching for intellectual turning points: progressive knowledge domain visualization. Proc. Natl. Acad. Sci. **101**(suppl 1), 5303–5310 (2004)

Duarte-Coronado, D., Tellez-Rodriguez, J., de Lima, R.P., Marfurt, K., Slatt, R.: Deep convolutional neural networks as an estimator of porosity in thin-section images for unconventional reservoirs. In SEG Technical Program Expanded Abstracts 2019 (pp. 3181–3184). Society of Exploration Geophysicists (2019)

Gudelek, M. U., Boluk, S. A., & Ozbayoglu, A. M. (2017, November). A deep learning based stock trading model with 2-D CNN trend detection. In 2017 IEEE Symposium Series on Computational Intelligence (SSCI) (pp. 1–8). IEEE.

Hosaka, T.: Bankruptcy prediction using imaged financial ratios and convolutional neural networks. Expert Syst. Appl. **117**, 287–299 (2019)

Jiang, H.: The application of artificial neural networks in risk assessment on high-tech project investment. In: 2009 International Conference on Business Intelligence and Financial Engineering, Beijing, pp. 17–20. IEEE (2009)

Kim, T., Kim, H.Y.: Forecasting stock prices with a feature fusion LSTM-CNN model using different representations of the same data. PloS One **14**(2) (2019)

Malkiel, B.G.: A random walk down Wall Street: including a life-cycle guide to personal investing. WW Norton & Company (1999)

Neely, A., Richards, H., Mills, J., Platts, K., Bourne, M.: Designing performance measures: a structured approach. Int. J. Oper. Prod. Manag. (1997)

Sarcià, S., Cantone, G., Basili, V.: A statistical neural network framework for risk management process. In: From the Proposal to its Preliminary Validation for Efficiency, pp. 168–177 (2007)

Sezer, O.B., Ozbayoglu, A.M., Dogdu, E.: An artificial neural network-based stock trading system using technical analysis and big data framework. In: Proceedings of the SouthEast Conference (2017)

Sim, K.S., Ting, F.F., Tan, Y.J.: Convolutional neural network improvement for breast cancer classification. Expert Syst. Appl. **120**, 103–115 (2019)

Song, S.K. Hong, S., Kim, S., Joh, M.: Globenet: convolutional neural networks for typhoon eye tracking from remote sensing imagery. arXiv preprint arXiv:1708.03417 (2017)

A Review and a Proposal About Socio-economic Impacts of Artificial Intelligence

Aysan Bashirpour Bonab, Ihor Rudko, and Francesco Bellini

1 Introduction

Artificial intelligence is not a new field of study. Formal institutionalization of AI as an academic discipline begun in the 1950s but the discussion about the capability to reproduce human skills already started well before with ancient Greece philosophers, passing through the fantasy of science fiction or the ideas of innovative mathematicians such as Leibnitz and Pascal. Since then it underwent at least three periods of accelerated development, above all in the methodology, intermitted with the disinterest towards the discipline due to the limited deployment of the first intelligent machines (Buchanan 2005).

Currently, things are changing at a much faster rate. By having at its disposal a huge amount of computing power, and almost limitless amount of cheap storage and access to the global network, artificial intelligence was able to abandon its predominantly theoretical framework and is about to become the truly pervasive technology on a global scale (Ransbotham et al. 2017). This makes of AI, as the leading experts in the field claim, a radical innovation destined to change the world as we know it today. Analogously with the discovery of electricity and the invention of the Internet, the consequences of the development and adoption of AI will be multiple. Since it is impossible to consider every single aspect of such a change, this work focuses mainly

A. B. Bonab · I. Rudko · F. Bellini (✉)
Department of Management, Sapienza University of Rome, Rome, Italy
e-mail: francesco.bellini@uniroma1.it

A. B. Bonab
e-mail: aysan.bsp@gmail.com

I. Rudko
e-mail: rudko.1449150@studenti.uniroma1.it

A. M. Dima and F. DÁscenzo (eds.), *Business Revolution in a Digital Era*,
Springer Proceedings in Business and Economics,
https://doi.org/10.1007/978-3-030-59972-0_18

on the economic consequences of advances in the field of artificial intelligence (2018; Chen et al. 2016; Furman and Seamans 2019).

More precisely, in the first part, we trace the developmental stages of the discipline and reported some evidences in favor of artificial intelligence as the key enabling technology of the new socio-economic system. Furthermore, we define weak artificial intelligence in order to better delimit the scope of our analysis. We provide then some concrete examples of the usage of AI in three economic sectors today: primary, secondary and tertiary. In the second part, we dwelled deeper with the systematic literature review by analyzing a couple of predictive studies regarding the socio-economic impact of the usage of artificial intelligence. In the concluding part of the paper we examine the possible relationship between AI usage by a firm and two indicators directly related to the increase in productivity, namely the yearly increase in profits and the yearly increase in revenues. While no particular relationship was found between variation in profits and AI usage (possibly due to minor methodological issues), the yearly increase in revenues resulted positively correlated with the increase in the deplyoment of AI.

2 Artificial Intelligence. Historical and Epistemological Profile

2.1 Artificial Intelligence as a New Technological Paradigm

For some years now the upcoming invalidity of Moore's law is hypothesized rather frequently (Ceruzzi 2005), especially regarding the materials currently used in the production of microchips. In fact, in 2016 Intel already declared that silicon-based transistors will continue to shrink only for another five years (Simonite 2016).

In the current state of affairs the Moore's law tends to become more obsolete with each passing year but the quantum computer, the one that will potentially be the first to solve NP (nondeterministic polynomial) complete class of problems in a reasonable amount time, is still largely a theorization. Considering the maturity of the hardware sector and the time needed for having a technological discontinuity, the new revolution in the world of IT will likely occur on the software side. Indeed, the software's potential has always been somewhat "neglected" and "compromised" in the frenetic competition of increasing the number of transistors on the unit of the surface of a microchip. But, according to Charles Simonyi, creator of Microsoft's most important application software package Office "the potential (of software) is much, much higher and has to do with coding knowledge in a deeper way" (Fallows 2013).

If optimization and continuous improvement of software are to be expected in the years to follow, artificial intelligence represents one of the most exciting and interesting aspects of this change.

Before proceeding with the more in-depth analysis of implications of AI development for the society and economic structure, a brief historical outline of the discipline can be traced, in parallel with the development of IT described previously.

Multiple steps towards the theorization of the discipline were made before and during the Second World War, especially by the British mathematician, logician and cryptographer Alan Turing whose hypothesis that any formal reasoning can be expressed by means of only two symbols, "0" and "1" was crucial for subsequent IT developments. This, together with the progress made in neurophysiology and cybernetics led researchers to believe in the possibility of building an electronic brain; but it was only in 1956, during a conference in New Hampshire dedicated to the development of intelligent systems that the expression "artificial intelligence" was first used. The main aspiration of the conference participants was to create machines capable of exhibiting a typically human way of reasoning (Buchanan 2005).

Throughout 1960s AI research in the United States was funded by the Department of Defense and there was a spread of interest in the development of AI all around the world. Expectations were rather optimistic. Herbert Simon, one of the founding fathers of the discipline and participant of the New Hampshire conference, declared that "machines will be able, within twenty years, to do any job that man can do" (McCorduck 2004). Unfortunately, the progress slowed down in Seventies when American government cut the funds for research and scientists clashed with the first epistemological difficulties: the reasoning capacity of existing artificial neural networks seemed doomed to remain limited to a mere syntactic manipulation of data without deeper understanding of the treated domains.

In the 1980s, interest in artificial intelligence development was revitalized, thanks above all to the commercial success of first expert systems, a form of AI capable of simulating the knowledge and skills of a human expert. The AI industry soon reached billions of dollars. Many companies flourished with the goal to design robots and expert systems specialized in certain tasks, But shortly after AI industry had its second decline in 1987, triggered by the market failure of Lisp Machines (first single-user commercial workstations engineered to run Lisp programmed software more efficiently) (Nilsson 2009).

At the beginning of the new millennium, as a direct consequence of the exponential growth of computational power and the increase in the available storage space, artificial intelligence started to be applied in the uncountable domains of human activity, from logistics to medical diagnosis. Deep Blue designed by IBM became the first machine to beat the world chess champion, Garry Kasparov, in a famous chess match of 1997 (McCorduck 2004). In the recent years, thanks to the almost ubiquitous spread of Internet, to an incessant data mining performed by giants of World Wide Web, to the availability of the databases of considerable size and to the possibility of distributing computing power over the network, researchers and engineers obtained new and powerful tools that allowed them to explore the infinite possibilities in the realm of AI development.

Considering the complexity of the discipline, it is not only the increase in the computational power of machines and the development of computer networks that have contributed to the advancements in the field of artificial intelligence. Branches of science such as cognitive psychology with its metaphor of the mind as a computer, and neurobiology, defined as a set of scientifically conducted studies on the nervous system, are bringing scientists closer to the understanding of the functioning of the human brain, shifting the ancient questions on the intelligence and consciousness from the realm of philosophical metaphysics to the more formal path of biological determinism. Even linguistics has much to offer for AI scholars: the more we know about the functioning of the natural language, its origins and evolutionary paths, the closer we are to the understanding of human consciousness. Knowledge derived from these disciplines is essential if we want to overcome the epistemological trap of weak artificial intelligence in the near future.

As can be seen in this brief historical overview, progress in the field of AI was never linear. Indeed, with at least two fairly long periods of indifference towards the discipline, its evolutionary path looks more like a sinusoid, each peak of which was triggered by some new revolutionary idea or invention. However, this trend seems to be destined to change soon. In fact, as stated in the recent report by Tractica, an American company that provides market research in the field of high technology, the total income from the sale of AI software products and services is forecasted to grow from $ 10.1 billion in 2018 to around 126 billion in 2025, showing an exponential type of growth trend. Artificial intelligence thus represents one of the most promising segments of the IT sector of the economy.

Indeed, according to Tractica's director of research, Aditya Kaul "AI has applications and use cases in almost every industry and is considered the next big technological shift, similar to past shifts like the industrial revolution, the computer age, and the smartphone revolution. [...] Artificial intelligence today represents the key technology of web-based IT companies that provide users with hyper-customized services following the AI-first strategy. [...] The rest of the market has yet to fully understand its use-value and subsequent implementation strategies" (Artificial Intelligence Market Forecasts 2019).

Distinguishing 333 specific use cases of AI and 28 sectors in which these could play an important role, Tractica report identifies three fundamental branches of artificial intelligence development: vision, learning and analytics. Analytics is a major driver for AI and is a continuation of business analytics and classical machine learning (ML) techniques. However, deep learning (DL)-based human perception derived from vision and language is a bigger driver for AI in the long run.

It is interesting to observe to what extent the most recent report of Tractica has revaluated its predictions. In only two years the prediction for the global revenue for the AI market has more than tripled, which further confirms that the role of artificial intelligence for the future of the economy is constantly underestimated, although in both cases the trends of growth seem to assume the exponential form.

2.2 Epistemological Limits of AI

Encyclopedia Britannica defines artificial intelligence as "the ability of a digital computer or computer-controlled robot to perform tasks commonly associated with intelligent beings" (Britannica, https://www.britannica.com/technology/artificial-intelligence). Meanwhile, John McCarthy, US computer scientist who coined the term in 1956 defines AI as "the science of making intelligent machines" (McCarthy et al. 2006).

Both definitions mention machines endowed with intelligence similar to that of human beings, more precisely the fluid intelligence, which unlike the crystallized one, perfectly implementable with enough storage space and access to the Internet, requires a certain procedural autonomy and the dexterity in solving completely new problems.

Zero difficulties arise from the first part of the expression: "artificial", that is a residual category with respect to the "natural", meaning something constructed, programmed or programmable, the feasible result achievable with the wealth of knowledge we already possess. However, epistemological complexities arise when we want to define the second part of the expression, "intelligence". Traditionally, for what concerns the human species, psychologists distinguish more than one type of intelligence. Howard Gardner, for example, identifies eight types: linguistic, logical-mathematical, spatial, bodily-kinesthetic, musical, interpersonal, naturalist and existential (Gardener 2000).

It would be rather simplistic to boil down human intelligence to the mere IQ score on the Stanford-Binet scale, that is, the ability to deal with problems by applying formal logic. If the main purpose of the AI algorithms is to imitate, at least partially, the biological intelligence of human beings, can the machine similar to Deep Blue be considered intelligent? In the case of chess-playing, the machine relies on algorithmic procedures that are usually very different from the ordinary human way of thinking. Unlike human, thanks to the enormous computational power, the machine can recursively calculate every possible outcome of the other player's move. The advances in the development of AI for the Chinese game of Go seem more promising because the number of possible outcomes is so high to require an unfeasible computing capacity, forcing the program to look for more complex solutions, based on heuristic techniques and, above all, to learn by making mistakes (Antonoglou et al. 2017).

However, no matter how good its performance is, artificial intelligence in the two above cases (the game of Go and chess) is still considered to be of the weak kind. In contrast to strong artificial intelligence (a term coined by the American philosopher John Searle) machines with weak AI lack self-awareness and are not able to recreate the thought processes like those of a human as they do not possess the infinite nuances of our mind. In his argument against the possibility of creating a strong AI in the future John Searle argues that any system capable of emulating human intelligence will only have the syntactic (grammatical) ability to process input data, without ever gaining the semantic understanding of it, that is, without ever understanding its deeper meaning (Searle 1980). So, theoretically, even a machine capable of passing the Turing Test is destined to remain an artificial intelligence of a weak type, a mere executor of the code with no ability for real thinking.

The epistemological trap of strong artificial intelligence seems far from being overcome (if it ever will). It is nonetheless clear that weak AI algorithms are getting more and more efficient and sophisticated, pervading every economic and social aspect of human activity: intelligent robots, expert systems, facial recognition systems, autonomous cars with AI for the first time responsible for ethical choices, and so on. The range of possible applications of weak artificial intelligence seems almost infinite. There is little doubt that society is facing a huge technological transformation. And the consequences of this transformation will soon follow. How will they be? "Technology is neither good nor bad," states historian Melvin Kranzberg "nor is it neutral" (Kranzberg 1985). Ultimately, it all depends on us and the way how we will manage it.

2.3 *Some Examples of the Use of AI in the Three Economic Sectors*

Before tackling the possible influence of AI on the economic systems of tomorrow, it may be appropriate to review the latest technological inventions based on artificial intelligence, already on the market or in the phases of development, following the traditional economic taxonomy, in the primary, secondary and tertiary sector respectively, in order to provide the subsequent analysis on some solid and concrete basis, anchored mainly to the current state of affairs.

2.3.1 Primary Sector

Reflecting on the sources of today's innovations, one rarely thinks of the primary sector. In reality, agriculture remains a fundamental economic activity, even though in recent years its contribution to GDP shows a decreasing trend. No wonder many may mistakenly consider the primary sector out of the reach of progress. There is however enough evidence that farmers are indeed preoccupied with rapidly renewing existing technologies and techniques, modernizing almost all agricultural production processes, once again proving the hypothesis of the AI being the enabling technology for the new technological revolution (Stoltzfus 2019).

Machine learning, deep learning, big data and the Internet of things are creating many new opportunities for the primary sector. Machine learning algorithms, for example, can access satellite data to better understand the dynamics of healthy crops growth. Pesticide manufacturing companies are currently developing image recognition technologies to identify and prevent problems arising from different species of pests. Some foresters use machine learning to better safeguard their plantations

(Patrício and Rieder 2018). Data and access to the data are therefore fundamental for the realization of the potential deriving from the use of AI.

The following list shows some of the most promising use cases of artificial intelligence in the today's primary sector to increase yields and reduce losses related to pests, as well as to the factors of anthropic and environmental origins.

- Precision farming, also known as satellite farming. It is the agriculture management strategy that makes use of GPS systems to optimize agricultural yields. Artificial intelligence algorithms can further improve the techniques adopted in precision farming by using available satellite data to make predictions of a different kind: where seeds will grow better, how good the ground conditions will be in the future, and so on.
- Harvesting. New technologies, such as the Harvest CROO Robotics strawberry picking machine, use artificial vision systems to identify fruits faster and pick them more efficiently. Those machines perform sophisticated directed movements to pick berries precisely by imitating human motor activity (Chen and Li 2019).
- Drones. Unmanned vehicles are equipped with precision sensors to perform different types of controls by flying over the fields. Farmers can use the collected data to improve their production models and strategies, reducing environmental risks and waste.
- Weed and pest control. The use of artificial intelligence guarantees farmers further improvement in weed control techniques. By using artificial vision, farmers can identify diseased plants and harmful weeds to eradicate them one at a time instead of spraying chemicals over the entire crop, therefore making food safer and saving huge amounts of money on insecticides and weedicides. One excellent example of this technology is the famous See and Spray AI model recently acquired by Deere & Company.
- Algorithms to increase agricultural yields. Firms are developing algorithms based on artificial intelligence to increase agricultural performance. By using complex mathematical models, these can guide farmers in their choices, therefore greatly increase yields.
- Chatbots. Intelligent voice assistants similar to Amazon's Alexa are able to interact with farmers to help them solve the most complex problems during sowing, weeding, and harvesting (Dharmaraj and Vijayanand 2018).

2.3.2 Secondary Sector

The secondary sector includes all industries that are related to the manufacturing of finished goods: mining, metallurgical, iron and steel, engineering, petrochemical, manufacturing, automotive, food, pharmaceutical, and so on. Although the vast majority of these have long been automated during the third industrial revolution (also known as the first digital revolution), the introduction of artificial intelligence in industrial processes had generated a new wave of automation and a further increase in productivity of such proportions that it led experts theorize the advent of the new industrial revolution, the so-called Industry 4.0. At the base of Industry 4.0 are the so-called CPS, cyber-physical systems, or physical systems integrated with computer systems that can interact with other CPS (Bellini and D'Ascenzo 2018). The nine technological pillars of a smart factory are defined enabling technologies by the Boston Consulting Group (Gerbert et al. 2015) and include, in alphabetical order:

- Additive manufacturing (or additive manufacturing systems). These are technologies, such as 3D printers, which provide additional flexibility to production processes, by creating components tailored to the needs of the client. Additive manufacturing introduces numerous and complex variables to monitor and control to obtain an acceptable level of precision in three-dimensional printing. Machine learning is used nowadays to improve printing efficiency and reduce costs (Savastano et al. 2019).
- Augmented reality. Those are AI-based systems that enrich human sensory perception through the means of electronically processed information. In the context of the smart factory, AR is used to support operators by providing real-time information during production. Artificial intelligence can be used in AR devices to provide the interface best suited to the user, completely synchronized and with ad hoc options for each operator. Furthermore, artificial vision algorithms are fundamental for the proper functioning of any augmented reality system (Fraga-Lamas et al. 2018).
- Autonomous robots (also known as advanced production systems). These technologies include materials handling systems and collaborative robots (or cobots), interconnected and able to learn from human operators by using machine learning algorithms.
- Big data and Analytics. The gathering of information and its subsequent processing (for optimization of production processes) are tasks that can be efficiently performed by machines equipped with some forms of artificial intelligence.
- Cloud and Cybersecurity. An increasing amount of available data requires secure systems for their management and processing and the systems that control processes are moving to over cloud platforms. Greater connectivity of industrial systems and production lines requires more complex security protocols. Computer security systems based on machine learning use data from previous cyber-attacks to respond with dexterity to new but somewhat similar threats (Lezzi et al. 2018). Considering that less complex types of attacks are the most common and are usually easy to avoid, it is likely that AI-based systems will be able to respond to these types of threats on their own, saving a considerable amount of resources of the company.
- Horizontal and vertical integration systems. An IT system will be fully integrated into each of the production phases, connecting all the operators in the production process.
- The Industrial Internet of Things. Each production element will be connected not only with other elements inside the factory but also to the elements outside the factory thanks to the use of Internet (Jeschke et al. 2017). This will allow companies to decentralize the decision-making process, with all the benefits that

can derive from decentralization (real-time responses, greater security and use of computational power distributed over the network).

- Simulation. Analyzing the physical world through a virtual model will allow operators to improve the quality of the products, simultaneously reducing the costs and time required for the actual setting of the machines.

Artificial intelligence, therefore, seems to be crucial for the effective and efficient functioning of the majority of the enabling technologies of Industry 4.0.

2.3.3 Tertiary Sector

The real technological revolution, however, is about to happen in the services sector. In fact, much of it still remains unautomated. But the peculiarity of artificial intelligence lies precisely in its ability to imitate the typically human way of thinking and behaving, including the delicate psychological aspects that are indispensable in the tertiary sector. Given the residual definition of the latter, the possible applications of AI in the sector are almost infinite. Below some of the use cases that are the ones that will be the most profitable in 2025 according to the Tractica report.

- Algorithmic trading. The financial sector is rapidly developing AI applications, both in the retail area and corporate finance, AI technologies are now used to search for new investment opportunities based on past trends and situations or for the advanced analysis of fraud and the computation of the risk (Banerjee et al. 2016),
- Static image recognition. In addition to being potentially useful in agriculture and industry, artificial vision can also be very profitable in the service sector. For example, it can be used to perform customer analysis by recording the logos or texts on products that the person consumes or for tagging images for their further classification (Zaforas 2017).
- More efficient healthcare. The health sector is among those with the highest potential for the implementation of AI technologies. Artificial intelligence is already being used to better plan personalized therapy, automatically interpret medical images (X-rays, angiograms, CT scans) and help doctors to make the most precise diagnoses (Yu et al. 2018).

3 Artificial Intelligence in the Economy of the Future

3.1 Further Epistemological Considerations

It seems necessary to further restrict the field of analysis to the only weak artificial intelligence, above all to shift the focus from the point of technological singularity to the more relevant and analyzable problems. The point of technological singularity is defined as the moment in the history of human development beyond which, according to the futurologists, it will be impossible to foresee any important outcome of technological progress. The singularity will be possible only when we succeed in completely emulating the human mind, by creating machines with the ability to supervise other machines, to design and to organizing them (Potapov 2018). However, this type of AI (not necessarily the strong AI) is still far from being developed, so any attempt to reason about it will be a mere futuristic speculation. To make a more truthful analysis of the implication of using AI in the near future, is therefore indispensable to limit the considerations only to the weak AI.

So far, we described artificial intelligence in a rather general way, considering it mainly as a branch of science. In the context of what is going to be analyzed, however, it is more convenient to look at AI under a slightly different lens. In fact, besides being the wide field of studies, artificial intelligence is also the final product, the technology that implements those studies. It is mainly a software implemented on a specific hardware support. The software that, unlike the usual computer programs, can modify its own source code and, therefore, can learn empirically (Vinge 1993).

If the main driver of today's technological revolution is information, the data management will become even more important in the future. Having access to a large amount of information is essential for the proper functioning of artificial intelligence algorithms that take advantage of a pre-existing and ever-growing structure of interconnected databases, especially now, in the era of social networks, when people deliberately and very often they unconsciously share every single aspect of their lives online. The intrinsic nature of the data will also change in a certain sense, becoming increasingly more dynamic, continuously updated by machines without any human intervention. Indeed, even now engineers and designers are not able to foresee how their intelligent creations will behave, because after a certain period of "schooling", by changing their source code several times, AI-based algorithms become mere black boxes whose activity can only be understood by analyzing the outputs resulting from specific inputs, as it is humanly impossible to decode the artificial neural network (Knight 2017).

3.2 Predictive Studies in the Field of AI. Full Automation of Labor

It is expected that the consequences of the development of artificial intelligence will be all-pervasive, from cognitive-psychological aspects to ways in which humans relate with each other and with the technology itself. In reality, this happened with every technological revolution of the past and it was never possible to fully forecast all the consequences of the technological paradigm in arrival. However, these predictions are always necessary, today perhaps more than ever, given a very high degree of substitutability between AI and the human workers.

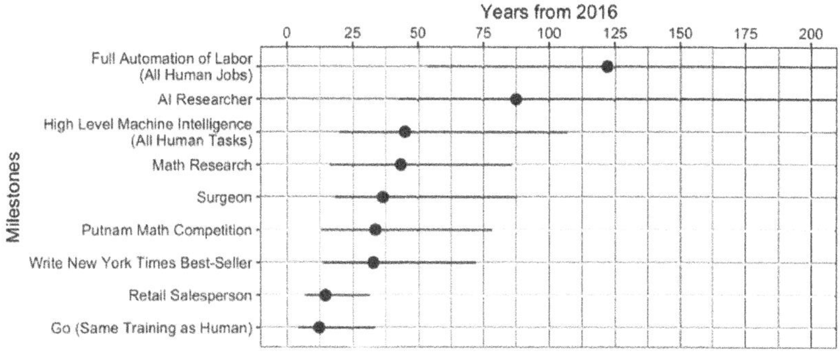

Fig. 1 The predicted onset of the full automation of labor. *Source* When Will AI Exceed Human Performance? Evidence from AI Experts (2017) (Intervals represent the range from the 25–75% probability of the event occurring, calculated from the mean of the individual predictions)

Multiple predictive studies have recently been made. Among the most important ones is the 2017 statistical survey made by the multidisciplinary group of scholars from the universities of Oxford and Yale. "Advances in the field of artificial intelligence", states the abstract, "will transform modern life by reshaping transportation, health, science, finance, and the military. To adapt public policy, we need to better anticipate these advances" (Dafoe et al. 2017). Having gathered the opinions of 352 researchers in the field of AI as a sample, the survey highlights the aggregate forecast for developing high-level machine intelligence (HLMI) within the next 100 year. High-level machine intelligence is defined as a point in the future "when unaided machines can accomplish every task better and more cheaply than human workers."

A subset of participants was asked logically similar questions concerning full automation of labor (FAL), intended as a complete replacement of people by machines in every working position. The forecasts obtained for full automation resulted much more projected towards the future than HLMI, with a 50% probability of reaching the FAL within 122 year and a 10% probability of reaching it within the next 65 year starting from 2016.

As can be seen in the Fig. 1, even if the full automation is still far from being reached, there are many working positions at risk, such as the surgeon, whose tasks, with an aggregate estimated probability of 50%, will be completely carried out by the machines within the next 35 year. "Advances in artificial intelligence will have massive social consequences", claims the study. "In addition to possible unemployment, the transition will bring new challenges, such as rebuilding infrastructure, protecting vehicle cyber-security, and adapting laws and regulations. New challenges, both for AI developers and policy-makers, will also arise from applications in law enforcement, military technology, and marketing."

Less drastic seem the conclusions of the same year study done by Accenture (Daugherty and Purdy 2016), one of the largest multinational business consultancy companies in the world. According to the Accenture report, the two traditional drivers of the economy, capital and labor, are no longer able to replicate the increase in

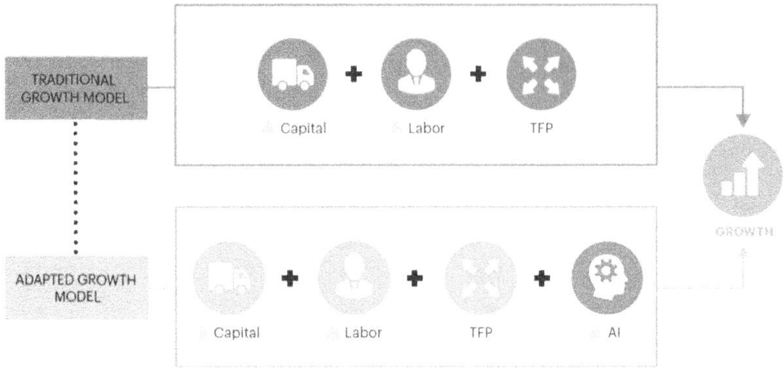

Fig. 2. New growth model proposed by Accenture (TFP is a total factor productivity). *Source* Daugherty and Purdy (2016)

prosperity that occurred in previous decades in most developed countries. Artificial intelligence, therefore, represents a new factor of production capable of transforming the basis of economic growth throughout the world (Fig. 2).

Little space in the research is devoted to the social cost of the estimated increase in growth rates, more specifically to the possible replacement of human operators in almost all working positions by intelligent machines. The report only briefly mentions the importance of "facing and anticipating the negative consequences of AI" by policy-makers. The authors remain confident that "a significant part of the economic growth from AI will come not from replacing existing labor and capital, but in enabling them to be used much more effectively". In fact, one of the basic assumptions of the AI growth model used in research presupposes a constant long-term employment rate, a postulate questioned by the results of the statistical survey examined previously.

3.3 AI in the Economy of the Future. Possible Problems and Solutions

It seems that the disappearance of a considerable amount of jobs is inevitable if artificial intelligence will become a dominant factor of production in the new technological paradigm. But this type of change does not represent a novelty with respect to the previous technological revolutions: there was a considerable intersectoral shift of workforce from agriculture to industry during the first two industrial revolutions, and then an intersectoral shift from the secondary to the tertiary sector during the first digital revolution (called sometimes the third industrial revolution in relation to the secondary sector only). The real novelty with respect to the previous technological revolution lies in the fact that AI represents a completely original factor of production (Korinek and Stiglitz 2017), a sort of hybrid between labor and capital that can potentially make most human operators completely obsolete. Therefore, no clear analogy can be drawn with respect to past technological shifts.

On the other hand, artificial intelligence can potentially become a source of enormous competitive advantage for every single type of business. It is, therefore, not conceivable for any State, at least in the current economic-political perspective of global capitalism, to prevent the development of artificial intelligence in any way just to keep the unemployment levels low. By doing so the State risk to suffer great losses in terms of competitiveness and growth, and to become disconnected from the global business network.

However, this does not mean that policy-makers should not intervene in any way. At first, they will be forced to reconsider the negative role that traditional macroeconomic theory attributes to unemployment, which may become so widespread as to be considered normal in the society and, absurdly, by contrasting unemployment growth the State will be running the risk to lower the rate of its GDP growth.

The long-term increase in productivity must normally be accompanied by an increase in global demand for goods and services. If this will not happen, that is if most of the unemployed population will not be endowed with the necessary means to satisfy their needs, the initial increase in productivity will soon become futile and so there will be no real economic growth. The role of the State appears to be central in this scenario, as only the State, by acting supra-partes, can efficiently transfer a part of wealth (not in the form of salary) from companies to citizens, a task that companies will not be able to tackle individually, given the free-rider type of behavior that tends to be adopted in the absence of an external regulator. Although there are still many debates on the subject, frequently of an ideological nature, it seems that some form of universal basic income (UBI) will be the only possible solution to the problem of the distribution of wealth in the hypothetical fully automated society (Hughes 2014).

The hypothesis of the upcoming full automation of labor makes universal basic income an even more desirable model to be taken into consideration. In fact, according to German economist Thomas Straubhaar "one of the strongest points for UBI comes from the rapid technological change" (Straubhaar 2017). However, despite the growing interest, with entrepreneurs of the caliber of Elon Musk and Mark Zuckerberg who have already expressed their support for UBI, the universal basic income remains a poorly explored social policy with the scarce empirical evidence.

The second, somewhat more optimistic economic outcome concerns the reduction of full-time working hours. This will be the case for tasks that are a bit more complex, more difficult to replace immediately with AI. In jobs of this type human abilities will be integrated with those of artificial intelligence and the tasks of individuals will be reduced more and more to the surveillance and control of the machines.

4 AI as a Component of Successful Business

In the perspective of the stated hypothesis of artificial intelligence being a possible candidate for becoming the enabling technology of the next technological paradigm shift, it seemed rather interesting to investigate how the adoption of artificial intelligence in the major businesses influence some corporate results, like the yearly variations in profits and revenues.

As a starting point of the analysis, 150 first companies from the 2019 Forbes Global 2000 list were extracted to form the basis of the dataset. The Forbes ranking of the most successful companies is based on a mix of four metrics: profits, sales, market value, and assets. By comparing the profits of 2019 and 2018 of the same ranked companies, a variation in revenues and profits were obtained, using simple expressions:

$$\text{Variation in Revenues} = \frac{\text{Revenues } 2019 - \text{Revenues } 2018}{\text{Revenues } 2018} \tag{1}$$

$$\text{Variation in Profits} = \frac{\text{Profits } 2019 - \text{Profits } 2018}{|\text{Profits } 2018|} \tag{2}$$

The absolute value in the denominator of Variation in Profits expression (2) is not conceptually correct as it may create some distortions in the computation and misleading results in some cases. However, the error can be considered acceptable, as the same methodology is frequently used in the analysis of growth metrics by analysts.

The problem arose with defining the unique unit of measurement of the intensity of the use of artificial intelligence in those companies, as information stated in individual reports is very scattered and cannot be easily compared among different companies. Therefore, a different criterion for comparison was adopted. AI Intensity index was defined as the ratio between the number of google search results in the News section of Google search engine of "*X artificial intelligence*" and the number of identical results for the search query "*X*", where *X* identifies the company name. So, for example, for Samsung Electronics the result obtained is 196.000/45,000,000 = 0.00436. The proposed index varies from 0 to 1. Theoretically, it is equal to zero if there are no articles in the press related to the usage of AI by the company. It is equal to one if all the news articles about the company mention artificial intelligence as well. In practice, many problems may be identified by using such index. The question may arise whether AI Intensity index properly captures the intensity of usage of artificial intelligence by companies rather than capturing the amount of attention that media devotes to the subject. Also, the results for the most famous companies (like Facebook or Apple) may be skewed due to the huge overall press coverage of them.

On the other hand, an index obtained in such a manner has the advantage of being a pure number, uninfluenced by the units of measurement, therefore making comparable the usage of artificial intelligence among very heterogeneous companies. The other advantage is, of course, the relative simplicity of obtaining of the results. The last one is particularly important, as it was noticed that the number of Google query results vary slightly from computer to computer and it is slightly different in different periods of the day. Therefore, even if the ratio itself tends to stay relatively

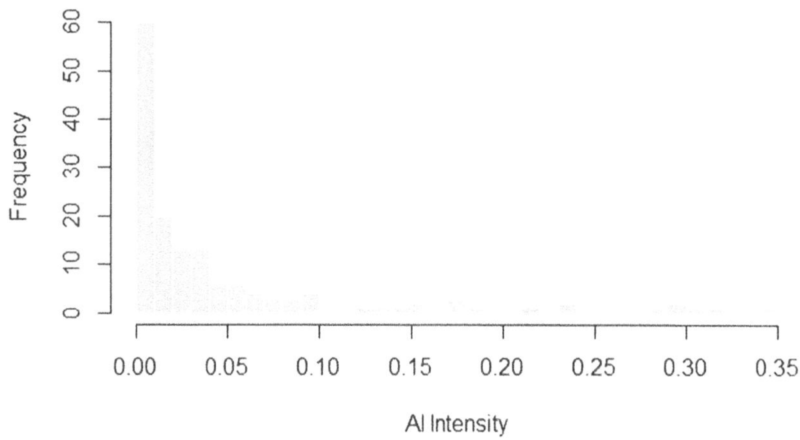

Fig. 3 The distribution of AI Intensity indexes in the dataset

stable, the calculation of the AI Intensity index was done by sitting on the same machine for the sake of the greater precision.

Overall, the distribution of AI Intensity indexes in the sample resulted to be highly asymmetric with a long right tail, with a mean value equal to 0.0464 and a median equal to 0.00423 (Fig. 3).

No hypothesis could have been formulated on the mean and the median of the AI Intensity index for the overall population of 2000 firms in the Forbes Global 2000 ranking as the non-random sample was formed by extracting first 150 companies from the list, therefore leaving a room for systematic errors in the estimations. However, such estimations were considered of no particular relevancy for purpose of the analysis.

The AI Intensity index was than correlated to the absolute Variation in Profits and absolute Variation in Revenues. The general assumptions for the distribution of error term (homoscedasticity and normality) were considered as given. Assumptions were further confirmed for the model having the absolute Variation in Revenues as a regressor by observing the distribution of residuals. The distribution of residuals resulted highly symmetric, with mean and variance centered around zero.

The distribution of residuals for the model having the absolute Variation in Profits as a regressor, however, resulted more asymmetric, with the median equal to −0.4432 (Figs. 4 and 5).

For the first model the fitted equation *Variation in Revenues* = *0.02252* + *1.51213*AI Intensity index* was obtained. The correlation index between Variation in Revenues and AI Intensity index resulted equal to 0.504, therefore the existence of modest linear relationship between two variables was hypothesized. Indeed, the relationship was confirmed by testing the hypothesis of the slope of the regression line being equal to zero. A t-test was used, and the obtained *p*-value of $4.46e^{-11}$ resulted significant enough to reject the assumption of the independence between Variation in Revenues and AI Intensity index.

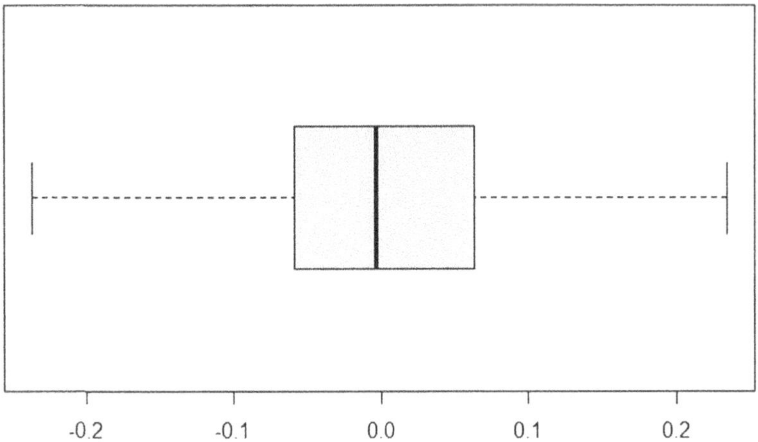

Fig. 4. Distribution of residuals for two models

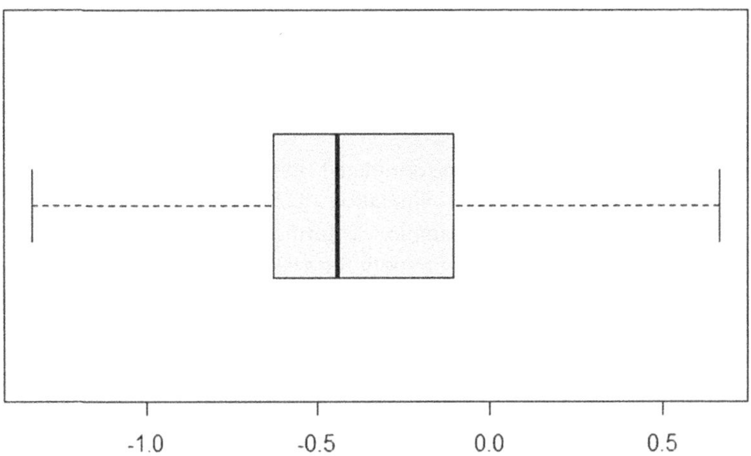

Fig. 5. Distribution of residuals for two models

The same procedure was repeated to model the relationship between the absolute Variation in Profits and AI Intensity index. The fitted equation *Variation in Profits = 0.6657–1.1335 *AI Intensity index* was therefore obtained. However, the weak negative correlation (−0.046) indicated no relationship of linear type between two variables. Indeed, a t-test was used, and the obtained *p*-value of 0.573273 for the test on the slope of regression line equal to zero resulted high enough to not allow the rejection of the hypothesis of independence between Variation in Profits and AI Intensity index (Figs. 6 and 7).[1]

[1]The analysis was developed by using RStudio.

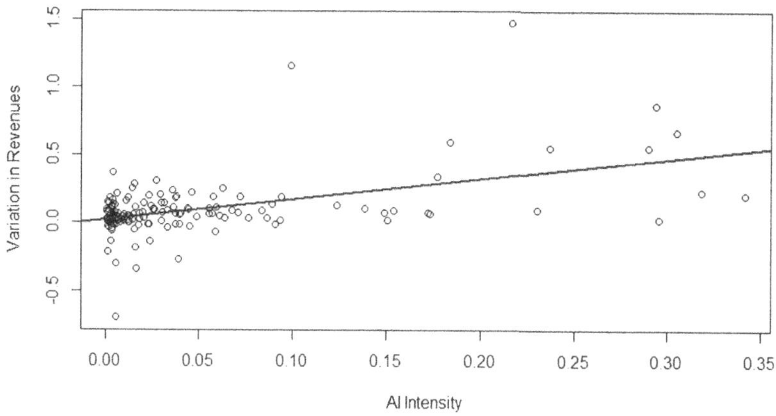

Fig. 6 Fitted model for variation in revenues with respect to AI intensity index

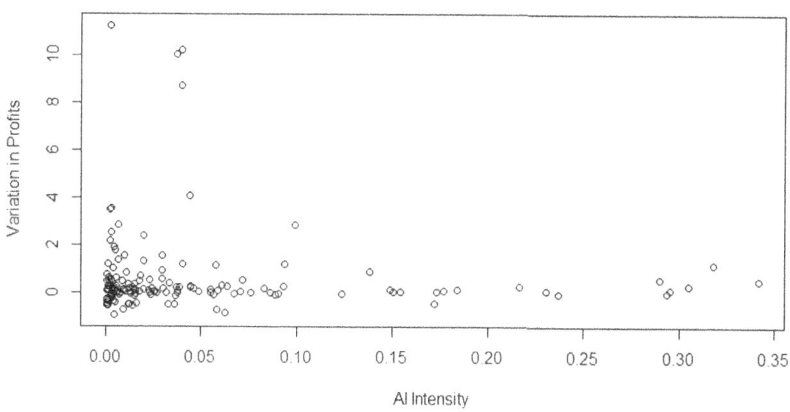

Fig. 7 Variation in revenues with respect to AI intensity index

It may not surprise that Variation in Profits for such big companies shows little to no correlation with the intensity of usage of AI. But the overall validity of the results may be undermined by the fact that the assumption of normality of error term seems to not hold for the Variation in Profits, as the distribution of residuals presented a certain degree of asymmetry. The asymmetry, on the other hand, may derive from the way in which the Variation in Profits index was calculated (as seen before, using the absolute value in denominator could potentially lead to biased results).

There is, however, a positive relationship between the absolute Variation in Revenues and the AI Intensity index in the model. Of course, given the reduced sample of firms and the multifactorial aggregated nature of Variation in Revenues index, further analysis is needed to be able to conclude that AI usage positively affects the flow of revenues of the companies. In the subsequent analysis bigger sample size must be considered.

The nature of the AI Intensity index as it was defined in the analysis requires further investigation as well. It remains unclear if the index is truly able to capture the intensity of the usage of artificial intelligence by companies in a meaningful way. Also, the implications of the volatility of the results (slightly different for different machines and in different time periods) should be necessarily tested.

5 Conclusions

Artificial intelligence has all the typical characteristics of the radical invention, capable of changing the modern socioeconomic framework. The apparent maturity of the key technologies of the first digital revolution provides further confirmation of this hypothesis. However, it must be emphasized that unlike the radical inventions of the past, AI possesses a completely original characteristic: it cannot be considered as a mere capital alone. Instead, it can be seen as the new factor of production, with the typical characteristics of both the labor and the capital, highly substitutable with the former. Indeed, growing unemployment rates can hardly be reversed in the future. Artificial intelligence is potentially a source of enormous competitive advantage, so companies will not be able to renounce it. Meanwhile, for more mechanically complex jobs and those that transcend the mere data analysis and require a bit of creativity, the integration between individual and artificial intelligence is to be expected, with the former having the task of controlling and to monitor the functioning of the latter, enriching the machine's capabilities with human feelings, empathy and also the beauty of human imperfection. The development of models and methodologies for measuring and steering the socio-economic impact of Artificial Intelligence is just at the beginning.

References

Antonoglou, I., Baker, L., Bolton, A., Chen, Y., Van den Driessche, G., Graepel, T., Guez, A., Hassabis, D., Huang, A., Hubert, T., Hui, F., Lai, M., Lillicrap, T., Schrittwieser, J., Sifre, L., Silver, D., Simonyan, K.: Mastering the game of Go without human knowledge. Nature **550**, 354–359 (2017)

Artificial Intelligence Market Forecasts (2019) Tractica rreport. Retrieved from https://tractica.omdia.com/research/artificial-intelligence-market-forecasts/

Banerjee, A., Hanna, R., Kreindler, G., Olken, B.A.: Debunking the stereotype of the lazy welfare recipient: evidence from cash transfer programs worldwide. World Bank Res. Observer **32**(2), 155–184 (2016)

Bellini, F., D'Ascenzo, F.: L'evoluzione dei modelli di produzione nella logica della co-creazione di valore. In: (a cura di): D'Ascenzo Fabrizio, Bellini Francesco, Produzione, Logistica e Trasformazione Digitale, pp. 1–23. PADOVA: CEDAM (2018). ISBN: 9788813366360

Buchanan, B.G.: A (very) brief history of artificial intelligence. AI Mag. **26**(4), 53 (2005). https://doi.org/10.1609/aimag.v26i4.1848

Ceruzzi, P.: Moore's law and technological determinism: reflections on the history of technology. Technol. Culture **46**(3), 584–593 (2005). Retrieved 23 June 2020, from www.jstor.org/stable/40060905

Chen, Y., Li, Y.: Intelligent autonomous pollination for future farming—a micro air vehicle conceptual framework with artificial intelligence and human-in-the-loop. In: IEEE Access, vol. 7, pp. 119706–119717 (2019). https://doi.org/10.1109/ACCESS.2019.2937171

Chen, N., Christensen, L., Gallagher, K., Mate, R., Rafert, G.: Global Econ. Impacts Assoc. Artif. Intell. **23** (2016)

Cockburn, I.M., Henderson, R., Stern, S.: The impact of artificial intelligence on innovation (Working Paper N. 24449; Working Paper Series). National Bureau of Economic Research (2018). https://doi.org/10.3386/w24449

Dafoe, A., Evans, O., Grace, K., Salvatier, J., Zhang, B.: When will AI exceed human performance? Evidence from AI experts. J. Artif. Intell. Res. **62**, 729–754 (2017)

Daugherty, P., Purdy, M.: Why Artificial intelligence is a future of growth. Accenture (2016)

Dharmaraj, V., Vijayanand, C.: Artificial intelligence (AI) in agriculture. Int. J. Curr. Microbiol. App. Sci. **7**(12):2122–2128 (2018). https://doi.org/10.20546/ijcmas.2018.712.241

Encyclopedia Britannica, "Artificial Intelligence". Retrieved from https://www.britannica.com/technology/artificial-intelligence

Fallows, J.: Why is software so slow? The Atlantic (2013). Retrieved from https://www.theatlantic.com/magazine/archive/2013/09/why-is-software-so-slow/309422

Fraga-Lamas, P., Fernández-Caramés, T. M., Blanco-Novoa, Ó., Vilar-Montesinos, M.A.: A review on industrial augmented reality systems for the industry 4.0 shipyard. In: IEEE Access, vol. 6, pp. 13358–13375 (2018). https://doi.org/10.1109/ACCESS.2018.2808326.

Furman, J., Seamans, R.: AI and the economy. Innov. Policy Econ. **19**, 161–191 (2019). https://doi.org/10.1086/699936

Gardener, H.: Intelligence Reframed: Multiple Intelligences for 21st Century. Basic Books, New York (2000)

Gerbert, P., Lorenz, M., Rüßmann, M., Waldner, M., Justus, J., Engel, P., Harnisch, M.: Industry 4.0: The Future of Productivity and Growth in Manufacturing Industries (2015). Accessed on 25 June 2020 from https://www.bcg.com/it-it/publications/2015/engineered_products_project_business_industry_4_future_productivity_growth_manufacturing_industries.aspx

Hughes, J.: A strategic opening for a basic income guarantee in the global crisis being created by AI, robots, desktop manufacturing and biomedicine. J Evol Technol **24**(1), 45–61 (2014)

Jeschke S., Brecher C., Meisen T., Özdemir D., Eschert T.: Industrial Internet of things and cyber manufacturing systems. In: Jeschke, S., Brecher, C., Song, H., Rawat, D. (eds.) Industrial Internet of Things. Springer Series in Wireless Technology. Springer, Cham (2017)

Knight, W. (2017). The dark secret at the heart of AI'11 April 2017. MIT Technol Rev. Retrieved from https://www.technologyreview.com/s/604087/the-dark-secret-at-the-heart-of-ai

Korinek, A., Stiglitz, J. E.: Artificial intelligence, worker-replacing technological progress and income distribution. NBER working paper, 24174 (2017)

Kranzberg, M. (1985) The Information Age: Evolution or Revolution? Information Technologies and Social Transformation, 35–53

Lezzi, M., Lazoi, M., Corallo, A.: Cybersecurity for industry 4.0 in the current literature: a reference framework. Comput. Ind. **103**, 97–110 (2018). https://doi.org/10.1016/j.compind.2018.09.004

McCarthy, J., Minsky, M.L., Rochester, N., Shannon, C.E.: A proposal for the dartmouth summer research project on artificial intelligence, August 31, 1955. AI Mag. **27**(4), 12 (2006). https://doi.org/10.1609/aimag.v27i4.1904

McCorduck, P.: Machines Who Think. A K Peters/CRC Press, Boca Raton (2004)

Nilsson, N.J.: The quest for artificial intelligence: a history of ideas and achievements. Cambridge University Press (2009). https://doi.org/10.1017/CBO9780511819346

Patrício, D.I., Rieder, R.: Computer vision and artificial intelligence in precision agriculture for grain crops: a systematic review. Comput. Electron. Agric. **153**, 69–81 (2018). https://doi.org/10.1016/j.compag.2018.08.001

Potapov, A.: Technological singularity: what do we really know? Information **9**, 82 (2018)
Ransbotham, S., Kiron, D., Gerbert, P., Reeves, M.: Reshaping business with artificial intelligence. MIT Sloan Manage. Rev. **59**(1), 1–17 (2017)
Savastano, M., Amendola, C., Bellini, F., D'Ascenzo, F.: Contextual impacts on industrial processes brought by the digital transformation of manufacturing: a systematic review. Sustainability **11**, 891 (2019)
Searle, J.: Minds, brains and programs. Behav. Brain Sci. **3**(3), 417–424 (1980)
Simonite, T.: Moore's law is dead. Now what? MIT Technol. Rev. (2016). Retrieved from https://www.technologyreview.com/s/601441/moores-law-is-dead-now-what
Straubhaar, T.: On the economics of a universal basic income. Intereconomics, 52–74 (2017)
Stoltzfus, J.: The 6 most amazing AI advances in agriculture. Techopedia, 7 Aug 2019. Retrieved from https://www.techopedia.com/the-6-most-amazing-ai-advances-in-agriculture/2/33177
Vinge, V.: The coming technological singularity: How to survive in the post-human era. In: Proceedings of the vision-21: interdisciplinary science and engineering in the era of cyberspace, Cleveland, OH, USA, pp. 11–22, 30–31 Mar 1993
Yu, K., Beam, A.L., Kohane, I.S.: Artificial intelligence in healthcare. Nat Biomed Eng **2**, 719–731 (2018). https://doi.org/10.1038/s41551-018-0305-z
Zaforas, M. (2017) Artificial intelligence as a service: image recognition, Paradigma. Retrieved from https://en.paradigmadigital.com/techbiz/artificial-intelligence-service-image-recognition

An Econometric Analysis of the Relationship Between Tourist Arrivals in Tourist Accommodation Structures in Romania and the Number of Overnight Stays

Mihai Dinu, Simona Roxana Pătărlăgeanu, Marius Constantin, and Adriana Tărăşilă

1 Introduction

The number of tourist arrivals in tourist accommodation structures is a key performance indicator which quantifies, to a certain extent, the tourists' interest (at both national and international level) in a certain destination, country, tourist objective etc. (Florescu 2019). Likewise, the number of overnight stays in such structures is a relevant indicator in measuring tourist interest (Popescu 2014). These two tourism specific indicators have a positive impact on the national economy, because tourism is one of the industries which can lead to economic growth and development.

The current research has the following objectives:

O_1: Quantifying the influence that the number of tourist arrivals in tourist accommodation structures had on the number of overnight stays in the year 2018, in all the counties of Romania;
O_2: Quantifying whether the relationship between the previously mentioned indicators was stronger or weaker in the case of Romanian tourists or in that of foreign tourists who arrived and spent the night in tourist accommodations structures in Romania in 2018.

The hypotheses formulated for this research were the following:

H_1: In Romania, at county level, the number of tourist overnight stays in tourist accommodation structures is highly influenced by the number of tourist arrivals;

M. Dinu (✉) · S. R. Pătărlăgeanu · M. Constantin · A. Tărăşilă
Bucharest University of Economic Studies, Bucharest, Romania
e-mail: mihai.dinu@eam.ase.ro

A. M. Dima and F. DÁscenzo (eds.), *Business Revolution in a Digital Era*,
Springer Proceedings in Business and Economics,
https://doi.org/10.1007/978-3-030-59972-0_19

H_2: Considering tourist typologies, in Romania, at county level, the number of tourist overnight stays in tourist accommodation structures is influenced more by the number of arrivals of foreign tourists than of Romanian ones.

The novelty that the present research brings to this field consists in identifying the intensity of the relationship between the two important tourism indicators: the number of tourists arriving in tourist accommodation structures and the number of overnight stays in such structures, the reference year being 2018 and the relationship being studied at county level (the data analysed are cross-sectional).

2 Literature Review

The economic growth within the EU block is generated by one of the industries which is constantly experiencing a complex evolution process: tourism (Gribincea 2015). The EU countries account for over 40% of the international tourists, which also contributes to Romania's economy, due to the fact that tourism generates income, workplaces, it fosters entrepreneurship and stimulates regional and rural development. (Bădulescu et al. 2018).

The underlying motivation of this research derives from the aspects included in the scientific literature with economic and social implications. If adequately supported, tourism can represent an important engine for economic development and a welfare generator, due to its contribution to the creation of workplaces, income increase, reduction of migration, turning to account of natural landscapes, protection of the natural environment and patrimony. (Davidescu et al. 2018). The direct contribution of tourism to the world gross domestic product is of 3.1%, while its total contribution is estimated at 10.2% (namely 7.6 trillion US dollars)—which is why tourism is a field of major interest in the world economy (Pascariu and Ibănescu 2018).

The year 2018 saw a certain amount of improvement in the national tourist activity, which led to an upsurge in the number of tourists in Romania. (Anghelache et al. 2018).

3 Research Methodology

The research method which best fits the requirements of this research is the quantitative one, simple linear regression, the approach being econometric. As a form of knowledge, econometrics comprises methods and techniques for analysing the dynamics of the variables in various fields of activity, as well as of the interconnections between/among the variables. (Anghelache et al. 2019). Econometrics involves a harmonious blend of theory, statistics and economic modelling and mathematical statistics. The simple linear regression model provides a way to observe and establish the existence or inexistence of correlations between two types of variables: a dependent or endogenous variable and an independent or exogenous variable (Gheorghiţă and Pătărlăgeanu 2006).

In order to validate or reject the hypotheses formulated for this research, the simple linear method was applied to the cross-sectional data, characterised by means of observations made at a certain moment of several entities referring to a single phenomenon.

The statistical data were taken over from the databases of the Romanian National Institute of Statistics on 31 December 2019. The variables analysed in this research were the following:

TUR105D—Overnight stays in tourist accommodation structures. This indicator is defined as follows: "A tourist overnight stay is the 24 h interval, starting from the hotel check in time, for which a person is entered into the records of the tourist accommodation structure and benefits from accommodation at the price corresponding to the occupied space, even if the actual duration of the stay is shorter than the mentioned interval. It also includes the overnight stays in supplementary beds paid by the clients." (Institutul Naţional de Statistică România 2019b). Annually, the National Institute of Statistics collects statistical data from the tourist accommodation structures with a capacity of minimum 5 beds and over.

TUR104B—Tourist arrivals in tourist accommodation structures. The definition of this indicator is the following: "The number of tourists accommodated in tourist accommodation structures includes all the people (either Romanian or foreigners) who are travelling outside their place of residence, for a period below 12 months and who are spending at least one night in a tourist accommodation structure in tourist areas throughout the country, the main reason of the trip being different than that of performing a paid activity in the visited sites." (Institutul Naţional de Statistică România 2019a).

The endogenous (dependent, response) variable is TUR105D—Overnight stays in tourist accommodation structures, while the exogenous (independent, explanatory) variable is TUR104B—Tourist arrivals in tourist accommodation structures.

The two research hypotheses will be validated or rejected after applying the simple linear regression methodology to the above-mentioned indicators, in the situation in which the data are of the cross-sectional type. The year for which the analysis was carried out was 2018 and the area covered is that of the 42 counties in Romania (41 plus the Bucharest municipality).

The standard deviation presented higher values as compared to the mean, a phenomenon justified by the high tourist attractiveness of certain counties such as Constanţa (where there was the maximum number of overnight stays, namely 5,010,766, of foreign and Romanian tourists in 2018), Braşov, Cluj or Sibiu, compared to other counties with low tourist attractiveness—for example Teleorman (where there was the minimum number of overnight stays in 2018, i.e. 8673, of foreign and Romanian tourists).

Skewness is an important indicator because it reflects the assymmetry of data distribution around the mean. A normal distribution is as close as possible to zero. In our case, the distribution is not normal and one can notice the positive assymmetry

Table 1 Descriptive statistics referring to the values of the analysed indicators at (cross-sectional) county level, the reference year being 2018

	Total (Romanian and foreign tourists)		Romanian tourists		Foreign tourists	
	TUR105D	TUR104B	TUR105D	TUR104B	TUR105D	TUR104B
Mean	682,017.00	307,265.00	555,122.00	240,678.00	126,895.00	66,586.00
Median	373,512.00	178,849.00	304,516.00	140,835.00	34,896.00	14,688.00
Maximum	5,010,766	2,080,229	4,818,638	1,249,667	2,061,184	1,210,580
Minimum	18,673	10,609	16,899	9,661	1,774	948
Standard deviation	970,889.00	410,315.00	821,941.00	281,858.00	321,001.00	186,941.00
Skewness	2.9025	2.7371	3.68280839	2.24721188	5.40612674	5.65410141
Kurtosis	11.9585	10.8669	18.7025843	7.86762434	32.9716164	35.0553188
Jarque-Bera	199.4234	160.7471	526.441061	76.8138204	1776.60458	2021.9831
Probability	0.0000	0.0000	0.0000	0.0000	0.0000	0.0000
Sum	28,644,742	12,905,131	23,315,138	10,108,509	5,329,604	2,796,622
Observations	42	42	42	42	42	42
Year	2018	2018	2018	2018	2018	2018

(the Skewness values are above zero), which is caused by much higher values than the mean in certain counties (for example Braşov).

Kurtosis is an indicator which reflects the flatness or curving of a distribution as compared to a normal distribution. In case of a normally distributed series, the Kurtosis value is 3. This criterion is not observed by the cross-sectional series analysed in Table 1. It can be seen that irrespective of the tourist category, the distribution of the series is leptokurtic (the Kurtsis value is above 3) and thus the peaks are thin and high.

Therefore, the analysed indicators do not have a normal distribution when the analysis comprises all the 41 counties of Romania plus the Bucharest municipality. In order to counter this phenomenon, we have divided the counties into two categories: counties with high tourist attractiveness and counties with low tourist attractiveness, depending on the number of overnight stays in tourist accommodation structures.

The second category, of the counties with low tourist attractiveness, includes 21 counties: Teleorman, Giurgiu, Călăraşi, Vaslui, Olt, Vrancea, Botoşani, Sălaj, Satu Mare, Galaţi, Ialomiţa, Bistriţa-Năsăud, Buzău, Gorj, Mehedinţi, Dolj, Brăila, Ilfov, Dâmboviţa, Alba and Hunedoara.

After dividing the counties into the two categories, the series started to have a distribution closer to normal, but there are still irregularities.

The value of the Skewness indicator is moderate, in the sense that it stays around the 0.5 threshold. In the case of foreign tourists, the positive assymmetry persists.

Table 2 Descriptive statistics referring to the values of the analysed indicators for the 21 counties with low tourist attractiveness (cross-sectional analysis), reference year—2018

	Category: counties with low tourist attractiveness					
	Total (Romanian and foreign tourists)		Romanian tourists		Foreign tourists	
	TUR105D	TUR104B	TUR105D	TUR104B	TUR105D	TUR104B
Mean	168,969.81	87,707.48	146,781.05	75,684.33	22,188.76	12,023.14
Median	170,308.00	93,355.00	164,913.00	79,979.00	14,002.00	6439.00
Maximum	369,286	198,936	343,717	171,363	108,536	80,010
Minimum	18,673	10,609	16,899	9661	1774	948
Strandard deviation	102,569.80	56,591.06	89,728.77	45,229.62	24,124.10	17,283.51
Skewness	0.4407	0.6863	0.5349	0.4846	2.6061	3.3807
Kurtosis	−0.6420	−0.2930	−0.3316	−0.3595	8.1248	12.8560
Jarque-Bera	1.1050	1.6360	1.1060	0.9730	52.3790	117.0480
Probability	0.5750	0.4410	0.5740	0.6140	0.0000	0.0000
Sum	3,548,366	1,841,857	3,082,402	1,589,371	465,964	252,486
Observations	21	21	21	21	21	21
Year	2018	2018	2018	2018	2018	2018

According to the values of the Kurtosis indicator in Table 2, there is a normal distribution as far as the foreign tourists are concerned (Kurtosis close to 3, the ideal value), but a platykurtic one for the other categories of tourists (HIS Markit 2017).

Even under these circumstances, the data have a distribution which is closer to normal than when all the counties in Romania were analysed together.

The category of counties with high attractiveness includes 18 counties, with the highest number of overnight stays: Arad, Bacău, Tulcea, Argeş, Neamţ, Maramureş, Harghita, Covasna, Iaşi, Caraş-Severin, Timiş, Sibiu, Suceava, Mureş, Cluj, Prahova, Vâlcea, Bihor. A limitation of this study is the fact that the counties of Braşov and Constanţa, as well as the Bucharest municipality, were excluded from this category, since their attractiveness is much above the category average and it would determine an abnormal distribution.

Similarly, in the case of the counties with high tourist attractivenes the value of the Skewness indicator is moderate, meaning that it stays around the 0.5 threshold, although it displays a tendency towards positive assymmetry in the case of foreign tourists. According to the Kurtosis indicator values in Table 3, there is a normal distribution when it comes to the foreign tourists (close to the ideal value of 3), almost normal for Romanian tourists and moderately platykurtic for all tourists (irrespective of the category).

Given the descriptive statistics analysis, we consider that the data have a distribution close to normality, with the above-mentioned observations.

Table 3 Descriptive statistics referring to the values of the analysed indicators for the 18 counties with high tourist attractiveness (cross-sectional analysis), reference year—2018

	Category: counties with high tourist attractiveness					
	Total (Romanian and foreign tourists)		Romanian tourists		Foreign tourists	
	TUR105D	TUR104B	TUR105D	TUR104B	TUR105D	TUR104B
Mean	776,538.39	349,463.89	654,577.67	290,390.72	121,960.72	59,073.17
Median	652,546.50	294,416.50	546,300.00	247,085.00	88,368.50	51,325.50
Maximum	1,523,648	656,508	1,372,314	514,921	308,047	159,325
Minimum	377,738	119,372	297,735	106,684	21,320	8,645
Strandard deviation	385,072.05	169,639.27	346,804.76	136,692.50	95,070.59	45,202.57
Skewness	0.5670	0.4240	0.8660	0.3950	0.8270	0.8170
Kurtosis	1.9570	1.7970	2.6360	1.7040	2.4040	2.7680
Jarque-Bera	1.7800	1.6250	2.3500	1.7280	2.3190	2.0470
Probability	0.4100	0.4430	0.3080	0.4210	0.3130	0.3590
Sum	13,977,691	6,290,350	11,782,398	5,227,033	2,195,293	1,063,317
Observations	18	18	18	18	18	18
Year	2018	2018	2018	2018	2018	2018

4 Results and Discussions

The simple linear regressive model was applied six times to the processed categories of cross-sectional data relative to the year 2018. We started off with the category of counties with low tourist attractiveness, to which the linear regressive model was applied three times: to all tourists (foreign and Romanian), then to Romanian tourists, and finally only to foreign tourists (Table 4).

In order to obtain the estimates, the least square method was used. The variables were processed in the EViews 10 software program: Student Version Lite, a useful tool in quantitative research.

The R-squared coefficient of determination has high values. The exogenous variable (arrivals of tourists in tourist accommodation structures) for all tourists (foreign and Romanian) explains 84.4% of the overnight stays in tourist accommodation structures in the counties with low tourist attractiveness in 2018, in Romania. However, as far as the foreign tourists are concerned, 94.55% of their overnight stays are explained by their arrivals. Thus, the relationship between the two indicators is stronger in the case of foreign tourists than in that of Romanian tourists (determination coefficient 83.46%).

According to the data in Table 5, the t-Statistic associated probability for the exogenous variable is zero in all the three situations analysed. In spite of this, the probability associated to the free coefficient is higher than the 0.05 limit in the case of Romanian tourists and overall (irrespective of the tourist category).

Table 4 The result of applying the simple linear regression method to the counties with low tourist attractiveness (cross-sectional), by tourist category, reference year—2018

	Category: counties with low tourist attractiveness		
	Total (Romanian and foreign tourists)	Romanian tourists	Foreign tourists
R-squared	0.844372	0.834653	0.945580
Adjusted R-squared	0.836181	0.825951	0.942716
S.E. of regression	41,515	37,434	5773
Sum squared resid	32,745,911,037	26,624,979,414	633,414,082
Log likelihood	−252.056	−249.883	−210.630
F-statistic	103.09	95.91	330.14
Prob (F-statistic)	0.000000	0.000000	0.000000
Mean dependent var	168,970	146,781	22,188
S.D. dependent var	102,570	89,729	24,124
Akaike info criterion	24.1959	23.9889	20.2505
Schwarz criterion	24.2954	24.0884	20.3499
Hannan-Quinn criter	24.2175	24.0105	20.2721
Durbin-Watson stat	2.6191	2.8077	1.8463

Table 5 Simple linear regression equation in the year 2018, for the counties with low tourist attractiveness, by tourist category

	Category: counties with low tourist attractiveness				Prob
	Estimation equation: overnight stays = C(1) + C(2)*Arrivals + ε				
	Variable	Coefficient	Std. Error	t-Statistic	
Total tourists	C	22,894.90	17,001.79	1.346617	0.1939
	Arrivals	1.665478	0.164036	10.153100	0.0000
OVERNIGHT STAYS = 22,894.9 + 1.66*ARRIVALS + ε					
Romanian tourists	C	9608.32	16,214	0.592568	0.5605
	Arrivals	1.812432	0.185067	9.793364	0.0000
OVERNIGHT STAYS = 9608.3 + 1.81*ARRIVALS + ε					
Foreign tourists	C	5870	1547	3.793723	0.0012
	Arrivals	1.357277	0.074700	18.169720	0.0000
OVERNIGHT STAYS = 5,870 + 1.35*ARRIVALS + ε					

Taking into account the results displayed in Table 5, only the equation of the estimate corresponding to the overnight stays of foreign tourists is considered valid. In this case, in 2018, in the counties with low tourist attractiveness in Romania, one can notice that if the number of arrivals of foreign tourists increases by one unit, then the number of overnight stays in tourist accommodation structures goes up 1.35 times.

According to the data centralised in Table 6, if we look at the residual mean (zero), the residual distribution is normal irrespective of the tourist category. There is a tendency towards a positive assymmetry (the Skewness value is above the ideal zero threshold, but it is situated below 1). The Kurtosis values confirm the residual normality in the case of Romanian tourists, but also overall. In the case of foreign tourists, the Kurtosis value (2.17) shows a slightly platykurtic residual distribution, but this is acceptable as long as the analysis included only 21 observations. In all three cases, the Jarque-Bera indicator shows a slight deviation from the ideal situation (normal residual distribution), when the indicator is zero. The Probability indicator has values above 0.05, which is desirable. The Prob. F indicator in the White test reflects the homoscedasticity of the residuals in all three tourist categories (Prob. F value above 0.05 in all cases), which is characteristic of a normal residual distribution.

Further on, we analysed the category of counties with high tourist attractiveness (Table 7).

Similar to the category of counties with low tourist attractiveness, the R-squared determination coefficient also displays high values in the case of the counties with high tourist attractiveness. In Romania, in 2018, the number of overnight stays in tourist accommodation structures is explained in a proportion of 68.82% by the exogenous variable (tourist arrivals in tourist accommodation structures) for all tourists (both Romanian and foreign). However, in the case of foreign tourists, the number of overnight stays in tourist accommodation structures is explained to a

Table 6 Residual analysis when simple linear regression is applied to the category of counties with low tourist attractiveness, by tourist category, reference year—2018

	Category: counties with low tourist attractiveness		
	Residuals analysis		
	Total (Foreign and Romanian tourists)	Romanian tourists	Foreign tourists
Skewness	0.5154	0.7374	0.8332
Kurtosis	3.0125	3.3837	2.1780
Jarque-Bera	0.9302	2.0323	3.0205
Probability	0.6280	0.3619	0.2208
Observations	21	21	21
Year	2018	2018	2018
The White Test (Homoscedasticity/Heteroscedasticity)			
F-statistic	0.3681	0.8200	2.7209
Prob. F	0.6972	0.4562	0.0928
Prob. Chi-Square	0.6620	0.4161	0.0874

Table 7 The result of applying the simple linear regression method to the counties with high tourist attractiveness (cross-sectional), by tourist category, reference year—2018

	Category: counties with high tourist attractiveness		
	Total (Romanian and foreign tourists)	Romanian tourists	Foreign tourists
R-squared	0.688218	0.647111	0.897659
Adjusted R-squared	0.668732	0.625055	0.891263
S.E. of regression	221,631	212,358	31,350
Sum squared resid	785,929,363,828	721,534,726,064	15,725,001,628
Log likelihood	−246.039	−245.269	−210.834
F-statistic	35.32	29.34	140.34
Prob(F-statistic)	0.000021	0.000057	0.000000
Mean dependent var	776,538	654,577	121,960
S.D. dependent var	385,072	346,804	95,070
Akaike info criterion	27.5599	27.4744	23.6483
Schwarz criterion	27.6588	27.5733	23.7472
Hannan-Quinn criter	27.5735	27.4880	23.6619
Durbin-Watson stat	1.1528	1.3005	2.2250

higher extent (89.76%) by their arrivals. Thus, the relationship between the two analysed indicators is stronger in the case of foreign tourists than of Romanian tourists (determination ratio: 64.71%).

According to the data in Table 8, the t-Statistic associated probability for the independent variable is zero, no matter the tourist typology. Nevertheless, the probability

Table 8 Simple linear regression equation in 2018, for the category of counties with high tourist attractiveness, by tourist category

	Category: counties with high tourist attractiveness				Prob
	Estimation equation: overnight stays = C(1) + C(2)*Arrivals + ε				
	Variable	Coefficient	Std. Error	t-Statistic	
Total tourists	C	118,455.00	122,438.00	0.967468	0.3477
	Arrivals	1.883123	0.31678	5.942892	0.0000
OVERNIGHT STAYS = 118,455 + 1.88*ARRIVALS + ε					
Romanian tourists	C	61,908.00	120,321	0.514524	0.6139
	Arrivals	2.040938	0.37679	5.416643	0.0001
OVERNIGHT STAYS = 61,908 + 2.04*ARRIVALS + ε					
Foreign tourists	C	4246	12,382	0.342930	0.7361
	Arrivals	1.992686	0.168208	11.846530	0.0000
OVERNIGHT STAYS = 4,246 + 1.99*ARRIVALS + ε					

associated to the free coefficient is much higher than the 0.05 limit in all situations, which offers stability to the overnight stay estimation equation in relation to arrivals. This is justified by the tourist performances of counties such as Prahova (with a total of 1,284,823 overnight stays and 567,877 arrivals) and the limited attractiveness of other counties (Arad: with a total of 377,738 overnight stays and 217,448 arrivals), both belonging to the category of counties with high tourist attractiveness, from the perspective of the overnight stays in tourist accommodation structures indicator. Within this category, the values recorded in 2018 for the most successful counties from the tourist point of view are generating shocks in the mediums of the two analysed indicators.

With reference to the residuals in the case of the category including counties with high tourist attractiveness, if we consider the residual mean (zero), then the residual distribution is normal (irrespective of the tourist typology). However, the distribution is not normal since one can notice the residuals' positive symmetry confirmed by the positive values of the Skewness indicator. Likewise, the Kurtosis values indicate the fact that the residuals are not evenly distributed, the values above 3 indicating the leptokurtic character. In all three cases, the Jarque-Bera indicator deviates from the ideal situation (normal residual distribution) where the indicator has a value equal to zero. The Probability indicator has values higher than 0.05—which is desirable (Table 9).

The Prob. F indicator in the White test reflects the homoscedasticity of the residuals (which is characteristic of the normal distribution) only for Romanian tourists, as well as overall (Romanians and foreigners together), since Prob. F is higher than 0.05. In the case of foreign tourists, the heteroscedasticity of the residuals is confirmed, this being an unfavourable situation for the model (0.0035 < 0.05).

Table 9 Residual analysis in the case of applying simple linear regression to the counties with high tourist attractiveness by tourist category, reference year—2018

	Category: counties with high tourist attractiveness		
	Residuals analysis		
	Total (Foreign and Romanian tourists)	Romanian tourists	Foreign tourists
Mean	0.0000	0.0000	0.0000
Skewness	1.1601	1.2904	0.1775
Kurtosis	3.7315	4.0205	3.9876
Jarque-Bera	4.4390	5.7846	0.8260
Probability	0.1086	0.0554	0.6617
Observations	18	18	18
Year	2018	2018	2018
The White Test (Homoscedasticity/Heteroscedasticity)			
F-statistic	0.9373	0.9969	8.4573
Prob. F	0.4135	0.3922	0.0035

5 Conclusions

Tourism represents a source of income at both county and country level. The development of tourism results in jobs being created and preserved, in fostering entrepreneurship and stimulating regional and rural development (Drăgulănescu and Drăgulănescu 2013).

The present research focuses on the relationship between two important indicators in the tourism industry. The objectives of the research were reached by applying the simple linear regressive method on cross-sectional data taken over from the Romanian National Institute of Statistics.

The two research hypotheses were validated. In Romania, at county level, the number of overnight stays in tourist accommodation structures is strongly influenced by the number of tourist arrivals. Also, considering the tourist typology, the number of tourist overnight stays in tourist accommodation structures is more strongly influenced by the number of tourist arrivals in the case of foreign tourists as compared to Romanian tourists.

The extent to which the number of overnight stays is influenced by the number of arrivals cannot be accurately quantified in the form of a linear regression equation because the cross-sectional series (at county level, in 2018) do not have a normal distribution, neither by tourist typology, nor when the counties are divided into two categories, depending on their tourist attractiveness.

The only simple linear regression equation which is closer to an applicable form refers to the foreign tourists who arrive and spend the night in counties with low tourist attractiveness. Based on the cross-sectional data for the year 2018 and according to the linear regression equation, the increase by a unit of the number of foreign tourists arrivals in tourist accommodation structures in Romania triggers the increase in the number of overnight stays in the respective county of 1.35 times, when the number of overnight stays is explained in a proportion of 94.55% by the number of arrivals of the foreign tourists.

The lack of accuracy of the simple, cross-sectional linear regression equations created on the basis of the tourist indicators recorded at county level in Romanian in the year 2018 is due to the very big discrepancies in the tourist activity of the various counties.

This study can be extended by designing a county typology depending on their tourist activity and on other criteria relevant to the research. Grouping the counties by typology, based on common criteria, might facilitate a more in-depth analysis of the relationship between the number of overnight stays and the number of arrivals of tourists at county level, on condition the series of data related to these indicators have a normal distribution.

Annexes

See Figs. 1, 2, 3 4, 5 and 6.

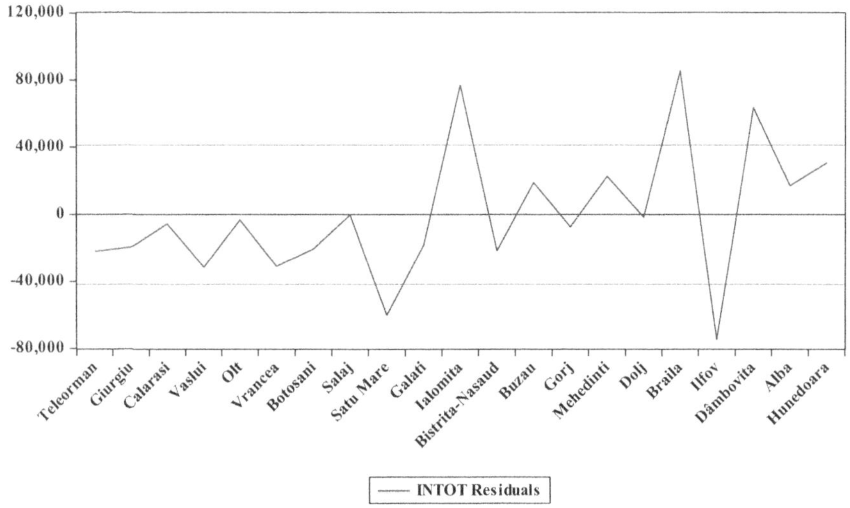

Fig. 1 Distribution of residuals when simple linear regression is applied to the category of counties with low tourist attractiveness, total tourists (Romanian and foreign), reference year: 2018

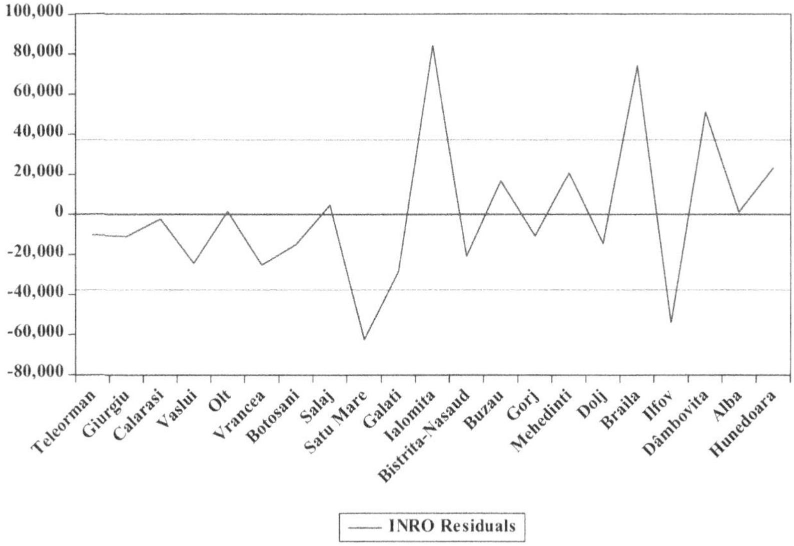

Fig. 2 Distribution of residuals when simple linear regression is applied to the category of counties with low tourist attractiveness, Romanian tourists, reference year: 2018

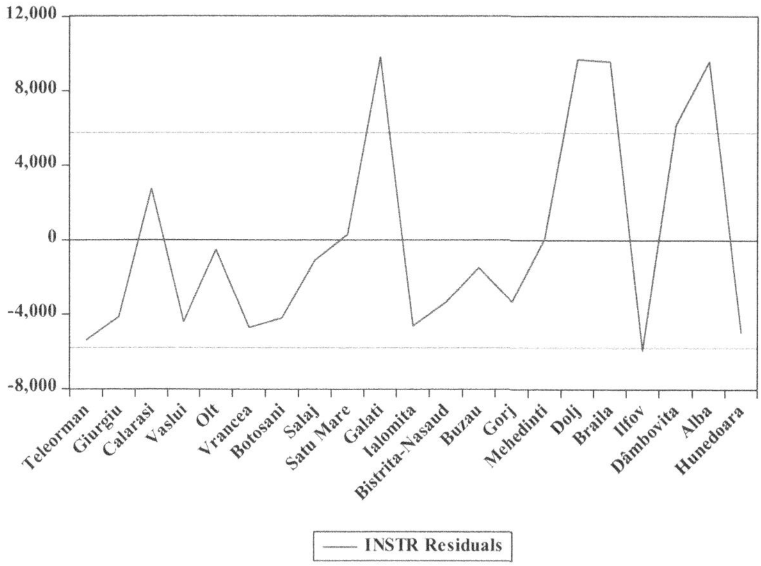

Fig. 3 Distribution of residuals when simple linear regression is applied to the category of counties with low tourist attractiveness, foreign tourists, reference year: 2018

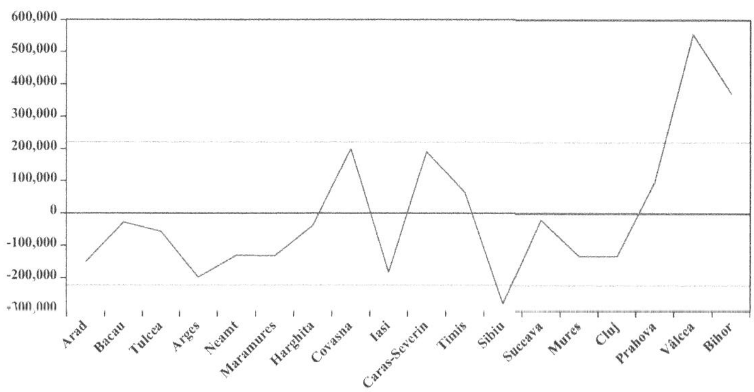

Fig. 4 Distribution of residuals when simple linear regression is applied to the category of counties with high tourist attractiveness, total tourists (Romanian and foreign), reference year: 2018

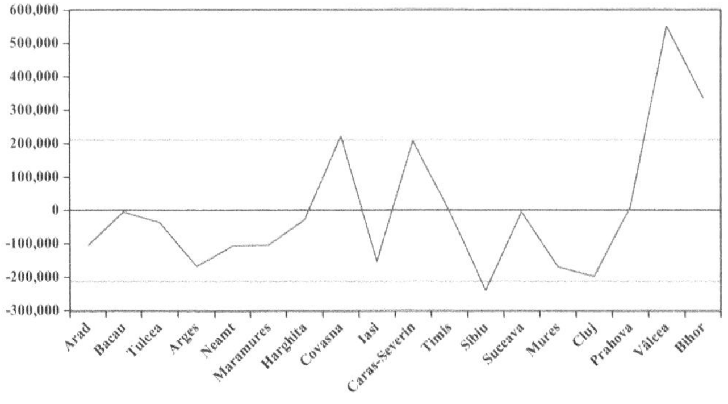

Fig. 5 Distribution of residuals when simple linear regression is applied to the category of counties with high tourist attractiveness, Romanian tourists (2018)

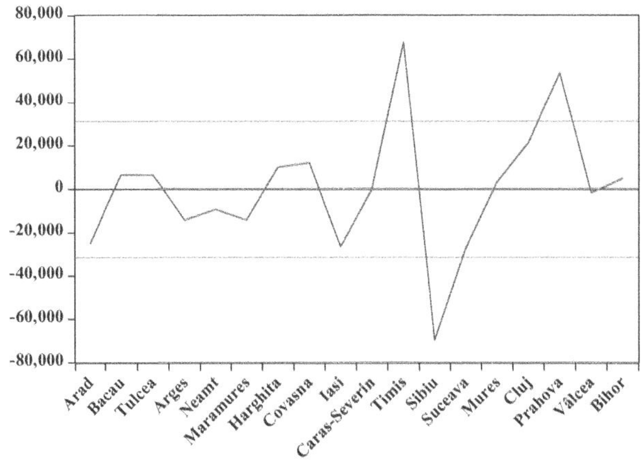

Fig. 6 Distribution of residuals when simple linear regression is applied to the category of counties with high tourist attractiveness, foreign tourists (2018)

References

Anghelache, C., Anghel, M.G., Samson, T.: Perspectiva evoluţiei turismului în anul 2018. Revista Română de Statistică - Supliment (2018)

Anghelache, C., Petre (Olteanu), A., Olteanu, C.: Unele concepte şi modele econometrice de analiză a performanţei macroeconomice. Revista Română de Statistică – Supliment (2019)

Bădulescu, A., Bădulescu, D., Simuţ, R.: Relaţia complexă dintre cererea turistică internaţională şi creşterea economică: o analiză la nivelul ţărilor Europei Centrale şi de Est. Amfiteatru Economic **20**(Special No. 12), 982–997 (2018)

Davidescu, A.A., Strat, V.A., Grosu, R.M., Zgură, I.D., Anagnoste, S.: Dezvoltarea la nivel regional a turismului rural din România. Amfiteatrul Economic **20**(Special No. 12), 854–869 (2018)

Drăgulănescu, I. V., Drăgulănescu, N.: Creştere, dezvoltare şi durabilitate. Roman. Statistical Rev. **10**, 46–59 (2013)

Florescu, G. I.: Cercetări privind optimizarea managementului hotelier şi al sistemelor de restauraţie, în baza principiilor dezvoltării sustenabile (2019)

Gheorghiţă, M., Pătărlăgeanu, S.R.: Econometrie, Editura ASE (2006)

Gribincea, A., Sava, E., Bîrcă, I.: Turismul internaţional - evoluţie în condiţiile de piaţă (2017)

HIS Markit: EViews 10 User's Guide (2017)

Institutul Naţional de Statistică România: TUR104B - Sosiri ale turistilor in structuri de primire turistica cu functiuni de cazare turistica, pe tipuri de structuri, tipuri de turisti, pe macroregiuni, regiuni de dezvoltare si judete. TEMPO Online. http://statistici.insse.ro:8077/tempo-online/#/pages/tables/insse-table. Last accessed 31 Dec 2019

Institutul Naţional de Statistică România: TUR105D - Innoptari in structuri de primire turistica pe tipuri de structuri, tipuri de turisti, macroregiuni, regiuni de dezvoltare si judete. TEMPO Online. http://statistici.insse.ro:8077/tempo-online/#/pages/tables/insse-table. Last accessed 31 Dec 2019

Pascariu, G.C., Ibănescu, B.C.: Determinanți și implicații ale efectului multiplicator al turismului în economiile UE. Către un model centru-periferie? Amfiteatru Economic **20**(Special No. 12), 982–997 (2018)

Popescu, D.: Abordări contemporane şi provocări ale turismului durabil. Amfiteatrul Economic, XV **I**(8), 827–829 (2014)

The Role of Chatbots in End-To-End Intelligent Automation and Future Employment Dynamics

Sorin Anagnoste, Isabelle Biclesanu, Fabrizio D'Ascenzo, and Marco Savastano

1 Introduction

Digital improvements and new technologies are being created at a rapid pace, companies becoming more efficient in their use of resources, expanding human capability, and creating jobs that are better fit for human characteristics.

Achieving integration and efficiency through digitization enables well-run companies to bring forward new, digital value propositions, while rapidly innovating their products or services.

However, technology should always be used in an ethical way, companies having to consider the employees' skills and workflows when adopting automation solutions, by planning and integrating the automated workforce along with managing the impact on the humans and creating new career paths (Anagnoste 2017).

As the use of robots and sophisticated software is proliferating worldwide, verbal communication, a basic function of humans, is becoming the link in human-to-robot, and even robot-to-robot, cooperation.

S. Anagnoste · I. Biclesanu (✉)
Faculty of Business Administration in Foreign Languages, Bucharest University of Economic Studies, Bucharest, Romania
e-mail: isabelle.bn@pm.me

S. Anagnoste
e-mail: sorin.anagnoste@fabiz.ase.ro

F. D'Ascenzo · M. Savastano
Faculty of Economics, Management Department, Sapienza University of Rome, Rome, Italy
e-mail: fabrizio.dascenzo@uniroma1.it

M. Savastano
e-mail: marco.savastano@uniroma1.it

A. M. Dima and F. DÁscenzo (eds.), *Business Revolution in a Digital Era*,
Springer Proceedings in Business and Economics,
https://doi.org/10.1007/978-3-030-59972-0_20

Modern chatbots allow for a natural interaction between the users and the digital systems inside organizations, as humans of all ages are increasingly more comfortable with the convenience provided by technology.

Millennials and Gen Z are especially attracted to messaging app communication with ~70% of the 4000 18–34 year olds surveyed (USA, UK, Japan, Australia, Germany and France) saying that they would prefer messaging over a phone call (LivePerson 2017). Furthermore, the same research shows that phones are becoming an extension of one's self, the younger generations preferring to communicate digitally, rather than in person.

In the last years, huge investments have been devoted by several companies to developing and continuously improving intelligent personal assistants (IPAs), such as Apple's Siri, Microsoft's Cortana, Google Assistant, and Amazon's Alexa. These IPAs are often deployed on mobile devices and are designed to answer a wide range of questions. Not only are these applications able to passively respond to requests, but they can also proactively anticipate user needs and provide on time assistance without the need of explicit requests from the user (Sarikaya 2017; Shum et al. 2018).

The article aims to help organizations take better digital transformation decisions, in view of the lack of awareness about modern chatbots' existence or capabilities that is manifesting in the business world. In order to achieve this research objective, the following research question arises: what are the factors that stimulate the successful adoption of innovative automation solutions by companies?

2 Contextual and Literature Overview

Physical and software robots alike work alongside humans to create a world that was a matter of science-fiction for many years.

As a result, automation's perpetual evolution and environmental complexity bring an undeniable series of challenges. However, if implemented timely and ethically, automation comes with impressive opportunities, both at company and society levels.

2.1 Global Automation Estimations

Predicting the impact and potential of automation around the world proves itself to be a difficult task. Still, researchers agree on scenarios in which both physical and software automation technologies will continue to shape the socio-economic and industrial systems (Ribeiro and Björkman 2017).

The speed and extent of automation technologies implementation inside companies depend on various factors, for instance, the existence and utility of the technologies needed for automating the tasks, the return on investment on the company's side, laws, regulations, social acceptance aspects etc. An important factor with a direct impact on the implementation of these technologies by companies is the technology-related entrepreneurial orientation, as argued by Oronsky and Chathoth (2007) in their paper concerning the decision-making process for IT technology adoption in the restaurant industry.

Moreover, the automation potential varies from country to country, as the sectorial makeup and its occupational distribution differ for each economy.

In addition, demographic trends (e.g. aging populations, higher average level of education) accentuate the adoption of automation inside industries with greater opportunity of using such technologies, as companies are filling the gap created by the scarcity of suitable middle-aged workers by using robots (Acemoglu and Restrepo 2018).

The Organization for Economic Co-operation and Development (OECD 2018) states that a high risk for automation is hovering over approximately 14% of the jobs in the member countries, some regions within them nearing 40% (e.g. West Slovakia), and being as low as 4% in others (e.g. Oslo region).

Nonetheless, at a global level, all currently automatable activities by employing available technologies (determined based on four criteria for automation: accepting input, delivering output, information processing, physical movement), translate into approximately \$15.8 trillion in wages and 1.1 billion FTE's (McKinsey Global Institute 2017), with China, India, Japan and the United States pertaining to over 50% of each.

As seen in Fig. 1, McKinsey Global Institute's analysis (2017) done for 46 countries, representing 80% of the global workforce, predicts that automation's level in today's, known, work activities is expected to reach 50% by 2055, considering a generous ±20 year window. This consists of less than 5% occupations being fully automatable, and about 60% having at least 30% automatable activities.

As a result of automation, the job market will be subjected to four categories of effects: (1) the disappearance of some roles, (2) the transformation of the task composition for others, (3) new roles driven by the constant technological advancements and (4) an increase in demand for existing jobs that sustain the emerging technologies.

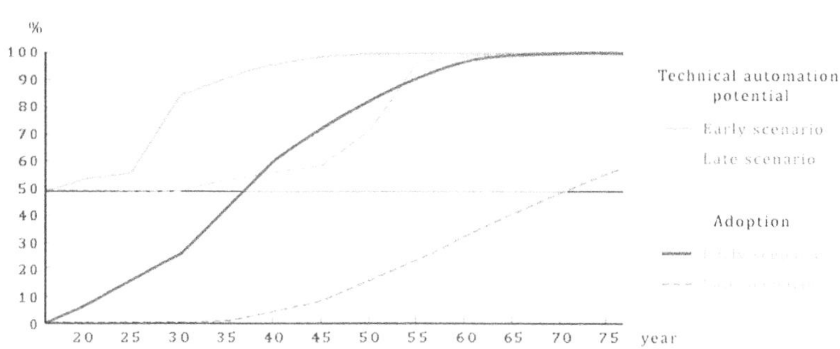

Fig. 1 Technical automation potential and adoption in known work activities. *Source* Adapted from McKinsey Global Institute (2017)

Extrapolating the trends resulted from a survey covering companies from 12 industry clusters, collectively representing 70% of global GDP, the World Economic Forum (2018) estimates that, by 2022, around 75 million roles may become redundant as a result of automation, while 133 million new roles may appear. The same report states that, for the sample covered, 29% of total task hours were executed by machines in 2018, this level being expected to reach 42% by 2022.

Currently, occupations requiring a high level of education (i.e. graduate degree or above), supervision responsibilities, creativity and intellectual reasoning skills have a lower automation potential compared to other areas, as robots are still unable to reach human performance and flexibility on complex tasks where expertise, imagination and human wisdom are needed (e.g. education, health, management, art). Nonetheless, as artificial intelligence develops, automation will be able to cover with better accuracy these highly sophisticated tasks.

In contrast, predictable and repetitive physical and mental tasks have the highest potential for automation, a 29 countries analysis done by PwC (2018) estimating that, by mid 2030s, 34% of the jobs done by men and 26% of the jobs done by women could be automated, low and medium level education workers being the most affected—with 44% and 36% respectively.

For companies, automation initiatives may be met with cultural resistance, as jobs are the primary means of earning money, and redistributing them between humans and robots may create mistrust, skill shortcomings and frustration.

Vermeulen et al. (2018) studied the projected impact of automation on employment. The authors analyzed occupations affected by automation (e.g. by the introduction of robotics and AI) to find out which and how several sectors and occupations face employment shifts. By studying different macro-level scenarios on employment, they found that mankind is facing "the usual structural change"—transformations similar to those triggered by the previous industrial revolutions—rather than the so called "end of work". Thus, historical evidence supports the perspective of an economically and socially sustainable future with a high level of employment for a skilled workforce, in which the recent wave of automation is merely a period of transition with temporary technological unemployment (Mokyr et al. 2015; Vermeulen et al. 2018).

On the rise of automation, future employees may need different skillsets, an adjustment to the new job market trends becoming a necessity for the education system and company trainings, which will need to encompass new technologies, as well as encourage lifelong learning and the acquisition of adaptability promoting skills, such as problem solving, self-development, communication and conflict resolution.

Moreover, having both depth and breadth of knowledge is considered an essential determining factor for long-term career success (Hart Research Associates 2015), as are the ability to communicate effectively, work in teams, have ethical judgment, critical thinking, analytical reasoning and decision making abilities.

2.2 Software Automation and Beyond

Robotic process automation (RPA) is one of the basic steps in digital transformation, as it efficiently deals with repetitive, rules-driven, tasks without the need of transforming the existing IT systems, as it replicates the manual workflows involved.

It is the prevalent automation technology already in use, followed by manufacturing robots, AI and cognitive services, reports Deloitte (2019). However, almost 75% of the respondents stated that their organizations are not yet ready to address the impact of these technologies in reskilling and job redesign.

The RPA market is estimated to reach $16.4 billion by 2023, with $4.2 billion for RPA software market and $12 billion for RPA services (Forrester Research, Q4 2019), UiPath being the leading RPA provider, based on strategy, offering and market presence.

Using RPA alone, time savings between 40 and 80% could be achieved for functions such as human resources, source to pay, order to cash, or tax (Anagnoste 2018a). Furthermore, 100% automation could be attained for some tasks by deploying RPA, cognitive intelligent automation, chatbots and artificial intelligence (Anagnoste 2018a).

Thus, aiming at intelligent automation, companies could integrate software robots and artificial intelligence (AI) to create self-learning systems that are equipped to perform tasks end-to-end, and efficiently address multiple decision points, without human assistance.

A tremendous commercial opportunity is attributed to artificial intelligence, as it has the potential to impact the global GDP by 2030 with +14%, the equivalent of an additional $15.7 trillion (PwC 2017). This should be the result of the speculated level of (1) productivity gains and (2) higher demand for AI products and services.

Businesses could increase revenues by almost 40% in the 2018–2022 period by investing in human-machine collaboration and artificial intelligence, resulting an additional $4.8 trillion profits at a global level, and, during the next three years, 74% of the 1,200 executives surveyed are planning to use AI to a large extent (Accenture 2018b).

Companies will have no choice but to follow the automation path, with big organizations creating Centers of Excellence (CoE) as the most efficient way of managing their robots, and the limited and expensive knowledge available (Anagnoste 2018b).

The Artificial Intelligence Index Report (Stanford HAI 2019), states that compute power has been doubling every 3.4 months since 2012, more than half of the large companies surveyed are using AI in at least one business area, and chatbots were in the top ten AI startups to receive funding in the last year—as illustrated in Fig. 2.

Within the context of a growing acceptance and use of automation, as well as remarkable advancements in artificial intelligence (e.g. deep learning algorithms (DL), natural language processing and generation (NLP and NLG), automatic speech recognition, computer vision etc.), new generations of chatbots are evolving and, as research suggests, chatbots are here to stay.

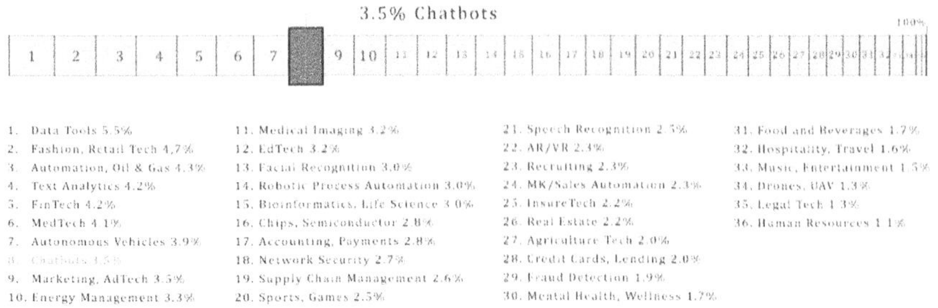

Fig. 2 Global AI startups that have received funding between July 18 and July 19. *Source* Based on data from Stanford HAI (2019)

3 Methodology

This research paper provides valuable business insights, being constructed around a thorough literature review, author contributions and an in depth case study, thus achieving its objective of helping organizations take better, informed digital transformation decisions.

The literature review covers the context of digital transformation, the benefits of automation technologies and the challenges in redefining labor and education for the employee of tomorrow. It makes a particular emphasis on software automation and completes the points made by the authors throughout the chapter.

Chatbots' role in end-to-end intelligent automation is presented step-by-step, from the drivers for enterprise chatbot adoption, their existing and future market size, main players, related technologies, their capabilities and areas of deployment, to the chatbot implementation steps and return on investment.

The case study investigates a high performing enterprise AI chatbot authoring platform, starting with their products' particularities, and concluding with the results achieved by one of their chatbots, deployed for an important healthcare industry client for their team of approximately 200 managers. The results serve as an example of the chatbots' value, even for a lower chatbot necessity area, such as management. The case study is based on a carefully analyzed nondirective interview with factual questions that leave small room for subjectivity, and the graciously provided files, completing everything that was discussed.

4 Chatbots

Even if chatbots have appeared for the first time in 1964, they've only started to develop more rapidly during the past few years, as other digital advancements were needed to improve their algorithms.

Now, conversational bots are one of the leading technology trends, impressive software that simulate human conversation using different input and output methods (e.g. text, voice), able to search the Internet or connect to enterprise systems, and perform various tasks depending on their purpose in the organization.

Modern chatbots' place in end-to-end automation and digital transformation is the result of multiple business, social and technology drivers.

For instance, the developments in artificial intelligence, are making possible the production of self-learning chatbots that deliver human-like conversations, and, in view of the proliferation of automation's use worldwide, chatbots have also the ability to connect to the other software systems inside the organization.

Moreover, messaging platforms are becoming a major communication channel worldwide, along with a raising customer demand for self-services, and 24/7 availability. In the context of AI-enhanced sales automation, the ability to react naturally to inputs represents a fundamental building block for more intimate and trusting brand relationships as well as more positive brand experiences and image. Indeed, introducing chatbots into consumers' shopping processes leads to more intimate consumer-brand relationships, greater trust, and improved upsell opportunities (Hildebrand and Bergner 2019). Likewise, the fast-paced world, filled with huge amounts of data, is driving our will to get error-free answers instantly.

Besides, humans have an innate desire to communicate, which is now becoming possible in a natural way, with their own creation, the robots.

4.1 The Chatbot Market and Technologies

Composed of intelligent virtual assistants and chatbots, the conversational AI market is anticipated to reach $15.7 billion by 2024, from an estimated $4.2 billion in 2019, as pictured in Fig. 3 (Markets and Markets 2019a). Its chatbot component is expected to grow at a 29.7% compound annual growth rate (CAGR), going from an estimated global market size of $2.6 billion in 2019 to $9.4 billion by 2024 (Markets and Markets 2019b).

The chatbot market is cloud dominated, however, since some clients have to account for strict security and privacy regulations (e.g. finance, health), hybrid and on-premise deployments are possible.

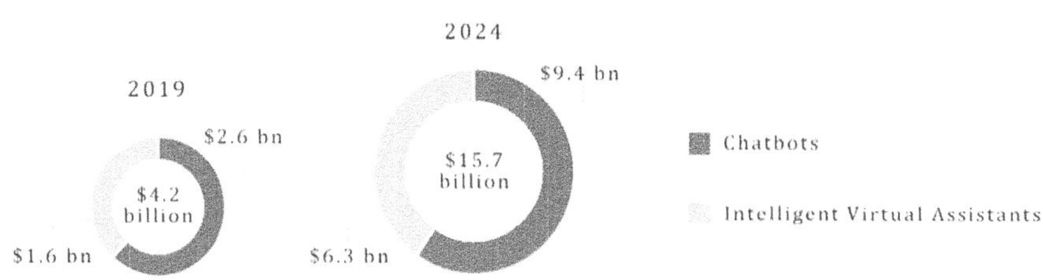

Fig. 3 Conversational AI market—2024 forecast. *Source* Based on data from Markets and Markets (2019a; b)

Chatbots can be developed for internal use (e.g. human resources), or external communication (e.g. customer service), and the same chatbot can be integrated with multiple channels. The channels could range from basic website or e-mail integrations, to Microsoft Teams, Slack, Cisco Spark, Facebook Messenger, WhatsApp, WeChat, Telegram, virtual assistants, phone calling etc.

The main part of a chatbot is the agent (i.e. natural language understanding module), trained to intent match and act accordingly. Depending on the enterprise systems' configuration, it can be connected to them directly or through an RPA robot.

Forrester (2018) has selected 7 conversational computing platforms based on the existence of 3 mandatory criteria (1) providing an end-to-end conversational solution, (2) offering standalone development tools to build customized chatbots, and (3) their relevance to Forrester clients indicated by their requests. Accounting for the strength of the offering and the strength of strategy, IBM (IBM Watson) was declared the leader, followed by Google (Dialogflow), Amazon (Amazon Lex), Microsoft (Microsoft Bot Framework, Azure Bot Service) and Nuance Communications as strong performers. Oracle (Oracle Intelligent Bots) was declared a contender and Rulai a challenger. Notably, Google, Amazon and Microsoft had the biggest market presence among them (Fig. 4).

Other major providers of conversational platforms on the global market are: Artificial Solutions, Creative Virtual, Facebook, Kore.ai, Salesforce, Pandorabots etc.

Most chatbots deployed on the market are simple, declarative, chatbots providing an interactive structure with conversational menus. Users can take action (e.g. approve a document) using buttons inside the chatbot. Advanced, conversational, chatbots employ complex NLP and NLG, machine learning and other AI capabilities.

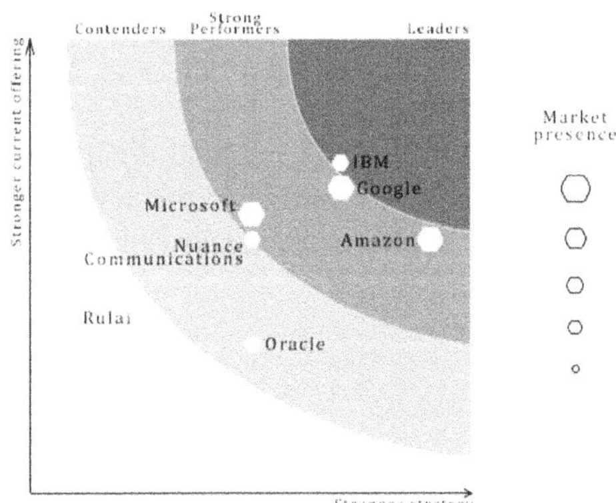

Fig. 4 Top seven conversational computing platforms Q2 2018. *Source* Adapted from Forrester (2018)

Table 1 Chatbot utility by industry and business function. *Source* Authors' research

Industry \ Function	CS	Sales	MK	HR	IT	Fin.	Supply Chain
Retail	high	medium	high	high	low	low	low
Cons. goods and services	high	medium	high	high	low	low	low
Electronics and high-tech	high	medium	high	high	high	medium	low
Industrial equipment	medium	medium	low	high	medium	medium	low
Utilities	high	medium	low	high	high	medium	low
Banking	high	medium	low	high	high	high	low
Insurance	high	medium	medium	high	high	high	low
Healthcare	high	low	medium	high	low	low	low
Communications	high	medium	medium	high	high	low	low

Chatbot implementation potential

low ▒ ▓ █ high

4.2 *Business Implementation and Return on Investment*

Chatbots can be deployed for any industry and any business area where their use is relevant and the basic technical requirements for implementation exist.

Customer service (CS), customer relationship management (CRM), sales, and marketing (MK) were the main points were chatbots were implemented, determined an Accenture research (2018a) done for mostly business-to-consumer companies (76.7%) with at least $500 million annual revenue, and covering nine industries—retail, consumer goods and services, electronics and high-tech, industrial equipment, utilities, banking, insurance, healthcare, communications.

These industries' chatbot implementation potential was assessed in Table 1.

Concerning the trust consumers have in AI chatbots for different sectors, a survey from Drift (2019) looking at chatbot engagement found that 40% of respondents (US-based consumers) said they used chatbots to engage with retailers in some way or another, their interactions for retail being the highest among the analyzed industries, as pictured in Fig. 5.

Some examples of chatbot roles leveraging repetitive or tedious work, structured by business area are presented in Table 2, based on authors' research.

For banking, $7.3 billion operational cost savings are expected by 2023, up from $209 million in 2019, the result of 862 million hours saved in 2023 due to a dramatic increase in successful chatbot interactions (Juniper 2019a). Moreover, using chatbots and AI for automating post-incident data collection, could save insurance companies around $1.3 billion in 2023 for life, health, property and motor insurance (Juniper 2019a).

As for retail, the migration of customer interactions from other channels to chatbots will be responsible for around $112 billion sales revenues by 2023, from $7.3

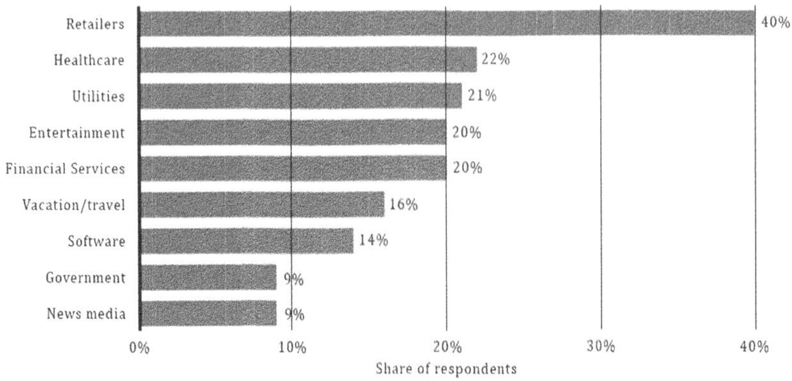

Fig. 5 Share of consumers who have used chatbots to engage with companies in the United States as of 2019, by industry. *Source* Adapted from Drift (2019)

billion in 2019, the process optimization reducing annual costs for retail with around $439 million globally in 2023 (Juniper 2019b).

As illustrated in Fig. 6, the following steps should be considered for a chatbot implementation: (1) where is the need for a chatbot (2) mapping process flows that should be automated and the enterprise systems involved, (3) deciding on the interaction channel/s, (4) defining the assessment criteria for choosing the right chatbot provider to work with, (5) technical requirements and regulatory constraints, (6) setting realistic goals, (7) use case validation, (8) MVP development, pilot deployment and rounds of testing, (9) chatbot launch, (10) assigning a team member to check the dashboard and make regular updates.

Some useful KPIs for assessing the chatbot are: self-service completion rate, number of escalations, user satisfaction, reuse rate, total and active users, new user attraction rate, active users per channel, total messages per channel, total conversations, live conversations, average session length, top requests, intents not recognized, fallback rate, security violations.

The payback period of the chatbot solution depends on its ability to satisfy the users' requests, and the quality of its (manual or self-learning) updates. Nonetheless, 91% of the companies that have already implemented bots expect a one-to-five times return on investment within the first year (Accenture 2018a).

5 Case Study

Druid is a high-performing AI startup, a no-code enterprise chatbot authoring platform, winner of international chatbot development competitions.

Currently, Druid is valued at over 8 million EUR, and, as a result of the planned expansion in the United States of America, its valuation is expected to reach 20

Table 2 Examples of chatbot roles by business area. *Source* Authors' own research

Business area	Role leveraging some repetitive or tedious tasks
Customer service	Answering FAQs
	Resolving requests (*e.g. product returns*)
Sales	Providing the sales personnel with information regarding their schedule, clients, the company's products, stock, suppliers etc
	Reservations and appointments
Marketing	Providing recommendations (proactively or reactively)
	Data collection (creating customer profiles)
Human resources	Answering FAQs
	Recruitment screenings and onboarding
	Getting feedback (*e.g. satisfaction*)
	Sending personalized messages to employees on special occasions
	Resolving HR requests (*e.g. vacation*)
	Training enrollment and in-module quiz administration
IT support	Answering FAQs
	Access provisioning and password resets
	Creating reports and alerts on tickets
Finance	Financial approvals
	Delivering information and alerts
	Creating or sending reports
Procurement	Answering queries regarding purchasing orders and invoices
	Contract and policy information access
Employee virtual agent (intranet and assistant manager)	Task monitoring, requests approvals, scheduling
	Time management (*e.g. asking to complete employee performance reviews or other forms when it sees the employee has a window*)
	Delivering internal news
	Knowledge management

million EUR in the next round of investments (envisioned for 2020), when it is intending to raise another 8–10 million EUR capital (Druid 2019).

Druid's clients come from a wide range of areas, including, but not limited to, banking, insurance, healthcare providers and drug stores, oil and gas, communications, consumer goods, industrial goods, media and entertainment etc.

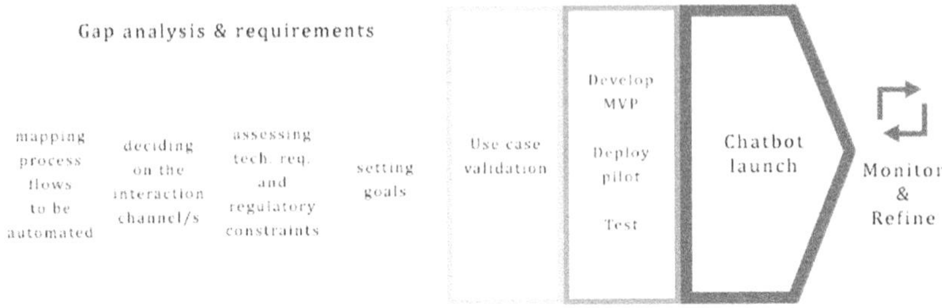

Fig. 6 Chatbot implementation steps. *Source* Authors' own research

Overall, a high demand for chatbots has been seen in industries having a large number of internal or external chatbot end-users (e.g. banking, healthcare, retail, services etc.), and especially in the human resources and customer services departments.

The platform is built upon Microsoft Bot framework, adding its own features, such as a conversation designer, enterprise-app connectors (e.g. for CRM, ERP, HRIS, databases etc.), enhanced NLP and optical character recognition (OCR) engines, named-entity-recognition (NER), route to human functionality, and many more.

Able to interact on multiple channels and mix languages within the same conversation, the chatbots are equipped with +250 pre-built skills for fast deployment, and others can be created depending on the client's needs.

Druid is enhancing the features of the RPA and business applications by giving them conversational capabilities, either beginning with a human query or asking the user for action when an RPA robot is requiring human intervention, and getting back to the robot with the feedback.

Druid's chatbot solutions are made possible through their internal consulting team, through referrals, and through their implementation partners that undergo a complex onboarding process.

Their chatbots come with dashboards for bot analytics and conversation history, providing the client with insights into their performance and new conversation flows to be integrated into the chatbot. The no-code platform makes it accessible for the client's employees to update the chatbot themselves, without the need for a programming background.

For an implementation, the following are typically considered: (1) client's needs, (2) if there are other chatbot functionalities that should be developed for the specific needs, (3) type of deployment (i.e. cloud/hybrid/on-premise), (4) pricing and (5) infrastructure.

The current pricing model involves (1) a one-time cost for licensing (i.e. platform access), (2) monthly payment per chatbot (three categories, depending on complexity—Junior, Manager and Partner), (3) change requests development cost (if further functionalities are necessary for the client), and (4) implementation cost (Fig. 7).

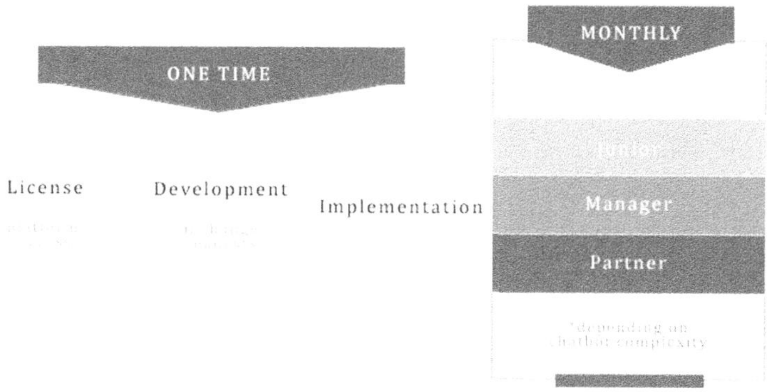

Fig. 7 Druid's current pricing model. *Source* Based on information from Druid

The results are measured based on the type of the process being optimized/automated, and can broadly be defined as: (1) reductions: time, workload, resources; and (2) growth: satisfaction, quality.

Management Chatbot Results for Healthcare Industry

An example of the value of five minutes is expressed through the results achieved by a Druid chatbot deployed in the management department of a prominent healthcare provider.

The customer was looking for increasing the management team's productivity and a better collaboration between the medical, sales and customer care employees, by adopting a simplified, mobile, user experience.

This was addressed by implementing an AI chatbot to assist with approvals (e.g. budget, meetings, contracts, salaries, medical leaves etc.) and communicate decisions. The chatbot knows the organizational structure, the names and roles, understanding the context of the question and replying accordingly. Through machine learning (ML) it is able to pick up on the preferences and internal rules, knowing when the meetings should be, or when to send a budget report.

Using a hybrid deployment (on cloud with RPA connector on-premise), and linked to the internal enterprise apps (e.g. CRM, ERP), it can be accessed directly from the phone, through Microsoft Teams.

The AI chatbot allows to save five-to-ten minutes per day for each manager, and, for a team of 200 managers, the results are more than 100.000 EUR per year of tasks done by the chatbot, while the managers are free to work on higher added value activities. This was illustrated in Fig. 8.

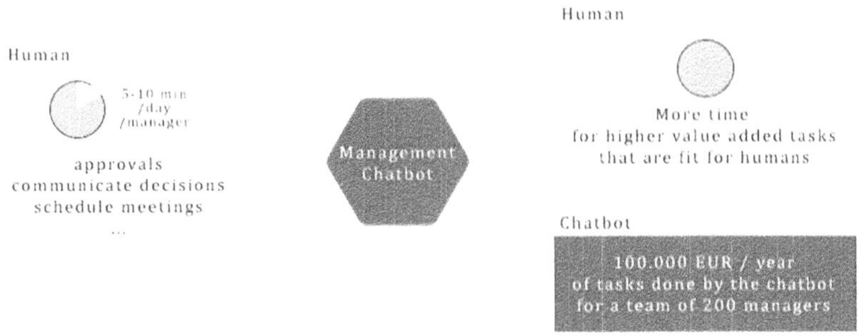

Fig. 8 Druid chatbot results for healthcare provider. *Source* Based on information from Druid

6 Conclusions

Automation is not new and it will most certainly not disappear due to dystopian fears. Instead, it is expected to continue to add both its challenges and contribution to society, reshaping the human labor as other disruptors did throughout history.

If timely and ethically embarking on the automation journey, companies could attract impressive financial opportunities, by using the right combination of technologies, and a good management of the costs and risks involved.

Digital transformation is opening up new possibilities for implementing artificial intelligence and other solutions inside organizations, and, due to their features and some key business, social and technology drivers, chatbots are taking their part in end-to-end automation.

Recognizing high availability, accuracy and speed as generators for better business results, companies are creating a growing market for chatbots, as they are promptly improving the interaction models inside and outside companies.

The highest returns are achieved where volume processes are, and, even if the costs for chatbot solutions could reach tens of thousands of EUR, with a good strategy, chatbots can deliver cost optimization within less than a year.

The rise of automation is reshaping society, existing business models and employment dynamics, letting humans work in new and exciting ways. The present study brings original contributions and business insights aimed at encouraging companies to take well-thought-out digital transformation decisions, enabling themselves to compete in the global economy.

The limitations of the paper are given by the qualitative nature of the research, however, the case study was constructed on factual data, and the carefully provided author contributions were thoroughly checked against the literature. Therefore, the paper has no place for researcher or interviewee subjectivity.

The study creates insight for future research on chatbots and automation, especially given the rapidly evolving technological environment and the constant changes in demographics and consumer behavior.

In the not-so-distant future, ethically employing highly-developed artificial intelligence may result in conversational agents that assist humans in numerous areas, and communicate through psychologically pleasing, seemingly human interactions that create trust, kindle emotions and achieve loyalty.

References

Accenture: Chatbots are here to stay. So what are you waiting for? (2018a). Retrieved from https://www.accenture.com/_acnmedia/pdf-77/accenture-research-conversational-ai-platforms.pdf

Accenture: Reworking the revolution: are you ready to compete as intelligent technology meets human ingenuity to create the future workforce? (2018b). Retrieved from https://www.accenture.com/_acnmedia/pdf-69/accenture-reworking-the-revolution-jan-2018-pov.pdf

Acemoglu, D., Restrepo, P.: Demographics and automation. National Bureau of Economic Research—NBER, Working Paper No. 24421 (2018). Retrieved from https://www.nber.org/papers/w24421.pdf

Anagnoste, S.: Robotic automation process—the next major revolution in terms of back office operations improvement. In: Proceedings of the International Conference on Business Excellence, vol. 11, no. 1, pp 676–686 (2017). Retrieved from https://content.sciendo.com/view/journals/picbe/11/1/article-p676.xml?rskey=i1zHDg&result=2

Anagnoste, S.: Robotic Automation Process—The operating system for the digital enterprise. In: Proceedings of the International Conference on Business Excellence, vol. 12, no. 1, pp. 54–69 (2018a). Retrieved from https://content.sciendo.com/view/journals/picbe/12/1/article-p54.xml?lang=en&tab_body=pdf

Anagnoste, S.: Setting up a robotic process automation center of excellence. Manage. Dyn. Knowl. Econ. **6**(2), 307–322 (2018b). Retrieved from https://www.researchgate.net/publication/326141509_Setting_Up_a_Robotic_Process_Automation_Center_of_Excellence

Deloitte: Leading the social enterprise: reinvent with a human focus—2019 Deloitte global human capital trends (2019). Retrieved from https://www2.deloitte.com/content/dam/Deloitte/cz/Documents/human-capital/cz-hc-trends-reinvent-with-human-focus.pdf

Drift: State of conversational marketing (2019). Retrieved from https://www.slideshare.net/DriftHQ/state-of-conversational-marketing-2019-free-report

Druid: Early game ventures invests in DRUID at over 8 mil. EUR valuation (2019). Retrieved from https://www.druidai.com/druid-investment-early-game/

Forrester Research: The forrester new wave™: conversational computing platforms, Q2 2018 the seven providers that matter most and how they stack up (2018). Retrieved from https://www.forrester.com/report/The+Forrester+New+Wave+Conversational+Computing+Platforms+Q2+2018/-/E-RES137816

Forrester Research: The forrester wave™: robotic process automation services, Q4 2019: the 13 providers that matter most and how they stack up (2019). Retrieved from https://www.forrester.com/report/The+Forrester+Wave+Robotic+Process+Automation+Q4+2019/-/E-RES147757

Hart Research Associates: Falling short? college learning and career success (2015). Retrieved from https://bit.ly/2vNt7QE

Hildebrand, C., Bergner, A.: AI-driven sales automation. Using chatbots to boost sales. NIM Market. Intel. Rev. **11**(2), 36–41 (2019). Retrieved from https://content.sciendo.com/configurable/contentpage/journals$002fnimmir$002f11$002f2$002farticle-p36.xml

Juniper Research: Bank cost savings via chatbots to reach $7.3 billion by 2023, as automated customer experience evolves (2019a). Retrieved from: https://www.juniperresearch.com/press/press-releases/bank-cost-savings-via-chatbots-reach-7-3bn-2023

Juniper Research: Chatbot interactions in retail to reach 22 billion by 2023, as AI offers compelling new engagement solutions (2019b). Retrieved from https://www.juniperresearch.com/press/press-releases/chatbot-interactions-retail-reach-22-billion-2023

LivePerson: The digital lives of Millennials and Gen Z (2017). Retrieved from https://www.liveperson.com/resources/reports/digital-lives-of-millennials-genz/

Markets and Markets Research: Conversational AI Market by Component (Platform and Services), Type (IVA and Chatbots), Technology, Application (Customer Support, Personal Assistant, and Customer Engagement and Retention), Deployment Mode, Vertical, and Region—Global Forecast to 2024 (2019a). Retrieved from https://www.marketsandmarkets.com/Market-Reports/conversational-ai-market-49043506.html

Markets and Markets Research: Chatbot Market by Component (Solutions and Services), Usage (Websites and Contact Centers), Technology, Deployment Model, Application (Customer Support and Personal Assistant), Organization Size, Vertical, and Region—Global Forecast to 2024 (2019b). Retrieved from https://www.marketsandmarkets.com/Market-Reports/smart-advisor-market-72302363.html

McKinsey Global Institute: A future that works: automation, employment and productivity (2017). Retrieved from https://mck.co/2Tzxs3F

Mokyr, J., Vickers, C., Ziebarth, N.: The history of technological anxiety and the future of economic growth: is this time different? J. Econ. Persp. **29**(3), 31–50 (2015). https://doi.org/10.1257/jep.29.3.31

Organization for economic co-operation and development—OECD: Job Creation and Local Economic Development 2018: Preparing for the Future of Work/Création d'emplois et développement économique local (2018). Retrieved from https://read.oecd-ilibrary.org/employment/job-creation-and-local-economic-development-2018/summary/french_4fdca3a0-fr#page1

Oronsky, C., Chathoth, P.: An exploratory study examining information technology adoption and implementation in full-service restaurant firms. Int. J. Hospital. Manage. **26**(4), 941–956 (2007). https://doi.org/10.1016/j.ijhm.2006.04.001

PricewaterhouseCoopers—PwC: Sizing the prize: What's the real value of AI for your business and how can you capitalize? (2017). Retrieved from https://www.pwc.com/gx/en/issues/analytics/assets/pwc-ai-analysis-sizing-the-prize-report.pdf

PricewaterhouseCoopers—PwC: Will robots really steal our jobs? An international analysis of the potential long term impact of automation (2018). Retrieved from https://www.pwc.co.uk/economic-services/assets/international-impact-of-automation-feb-2018.pdf

Ribeiro, L., Björkman, M.: Transitioning from standard automation solutions to cyber-physical production systems: an assessment of critical conceptual and technical challenges. IEEE Syst. J. **12**(4), 3816–3827 (2017). https://doi.org/10.1109/JSYST.2017.2771139

Sarikaya, R.: The technology behind personal digital assistants: an overview of the system architecture and key components. IEEE Signal Process. Mag. **34**(1), 67–81 (2017). https://doi.org/10.1109/MSP.2016.2617341

Shum, H., He, X., Li, D.: From Eliza to XiaoIce: challenges and opportunities with social chatbots. Front. Inf. Technol. Electron. Eng. **19**(1), 10–26 (2018). Retrieved from https://arxiv.org/ftp/arxiv/papers/1801/1801.01957.pdf

Stanford Human-Centered Artificial Intelligence HAI: Artificial Intelligence Index Report (2019). Retrieved from https://hai.stanford.edu/sites/g/files/sbiybj10986/f/ai_index_2019_report.pdf

Vermeulen, B., Kesselhut, J., Pyka, A., Saviotti, P.: The impact of automation on employment: just the usual structural change? Sustainability **10**(5), 1661 (2018). https://doi.org/10.3390/su10051661

World Economic Forum: The Future of Jobs Report (2018). Retrieved from https://www3.weforum.org/docs/WEF_Future_of_Jobs_2018.pdf

Price Probability Predictor. Capital Investments Assisted by a Probability Field

Cristian Păuna

1 Introduction

Capital investment has become a sustained and collective activity nowadays. An impressive number of market participants are buying and selling every day to make a profit. Private or public investment funds, financial companies, professional investors, traders, or just speculating people, all are part of an unstopped dispute with the price action. Using different strategies, everyone tries to predict the price evolution in order to buy cheap and sell more expensive. After the global scale of the electronic trading systems implementation, access to the capital markets is at a couple of clicks distance. This fact has increased the liquidity in all markets and also has grown the price volatility once the psychological factors can influence the market price behavior in seconds.

The question this chapter will answer to is: how much is the current probability for price growth in the next period of time? The interest in an accurate answer at this question is huge. Studying a probability field for price growth in a specific market will permit us to exit investments when the probability is low, and to initiate new positions when the probability is high. Moreover, a lower price growth probability can avoid buying near the maximal price levels and will inform investors to wait until the market presents a significant decrease. The evolution of a price probability field will also give us additional information about market behavior. The Ph.D. research behind this paper has found a probability prediction function, based only on the price time series that will give us the answer to the formulated question. It is called here as the Price Probability Predictor.

Paper financed by Algorithm Invest (https://algoinvest.biz).

C. Păuna (✉)
Economic Informatics Doctoral School, Academy of Economic Studies, Bucharest, Romania
e-mail: cristian.pauna@ie.ase.ro

A. M. Dima and F. DÁscenzo (eds.), *Business Revolution in a Digital Era*,
Springer Proceedings in Business and Economics,
https://doi.org/10.1007/978-3-030-59972-0_21

In the electronic trading environment, a significant part of the investment orders is made and sent today by automated decision-making computer software. The online price quotes transmission permits today a real-time price analysis through advanced mathematical algorithms to fundament the investment decisions. A simple trading strategy is not useful today if it can not be set in the algorithmic trading environment. One of the highest advantages of the Price Probability Predictor is the fact that it can be automated. Based on the revealed function, automated trading signals and limit conditions can be built and incorporate in any algorithmic trading software system, for any market.

In the last part of this chapter, real capital investment results will be included, in order to qualify the presented trading methodology and to compare it with other similar mathematical models. At the end of this paper has found that the Price Probability Predictor is a reliable probability field for a price growth that can be used with excellent results to build a stable investment strategy and also to optimize the capital efficiency of any other strategy. Any reader will find the originality and universality of the presented method.

2 Literature Review

There are few studies in the literature about price growth probability even the probability term appears in many titles of trading books. The most are trying to estimate the probability that the price will touch a precise level in the future. The author of the current research has decided not to cite any of these studies. During the research conducted behind this paper, it was found that in more than 2200 trading books and papers read, no probability field method with sustained and repetitive characteristics when it is about the algorithmic capital investment was found. Several studies indicate entry points in the market based on probability estimate but have no criteria for a technical exit decision. Other studies are made for particular markets, having no proved possible generalization. There are no reasons to cite uncompleted strategies or unproved price probability models. This will be the gap filled by the current paper.

Regarding the subject of capital investment strategies that can be automated, working and proved models for the stock markets can be found in (Connors 1999; Connors and Sen 2004; Bernstein and Bernstein 2008; Connors and Alvarez 2009a; b). Even these papers are not presenting the ways to automate the included strategies; it remains excellent references for stock markets investment strategies. The currency market trading strategies are also a very actual subject. Effective and proved strategies that can be automated can be found in (Cheng 2007; Lien 2009, 2011; Volman 2011). Particular approaches for the commodity markets can be found in (Kleinman 2009; Jagerson and Hansen 2011). Important psychological strategies that can be easily adapted with any technical analysis investment strategy can be found in (Pring 1992; Kiev 2008; Ward 2010). Some working mathematical models that can be adapted for algorithmic trading can be found in (Focardi and Fabozi 2004). A particular approach for risk management techniques that can be used in automated decision-making systems for capital investments can be found in (Vince 1992). Mathematical models especially designed and optimized for algorithmic trading with proved and sustained results in real capital investments can be found in (Păuna and Lungu 2018; Păuna 2018a, 2019a, b, c, d, e, f, 2020).

3 Price Probability

3.1 Price Probability Field

In this paper, we will call a price probability field an analytical function that will give us a measure for price growth in the next time periods. The current research will present how a price probability field can be built, how it can be optimized to estimate a precise price growth, and how three different types of price probability fields can be combined in order to obtain a more accurate mathematical model. Besides, in the second part of this paper, automated trading signals and limit conditions will be built using the price probability field introduced to present how this model can be used in automated capital investment software systems.

To clarify the notion of the price probability growth, we will say that a price presents zero probability for growth with an established value in the future if the price never riches that value before to decrease with at least the double of that value. Similarly, a price has a 100% probability for increase with a specified value if it will touch that value in the future time before to decrease with the double of value considered. The definitions above are the hypothesis for this study. The probability field can be defined in different other modes. The current research has established that comparing a price increase with the double of his decrease gives us the best capital efficiency in the model that will be presented further. An additional requirement for a price probability field is to be continuously defined in all the time price series definition intervals. In other words, the price probability field has to give us the probability value for price growth at any moment of time.

3.2 Probability Through Price Cyclicality Function

The Price Probability function was introduced in (Păuna and Lungu 2018). It was proved that a very strong and direct correlation exists between this function and the price movement. The function is defined in [0; 100] intervals and has minimal points near the minimal price levels, and maximal values correlated with the maximal price levels. We will define the probability field through Price Cyclicality Function the next function:

$$PRO_{PCY} = \phi \cdot (100 - PCY)/100 \quad (1)$$

where *PCY* is the Price Probability Function, and φ is a functional parameter that will be optimized for each capital market analyzed, depending on the way of how the price probability field is defined, as we will see. Once the *PCY* function is defined in [0; 100], the PRO_{PCY} function will be defined in [0; 1] and will be inversely proportional to the price evolution. When PRO_{PCY} has a minimal point, this means the probability for a price increase is at a minimum, and the price will not make significant up movements. Similarly, when the PRO_{PCY} makes a maximum, the probability for price growth is at maximum, a significant price increase being expected in that market.

For each market, depending on the price probability field definition, the φ factor will be computed using the historical price evolution. For example, the probability for a 200 points price increase after a maximal value of the probability field, using the PCY function with 20 time intervals period, and 20 and 50 periods for the weighted moving averages used, on a daily time price series of DAX30 Index market, is 98.75%. This means, for the specified market, the 200 point growth price probability field is defined by $\varphi = 0.9875$.

The value $\varphi = 0.9875$ was found computing the PCY function and analyzing the price evolution for the historical time price series of the DAX30 Index market between 2010 and 2019. Considering all the cases when the PCY function made a minimal point lower than 10, 1.25% of cases were not true. In 1.25% of cases, after a minimum point of the PCY function, the price made a lower movement with more than 400 points before to rich an up value with 200 points. In this way can be computed the φ parameter for any type of probability field using any kind of function. To compute the Formula (1), the PCY function with n period will be defined by the recurrence formula:

$$PCY_i = \alpha(\Delta_i - PCY_{i-1}) + PCY_{i-1} \text{for } i \geq 0 \text{ with } PCY_0 = 0 \quad (2)$$

where α defines the gradient of the *PCY* function, and

$$\Delta_i = \frac{\max_i - \xi_i}{\max_i - \min_i}, \xi_i = Ma_i - ma_i \quad (3)$$

$$\max_i = \max_{k=i}^{i-n}(Ma_k - ma_k), \max_i = \max_{k=i}^{i-n}(Ma_k - ma_k) \quad (4)$$

using Ma_k and ma_k as two weighted moving averages with different periods (Cox 1969).

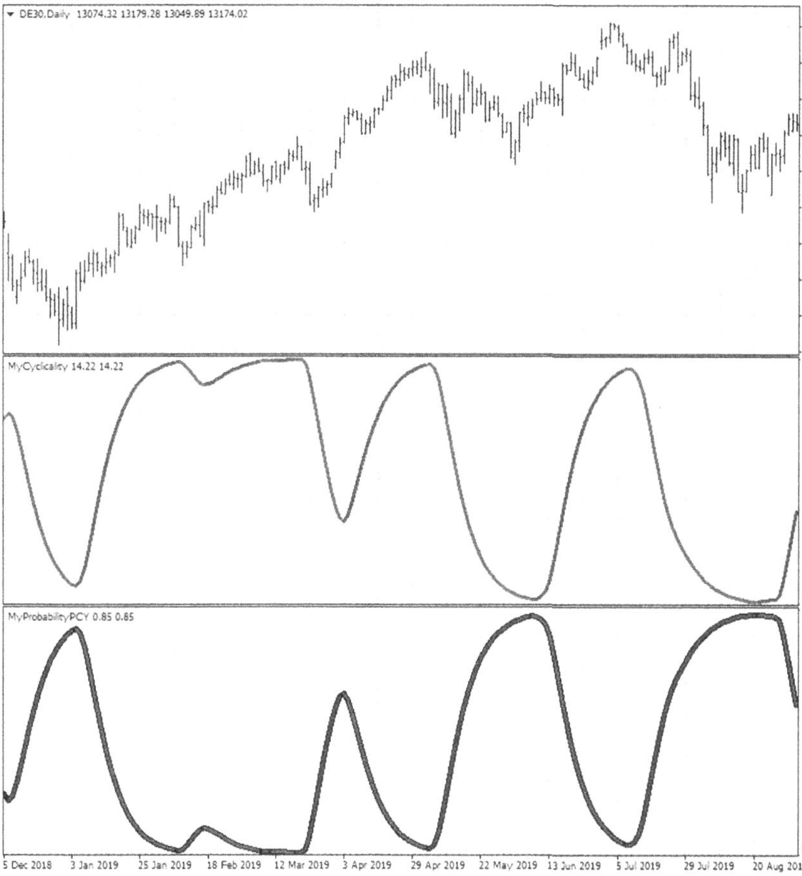

Fig. 1 Price probability field using the price cyclicality function for DAX30 index market

3.3 *Probability Through Price Smoothed Heikin-Ashi Transform*

Smoothed Heikin-Ashi price transform is analytically defined in (Păuna 2018):

$$\begin{cases} \overline{Oha_i} = \left(\overline{O}_{i-1} + \overline{C}_{i-1}\right)/2 \\ \overline{Lha_i} = \min(\overline{L}_i, \overline{O}_i, \overline{C}_i) \\ \overline{Hha_i} = \max(\overline{H}_i, \overline{O}_i, \overline{C}_i) \\ \overline{Cha_i} = \left(\overline{O}_i + \overline{H}_i + \overline{L}_i + \overline{C}_i\right)/4 \end{cases} \tag{5}$$

in which $\overline{O_i}$, $\overline{H_i}$, $\overline{L_i}$ and $\overline{C_i}$ are the averages values of open, high, low, respectively close price levels into a specified M number of time intervals. During this research, it was found that this price function has a direct and positive correlation with the price evolution. Measuring the price evolution after the moment when $\overline{H_i} > \overline{O_i}$, a significant price growth probability was found.

The probability field through the Smoothed Heikin-Ashi price transform will be defined analyzing the cyclicality of $\overline{O_i}$ and $\overline{H_i}$ price series:

$$PRO_{SHA} = \psi \cdot (100 - SAH)/100 \tag{6}$$

where

$$SHA_i = \beta(\Sigma_i - SHA_{i-1}) + SAH_{i-1} \text{for}\, i \geq 0\, \text{with}\, SHA_0 = 0 \tag{7}$$

where β defines the gradient of the *SHA* function with m period, and

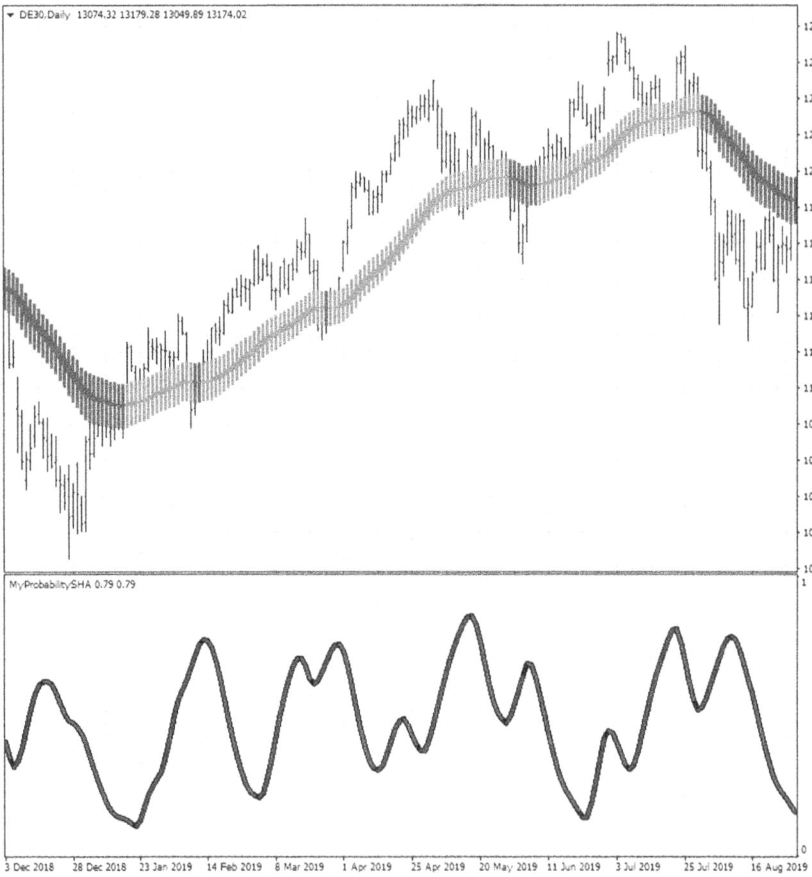

Fig. 2 Price probability field using the smoothed Heikin-Ashi for DAX30 Index market

$$\Sigma_i = \frac{\max_i - \zeta_i}{\max_i - \min_i}, \zeta_i = Ma_i - ma_i \quad (8)$$

and the maximal and minimal functions are computed using $\overline{O_i}$ and $\overline{H_i}$:

$$\max_i = \max_{k=i}^{i-m}\left(\overline{H_k} - \overline{O_k}\right), \max_i = \max_{k=i}^{i-m}\left(\overline{H_k} - \overline{O_k}\right) \quad (9)$$

The price probability field measuring the chances for 200 point price increase after $\overline{H_i} > \overline{O_i}$ on a daily time price series of DAX30 Index market is presented in Fig. 2. The functional parameters β and ψ can be found using the historical time price series of any market. β will define the gradient of the probability field, and ψ will define the maximal probability value measured in the historical time price series.

As a first observation, the probability variation in Fig. 1 and the probability field in Fig. 2 have significantly different evolutions. There are some time intervals when both series take maximal or minimal probability values. An important note is that the two functions are measuring the same phenomenon, which is the price increase with 200 points, but using different methods. Later in this paper, we will see how two or more probability fields can be combined in order to obtain a better capital efficiency.

3.4 Probability Through Price Prediction Line and Trigonometric Price Line

The Price Prediction Line is a function introduced in (Păuna 2019d). It represents the back transformation into the price space of the Price Cyclicality Function, using the formula:

$$PPL_i = PCY_i \cdot \left(P\max_i - P\min_i\right)/100 + P\min_i \quad (10)$$

where the terms $P\min_i$ and $P\max_i$ represent the minimum and respectively maximum price values on the current monotony interval of the Price Cyclicality Function. The Price Prediction Line is figured with a dotted line in Fig. 3.

The Trigonometric Price Line is a price interpolation line using trigonometric functions, presented in (Păuna 2020). The analytical function is given by the form:

$$p(t_i) = \alpha_0 + \sum_{k=1}^{N} \alpha_k \cos(k \cdot t_i) + \sum_{k=1}^{N} \beta_k \sin(k \cdot t_i), i \in \overline{1, N} \quad (11)$$

where α_k and β_k coefficients are computed solving the N equation system, based on the fact that the values $p(t_i)$ are known for the last time moment t_i in the price history series.

The Trigonometric Price Line is figured in the Fig. 3 over the price evolution with continuous red and blue lines. During the Ph.D. research behind this chapter, it was found that the intersections between the Price Prediction Line and trigonometric Price Line have an important significance. Once the Trigonometric Price Line values exceed the Price Prediction Lines values and both functions are increasing, the price will make a significant up evolution. To define a price probability grow field we will apply the same technique presented above, considering the cyclicality between the two functions:

$$PRO_{PPLTPL} = \omega \cdot (100 - PPLTPL)/100 \tag{12}$$

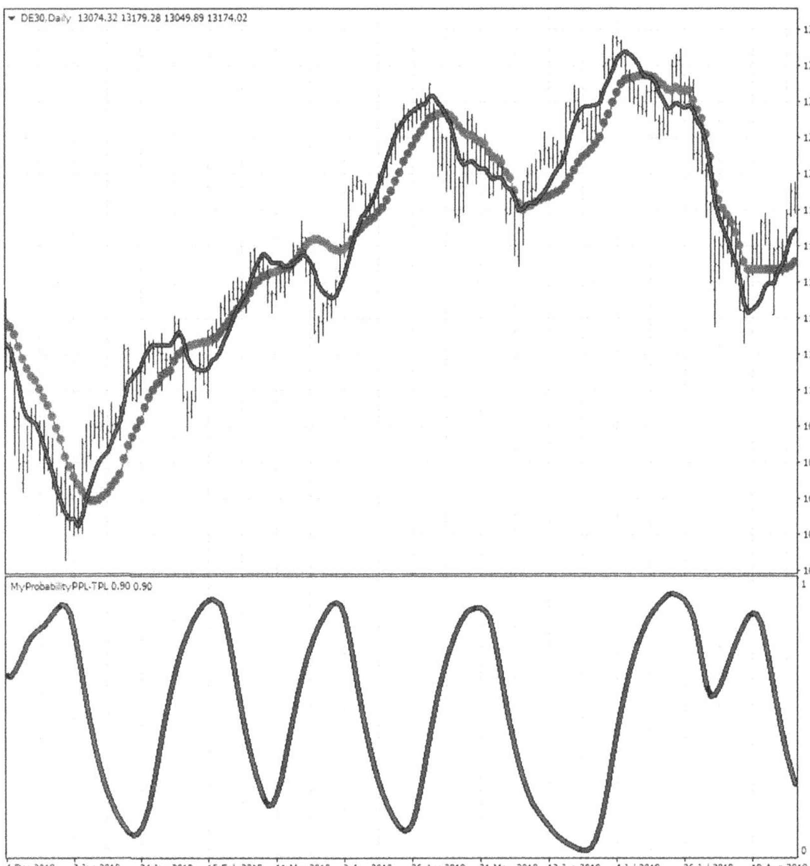

Fig. 3 Price probability field through price prediction line and trigonometric price line

where

$$PPLTPL_i = \gamma(\Sigma_i - PPLTPL_{i-1}) + PPLTPL_{i-1} \text{ for } i \geq 0 \text{ with } PPLTPL_0 = 0 \quad (13)$$

where γ defines the gradient of the *PPLTPL* function with p period, and

$$\Pi_i = \frac{\max_i - \pi_i}{\max_i - \min_i}, \pi_i = TPL_i - PPL_i \quad (14)$$

and the maximal and minimal functions are computed this time using PPL and TPL:

$$\max_i = \max_{k=i}^{i-p}(TPL_k - PPL_k), \max_i = \max_{k=i}^{i-p}(TPL_k - PPL_k) \quad (15)$$

The price probability field through Price Prediction Line and trigonometric Price Line is presented in Fig. 3 for the same example of the DAX30 Index market.

3.5 Price Probability Predictor

This research has found that a simple average of the three probability field presented above, will produce a more stable probability function that is giving us a better capital efficiency when trading signals are computed using it. This is called the Price Probability Predictor (PPP) and it is given by the relation:

$$PPP = (PRO_{PCY} + PRO_{SHA} + PRO_{PPLTPL})/3 \quad (16)$$

The results of the Price Predictor Probability function for a 200 points chance of price increase on a daily time price series of DAX30 Index market are presented in Fig. 3. The n, m, and p periods of PCY, SHA and PPLTPL functions are also at our disposal to be optimized for each analyzed market. In Fig. 4 was used $n = m = p = 5$.

To prove that the Price Probability Predictor is in a inverse and strong correlation with the price action, the Pearson correlation coefficient (Andrei 2003) was computed for a significant number of capital markets. Values between (−0.999) and (−0.537) were obtaind for 4-h and daily timeframes for the next markets: Frankfurt Stock Exchange Deutscher Aktienindex DAX30, New York Stock Exchange Dow Jones Industrial Average Index DJIA30, Financial Times London Stock Exchange Index FTSE100, Cotation Assistée en Continu Paris Stock Exchange Index CAC40, Swiss Market Index SMI20, Standard and Poor's Index S&P500, National Association of Securities Dealers Automated Quotations NASDAQ100, Tokyo Stock Exchange

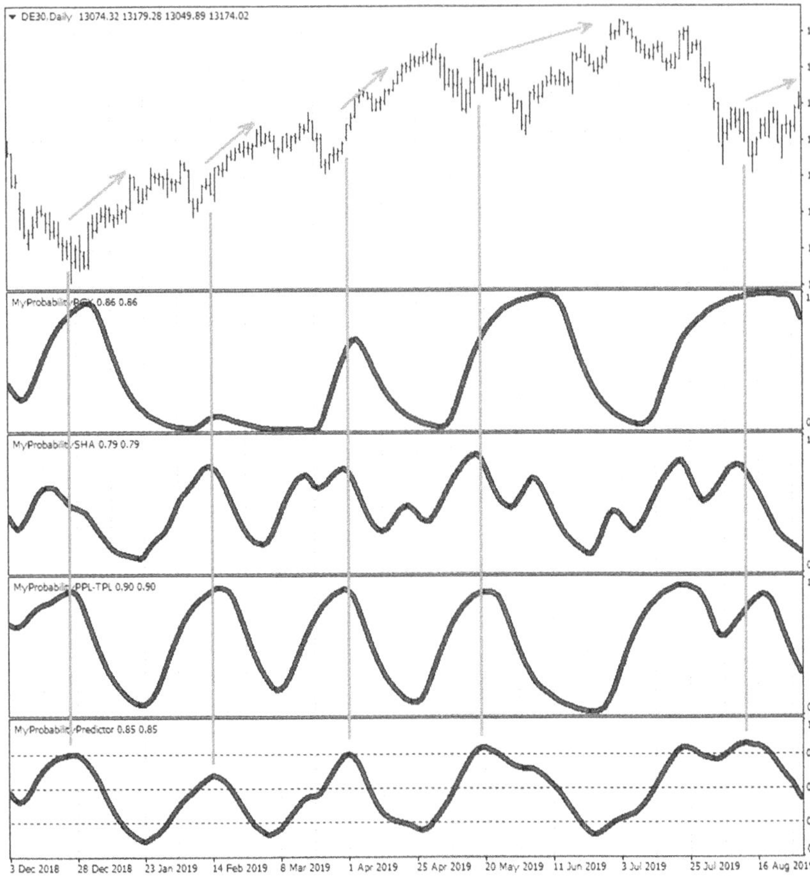

Fig. 4 Price probability predictor for DAX30 index market

index NIKKEI225, and Australian Security Exchange Index ASX200, spot price of gold XAUUSD, and Brent crude oil. For currency pairs markets, values between (−0.972) and (−0.518) were obtained for 4-h and daily timeframes for all major currencies pairs. These results confirm that the Price Probability Predictor is in an inverse and strong correlation with the price tendency. Based on this fact, after a maximum point of the Price Probability predictor, the price will make a significant up movement.

4 Automated Trading Signals and Limit Conditions

Two types of entry automated trading signals can be built using the Probability Price Predictor. The first type follows the maximal points made by the *PPP* function and will generate one market entry after a maximal point if the *PPP* values are higher than a profitability limit level:

$$\text{Buy Signal}_i = (PPP_i < PPP_{i-1}) \wedge (PPP_{i-1} < PPP_{i-2}) \wedge (PPP_i > \lambda) \quad (17)$$

where λ filter the signals in order to ignore entries when the price growth probability is lower, in case the *PPP* function makes a local maximal point at lower values; usually $\lambda = 0.5$.

The second type of automated trading signals that can be built with the PPP function is adapted for more volatile markets, initiating multiple entries each time when the price decrease with a specific δ value:

$$\text{Buy Signal}_{ik} = (PPP_i > PPP_{i-1}) \wedge (PPP_i \geq \theta) \wedge (p_k < p_{k-1} - \delta) \quad (18)$$

with $1 \leq k \leq N$, where i denotes the time interval, and k denotes the number of opened trade. In Formula (17), the first price entry p_1 is made for $PPP_i = \theta$, hen the market probability riches for the first time θ value on an ascending probability interval:

$$\text{Buy Signal}_{i1} = (PPP_i > PPP_{i-1}) \wedge (PPP_i = \theta) \quad (19)$$

In Formula (17), N is the maximal number of simultaneously opened trades, having the purpose of limiting capital exposure,N will make possible risk management. The θ, δ, and N factors are at the investors' disposal; all can be optimized depending on the traded market and on the timeframe used for price analysis.

The exit conditions using the Price Probability Predictor function must be related with the probability field definition considered in the built model. If the probability field was computed for a price growth of 200 points, a target higher that this value will have no sense. Moreover, to be safe of the unpredictable market behavior, using a target lower than the target considered building the probability field is recommended. As conclusion, the first exit criteria is a price increase with a Δ distance than the price level met in the maximal interval of the PPP function, noted here as Ω:

$$\text{Exit Buy Signal}_i = (p_i \geq \Omega + \Delta) \quad (20)$$

The exit condition made with Formula (20) can be used for one entry made with (17) or for multiple market entries by Formula (18). During this research was found that a better exit condition is met using the Average True Range (ATR) function introduced in (Wilder 1978). This will take into consideration the market volatility change during the investment process. The exit decision can be automated using the relation:

$$\text{Exit Buy Signal}_i = (p_i \geq \Omega + ATR_i) \quad (21)$$

if ATR value is less than the target considered for the price probability field definition. Formula (21) will generate exit decisions faster that (20), the capital will stay shorter allocated in the trades, and the investment efficiency will be significantly improved.

Limit conditions built using the PPP functions can be used to improve any other investment strategy. Entries made by any mathematical or empirical trading model can be filtered using the Price Probability Predictor. The capital efficiency can be improved allowing only entries when the price growth probability is higher than a minimal limit:

$$\text{Limit Condition}_i = (PPP_i > \Theta) \tag{22}$$

Moreover, an increase in the price probability field values will be a positive condition:

$$\text{Limit Condition}_i = (PPP_i > PPP_{i-1}) \wedge (PPP_i > \Theta) \tag{23}$$

In the same idea, exit conditions applied to trades opened with any other trading strategy can be built when the price growth probability is decreasing under a specific level:

$$\text{Exit Condition}_i = (PPP_i < PPP_{i-1}) \wedge (PPP_i < \Xi) \tag{24}$$

where the parameters Θ and Ξ can be optimized for each traded market and for each timeframe used for the price analysis.

5 Results

In this section, trading results obtained with the signals presented in the last part will be presented in order to prove the functionality of the method introduces in this paper and to get the possibility to compare the results with other investment strategies.

The automated signals made by relation (17) were traded for Frankfurt Stock exchange Deutscher Aktienindex DAX30 market between 1 January 2019 and 31 December 2019. The Price probability predictor was optimized for a price increase with 200 points after a maximal probability evolution, using the DAX30 historical time price series between 1 January 2010 and 31 December 2018. The cross-over validation is used in this example, once the optimization interval does not contain the time interval in which the results are. In Fig. 5 is presented the capital evolution due to signals (17), for a particular value of $\lambda = 0.5$, using a 4-h timeframe.

In 12 months, signals (17) have obtained a risk to reward ratio of 1:2.64 in a total number of 39 profitable trades. There was no losing trade, and the most extended trade last 475 h. The results were obtained with DaxTrader (Păuna 2010), an automated capital investment software using the Price Probability Predictor to build automated

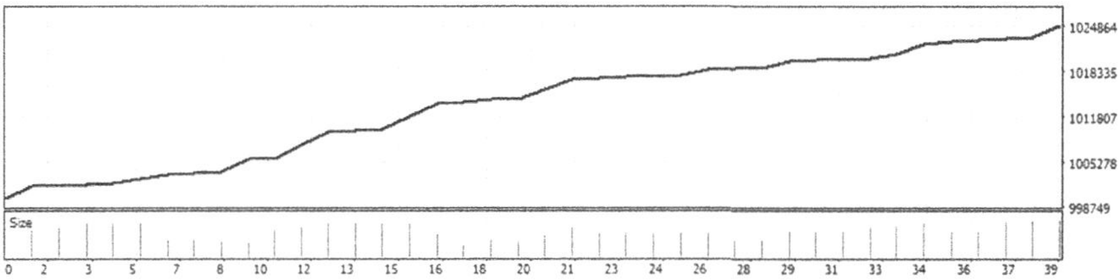

Fig. 5 Trading results obtained with (17) automated signals for DAX30 Index

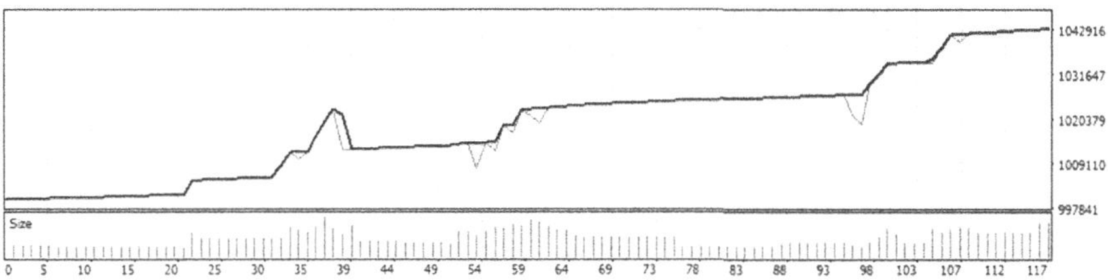

Fig. 6 Trading results obtained with (18) automated signals for DAX30 Index

capital investment signals. The risk and capital management were assured using the "Global Stop Loss" method (Păuna 2018d) with a maximal risk level of 1%.

A significantly large number of trades were made by the signals built with (18) formula for $\theta = 0.75$ and $\delta = 100$ points. The results obtained with the same automated trading software are presented in Fig. 6. In this case, it was obtained a risk to reward ratio of 1:2.32, and the longest trade last 522 h. In this second case, a maximal risk level of 2% of the available capital was used. In this case, two positions were closed with losses, 2 from 117 trades made, meaning a percentage of success equal with 98.29%.

The results above are better understood is both signals are used together. Using the (17) and (18) automated trading signals for the 2019 period applied for the DAX30 Index market, with a maximal risk level of 2% of the available capital, a risk to reward ratio of 1:4.96 was obtained. This is an excellent result, proving that the Price Probability Predictor is a reliable and profitable model to build trading signals on the capital market.

Another important observation is regarding the specificity of the trades opened with signals built with Price Probability Predictor. The Quality Trading Coefficient (Păuna 2018e) of 98% of trades above has a positive and higher value in the interval [0.52; 0.96]. This means the trades opened when the probability for a price increase is higher are trades that are evolving fast and constant to the designed target. The values obtained for the Quality Trading Coefficient classify the investment methodology using price Probability predictor in the top trading strategies presented in the Ph.D. research behind this chapter.

6 Conclusions

Price Probability Predictor is a technical indicator built using the time price series and several particular functions as Price Cyclicality Function, Smoothed Heikin-Ashi price transformation, Price Prediction Line, and Trigonometric Price Line. An analytical mathematical model links all of these functions into a continuous probability field, measuring the chance for price growth in the next time intervals. The model includes several functional parameters that can be optimized for each market in order to define the function to indicate the probability of price increase with a specified value.

The Price Probability Predictor can be used to build reliable trading signals and limit conditions to automate the investment activity. It can be optimized for any analyzed capital market and for any timeframe used. During this research, the model was tested with excellent results for a considerable number of financial markets: Frankfurt Stock Exchange Deutscher Aktienindex DAX30, New York Stock Exchange Dow Jones Industrial Average Index DJIA30, Financial Times London Stock Exchange Index FTSE100, Cotation Assistée en Continu Paris Stock Exchange Index CAC40, Swiss Market Index SMI20, Standard and Poor's Index S&P500, National Association of Securities Dealers Automated Quotations NASDAQ100, Tokyo Stock Exchange index NIKKEI225, and Australian Security Exchange Index ASX200. For more volatile markets as spot gold (XAUUSD) and currency markets, the signals built with the PPP function must be filtered by additional limit conditions imposed with the Price Cyclicality Function (Păuna and Lungu 2018).

Due to how the Price Probability Predictor function is defined and optimized, it measures the price increase chance. The presented function is also an excellent tool for educational purposes. When the values of the PPP field are high, the function indicates a higher price growth probability. Besides, when the PPP function has lower values, it will mean a lower chance for price growth, but not a higher chance for a price decrease. Based on this particular observation, any capital trading or investment strategy can be filtered and improved using the Price Probability Predictors to reduce the allocated risk, to reduce the time spent into a trade, and, consequently, to increase the capital efficiency.

The Price Probability Predictor function was designed for automated trading systems. Even the mathematical model is a complex one, the computational power needed to build the function is a reasonable one. It can be built-in real-time with low latency and can be included in any automated capital investment software system.

The Price Probability Predictor function has a high degree of efficiency in improving the results of any other trading strategy. Due to this fact, in the research behind this article, the PPP function assists any automated capital investment decision. Also, it can be used for manual investment decisions. Any investor using the PPP function can simply choose to invest in a market with an 85% price increase probability and to exit from markets indicating only a 20% price growth chance or a decreasing probability evolution. With all the facts presented, the Price Probability

Predictor is a reliable investment indicator, giving us the possibility to measure the chance to record a profit in any market on the next time interval.

References

Andrei, T.: Statistică și econometrie, Romania: Editura Economică, București (2003). ISBN: 973-590-764-X

Bernstein, J., Bernstein, E.: Stock market strategies that work. McGraw Hill (2008). ISBN: 0-07-140633-6. https://doi.org/10.1036/0071406336

Cheng, G.: 7 Winning strategies for trading forex. Real and actionable techniques for profiting from the currency markets. Hariman Trading, GB (2007). ISBN: 978-0-857190-90-1

Connors, L.A.: Best trading patterns. Best Prof. Trade. J. M. Gordon Publishing Group, US (1999). ISBN: 0-9650461-0-2

Connors, L., Alvarez, C.: Short term trading strategies that work. In: A Quantitative Guide to Trading Stocks and ETFs. Trading Markets Publishing Group, US (2009a). ISBN: 978-0-0919239-0-1

Connors, L., Alvarez, C.: High Probability ETF Trading—7 Professional Strategies to Improve Your ETF Trading. Connors Research, US (2009b). ISBN: 978-0-615-29741-5

Connors, L., Sen, C.: How Markets Really Work—A Quantitative Guide to Stock Market Behavior. Connors Research Group, US (2004). ISBN 978-0-9755513-1-8

Cox, Sir, D.R.: Prediction by exponentially weighted moving averages and related methods. J. R. Stat. Soc. Ser. B **23**(2) (1969)

Focardi, S.M, Fabozi, F.J.: The mathematics of financial modeling and investment management. Wiley (2004). ISBN: 0-471-46599-2

Jagerson, J., Hansen, S.W.: All about investing in gold. McGraw Hill (2011). ISBN: 978-0-07-176834-4

Kiev, A.: Mastering Trading Stress. Wiley (2008). ISBN: 978-0-470-18168-3

Kleinman, G.: The new commodity trading guide. Breakthrough strategies for capturing market profits. Pearson Education (2009). ISBN: 978-0-13-714529-4

Lien, K.: Day trading and swing trading the currency market. In: Technical and Fundamental Strategies to Profit the Market Moves. Wiley (2009). ISBN: 978-0-470-37736-0

Lien, K.: The little book of currency trading. In: How to Make Big Profits in the World of Forex. Wiley, US (2011). ISBN: 978-0-470-77035-1

Păuna, C.: Reliable signals based on fisher transform for algorithmic trading. Timișoara, Romania Timișoara J. Econ. Business **11**(1) (2018a). ISSN: 2286-0991. West University of Timișoara. https://doi.org/10.2478/tjeb-2018-0006. Available at https://tjeb.ro

Păuna, C.: Low risk trading algorithm based on the price cyclicality function for capital markets. In: Bucharest, Romania: 13th International Conference on Business Excellence (2019a). https://doi.org/10.2478/mmcks-2019-0006

Păuna, C.: Additional limit conditions for breakout trading strategies. Bucharest, Romania Inform. Econ. J. **23**(2) (2019b). https://doi.org/10.12948/issn14531305/23.2.2019.03. Available at https://revistaie.ase.ro

Păuna, C.: A prediction model using price cyclicality function optimized for algorithmic trading in financial markets. Int. J. Comput. Inf. Eng. **13**(4). World Academy of Science, Engineering and Technology, Athens, Greece (2019c). Available at https://publications.waset.org/author/cristian-pauna

Păuna, C.: Price prediction line. Investment signals and limit conditions applied for the German financial market. Int. J. Comput. Inf. Eng. **13**(9). World Academy of Science, Engineering and Technology, Rome, Italy (2019d). Available at https://publications.waset.org/author/cristian-pauna

Păuna, C.: Silent market indicator. Methodology to avoid the risk in no significant price movements. Timișoara, Romania Timișoara J. Econ. Business **12**(1) (2019f). ISSN: 2286-0991. https://doi.org/10.2478/tjeb-2018-0009. Available at https://tjeb.ro

Păuna, C.: Capital and risk management for automated trading systems, Romania. In: Proceedings of the 17th International Conference on Informatics in Economy, pp 183–188 (2018d). Available at https://pauna.biz/ideas

Păuna, C.: DaxTrader automated trading system, online software presentation (2010). Available at https://pauna.biz/daxtrader

Păuna, C.: Smoothed Heikin-Ashi algorithms optimized for automated trading systems. In: Graz, Austria: Proceeding of the 2nd International Scientific Conference on IT, Tourism, Economics, Management, and Agriculture, ITEMA 2018. Graz University of Technology (2018c). Available at https://itema-conference.com

Păuna, C.: Reliable signals and limit conditions using trigonometric interpolation for algorithmic capital investments. In: Proceedings of 7th Business Systems Laboratory International Symposia Conference, BSLAB (2020). Available at https://pauna.biz/ideas

Păuna, C.: Data mining methods on time price series for algorithmic trading systems. Bucharest, Romania Inform. Econ. J. **23**(1)(2019e). ISSN: 1453-1305. https://doi.org/10.12948/issn14531305/23.1.2019.03. Available at https://revistaie.ase.ro

Păuna, C.: Reliable signals and limit conditions for automated trading systems. Iași, Romania Rev. Econ. Business Stud. **XI**(2) (2018b). ISSN: 1843-763X. Alexandru Ioan Cuza University Press. https://doi.org/10.1515/rebs-2018-0070. Available at https://rebs.feaa.uaic.ro

Păuna, C.: The quality trading coefficient. General formula to qualify a trade and a trading methodology. Bucharest, Romania Inform. Econ. J. **22**(3) (2018e). ISSN: 1453-1305. https://doi.org/10.12948/issn14531305/22.2.2018.04. Available at https://revistaie.ase.ro

Păuna, C., Lungu, I.: Price cyclicality model for financial markets. Reliable limit conditions for algorithmic trading. Bucharest Romania Econ. Comput. Econ. Cybern. Stud. Res. J. **52**(4) (2018). ISSN: 1842-3264. https://doi.org/10.24818/18423264/52.4.18.10. Available at https://ecocyb.ase.ro

Pring, M.J.: Investment psychology explained. Wiley (1992). ISBN: 9780471557210

Vince, R.: The mathematics of money management: risk analysis techniques for traders. Wiley (1992). ISBN: 0-471-54738-7

Volman, B.: Forex price action scalping. An in-deep look into the field of professional scalping. Light Tower Publishing. ISBN: 978-90-9026411-0

Ward, S.: High performance trading. In: 35 Practical Strategies and Techniques to enhance Your Trading Psychology and Performance. Hariman House, GB. ISBN: 978-1-905641-61-1

Wilder, J.W.: New Concepts in Technical Trading Systems. Greensboro, Trend Research (1978). ISBN 978-0-89459-027-6

Time Management and Time Utilization for Urology Surgeons, a Step in Implementing Social Responsibility, a Theoretical and a Practical Approach

Luminița-Mihaela Dumitrașcu, Liliana Feleagă, and Bogdan-Ștefan Ionescu

1 Introduction

Corporate social responsibility emerged in the United States of America, being introduced by Howard Bowen, in 1953, in his "Social Responsibilities of the businessman." The literature presents a wide range of definitions (Philip 2007).

Corporate social responsibility could play an important role in hospitals. Examples of some positive impact and opportunities to perform and implement corporate social responsibility in the health sector are: health promotion activities, manufacturing health safety goods, research, innovation, collaboration among different health institutions, charity, fundraising, volunteering, health campaigns, selling and manufacturing drugs at a low price for vulnerable people and reducing treatment cost for them, improving health infrastructure, community partnerships. Social responsibility actions are considering: encouraging feedback in terms of social responsibility; the evolution of managerial skills in terms of social responsibility; stimulating the adoption of corporate social responsibility strategies; transparency of corporate social responsibility practices, which also contributes to their improvement, but is useful in the positioning and comparing results.

2 Literature Review

Organizations have as main objective the profit, that is usually connected with efficiency, productivity, innovation, value-added to the company, but people are more

L.-M. Dumitrașcu (✉) · L. Feleagă · B.-Ș. Ionescu
Bucharest University of Economic Studies, Romana Square, No. 6, 010374 Bucharest, Romania
e-mail: mihaela.dumitrascu@cig.ase.ro

A. M. Dima and F. DÁscenzo (eds.), *Business Revolution in a Digital Era*,
Springer Proceedings in Business and Economics,
https://doi.org/10.1007/978-3-030-59972-0_22

interested in social responsibility issues, no matter the sector of activity. In medicine, we observe economic influence. Some studies discovered what are the profession-related competencies (Xiangyun et al. 2019). The items are clustered within interpersonal competencies (collaboration, communication, adaptability, positive feedback, interdependency), cognitive skills (reflectivity, analysis, critical thinking, problem-solving, ability to see in perspective, curiosity, creativity), work-related skills (dedication, perseverance, leadership, focus, self-management, discipline, stress-management, improvisation, time-management, planning organizing), professionalism (ability to recognize health needs of the community, quality healthcare, education of patients, empathy, ethics, integrity, responsibility, respect, empathy, humanity, ethics) (Veloski et al. 2005; MacKenzie 2007; Blackall et al. 2007; Du Preez et al. 2007; Klemenc-Ketis and Vrecko 2014; Ho and Al-Eraky 2016).

The structure of a physician's workday changed in recent years, on hours worked per week, implementation of electronic medical records, administrative tasks and increase of volume of clinical data. Information technology is used in the health care sector and have both positive and negative effects (share medical data and make them be available, increase the time spent by physicians on administrative tasks, decrease the time spent by the physician with the patient) (Poissant et al. 2005; Amankra et al. 2016; Alkureishi et al. 2016; Ratanawongsa et al. 2016). Researchers discovered that physicians use 50% of their time using computers. This trend can be interpreted like less time spent in face to face meetings with patients, decrease physician and patient satisfaction, have an impact on health promotion and can conduct to medical malpractice (Westbrook et al. 2008; Ammenwerth et al. 2009; Shanafelt et al. 2016; Dugdale et al. 1999).

Among all the resources time is the most important. It cannot be defined, saved, bought or stored. As responsibilities increase, physicians lead stressful lifestyles and need to learn new skills with impact on their time, practice and lifestyle.

There are many challenges regarding time management of physicians reported in different studies (Crosby 2004; Dugdale et al. 1999). Other studies bring into spotlights the problem of improving time management skills of physicians (Crosby 2004; Dugdale et al. 1999; Jackson 2009; Lowenstein 2009; Riba et al. 2007). Successful physicians seem to have limited time available but are actually about the management of it. The limited-time is the main cause of burnout depression, suicide (Shanafelt et al. 2012).

Surgeons have been subject to different pressures in the past decade, referring to cost-cutting, regulations, transition to electronic health records (Friedberg et al. 2013; Babbott et al. 2014). To achieve efficiency and productivity surgeons should find a balance between family, career, hobbies and other activities. Days on the surgery room can get very busy, each day can look different, but being organized and efficient helps to stay on top (Dyrbye and Shanafelt 2011).

Not only time management is important, but also the management of responsibilities. In this regard there is The Time Management Matrix Technique (TMMT) that provides an overview of the responsibilities (Covey et al. 1996; Covey1990; Christie 2009; Brunicardi and Hobson 1996) and classify each responsibility as urgent, non-urgent, important, non-important. It is important to discover the most productive individual time for focusing (Taylor 2010), with the highest energy, creativity and if it is possible sufficient uninterrupted time (Lowenstein 2009).

The present research aims to compare the time dedicated to consultations, surgery, research versus free time to improve time management techniques, to increase the awareness of the importance of time management of surgeons, to stimulate future research, to stimulate to incorporate within department social responsibility and sustainability trainings, actions and activities.

A study investigated how family physicians spent their time within a workday, by using time-motion techniques, for 11 physicians (82% men vs. 68%). Data collected refers to 203 h of work. The average workday was 8.6 h. Face to face time with patients represents 55% of the day (Gottschalk and Flocke 2005). There are studies that investigated the time allocation of physicians of different specialities (family medicine, internal medicine, cardiology, orthopedic surgery) (Sinsky et al. 2016). Other investigated the time allocation. The technique used was time-motion direct observation. The sample consists of 80 interns from 6 US universities, 55% men 28,7 year average data were gattered from March 10 to May 31 2016 and a total of 2173 h. 66% of the time was spent on patient care, documentation 44% multitasking 16%. Time allocation is split within patient time, research and multitasking, the limit of the study is given by the daytime activity analyzed (Gabow et al. 2006).

3 Methodology

We conducted an observational study within the Department of Urology of Carol Davila University Emergency Military Hospital, the only university hospital out of 11 Military hospitals in Romania. Eight surgeons were recruited using stratified nonprobability sampling based on predetermined categories (specialty and geographic location).

The study was based on direct observation using a time and motion approach during office hours and on a self- reported diary. All data were collected from 1st of October 2019 to 1st of December 2019 on weekdays. All physicians working in Urology Department were eligible for inclusion. There were no exclusion criteria. No patient or health information was recorded. We did not count the number of patients seen per hour. There are situations when tasks could be conducted at the same time. Collected data were reviewed and tasks were aggregated to calculate the total time spent at work. Descriptive statistics are presented to show how physicians spent their time and which are the main activities developed. All physicians are men. They were aged from 35 to 66 year old. We choose a department only with men because was demonstrated in previous studies that female physicians have less influence at work (Jansson von Vultée and Arnetz 2004). Physicians' activity usually starts at 8 am and end at 15:00. Teaching activity takes place on eight weeks per year and may be overlapped on surgery activity. The average number of on duty per surgeon is 4 per month with an extended activity of 36 h. Each participant reported the type of activity developed and the time interval they were carrying out (Fig. 1). We included the workday, but we excluded on-call duties. A statistical analyze was performed in to estimate the proportion of work time of surgeons. Blyth Still Casella confidence intervals and Agresti Min confidence intervals were estimated because we obtained differences between subgroups (Blyth and Still 1983; Casella 1986; Agresti and Min 2001).

4 Result and Discussions

Most of our findings are in accordance with the literature. (Block et al. 2013; Fletcher et al. 2012; Westbrook et al. 2008; Ammenwerth et al. 2009). Our results suggest the need to reorganize the work to fit the artificial intelligence era. (Wachter 2016; Guarisco et al. 1994; Gillanders and Heiman 1971; Gopal et al. 2005).

A total of 3136 h of work time were collected. Surgeons spent most of their work time in interventions, but also on direct patient care and teaching activities. Results provided a basis for future research on time management to increase the responsibility, efficiency, and productivity, to ensure a work-life balance and to calculate the cost of health care interventions.

All activities developed by surgeons during one day were grouped within 5 categories:

1. Research (literature review, searching scientific data to improve patient management, reading scientific papers, developing studies, reading websites, discussion with a senior physician for the best decision on patient management, collecting information, attending conferences, paper review, writing articles, books, developing academic research, receiving training, self preparation, documentation, work on computer or on paper, information seeking, tests, medication order)
2. Surgery
3. Teaching (sharing information, teaching activities, lectures, tutorials, practice, laboratories, talking with students, assessment of students, supervision)
4. Consultation (examination, assessing, planning, seeking for information and recording details about the patient disease, test results, medication order, administrative tasks, physical examination of patients, assessment, planning, discussing, looking for information in the paper record, computer archive, other medical record, other documents provided by the patient, clinical examination, communication with patient, anamnesis, prescription of treatment, writing notes, writing medical reports, examination results and letters, writing hospitalization reports, preparation of the documents, writing voucher for radiography, RMN, laboratory tests, other specialized consultation, booking appointments, phone calls, discussion with a senior physician, communication with family of the patient or close relatives, collecting information and opinions, listening to the patient, delivering therapeutic orientations, patient educational therapy, different procedures, emergency situations, transfer to other department)

5. Other activities (scheduling meetings, seminars, personal time in restrooms, breaks, eating, personal phone calls, conferences participation, travel between examination rooms or other locations, scheduling staff meetings, patient care discussions not in the presence of the patients, patients rounds, daily medical round of inpatients the physician is in charge of, review, clinical examination, prescription of treatment, letters, anamnesis, different procedures, meetings between professionals in order to discuss special cases, receiving training, self preparation, answering professional emails, food, rest, private use of computer and telephone, transit time to another activity or office restroom breaks).

Research and teaching are specific activities developed only by those that have an academic career. Tasks could be conducted in parallel, using multitasking, for example, a physician could read documents within consultations, or could review documents while transiting.

Only 25% of surgeons dedicated their time to each activity. 12% of surgeons has no military degree (Fig. 2). 25% of them are involved in research activity and only 37.5% of them have developed teaching activities, knowing that only 50% of them have an academic position (Fig. 4). We observed a significant time shared for different tasks between physicians. There are no such differences between surgeons regarding the time dedicated to consultations or teaching.

The study performed used the direct observation of time and motion during office hours and a self-reported diary for after-hours work. All direct observation data were collected on weekdays between 7 am and 24. Work at home and travel outside the hospital were not excluded. We did not measure the number of patients seen per hour or per day their medical complexity or the quality of the care provided. We allow recording two tasks in parallel.

The confidence level is so high, 27.45% because only 6% of surgeons are involved in research activities since 81.22% of surgeons do not have teaching activities. In the

Surgeon	Research	Surgery	Consultations	Other activities	Other	Maximum likelihood estimator: Blyth-Still-Casella intervals (95% CI) %
1	15,31%*	30,61%	15,31%	30,61%	8,16%	11,13% - 28,87%
2	0,00%	20,41%	5,10%	5,10%	69,39%	5,50% - 55,72%
3	0,00%	30,61%	5,10%	14,29%	50%	12,72% - 48,50%
4	20,41%	35,71%	5,10%	9,18%	29,60%	19,20% - 42,02%
5	0,00%	30,61%	4,08%	17,35%	47,96%	13,33% - 47,89%
6	0,00%	35,71%	5,10%	14,29%	44,90%	13,52% - 47,70%
7	0,00%	30,61%	5,10%	25,51%	38,78%	15,96% - 45,26%
8	0,00%	30,61%	10,20%	11,22%	47,97%	13,82% - 47,40%

Fig. 1 Work time of surgeons among types of activities percentage with maximum likelihood estimator Blyth Still Casella intervals. *Source* Authors' own projection

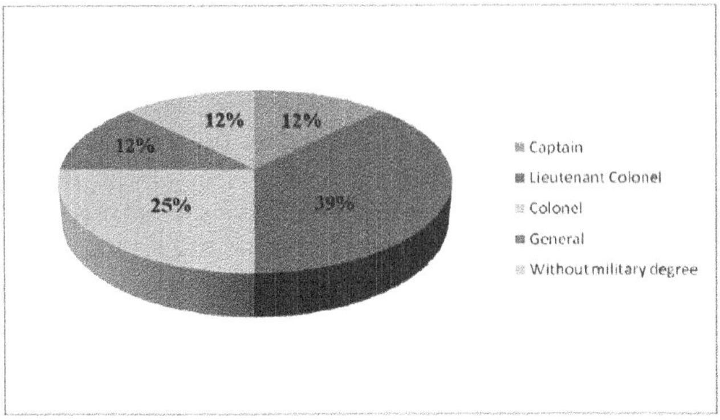

Fig. 2 Distribution of military degree of surgeons. *Source* Authors' own projection

Variable	Minimum, h	Maximum, h	Average, h
Research	0	80	17,5
Surgery	80	140	120
Teaching	0	140	52,5
Consultations	16	60	27
Other activities	20	120	62,5

Fig. 3 Results of study on work time of surgeons among types of activities. Number of hours with teaching activities. *Source* Authors' own projection

health-related publications. A 95% confidence interval is most often used, but this is an arbitrary value, and other confidence levels can be selected (Fig. 5).

Figure 3 illustrates the distribution of work time of surgeons among each type of activities (average work time per day in total) and starting from here we developed a graph representation of the distribution of work time on different hours of the day (Fig. 5).

During office hours surgeons spent half of their activity on surgery (42.93%) and on research less time, 6%. This is because not all of them are involved in teaching activities. Significant differences were found in work time spent on the research because such activities are mandatory for academic staff only. The low interest of involving in research activities may give an alarm sign to decision makers to increase the budget allocated in this regard. Surgeons that have research and an academic career are contributing to the best understanding of the disease and they come to innovative therapies (Goldstein et al. 2019). Surgeons contributions to knowledge are unique. Here we can mention that nine surgeons obtained the Nobel Prize for their scientific activity (Toledo-Pereyra 2006). As their field of interest is complex, the

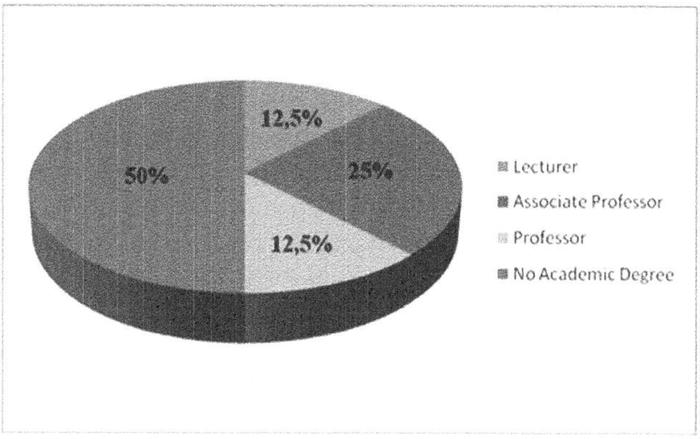

Fig. 4 Distribution of academic activity. *Source* Authors' own projection

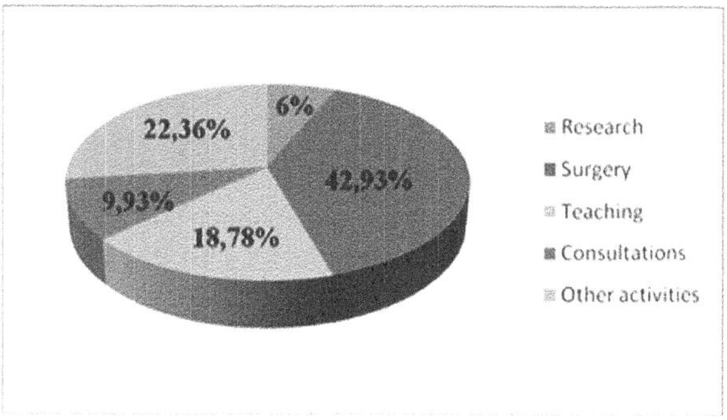

Fig. 5 Distribution of work time of surgeons among each type of activities. *Source* Authors' own projection

surgeons research in multidisciplinary teams. (Keswani et al. 2017). Surgeons receive fewer research grants than their nonsurgical colleagues. This means an increase in competition. (Mann et al. 2008; Rangel et al. 2002; Hu et al. 2015). The study has also some limits: the selected period might not have been representative, seeing that from one time to another there are differences and we did not link activities with the age and time spent on it, because the sample was not controlled for age, seeing that previous studies do not consider this to be a predictor of higher workload.

5 Conclusions

Time and motion studies are better than using other methods such as interviews or questionnaires because they are objective and avoid bias.

Organizations are involved in different research studies to decrease the daily volume and time of work. It is important to have a happy and productive employee rather than an exhausted one or one that makes mistakes. After the industrial revolution Robert Owen, launched in 1817 the slogan "Eight hours labor, eight hours recreation, eight hours rest" to assure a balance of a working day. Henry Ford moved from 6 days week to 5 days to increase the productivity of his employees. The working day is influenced by biological factors. Working 8 h a day is oxymoronic with the way our body works because it is unable to be productive, it reacts differently due to many factors, such as diet, hormones, exposure to temperature and specific biorhythm. This is why we are more productive, at different times on the day. The human body has two productivity peaks in a day, mid-late morning (to think), after waking up to 1 pm and after 9 pm (creativity), not very productive until 3–4 (little concentration), reactivates and reaches a maximum of productivity until 5–6 pm (physical tasks). This is not a general rule for everybody, because it depends on sleeping hours, eating hours and other factors.

Working more than 8 h a day increase with 40% the risk of heart and stress disease, headaches, according to The Laboratory on Health and Safety in the UK. Some studies demonstrated that only 52 min with 17-min break, we are concentrated or maybe maximum 90 min.

The study was performed within one hospital, but this is not a limitation, seeing that most other published researches were also conducted in a single hospital. Replicating our study or comparing with another sector of activity would be interesting as future research directions.

We suggest improving physicians' time allocation, by delegation of administrative tasks to focus on medical activities, optimizing documentation supports, placing medical assistants to enter data into medical system program, live-streaming consultations, diagnosis simulator on website for non-emergency patients.

Strategies to improve the time utilization on surgeons by taking into considerations aspects of social responsibility could refer to social climate (networking, brainstorming, support, team spirit, pleasant work atmosphere, skills development (learning new skills, working time is enough for developing and research), work satisfaction (harmony at work-place, stimulating, proud), energy (concentrating, rest, stimulated), self-esteem (positive approach, positive attitude, qualities), implication, involvement, participation (time to plan work tasks, multitasking, influence on the work situation, on work hours), efficiency work available to match deadline, optimally use of resources, all employees have the same goals, feedback on performance, career development support, emotionally supportive of the leader, engaging in skills development.

Social responsibility of surgeons represents the obligation and commitment of surgeons to protect and improve the society's welfare. They have the moral obligation to solve social problems and save the lives of the people, efficient and effective employees: they need to have the best skills and competencies, precautionary measure: refers to cost-efficiency, resources, such as material, financial, time, better organizational environment: surgeons could perform better and could offer a superior quality of their services.

Healthcare should focus on integrative and preventive approach (Chouchane et al. 2011). Physicians should learn to become more effective and more efficient to better manage the personal-professional balance. The main principles of time management are Pareto's Principle and Parkinson's Law. A set of tasks should be grouped by using ABC method, described by Alan Lakein of their importance, where A is the activity of highest importance. In this way, we force on priorities (Lakein 1973). Another technique is the time management matrix technique TMMT, described by Steve Covey. We should focus on the control of personal actions than scheduling time (Covey 1989; McLauchlan 1997). The technique places time-consuming actions into one quadrant of activity (I important and urgent, II important and not urgent, III not important and urgent, IV not important and not urgent). It is also called Eisenhower Method.

Pareto analysis mentions that 80% of tasks (with higher priority) can be completed in 20% of the available time and the remaining 20 in 80% of the time.

POSEC method is an acronym for "Prioritize by Organizing, Streamlining, Economizing and Contributing". There are different tasks that take more or less time to be accomplished: very small, less than 5 min, small, 5–10 min, require minimal concentration, medium, 30–60 min, require concentration, large >1 h, require maximal concentration and uninterrupted time.

Another technique is Natural Laws technique, that asserts that maximal productivity is achieved by using time records.

GTD Getting Things Done introduced by David Allen considers to finish the small tasks and the bigger ones to be divided into more smaller tasks. There is a time management method that can help us focus. It was invented by Francesco Cirillo in 1990s. The name is Pomodoro and comes from the tomato-shaped timer used by him to tracks his work.

It is important to have a positive atmosphere at work for both patients and physicians, to improve the working conditions that contribute to both professional and individual satisfaction and well being. Time management has an impact on both professional and personal satisfaction and increase productivity. Poor time management implementation may lead, in some cases, to depression, suicide and burnout for physicians (Shanafelt et al. 2012). Larger longitudinal studies are needed to be developed to discover how surgeons cope with time constraints in different countries.

References

Agresti, A., Min, Y.: On small-sample confidence intervals for parameters in discrete distributions. Biometrics **57**, 963–971 (2001)

Alkureishi, M.A., Lee, W.W., Lyons, M., Press, V.G., Imam, S., NkansahAmankra, A., et al.: Impact of electronic medical record use on the patient-doctor relationship and communication: a systematic review. J. Gen. Intern. Med. **31**, 548–560 (2016)

Ammenwerth, E., Spotl, H.P.: The time needed for clinical documentation versus direct patient care. A work-sampling analysis of physicians' activities. Methods Inf. Med. **48**, 84–91 (2009)

Arnet, P.J.V.B.: The impact of management programs on physicians' work environment and health. J. Health Org. Manage. **18**(1), 25–37 (2004)
Babbott, S., Manwell, L.B., Brown, R., Montague, E., Williams, E., Schwartz, M., et al.: Electronic medical records and physician stress in primary care: results from the MEMO study. J. Am. Med. Inform. Assoc. **21**, e100–e106 (2014)
Blackall, G., Melnick, S., Shoop, G., George, J., Lerner, S., Wilson, P., Pees, R., Kreher, M.: Professionalism in medical education: the development and validation of a survey instrument to assess attitudes toward professionalism. Med. Teach. **29**(2–3), e58–e62 (2007)
Block, L., Habicht, R., Wu, A.W., et al.: In the wake of the 2003 and 2011 duty hours regulations, how do internal medicine interns spend their time? J. Gen. Int. Med. 1042–1047 (2013)
Blyth, C.R.: Still HA binomial confidence intervals. J. Am. Stat. Assoc. **78**, 108–116 (1983)
Brunicardi, F.C., Hobson, F.L.: Time management: a review for physicians. J. Natl. Med. Assoc. **88**, 581–587 (1996)
Casella, G.: Refining binomial confidence intervals. J. Stat. Rev. Can Stat. **14**, 113–129 (1986)
Chouchane, L., Mamtani, R., Al-Thani, M., Al-Thani, A., Ameduri, M., Sheikh, J.: Medical education and research environment in Qatar: a new epoch for translational research in the Middle East. J. Transl. Med. **9**(1), 16 (2011)
Christie, S.: Effective time management skills for doctors. Developmedica, Nottingham (2009)
Covey, S.: The Seven Habits of Highly Effective People. Simon & Schuster, New York, NY (1989)
Covey, S.R.: The 7 Habits of Highly Effective People. Simon & Schuster Ltd, London (1990)
Covey, S.R., Merrill, A.R., Merrill, R.R.: First things first. Free Press (1996)
Crosby, J.W.: Ten time-management tips for family physicians. CMAJ **170**, 949–950 (2004)
Dugdale, D.C., Epstein, R., Pantilat, S.Z.: Time and the patient-physician relationship. J. Gen. Int. Med. **14**(Suppl 1), S34-40 (1999)
Du Preez, R.R., Pickworth, G.E., Van Rooyen, M.: Teaching professionalism: a South African perspective. Med. Teach. **29**(9–10), e284–e291 (2007)
Du, X., Kassab, S.E., Al-Moslih, A.M., Abu-Hijleh, M.F., Hamdy, H., Cyprian, F.S.: Identifying essential competencies for medical students. J. Appl. Res. High. Educ. (2019)
Dyrbye, L.N., Shanafelt, T.D.: Physician burnout: a potential threat to successful health care reform. JAMA **305**, 2009–2010 (2011)
Fletcher, K.E., Visotcky, A.M., Slagle, J.M., Tarima, S., Weinger, M.B., Schapira, M.M.: The composition of intern work while on call. J. Gen. Int. Med. **27**(11), 1432–1437 (2012)
Friedberg, M., Chen, P.G., Van Busum, K.R., Aunon, F., Pham, C., Caloyeras, J., et al.: Factors Affecting Physician Professional Satisfaction and Their Implications for Patient Care, Health Systems and Health Policy. RAND, Santa Monica, CA (2013)
Gabow, P.A., Karkhanis, A., Knight, A., Dixon, P., Eisert, S., Albert, R.K.: Observations of residents' work activities for 24 consecutive hours: implications for workflow redesign. Acad. Med. **81**(8), 766–775 (2006)
Gillanders, W., Heiman, M.: Time study comparisons of 3 intern programs. J. Med. Educ. **46**, 142–149 (1971)
Goldstein, A.M., Blair, A.B., Keswani, S.G., Gosain, A., Morowitz, M., Kuo, J.S., Levine, M., Ahuja, N., Hackam, D.J.: Basic science committee of the society of university surgeons. A roadmap for aspiring surgeon-scientists in today's healthcare environment. Ann. Surg. **269**(1), 66–72 (2019)
Gopal, R., Glasheen, J.J., Miyoshi, T.J., Prochazka, A.V.: Burnout and internal medicine resident work-hour restrictions. Arch. Int. Med. **165**, 2595–2600 (2005)
Gottschalk, A., Flocke, S.A.: Time spent in face-to-face patient care and work outside the examination room. Ann. Fam. Med. **3**(6), 488–493. https://doi.org/10.1370/afm.404. PMID: 16338911; PMCID: PMC1466945. (2005)
Guarisco, S., Oddone, E., Simel, D.: Time analysis of a general medicine service: results from a random work sampling study. J. Gen. Int. Med. **9**(5), 272–277 (1994)
Ho, M.J., Al-Eraky, M.: Professionalism in context: insights from the United Arab Emirates and beyond. J. Grad. Med. Educ. **8**(2), 268–270 (2016)

Hu, Y., Edwards, B.L., Brooks, K.D.: Recent trends in National Institutes of Health funding for surgery: 2003–2013. Am. J. Surg. **209**, 1083–1089 (2015)

Jackson, V.P.: Time management: a realistic approach. J. Am. Coll. Radiol. **6**, 434–436 (2009)

Keswani, S.G., Moles, C.M., Morowitz, M., et al.: The future of basic science in academic surgery: identifying barriers to success for surgeon-scientists. Ann. Surg. **265**, 1053–1059 (2017)

Klemenc-Ketis, Z., Vrecko, H.: Development and validation of a professionalism assessment scale for medical students. Int. J. Med. Educ. **5**, 205–211 (2014)

Lowenstein, S.R.: Tuesdays to write … a guide to time management in academic emergency medicine. Acad. Emerg. Med. **16**, 165–167 (2009)

MacKenzie, C.R.: Professionalism and medicine. HSS J. **3**(2), 222–227 (2007)

Mann, M., Tendulkar, A., Birger, N.: National Institutes of Health funding for surgical research. Ann. Surg. **247**, 217–221 (2008)

McLauchlan, C.: Time management. J Accident Emerg. Med. **14**, 345–346 (1997)

Philip, L.C.: The evolution of corporate social responsibility. Bus. Horiz. 50(6):449–454 (2007)

Poissant, L., Pereira, J., Tamblyn, R., Kawasumi, Y.: The impact of electronic health records on time efficiency of physicians and nurses: a systematic review. J. Am. Med. Inform. Assoc. **12**, 505–516 (2005)

Rangel, S.J., Efron, B., Moss, R.L.: Recent trends in National Institutes of Health funding of surgical research. Ann. Surg. **236**, 277–286 (2002)

Ratanawongsa, N., Barton, J.L., Lyles, C.R., Wu, M., Yelin, E.H., Martinez, D.: Association between clinician computer use and communication with patients in safety-net clinics. JAMA Int. Med. **176**, 125–128 (2016)

Riba, M.B., Riba, A., Riba, E.: Life as a balance beam: practical ideas for balancing work and home. Acad. Psychiatry **31**, 135–137 (2007)

Shanafelt, T.D., Boone, S., Tan, L., Dyrbye, L.N., Sotile, W., Satele, D.: Burnout and satisfaction with work-life balance among US physicians relative to the general US population. Arch. Int. Med. **172**, 1377–1385 (2012)

Shanafelt, T.D., Dyrbye, L.N., Sinsky, C., Hasan, O., Satele, D., Sloan, J.: Relationship between clerical burden and characteristics of the electronic environment with physician burnout and professional satisfaction. Mayo Clin. Proc. **91**, 836–848 (2016)

Sinsky, C., Colligan, L., Li, L., Prgomet, M., Reynolds, S., Goeders, L.: Allocation of physician time in ambulatory practice: a time and motion study in 4 specialties. Ann. Int. Med. **165**, 753–760 (2016)

Taylor, R.: Medical Wisdom and Doctoring: The Art of 21st Century Practice. Springer, New York (2010)

Toledo-Pereyra, L.H.: Nobel Laureate surgeons. J. Invest. Surg. **19**, 211–218 (2006)

Veloski, J., Fields, S., Boex, J., Blank, L.: Measuring professionalism: a review of studies with instruments reported in the literature between 1982 and 2002. Acad. Med. **80**(4), 366–370 (2005)

von Vultée, P.J., Arnetz, B.: The impact of management programs on physicians' work environment and health. J. Health Organ. Manage. **18**(1), 25–37 (2004)

Wachter, R.M.: Annals for hospitalists inpatient notes—hospitalists and digital medicine—overcoming the productivity paradox. Ann. Int. Med. **165**, HO2–HO3 (2016)

Westbrook, J.I., Ampt, A., Kearney, L., Rob, M.I.: All in a day's work: an observational study to quantify how and with whom doctors on hospital wards spend their time. Med. J. Aust. **188**, 506–509 (2008)

Challenges and Controversies Related to IFRS 15 Implementation

Valentin Ioan Usurelu, Adriana Dutescu, and Robin Jarvis

1 Introduction

Modern economies rely on cross-border transactions and the free flow of international capital. More than a third of all financial transactions occurs across borders, and that number is expected to grow. IFRS Standards address this challenge by providing a high quality, internationally recognized set of accounting standards that bring transparency, accountability and efficiency to financial markets around the world.

Engineering & Construction (E&C) entities may need to change their revenue recognition policies and practices as a result of the new revenue recognition standard, IFRS 15 Revenue from Contracts with Customers. The new standard is a result of a joint project issued by the International Accounting Standards Board (the IASB) and the Financial Accounting Standards Board (the FASB) (collectively, the Boards).

While many of the concepts in the new model are consistent with those in current IFRS's conceptual framework and the recognition of revenue from construction contracts in IAS 11, the requirements related to certain elements of E&C contracts will change. In addition, IFRS 15 Revenue recognition from contracts with customers introduces a number of new disclosure requirements that E&C entities will need to evaluate. The most notable change for E&C contracts is that under IAS 11, recognition of revenue and profits on a percentage of completion basis was required where an

V. I. Usurelu (✉) · A. Dutescu
Bucharest University of Economic Studies, Bucharest, Romania
e-mail: valiusurelu@yahoo.com

A. Dutescu
e-mail: adriana.dutescu@ase.ro

R. Jarvis
Brunel University, London, UK
e-mail: robin.jarvis@brunel.ac.uk

A. M. Dima and F. DÁscenzo (eds.), *Business Revolution in a Digital Era*,
Springer Proceedings in Business and Economics,
https://doi.org/10.1007/978-3-030-59972-0_23

Table 1 Size of IFRS 15

	Existing IASs	IAS 11	IAS 18	SIC 31	IFRIC 13,15,18	IFRS 15
Standard	33	11	10	1	11	39
Application guidance	1	–	–	–	1	17
Transition guidance	–	–	–	–	–	2
Amendments to other standards	–	–	–	–	–	26
Illustrative examples	21	4	8	–	9	82
Basis for conclusions	22	–	–	2	20	175
Total Pages	**77**	**15**	**18**	**3**	**41**	**341**

Source Author's own research

arrangement met the definition of a construction contract. Under IFRS 15, progressive revenue recognition will only be permitted where the enforceable contractual rights and obligations satisfy certain criteria. There is no automatic right to recognize revenue on a progressive basis for construction contracts.

Considering the complexity of the approaches resulting from the IFRS 15 standard, a short comparative analysis is performed on the content (number of pages) in order to illustrate that the new standard brings in a technical perspective many guidelines, many illustrative examples for the final product to contain as few inconsistencies as possible.

In our country, Romania, only listed companies are required to adopt IFRS standards for individual annual financial statements, according to the Order of the Ministry of Public Finance 2844/2016, Order of the Ministry of Public Finance 881/2012 and the Order of the National Bank of Romania 8/2019.

Following the worldwide trend of applying IFRS 15, Romanian companies should be encouraged to adopt the provisions of the new standard on a voluntary basis in order to generate a unified practice and a consolidated accounting at global level.

Our analysis wants to determine the implications that IFRS 15 has on constructions entities. There are critical judgements at contract inception and also during the contract life cycle.

2 Literature Review

The seven wave's convergence agenda of Norwalk's developed high quality, compatible standards revenues recognition included. This topic was one of the latest under the spot light, due to the importance of revenues recognition on performance models and investor's decisions, not to speak about the revenues susceptibility of manipulation. The outcome was the creation of new, common, enhanced standard, rather than removing the differences from the existent standards on both jurisdictions. (Duțescu and Ușurelu 2018).

Board members of the IASB believe "that the approach to revenue recognition that we have developed will provide a more consistent basis for reporting revenue and produce accounting that more closely matches the underlying economics of transactions" (Cooper 2010).

Nevertheless, the devil is in details. Weaknesses and inconsistencies in the existing revenue guidance often lead to different accounting effects for economically similar transactions. With revenue as the "top line" matrix and its importance in supporting material decisions, the issuance of IFRS 15 is a significant milestone in financial reporting.

To better understand and correctly apply the principles presented in IFRS 15, all relevant transactions will be subject of professional judgement and depend on consistent application of the principles for similar transactions. A previous research predicted that the IFRS 15s effects on the amount and timing of revenue recognition will differ depending on the type of company, the transaction, the sector (industry) and the jurisdiction (McConnell 2014). In few other cases, there will be no change to the amount and timing of revenue recognition. In other cases, there will be changes and those changes could be significant, such as the termism and volatility of revenue recognition (Grigoroi 2017).

Analysis of the revenue's trend is relevant for past performance assessment, as well as for predicting future revenue and cash flows (Knorová 2016). In some cases, revenue is preferred due to its more steady and consistent character, rather than expenses or earnings and its usage in evaluating the firms with losses (Wagenhofer 2014).

In general, countries which have chosen a standard by standard implementation. Method demonstrate an improvement in the relevance of accounting information (Ouezzani and Alami 2014). Furthermore, techniques and models used by researchers in analyzing the effect of IFRS adoption on accounting quality would influence the findings. (Koch et al. 2014).

Peters presented the challenges of transition to IFRS 15 as an opportunity for the investors to understand the underlying business, the quality of the earnings and the relationship of the company with its customers. More than that, Peters suggested that investors should formulate some expectations regarding the new amounts generated by the standard implementation and if these expectations are not met or properly disclosed in the financial statements, to require clarifications from company's executives (Peters 2018).

The most notable change for construction contracts is that under IAS 11, the recognition of revenues and profits was performed on a percentage of completion basis that was required where an arrangement met the definition of a construction contract. Under IFRS 15, progressive revenue recognition will only be permitted where the enforceable contractual rights and obligations satisfy certain criteria. There is no automatic right to recognize revenue on a progressive basis for construction contracts.

Also, IAS 11 prescribed how to account for foreseeable contract losses. This guidance is not contained in IFRS 15 and accordingly loss-making projects are now accounted for as 'onerous' contracts under IAS 37 Provisions, Contingent Liabilities and Contingent Assets. This change could have an impact when losses from loss-making projects are recognized and, on the way, these are measured. (KPMG 2014).

The construction industry has lost its contract accounting 'rule book'. The updated IFRS 15 guidance is likely to introduce considerable professional judgments in the accounting systems of construction companies, due to the specific nature of construction contracts.

3 Methodology

The objectives of this article are to analyze the accounting, fiscal and legal patterns and implications resulting from the application of IFRS 15 by E&C entities.

Starting from the previsions IFRS's requirements, from the opinions and studies carried out by researchers in this particular areas, practical examples regarding the difficulties encountered by E&C entities in the process of implementing and the resulting economic aspects, we have decided to use the content analysis method, applied to the relevant literature and cases. We were seeking the answers to the following research questions, based on the contractual period:

1. What costs should be capitalized during the bid process?
2. Can construction accounting be done at the contract level?
3. When does a contract generate revenue?
4. What costs of fulfilling a contract can be capitalized?
5. How should a contractor measure the contract's progress?
6. What strategy should be applied in the construction industry in relation to pricing?
7. What are the implications of variations and contractual complaints under the accounting system?
8. Does IFRS 15 provide specific guidance on loss-making contracts?

Limitations: The comparability between the states was not covered in this study, nor were the differences between IFRS 15 and ASC 606, as the access to accounting information regarding construction companies was restricted. However, this theme can be used for any future research.

4 Results and Discussions

Comparison of the Previous and Actual standard's Requirements, Conceptual Framework, Amendments, Clarifications, and Examples.

Entities in the construction industry have historically implemented their own accounting policy (based upon IAS 11 Building Contracts), which included specific rules on the recognition of construction contract earned. Now the new standard has been replaced by IFRS 15 Revenue from Contracts with Customers that requires a new set of policies. The direct outcome of this will be in form of additional complexities for accountants, for managers, owners, investors, and other accounting information users.

Investors should take the time to understand IFRS 15, consider how it applies to the companies, and to be able to follow and analyze the disclosures that those companies will provide.

Compared with existing guidance, the disclosure requirements of IFRS 15 are clear, therefore we seek to determine the impact of applying this guidance, in order to enhance the relevance of the information.

4.1 The First Set of Questions Relate to the Topic of Critical Judgements at Contract Inception. Pre-contract Costs.

Question 1: What costs should be capitalized during the bid process?

Incremental costs of obtaining a contract are costs that are incurred only as a result of winning a contract (e.g. a sale commission). This focus on purely incremental cost that exists in current IFRS; however, it is a new approach in contract accounting.

Under the legacy of IAS 11 it was not just these costs that are incremental, but a wide range of other pre-contract costs were permitted to be capitalized, when the contract will probably be obtained.

The new standard permits the capitalization of only the incremental costs of contract and contract fulfilment costs when these categories of costs are expected to be recuperated. Otherwise in the case of not meeting these criteria the costs are expensed as incurred.

Although it appears that there is no significantly differentiation between 'probable' term and 'expected to be recovered' formulation, the tests required by the incremental costs criteria may impact the profit timing report and subsequently unify the practice and generate a more consistent accounting disclosure.

Next question is in the parameter of the contract performance obligations:

Question 2: Can construction accounting be done at the contract level?

IFRS 15 includes additional guidance to help determine whether these criteria are met. Indicators that a performance obligation is separately identifiable include the following (IFRS 15, paragraph 29):

- the entity does not provide a significant service of integrating the good or service with other goods or services promised in the contract;
- the good or service does not significantly modify or customize another good or service promised in the contract; or

- the good or service is not highly dependent on, or highly inter-related with, other goods or services promised in the contract.

Entities will have to exercise their judgment and report their conclusion that the various elements of the construction contract are strongly interrelated and that a comprehensive implementation function is undertaken to account for the contract as a single performance obligation. If the company is unable to demonstrate the interrelationship between the components, it may need to recognize revenue from numerous performance obligations.

Next topic relates to the way revenues should be disclosed: over time or at a point in time?

Question 3: when does a contract recognize revenue?

An entity recognizes revenue over time if one or more of the following criteria are met (IFRS 15, paragraph 35):

- the customer simultaneously receives and consumes the benefits provided by the entity's performance as the entity performs (routine or recurring services);
- the entity's performance creates or enhances an asset that the customer controls as the asset is created or enhanced (building an asset on a customer's site);
- the entity's performance does not create an asset with an alternative use to the entity and the entity has an enforceable right to payment for performance completed to date(Building a specialized asset that only the customer can use, or building an asset to a customer order).

Impact of revenue recognition at a point in time.

While there is no automatic right to progressive revenue recognition, over time performance obligations to provide construction services should usually be satisfied. As they are created or improved, customers also control the assets.

Therefore, suppliers will often have contractual and realistic restrictions on the transition of property to another company and will be entitled to receive costs incurred and a reasonable profit margin from the customer if the customer cancels the contract for reasons other than the no-performance of the organization. Of transactions currently accounted for using the completion method level, management will need to review contracts against the new criteria to determine if revenue should be recognized over time or at a point in time. If the contract agreements do not require revenue to be slowly recognized, instead revenue is recognized on the change of ownership at a specific point in time, which is likely to be close to completion for a building project. Entities should understand the nature of their construction contracts and the potential impact that may have on the identification of revenue and profit.

4.2 Critical Judgements During the Contract Lifecycle - Contract Costs Are the Following Topic:

Question 4: What costs of fulfilling a contract can be capitalized?

Both IAS 11 and IFRS 15 offer guidelines on costs that are expensed; however, the details of the guidance's framework differ. Contractors should consider the guidance fulfilment costs when deciding whether to capitalize on costs.

Question 5 relates to the contract progress:

5. *How should a contractor measure contract progress?*

For each obligation performed over time, an entity implements a single method of measuring the progress and extends the approach continuously with similar performance obligations and in similar circumstances.

While the available methods for assessing the amount of work done to date and the revenue to be recognized under IFRS 15 do not seem to vary, the company should decide whether an input or output system adequately describes the performance under the contract. Many companies will therefore need to adjust strategies for measuring progress under IFRS 15, resulting in either a deferment or acceleration in revenue and profit compared to current practice.

How to measure revenue: variable consideration

Question 6. What strategy should be applied in the construction industry in relation to pricing?

An entity uses one of the following methods to estimate the total variable contract price to determine the amount of consideration that it claims to be entitled to (IFRS 5, paragraph 53):

- the expected value—the sum of probability-weighted amounts in a range of possible consideration amounts; or
- the most likely amount—the single most likely outcome of the contract (which may be more appropriate if the transaction amount only has two possible outcomes, e.g. when there is a success fee that either will or will not be receivable).

Constraining the amount of revenue recognized—Factors indicating that including an estimate of variable consideration in the transaction price could result in a significant revenue reversal include, but are not limited to, the following:

- the amount of consideration is highly susceptible to factors outside the influence of the entity (for example, the judgement of third parties);
- the uncertainty about the amount of consideration is not expected to be resolved for a long period of time;
- the entity has a practice of either offering a broad range of price concessions or changing the payment terms and conditions of similar contracts in similar circumstances;
- the entity's experience with similar types of contracts is limited or has limited predictive value; or
- the contract has a large number and high variability of possible consideration amounts.

Contract modifications

Question 7: What are the implications of variations and contractual complaints under the accounting system?

The requirement for IFRS 15 to approve a contract modification does not appear to include explicit guidance as in IAS 11. This new requirement may result in revenue from contract modifications being recognized later under IFRS 15 than would have been the case under IAS 11. The requirement adjustment illustrates the standard's general approach that an entity accounts for enforceable rights and obligations resulting from contracts. In many cases, a change in scope may be approved, but the change in price may not. In these situations, revenue measurement will be governed by the variable consideration guidelines.

Loss-making contracts

Question 8: Does ifrs 15 provide specific guidance on loss-making contracts?

Under IAS 37, when defining onerous contracts and calculating the necessary clause, an individual recognizes only the 'unavoidable costs' of performing an obligation. IAS 37 does not clarify what' unavoidable costs' actually meant. Whether the IASB expects a shift of accounting of loss-making construction contracts and whether it assumes the expected costs of meeting a duty are equal to contract costs under IAS 11 is uncertain.

For example, construction entities with full-time employees may not be required to include these staff costs in the calculation of an onerous contract; however, construction entities employing subcontractors to fulfil duties may be required to include these costs in their estimates. Costs that are not deemed foreseeable are billed as incurred because they are assumed to be the costs of the company. The distinction between what it is and it is not considered inevitable can have a significant impact on whether a contract is considered onerous and how it is measured as a contract loss.

4.3 Evaluation of Changes that Occurred in the First year of Mandatory Implementation of the New Standard

We have addressed also the challenges and controversy that may occurred in the first year of IFRS 15s mandatory implementation and we focused on one of the most important construction corporate groups in European Union: Actividades de Construccion Y Servicios (ACS), Porr and Strabag. These corporations, that according to the specific requirements, report based on the new standard from 01 January 2018, 2017 being the last period under the superseded standards.

ACS, and Strabag are part of the Top 10 most important construction companies in Europe, with ACS occupying second place and Strabag 6th place, in an article published by KHL.com. According to letsbuild.com, Porr is one of the most important construction company in Austria.

The data used in this study have been extracted from the annual financial statements of each company on their official website.

It is expected that the adoption of IFRS 15 to significantly affect the measurement of key performance indicators for companies. Table 2 shows the effect of the adoption of IFRS 15 on revenue, costs, and net profit for the fiscal year 2018.

Table 2 Changes generated in the first year of the new revenue recognition standard mandatory implementation

Key financial and accounting numbers for corporate group (TEUR)				
		ACS	Porr	Strabag
Revenue	2017	34,898,213.00	4,292,886.00	13,508,725.00
	2018	36,658,516.00	4,959,109.00	15,221,832.00
	Change (%)	**5.04%**	**15.52%**	**12.68%**
Gross profit	2017	1,416,674.00	90,219.00	448,357.00
	2018	1,650,480.00	92,324.00	558,215.00
	Change (%)	**16.50%**	**2.28%**	**24.50%**
Margin (%)	2017	4.06%	2.10%	3.32%
	2018	4.50%	1.86%	3.67%
	Change (%)	**10.91%**	**−11.41%**	**10.49%**
Net profit (loss)	2017	802,010.00	63,691.00	292,364.00
	2018	915,021.00	66,195.00	362,784.00
	Change (%)	**14.09%**	**3.93%**	**24.09%**
Margin (%)	2017	2.30%	1.48%	2.16%
	2018	2.50%	1.33%	2.38%
	Change (%)	**8.61%**	**−10.03%**	**10.12%**
Cash flow	2017	6,319,318.00	358,707.00	2,789,687.00
	2018	6,966,457.00	319,674.00	2,384,343.00
	Change (%)	**10.24%**	**−10.88%**	**−14.53%**
Equity	2017	5,164,029.00	551,166.00	3,397,719.00
	2018	6,055,705.00	571,646.00	3,653,773.00
	Change (%)	**17.27%**	**3.72%**	**7.54%**
Assets	2017	31,339,475.00	2,884,790.00	11,054,123.00
	2018	34,295,358.00	3,114,736.00	11,621,448.00
	Change (%)	**9.43%**	**7.97%**	**5.13%**
Earnings per share	2017	2.27	2.09	2.72
	2018	2.94	2.17	3.45
	Change (%)	**29.52%**	**3.83%**	**26.84%**

Source Author's own research

In general, results indicate a significant increase in gross profit, and net profit. Applying the IFRS 15 seems to signal that the entity is disclosing high-quality accounting information which is important and crucial to the development of listed firms.

This overall increase could be explained by revenue increase and/or costs decrease. That is, IFRS 15 allows the "over time recognition" of revenue in certain situations. For example, ACS, PORR and STRABAG performance obligations are met over time, and not at one specific time, since the client simultaneously receives and consumes the benefits provided by the performance of the entity as the service is provided.

An increase in the gross profit and therefore in the net income, would.

be explained by a decrease in costs as measured by the new guidance of IFRS 15. In the ACS Group, income is recognized, as a general rule, according to the "Output Method," which corresponds to the measurement of the work executed through the valued ratio or "valued unit of work," by which the recognized revenue corresponds to the work units executed according to the price assigned to them, in accordance with that established under IFRS 15, which replaces IAS 11.

In the project development business, the first-time adoption of IFRS 15 results in changes to the point in time when revenue is recognized. IFRS 15 requires revenue to be recognized over time if a contractual agreement excludes the possibility of any alternative use and there exists a right to payment including profit margin on the work performed. These conditions are always met if real estate projects are sold already prior to their completion.

In 2018 the consolidated revenue of the ACS Group climbed by EUR 1.760.3 m, to EUR 36,658.5 m. In accordance with the table above, the rise in revenue was 5.04%. Total revenue from the Services area amounted to EUR 98,101 thousand, relating to international operations in 2018 and EUR 84,535 thousand in 2017, representing 6.5% and 5.8% respectively. Contract durations varies depending on the different areas of activity, with the average duration of contracts for construction activities ranging between 1 and 5 yr, maintenance construction and services up to 10 yr, and the construction and operation of concessions up to 30 yr. The gross profit increased by 16.50% to € 1.650.4 Mio., which corresponds to an EBIT margin of 4.50% after 4.06% in 2017. As of 31 December 2018, the ACS Group's assets stood at EUR 34,295.3 m and thereby rose by 9,43% against the previous year as the result of the increase in revenue and the acquisition.

In 2018 the consolidated revenue of the PORR Group climbed by EUR 666.2 m to EUR 4959.1 m. The rise in revenue of 15.52% was slower than the increase in production output as there was a disproportionately strong rise in output from consortiums. The PORR Group's other operating income increased more slowly than revenue, climbing by 7.6% to EUR 183.9 m. In comparison to 2017 this contained higher charges passed on to associates—especially for projects in Qatar—as well as income from the sale of assets. A counter effect to this increase came from the decline in other operating expenses, which in 2017 included damages received in the course of realizing construction contracts, as is common in the industry. The gross profit increased by 2.28% to € 92.32 Mio., which corresponds to an EBIT margin of 2.10% after 1,86% in 2017. As of 31 December 2018, the PORR Group's assets stood at EUR 3114.7 m and thereby rose by 7.97% against the previous year as the result of the increase in revenue and the acquisition.

The consolidated group revenue for the Strabag 2018 financial year amounted to € 15,221.83 Mio.. This corresponds to a plus of 12.68%—similar to the output volume. The ratio of revenue to output increased slightly to 93% after spending several years at 92%. The gross profit increased by 24.50% to € 558.21 Mio., which corresponds to an EBIT margin of 3.67% after 3.32% in 2017. Even when adjusted for the non-operating step-up profit, the EBIT grew by 12% with an EBIT margin of 3.32%. The earnings improvement is attributable to the International + Special Divisions segment. The property and facility services and real estate development businesses continued to make very positive contributions to the earnings, while burdens from large, loss-making projects in the international area were absent.

As of 31 December 2018, the PORR Group's assets stood at EUR 11,621.4 m and thereby rose by 5.13% against the previous year as the result of the increase in revenue and the acquisition.

5 Conclusion

Construction industry must now pay attention to the new standard on revenue recognition. We believe that the complex nature of its model-business and contracts generate exceedingly difficulties applying for the construction industry. It is much more complex than the legacy accounting standard and can change the income recognition pattern and profit pattern for construction industry significantly.

Many challenges exist when revenue transactions are recorded under the new standard, related to when, whether and how to recognize it, taking into account that entities need to assure that all facts included in one particular transaction are known and have been analyzed.

While revenue recognition is retained under IFRS 15, similar to the completion stage of accounting under IAS 11, the criteria for achieving this outcome have changed. Contractors will have to consider their contractual terms in order to assess whether they can continue to recognize revenue over time, as failure to do so may result in significant revenue delays.

There are also changes in the revenue calculation involving a portion of a variable consideration or a contract modification compared to IAS 11 which can affect the recognition and timing of revenues. The devil really is in the detail.

With the help of the relevant literature, we have tried to set out the main objectives of the program for establishing convergence standards and to look for the most important opportunities and challenges that it has brought within the companies in the construction industry. We hope that our findings would shape the research perspectives in order to achieve a better understanding of the impact of IFRS 15.

We have investigated, in our research, the way IFRS 15 changes various business patterns and financial information disclosure within the annual report, specifically in the real estate sector. Same patterns were withdrawn from the analysis, based upon the construction sector: e.g. operating revenues are improving, alongside with specific costs incremental: the new pattern of the financial statements' disclosure, specifically on the income statement side and explanatory notes, is more complex and comprehensive. The capitalized cost of the biding process are more adequately analyzed during the process, the revenue recognition becomes a more consistent and unbiased process, the assessment of the progress of the contract will requiring a more business model oriented approach and professional judgment on pricing will be affected accordingly. Loss making contracts are still unsolved and under the close scrutiny.

The construction sector (real estate) was one of the most impacted area by the enforcement in global financial reporting convergence of IASB-IFRS 15 and FASB. If we link this impact with the effects of the COVID 19 crisis, the outcome is not too encouraging (statistics show that the real estate investments had declined by 5% just during the first quarter of 2020, being the first quarter of drop in 11 yr).

The topic of our research offers a different perspective on how IFRS 15 application should be looked at, from the perspective of construction sector (real estate). The limitations of our research are based upon the small number of tested companies within the sector and the COVID 19s impact, that we have not taken into consideration when starting the research investigation. Further investigation will scrutinize all these aspects, considered crucial in the further sustainability and development of the sector.

We think our research provides a value-added practical contribution to the literature concerning the IFRS 15s implementation, being aware of its limitations and potential.

References

Cooper, S.: Revenue recognition and your mobile phone. Retrieved from https://www.ifrs.org (2010)

Duțescu, Ușurelu.: The seventh wave of Norwalk Agreement's convergence Roadmap (2018)

Dutescu, A.: Accouting Information and Capital Markets. Editura Eonomica, Bibliotaca de contabilitate, Bucharest (2000)

Grigoroi, L.: Revenue from contracts with customers: Key aspects of IFRS 15. Jurnal ECONOMICA No. 4 (102). Retrieved from https://oaji.net/articles/2017/1425-1519732377.pdf (2017)

IASB: The Conceptual Framework for Financial. IFRS Foundation, London (2010)

IFRS Foundation. (n.d.). The Norwalk Agreement. Retrieved from https://archive.ifrs.org: https://archive.ifrs.org/Use-around-the-world/Global%20convergence/Convergence-with-US-GAAP/Documents/Norwalk_agreement.pdf

Knorová, K.: Do Czech companies disclose revenue in accordance with IFRS requirements? Euro Fin Account J 69–84 (2016). Retrieved from https://hdl.handle.net/10419/187745

Koch, C., Nilsson, O., Jansson, A.: An empirical study of the method effect in analysing the adoption of IFRS. Account Fin Res **3**(2) (2014)

KPMG.: kpmg.com/ifrs/, Impact on the construction industry of the new revenue standard (2014)

McConnell, P.: Revenue Recognition: Finally, a Standard Approach for all. Retrieved from https://www.ifrs.org (2014)

Ouezzani, Alami.: The effects of various choices of IFRS implementation on the relevance of accounting information. Account Fin Res **3**(2 (2014)

Peters, J.: Revenue Recognition: Top 10 Questions Investors Should Ask About the Adoption of The New Standard. Retrieved from https://www.cfainstitute.org/en/advocacy/policy-positions/revenue-recognition-top-10-questions-investors-should-ask-about-the-adoption-of-the-new-standard (2018)

Wagenhofer, A.: The role of revenue recognition in performance reporting. Account Bus Res **4**, 349–379 (2014). Retrieved from https://www.icaew.com/-/media/corporate/files/events/2013/regions/london/alfred-wagenhofer-ifbm-recognition.ashx

International Accounting Standards Board [IASB].: IFRS 15 Revenue from Contracts with Customers 2014)
International Accounting Standards Board [IASB].: IAS 11 Construction Contracts (1993)
International Accounting Standards Board [IASB].: IAS 18 Revenue Recognition (1993)
https://www.letsbuild.com/blog/biggest-construction-companies-in-europe. Last Accessed 20 May 2019
https://www.grupoacs.com/shareholders-investors/annual-report/. Last Accessed 20 May 2019
https://porr-group.com/en/investor-relations/reporting/group-reports/. Last Accessed 20 May 2019
https://www.strabag.com/databases/internet/_public/content.nsf/web/EN-STRABAG.COM-GB.html. Last Accessed 20 May 2019
https://www.khl.com/construction-europe/top-10-european-construction-companies-2019/139997.article. Last Accessed 20 May 2019

The Optimal Definition of an Institution Using Analytic Hierarchy Process

Andrei Răduțu

1 Introduction

The hypermarkets and supermarkets' market is considered to be one of the most important and attractive in Romania, the big players competing in 2018 for a slice, as big as possible from the 89 billion RON (Economica.net 2019). The modern food trade in Romania, currently known today by means of this market, started in 1995, when the big players opened their first stores and expanding progressively since then.

This market is represented by dynamism, evolving continuously through the development and expansion of the big players networks in the market throughout the country, respectively through purchases and products and services' continuous improvement, offered to consumers. As the analysis focuses on certain key aspects, it can be said that the role of hypermarkets and supermarkets has undoubtedly become an essential one in Romania, these now managing to become the alternative of products supply for about 83.6% of Romania's population, according to a study made by Revista Progresiv in 2015. The same research also underlines the fact that two thirds of the consumers consider that Romanian food products have a higher quality than those from abroad. Taking this into account, as well as the regulations imposed by the Romanian authorities in 2016 (Law 150/2016), according to which 51% of the total area dedicated for the sale of certain categories of food products should be made by a supply chain constituted by local producers, the payment term to the suppliers not being longer than 30 days, according to the negotiated contract and even 7 calendar days for fresh food products and the elimination of the shelf charges, the hypermarkets and supermarkets focused on establishing partnerships with farmers, local producers, and agri-food companies.

A. Răduțu (✉)
The Bucharest University of Economic Studies, 010731 Bucharest, Romania
e-mail: radutuandrei@yahoo.com

A. M. Dima and F. DÁscenzo (eds.), *Business Revolution in a Digital Era*,
Springer Proceedings in Business and Economics,
https://doi.org/10.1007/978-3-030-59972-0_24

In 2017, according to the "Retailer Scorecard" report, which represents the first such in-depth study concerning the Romanian retail market in terms of the environmental performance of the product portfolio of the most important retailers, WWF Romania analyzed in 2016, a series of indicators involving the sustainability policies implemented, as well as the certified or local products available for sale to final consumers. The study involved the main chains of hypermarkets and supermarkets in Romania, only 5 of the 11 retailers obtaining a score of over 50%.

Analyzing the regulations and conclusions of the aforementioned study, as well as the challenges of the agricultural field, the lack of a vision with clear and coherent objectives, of an implementation plan, of leadership abilities and working teams to put it into practice, the economic context, the poorly developed infrastructure, the rather deficient relationships between customers and local suppliers, respectively the needs existing in the market, hypermarkets have felt the need for an optimal way by which these dimensions could be developed and correlated as an activity which to be advantageous for every stakeholder.

Thus, the establishment of the Regional Agricultural Centers, as optimally defined agricultural institutions, that will sustainably fulfill a series of necessary functions, represents a proposal of the large chains of hypermarkets and supermarkets, designed to successfully overcome the obstacles encountered so far. The integration of multicriteria decision-making methods, as well as the methods and techniques of continuous improvement—KAIZEN™, constitute the foundation of a sustainable management system, which is advantageous for every stakeholder, and which leads to the optimal development of the agricultural field.

2 Literature Review

The specialized literature illustrates a series of good practices regarding the approaches and initiatives of optimally defining and functioning of the different types of economic institutions or organizations meant to facilitate the good organization and development of the agricultural field, through the use of multicriteria decision-making methods (MCDM).

Starting from the need of optimum definition of an agricultural institution, which to be integrated into the economic and social environment, thus contributing to the development of the agri-food market in the context of the implementation of the Common Agricultural Policy, Popescu (2014) stresses the importance of cooperation and association in agriculture, especially considering the experiences of Romania within different political regimes. Popescu and Agapie (2015) analyze how an optimally defined institution in the agricultural field should be realized, starting from the improvement opportunities that this field has in Romania, such as the lack of an infrastructure, which to serve as smooth functioning of the flows, property rights, market integration and use of the existing know-how of each major category of experts in the field. Having the help of experts in the field, by using an AHP decision model, the authors defined and evaluated the main risks that these institutions (called

"Agricultural Chambers") may have, also emphasizing the essential way in which the local knowledge transfer should be realized, in the vision of reaching the common goal.

In the context of the agricultural field development in Romania, Răduțu and Pop (2018) introduced for the first time the connection between the risks associated with the management functions and the financial risk, two of the most important topics for any entity that wishes to achieve performance. Thus, from the perspective of an optimal institution, having the objective of well-functioning, the approach of implementing various financing projects, while also having sustainable decision-making processes, the authors illustrated the connections between these risks, as well as the recommendations necessary to reduce them through an ANP decision model, having as input the experts and managers of a company that wants to implement a EU financed project.

Parra-Lopez et al. (2008) use ANP to create a decision model for identifying the answers regarding the functions that the agricultural field should have according to the general public opinion, how they could be useful to the population and especially how the public preferences could be integrated in the performance evaluation of the agricultural sector in the Netherlands. A similar approach has been performed in Spain, for bringing together the economic, social and environmental functions of the agricultural sector. In this concern, Kallas et al. created an AHP model in (2007) to investigate whether the population is considering the implementation of a multifunctional agriculture.

A very good initiative can be noticed regarding the research and analysis of the public decision-making processes in agriculture from Chile performed by Braunschweig et al. (2001). Following also the premises of an optimal institution definition, the authors identify and elaborate the most important criteria and alternatives in this concern, starting from the national agricultural development objectives and continuing with the specific ones such as availability and resource allocation, clients' needs, research alternatives, as well as the time frame planning which should be needed for implementation.

Regarding the activities or functions similar to those to be described by the AHP hybrid decision-making model for Regional Agricultural Centers, Adeyeye et al. (2019) are studying how the educational, training and research component of the "Agricultural Services and Training Center" from Plateau State should be developed using new media tools (e.g. phones, tablets and other tools designed to facilitate interaction with the user) for carrying out their activity. The educational and research function was also studied by Souza and Gomez (2015), who wanted to identify a series of performance indicators, meant to support sustainable decision-making in the agricultural field in Brazil, through the "Agricultural Research Centers". Their analysis was approached through the involvement of 37 such centers, defining a series of input variables (for example: operational costs, labor force and capital costs), as well as the result variables, these being aggregated through non-parametric multi-variable analysis. This study contributed to facilitating the knowledge and technology transfer within the agricultural field and implicitly to research increase, by carrying out more scientific articles in this regard.

Adding also the component of sustainable management system performance of continuous improvement—KAIZEN™ (which is translated as "change for the better" or "continuous improvement"), one of the best practices took place in Portugal, where the company Sonae MC, started such an initiative in 2007 (Imai 2012; de Campos, 2016). After a preliminary visit, the needs expressed by the management team, aligned with the diagnostic analysis performed, constituted the foundation for a continuous improvement project, in collaboration with Kaizen Institute. The program started with fundamental activities regarding the optimum designing of workplace in the warehouse area, by raising awareness regarding the differences between value-added activities versus those containing waste (Muda). Next, the "5S" method has led the change management way in order to exploit the opportunities for improvement in clear objectives, whereby each object has its place well-defined, in such a way in which the search time is minimal, while the storage space is well-organized. If the application of these methods had an immediate effect on increasing the employees' motivation, as they were empowered to optimally define their workplace and workspace, another component of the KAIZEN™ implementation within Sonae MC supermarkets was the expansion of the best practices and continuous improvement principles to other stores of the company, from all over the country (Imai 2012; de Campos 2016).

Through these best practices sharing and the analysis performed by each location separately, the stores started to consistently apply the fundamental methods, in the quest of obtaining good results and benefits. Through this project, several significant objectives within this field were also achieved, such as increasing safety, decreasing the inventories, which had positively influenced the company's profitability indicators (Imai 2012; de Campos 2016).

Among the results and benefits obtained by implementing the KAIZEN™ methods and techniques there can be mentioned: high degree of motivation and employees involvement, simplification of operations of any kind, eliminating unnecessary time and implicitly increasing the productivity of employees, quality and customer satisfaction, as well as positive results of economic performance indicators (turnover, profitability, etc.).

3 Methodology

The American professor Thomas L. Saaty addressed the issue of a sustainable way of taking decision by creating the multi-criteria measurement theories, described by Analytic Hierarchy Process (AHP) and Analytic Network Process (ANP). These methodologies, which were developed more than fifty years ago, have been successfully applied during the time he worked as chief researcher at the Pentagon, in order to identify various solutions of high complexity to the problems of national defense and security.

In his approach, he designed applications in practically every field of activity, with a special interest in economics, social sciences and research regarding their effect on human values. Saaty and Vargas (2001) consider that, by applying these two techniques, the decision-makers receive a sustainable help regarding the decision-making process, they are organizing their thoughts better and, finally, they become more prone to what they represent. The advantages of this approach are significant and can lead to relevant expansions and developments. Since the introduction of these methods and until the present moment, various such applications have been developed around the world and many companies have implemented them for developing expert decision systems. Also, the interest for these methodologies is also increased among researchers from all fields (for example: economics, physics, mathematics, agriculture, etc.), they succeeding in developing applications for identifying answers to a series of high complexity and sensibility concepts.

Professor Saaty's multicriteria decision-making methods could be perceived as having several components. Although usually in econometric analysis, criteria and alternatives can be compared in monetary units, there are certain parameters that cannot be compared and evaluated in a relevant way, because of their tangible and intangible character. The AHP and ANP theories have a relevant scale with nine intensities of preference that manage to solve this difficulty, with the purpose of identifying the comparative importance of specific alternatives (Table 1). The tangible elements are considered by the authors as part of the objective reality (having rather a measurable character), whereas the intangible (or more difficult to measure) elements take into account the aspects that characterize a person (values, opinions, beliefs or feelings), which can be attributed to more subjective concepts (Saaty and Vargas 2001).

The main elements that constitute an analytic hierarchy process or an analytic network process model are the clusters (the group), the nodes (the specific item, part of a cluster) and the specific connections. Each model is evaluated by the decision makers, who are expressing the intensities of preference, by comparison, and implicitly, by quantifying these intensities using the numerical scale described in Table 1. The fundamental element in the construction of any model, whether in the form of hierarchy or network, is the node. This is a concept, similar to the point of a graph, that identifies a tangible or intangible aspect, which is relevant and significant for taking a decision or reaching an objective. Several nodes, which share an affinity, that could conceptually influence the decision-making process, form a cluster. Between nodes, influence relations can be also defined and illustrated, determining exactly which node will have an influence (source), and which are the nodes on which the source node will have an impact, and which will be connected with them. By determining these connections, the preferences and the evaluation of their intensity are judged by the decision maker, by considering the perspective of the source node and it is evaluated on a linguistic scale. This is subsequently correlated with the steps in Saaty's fundamental scale, and comparative preferences are noted in a decision matrix, which includes various specific mathematical principles and properties.

Following the assessments of experts' preference intensities, the priority vectors of the decision matrix are computed. Priority vectors are subsequently introduced and synthetized into other matrix-type structures, which are processed like stochastic matrixes. Considering the notions defined above, the logical procedure for obtaining

Table 1 Saaty fundamental scale

Value of perceived importance	Definition	Interpretation
1	Equal importance	Equally perceived importance between two elements
2	Weak importance	
3	Moderate importance	Slightly perceived importance for one activity over the other
4	Moderate plus importance	
5	Strong importance	Strongly perceived importance for one activity due to the experience and judgement
6	Strong plus importance	
7	Very strong or demonstrated importance	Very strong importance for one activity over the other, its dominating trait being observable in practice
8	Very, very strong importance	
9	Extreme importance	The evidence is favoring one activity over another with the highest possible order of affirmation
Reciprocals from above	If the activity i has one of the above non-zero numbers assigned to it when compared with activity j, then j has the reciprocal value when compared with i	A reasonable and logic assumption
Value of perceived importance	Definition	Interpretation

Source Saaty and Vargas (2006)

an adequate answer to a problem or decision purpose, as explained by the founders of the method, is represented by defining and organizing it in a logical structure. With AHP, one can take this specific problem and break it down, using a top-down approach (in the form of a hierarchy), while by ANP, the reverse effects can be studied through a network. Professor Saaty states that the classical way of creating such a hierarchy or network is represented by its organization in a model with at least three clusters (Fig. 1).

As previously described, the establishment of the Regional Agricultural Centers is represented by the proposal of the main chains of hypermarkets and supermarkets from Romania, in order to fulfill a series of functions and needs within the market, which are currently missing, such as the harmonization of the supply chains, a sustainable retail market for local producers, a supply market for the retail area and agri-food companies, a supply market with quality Romanian products for any person, etc. In this regard, an interview was conducted through a focus group, which brought together the management teams of the main chains of hypermarkets and

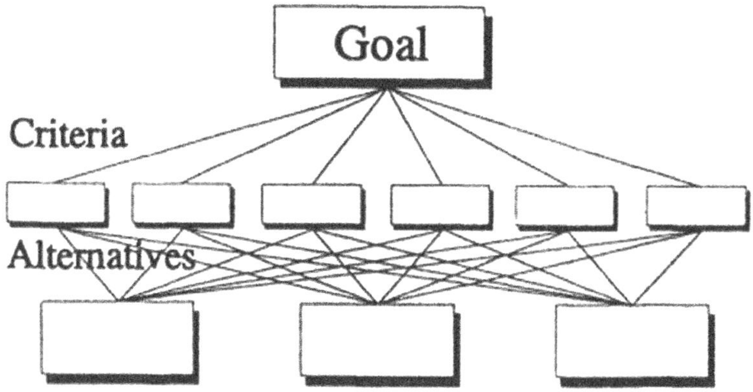

Fig. 1 A model with three clusters. 2001 *Source* Saaty and Vargas

supermarkets from Romania, through which this objective was debated. Using the expertise of each present member, each element that could influence the creation of such an optimal institution, called "Regional Agricultural Centers", was written using the multicriteria decision-making methodologies, on a large "whiteboard". These elements (nodes) became the gross fundament of what will be called the AHP hybrid decision-making model of the Regional Agricultural Centers. Through the following steps, each of these elements were debated and agreed, while those considered unnecessary were eliminated, the next step consisting, according to the multicriteria decision-making methodology, in defining the clusters by associating the nodes that have common affinities, as well as connections between these nodes. This AHP conceptual model has become a hybrid one because it illustrates a series of properties that belong to a hierarchy, having the decisional objective of optimally defining such an institution in the agricultural field, criteria, sub-criteria (which are influenced by the decision objective), as well as alternatives (the functions that the Regional Agricultural Centers should perform), but also elements related to a network, as the alternatives also influence, at their turn, a series of criteria.

After this stage of model definition and agreement was completed, the next one was represented by the individual evaluation of the model by two top management representatives (for example: general managers, operational managers, supply managers, human resources managers, etc.) for each of the main chains of hypermarkets and supermarkets, which, as described in the previous section, hold a majority share in the retail market, as well as by two representatives of the middle management (for example: production manager, finished goods products manager, project manager, etc.), some of them also leading KAIZEN™ continuous improvement projects.

In what it concerns the KAIZEN™ methods and techniques for creating a culture of performance and a sustainable management system within an organization, as the next section will illustrate, the model included also two clusters in this concern, that the experts should evaluate also regarding the definition of Regional Agricultural Centers. While one cluster is composed by the main pillars necessary for defining and designing such a management system of performance, the second one comprises a series of methods and techniques, which are fundamental for achieving the objective defined by the experts.

The model evaluation was performed individually, using the "multi-actor" approach, like in European financed projects, which defines a real problem faced by the field representatives, to which participants are trying to solve, according to the individual specific set of skills and experience. Subsequently, these assessments were aggregated, according to the multicriteria decision-making rules, using the geometric mean, and the results, respectively the most important functions that the Regional Agricultural Centers should perform, represented their synthesis (aggregated priority vectors).

4 Results and Discussions

Complying with the principles and rules described above, the AHP multicriteria hybrid model has been designed, in order to address in a specific way the objectives and needs analyzed, specific to the Regional Agricultural Centers (Table 2).

The AHP multicriteria hybrid model contains 9 clusters (groups of decision problem, criteria, sub-criteria or alternatives), each representing a series of elements with a common theme, which are part of the optimal definition regarding the well-functioning of the Regional Agricultural Centers. At their turn, the clusters are made up of individual nodes, which describe their specificity, as well as their importance in the decision problem definition. The nodes' connections are made through hierarchical (when between two clusters there is only one top-down connection) and network relationships (when between two clusters there are bilateral connections, both top-down, as well as "bottom-up"). Below, there can be illustrated the AHP conceptual model designed in the Super Decisions software (Fig. 2).

The experts (representatives of the management teams of the main chains of supermarkets and hypermarkets in Romania) evaluated and validated the AHP multicriteria hybrid model, for optimally define the Regional Agricultural Centers. Every expert introduced his data by completing the perceived importance from the point of view of each of the source reference points, through questionnaires, by pairwise comparisons in the software "Super Decisions".

After the experts evaluated their intensities of preference for each pairwise comparison of the AHP multicriteria hybrid model, their results were aggregated according to the multicriteria decision-making methodology, using the geometric mean. The results are illustrated below in Table 3.

While the column "Raw" represents the nominal values of the synthesized priority vector, described above, the column "Normal" represents the normalization of these values or their proportions. The "Ideals" values, as illustrated by the name, offers a perspective to the decision-maker, considering the best alternative as a point of reference and comparing it with the other alternatives.

Table 2 Clusters and nodes of the AHP multicriteria hybrid model

Cluster	Nodes
C1. Regional Agricultural Centers	C1N1. Optimal Definition of the Regional Agricultural Centers
C2. Defining Aspects of the Regional Agricultural Centers	C2N1. Resource Allocation
	C2N2. Major Parties Involved
	C2N3. Necessary Resources
	C2N4. Implementation of a Performant Management System
C3. Stakeholders	C3N1. Farmers
	C3N2. Supermarkets
	C3N3. Citizens
	C3N4. Romanian State
	C3N5. Agri-food Companies
	C3N6. Professional Schools
	C3N7. Universities
C4. Technical Necessary and Promotion of Regional Agricultural Centers	C4N1. Defining the Number of Locations
	C4N2. Defining the Necessary Machinery and Equipment
	C4N3. Products and Services Offered Promotion
	C4N4. Defining the Number of Employees
	C4N5. Defining the Employee Profile
C5. Regional Agricultural Centers Financing Method	C5N1. Financing by European Funds
	C5N2. Tax Exemptions of the Users of Regional Agricultural Centers
	C5N3. Self-Financing (Products' Processing and their Sale)
	C5N4. Financing from the Romanian State
	C5N5. Sponsorships
C6. Definition of a Continuous Improvement Management System	C6N1. Strategic Management
	C6N2. Operational Management
	C6N3. Technology Management
	C6N4. Flow Management
	C6N5. Quality Management
	C6N6. KAIZEN™ Fundamentals
	C6N7. KAIZEN™ Sustaining
C7. Continuous Improvement Methods	C7N1. Defining the Vision and Mission
	C7N2. Defining the Management System
	C7N3. Defining the Strategic Objectives

(continued)

Table 2 (continued)

Cluster	Nodes
	C7N4. Production Planning
	C7N5. Daily Performance Analysis
	C7N6. Defining the Roles and Responsibilities
	C7N7. Kobetsu KAIZEN™ Projects
	C7N8. Improvement the Equipment Effectiveness
	C7N9. Planning the Client – Supplier Flows
	C7N10. Optimal Definition of the Internal Flows
	C7N11. MAQ Implementation
	C7N12. Muda Identification and Elimination
	C7N13. Problem Solving Story in 4 Steps Application
	C7N14. 5S Implementation
	C7N15. Standardization
	C7N16. Visual Management Implementation
	C7N17. Suggestion System Implementation
	C7N18. Creating a Continuous Improvement Internal Team
C8. Regional Agricultural Centers Performance Indicators	C8N1. Increasing the Proportion of High-Quality Ecologic Products
	C8N2. Equipment Availability for Production
	C8N3. Increasing the Presence of the Romanian Products on the Local and International Market
	C8N4. Increasing the Supermarkets and Agri-food Companies Motivation to Become Regional Agricultural Centers Clients
	C8N5. Increasing the Trust within the Regional Agricultural Centers Products
	C8N6. Increasing the Motivation of the Regional Agricultural Centers Motivation
	C8N7. Increasing the Farmers and Local Producers Motivation to use the Regional Agricultural Centers
	C8N8. Good Organization of Flows and Activities of Regional Agricultural Centers
Alternatives	A1. Market (Selling Products) for Local Producers
	A2. Place for Processing Agri-food Products

(continued)

Table 2 (continued)

Cluster	Nodes
	A3. Supply Market for Companies and Supermarkets with Fresh Products
	A4. Supply Market for the Romanian State for Export
	A5. Supply Market with Products for Every Citizen
	A6. Practice for Agri-food Field Professionals

Source Author own research using Super Decisions software

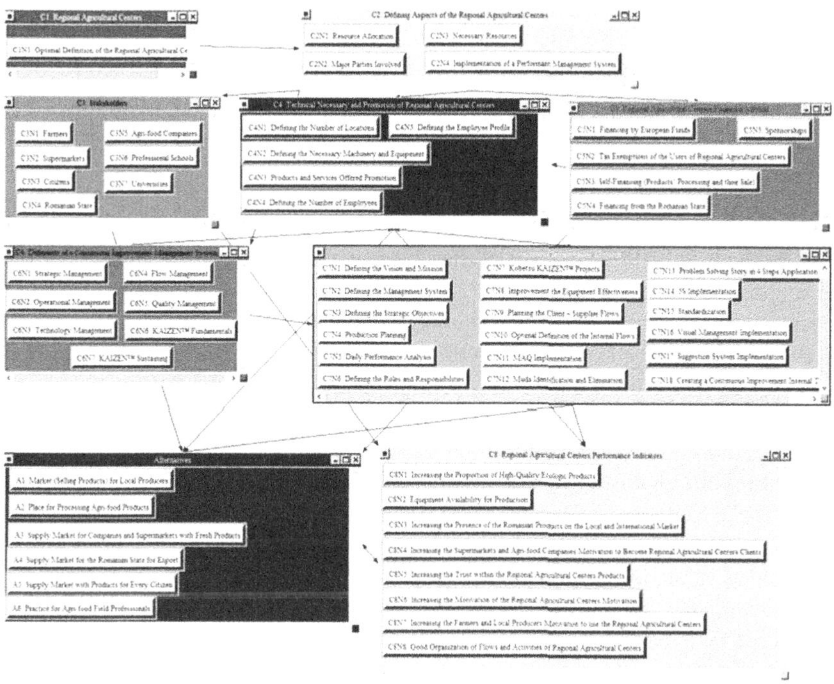

Fig. 2 AHP multicriteria hybrid model illustrated in super decisions. *Source* Author own research using Super Decisions software

According to the aggregation of expert opinions, the most important function that the Regional Agricultural Centers should have is "A3. Supply market for companies and supermarkets with Fresh products" (26.20%). It can be therefore stated, based on the experts' opinions, that a large part of the population consuming agri-food products would be interested to have more qualitative local products in hypermarkets and supermarkets, and these should serve also as raw materials for processing. The second most important considered alternative is "A6. Practice for Agri-food Field

Table 3 Synthetized Priority Vectors for the AHP Multicriteria Hybrid Model

Functions	Ideals	Normals	Raw
A1. Market (selling products) for local producers	0.535518	0.140327	0.125769
A2. Place for processing agri-food products	0.731775	0.191754	0.171860
A3. Supply market for companies and supermarkets with fresh products	1.000000	0.262040	0.234854
A4. Supply market for the Romanian state for export	0.416433	0.109122	0.097801
A5. Supply market with products for every citizen	0.323418	0.084748	0.075956
A6. Practice for agri-food field professionals	0.809063	0.212007	0.190012

Source Author own research using Super Decisions software

Professionals" (21.20%). This function, being an educational one, should serve as a training for the next generation of specialists in the field, therefore, the Regional Agricultural Centers should become so-called excellence centers in training and applying the agricultural knowledge, so that it will ensure a very good correlation with the market requirements, as well as with the program and curriculum offered by the schools. Professionals and faculties in the field. The next most important function that this type of institution should fulfill was "A2. Place for Processing Agri-food Products" (19.17%), an aspect that illustrates the perceived utility of Regional Agricultural Centers for consumers, through the creation of their own customized products, having all the necessary equipment and tools available. The "A1. Market (Selling Products) for Local Producers" alternative was perceived as next in importance (14.03%) by the experts, the local producers having the opportunity to use the services offered by the Regional Agricultural Centers as a market and becoming therefore, more motivated to consolidate and expand their business in this field and contribute with quality products, as their need is finally fulfilled. The alternative "A4. Supply Market for the Romanian State for Export" (10.91%) illustrates that the still not capitalized potential of the Romanian agriculture could start to provide more added value, by selling quality agri-food products in the European space and beyond, while the "A5. Supply Market with Products for Every Citizen" (8.47%), was considered by experts as having a rather low importance as an activity for Regional Agricultural Centers. However, this alternative illustrates that the Regional Agricultural Centers should provide also a utility at the individual level, for offering added value to any consumer, and it should be designed in such a way in which to meet their requirements.

Continuing the results description, the sensitivity analysis is illustrating how the focus on one criterion or sub-criterion of the AHP Multicriteria Hybrid Model can influence the alternatives intensity of preference. In this concern, the way in which variation of importance of a certain criterion, in the context of the whole decision model, is changed by a certain percentage, influencing the priorities associated with the defined alternatives, is calculated and illustrated in Super Decisions software. The value of the alternatives resulting from the synthesis of the priority vectors within a decision model is associated with a control parameter, which has the value 0.5.

Thus, if it is aimed to study the sensitivity analysis for a specific node, by awarding a greater importance, for example by 50%, then the value of the control parameter will be changed in the Super Decisions software by increasing it from the reference point (0.5) to the specific degree (in this case, becoming 0.75). Similar, for a sensitivity analysis study of a specific node having a decreased importance, the control parameter will be changed accordingly.

In this regard, Fig. 3 illustrates an example of such sensitivity analysis of alternatives, with respect to "C8N7. Increasing the motivation of farmers and local producers to use the Regional Agricultural Centers" criterion. The reference value starts from parameter 0.5, the values of the alternatives priority vectors being the following: 0.095 for "A1. Market (Selling Products) for Local Producers", 0.122 for "A2. Place for Processing Agri-food Products", 0.160 for "A3. Supply Market for Companies and Supermarkets with Fresh Products", 0.163 for "A4. Supply Market for the Romanian State for Export", 0.240 for "A5. Supply Market with Products for Every Citizen", respectively 0.220 for "A6. Practice for Agri-food Field Professionals".

By awarding more importance to the C8N7 criterion (the new analysis parameter becoming 0.75), it can be observed that the alternatives will illustrate another degree of sensitivity (Fig. 4).

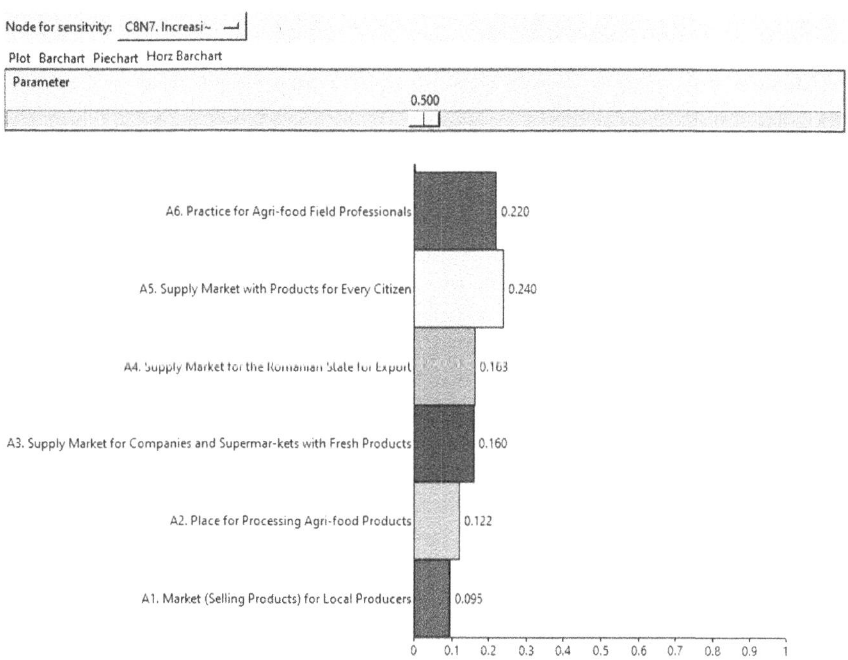

Fig. 3 Sensitivity of alternatives concerning the "C8N7. Increasing the motivation of farmers and local producers to use the Regional Agricultural Centers" criterion. *Source* Author own research using Super Decisions software

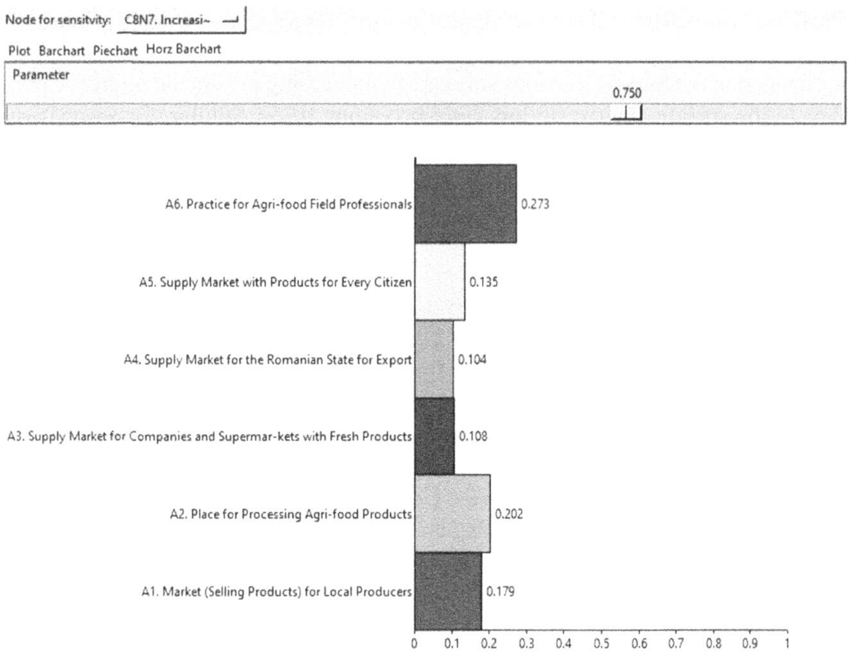

Fig. 4 Sensitivity of alternatives with respect to a 50% increase of importance of the "C8N7. Increasing the motivation of farmers and local producers to use the Regional Agricultural Centers" criterion. *Source* Author own research using Super Decisions software

Following the 50% increase in the importance of the criterion referring to the motivation of farmers and local producers for using the Regional Agricultural Centers, Table 4 illustrates the sensitivity rate of variation of the functions that should offer value to such an institution.

It can he therefore observed that by awarding 50% more importance to the criterion "C8N7. Increasing the motivation of farmers and local producers to use the Regional Agricultural Centers", the importance of "A1. Market (Selling Products) for Local Producers" would increase with 88.42%, "A2. Place for Processing Agri-food Products" with 65.57%, and "A6. Practice for Agri-food Field Professionals" with 24.09%. The "A3. Supply Market for Companies and Supermarkets with Fresh Products", "A4. Supply Market for the Romanian State for Export" and "A5. Supply Market with Products for Every Citizen" alternatives register a decrease of the perceived importance with 33.12%, 36.80%, respectively 44.16%, in the same circumstances. As illustrated, considering the experts' opinions, the effect of increasing the farmers' motivation is having a significant importance for the local producers (A1), an important one for the activity of processing the agri-food products (A2) and a medium one for the new professionals' development (A6).

Table 4 Sensitivity rate of variation of the alternatives with respect to a 50% increase in the importance of the "C8N7

Node C8N7	Reference (parameter 0.5)	Increase with 50% of the importance of C8N7 criterion	Variation rate	Variation rate (%)
A1. Market (Selling Products) for Local Producers	0.095	0.179	$\frac{0.179-0.095}{0.095}$	+88.42
A2. Place for Processing Agri-food Products	0.122	0.202	$\frac{0.202-0.122}{0.122}$	+65.57
A3. Supply Market for Companies and Supermarkets with Fresh Products	0.160	0.107	$\frac{0.107-0.160}{0.160}$	−33.12
A4. Supply Market for the Romanian State for Export	0.163	0.103	$\frac{0.103-0.163}{0.163}$	−36.80
A5. Supply Market with Products for Every Citizen	0.240	0.134	$\frac{0.134-0.240}{0.240}$	−44.16
A6. Practice for Agri-food Field Professionals	0.220	0.273	$\frac{0.273-0.220}{0.220}$	+24.09

Increasing the motivation of farmers and local producers to use the Regional Agricultural Centers" criterion. *Source* Author own research using Super Decisions software

Therefore, it can be stated that when stakeholders would like to focus on the aforementioned activities, the farmers' motivation should become the main pillar for this development.

While using sensitivity analysis, one could very easily identify what the impact of increasing or decreasing the importance of a criterion will be. Also, generically, personnel and stakeholder's motivation represent a key element for offering value and it should become the core of such an optimum institution and of other organizations.

5 Conclusions

Defining an optimal institution such as the Regional Agricultural Centers is represented by a series of activities that ensure the sustainable implementation of a decision-making system, as well as of an efficient management system in the agricultural field.

Starting from the need of developing an optimal way of organizing such an institution in this field, based on the needs expressed by the main chains of hypermarkets and supermarkets from Romania, by taking into account the objectives defined in the introduction of this paper, the definition of such an institution from the agricultural field followed a series of logical steps, being explained both the methodologies used, their use and the results to which they are leading, together with the potential benefits obtained.

Through the multicriteria decision-making methodologies, it was possible to connect the interests of the major stakeholders interested in defining the activities and functions that an optimal institution from the agricultural field, such as the Regional Agricultural Centers, should perform and the performances that can be obtained, in order to reduce and progressively eliminate the obstacles related to the absence of a clear vision of consolidation and development in the field, the lack of infrastructure, respectively to develop of a sustainable customer-supplier relationship, which to be advantageous for the final client. Also, considering the large proportion of the Romanian population, which are clients of the hypermarket and supermarket chains, the quality requirements of the food products, as well as the regulations regarding the fact that 51% of the total area specific for the sale of certain categories of food products should be made by having a supply chain made up of local producers, the decision-making model provided assistance and benefits for all stakeholders. This approach of developing a decision-making model (AHP multicriteria hybrid model) with the help of a group of experts and identifying the clusters of criteria and sub-criteria, through its objective, as well as the specific alternatives is innovative for the agricultural field in Romania. By each expert evaluation of the AHP multicriteria hybrid model, important aspects could be identified, which are related to the way of involvement within such a project, of resource allocation, of the functions that should be useful for each major stakeholder category and their importance, a series of performance criteria, as well the definition of a performance management system, based on the continuous improvement principles (KAIZEN™).

The use of the two methodologies for optimally definition of the core of such an agricultural institution that has as a goal to obtain the common good for citizens, farmers, companies, hypermarkets and supermarkets and even for the country, represents an innovative approach for the achievement of sustainability and performance in the agricultural field.This approach can be extended, through the experts, stakeholders and management teams interested in this subject from the regional level, to the national one, by taking into account the challenges and opportunities stipulated by the Common Agricultural Policy (CAP), for obtaining a sustainable and reliable management system, at local, regional, national and even international level.

References

Adeyeye, B., Amodu, L., Odiboh, O., Okorie, N., Adesina, E., Yartey, D., Ekanem, T.: Data on new media use for agricultural training and research at Agricultural services and training centre (ASTC). Data Brief **22**, 181–184 (2019)

Braunschweig, T., Janssen, W., Rieder, P.: Identifying criteria for public agricultural research decisions. Res. Policy **30**, 725–734 (2001)

Kallas, Z., Gómez-Limón, J.A., Hurle, J.B.: Decomposing the value of agricultural multifunctionality: combining contingent valuation and the analytical hierarchy process. J. Agric. Econ. **58**(2), 218–241 (2007)

De Campos, C., Sonae, M.C.: The road model of kaizen, presented as part of the requirements for the award of a Master's Degree in Management from the NOVA. School of Business and Economics (2016).

Economica.net, https://www.economica.net/kaufland--liderul-pietei-comertului-alimentar-din-romania--incepe-sa-piarda-din-cota-de-piata--isi-imparte-prima-pozitie-cu-carrefour_167351.html. Last Accessed 19 June 2019

Imai, M., Gemba Kaizen, A.: Common Sense Approach to a Continuous Improvement Strategy 2, McGraw Hill, USA (2012)

Parra-López, C., Groot, J.C.J., Carmona Torresa C., Rossing, W.A.H.: Integrating pub-lic demands into model-based design for multifunctional agriculture: an application to intensive Dutch dairy landscapes, Ecol. Econ. (67), 538-551 (2008)

Popescu, G.: Cooperația în agricultură, de la argument istoric la transferul de cunoaștere. București: Editura Academiei Române, ISBN 978-973-27-2327-2 (2014)

Popescu G., Agapie A.: Social Innovative policies within local knowledge transfer in Romanian agriculture. In: 4th International Conference Competitiveness of Agri-Food and Environ-mental Economy, CAFEE, pp. 414-419. Bucharest (2015)

Răduțu, A., Pop, I.D.: Innovative social policies for the Romanian agriculture. Int. J. Acad. Res. Bus. Soc. Sci. **8**(5), 417–435 (2018)

Revista Progresiv, https://revistaprogresiv.ro/articole/aproape-84-dintre-romani-cumpara-din-supermarketuri-hypermarketuri-cashcarry-si-magazine-de. Last Accessed 27 Sept 2018

Saaty, T. L., Vargas, L. G.: Models, Methods, Concepts & Applications of the Analytic Hierarchy Process. Springer Science+Business Media, New York (2001)

Saaty, T. L., Vargas, L. G.: Decision making with the analytic network process. In: Economic, Political, Social and Technological Applications with Benefits, Opportunities, Costs and Risks. Springer Science+Business Media, New York (2006)

Souza, G., Gomes, E.G.: A performance measure to support decision-making in agricultural research centers in Brazil. Procedia Comput. Sci. **55**, 405–414 (2015)

WWF Retailer Scorecard https://d2ouvy59p0dg6k.cloudfront.net/downloads/retailer_scorecard_2016_wwf_ro_20_feb_2017.pdf. Last Accessed 11 June 2019

Romanians' Perceptions Regarding the Drivers of Social Venture. Evidence Based on AGER Data

Carmen Păunescu and Fabrizio D'Ascenzo

1 Introduction

For many decades, entrepreneurship and making profit were seen interchangeable and almost impossible to separate. It has been widely assumed that entrepreneurs were perceived as mostly commercially driven and profit-oriented, with dividends shared among company shareholders. Recently, the emergent literature was beginning to question this representation of entrepreneurship and entrepreneurs and discussion about society impact of entrepreneurial actions has been brought into the front page (Sepulveda 2015; Farmer et al. 2016).

Austin et al. (Austin et al. 2006) distinguished between two types of entrepreneurship, one with a for-profit orientation and the other one driven by society needs. In their paper, for-profit entrepreneurship represents the identification, evaluation, and exploitation of opportunities that result in profits for shareholders. On the other hand, social entrepreneurship refers to the identification, evaluation, and exploitation of opportunities that result in social value for community. Other scholars took this theory forward and explained how the two types of entrepreneurship work for a higher education institution (Păunescu and Cantaragiu 2012). However, for-profit and social entrepreneurship should not be put in contrast. Rather they should be more accurately conceptualized as ranging from a purely social nature to an economic one.

The present paper aims to explore the perceptions of Romanians regarding the business purpose of their new venture, and further to investigate the factors that drive their desire to start a social-oriented new venture. The study relies on the Amway Global Entrepreneurship Report (AGER)˘ (AGER 2018) dataset. The paper starts

C. Păunescu (✉)
Bucharest University of Economic Studies, Romana Square 6, 010374 Bucharest, Romania
e-mail: carmen.paunescu@ase.ro

F. D'Ascenzo
University of Rome Sapienza, Aldo Moro Square 5, 00185 Rome, Italy

A. M. Dima and F. DÁscenzo (eds.), *Business Revolution in a Digital Era*,
Springer Proceedings in Business and Economics,
https://doi.org/10.1007/978-3-030-59972-0_25

with a brief review of the literature and identification of the problem investigated. Then it explains the methodology used to analyse the driving factors which will influence the individuals' desire to start a new venture with a social purpose. Finally, analysis is conducted on selected data and conclusions are drawn based on results.

2 Social Versus Profit Nature of a Business

2.1 Distinguishing Between For-Profit and Social-Oriented Business

According to the annual activity report issued by the European Network of Social Integration Enterprises (2017), which brings together different local and national structures and types of social economy organizations with integrative purpose, social enterprises act as a core pillar of the economic domain. The report acknowledges that 65% of the individuals that are subjects to the integrative process face encouraging results after being the beneficiaries of these entities. These results refer to either managing to successfully identify a workplace, initiating a career on their own or managing to reach a training for their further occupation.

Due to its positive aid provided towards the alleviation of social, economic and environmental issues, entrepreneurship has gained a wide interest from the researchers' side and as a consequence, its benefits and challenges were highly discussed in the specialty literature. As per Halkias and Thurman (2012), the alleviation of human poor living conditions, their low life quality as well as the reduction of poverty cannot be undertaken at the society level in the absence of the entrepreneurship contribution, irrespective of the fact that a certain state is a developed or developing one.

The specialized literature provides a large variety of definitions of commercial vs. social entrepreneurship or for-profit vs. social-oriented business. In general, the evolving definition of entrepreneurship involves individuals who are driven to act on opportunities and/or environmental catalysts by employing innovative processes in the face of limited resources (Schaper and Volery 2007). Ulhøi (2005) defined business or commercial entrepreneurship as being an ability to recognize a business opportunity and a risk-willingness to exploit entrepreneurial opportunities. The outcome of entrepreneurial activities may lead to profit for shareholders, job creation and, therefore, to economic growth (Bellini et al. 2019). As such, commercial entrepreneurship refers to those actively involved in starting a business which is grounded in a for-profit objective.

In contrast, social entrepreneurship is defined as ability to start a business which has a social or environmental objective in either the non-profit, for-profit or government sectors, whose surpluses are principally reinvested for that purpose in the business or community (Dees and Anderson 2003). Social entrepreneurship comes as a viable solution for the resolution of disturbing societal issues and the formation of a sustainable society (Ulfah and Dhewanto 2015). Efi and Etim (2014) state that social entrepreneurship has various sources of competitive advantage in comparison with governmental institutions and even private businesses. Thus, social entrepreneurs are less constrained in their activity, they can respond at a faster pace, can utilize a diverse set of alternative courses of action, and can make their projects fit the inner needs of a community (Efi and Etim 2014). Furthermore, the resolutions supplied by social businesses reflect sustainability and seem to be a suitable reaction to the nowadays societal problems (Yunus et al. 2012).

In Romania, entrepreneurship became in the last years more and more celebrated in the media and encouraged through government policies (e.g., Startup Nation 2019 and 2020, Startup Plus). These efforts came as a result of decreasing number of active companies at national level in all regions (except the capital city), and an increasing number of companies that were becoming inactive.

According to AGER (2018) report for Romania, entrepreneurship in the younger generation seems more of a mindset than an occupation, while for middle aged and elders more of a necessity-driven decision rather than an opportunity. Young generation think of entrepreneurship more as a way to become independent, have better balance between work and personal life, and have a self-fulfilling, creative and flexible work, where they can realize their own ideas.

Young people with less work experience and personal wealth compared to older persons and also less likely to have families and children are more flexible in their decision-making, being willing to change the place of living, studying and working, by going abroad (AGER 2018). However, they might be reluctant to take the risk of business start-up or commitment to self-employment. Instead, attraction to entrepreneurial activities can be enhanced through the use of ICT, social media, new marketing tools, mobile applications and new technology, with potential application to traditional industries, which are skills mastered by young people.

On the other hand, older people benefit from the advantage of having a longer professional experience and, potentially, important financial, human and social capital for successfully starting and running their own business (AGER 2018). Older people in Romania who lost their jobs have a harder time finding new jobs and display a low interest in entrepreneurship at the same time. Moreover, women feel often unskilled or lack leadership skills for self-employment as they have spent a long time doing a routine job, and, on the other hand, they feel that the economic environment is not beneficial to them (AGER 2018). Women and older generation with families and children views entrepreneurship as more necessity driven.

The entrepreneurship education offered by higher education institutions has been significantly improving over the past years. However, in many cases university education still lacks actual application and puts emphasis on classroom instruction, making it difficult for the students to explore real-life situations. Also, difficulties faced with acquiring resources for entrepreneurship make this occupation less attractive to young entrepreneurs and this might explain a large fall in the desire for starting a business. Even so, many university students start their ventures while being students, so they are more ready to be entrepreneurs and have more optimistic future prospects for entrepreneurship.

2.2 What Fuels an Entrepreneur to Start a Social Venture?

The business purpose means the reason why a new venture is created. The study of van der Paauw (Paauw 2016) underlines that the choice of the business purpose and overall strategy is decisive for how managerial practices are enacted, how the set objectives will be delivered and how external risks are fought against, ultimately shaping success. Reasons to start a business are various, from making money, to gaining benefits for stakeholders, and to helping others and gaining satisfaction for them. To understand the business purpose, companies evaluate their mission and the marketplace. A profit-oriented business usually makes money in the marketplace by selling a product or service to the public and acquiring funds through sales. A social-oriented business distinguishes in the marketplace through its vision and mission (Păunescu and Evans 2018). It exists for educational or charitable reasons, and from which its shareholders do not benefit financially. Any money earned must be retained by the company, and used for its own expenses, operations, and programs.

A social enterprise is also a business, but one with strong values, among which the most important ones are the primacy of social objectives over capital and the investment of surpluses in sustainable development projects (Păunescu and Evans 2018). Also, as they work in the global economic environment, social businesses have to comply with performance objectives despite their social aims. They must embrace the best practices of the for-profit world in order to survive (Ohana and Meyer 2010). In fact, the social business arose from the business enterprise model, with a change in objectives and, as consequence, some of the processes and practices must also be applied.

Since the social entrepreneur is the engine of social entrepreneurship, several studies were performed to grasp the motivational factors of this person in carrying out this kind of actions (Păunescu et al. 2018; Mottiar et al. 2018). Gabarret et al. (Gabarret et al. 2017) present four possible sources of motivation: external ones, meaning financial incentives, internal ones, for instance the acknowledgment of having completed a certain innovation action, the wish of being self-governed, and the fourth source of motivation, having previously been ruled out from the work-force. Boluk and Mottiar (2014) bring also similar supportive evidence for the social entrepreneurs' own concerns and needs as a catalyst for conducting social change.

Given the fact that not only the motivation that fuels the social entrepreneurs is important to look at in establishing their future success, literature gives importance to how personality attributes drive this output. Thus, İrengün and Arıkboğa (2015) have found out that a great extroversion degree of the social entrepreneurs is able to support the survivability of their social venture through the formation of social networks and partnerships that help them attract the needed capital for development. Reflecting on the social entrepreneurs' creativity degree and acceptance of failure, Ip et al. (Ip et al. 2018) claim that it is an accelerator for their wish to pursue entrepreneurship activities. Additionally, such studies approaching personality attributes (Salhi 2018) reveal that the locus of control held by the social entrepreneurs and the efforts put, including the time dedicated, or in other words, their assumption that their results are impacted by the activities they undertake and self-characteristics, create a positive impact on their willingness to perform societal business.

Literature notes different other aspects that can either diminish or boost the success of social entrepreneurs, such as their competence in noting previously un-tackled community gaps and their risk approach (Gandhi and Raina 2018), their leadership abilities, expertise, educational background and competences with respect to social innovation (Faruk et al. 2016; Pangriya 2019), and their partnerships with external stakeholders which deliver support in reaching financing and constructing the business plan (Ratinho et al. 2020). Based on these arguments we state the following:

H1: There is a strong positive correlation between the skills and resources necessary to develop a new business idea and the desire to start a social venture.

H2: The higher is the ability to raise money for own business idea, the greater is the desire to start a social-oriented new venture.

H3: The higher is the willingness to take the risk of failing the greater exhibits the desire to start a social-oriented new venture.

H4: There is a strong positive correlation between the willingness to sacrifice own free time to work on the business idea and the desire to start a social venture.

3 Methodology

The paper attempts to explore the perceptions of Romanians regarding the business purpose of their new venture and to understand what factors drive their desire to start a social-oriented new venture and to consider entrepreneurship as a career opportunity. The research questions are two-folded: (1) Do Romanians display a strong preference for a social-oriented vs. profit-oriented new venture? (2) What are the key drivers of starting a social-oriented new venture? To answer the questions, the study uses the Amway Global Entrepreneurship Report (AGER) data (AGER 2018) for Romania. Since 2011 globally and 2013 in Romania AGER has been examining different aspects of entrepreneurship in order to make it more encouraging and accessible to anyone interested to pursue a self-employment career. Each year the study was carry out globally by the prestigious marketing research institute GfK Consumer Experiences, Nuremberg, Germany, covering 44 nations in the latest AGER edition. In case of Romania, a representative target group of population—1000 males and females aged 15+ —was selected from the universe of the Romanian population. The study was carried out within the framework of an omnibus survey with the data collected in-person and through telephone interviews. The selection procedures used ensured a representative sample. The data were collected using a fully structured questionnaire, with the interviewers having to follow the questions in the given order and wording. The omnibus survey used a stratified sample with the population divided into subgroups who all shared a similar characteristic. Period of fieldwork lasted from 21 April 2017 to 12 May 2017. The total number of valid questionnaires, filled in by Romanian respondents and analysed in the AGER report, was 1038, with a population sample including: youngsters (n = 219), seniors of 60 + years (n = 298), females (n = 531), males (n = 507), low income population with a monthly household net income lower than 1000 RON (n = 155), university degree (n = 191), and working persons (n = 511).

To test the research hypotheses the paper employs descriptive statistics, Pearson bivariate correlation and linear regression. For this purpose, the population sample analyzed in the paper include only the respondents who perceive themselves as being willing to start a social-oriented new venture (n = 531). The measured variables include the dependent variable, desire to start a social venture and embrace entrepreneurship as a career opportunity (*Desire to start a social venture*), and four independent variables: (1) holding the necessary skills and resources to start a business (*Skills and resources*), (2) ability to raise money for own business ideas (*Raise money*), (3) willingness to take the risk of failing (*Risk of failing*), and (4) willingness to sacrifice own free time to work on the business idea (*Sacrifice free time*). All the variables have been measured through nominal scales, with two levels of measurement, '*Yes*' and '*No*'.

4 Results

The following paragraphs present and discuss the main results of the research.

Analysis of the individuals' perceptions regarding the new venture purpose, based on the AGER (AGER 2018) data at global, EU and country level, shows that Romanians have greater proclivity for starting a social-oriented business (51%) relative to EU or global level (40% each) (see Fig. 1). This can be explained by a long and more recent history, where humanistic and social values were strongly appreciated and valued in society.

Analysis of the demographic characteristics of the Romanian respondents reveals that women (55%), persons over 35 yr (more than 52%) and persons with university degree (56%) are more likely to start a social-oriented new venture, while men (53%)

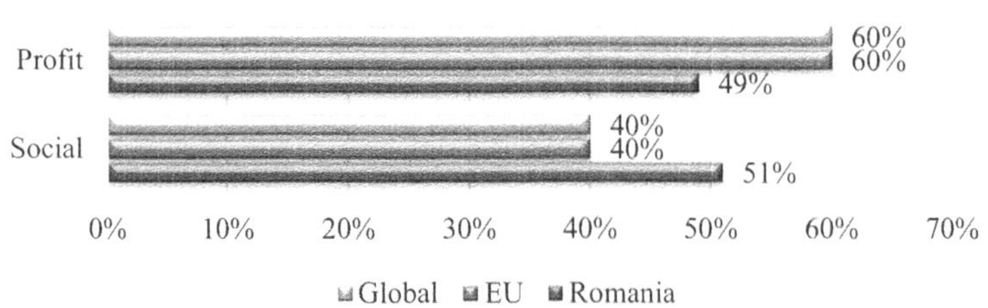

Fig. 1 Purpose of business in Romania versus EU and global level. Source Processed based on AGER (2018) data

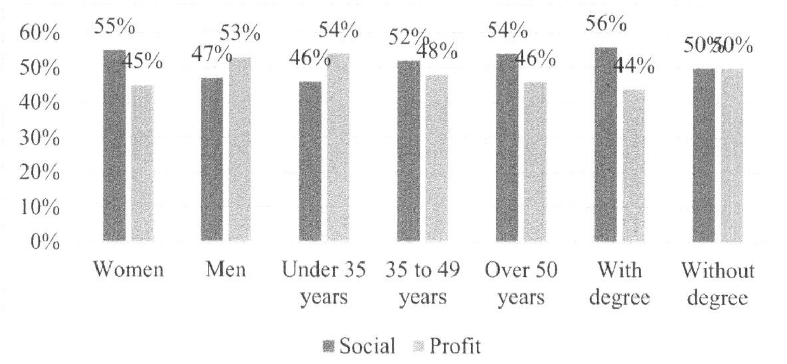

Fig. 2 Respondents' demographics and their perception regarding the business purpose. Source Processed based on AGER (2018) data

and youngsters (54%) have more proclivity for starting a profit-oriented business (see Fig. 2.

The further results presented in the paper refer to the sample of population from Romania who is willing to consider starting a social-oriented new venture. The descriptive statistics of the sample (n = 531) are presented in Table 1. To attain a statistical perspective of the desire to start a social venture phenomenon in this country, the analysis employs two statistical tools, mean and standard deviation. The mean represents the average value of the given data group, while the standard deviation indicates the departure of the given data observations from the mean of the data set (Lee et al. 2015). Analyzing the descriptive statistics from Table 1, it shows that there are two variables included in the study with a mean score ≥ 0.3, namely ability to raise money for own business ideas and willingness to sacrifice own free time to work on the business idea, which means that they highly account for an increased desire to start a social venture. Also, the standard deviation for all the variables is lower than the middle point, meaning that the values in the statistical data set are close to the mean of the data set, and, therefore, these variables are highly reliable (Păunescu et al. 2018).

Furthermore, to ensure that the data analyzed in the paper is defined by reliability and consistency, a Cronbach Alpha test operation was put in place. The greater the value displayed by the coefficient is, the bigger the likelihood that the assessed variables offer quantitative hints on the model exhibits (Bujang et al. 2018). The Cronbach Alpha indicator has a value of 0.806, hence we may conclude that the analyzed data presents a high degree of reliability and analysis is relevant.

To depict a primary phase influence of the independent variables upon the dependent one, desire to start a social venture, the paper employs a Pearson bivariate

Table 1 Descriptive statistics

	N	Min	Max	Mean	Standard deviation
	Statistic	Statistic	Statistic	Statistic	Statistic
Desire to start a social venture	531	0	1	0.23	0.422
Skills and resources	531	0	1	0.19	0.394
Raise money	531	0	1	0.33	0.469
Risk of failing	531	0	1	0.25	0.433
Sacrifice free time	531	0	1	0.36	0.482
Valid N (listwise)	531				

Source Author's own processing based on AGER (AGER 2018) data

correlation test. Analysis of correlations (see Table 2) shows that there are significant strong positive correlations between all measured variables. Thus, all the defined independent variables prove to reflect a high degree of influence upon the dependent

Table 2 The Pearson bivariate correlation testing for the research hypotheses

		Desire to start a SV	Skills & resources	Raise money	Risk of failing	Sacrifice free time
Desire to start a social venture (SV)	Pearson	1	0.415**	0.421**	0.427**	0.516**
	Sig. (2-tailed)		0.000	0.000	0.000	0.000
	N	531	531	531	531	531
Skills & resources	Pearson		1	0.425**	0.377**	0.401**
	Sig. (2-tailed)			0.000	0.000	0.000
	N		531	531	531	531
Raise money	Pearson			1	0.488**	0.523**
	Sig. (2-tailed)				0.000	0.000
	N			531	531	531
Risk of failing	Pearson				1	0.528**
	Sig. (2-tailed)					0.000
	N				531	531
Sacrifice free time	Pearson					1
	Sig. (2-tailed)					
	N					531

Source Author's own processing based on AGER (AGER 2018) data
**Correlation is significant at the 0.01 level (2-tailed).

Table 3 Regression model summary[b]

Model	R	R^2	Adjusted R^2	SE of the Estimate	Change Statistics				
					ΔR^2	ΔF	df1	df2	Sig. F Change
1	0.587[a]	0.344	0.339	0.343	0.344	68.911	4	525	0.000

Source Author's own processing based on AGER (AGER 2018) data
[a]Predictors (Constant), Sacrifice free time, Skills and resources, Risk of failing, Raise money
[b]Dependent Variable: Desire to start a social venture

variable, showing significance at the $p < 0.01$ confidence level. As such, the higher the individuals' willingness to sacrifice their own free time to work on the business idea (r = 0.516), the greater their desire to start a social venture. Also, the higher the individuals' willingness to take the risk of failing (r = 0.427), the greater their desire to start a social venture. Moreover, the higher the individuals' capability to raise money for their business idea (r = 0.421) and other capabilities and resources (r = 0.415), the greater their desire to start a social venture.

Furthermore, the research employs a linear regression analysis to identify the linkage manifested in between the variables, and to forecast the value that the dependent variable will have contingent on the independent variable's value (Kumari and Yadav 2018). The regression model summary is presented in Table 3. Checking the R^2 value in the third column, it may be observed that the model, meaning *Sacrifice free time, Skills and resources, Risk of failing* and *Raise money*, explains 34.4% of the variance in the desire to start a social-oriented new venture. This is a statistically significant contribution, as indicated by the Sig. F Change value for this line (<0.001). The ANOVA results show that all the variables are significant predictors of the desire to start a social venture ($F = 68.911$, $p < 0.001$), and that the model has a good fit (see Table 4).

To find how well each of the variables predicts the dependent variable, the coefficients are studied. The coefficients (see Table 5) show that all the analysed variables are significant positive predictors of the desire to start a social venture. In addition, the model of regression shows that a 1-unit increase in the willingness to sacrifice

Table 4 ANOVA[a]

Model		Sum of Squares	df	Mean Square	F	Sig
1	Regression	32.411	4	8.103	68.911	0.000[b]
	Residual	61.809	526	0.118		
	Total	94.220	530			

Source Author's own processing based on AGER (AGER 2018) data
[a]Dependent Variable: Desire to start a social venture
[b]Predictors: (Constant), Sacrifice free time, Skills and resources, Risk of failing, Raise money

Table 5 Coefficients[a]

Model		Unstandard. Coeff		Stand. Coeff	t	Sig	Correlations			Collinearity statistics	
		B	Std. Error	Beta			Zero-order	Partial	Part	Tolerance	VIF
1	(Constant)	0.027	0.020		1.393	0.164					
	Skills and resources	0.206	0.043	0.192	4.748	0.000	0.415	0.203	0.168	0.759	1.317
	Raise money	0.100	0.040	0.111	2.493	0.013	0.421	0.108	0.088	0.629	1.589
	Risk of failing	0.134	0.043	0.138	3.140	0.002	0.427	0.136	0.111	0.646	1.548
	Sacrifice free time	0.269	0.040	0.307	6.802	0.000	0.516	0.284	0.240	0.611	1.637

Source Author's own processing based on AGER (AGER 2018) data
[a]Dependent Variable: Desire to start a social venture

own free time to work on the business idea will result in a 0.269 unit increase in the desire to start a social venture ($p < 0.001$). Also, a 1-unit improvement of skills and resources necessary to start a business will result in a 0.206 unit increase in the desire to start a social venture ($p < 0.001$). Therefore, any effort made by the individuals, either it is skills, time or other capabilities, to work on their business ideas will result in the enhancement of their desire to start a social business. The standardized beta values indicate that all variables ($\beta = 0.581$, t (119) = 6.901) have a significant impact on the desire to start a social-oriented new venture, stronger for *Sacrifice free time* ($\beta = 0.581$, t (119) = 6.901), and moderate to lower for *Skills and resources* ($\beta = 0.581$, t (119) = 6.901), *Risk of failing* ($\beta = 0.581$, t (119) = 6.901) and *Raise money* ($\beta = 0.581$, t (119) = 6.901).

The values of VIF (*variance inflation factor*) close to 1 indicate that there is no collinearity found between the independent variables and, as such, in the regression model all predictor variables can independently predict the value of the dependent variable. Therefore, based on the results obtained, all the research hypotheses H1–H4 have been successfully confirmed.

5 Conclusions

The paper explored the perceptions of Romanians regarding their preferences for a profit-oriented or social-oriented new venture purpose. Also, the paper discussed the factors that drive their desire to start a social-oriented new venture and consider entrepreneurship as a career opportunity. The results of the research indicate that Romanians have a higher proclivity for starting a social-oriented new venture relative to average EU and average global level. Also, the research results show that all the variables analyzed in the paper are significant positive predictors of the desire to start a social venture. While the individuals' willingness to sacrifice their own free time to work on the business idea proved to have a strong significant impact on the desire to start a social-oriented new venture, the other factors, namely holding the necessary skills and resources to start a business, willingness to take the risk of failing and ability to raise money for own business ideas, have a moderate to low significant impact on the desire to start a social venture.

Despite the consistent need for social enterprises at the level of Romania, European Commission (2014) claims that this field is still under-acknowledged and thus the attainability of financing sources, as well as procuring pecuniary resources from public sources, private financing, etc. is a delicate aspect as it is scarce. Additionally, social enterprises do not hold a competitive ranking by comparison with profit-oriented organizations when speaking about reaching public funding projects, disregarding certain European Social Fund grants. Also, existing social enterprises in Romania are often struggling to ensure their survival due to many constraining factors that they undergo. In line with the research findings, the researchers assert that Romanian local institutions, even the ones with statistical function, need to track data regarding social enterprises to better understand their behavior and actions undertaken, as well as the social impact they create, and to focus on their needs, with priority and no any criteria for differentiation.

Limitations of the current research are determined by the nature and type of the variables used to determine individuals' perception towards creation of a profit- or social-oriented new venture. Also, the data analyzed in the paper are limited to one country. Future research could focus, for example, on a multi-country analysis and various other factors which influence the decision to start a new venture with social purpose, to allow the policy makers to better sustain the social entrepreneurship sector of economy, which will generate sustainable economic growth. There is insufficient knowledge on the degree to which the supportive procedures implemented by state institutions will manage to make social entrepreneurial innovation to be intensified (Chen et al. 2018). Moreover, future research should investigate the driving factors for the decision to start a social venture in close connection with the fields of activity where the social danger exists, either it is employment field exclusion, the inappropriateness of income, a reduced accessibility of education and healthcare, as well as the considerable presence of people belonging to vulnerable groups.

References

AGER: Amway Global Entrepreneurship Report 2018. https://www.amwayglobal.com/amway-global-entrepreneurship-report/. Last Accessed 28 April 2020

Austin, J., Stevenson, H., Wei-Skillern, J.: Social and commercial entrepreneurship: same, different of both? Entrepre. Theory Pract. **30**(1), 1–22 (2006)

Bellini, F., Dulskaia, I., Savastano, M., D'Ascenzo, F.: Business models innovation for sustainable urban mobility in small and medium-sized european cities. Management & marketing. Chall Knowl Soc **14**(3), 266–277 (2019)

Boluk, K.A., Mottiar, Z.: Motivations of social entrepreneurs: blurring the social contribution and profits dichotomy. Soc. Enterprise J. **10**(1), 53–68 (2014)

Bujang, M.A., Omar. E.D., Baharum, N.A.: A review on sample size determination for Cronbach's alpha test: a simple guide for researchers. Malays. J. Med. Sci. **25**(6), 85–99 (2018)

Chen, J., Yin, X., Mei, L.: Holistic innovation: an emerging innovation paradigm. Int. J. Inn. Stud. **2**(1), 1–13 (2018)

Dees, J.G., Anderson, B.B.: For-profit social venture, Dublin, Ireland: Senate Hall Academic Publishing. Spe. Iss. Int. J. Entrepre. Educat. **2**(1), 1–26 (2003)

Efi, A.E., Etim, E.O.: Social entrepreneurship: a panacea for correcting economic growth and development paradoxes in less developing countries–a case of Nigerian economy. Acad. J. Interdiscipl. Stud. **3**(4), 485–491 (2014)

ENSIE: European network of social integration enterprises. Annual Report 2017, https://www.ensie.org/activity-reports. Last Accessed 25 April 2020

European Commission: A map of social enterprises and their eco-systems in Europe–Country Report Romania (2014). https://ec.europa.eu/social/BlobServlet?docId=13095&langId=en. Last Accessed 12 March 2020

Ezzi, F., Zouari-Hadiji, R., Jarboui, A.: CSR categories and R&D investment: The moderates' role of managerial emotional intelligence. Management & marketing. Chall. Knowl. Soc. **15**(1), 17–37 (2020)

Farmer, J., De Cotta, T., McKinnon, K., Barraket, J., Munoz, S.A., Douglas, H., Roy, M.J.: Social enterprise and wellbeing in community life. Soc. Enter. J. **12**(2), 235–254 (2016)

Faruk, M., Hassan, N., Islam, N.: Factors influencing the development of social entrepreneurship in Bangladesh, https://papers.ssrn.com/sol3/papers.cfm?abstract_id=2856210 (2016). Last Accessed 14 March 2020

Gabarret, I., Vedel, B., Decaillon, J.: A social affair: Identifying motivation of social entrepreneurs. Int. J. Entrepreneur. Small Bus. Indersci. **31**(3), 399–415 (2017)

Gandhi, T., Raina, R.: Social entrepreneurship: the need, relevance, facets and constraints. J. Global Entrepreneur. Res. **9**, Article no. 9, (2018).

Halkias, D., Thurman, P.W.: Entrepreneurship and sustainability: Can business really alleviate poverty? Int. J. Soc. Entrepreneur. Inn. **1**(4), 419–427 (2012)

Ip, C.Y., Liang, C., Wu, S.C., Law, K.M.Y., Liu, H.C.: Enhancing social entrepreneurial intentions through entrepreneurial creativity: a comparative study between Taiwan and Hong Kong. Creativity Res. J. **30**(2), 132–142 (2018)

İrengün, O., Arıkboğa, Ş.: The effect of personality traits on social entrepreneurship intentions: a field research. Procedia Soc. Behav. Sci. **195**, 1186–1195 (2015)

Kumari, K., Yadav, S.: Linear regression analysis study. J. Pract. Cardiovasc. Sci. **4**, 33–36 (2018)

Lee, D.K., In, J., Lee, S.: Standard deviation and standard error of the mean. Korean J. Anesthesiol. **68**(3), 220–223 (2015)

Mthembu, A., Barnard, B.: Social entrepreneurship: objectives, innovation, implementation and impact on entrepreneurship. Expert J. Bus. Manag. **7**(1), 147–177 (2019)

Mottiar, Z., Boluk, K., Kline, C.: The roles of social entrepreneurs in rural destination development. Ann. Tourism Res. **68**(1), 77–88 (2018)

Ohana, M., Meyer, M.: Should I stay or should I go now? Investigating the intention to quit of the permanent staff in social enterprises. Euro. Manag. J. **28**, 441–454 (2010)

Pangriya, R.: Hidden aspects of social entrepreneurs' life: a content analysis. J. Global Entrepreneur. Res. **9**, Article no. 66 (2019).

Pathak, R.R., Poudel, B.R., Acharya, P.: Social enterprise and social entrepreneurship: conceptual clarity and implication in Nepalese Context. Nepal Comm. Campus (NCC) J. **3**(1), 143–152 (2018)

Păunescu, C., Evans, R.: The role of social enterprises at European level. In: Dima, A.M. (ed). Doing Business in Europe. Economic Integration Processes, Policies, and the Business Environment, pp. 235–254. Springer International Publishing (2018)

Păunescu, C., Cantaragiu, R.: Entrepreneurship in higher education: commercial or social? In: Proceedings of the 18th IGWT Symposium Technology and Innovation for a Sustainable Future: A Commodity Science Perspective (CD), Edited by Roberto Merl, pp. 1–12. IGWT, Rome (2012)

Păunescu, C., Popescu, M.C., Duennweber, M.: Factors determining desirability of entrepreneurship in Romania. Sustainability, 10(11), Article Number: 3893 (2018)

Ratinho, T., Amezcua, A., Honig, B., Zeng, Z.: Supporting entrepreneurs: A systematic review of literature and an agenda for research. Technol. Forecast. Soc. Change, **154** (2020)

Salhi, B.: Impact of personal motivation on the intention and behaviour of social entrepreneurs. J. Entrepreneur. Educ. **21**(1), 1–15 (2018)

Schaper, M., Volery, T.: Entrepreneurship and small business–a Pacific Rim perspective. Wiley , Australia Sidney (2007)

Sepulveda, L.: Social enterprise-a new phenomenon in the field of economic and social welfare? Soc. Policy Adm. **49**(7), 842–861 (2015)

Ulfah, W.N., Dhewanto, W.: Model in generating social innovation process: Case study in Indonesian community-based entrepreneurship. Int. Bus. Manag. **9**(1), 99–104 (2015)

Ulhøi, J.P. (2005). The social dimensions of entrepreneurship. Technovation, **25**(8), 939–946 (2005)

van der Paauw, C.: The critical success factors and barriers of social enterprises in the health and social care sector. https://nieuw.multivation.nl/wp-content/uploads/2016/09/Succes-factors-of-social-enterprises-in-health-and-social-care.pdf (2016). Last Accessed 12 April 2020

Yunus, M., Sibieude, T., Lesueur, E.: Social Business and big business: Innovative, promising solutions to overcome poverty? Field Actions Sci. Rep. **4**, 68–74 (2012)

The Current Context of the Smart City Concept Development. Case Study: Romania

Maria Alexandra Maassen, Adrian Dumitru Tantau, and Lenka Smekalova

1 Introduction

As the population and urban regions have developed tremendously in the past two decades, the concept of industry 4.0, which enabled the development of smart cities have become a necessity for managing the needs of the people, as well as the need for sustainability, urban efficiency in terms of organization and infrastructure especially and necessary resources for higher living standards. The industry 4.0 refers to the concept of smart factory, where networking and communication between smart digital devices with products, machines, tools, robots and people are the main focus, including elements Internet of Things, Industrial Internet, Smart Manufacturing and Cloud based Manufacturing (Vaidya et al. 2018). This has translated even in the educational field in terms of digitalization and networking of companies and the academic field (Dima and Ghinea 2016; Dima et al. 2017). It has also changed business models of corporations in all fields of activity in order to create value given new customer needs and the need for innovation, especially in the field of energy management in order to respect the sustainability principle (Păunescu and Blid 2016; Tantau and Khorshidi 2016). The industry 4.0 is considered the fourth industrial revolution and has changed the organization and control of the value chain of the life cycle of products and services in the sense of digitization and networking especially.

M. A. Maassen (✉) · A. D. Tantau
The Bucharest University of Economic Studies, Calea Grivitei, No. 2-2A, Bucharest, Romania
e-mail: maria.maassen@fabiz.ase.ro

A. D. Tantau
e-mail: adrian.tantau@fabiz.ase.ro

L. Smekalova
Faculty of Management and Economics, Tomas Bata University in Zlín, 5139 Zlín, Czech Republic
e-mail: smekalova@utb.cz

A. M. Dima and F. DÁscenzo (eds.), *Business Revolution in a Digital Era*,
Springer Proceedings in Business and Economics,
https://doi.org/10.1007/978-3-030-59972-0_26

These elements have enabled the smart cities development over the past decades. Furthermore, the industry 4.0 has enabled the development of the robotic automation process, which is revolutionizing the back office operations of companies and institutions already in the sense of automation of many activities, while people will perform only high value tasks (Anagnoste 2017).

While the smart city concept was created in the 1990s, followed by innovations in the field in the following period, the practical applications of the term have diversified up to the 21st century, including nowadays characteristics, such as: smart living, smart economies, smart people, smart governance, smart mobility, smart environment (Samih 2019). A definition of the smart city was provided by the Smart Cities Council, "A smart city is one that has digital technology embedded across all city functions" (Smart Cities Council 2020). This definition is by no means the only one in existence. Many studies have already been carried out that aim to define smart city and study its components from the (Giffinger et al. 2020) early ranking of European smart cities to (Neirotti et al. 2014) overview of smart city components and Albino et al. (2015) summary of smart city definitions.

The popularity of smart city concept is understandable given that in 2015 the European Union's urban population was 72% of the total population and is expected to increase to 80% by 2050 (Eremia et al. 2017).

In Romania in 2018 the urbanization degree was 54%, not significantly higher comparing to the level of 2008 of 53.57%. However the population in urban areas is expected to increase in the next years (Statista 2020).

One of the main current issues globally is the governance of smart cities by finding methods and applications, that ensure socio-techno synergy, which describe how new technologies can be implemented "in order to strengthen the quality and effectiveness of the government" (Meijer and Bolivar 2016).

The smart city concept has also stimulated competition and innovation on the market, especially for companies producing the smart city applications and devices. Thus, competition by encouraging companies, people and institutions to innovate and provide high quality products at competitive prices (Dima et al. 2018) has been proven to be of significant importance also in terms of developing smart city applications. An important aspect of the smart cities is also the reduction of greenhouse gas emissions, which is also a policy regulation for the European Union, namely a decrease of 40% of these emissions by 2030 (Tantau and Frăţilă 2018) as urban regions worldwide accounted in the last years for about 80% of these emissions (Eremia et al. 2017). In the EU, 80% of the energy consumption will be registered in big cities and their surroundings and therefore a high concentration of CO_2 emissions will be registered in these areas (EEA 2017).

Elements such as smart housing, smart grids are part of the smart city concept, that contribute to a more efficient and sustainable way of living and activity for people, institutions and companies. The concept of smart city, however, is more than just technology. The concept includes also governmental activities and is focused on people as well (Bolívar and Meijer 2016; Oliveira and Campolargo 2015).

According to Wadhwa (2020) regulations can also stimulate the development of some main elements of the smart city concept for futuristic cities, such as: data management, including intellectual property rights, proper data handling, and physical storage and distribution requirements, as well as issues relating to safety of its citizens. Also the smart city concept stimulates the development of production of services, but also goods through knowledge intensive activities, namely the knowledge economy (Brătianu 2017), which has also intensified in the last two decades especially.

The objective of the present article was to inquire some of the main smart city applications, in terms of technology factors, currently used in Romania, as well as expected trends for the next five years. The novelty of the study lies in the fact that it offers an overview regarding the smart city implementation based on the sample of selected participants from different urban regions, but especially Bucharest, which was not previously presented in other studies.

2 Literature Review

The cities currently play a significant role, as urbanization degrees are expected to increase for the next years. This will make it necessary to find more efficient and sustainable ways to develop different elements, especially in terms of infrastructure and urban modeling, in order to satisfy the population needs, but also to balance these needs with the need for sustainability, pollution decrease and higher urban standards. Trindade et al. (2017) mention population increase, rapid urbanization, high private motor vehicle dependency, deregulated industrialization, and mass livestock production as main elements that have made it necessary to develop the smart city concept and especially in connection with the need of ensuring sustainability for the future.

According to Stokes et al. (2015) there are six main elements of the smart city concept:

1. The utilization of networked infrastructure to improve economic and political efficiency and enable social, cultural, and urban development;
2. An underlying emphasis on business-led urban development;
3. A strong focus on the aim of achieving the social inclusion of various urban residents in public services;
4. A stress on the crucial role of high-tech and creative industries in long-run urban growth;
5. Profound attention to the role of social and relational capital in urban development;
6. Social and environmental sustainability as a major strategic component.

Smart cities are defined as cities with enough advanced progress, ensuring quality of life, competitiveness, resource availability for present and next generations (Gocmen and Erol 2018).

Other authors describe people, technology and institutions as three main factors of smart cities, each having their own contribution to the development of this concept as illustrated in Fig. 1. These elements were also confirmed by the study of Myeong

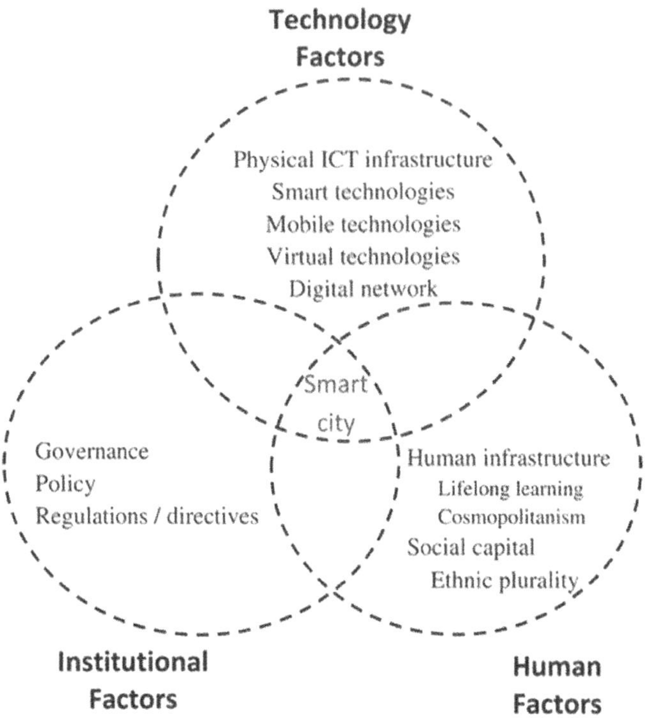

Fig. 1. Technology, Institutional and Human factors as key elements of the smart city concept. *Source* Nam and Pardo (2011)

et al. (Myeong et al. 2018).

Furthermore, Samih (2019) mentions another classification of smart city elements, that confirm the ones of Nam and Pardo (2011), respectively: smart living, smart economies, smart people, smart governance, smart mobility, smart environment.

Energy efficiency, emissions reduction, better infrastructures for reducing number of accidents, air pollution, transport, congestion and interconnectivity of applications of smart city elements are some of the main reasons for investments in smart mobility solutions, which are essential to the development of futuristic smart cities (Chen et al. 2017). The authors mention the importance of Intelligence Transportation Systems (ITS), with examples, such as smart parking, smart bike renting through cell phones, autonomous driving and which are classified into three categories (Chen et al. 2017):

- People centric, aiming to improve people's travel experience and quality of life
- Data-driven, which includes not only the data traditional ITS collect through CCTV cameras, sensors, and detectors from roads, vehicles, etc., but also additional data sources such as real-time location of buses and taxis, activity records of mobile phones, smart cards, social networks, webpage view and click, shopping and credit cards, and various other user-generated information.

- Powered by bottom-up innovations, possible through data availability and stimulating new business models, jobs, innovation, low cost public services, entrepreneurship and other benefits. For example, digital maps or navigation applications, such as Google maps or Waze.

In transport sector there is a high potential to be developed in smart cities. New behavior attitudes are very important for smart cities: (i) less travel (reduction in total vehicle-distance traveled), (ii) modal shift (users switch to a less energy-intensive mode), and (iii) reduction of per-km energy consumption (fewer stops, faster speed) in the short term.

Thus, smart mobility as part of technology factors from the classification of Nam and Pardo (2011) has revolutionized how the mobility system is organized and can function and practically, implies solving transport issues interconnected with elements such as, housing, environment, energy, health, public security, economy development, information technology (Docherty et al. 2018). These factors will also be inquired in the practical part of the research in this paper.

From the institutional factors of Fig. 1 governance, policy and regulations contribute to the smart city concept development as well. According to Tomor et al. (2019) smart governance, defined as technology-enabled collaboration between citizens and local governments to advance sustainable development, including elements, such as: e-governance participation, e-governance sustainability, citizen e-participation urban sustainability, smart city participation sustainability, city participation ICT sustainability, governance e-collaboration citizen sustainability, smart city citizen sustainability, e-participation co-creation sustainability and collaborative e-governance. The authors underline the importance of the government's commitment, motivation and responsiveness to the citizens' needs and perspectives in the matter of developing smart cities, as well as the importance of involving citizens for development of efficient policy decisions of governments and use of technology such as communication platforms, municipality websites, blogs where citizens and municipalities can communicate with each other. Regulations and policies such as the one imposing a decrease of 40% of greenhouse gas emissions in the European Union by 2030 also stimulate the smart city concept development, through elements such as for example smart housing (Bolívar and Meijer 2016). So do the public sector initiatives that foster innovative behavior among companies and various schemes allowing better accessibility to finance and stimulation of entrepreneurial environment (Hvolkova et al. 2019; Belas et al. 2019).

Human factors, another element from the classification of Nam and Pardo (2011) from Fig. 1 and Myeong et al. (2018) includes factors linked to the necessity of knowledge development in people, such as lifelong learning, ethnic plurality and social capital. The universities and other higher learning institution are inevitably tied to the human potential of smart cities. In this context universities adopting innovative approaches to management and learning and cooperating with other actors involved in creation of smart city is necessary (Grimaldi and Fernandez 2017; Bileviciute et al. 2019).

Therefore in order to define and design a Smart City there are two major things to look for: first there is a need to consider the smart efficient use of resources, which means providing good services with the minimum of negative impact on the environment. This can ensure a healthy environment and thus a good life quality for the inhabitants of the Smart City. Second, there is the component of using IT&C solutions based on advanced algorithm and control techniques, Computational Intelligence and machine learning for improving the life quality in smart cities (D'Ascenzo et al. 2019).

Essentially, smart city represents a complex concept, that has been understood primarily in its technological dimension and this understanding has been expanding to other dimensions such as people, institutions or governance which are now, too, fixed components of equal importance (Mora et al. 2017). World-wide cities adopt strategies whose objective is to make them smart or at least smarter than they are now with emphasis on incorporating technologies in order to improve quality of life (Castelnovo et al. 2016).

3 Methodology

In order to ensure a practical approach, the Delphi method based on two rounds of interviews and questionnaires was implemented. The two rounds were organized as followed (Häder 2009): first the topic of the research and the questions for the questionnaires and interviews were prepared, the selection of participants, the distribution of questionnaires with the first part of the research questions to the participants and interviews, analysis and a report of the answers, feedback to the users, the distribution of the second part of the research questions, analysis and report of the answers, feedback, final report with all the answers based on which the paper was written.

There were 61 participants selected for the research, mostly residing in Bucharest (72%), while the rest were from other cities, such as Brasov, Constanta and Deva mostly. The persons were members of the Faculty of the Business Administration from the Bucharest University of Economic Studies or persons connected to the faculty or its members. The confidence level used as a criteria is 95% for the margin of error we used the following parameters. Population of the cluster(the members and connected persons of the Faculty of Business Administration of the Bucharest University of Economic Studies) is approximately between 900–1000 persons. The margin of error is $+12, -12\%$ according to the standard Cochran's Formula.

The research took place between 1st March 2019 and 10th July 2019.

The first part of the study focused on analyzing which Smart city applications, included in technology factors from the classification of Nam and Pardo (2011), participants use while in the city of residence and which they use at their own home and workplace or study place, while the second part of the study inquired the willingness of respondents to contribute financially to develop the infrastructure of the city with smart city tools, as well as existing programs or trainings at the work or study place for education on the smart city tools.

Regarding the age of the participants 33% were between 18 and 20 yr old, 61% were between 21 and 35 yr old and the rest were above 55 yr old. 72% of the respondents were students, one person was retired and the rest were employees or freelancers.

4 Findings and Analysis

In the first part of the research respondents were asked which Smart City applications launched by the city hall of Bucharest they are using if it was the case or if they use any other ones available for their city of residence. 44% of the participants mentioned they used the Info STB application for identification of public transport schedules and routes, while 10% used the Parking Bucharest application for identification of public parking places of the city hall and 18% used the Traffic alert Bucharest, which signalizes obstacles, accidents and emergencies on the roads. Most respondents mentioned at least two of these applications as being used by them currently. An interesting fact was that 41% of the respondents did not use these applications yet.

Regarding the smart city and industry 4.0 applications noticed in the city of residence by participants most citizens mentioned smart transport devices and applications, such as bicycle rentals (71%), as well as systems to recharge electric cars (54%), as shown in Fig. 2. For example, in Bucharest, most respondents mentioned the bicycle rentals I'Velo as one of the most used bicycle sharing centers, where users can also have subscriptions and can rent a bicycle and leave the bicycle in any of their centers throughout Bucharest. Through this method, users must not return to the initial location to leave the bicycle and can leave it at another bicycle sharing center closer to the location where they intend to go further.

Smart traffic lights were also mentioned by 18% of the respondents as being present in their city of residence. These type of traffic lights are practically traffic lights with sensors and artificial intelligence, that send signals and can adapt to traffic conditions in order to decrease idle time for cars and pedestrians and intelligently route the traffic. The respondents, who mentioned these types of smart city devices were from Bucharest.

Besides Bucharest, in Romania, the city of Cluj-Napoca and the city of Alba-Iulia are pilot projects of smart cities, with IT applications, applications on energy efficiency and in transportation. Cluj-Napoca aims to be a smart city. In order to achieve this status, the city focuses on the reduction of pollution and noise, on efficient parking support by technology and on a good public transportation system supported by technology to give accurate information to the users. The city aims to be a clean city, with less pollution and therefore it has as a goal public transportation by means of electric buses (D'Ascenzo et al. 2019).

The next inquired aspect was which industry 4.0 tools do the research participants use at home. Most participants had already a home automation system, which enables practically automating the possibility to control items around the house such as a smart TV or smart home surveillance cameras, as shown in Fig. 3 28% of the

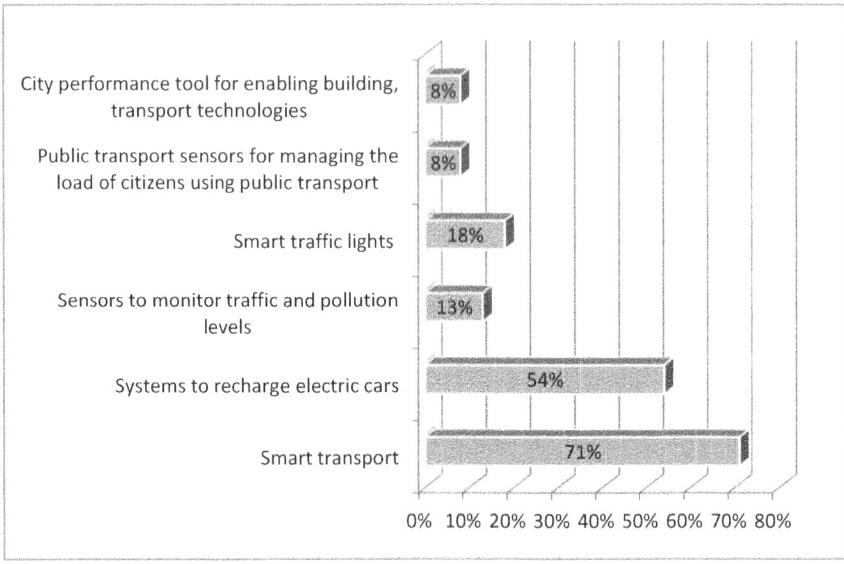

Fig. 2. Industry 4.0 and Smart city tools noticed by respondents in the city of residence. *Source* Authors' own research

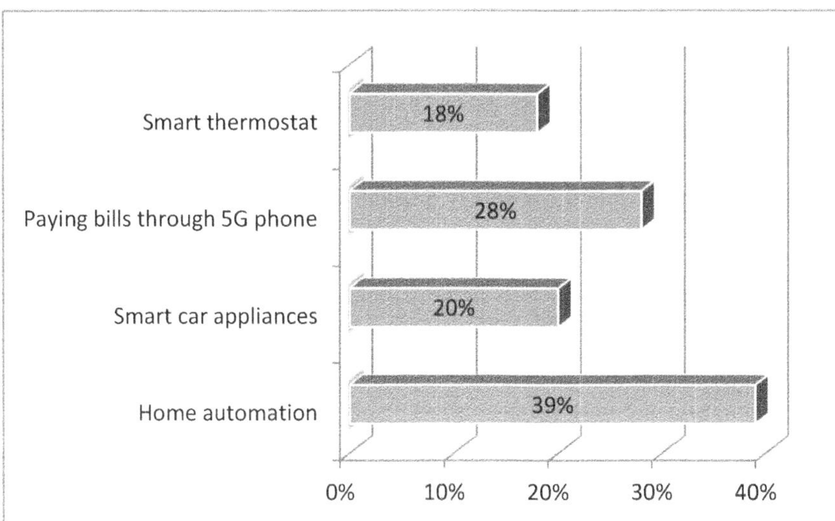

Fig. 3. Industry 4.0 and Smart city tools used by respondents at home. *Source* Authors' own research

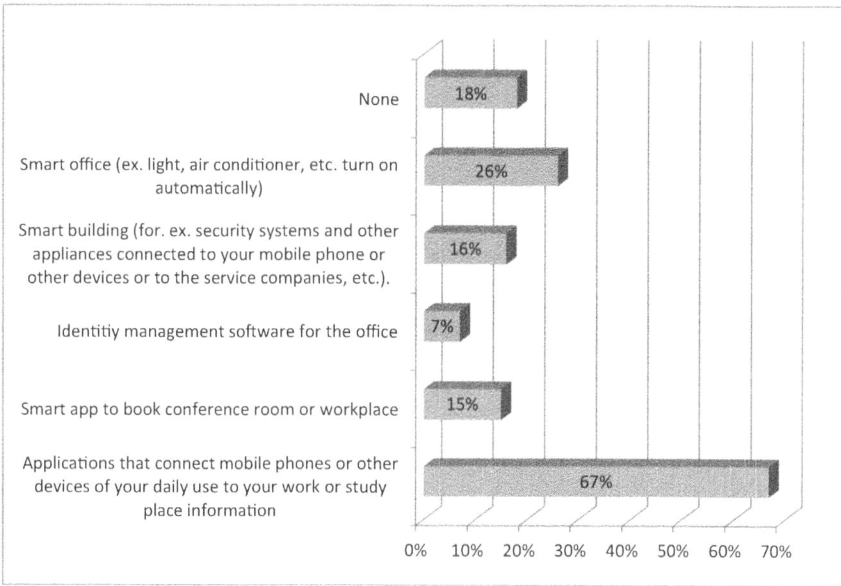

Fig. 4. Industry 4.0 and Smart city tools used by respondents at workplace/study place. *Source* Authors' own research

participants were paying bills through the 5G phone and 20% were using smart car appliances, such as mobile applications managing the car. 15% of the respondents also mentioned they had smart thermostats as smart devices in their homes.

Another aspect inquired was the smart city or industry 4.0 applications used at the workplace or study place of the participants. Most participants used applications, that connect mobile phones to their work or study place (67%) as shown in Fig. 4. Only 18% of the respondents did not use any of these. 26% of the participants mentioned smart office applications, such as lights turning on automatically and 7% identity management software for the office, such as facial recognition.

The second part of the study focused on the willingness of participants to financially support the installment of smart city tools for the infrastructure of the city, as well as the costs they already pay for the used applications and existing programs they attend for informing themselves on the smart city.

The first aspect of the second part of the research was the willingness of respondents to contribute to the installment of smart city apps for the infrastructure of the city. 77% of the respondents were specifically willing to contribute financially to this aspect, 18% were not willing to pay anything for it, while the rest did not think about it or had another answer, as shown in Fig. 5. 31% of the respondents willing to contribute mentioned they would offer between 5 and 10 Euro per year, while 25% mentioned they would contribute between 10 and 50 Euro per year.

The participants also mentioned what they spend monthly for the Smart city tools they use. 80% mentioned they did not have any costs with them, 5% mentioned costs

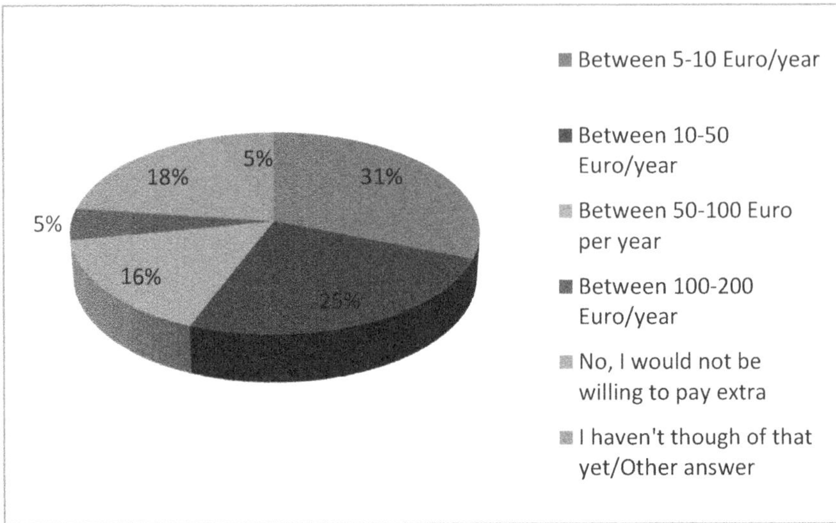

Fig. 5. Financial contributions participants would be willing to offer per year for improvement of the city's infrastructure through Smart City tools. *Source* Authors' own research

between 2 and 5 Euro per month, 10% mentioned costs between 5 and 10 Euro per month and 5% between 10 and 20 Euro per month. Thus, there were already many existing smart city applications, that were cost free and used by the respondents.

Regarding trainings or programs informing citizens of the Smart City tools only 4% of the participants mentioned they had or had attended such classes at work or the study place, especially through online platform for courses or through homework and exam planning platforms. 60% did not know if any of such training courses existed, while 36% mentioned they did not have such training courses at work or at the study place. Most respondents mentioned there is still need for more informing sources on such applications and devices for the population to be informed and to increase efficiency of the usage. Many participants to the study mentioned that many people in Romania use the smart city applications, but are not aware that these are smart city apps and they should be more informed on the term, as well as more existing industry 4.0 and smart city applications.

5 Conclusions

As a main conclusion most participants of the study were involved in the usage of some type of smart city applications, whether they used smart transport, smart parking or smart home applications. Most participants (71%) of the study notice methods of smart transport in their city of residence, while systems of charging electric cars were also noticed by 54% of the respondents. Regarding the most used applications at home most participants mentioned home automation systems (39%) and paying bills through 5G phone (28%). The study revealed also a high interest of the respondents to contribute to installing smart city applications for their city of residence: 56% were willing to pay between 5 and 50 Euro/year, while 16% were willing to pay 50–100 Euro/year for modernization of the city infrastructure with these smart city applications.

However, the informing about the smart city applications remains quite limited in Romania, as mentioned by respondents, where 60% of them mentioned they did not know of any of such trainings regarding such tools. The smart city concept has evolved also in Romania in the past decade with smart city applications within the city, at homes, workplaces and study places and is expected to be improved further. There is still need of more trainings or informing for the population, as most smart city and industry 4.0 applications are used, but not known as smart city or industry 4.0 applications.

The trend of urbanization globally is expected to contribute to the development of more smart city and industry 4.0 tools, especially in terms of city infrastructure, work and home automation and interconnected systems, but also in other sectors, such as health and economy. The positive effects of the smart city tools and the industry 4.0 are already perceived worldwide by the population, companies and institutions, as they contributed to better interconnectivity of devices, information, processes and better dynamics of action for the necessary objectives of the population. The major contributions of implementing the industry 4.0 elements in smart city application developments, home and workplace automation, as well as other automation of processes, such as in companies and institutions is expected to bring further advantages, such as reduced time consumption on activities, which can be performed automatically by digitalized devices or software and focus on main high value activities for people, decreased costs as technology costs decrease over time, better results and more competitive advantage. Smart city applications, as well as many industry 4.0 applications are already free of charge or have low costs, which makes them accessible to a large number of users and other costly applications are also expected to decrease in costs in the future. Thus, the industry 4.0 and the smart city concept are the basis for a sustainable and more efficient way of action for people, companies and institutions in terms of time, costs and results, as well as in terms of automation of unnecessary workload for people. This will lead to more time for high value activities for people and other types of jobs.

A future objective of the present study is to further inquire new applications of the industry 4.0 and smart city applications in the next years, as well as their implementation in different fields of activity in Romania, as well as in other European Union countries. Furthermore, to inquire which social, environmental or economic elements will be the major factors of influence for developing new applications for this new field in terms of improving interconnectivity of people, devices and several fields.

References

Albino, V., Berardi, U., Dangelico, R. M.: Smart cities: definitions, dimensions, performance, and initiatives. J. Urban Technol. **22**(1), 3–21 (2015). ISSN 1063–0732

Anagnoste, S.: Robotic automation process—the next major revolution in terms of back office operations improvement. In: Dima, A.M. (eds.) The 11th International Conference on Business Excellence 2017, Proceedings of the 11th International Conference on Business Excellence, vol. 11(1), pp. 676–686. De Gruyter, Germany (2017)

Belas, J., Belas, L., Cepel, M., Rozsa, Z.: The impact of the public sector on the quality of the business environment in the SME segment. Adm. Si Manage. Pub. **2019**(32), 18–31 (2019)

Bileviciute, E., Draksas, R., Nevera, A., Vainiute, M.: Competitiveness in higher education: the case of university management. J. Compet. **11**(4), 5–21 (2019)

Bolívar, M.P.R., Meijer, A.J.: Smart governance: using a literature review and empirical analysis to build a research model. Soc. Sci. Comput. Rev.s **34**(6), 673–692 (2016)

Brătianu, C.: The knowledge economy: the present future. Manage. Dyn. Knowl. Econ. **5**(4), 477–479 (2017)

Castelnovo, W., Misuraca, G., Savoldelli, A.: Smart cities governance. Soc. Sci. Comput. Rev. **34**(6), 724–739 (2016)

Chen, L., Ardila-Gomez, A., Frame, G.: Achieving energy savings by intelligent transportation systems investments in the context of smart cities. Transp. Res. **54**, 381–396 (2017)

D'Ascenzo F., Tantau A., Savastano M., Santa A.: New energy policies for smart cities - a comparison among smart cities in the European Union. In: Proceedings of the 13th International Conference on Business Excellence, pp. 1140–1149, De Gruyter, Germany (2019)

Dima, A.M., Ghinea, V. A model of academic leadership. In: Proceedings of the 12th European Conference on Management, Leadership and Governance, Acpil (2016).: https://books.google.ro/books?hl=uk&lr=&id=S7LqDQAAQBAJ&oi=fnd&pg=PA61&ots=kYk1OwXNyn&sig=kR9Oo3X-t1_DDgTJlvYfksFV68k&redir_esc=y#v=onepage&q&f=false

Dima, A.M., Hadad, S., Luchian, I.: Review on the dimensions of business-university alliances. In: Proceedings of the 11th International Conference on Business Excellence, pp. 64–73. De Gruyter, Germany (2017).

Dima, A.M., Cantaragiu, R., Istudor, L.G.: The Relationship between Competition Policy and Innovation in the European Business Environment. Springer, Cham (2018)

Docherty, I., Marsden, G., Anable, J.: The governance of smart mobility. Transp. Res. Part A Policy and Practice **115**, 114–125 (2018)

EEA.: https://www.eea.europa.eu/themes/urban/intro. Last Accessed on 3 2020

Eremia, M., Toma, L., Sanduleac, M.: The smart city concept in the 21st century. Proced. Eng. **181**, 12–19 (2017)

Giffinger, R., Fertner, C., Kramar, H., Kalasek, R., Milanović, N., Meijers, E.: www.smart-cities.eu/download/smart_cities_final_report.pdf. Last Accessed on 2 2020

Gocmen, E., Erol, R.: The transition to industry 4.0 in one of the Turkish logistics company. Int. J. 3D Printing Technol. Digital Indus. **2**(1), 76–85 (2018)

Grimaldi, D., Fernandez, V.: The alignment of university curricula with the building of a smart city: a case study from Barcelona. Technol. Forecast. Soc. Chang. **123**, 298–306 (2017)

Häder, M.: Delphi Befragungen: Ein Arbeitsbuch. VS Verlag, Wiesbaden (2009)

Hvolkova, L., Klement, L., Klementova, V., Kovalova, M.: Barriers hindering innovations in small and medium-sized enterprises. J. Compet. **11**(2), 51–67 (2019)

Meijer, A., Bolivar, M.P.R.: Governing the smart city: a review of the literature on smart urban governance. Int. Rev. Adm. Sci. **82**(2), 392–408 (2016)

Mora, L., Bolici, R., Deakin, M.: The first two decades of smart-city research: a bibliometric analysis. J. Urban Technol. **24**(1), 3–27 (2017)

Myeong, S., Jung, Y., Lee, E.: A Study on Determinant Factors in Smart City (2018)

Nam, T., Pardo, T.A.: https://inta-aivn.org/images/cc/Urbanism/background%20documents/dgo_2011_smartcity.pdf. (2011). Last Accessed 02 2020

Neirotti, P., De Marco, A., Cagliano, A.C., Mangano, G., Scorrano, F.: Current trends in smart city initiatives: some stylised facts. Cities **38**, 25–36 (2014)
Oliveira, Á., Campolargo, M.: From smart cities to human smart cities. In: Proceedings of the Annual Hawaii International Conference on System Sciences, pp. 2336–2344. IEEE, Kauai (2015)
Păunescu, C., Blid, L.: Effective energy planning for improving the organization's energy performance. Manage. Mark. Challenges Knowl. Soc. **11**(3), 513–531 (2016)
Samih, H.: Smart cities and internet of things. J. Inf. Technol. Case Appl. Res. **21**(1), 3–12 (2019)
Smart Cities Council.: https://smartcitiescouncil.com/smart-cities-information-center/definitions-and-overviews. Last Accessed 03 2020
Statista, https://www.statista.com/statistics/455918/urbanization-in-romania/. Last Accessed 02 2020
Stokes, P., Larson, M., Russell, N., Adderly, S., Moore, N., Mathews, M., Smith, S., Lichy, J., Scott, P., Ward, T., Brindley, C.: Smart cities'—dynamic sustainability issues and challenges for 'Old world' economies: a case from the United Kingdom. Dyn. Relat. Manage. J. **4**(2), 3–22 (2015)
Tantau, A., Frăţilă, C.L.: Entrepreneurship and Business Development in the Renewable Energy Sector. IGI Global, USA (2018)
Tantau, A., Khorshidi, M.: New business models for state companies in the oil industry. Manage. Mark. Challenges Knowl. Soc. **11**(3), 484–497 (2016)
Tomor, Z., Meijer, A., Michels, A., Geertman, S.: Smart governance for sustainable cities: findings from a systematic literature review. J. Urban Technol. **26**(4), 3–27 (2019)
Trindade, E., Marcus, H., Costa, E., Marques, J., Bastos, R., Yigitcanlar, T.: Sustainable development of smart cities: a systematic review of the literature. J. Open Innovation Technol. Mark. Complexity **3**(10), 1–14 (2017)
Vaidya, S., Ambad, P., Bhosle, S.: Industry 4.0-A glimpse. Proced. Manuf. **20**, 233–238 (2018)
Wadhwa, M.: Understanding the Impact of Smart Cities and the Need for Smart Regulations. https://ssrn.com/abstract=2908299 or http://dx.doi.org/https://doi.org/10.2139/ssrn.2908299. Last Accessed 03 2020

Impact of National Culture in Reaction to Service Failures

Raquel Ribeiro and Raquel Meneses

1 Introduction

The good performance of a service is fundamental to consumer satisfaction, but service failures are inevitable (Zeithaml et al. 1990). The result of a negative service "encounter" lead to the dissatisfaction expression in several ways (Singh 1988; Rogers et al. 1992).

With increasing globalization and the growing interest of service companies to expand into other markets, the role of culture in the service delivery process has become increasingly important (Zhang et al. 2008). In addition, the inward export, comes in the need for consumers from different countries to move to the country of origin of the company to receive a service (Montanari et al. 2019). As such, companies need to deal with simultaneous demands, which makes it necessary to understand the different cultures in service interactions. It is important to note that the "literature on the influence of culture on service experience indicates existence of cross-country differences" (Schoefer et al. 2019).

When a service failure occurs, the consumer behavior is influenced by their culture (Chan and Wan 2008). Thus, it is necessary customer support services understand the implications of the cultural values. (Schoefer et al. 2019). Also, the degree of "power" of the service provider impacts on failure reactions in certain cultural dimensions (Furrer et al. 2000).

Little has been done to examine the effects of culture on service failures and consumer behaviors after a failure (Ngai et al. 2007; Yuksel et al. 2006; Zhang et al.

R. Ribeiro · R. Meneses (✉)
School of Economics and Management, University of Porto, Porto, Portugal
e-mail: raquelm@fep.up.pt

R. Ribeiro
e-mail: m_raquel22@hotmail.com

A. M. Dima and F. DÁscenzo (eds.), *Business Revolution in a Digital Era*,
Springer Proceedings in Business and Economics,
https://doi.org/10.1007/978-3-030-59972-0_27

2008). In addition, there seems to be only one study that studies the influence of the "power" of the service provider in different cultures (Furrer et al. 2000).

The present study intends to fill a gap in the literature, aiming to analyze the impact of two dimensions of Hofstede cultural typology (Power distance and masculinity vs feminility, in the reaction to a service failure. In addition, it is intended to test whether the degree of "power" of the service provider has implications for the reactions between individuals with different cultures. We chose these two dimensions because they are more related to the power sensation.

2 Literature Review

Service failures are unavoidable due, mainly, to human involvement, which implies the inseparability of service production and delivery. It is impossible to review the quality of the service before the delivery (Hess et al. 2003).

There are several models of consumer complaint behaviors (Hirschman 1970; Singh 1988; Boote 1998; Velázquez et al. 2006). However, these were created long before there were certain online channels, such as Facebook or complaint websites, and therefore did not include certain responses, which have been increasingly referred to as very relevant (Mattila and Wirtz 2004; Andreassen and Streukens 2013; Tronvoll 2012; Ergün and Kitapci 2018).

The categories of complaints are reflected in consumer behavior in a variety of ways.

Direct service complaint can be done by voice (face-to-face or telephone) to the service provider or the service manager, or in writing (via letter, email (Mattila and Wirtz 2004) or suggestion boxes (Heung and Lam 2003)). Voice complaint happens when consumers seek compensation for failure, while written complaint occurs when they are intended to alleviate the frustration caused by the failure (Mattila and Wirtz 2004).

Direct consumer complaints are very important, since they provide feedback on the service (Homburg and Fürst 2005). However, only few consumers do that (Stauss and Seidel 2008). Communication to third parties seeks the help of third parties to deal with the incident, through legal action or just to communicate their dissatisfaction to others, such as communication to consumer advocacy agencies or through the media (Singh 1988; Liu and McClure 2001; Kim et al. 2010).This behavior can represent considerable costs for companies, regulatory intervention and big reputational problems (Singh 1989).

The word-of-mouth seems more subtle; it could be completely anonymous, avoiding confrontations (Schoefer et al. 2019). At the same time, it is seen as one of the most persuasive and effective forms of communication (Marney 1995; Henricks 1998) and is, therefore, one of the most negative consequences of post-failure, for the company. This effect can be even more devastating thanks to the Internet.

The Internet has the power to multiply the effects of word-of-mouth, as it has a great impact, not only on the number of people that can be influenced, but also on the speed of information dissemination (Cantallops and Salvi 2014).

Abandonment of the service and choose a competitor is a response in which the dissatisfied consumer, voluntarily, chooses to terminate the relationship with the service provider and switch to another service (Singh 1988; Rogers et al. 1992).

This behavior is a destructive act for the organization, since the consumers leave the company without knowing what has failed.

Boycott combines two of the previous behaviors: abandonment of the service, since consumers interrupt the relationship with the company (Hirschman 1970), and communication through word-of-mouth, since these collective actions intend to express discontent and anger (Hoffmann 2014).

Retaliation includes actions that create costs or losses for the company. This study will not examine retaliatory behavior because it is illegal. Do nothing means ignoring the dissatisfaction arising from failure (Rogers et al. 1992), and it is the most common response to dissatisfaction (Oliver 1997).

This non-action can have several reasons: the hope that things will improve in the future; high costs of changing service; lack of better alternatives; etc.

2.1 National Culture

A service provider may have to deal with totally different clients, who require different approaches, because they have different personalities or different cultures.This study only studies two Hofstede cultural dimensions; Power distance and Masculitnity vs feminility, as these two dimensions are related with power and tolerance.

Cultures with High Power Distance (CHPD) tolerate high social inequalities, accept income differences, and the distribution of power. In cultures with Low Power Distance (CLPD), people strive to balance the distribution of power and seek justification for this inequality. It is expected that people will all be treated equally, and that power be shared among individuals of different hierarchical levels (Brettel et al. 2008).

Cultures with Masculinity (CM) are societies where the dominant values are success, money and material. The assertive, competitive side and the little concern with the feelings of others, characterizes these societies better. Cultures with Femininity (CF) are societies where the dominant values are the protection of others and the quality of life. The modest side, which is oriented towards relations and solidarity, characterizes better these societies.

2.2 National Culture and Reactions to Service Failures

Consumers from different cultures present different reaction to service failures (Huang et al. 1996; Liu and McClure 2001; Chan and Wan 2008).

Cultures with High Power Distance (CHPD)/Cultures with Low Power Distance (CLPD).

According to Furrer et al. (2000) in a CHPD, the consumer may feel "powerful" or "weak" in relation to the service provider. Donthu and Yoo (1998) stated that consumers are "weak" when the service requires a high degree of professional knowledge on the part of the service provider (eg. Doctors, lawyers). In services where the service provider is considered to have a lower status (eg. in hotels, restaurants), consumers in these societies consider themselves as more "powerful" than the service provider (Mattila 1999).

During the interaction of the service, a consumer who considers himself to be "powerful" tends to complain directly, when a service failure occurs (Furrer et al. 2000) and to engage in public and legal actions (Ngai et al. 2007).

When the consumer is "weak", consumers acknowledges that they do not have the skills and knowledge on the subject (Tsoukatos and Rand 2007), and when a service failure occurs, "weak" clients of a CHPD are less likely to complain (Jahandideh et al. 2014) and to tolerate poor service, due to their tolerance for inequalities (Donthu and Yoo 1998; Heung and Lam 2003). They prefer word-of-mouth or to do nothing, even when unsatisfied (Huang et al. 1996; Yuksel et al. 2006; Ergün and Kitapci 2018).

In CLPD, all the people are treated indistinctly, they all have the same "degree of importance" (Ngai et al. 2007). So, individuals in these societies are more likely to complain on the spot or to abandon when a failure occurs (Huang et al. 1996), because complaining is understood as a consumer right and is not seen as a challenge to authority. (Ngai et al. 2007).

Thus, three hypotheses are proposed:

H1a: Consumers belonging to cultures with high power distance react differently, to a service failure, from consumers belonging to cultures with low power distance.

H1b: Consumers belonging to cultures with high power distance react differently, between a "powerful" service failure and a "weak" service failure.

H1c0: Consumers from cultures with low power distance react in the same way, between a "powerful" service failure and a "weak" service failure.

Cultures with Masculinity (CM)/Cultures with Femininity (CF).

CM people have high expectations of service and attach great value to good service. These individuals have higher levels of dissatisfaction and attitudes of disloyalty to service. In case of failure, they do more complaints on the spot, because of the demand for material compensation (Kindel 1983) and share dissatisfaction with consumer advocacy agencies who fight for their rights (Yuksel et al. 2006).

On the other hand, CF people, where there is more tenderness and sympathy for others, adopt more moderate behaviors in critiques and evaluations (Erdmann and Crotts 2000). Furthermore, Samaha et al. (2014) argue that CF are more concerned with relationships, increasing WOM behavior.

This results in the hypothesis H2.

H2: Consumers from cultures with masculinity react differently, to a service failure, from consumers belonging to cultures with femininity.

3 Methodology

For this study, two services were used: a weak service - restaurant (Furrer et al. 2000; Mattila 1999) and a power service—lawyer service (Chan and Wan 2007, 2008; Furrer et al. 2000).

To identify the main failures and the main consumer reactions after service failures we performed ten exploratory interviews. Used to elaborate the scenarios. Subsequently, it was used the online questionnaire method to identify the cultural differences in the reactions to services failures. The questionnaire was translated to English, Spanish, French, German, Italian and Chinese, by native people and sent to US, Brazil, Portugal, Spain, France, Germany, Italy, Austria, Finland, South Africa, China and Australia. Two scenarios were used (see table 1): failures in a restaurant service and failures in a lawyer service.

After the presentation of each scenario, the respondents were asked to rate, on a Likert scale from 1 to 7, what would they do if the situation happen to them. The development of behavioral expressions was based on the studies by Singh (1988), Huefner and Hunt (2000), Liu and McClure (2001), Volkov et al., (2002) and Kitapci and Dortyol (2009), previously performed and the expressions based on the previous qualitative study were adapted.

In order to analyze the culture of the countries, this study uses the cultural indexes developed by Hofstede. Since these are continuous values, the countries whose index

Table 1 Scenarios presented in the questionnaire

Power	Scenario
Weak	**Think of a restaurant where you often dine. Imagine that the following scenario occurs to you:** You decide to go to dinner at your usual restaurant. You are already at the table and already chose the meal that you will ask. After asking the employee for the chosen meal, you had to wait more than 1h30m for the food to arrive, and there were few customers in the restaurant. When the food arrived, it did not contain all the ingredients described on the menu
Powerful	**Think (or imagine) your usual lawyer, whom you turn to whenever you need help. Imagine that you have the following situation:** You decide to consult your usual lawyer to resolve a personal problem. He tells you that he can come up with a solution within 2 weeks. Only three months later, the lawyer presented the resolution of the case. In the end, when you read the work, you realized that the lawyer, who did not want to refuse the case, had no specialization in the matter in question and, therefore, presented a poor-quality work

was between 35 and 65, were remove from the analysis of each cultural dimension, since the aim is to analyze the low and high level of each cultural dimension.

A total sample of 631 responses was obtained, 565 valid. A non-probability sampling technique (based on convenience) was used. Different schools from different countries were contacted to collaborate. As this study is based on hypotheses testing, the minimum size for any country sample size is 30 (as from 30 subjects, the distribution could be considered Normal).

4 Results and Discussions

Among the respondents, 40 belong to France, 48 belong to South Africa, 57 to Italy, 56 to Portugal, 63 to China, 58 to Germany, 33 to Australia, 35 to Austria, 41 to Brazil, 35 to Spain, 36 to the USA and 63 to Finland. The levels of each cultural dimension are detailed, by country, in Table 1. 66.19% of the respondents are female. Regarding the age, average of about 25 yr was obtained. About 78% of the total sample has higher education and 21% have the secondary education (Table 2).

In terms of household income, 36.46% respondents consider that they are in the average of their country and 26.37% consider that they are above.

Demographic variables were included as control variables.

Table 2 Cultural dimension

Cultural dimensions index countries	Distance to power	Masculinity/feminility
Germany	35	66
Brazil	69	49
Spain	57	42
France	68	43
Finland	33	**26**
Italy	50	70
Portugal	63	31
China	**80**	66
Austria	**11**	**79**
USA	40	62
South Africa	49	63
Australia	36	61

4.1 Factorial Analysis

In order to perform exploratory factorial analysis, all the variables of each scenario, representing each behavior, were joined. Through this analysis it was possible to generate 3 factors.

Commonalities below 0.5 should be withdrawn from the study. The reaction "Forget the incident and do nothing" presented a commonality of 0.259, so it was removed and will be treated, later, as a category of single expression.

Hair et al. (2006) argue that factorial weights above 0.7 are considered significant and indicative of a well-defined structure and that values above 0.5 are considered acceptable. All items in this analysis have values above 0.5, ranging from 0.626 to 0.841.

For the Cronbach's Alpha, all factors of the study presented a value between 0.702 and 0.837, which confirms the consistency and reliability of the scale.

Factor 1—Actions Directed to the Service:

Many authors consider, as a category of complaint, the direct response to the service, by voice (Singh 1988; Liu and McClure 2001; Volkov et al. 2002; Kim et al. 2010). However, it has already been mentioned the need to consider other channels, such as e-mail, letter or suggestion box, as a form of communication of dissatisfaction with the company (Heung and Lam 2003; Mattila and Wirtz 2004). Factor 1 encompasses these options and, therefore, will be called "Actions directed to the service". These can be explained by the demand for economic or material compensation, or by the willingness to help the company to realize and correct the problem permanently (Emir 2011).

Factor 2—Private Actions:

Some authors identify the word-of-mouth (Chan and Wan 2008; Ergün and Kitapci 2018), boycott and abandonment (Liu et al. 2001; Kitapci and Dortyol 2009; Ergün and Kitapci 2018) as a category of private response by the consumer. Also, in this study, the offline word-of-mouth, abandonment of service and offline boycott make up a factor. This factor will be called "Private actions", since it includes private actions related to the consumer himself, with friends, family and acquaintances (Singh 1988).

These actions do not allow the company to realize what has failed, but relieve frustration and prevent friends, acquaintances, family members and the own person from going through the same situation again.

Although Park et al. (2014) have suggested the inclusion of online behaviors in private responses, in this study, online reactions are not part of the category "Private actions", since they are available to everyone, including the company itself (Tronvoll 2012).

Factor 3—Public Actions:

Communication to third parties includes a formal complaint to a regulator entity, communication to a consumer protection agency, and dissemination the dissatisfaction to the media. In this study, these behaviors related to third-party communication are a factor in conjunction with behaviors related to online word-of-mouth and online boycott. This is explained by the common goal of spreading dissatisfaction

Table 3 MANCOVA—Comparisons of the reactions between individuals of CLPD and CHPD, in the various scenarios

Scenario 1 (restaurant)	Mean CLPD	Mean CHPD	Mean difference	F	St. Error	Sig
Actions directed to service	3.642	4.201	−0.559*	13.156	0.154	0.000
Private actions	4.527	4.891	−0.364*	4.077	0.180	0.044
Public actions	1.501	2.221	−0.721*	32.365	0.127	0.000
Do nothing	4.242	3.353	0.890*	16.568	0.219	0.000
Scenario 2 (lawyer)						
Actions directed to service	5.884	5.311	0.572*	9.618	0.184	0.002
Private actions	5.444	4.892	0.553*	7.733	0.199	0.006
Public actions	1.800	2.213	−0.413*	6.258	0.165	0.013
Do nothing	2.673	2.786	−0.114	0.319	0.201	0.573

*Significant mean difference at the 0.05 level

to the public as a form of warning, by seeking compensation, or simply by relieving frustration caused by failure (Singh 1988).

For the "Do nothing" category, which was analyzed with a unique expression, there are no reliable estimates to be made.

4.2 Results

To test the differences between the two groups of each cultural dimension, MANCOVA were used. In order to analyze the differences between the powerful and weak services, in the cultural dimensions Power Distance, ANCOVA of Repeated Measures were performed.

Cultures with Low Power Distance Versus Cultures with High Power Distance

In order to compare the two groups of this cultural dimension, MANCOVA tests were performed (Table 3). In all scenarios, significant statistically differences were found between the two groups. Thus, the hypothesis H1a was confirmed.

The people of CHPD consider that they have less "power" to go directly to a powerful service (lawyer), and they do not dare to engage in private actions about a service they do not have knowledge of (Emerson 1962), so they show less involvement in actions directed to service and private actions on powerful services than CLPD people. On the other hand, in restaurants' services, people from CHPD consider themselves more "powerful" than the service provider and, therefore, show a greater involvement in directed to service and private actions than CLPD. The fact that CHPD individuals tend more toward public actions at all services than CLPD individuals

Table 4 ANCOVA tests of repeated measures—Comparison of CLPD and CHPD individuals' reactions between "weak" and "powerful" services

Power distance index	Actions directed to service	Mean	Actions directed to service	Mean	Mean difference	St. Error	Sig
CLPD	Scenario 1-weak	3.642	Scenario 2-powerful	5.884	−2.241*	0.129	0.000
CHPD	Scenario 1-weak	4.201	Scenario 2-powerful	5.311	−1.110*	0.134	0.000
Power distance index	Private actions	Mean	Private actions	Mean	Mean difference	St. Error	Sig
CLPD	Scenario 1-weak	4.527	Scenario 2-powerful	5.444	−0.918*	0.115	0.000
CHPD	Scenario 1-weak	4.891	Scenario 2-powerful	4.892	−0.001	0.120	1.000
Power distance index	Public actions	Mean	Public actions	Mean	Mean difference	St. Error	Sig
CLPD	Scenario 1-weak	1.501	Scenario 2-powerful	1.800	-0.299*	0.084	0.003
CHPD	Scenario 1-weak	2.221	Scenario 2-powerful	2.213	0.008	0.088	1.000
Power distance index	Do nothing	Mean	Do nothing	Mean	Mean difference	St. Error	Sig
CLPD	Scenario 1-weak	4.242	Scenario 2-powerful	2.673	1.570*	0.146	0.000
CHPD	Scenario 1-weak	3.353	Scenario 2-powerful	2.786	0.566*	0.152	0.001

*Significant mean difference at the 0.05 level

may be explained by the need for them to call upon competent entities to solve the problem (Patterson et al. 2006).

In order to understand if the reactions of the individuals of CHPD and CLPD differ between "powerful" and "weak" services, ANCOVA Tests of Repeated Measures were performed (Table 4). The hypothesis H1b was partially confirmed, since the individuals of CHPD present significant statistically differences between "powerful" and "weak" services, but only in actions directed to service and the option of doing nothing.

Although this hypothesis was partially confirmed, the results were not as expected. According to Mattila (1999) and Furrer et al. (2000), consumers of CHPD expect an excellent treatment from weak services and so, tend to complain directly, while in a powerful service, they consider that they have less knowledge than the service provider and, thus better tolerate a service failure (Donthu and Yoo 1998; Heung and Lam 2003).

However, in this study, these individuals engage more in actions directed to service in powerful services, than in weak services that fail. In turn, they also tend more to do nothing in a weak service that fails than in a powerful service that fails. The explanation may be because of the worse implications that failures in lawyers' services may have.

The H1c0 hypothesis was not confirmed, since the CLPD individuals present significant statistically differences between "powerful" and "weak" services.

It was expected that CLPD individuals did not present differences between powerful and weak services, since they consider that all have the same "degree of importance" (Brettel et al. 2008). However, in this study this did not happen, and the greater involvement in actions directed to service, private and public actions after failures in powerful services than in weak ones, and the greater intention of doing nothing in weak rather than powerful services can be once again, due to the fact that a failure in a lawyers' service could lead to greater losses to the consumer.

Cultures with Femininity (CF) versus Cultures with Masculinity (CM).

In order to understand if there are differences in the reactions to service failures, between CM and CF individuals, MANCOVA tests were performed (Table 5). In all scenarios, there were statistically significant differences between the two groups. Thus, the H2 hypothesis was confirmed.

This hypothesis was confirmed; however, the literature review suggested another type of reactions between these two groups. According to Kindel (1983) and Huang et al. (1996), CM individuals are more predisposed to complain on the spot and to third parties for the demand for material compensation, while CF individuals are less likely to complain on the spot.

In this study, CF individuals (eg. Finland and Portugal) showed greater involvement in private actions (all services), in public actions (services 1 and 2, and in actions directed to service (services 1) than CM individuals (eg. Austria and Italy).

Table 5 MANCOVA—comparison of the reactions between CF and CM individuals, in the various scenarios

Scenario 1	Mean CF	Mean CM	Mean difference	F	St. Error	Sig
Actions directed to service	4.145	3.651	0.493*	14.015	0.132	0.000
Private actions	4.883	4.430	0.453*	8.514	0.155	0.004
Public actions	1.952	1.730	0.222*	4.144	0.109	0.043
Do nothing	3.733	4.027	−0.294	2.364	0.191	0.125
Scenario 2						
Actions directed to service	5.785	5.540	0.245	2.521	0.154	0.113
Private actions	5.524	5.163	0.361*	4.712	0.166	0.031
Public actions	2.348	1.818	0.529*	14.064	0.141	0.000
Do nothing	2.563	2.731	−0.169	0.904	0.177	0.342

*Significant mean difference at the 0.05 level

The explanation for this result may be that, since CF individuals are orientated towards relationships and the protection of others (Hofstede 1991), their greater involvement in reactions after failures is due to the interest in helping the provider of the restaurant's service to improve service in the future, or to warn other individuals not to go through the same negative experience.

5 Conclusion

When comparing the local vs external client, managers must identify the cultural dimension in which they differ most in order to be able to base the findings of this research and adapt the strategies to one another, through the cultural differences presented.

Yuksel et al. (2006) found that complaining directly to the employee or manager may indicate a greater intention to return to service, rather than abandoning. Through this study, it is possible to state that, in services similar in nature to restaurant services (weak services), people from cultures with Low Power Distance, and Masculinity are less involved in these direct actions than their counterparts. On the other hand, in services of a nature like lawyer services (powerful services), people from cultures with High Power Distance are less involved in these direct actions than their counterparts. To encourage, to the maximum, actions directed to service, in detriment of private, public actions and the option of doing-nothing, service managers should provide varied and simple complaint options.

Private actions do not allow companies to have the opportunity to perceive customers' dissatisfaction and, therefore, do not allow companies to improve the procedures, which led to the failure. With this study, it is possible to perceive that people of cultures with Femininity are more involved in these private actions, in all services, than their counterparts. In services of a similar nature to restaurant (weak service), people of cultures with High Power Distance are more involved in these actions than their counterparts. In services with a nature like those of lawyer services (powerful services), people from cultures with Low Power Distance are more involved in these actions, than their counterparts. Since this is an action that the company cannot uncover, if direct complaints are more encouraged in these cultures, the service provider has an opportunity to remedy the situation, recover the willingness to repurchase (Richins 1983) and incentive the positive word-of-mouth, since people who share the negative experience are also the ones who share a more positive experience (East et al. 2007).

Public actions, although they may be perceivable by companies and allow them to discover what has failed, have a very high power because, given the effectiveness of third parties (Singh 1989) and the increasing effect of communication technologies (Anderson and Zemke 2003), any such action can have a devastating effect on the company image.

People from cultures with High Power Distance showed greater involvement in public actions than their counterparts. In services of a similar nature to restaurant service (weak service). In services with nature like lawyer services (powerful services), people of cultures with Femininity require more caution. Thus, in order to avoid public actions, managers should develop strategies that help the client to immediately alleviate the frustration caused by the failure, such as for example, by submitting online satisfaction questionnaires, shortly after the purchase of the service, and demonstrating good problem-solving skills.

Regarding the option of doing nothing, although apparently not harmful to the company, may represent losses of recovery opportunities. Managers should know that those who are most prone to do nothing in services like restaurants (weak service) are people from cultures with Low Power Distance. Thus, these are the individuals that seem to show a greater tendency for loyalty, and these are the ones that the company should most encourage to convey to the company what has failed, for example, by encouraging writing in suggestion boxes, or by providing a touch-screen in the establishment, which require little time and no cost.

References

Anderson, K., Zemke, R.: Delivering Knock Your Socks Off Service, vol. 18. AMACOM Div American Mgmt Assn. (2003)

Andreassen, T.W., Streukens, S.: Online complaining: Understanding the adoption process and the role of individual and situational characteristics. Manag. Serv. Qual.: Int. J. **23**(1), 4–24 (2013)

Boote, J.: Towards a comprehensive taxonomy and model of consumer complaining behaviour. J. Consum. Satisfaction Dissatisfaction Complaining Behav. **11**, 140–151 (1998)

Brettel, M., Engelen, A., Heinemann, F., Vadhanasindhu, P.: Antecedents of market orientation: a cross-cultural comparison. J. Int. Mark. **16**(2), 84–119 (2008)

Cantallops, A.S., Salvi, F.: New consumer behavior: a review of research on eWOM and hotels. Int. J. Hosp. Manage. **36**, 41–51 (2014)

Chan, H., Wan, L.C.: Consumer responses to service failures: a resource preference model of cultural influences. J. Int. Mark. **16**(1), 72–97 (2008)

Donthu, N., Yoo, B.: Cultural influences on service quality expectations. J. Serv. Res. **1**(2), 178–186 (1998)

East, R., Hammond, K., Wright, M.: The relative incidence of positive and negative word of mouth: a multi-category study. Int. J. Res. Mark. **24**(2), 175–184 (2007)

Emerson, R. M.: Power-dependence relations. American sociological review, 31–41 (1962)

Emir, O.: Customer complaints and complaint behaviours in Turkish hotel restaurants: an application in Lara and Kundu areas of Antalya. Afr. J. Bus. Manage. **5**(11), 4239–4253 (2011)

Ergün, G.S., Kitapci, O.: The impact of cultural dimensions on customer complaint behaviours: an exploratory study in Antalya/Manavgat tourism region. Int. J. Cult. Tour. Hosp. Res.s **12**(1), 59–79 (2018)

Furrer, O., Liu, B.S.C., Sudharshan, D.: The relationships between culture and service quality perceptions: basis for cross-cultural market segmentation and resource allocation. J. Serv. Res. **2**(4), 355–371 (2000)

Hair, J.F., Black, W.C., Babin, B.J., Anderson, R.E., Tatham, R.L.: Multivariate data analysis. In: Uppersaddle River. Pearson Prentice Hall, NJ (2006)

Henricks, M.: Spread the word. Entrepreneur **26**(2), 120–125 (1998)

Hess, R.L., Jr., Ganesan, S., Klein, N.M.: Service failure and recovery: the impact of relationship factors on customer satisfaction. J. Acad. Mark. Sci. **31**(2), 127–145 (2003)
Heung, V.C., Lam, T.: Customer complaint behaviour towards hotel restaurant services. Int. J. Contemp. Hosp. Manage. **15**(5), 283–289 (2003)
Hirschman, A.O.: Exit, Voice, and Loyalty: Responses to Decline in Firms, Organizations, and States, vol. 25. Harvard University Press (1970)
Hoffmann, S.: Does national culture impact consumer boycott prevalence? A multi-country study. Euro. J. Int. Manage. **8**(2), 141–159 (2014)
Hofstede, G.: Cultures and Organizations: Software of the Mind. McGraw-Hill, London; New York (1991)
Homburg, C., Fürst, A.: How organizational complaint handling drives customer loyalty: an analysis of the mechanistic and the organic approach. J. Mark. **69**(3), 95–114 (2005)
Huang, J.H., Huang, C.T., Wu, S.: National character and response to unsatisfactory hotel service. Int. J. Hosp. Manage. **15**(3), 229–243 (1996)
Huefner, J., Hunt, H.K.: Consumer retaliation as a response to dissatisfaction. J. Consum. Satisfaction Dissatisfaction Complaining Behav. **13**, 61–82 (2000)
Jahandideh, B., Golmohammadi, A., Meng, F., O'Gorman, K.D., Taheri, B.: Cross-cultural comparison of Chinese and Arab consumer complaint behavior in the hotel context. Int. J. Hosp. Manage. **41**, 67–76 (2014)
Kim, M., Wang, C., Mattila, A.S.: The relationship between consumer complaining behavior and service recovery: an integrative review. Int. J. Contemp. Hosp. Manage. **22**(7), 975–991 (2010)
Kindel, T.I.: A partial theory of Chinese consumer behavior: marketing strategy implications. Hong Kong J. Bus. Manage. **1**(1), 97–109 (1983)
Kitapci, O., Dortyol, T.: The differences in customer complaint behaviour between loyal customers and first comers in the retail banking industry: the case of Turkish customers. Manage. Res. News **32**(10), 932–941 (2009)
Liu, B.S.C., Furrer, O., Sudharshan, D.: The relationships between culture and behavioral intentions toward services. J. Serv. Res. **4**(2), 118–129 (2001)
Liu, R.R., McClure, P.: Recognizing cross-cultural differences in consumer complaint behavior and intentions: an empirical examination. J. Consum. Mark. **18**(1), 54–75 (2001)
Marney, J.: Selling in tongues. Mark. Maga. **100**(38), 14–14 (1995)
Mattila, A.S.: The role of culture in the service evaluation process. J. Serv. Res. **1**(3), 250–261 (1999)
Mattila, A.S., Wirtz, J.: Consumer complaining to firms: the determinants of channel choice. J. Serv. Mark. **18**(2), 147–155 (2004)
Montanari, M.G., Giraldi, J.D.M.E., Galina, S.V.R.: Relationship between country brand and internationalization: a literature review. Benchmarking: Int J. **27**(7), 2148–2165 (2019)
Ngai, E.W., Heung, V.C., Wong, Y., Chan, F.K.: Consumer complaint behaviour of Asians and non-Asians about hotel services: an empirical analysis. Eur. J. Mark. **41**(11/12), 1375–1391 (2007)
Oliver, R.L.: Satisfaction: A Behavioral Perspective on the Consumer. Irwin-McGraw-Hill, New York (1997)
Park, S., Kim, K., O'Neill, M.: Complaint behavior intentions and expectation of service recovery in individualistic and collectivistic cultures. Int. J. Cult. Tour. Hosp. Res. **8**(3), 255–271 (2014)
Patterson, P.G., Cowley, E., Prasongsukarn, K.: Service failure recovery: the moderating impact of individual-level cultural value orientation on perceptions of Justice. Int. J. Res. Mark. **23**(3), 263–277 (2006)
Richins, M.L. Negative word-of-mouth by dissatisfied consumers: a pilot study. J. Mark. 68–78 (1983)
Rogers, J.C., Ross, S.C., Williams, T.G.: Personal values and purchase dissatisfaction response. J. Consum. Satisfaction Dissatisfaction Complaining Behav. **5**(1), 81–92 (1992)
Samaha, S.A., Beck, J.T., Palmatier, R.W.: The role of culture in international relationship marketing. J. Mark. **78**(5), 78–98 (2014)

Schoefer, K., Wäppling, A., Heirati, N., Blut, M.: The moderating effect of cultural value orientations on behavioral responses to dissatisfactory service experiences. J. Retail. Consum. Serv. **48**, 247–256 (2019)

Singh, J.: Consumer complaint intentions and behavior: definitional and taxonomical issues. J. Mark. 93–107 (1988)

Singh, J.: Determinants of consumers' decisions to seek third party redress: an empirical study of dissatisfied patients. J. Consum. Aff. **23**(2), 329–363 (1989)

Stauss, B., Seidel, W.: Discovering the "customer annoyance iceberg" through evidence controlling. Serv. Bus. **2**(1), 33–45 (2008)

Tronvoll, B.: A dynamic model of customer complaining behaviour from the perspective of service-dominant logic. Eur. J. Mark. **46**(1/2), 284–305 (2012)

Tsoukatos, E., Rand, G.K.: Cultural influences on service quality and customer satisfaction: evidence from Greek insurance. Manage. Serv. Qual. Int. J. **17**(4), 467–485 (2007)

Velázquez, B.M., Contrí, G.B., Saura, I.G., Blasco, M.F.: Antecedents to complaint behaviour in the context of restaurant goers. Int. Rev. Retail Distrib. Consum. Res. **16**(5), 493–517 (2006)

Volkov, M., Harker, D., Harker, M.: Complaint behaviour: a study of the differences between complainants about advertising in Australia and the population at large. J. Consum. Mark. **19**(4), 319–332 (2002)

Yuksel, A., Kilinc, U., Yuksel, F.: Cross-national analysis of hotel customers' attitudes toward complaining and their complaining behaviours. Tour. Manage. **27**(1), 11–24 (2006)

Zeithaml, V.A., Parasuraman, A., Berry, L.L., Berry, L.L.: Delivering quality service: balancing customer perceptions and expectations: Simon and Schuster (1990)

Zhang, J., Beatty, S.E., Walsh, G.: Review and future directions of cross-cultural consumer services research. J. Bus. Res. **61**(3), 211–224 (2008)

The Effect of Proper Complaint Handling on Customers' Satisfaction and Loyalty in Online Shopping

Bassam Tarhini and Dana Hayek

1 Introduction

"Due to the emergence of globalization and technology, online shopping has changed consumer behavior and organizations' marketing strategies.

However, with online shopping comes many challenges comprising of the difficulty to complain online due to lack of face-to-face interaction, Our objectives are: to understand how unsatisfied customers go about a problem they are facing with their purchase, to recognize the reason behind their complaints, to assess their expectations following the complaint, and what will be considered an effective service recovery system. This paper will examine the effect of online rapid complaint handling on customer loyalty, the impact of resilience and service recovery on world-of-mouth, and how fair compensation following a complaint will contribute to customer satisfaction and retention. The Lebanese market, online shopping practice is increasing rapidly with many products and services sold online and delivered to customers doorsteps. The challenge remains whether consumers can trust online transactions and how well online firms handle customer complaints and resolve their problems. It was shown that in order to create a loyal customer base, online sellers have to recover quickly from service failure, and rapidly handle customers' complaint, in order to avoid an escalated problem, and decrease customers' anger and frustration, which will in turn encourage them to deal with the same seller again, and become loyal. Also, online sellers have to be flexible when dealing with complaining customers,

B. Tarhini (✉)
The Bucharest University of Economic Studies, 6 Piata Romania, 1st district, 010374 Bucharest, Romania
e-mail: bassam.tarhini@liu.edu.lb

D. Hayek
Lebanese International University, Mazraa, MousaitbehBeirut 146404, Lebanon
e-mail: dana.hayek@liu.edu.lb

A. M. Dima and F. DÁscenzo (eds.), *Business Revolution in a Digital Era*,
Springer Proceedings in Business and Economics,
https://doi.org/10.1007/978-3-030-59972-0_28

which in turn, will spread positive word of mouth to their friends and relatives, letting them know how the seller resolved their problem, which might encourage other customers to deal with this seller, thus increasing customer base. Finally, to restore customers' satisfaction after service failure, online sellers should compensate fairly, by reaching an agreement with the customers on what makes them happy and satisfied again, in a customized, and sometimes, creative way. This might lead to customers' retention, increasing their trust and loyalty.

2 Literature

2.1 Factors Affecting Online Shopping Behavior

Liang and Lai (2000) suggested five steps that customers undertake when buying online starting with need recognition, online information search, evaluating several alternatives, choosing the best alternative, then finalizing the transaction.

While Chen (2009), stated four major motivators for online shopping including convenience, website design and characteristics, time saving and, security for money transactions.

2.2 The Lebanese Online Market

With the popularity of online shopping in Lebanon, slow Internet, slow delivery, and security concerns still prevent Lebanese from fully utilizing the Internet potential. Moreover, buyers lack trust for companies selling online, due to poor customer service and fraud. To overcome trust issues, some stores are allowing cash-on-delivery. According to Chelala and Ghalayini (2016) Lebanon has not passed any low to preserve privacy and protect personal data.

2.3 Customers' Complaining Behavior

Bougie et al. (2003) identified three major courses of action unsatisfied customers may take: complain to a public affairs party, switch to another vendor, or take no action. Understanding why unsatisfied customers complain is crucial to effectively solve their problems. Chebat et al. (2005) identified four purposes behind customers' complaints: obtaining compensation, vent anger, help improving the service, or spare future customers from similar unpleasant experience.

2.4 *Service Recovery Systems*

Service recovery is a concerted effort by a firm to correct a problem from service failure, and to retain customer's goodwill (Warden et al., 2003), following three major steps: easy complain mechanism, effective recovery, planned, empowered, and determined compensation strategies.

OK et al. (2007) stated that customers with solved problems are more satisfied than customers with no problems if the problem occurs one time. So the best strategy remains to do it right the first time (Kaufman 2000). Increased customer awareness of their bargaining power accompanied with the powerful role of the internet, complaining customers are increasing either to get compensated or vent anger (Hu and Mao 2013).

3 Methodology

This research used quantitative research method with a deductive reasoning approach, Furthermore, nominal scale was used to categorize demographical data while ordinal scale was employed to denote the degree of respondents' agreement to different questions, using Likert 5-point scale.

Self-constructed questionnaire method was employed to collect primary data. The population selected are people who have experienced online shopping in Lebanon. Probability simple random sampling technique was employed in order to create a highly representative sample of the population (Groves et al., 2004).

According to the sample size table by the research advisor, the population is 150 and our sample size will be 108 with 5% margin of error (Krejcie and Morgan 1970). However, since 8 respondents were unreachable, we end up with 100 respondents who completed our survey.

SPSS program was used to analyze the collected data from the questionnaire. Data was collected Summer of 2019 and was grouped into different categories, as shown in Table 1. Usually, to be significant, *p*-value should be less than 0.05 or 5% (Turner 2014).

4 Results and Discussions

Among 100 Lebanese online shoppers respondents, 34% respondents were males, and 66% respondents were females (Fig. 1).

Table 1 describes that, the female gender agreed on rarely receiving damaged orders while shopping online, with a *p*-value of 0.029 (n = 32 respondents), while males felt neutral (n = 16 respondents). Concluding that, females might be more careful while shopping online due to receiving rarely damaged orders. Overall results,

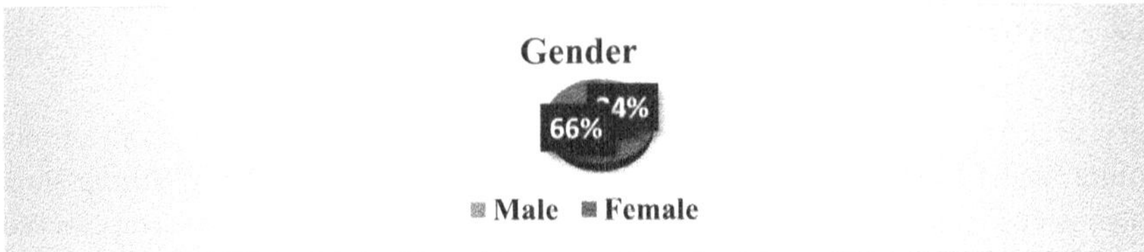

Fig. 1 Percentage of the male and female

Table 1 Gender cross tabulation

Count

		I rarely get a damaged order					Total
		Strongly disagree	Disagree	Neutral	Agree	Strongly agree	
Gender	Male	0	2	**16**	13	3	34
	Female	1	18	15	**29**	**3**	66
Total		1	20	31	42	6	100

Chi-square tests

	Value	df	Asymp. Sig. (2-sided)
Pearson chi-square	10.793[a]	4	**0.029**
Likelihood ratio	11.971	4	0.018
Linear-by-linear association	2.072	1	0.150
N of valid cases	100		

as illustrated in Fig. 2, show that, 5% respondents are between 15–20 yr old, 25% respondents are between 21–25 yr old, 46% respondents are between 26–30 yr old, 20% respondents are between 31–40 yr old, and 4% respondents are above 40 yr old.

Table 2 the age category of 15–20 yr old (n = 3 respondents), in addition to the age category of above 40 yr old (n = 3 respondents) disagreed about complaining to vent their anger when they encounter a problem while shopping online, while the age category of 21–25 yr old (n = 17 respondents), in addition to the age category of 26–30 yr old (n = 26 respondents) both agreed to this statement, and finally, the

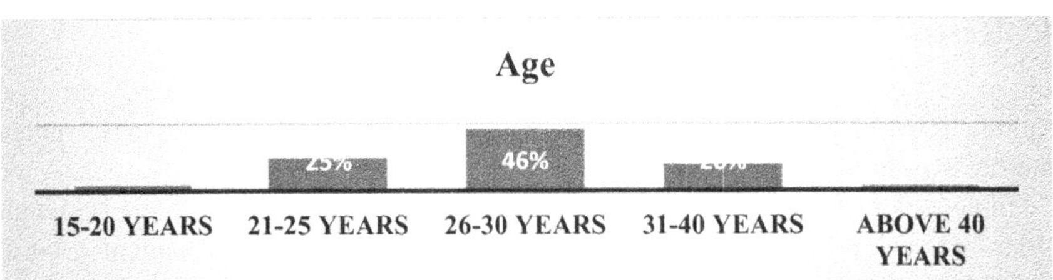

Fig. 2 Percentage of customers' age

Table 2 Age cross tabulation

Crosstab							
Count							
Age		I complain to vent my anger					Total
		Strongly disagree	Disagree	Neutral	Agree	Strongly agree	
	15–20 yr	**1**	**2**	0	2	0	5
	21–25 yr	0	4	4	**12**	**5**	25
	26–30 yr	2	8	10	**20**	**6**	46
	31–40 yr	0	2	**10**	7	1	20
	Above 40 yr	1	2	1	0	0	4
Total		4	18	25	41	12	100

Chi-square tests

	Value	df	Asymp. Sig. (2-sided)
Pearson chi-square	26.532[a]	16	**0.047**
Likelihood ratio	26.326	16	0.050
Linear-by-linear association	1.717	1	0.190
N of valid cases	100		

age category of 31–40 yr old felt neutral (n = 10 respondents), with a *p*-value of 0.047. We can conclude that, 15–20 yr old online shoppers might be careless or shy when encountering a problem, thus don't complain to vent their anger. Meanwhile, 21–25 and 26–30 yr old online shoppers, might be more enthusiastic or driven by their feelings of anger. In contrast, the above 40 yr of age don't complain to vent their anger, as they manage their anger wisely. Monthly income profile, presented in Fig. 3, shows that 15% respondents have a monthly income below \$500, 31% respondents have a monthly income between \$500 and \$1000, 47% respondents have a monthly income between \$1000 and \$3000, and 7% respondents have a monthly income above \$3000.

Table 3 respondents having a monthly income below \$500 disagreed that the online order always meets their expectations (n = 8 respondents), respondents having

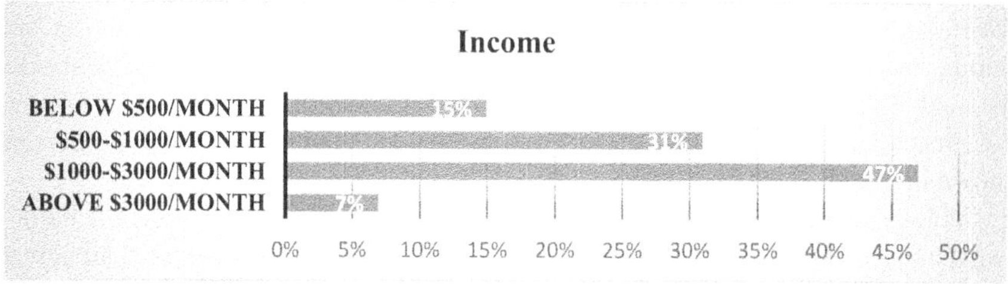

Fig. 3 Percentage of customers' monthly income

Table 3 Income cross tabulation 1

Count

		The online order always meets my expectations when received				Total
		Strongly disagree	Disagree	Neutral	Agree	
Income	Below \$500/month	**1**	**7**	5	2	15
	\$500–\$1000/month	2	13	**16**	0	31
	\$1000–\$3000/month	3	13	9	**22**	47
	Above \$3000/month	0	2	**4**	1	7
Total		6	35	34	25	100

Chi-square tests

	Value	df	Asymp. Sig. (2-sided)
Pearson chi-square	27.080[a]	9	**0.001**
Likelihood ratio	33.610	9	.000
Linear-by-linear association	5.965	1	.015
N of valid cases	100		

a monthly income between \$500 and \$1000 (n = 16 respondents), in addition to respondents having a monthly income above \$3000 (n = 4), both felt neutral, and finally, respondents having a monthly income between \$1000 and \$3000 agreed to this statement (n = 22 respondents), with a p-value of 0.001. We can conclude that customers with an income of \$500/month lack enough resources to shop from expensive online sellers, explaining why their order doesn't meet their expectations. On the other hand, customers with an income between \$1000 and \$3000/month might be more capable of shopping from expensive, more reputable online retailers, explaining why their online orders meets their expectations.

Table 4 respondents having a monthly income below \$500 (n = 6), in addition to respondents having a monthly income above \$3000 (n = 6) felt neutral when asked if they complain to vent their anger. On the other hand, respondents having a monthly income between \$500 and \$1000 (n = 23 respondents), in addition to respondents having a monthly income between \$1000 and \$3000 (n = 26 respondents), both agreed, with a p-value of 0.015. It can be concluded that online shoppers with a monthly income between \$500–\$1000 and \$1000–\$3000, might feel more frustrated about their money spent on an order that falls below their expectation, and finding complaining a good way to vent this anger. Among the 100 respondents, 3% respondents have a High School Degree, 53% respondents have a Bachelor's Degree, 40% respondents have a Master's Degree, and 4% respondents are Ph.D. holders, as shown in Fig. 4.

Table 5 respondents with High School Degree (n = 2 respondents), Bachelor's Degree (n = 39 respondents), and Master's Degree (n = 31 respondents), all agreed on complaining to the seller when they encounter a problem with their online order, while PhD holders (n = 2 respondents) felt neutral, with a p-value of 0.035. It

Table 4 Income cross tabulation 2

Count

		I complain to vent my anger					Total
		Strongly disagree	Disagree	Neutral	Agree	Strongly agree	
Income	Below $500/month	1	4	**6**	3	1	15
	$500–$1000/month	1	4	3	**18**	**5**	31
	$1000–$3000/month	2	9	10	**20**	**6**	47
	Above $3000/month	0	1	**6**	0	0	7
Total		4	18	25	41	12	100

Chi-square tests

	Value	df	Asymp. Sig. (2-sided)
Pearson chi-square	24.977[a]	12	**0.015**
Likelihood ratio	25.709	12	0.012
Linear-by-linear association	0.000	1	0.994
N of valid cases	100		

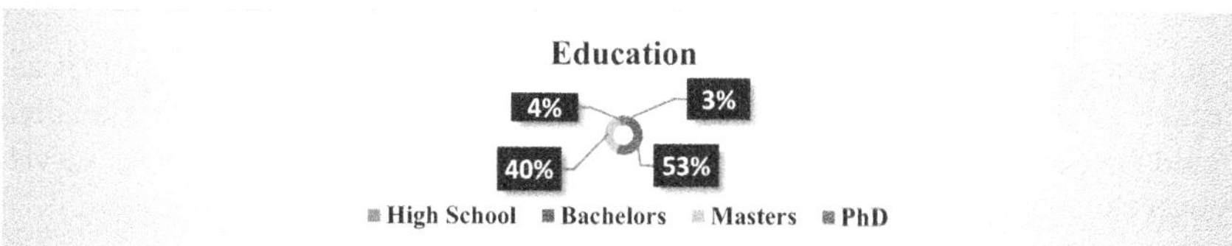

Fig. 4 Percentage of customers' education level

can be concluded that High School, Bachelor's, and Master's Degree holders might be knowledgeable about their power and rights as customers, encouraging them to complain when encountering any problem while shopping online (Table 6).

First 10 questions revealed that the majority of the Lebanese online shoppers still prefer traditional shopping (36%), maybe due to slow Internet, slow delivery, and lack of trust with online companies. Guarantees might encourage online shopping and regain trust. Moreover, the majority agreed on getting on-time delivery and rarely receiving damaged orders (39%). This shows that Lebanese online retailers are stepping ahead to avoid any delays or damages in delivered orders. However, the majority disagreed about receiving the correct order every time (38%), or if the order always meets their expectations (41%), and they consider complaining useless (37%). In these cases, trust issue rises again, where fraud is still the main obstacle preventing Lebanese online shopping from reaching its full potential. On the other hand, the majority who complain when encountering any problem agreed that they know where (49%) and to whom (73%) they complain, showing high level of awareness and knowledge. Finally, the majority stated that they mainly complain

Table 5 Education cross tabulation 3

Count

		I complain to the seller when i encounter a problem with my order					Total
		Strongly disagree	Disagree	Neutral	Agree	Strongly agree	
Education	High school	0	1	0	**2**	0	3
	Bachelors	1	8	6	**28**	**11**	54
	Masters	0	3	5	**19**	**12**	39
	PHD	1	0	**2**	1	0	4
Total		2	12	13	50	23	100

Chi-square tests

	Value	df	Asymp. Sig. (2-sided)
Pearson chi-square	22.267[a]	12	**0.035**
Likelihood ratio	16.137	12	0.185
Linear-by-linear association	0.085	1	0.771
N of valid cases	100		

to get a compensation (47%) and vent their anger (53%), with the consent that any mistake should not be repeated more than once (81%). Therefore, online retailers should encourage customers' complains, compensate, and follow a proper service recovery management.

Testing the hypothesizes,

H1: Rapid complaint handling affect positively customers' loyalty in online shopping.

Q11: When I complain, I expect the seller to respond quickly.

Q12: A rapid problem handling will encourage me to buy from the same seller again.

Q18: If the mistake is correctly handled by the online seller, I will definitely become a loyal customer.

Table 7 describes the relationship between Q11*Q12: p-value = 0.002 (significant), where 61% agreed that, when the online seller respond quickly to their complaint, they will buy from him again, implicating that, a rapid complaint handling might lead to customers' retention, increasing the chance of turning them into loyal ones.

Table 8 describes the relationship between Q11*Q18: p-value = 0.000 (significant), where 62% agreed that, when complaining, they expect the seller to respond quickly, which will leads to loyalty. This result focuses on the importance of time in complaint handling, where promptness can create a loyal customer base.

Table 9 describes the relationship between Q12*Q18: p-value = 0.000 (significant), where 66% agreed that quick resolution, will lead to retention and loyalty, which demonstrates that time is a critical factor in service recovery.

Table 6 Frequency for the respondents' agreement with each question of the survey

Questions	Percentage of Respondents				
	SA	A	N	D	SD
1. I prefer online shopping over traditional shopping.	4	25	35	30	6
2. I can get on-time delivery by shopping online.	5	34	30	25	6
3. I get the correct order every time.	2	33	27	33	5
4. I rarely get a damaged order.	6	42	31	20	1
5. Online order always meets my expectations when received (just like the picture).	1	25	33	35	6
6. I complain to the seller when I encounter a problem with my order.	23	50	13	12	2
7. If a problem occurs, I don't know where to file a complaint.	7	23	21	39	10
8. Complaining is useless and has uncertain consequences.	5	32	29	22	12
9. I complain to get a compensation.	11	36	31	17	5
10. I complain to vent my anger.	12	41	25	18	4
11. When I complain, I expect the seller to respond quickly.	18	56	19	4	3
12. A rapid problem handling will encourage me to buy from the same seller again.	32	42	12	9	5
13. When I face any problem online, I tell my friends and relatives about it.	34	55	7	2	2
14. When I face any problem when buying online, I spread the news on Social Media.	9	16	24	44	7
15. I let everyone know how the company resolved my problem.	15	55	22	6	2
16. In case of any mistake, the seller should compensate fairly, and with respect.	42	52	4	1	1
17. A clear, easy to follow complaining mechanism should be set by all online sellers.	43	43	12	1	1
18. If the mistake is correctly handled by the online seller, I will definitely become a loyal customer.	32	46	19	2	1
19. A mistake in online shopping should not be repeated more than once.	37	44	12	6	1
20. I am satisfied only if my problem is resolved properly.	42	48	6	3	1

Thus, based on the above results, H1 is accepted.

H2: Resilience in online shopping will lead to the spread of positive word of mouth, thus increasing the customer base.

Q13: When I face any problem when buying online, I tell my friends and relatives about it.

Q14: When I face any problem when buying online, I spread the news on Social Media Networks.

Q15: I let everyone know how the company resolved my problem.

Q16: In case of any mistake, the seller should compensate fairly, and with respect.

Q17: A clear, easy to follow complaining mechanism should be set by all online sellers.

Table 7 Q11*Q12 cross tabulation 4

Count

		A rapid problem handling will encourage me to buy from the same seller again					Total
		Strongly disagree	Disagree	Neutral	Agree	Strongly agree	
When i complain, I expect the seller to respond quickly	Strongly disagree	1	0	0	1	1	3
	Disagree	1	1	0	1	1	4
	Neutral	2	2	6	6	3	19
	Agree	0	5	5	31	15	56
	Strongly agree	1	1	1	3	12	18
Total		5	9	12	42	32	100

Chi-square tests

	Value	df	Asymp. Sig. (2-sided)
Pearson chi-square	36.464[a]	16	0.002
Likelihood ratio	33.223	16	0.007
Linear-by-linear association	9.832	1	0.002
N of valid cases	100		

Table 8 Q11*Q18 cross tabulation 5

Count

		If the mistake is correctly handled by the online seller, i will definitely become a loyal customer					Total
		Strongly disagree	Disagree	Neutral	Agree	Strongly agree	
When i complain, i expect the seller to respond quickly	Strongly disagree	1	0	1	1	0	3
	Disagree	0	0	1	1	2	4
	Neutral	0	0	7	8	4	19
	Agree	0	2	9	30	15	56
	Strongly agree	0	0	1	6	11	18
Total		1	2	19	46	32	100

Chi-square tests

	Value	df	Asymp. Sig. (2-sided)
Pearson chi-square	48.649[a]	16	0.000
Likelihood ratio	24.135	16	0.087
Linear-by-linear association	11.056	1	0.001
N of valid cases	100		

Table 9 Q12*Q18 cross tabulation 6

Count							
		If the mistake is correctly handled by the online seller, i will definitely become a loyal customer					Total
		Strongly disagree	Disagree	Neutral	Agree	Strongly agree	
A rapid problem handling will encourage me to buy from the same seller again	Strongly disagree	0	0	2	0	3	5
	Disagree	0	1	3	3	2	9
	Neutral	0	0	8	1	3	12
	Agree	0	1	5	30	6	42
	Strongly agree	1	0	1	12	18	32
Total		1	2	19	46	32	100

Chi-square tests

	Value	df	Asymp. Sig. (2-sided)
Pearson chi-square	53.111[a]	16	0.000
Likelihood ratio	51.819	16	0.000
Linear-by-linear association	6.159	1	0.013
N of valid cases	100		

Table 10 Q13*Q16 cross tabulation 7

Count						
		In case of any mistake, the seller should compensate fairly, and with respect				Total
		Disagree	Neutral	Agree	Strongly agree	
When i face any problem when buying online, i tell my friends and relatives about it	Disagree	0	2	0	0	2
	Neutral	0	3	3	1	7
	Agree	0	0	42	14	56
	Strongly agree	1	0	7	27	35
Total		1	5	52	42	100

Chi-square tests

	Value	df	Asymp. Sig. (2-sided)
Pearson chi-square	92.578[a]	9	0.000
Likelihood ratio	59.349	9	0.000
Linear-by-linear association	29.496	1	0.000
N of valid cases	100		

Table 11 Q14*Q16 cross tabulation 8

Count

		In case of any mistake, the seller should compensate fairly, and with respect				Total
		Disagree	Neutral	Agree	Strongly agree	
When i face any problem when buying online, i spread the new on social media networks	Strongly disagree	0	0	3	4	7
	Disagree	0	2	24	18	44
	Neutral	0	2	10	12	24
	Agree	0	1	13	2	16
	Strongly agree	1	0	2	6	9
Total		1	5	52	42	100

Chi-square tests

	Value	df	Asymp. Sig. (2-sided)
Pearson chi-square	21.719[a]	12	0.041
Likelihood ratio	18.227	12	0.109
Linear-by-linear association	0.941	1	0.332
N of valid cases	100		

Table 10 describes the relationship between Q13*Q16: p-value = 0.000 (significant), where 90% that tell their friends and relatives when facing a problem while shopping online, agreed that the online seller should compensate fairly, and with respect. This implicates that, online retailers should be resilient and flexible when recovering from service failure, to encourage customers to spread positive word of mouth, thus attracting new customers and increasing customer base.

Table 11 describes the relationship between Q14*Q16: p-value = 0.041 (significant), where 49% that don't spread the news on Social Media when facing a problem while shopping online, agreed that the online seller should compensate fairly, and with respect. This implicates that, those customers are not taking full advantage of the Internet's power to inform other online shoppers about their experience.

Table 12: respondents that spread the news to their friends and relatives when encountering any problem when buying online, agreed that a clear and easy to follow complaining mechanism should be set by all online shoppers reflecting their resilience and flexibility. This gives the impression that the online retailer is ready to be held accountable for any mistake, thus encouraging them to spread positive word of mouth, which might attract new customers and increase customer base.

Table 13 describes the relationship between Q14*Q17: p-value = 0.007 (significant), where 45% that don't spread the news on Social Media when facing any problem when buying online, implicating that they don't take advantage of the potential of the internet to increase awareness among other shoppers, agreed that a clear

Table 12 Q13*Q17 cross tabulation 9

Count

		A clear, easy to follow complaining mechanism should be set by all online sellers					Total
		Strongly disagree	Disagree	Neutral	Agree	Strongly agree	
When i face any problem when buying online, i tell my friends and relatives about it	Disagree	0	0	2	0	0	2
	Neutral	0	0	3	3	1	7
	Agree	0	0	5	33	18	56
	Strongly agree	1	1	2	7	24	35
Total		1	1	12	43	43	100

Chi-square tests

	Value	df	Asymp. Sig. (2-sided)
Pearson chi-square	41.298[a]	12	0.000
Likelihood ratio	34.176	12	0.001
Linear-by-linear association	10.264	1	0.001
N of valid cases	100		

Table 13 Q14*Q17 cross tabulation 10

Count

		A clear, easy to follow complaining mechanism should be set by all online sellers					Total
		Strongly disagree	Disagree	Neutral	Agree	Strongly agree	
When i face any problem when buying online, i spread the new on social media networks	Strongly disagree	0	0	0	1	6	7
	Disagree	0	0	6	21	17	44
	Neutral	0	0	2	9	13	24
	Agree	0	0	4	9	3	16
	Strongly agree	1	1	0	3	4	9
Total		1	1	12	43	43	100

Chi-square tests

	Value	df	Asymp. Sig. (2-sided)
Pearson chi-square	33.405[a]	16	0.007
Likelihood ratio	24.526	16	0.079
Linear-by-linear association	5.338	1	0.021
N of valid cases	100		

Table 14 Q15*Q16 cross tabulation 11

Count

		In case of any mistake, the seller should compensate fairly, and with respect				Total
		Disagree	Neutral	Agree	Strongly agree	
I let everyone know how the company resolved my problem	Strongly disagree	0	0	0	2	2
	Disagree	0	0	5	1	6
	Neutral	0	3	10	9	22
	Agree	0	2	36	17	55
	Strongly agree	1	0	1	13	15
Total		1	5	52	42	100

Chi-square tests

	Value	df	Asymp. Sig. (2-sided)
Pearson chi-square	31.761[a]	12	0.002
Likelihood ratio	32.583	12	0.001
Linear-by-linear association	1.161	1	0.281
N of valid cases	100		

and easy to follow complaining mechanism should be set by all online sellers, which will reflect their resilience and flexibility.

Table 14 describes the relationship between Q15*Q16: p-value = 0.002 (significant), where 67% that let everyone know how the company resolved their problem, agreed that the seller should compensate fairly and with respect, in case of any mistake. This gives the seller a chance to encourage customers to spread positive word of mouth since proper handling of mistake has more positive impact than not doing anything.

The relationship between Q15*Q17 had insignificant result.

Therefore, H2 is accepted.

H3: Fair compensation has a positive effect on customers' satisfaction and retention, following a complaint handling in online shopping.

Q16: In case of any mistake, the seller should compensate fairly, and with respect.

Q17: A clear, easy to follow complaining mechanism should be set by all online sellers.

Q20: I am satisfied only if my problem is resolved properly.

Table 15 describes the relationship between Q16*Q20: p-value = 0.000 (significant), where 87% agreed that in case of any mistake, the seller should compensate fairly, and with respect, which will restore their satisfaction. This implicates that service recovery process should be flexible and tailored according to each situation, in order to meet customers' expectations and recover their satisfaction.

Table 15 Q16*Q20 cross tabulation 12

Count

		I am satisfied only if my problem is resolved properly					Total
		Strongly disagree	Disagree	Neutral	Agree	Strongly agree	
In case of any mistake, the seller should compensate fairly, and with respect	Disagree	1	0	0	0	0	1
	Neutral	0	0	2	3	0	5
	Agree	0	2	3	**32**	**15**	52
	Strongly agree	0	1	1	**13**	**27**	42
Total		1	3	6	48	42	100

Chi-square tests

	Value	df	Asymp. Sig. (2-sided)
Pearson chi-square	124.760[a]	12	**0.000**
Likelihood ratio	32.795	12	0.001
Linear-by-linear association	21.052	1	0.000
N of valid cases	100		

Table 16 Q17*Q20 cross tabulation 13

Count

		I am satisfied only if my problem is resolved properly					Total
		Strongly disagree	Disagree	Neutral	Agree	Strongly agree	
A clear, easy to follow complaining mechanism should be set by all online sellers	Strongly disagree	1	0	0	0	0	1
	Disagree	0	0	0	1	0	1
	Neutral	0	0	3	6	3	12
	Agree	0	2	1	25	15	43
	Strongly agree	0	1	2	16	24	43
Total		1	3	6	48	42	100

Chi-square tests

	Value	df	Asymp. Sig. (2-sided)
Pearson chi-square	115.469[a]	16	0.000
Likelihood ratio	24.462	16	0.080
Linear-by-linear association	12.656	1	0.000
N of valid cases	100		

Table 16 describes the relationship between Q17*Q20: p-value = 0.000 (significant), were 80% agreed that a clear and easy to follow complaining mechanism should be set by all online sellers, because it gives the impression that the seller is ready to be held accountable for any mistake that could happen, which in turn, will lead to proper complaint handling and service recovery, resulting in the recovery of customers' satisfaction.

Therefore, H3 is accepted.

5 Conclusion

By analyzing the relationship between different survey's questions, significant correlations were found, resulting in the acceptance of the 3 hypothesizes. By analyzing questions 12, 18, and 20 from the questionnaire that is related to the impact of a prompt complaint handling process on customers' loyalty, we can conclude that a rapid, correct, and proper complaint handling, will restore customers' satisfaction (90%), encourage them to buy from the seller again (74%), and become loyal customers (78%). One of the most important factors in complaint handling is time. The process should be rapid, to restore customers' satisfaction and relief them from their anger and frustration, to avoid an escalated problem.

By analyzing questions 13, 14, and 15 from the questionnaire related to the impact of flexible and genuine complaint handling on encouraging complaining customers to spread positive word of mouth, we can conclude that most online shoppers, tell their friends and relatives when they encounter a problem while shopping online (89%), in addition to letting everyone know how the company resolved the problem (70%). In contrary, they don't spread the news on Social Media Networks (51%). From those findings, we can conclude that, most online shoppers will spread negative word of mouth when they encounter a problem, and positive word of mouth when their problem is correctly handled, mainly to their friends and relatives, maybe for altruistic reasons. But the majority don't spread negative word of mouth on Social Media Networks, which is a good thing for sellers, because this can go viral, locally and globally, within seconds, destroying the business. But it's bad for other online shoppers, due to lack of other customers' reviews and opinions. Not to forget that, spreading the news to friends and relatives also has a negative impact on businesses, especially if someone is an influencer in his community. For those reasons, online sellers should strive to avoid such problems, and prevent customer's from spreading negative word of mouth in their surroundings.

By analyzing questions 11, 16, 17, and 19 form the questionnaire related to the expectations of complaining customer from the sellers, in order to be satisfied, we can conclude that, complaining customers expect the seller to respond quickly (74%), fairly and with respect (94%), following an easy procedure (86%), and finally, not to repeat the same mistake again (90%). Hence, it can be concluded that, unsatisfied customers can easily shift to competitors. That's why, online sellers should meet customers' expectations, regarding complaint handling, in order to retain them and restore their satisfaction. When customers encounter a problem, they are angry and frustrated, that's why, as demonstrated earlier, time is a critical factor to restore their satisfaction, in addition to fairly compensating the time, money, and effort they spent, with respect and empathy, to relief them from their frustration. And most importantly, to avoid such incidence a second time, because it will be so hard to survive from it again.

References

Bougie, R., Pieters, R., Zeelenberg, M.: Angry customers don't come back, they get back: The experience and behavioral implications of anger and dissatisfaction in services. J. Acad. Mark. Sci. **31**(4), 377–393 (2003)

Chebat, J.C., Davidow, M., Codjovi, I.: Silent voices: why some dissatisfied consumers fail to complain. J. Serv. Res. **7**(4), 328–342 (2005)

Chelala, C., Ghalayini, L.K.: The impact of the lack of data protection regulations on the development of E-commerce in Lebanon (2016)

Chen, L.: Online Consumer Behavior: An Empirical Study Based on Theory of Planned Behavior. The University of Nebraska-Lincoln (2009)

Groves, R.M., Fowler, F.J., Couper, M.P., Lepkowski, J.M., Singer, E., Tourangeau, R.: Survey Methodology: Wiley Series in Survey Methodology. New York, USA, 43–198 (2004)

Hu, J., Mao, O.C.: Tmall, the Sky Cat: A Rocky Road toward Bringing Buyers and Suppliers Together. The Supply Chain Management Casebook: Comprehensive Coverage and Best Practices in SCM, p. 171 (2013)

Kaufman, R.: Up your service!: strategies and action steps to delight your customers now! (2000)

Krejcie, R.V., Morgan, D.W.: Determining sample size for research activities. Educ. Psychol. Measur. **30**(3), 607–10 (1970)

Liang, T., Lai, H.J.: Electronic store design and consumer choice: an empirical study. In: Proceedings of the 33rd Annual Hawaii International Conference on System Sciences, 10pp. IEEE (2000)

Ok, C., Back, K.J., Shanklin, C.W.: Mixed findings on the service recovery paradox. Serv. Ind. J. **27**(6), 671–686 (2007)

Turner, J.S.: A longitudinal content analysis of gender and ethnicity portrayals on ESPN's SportsCenter from 1999 to 2009. Commun. Sport **2**(4), 303–327 (2014)

Warden, C.A., Liu, T.C., Huang, C.T., Lee, C.H.: Service failures away from home: benefits in intercultural service encounters. Int. J. Serv. Indus. Manage. (2003)

The manufacturer's authorised representative in the EU is Springer Nature Customer Service Centre GmbH, Europaplatz 3, 69115 Heidelberg, Germany. If you have any concerns regarding our products, please contact ProductSafety@springernature.com

Printed and bound by CPI Group (UK) Ltd, Croydon, CR0 4YY

30/09/2026

02225234-0014